D1453593

British Roots
of Maryland Families II

British Roots
of Maryland Families
II

Robert W. Barnes

GENEALOGICAL PUBLISHING Co. Inc.

To Elizabeth Linton de Keyser

Contents

Introduction

It is with great pleasure and gratitude that I dedicate this book to Elizabeth Linton deKeyser, a good friend,who also volunteered to serve as copy editor for my manuscript.

As with the first volume of *British Roots* my intention has been to present material on the British origins of Maryland families. The second volume was made possible by new clues to origins of settlers that have come to light since the publication of the first volume, new sources that have made it possible to extend the research in Britain, and new finding aids that have made searching electronic sources possible.

Particularly helpful in my research were the marriage bonds and allegations published as part of the Harleian Society *Visitation* series. Marriages in parish registers usually give just the names of the parties and the date of marriage. Marriage bonds and allegations, however, contain a great deal of information about the ages, status, and parentage of the parties.

The families included in this work were chosen because (a) their home parish has been identified; (b) their families left descendants in the New World; and (c) most had arrived well before 1800. Some families are labeled "A Tentative Reconstruction" because some more work should be done to confirm the facts. I have tried to keep these tentative pedigrees to a minimum.

I have included the results of my own work and the work that has generously been made available by others such as Rick Saunders and Robert Hall. All those who have shared their work are acknowledged where their families have been discussed.

As I compiled the family histories, I was able to show connections with settlers in other colonies, and I specially enjoyed compiling the family of Robert and Mary (Atwater) Honywood, whose descendants settled in Maryland, Virginia, and New England.

This volume discusses the origins of 203 Maryland settlers (in a few cases, such as Nicholas Wyatt, it disproves the line published elsewhere). In addition, the connection to 120 settlers in other colonies (or states) is discussed.

Acknowledgments

Those researching Maryland families are fortunate in being able to work at several repositories. Under the direction of Dr. Edward C. Papenfuse and his staff, the Maryland State Archives is an outstanding place to research Maryland families. Michael Miller of the Maryland State Law Library oversees the work of another fine institution. It has been a pleasure to use the holdings of the George Peabody Branch of the Eisenhower Library of the Johns Hopkins University. Carolyn Smith and her people make research at "The Peabody" an enjoyable experience. I must thank the hardworking librarians of the Maryland Historical Society--Donna Williams, Francis O'Neill, and Robert Bartram--for always making me feel welcome, and assisting me. Thanks are also due to Judith Reid and the staff of the Local History and Genealogy Room of the Library of Congress.

I am also indebted to Michael Tepper, Joe Garonzik, and Eileen Perkins of the Genealogical Publishing Company for their patience, support, and for much technical assistance.

I am grateful to my friends Patricia Dockman Anderson, Jean Kolb Brandau, Dolly Zeigler, Robert K. Headley, and Allender Sybert for their patience while I rattled on about what to include or not include in the text.

If it were not for the excellent work of Peter Wilson Coldham, David Dobson, and Francis McDonnell in bringing many of the clues to British origins to light, this book might never have gotten off the ground.

Thanks are also due to my wife who put up with my slaving over the computer while I worked on the book.

Many individuals have contributed material for this book, and they are thanked in the text, but to all of them I again express my appreciation. I must give special thanks to Fredric Z. Saunders.

Additions and Corrections
to the First Volume of
British Roots of Maryland Families (1999)

The author is indebted to the following people (identified in the following items by initials) for submitting additions and corrections, in the form of additional data, correction of numbering, and other pertinent items. The author regrets the errors, and appreciates the kindness of the following:

BDK: Betty deKeyser of Pasadena, MD.
DM: David Morehouse of Hopkins, MN.
FZS: Fredric Z. Saunders, of Boulder, CO.
GER: George Ely Russell of Middletown, MD.
JBM: James B. McCurley of Baltimore, MD

THE ACTON FAMILY, p. 4: Ann Acton, dau. of Henry (2), m. James Dunning on 24 Jan 1720 (PGKG:1); Barbara Acton, dau. of Henry (2), m. William McPherson ("Kincheloe, McPherson, and Related Families, poss. available at MHS) (BDK).

ACTON: A ROYAL DESCENT, p. 5 The children of Robert Corbett (13) were baptized at longnor, Salop, not Longmoor (BDK).

THE ALLANSON FAMILY: Charles Allison, or Allanson, is said to have married Susanna Pusey. It is very clear Susanna Posey married Edward Philpott (FZS cites Charles Co., MD and Court and Land Q1:24-26).

As to Thomas Allanson (2), Fisher relied on an abstract of the will of Elizabeth Smyth who wrote her will in 1646, and did not consult the original will. I have a copy of the original, and it is very clear that of 1. John Allanson's children that only one was of age, and his son Thomas was a minor. John's son Thomas being a minor when the will was written, he cannot be identical to Thomas Allanson (2), who had children born by 1637 (FZS).

As for Thomas baptized in 1639 at St. Giles Cripplegate being identical to Thomas of MD, I admit this is a possibility, but nowhere close to being proved. There are too many London parishes that have not been abstracted to conclude the two are actually the same person. There is also no guarantee that he was born in London, only that he was there at the time he married. Many prosperous young men from other parts of England went to London is this time period for the business opportunities, and from there on to the Colonies (FZS).

THE ANDREWS FAMILY, p. 18: John (5), son of Edward (4); Edward (6), son of (4) (BDK).

THE BIRCKHEAD FAMILY, p. 55: Nehemiah (4), son of Christopher (2) (BDK).

THE BORDLEY FAMILY, p. 64: Thomas (4), son of (2), not (3) (BDK).

THE CHANDLER FAMILY (1), p. 108: Job Chandler (2), m. Ann, dau. of Adam and Sarah (Offley) Thoroughgood; see **THE OFFLEY FAMILY** on p. 346 (BDK).

THE CHASE FAMILY, p. 109: Rev. Thomas (4), son of Samuel (2), not (3) (BDK).

THE CHENEY FAMILY, p. 111: Richard (7), son of John (6), not (5) (BDK).

THE COKAYNE FAMILY, p. 123: Sir Edmund (8), son of (7); John (10), son of (9) (BDK).

THE DARNALL FAMILY, p. 151: Henry (7): his son PHILP was b. c1604 (BDK).

THE DAWSON FAMILY, p.154: William (5), m. 2nd, Elizabeth, dau. of Henry and Sarah (Turner) Marsden of Wennington; his son William was by this 2nd marriage (BDK).

THE DENT FAMILY, p. 157: John (6), prob. son of George (5), not (4) (BDK).

THE FITZALAN FAMILY, p. 193: John (7), son of Sir John (6) and Isabel (d'Aubigny), not Isabel (de Saye) (BDK).

THE GARDINER FAMILY, p. 204: Capt. Luke (7) son of Richard (5), not (6) (BDK).

THE GROOME FAMILY, p. 223: Daniel, son of Daniel (4), aid to be a guardian of Samuel (not; identity not sure) (BDK).

THE HALL FAMILY, p. 228: Thomas (2) was overseer of his father's will; John (3) son of Thomas (2) not (3) (BDK).

THE HANSLAP FAMILY, p. 231: Thomas (4), son of Nicholas (3); Thomas (5), son of Thomas (4); Joseph (7), son of Henry (6), not (8) (BDK).

THE HARDESTY FAMILY, p. 223: Grace (3), sister of Henry (2), not (1) (BDK).

THE HOSKINS FAMILY, p. 250: Add to Refs.: George Ely Russell. "Colonel Philip Hoskins of Charles Couny, Maryland," *NGSQ* 51 (1963): 26-31 (GER).

THE IRELAND FAMILY, p. 260: Edward (3), stated he was a native of the Island of Barbadoes (BDK).

THE MINSHULL FAMILY, p. 316: Jeffrey (7), son of Richard and Ellen, was bapt. 26 March 1620 in Wistaston Parish, Cheshire. Matthew Wise, in *Boston Family of Maryland*, 2nd ed., rev. (Charlotte: Delamar cl., 1986), p. 420, states that subsequent research, by genealogists of the College of Arms, London, has revealed that the Bishop's Transcripts of Wisaston Parish show that this Jeffrey was buried 16 June 1624 at the age four. Thus the parentage of the Jeffrey who settled in SO Co. has not been determined (JBM).

READE: George Reade was not the son of Thomas and Eleanor (Fenwick) Reade. Fisher was hasty in desiring to tie into an armorial family. First, George Reade had children baptized in Jan 1604/5, meaning he was married probably no later than early 1603/4. If he were the George baptized in Nov 1588, that would place his age as no more than barely 15 when he married, highly unlikely. I believe there are also records showing this

George Reade of Thomas went to either Cambridge or Oxford, I forget offhand which, and was an entirely different person.

As George Reade was an innholder in Holborn, I believe it more likely he was a different George Reade that was baptized there. A will made by a man of the same name as his possible father, was an innholder in an adjacent parish in London. He stated he had three sons, but unfortunately did not mention them by name in his will (FZS).

ROBERTS: The wording you list regarding Edward Roberts will is not technically correct. John Reade did not leave property to his nephew Edward ROBERTS. Edward Roberts will shows it is more precisely, he was due property of his grandfather George Reade, due to the death of his uncle John Reade. This is also born out by the will of George Reade, regarding dispostion of his son John's share if he died without issue. See George Reade's will and more details at my site [given above] (FZS).

ROBINS-CORNISH, pp. 378-380. Shortly after the publication of my article in the MGSB, I discovered on FHL microfilm 916997, an abstract of the Diocese of Exeter Marriage Bonds and Allegations. This contained the record of Edward Robins and Jane Cornish as you noted, listing the date of this document as 16 April 1630. The actual marriage date was probably shortly after this.

I notice in the section on Robins you did not correct this, leaving her name as Skinner, but did in the section under Cornish.

I disagree with Foose's statement that Jane would have been a sister to either Alice (Skinner) Ridgely's mother, possibly a Cornish, or to her father, Aquilla Skinner. He of course based this on the deposition of Rachel Freeborne, who stated that Jane was "aunt" to Alice Skinner. This and other depositions were microfilmed in 1988 by the LDS on microfilm 1526426, of miscellaneous documents of the Tiverton Baptist Church. Since Jane was not named in James Cornish's will, the conclusion was that she was a sister to Aquilla Skinner. In fact, she was sister to neither. The error comes from interpreting "aunt," as we would today. She was not an actual "aunt" but probably referred to as "aunt," from being an elder relative of Alice Skinner's.

As I noted in my article, the Bishop's Transcripts for many (really most) years at Tiverton are missing. With a distant relative, we have been having the original parish register read. Between that, plus numerous other appropriate PCC wills, a fairly good picture of the Cornish family has emerged, as has Jane's likely identity. Not only did James Cornish not name a daughter Jane, but he had no daughter of that name in the parish records. She is also not the Jane, daughter of Richard bapt. 6 Jan 1606/7 that Foose alluded to, for she was buried on 28 Oct 1608. James' brother George Cornish of London was armorial. Edward Robins and wife Jane had numerous children baptized in London, some at the same church that George Cornish attended. This was a very small church, especially for London, as most years there were only a couple dozen baptisms, compared to some London churches at which I have looked where there were 100 or more baptisms a month. It was undoubtedly through George Cornish that Edward Robins in London met George's relative Jane in Tiverton, Devon.

As a side result, some information regarding the Puddington family has been acquired. The identity of George Puddington is not certain, but appears that a sister of his married a brother of his wife Jane (Cornish) Robins (FZS).

The children of Edward Robins were baptized in London (FZS).

SKINNER, pp. 397-398. As I noted in my article, Harry Wright NEWMAN stated that Aquilla Skinner was the son of Richard Skinner. He mentioned it was from an American of Skinner descent who had found it. I have corresponded with that person, and he says that he had only sent Newman the abstract of the will of Richard Skinner, and that Newman jumped to the conclusion that the son Aquilla mentioned in the will of Richard was the same Aquilla that was the father of Alice. They were not.

There were two separate Aquilla Skinners: (1) one of Collumpton (various spellings), and the son of Richard, and (2) one of Tiverton, parentage unknown, that married Alice Cornish, daughter of James (FZS).

THE SLYE FAMILY, p. 400: Add to **Refs.**: George Ely Russell, "The Slye Family," *CSM* 29 (5) (1981): 1-4 (GER).

THE STRINGER FAMILY (2), p. 414: **1. SAMUEL STRINGER** was b. **c1636** not 1536. p. 414: Martha Stringer, dau. of **2. SAMUEL STRINGER**, was bapt. 12 Oct 1701.

THE STRANGMAN FAMILY, p. 413: George and Martha (Strangman) Wiseman were the parents of Jane Wiseman who m. James Nuthall of Rocheford, Essex; correction to footnote 87 (DM).

New Publications

In researching the material for this book I have come across several books and periodical articles which give at least one specific date and one specific place providing data on the British ancestry of Maryland settlers. This brief list is intended to assist those working on the families included.

N.B.: *MGSB* = (*Maryland Genealogical Society Bulletin*).
TAG = *The American Genealogist.*

BOARMAN
Dorman, John Frederick, "A Boarman-Brooke Marriage," *TAG* 47 (2) 196.

BOOTH
Barnes, Robert, "The Family of Bartholmew Booth," *MGSB* 38 (2) (Spring 1997) 202-208.

BOWLES
Loeser, Rudolf, "Hon. James Bowles of St. Mary's County," *MGSB* 38 (4) (Fall 1997) 471.
Loeser, Rudolf, "Hon. James Bowles of St. Mary's County; Additions," *MGSB* 41 (1) (Winter 2000) 96-101.

BROOKE. See BOARMAN.

CORNISH
Saunders, Fredric Z., "The Cornish Family of Tiverton, Devon, England," *MGSB* 41 (1) (Winter 2001) 51-100.

DASHIELL
Belser, Gale J., "Family Charts," *MGSB* 39 (1) (Winter 1998) 31-32.

DORSEY
Chaney, Nellie Owings, "Edward Dorsey - A Review and A Question," *MGSB* 38 (2) (Spring 1997) 210-215.

DOUGHTY
Brayton, John Anderson, "The Ancestry of the Rev. Francis Doughty of Massachusetts, Long Island, New Amsterdam, Maryland, and Virginia," *TAG* 77 (1) (January 2002) 1-17.

GORSUCH
Barnes, Robert, "Ancestor Chart of Charles Gorsuch, an Early Settler of Baltimore County, MD," *MGSB* 38 (1) (Winter 1997) 61-67.

HOLT

Poets, Michael A., "The Holt Brothers of Baltimore City," *MGSB* 41 (4) (Fall 2000) 491-519.

HOWARD

Howard, Joseph H., "Who Were Matthew Howard's Parents: A Revisit," *MGSB* 41 (4) (Fall 2000) 574-605.

JACKSON (of BA Co., MD)

Lester L. Jackson, Jr. *Descendants of Humphrey and Margaret Jackson (1592-1996) Derbyshire, England to St. Mary's County, Maryland.* Baltimore: Gateway Press,. Inc., 1996.

JACOB

Paul C. Reed. "The Claimed English Origin of John Jacob of Anne Arundel County, Maryland," *TAG* 67 (3) (July 1992), p. 176.

LAYFIELD

Patricia Law Hatcher, "'Mother Nottle,' A Correction to the Ancestry of George and Samuel Layfield of Maryland," *TAG* 77 (1) (January 2002) 18-24.

MACCUBBIN

Leogrande, William M., and Jerome F. Collins, "The Maccubbin Family of Montgomery County," *MGSB* 37 (1) (Winter1996) 67-92.

RAILLY

Ports, Michael A., "William Railly of Baltimore City, Maryland," *MGSB* 41 (1) 3-18.

ROBINS

Saunders, Fredric Z., "Edward Robins: Corrections to His English Ancestry and Identification of His Wife Jane Skinner," *MGSB* 37 (2) (Spring 996) 169-186.

SEYMOUR

Loeser, Rudolf, "Hon. James Bowles of St. Mary's County," *MGSB* 38 (4) (Fall 1997) 471.

SKINNER

Saunders, Fredric Z., "Edward Robins: Corrections to His English Ancestry and Identification of His Wife Jane Skinner," *MGSB* 37 (2) (Spring 996) 169-186.

SOMERSET

Barnes, Robert, "The Search for Maria Johanna - The Smith Somerset Marriage," *MGSB* 37 (3) (Summer 1996) 299-303.

WALKER

"Walker-Cradock Bible Entries," *MGSB* 39 (4) (Fall 1998) 530-532.

WARING

Coddington, John Insley, "Ancestors and Siblings of Sampson Waring of Shrewsbury, Co. Salop, and Calvert Co., Md." *TAG* 53 (4) 207-209.

WELLS

Chaney, Nellie Owings, "Of Sackcloth and Ashes-The Wells/White Marriage," *MGSB* 37 (2) (Spring 1996) 145-153.

Trabue, James, "A Reconsideration of the Wells-White Marriage," *MGSB* 40 (1) (Winter 1999) 3-25.

WHITE

Chaney, Nellie Owings, "Of Sackcloth and Ashes-The Wells/White Marriage," *MGSB* 37 (2) (Spring 1996) 145-153.

Trabue, James, "A Reconsideration of the Wells-White Marriage," *MGSB* 40 (1) (Winter 1999) 3-25.

List of Settlers

Some of these individuals are mentioned in more than one place in the text, so consult the index for the page(s) where they are mentioned. Note that some of these individuals have had their European ancestry disproved.

Settlers in Maryland

Alba, Pierre, of MD
Allanson, Mary Roberts of MD
Anderton, John, of MD
Ange, Francis, of VA and MD
Anketill, Francis, of MD
Athy, George, of MD
Attwood, George, of MD
Auchterloney, John, of MD
Auchterloney, Patrick, of MD
Barber, Dr. Luke, of MD
Beard, Rachel Robins, of MD
Belt, Humphrey, of MD (disproven)
Bigland, Ralph, of MD
Billingsley, Francis, of VA and MD (line corrected)
Billingsley, James, of VA and MD (line corrected)
Billingsley, John, of VA and MD (line corrected)
Billingsley, Thomas, of VA and MD (line corrected)
Billingsley, William, of VA and MD (line corrected)
Birch, Ann, of MD
Birnie, Clotworthy 18, of MD
Blakiston, George, of MD
Blakiston, Nehemiah, of MD
Bland, Thomas, of MD
Boardman, Francis, of MD
Bone, Robert, of MD
Boteler, Capt. John, of MD
Boteler, Thomas, of MD
Bowdle, Thomas, of MD
Brooke, Mary Baker, of MD
Brown, David, of MD
Brown, Peregrine, of MD
Brown, Thomas, of MD
Bruce, Andrew, of MD
Bruce, Charles, of MD
Bruce, Normand, of MD
Bruce, Selkrig, of MD
Bruce, William, of MD
Bryan, William, of MD
Burch, Thomas, of MD

Burgess, Elizabeth Robins, of MD
Burgess, Henry, of MD
Burgess, William, of MD
Burroughs, Nathaniel, of MA and MD
Calvert, Cecil, 2nd Baron of Baltimore
Calvert, Lady Anne Arundell, of MD
Campbell, James, of MD
Carlisle, Dr. John, of MD
Chalmers, Col. Charles, of MD
Chalmers, George, of MD
Chalmers, Rev. Walter, of MD
Chandlee, William, of MD
Cheney, Dr. Andrew Francis, of MD
Cheney, Richard, of AA Co., MD
Cheseldyne, Kenelm, of MD
Clark, Ann, of MD
Clifton, James, of MD and VA
Codd, Col. St. Leger, of MD
Conn, Rev. Hugh, of MD
Cooke, Andrew, of MD
Cornish Jane, of VA and MD
Cracknell, John, of MD
Cunningham, David, of MD
Dalyzell, John, of MD
Darnall, Anne Talbot, of MD
Dorsey, Edward, of MD
Drunckord, James, of MD
Dunbarr, John, of MD
Eburnathy, James, of MD
Eburnathy, John, of MD
Eburnathy, Thomas, of MD
Edelen Family of MD
Edgar, Richard, of MD
Eltonhead Family of VA and MD
Erskine, Janet Brown, of MD
Eyre, Francis, of MD
Fenwick, Cuthbert, of MD
Fleete, Capt. Henry, of VA and MD
Fleete, Capt. Henry, of MD and VA
Frisby, James, of MD
Frisby, Peregrine, of MD
Frisby, Thomas, of MD
Godby, Jasper, of MD
Goodhand, Christopher, of MD
Gordon, Alexander, of MD
Gordon, Capt. George, of MD
Gorsuch, Anne Lovelace, of VA and MD
Greene, Gov. Thomas, of MD
Gutteridge, Edward, of MD
Hardesty, Francis, of MD

Hardy, Henry, of MD
Harrington, John, of MD
Hicks, Capt. John, of MD
Hicks, Thomas, of MD
Hill, Clement, the Younger, of MD
Hill, Clement, the Elder, of MD
Hopkins, Matthew, of MD
Howard, Michael, of MD
Huett, John, of MD
Hurst, Andrew, of MD
Hurst, John, of MD
Hurst, Richard, of MD
Hyde, Henry, of MD
Inch, John, of MD
Ireland, Joseph, of MD
Israel, John, of MD
Key, Henry, of MD
Key, Philip, of MD
Key, William, of MD
King, Elias, of MD
Laking, Abraham, of MD
Lamphier, Elizabeth Going of MD
Lamphier, Thomas, of MD
Layfield, George, of MD
Layfield, Samuel, of MD
Lenman, William, of MD
Lewgar, Anne [, ?,], of MD
Lewgar, John, of MD
Lowe, Henry, of MD
Lowe, John, of MD
Lowe, Nicholas, of MD
Lowe, Thomas, of MD
Macdonald, Elizabeth Sedley, of MD
Macdonald, Elizabeth Sedley, of MD
MacPherson, Donald, of MD
Magruder, Alexander, of MD
Magruder, John, of MD
Marbury, Elizabeth, of MD
Marbury, Eusbeius, of MD
Marbury, Francis, of MD
Marbury, Martin, of MD
McCubbin, John, of MD
Merriken, Hugh, of MD
Merriken, John, of MD
Merriken, Joshua, of MD
Neale, Capt. James, of MD
Nevitt, Richard, of MD
Nicholson, James, of AA Co., MD
Nicholson, Joseph, of KE Co., MD
Noble, Thomas, of MD

Norris, Thomas, of MD
Nourse, James, of PA and MD
Offley, Michael, of MD and DE
Payne, Flayle, of MD
Peale Family, of MD
Penruddock, Anthony, of MD
Priestley, Edward, of MD
Pye, Charles, of MD
Pye, Mary Elizabeth,, of MD
Randall, Benjamin, of MD
Reresby, John, of MD
Reynolds, Ebenezer, of MD
Roberts, Edward, of MD
Roberts, William, of MD
Savory, William, of MD
Scott, Abraham, of MD
Sewell, Henry, of MD
Showel, Thomas Roades, of MD
Skinner, Alice, of MD
Smith, Maria Johanna Somerset, of MD
Smith, Robert, of MD
Smithson, George, of MD
Smithson, Thomas, the Elder, of MD
Smithson, Thomas, the Younger, of MD
Sorrell, Richard, of MD
Sparks, John, of MD
Sparks, George, of MD
Sprigg, Thomas, of VA or MD
Stewart, Dr. George Hume, of MD
Stewart, William, poss. of MD
Storer, Anne, of MD
Talbott, John, of MD
Taylor, Michael, of MD
Taylor, Philip, of MD
Thomas, Anna Bevan Braithwaite, of MD
Thomas, Christopher, of VA and MD
Thompson, Ann Rous of MD
Thornborough, Jane, of MD
Thornborough, Roland, of MD
Thornborough, Samuel, of MD
Tilghman, "Admiral" Samuel of MD
Tolson, Francis, of MD
Tomlins, James, of MD
Tubman, George, of MD
Waring, Sampson, of MD
Warren, Humohrey, of MD
Whichcote, Paul, of MD
White, Frances, of MD
White, Frances, of MD
White, Jerome, of MD

White, Jerome, of MD
Wintour, Edward, of MD
Wintour, Frederick, of MD
Wintour, Robert, of MD
Wiseman, Alice Capell, of MD
Wiseman, Robert, of MD
Wiseman, Robert, of MD
Workman, Anthony, of MD
Workman, William, of MD
Worthington, Capt. John, of MD
Wyatt, Nicholas, of MD
Wyvill, Marmaduke, of MD
Wyvill, William, of MD
Yate, George, of MD

Settlers in Other Colonies

Abbott, Anne Mauleverer, of NJ
Aglionby, John (Yates), of VA
Alden, Eleanor Willis, of VA
Bacon, Nathaniel, of VA
Barclay, John, of NJ
Barclay, Robert, of NJ
Barham, Capt. Charles, of VA
Berkeley, Frances Culpeper Stephens, of VA
Bland, Edward, of VA
Bland, Frances, of VA
Bland, Giles, of VA
Bland, Jane, of VA
Bland, Theodorick, of VA
Blennerhasset, Herman, of VA
Bohun, Edmund, of SC
Bradford, Dorothy May, of MA
Browne, Nathaniel, of CT
Bysshe, Ursula, of VA
Carlisle, John, of VA
Carteret, Philip, of NJ and NC
Claiborne, Elizabeth Boteler, of VA
Clarke, Jeremy, of RI
Clerke, Jeremy, of RI
Clopton, William, of VA
Clopton, William, of New Eng.
Coke, John, of VA
Cope, Edward, of America
Cope, Oliver, of PA
Cotymore, Rowland, of VA
Cromwell, Philip, of Salem, MA
Cromwell, Thomas, of Salem, MA
Culpeper, Capt. Alexander, of VA

Culpeper, John, of NC and SC
Curwen, Capt. George, of Salem, MA
Daggett, Mary Clopton, of New Eng.
Dale, Elizabeth Throckmorton, of VA
Danby, Ann Culpeper, of VA
Digges, Dudley, of VA
Dumaresq, Philip, of MA
Emmet, Thomas Addis, of NY
Fairfax, Hon. William, of VA
Fairfax, Thomas, Lord, of VA
Fenwick, George, of CT.
Filmer, Major Henry, of VA
Hogben, Dorothea Scott Gotherson, of NY
Honywood, Sir Philip, of VA
Horsmanden, Col. Walter, of VA
Humphrey, Ann
Hyde, Edward, E. of Clarendon, Gov. of NY
Hyde, Edward, of NY and NJ
Hyde, William, of Norwich, CT
Isham, Henry, of VA
Jeffreys, Sir Jeffrey, of VA
Kempe Family of VA
Kirkbride, Joseph, of PA
Layne, Alice, of VA
Lloyd, Thomas, of PA
Lloyd, Thomas (the younger), of America
Lyddall, Capt. George, of VA
Lynde, Aimon, of MA
Marbury family of New England
Marbury, Anthony, of St. Kitts.
Marbury, Eusebius, of VA
May, Dorothy, of MA
Montagu, Lord Charles Greville, of SC
Moody, Lady Deborah Dunch, of NY
Moryson, Francis, of VA
Moryson, Gov. Francis, of VA
Nelson, Philip, of New Eng.
Nelson, Thomas, of New Eng.
Nevitt, Hugh, of VA
Offley, David, of Boston, MA
Oglethorpe, James Edward, of GA
Oxenbridge, Rev. John, of MA
Pelham, Herbert, of New Eng.
Pelham, Herbert, of New Eng.
Peyton, Major Robert, of VA
Priestley, Joseph of PA
Randolph Family of VA
Read, John, of MA
Read, Wlliam, of CT
Reynolds, William, of MA or RI

Reynolds, Henry, of NJ
Robins, Edward, of VA
Robins, Obedience, of VA
Saltonstall, Muriel Gurdon, of MA
Sandys, George, of VA
Sherman, Mary Launce, of MA
Skipwith Family of VA
Smith, Martha Bacon, of VA
Sorrell, Edward, of VA
Sorrell, John, of VA
Sorrell, Robert, of VA
Sorrell, Thomas, of VA
Sorrell, Timothy, of VA
Sprigg, Katherine, of VA
Stephens, Mary Newdigate, of GA
Talbot, Peter, of MA
Thompson, Alice Freeman, of CT
Thompson, Anthony, of CT
Thornborough, Thomas, of VA
Throckmorton, Gabriel, of VA
Throckmorton, John, of RI
Throckmorton, Kenelm, of VA
Throckmorton, Robert, of VA
Throop, William, of MA
Vane, Gov. Sir Henry, of MA
Waller, Col. John, of VA
West, John
Willis, Thomas, of VA
Wilsford, Capt. Thomas, of VA
Wingfield, Thomas, of VA
Winthrop, Gov. John, of MA
Woodroffe, Thomas, of NJ
Wyatt, Sir Dudley, of VA
Wyatt, Edward, of VA
Wyatt, Gov. Sir Francis, of VA
Wyatt, George, of VA
Wyatt, Margaret Sandys, of VA
Yates, John, of VA

British Roots
of Maryland Families II

THE AGLIONBY FAMILY

Refs.: A; "Aglionby, late of Nunnery." *BLG* 1906, 8. B: "Aglionby of Carlisle," *CWfO*:1. C; "Aglionby of Drawdykes and Nunnery." *CFAH*:2-3.

ARMS: (of Aglionby) Argent, two bars and in chief, three martlets Sable. **CREST**: A demi-eagle displayed Or (A; B states that "no proof was made of these arms.").

ARMS: (of Yates): ... , a chevron ... , between three gates .... (*CFAH*:178).

1. EDWARD AGLIONBY of Aglionby, was Sheriff of Cumberland, 36 Henry VIII, and was the father of (A): JOHN.

2. JOHN AGLIONBY, of Carlisle, son of Edward (1), m. [-?-], dau. of Richard Salkeld of Corby Castle, Co. Cumberland. They were the parents of (A; B): EDWARD.

3. EDWARD AGLIONBY, of Carlisle, son of John (2), m. Elizabeth, dau. of Cuthbert Musgrave of Crookedyke, Co. Cumberland (A: B). Edward and Eliza-beth were the parents of (A; B): EDWARD; JOHN, D.D., Principal of St. Edmund's Hall, Oxford, and Chaplain in Ordinary to King James I; and DOROTHY, m. Alan Blennerhasset of Carlisle.

4. EDWARD AGLIONBY, son of Edward (3) and Elizabeth, d. 1648.(A). He m. Jane, dau. of Henry Brougham of Blackwell Hall, Cumberland (A; B).

Edward was the father of (A; B): JOHN; and MARY, m. John Stamford of Askham, Co. Cumberland.

5. JOHN AGLIONBY, son of Edward (4) and Jane, was b. 1610 (age 55 on 28 March 1655), and m. Margery, dau. of Christopher Richmond of Highhead Castle, by his wife Elizabeth, dau. of Anthony Chaytor of Croft.

John Aglionby took part in the defense of the City of Carlisle in 1644-5 against the Parliamentary forces, and when the city surrendered, he was imprisoned (A).

John and Margery were the parents of (A: B): JOHN; HENRY; CHRISTOPHER; RICHARD, m. and had issue; GEORGE; JANE; ISABEL; and MARY.

6. JOHN AGLIONBY, son of John (5) and Margery, was b. 1642 (age 23 on 28 March 1665) and d. 1717. He m. Barbara, dau. of John Patrickson of Calder Abbey. He was one of the King's Counsel and Recorder of Carlisle. In 1686 he exchanged DrumburghCastle and Manor, with Sir John Lowther, Bart., for the estate of Nunnery, and manor of Armathwaite, in the parish of Ainstable, Cumberland (A).

John and Barbara were the parents of (A: B): JOHN; and BRIDGET, m. George Watson of Goswick Castle, Co. Durham.

7. JOHN AGLIONBY, of Nunnery, son of John (6) and Barbara, was b. c1663 (age 2 on 28 March 1665) (A). He m. Dinah, dau. and coheir of Rev. Richard Stodart. They were the parents of (A): HENRY.

8. HENRY AGLIONBY, of Nunnery, M.P. for Carlisle, temp. George I, son of John (7) and Dinah, was b. 1684, and d. 1759. He m. Elizabeth, youngest sister of Sir Wilfred Lawson, Bart. Henry was Sheriff of Co. Cumberland in 1733. He and his wife were the parents of (A): HENRY.

9. HENRY AGLIONBY, son of Henry (8) and Elizabeth, was b. 1715 and d. 1770. He m. Anne, 4th dau. of Sir Christopher Musgrave, Bart., of Edenhall, and a descendant of King Edward III (*RD500*:174). She d. in 1780 (A).

Henry and Anne were the parents of (A: Sir CHRISTOPHER; ELIZABETH, m. [-?-] Bamber; JULIA, d. unm.; ANNE, m. Rev. Samuel Bateman; and MARY.

10. MARY AGLIONBY, dau. of Henry (9) and Anne, m. John Orfeur Yates of Skirwith Abbey, Cumberland. They were the parents of (A): FRANCIS, assumed the name of Aglionby; and JOHN, **settled in VA**, m. Julia Lovell and had issue.

THE ALBA FAMILY

1. ABEL ALBA m. Esther [-?-]. They were the parents of at least three children, baptized at the French Huguenot Church in Threadneedle St., London (IGI): PIERRE, bapt. 1 Dec 1689; JEAN, bapt. 16 Feb 1696; and PIERRE, bapt. 6 Nov 1698.

2. PIERRE ALBA, son of Abel (1) and Esther, was bapt. 6 Nov 1698 at the French Huguenot Church in Threadneedle St., London (IGI). He is almost certainly the Peter Alba, 18, of Stepney, Mddx., on 31 July 1718 bound himself to serve John Dykes of London, victualer, for 5 years in MD (*LEMK*:2).

On 26 May 1758 Peter "Albee" was listed as a debtor in the administration account of John Lamar of PG Co. (MDAD 41:454).

THE ANDERTON FAMILY

Refs.: A: "Anderton of Birchley," *Visitation of Lancashire by Sir William Dugdale, 1664-5. Chetham Society* 84:5.

Internet Postings: The will was posted by Alan Anderton on the Rootsweb ANDERTON-L Mailing List over two postings:
http://archiver.rootsweb.com/th/read/ANDERTON/2001/ and
http://archiver.rootsweb.com/th/read/ANDERTON/2001-04/0986774338
Anthony Anderson also posted the will at:
http://genforum.genealogy.com/anderton/massages/209.hrml

The author is indebted to several Anderton researchers, who have generously shared material with him. They are: Alan Anderton of Bargo, NSW, Australia, Anthony Anderton (BA Hons) pf Manchester, Lancs., Eng., Linda Eaton of Ogden, UT, and Parker Todd and Rachel Sawyer of MD.

ARMS: Sable, three shackbolts Argent, a canton Or. **CREST**: A stork Proper.

1. LAWRENCE ANDERTON, descended from a third son of Anderton of Anderton, Lancs., was the father of (A): CHRISTOPHER.

2. CHRISTOPHER ANDERTON, of Lostock, son of Lawrence (1), m. Dorothy, dau. of Peter Anderton of Anderton (who died 1561), by his wife [-?-], dau. of Greenhaugh of Bradlesham, Lancs.
Christopher and Dorothy were the parents of (A): JAMES, d. s.p.; THURSTAN, d. s.p.; CHRISTOPHER of Lostock; ROGER, of Birchley; ELIZABETH, m. Thomas Tildesley of Morleis, Lancs.; ANNE, m. Roger Bradshaw of the Haigh, Lancs.; DOROTHY, m. [-?-] Tompson of Ashall, Yorks.; ISABELL, m. [-?-] Rockley of Rockley, Yorks.; and ALICE, m. John Orrell of Turton, Lancs.

3. ROGER ANDERTON of Birchley, Lancs., son of Christopher (2) and Dorothy, was b. 1570 and d. 1640. He m. Anne, dau. of Edward Stanford of Perryhall, Staffs., by whom he was the father of (A; dates of birth suggested by Anthony Anderson): JAMES, b. 1616/7, age 47 on 22 Sep 1664, d. 1679, m. Anne, dau. of Walter Blount of Sodington, Co. Wigorn, Bart.; CHRISTOPHER, b. 1618, d. by Sep 1664 unm.; THURSTON, b. 1619, d. 1643, unm.; ROGER, a priest, b. 1621, d. 1696; EDWARD, a priest, b. 1623, d. 1685; DOROTHY, a nun, b. c12624, d. by 1653; ROBERT, a priest, b. 1625, d. 1685; ANNE, a nun, b. 1626, d. 1664; JOHN, b. c1628; ELIZABETH, a nun, b. 1629, d. 1700; MARY, a nun, b. 1630, d. 1683; and WILLIAM, b. 1631, d. by 1637.

4. JOHN ANDERTON, 7th son of Roger (3) and Anne, was b. c1628, and m. by 1664 Gertrude, dau. of [-?-] Smith. Gertrude's mother may have been Jane Fenwick Smith Taylor Eltonhead.
On 29 Sep 1649 Gertrude and Jane, daus. of Thomas Smith, dec., recorded their cattle mark (*ARMD* 4:507). Thomas Smith had been put to death in a rebellion on Kent Island. His estate was delivered to his widow, Jane, for the use of her two young daughters. By 1667/8, the land was now in dispute by Gertrude, wife of John Anderton, and dau. of said Thomas Smith (*ARMD* 57:249).
Jane Fenwick Smith Taylor Eltonhead died leaving an undated will recorded on 28 Feb 1659. She named her eldest son Thomas Taylor, her dau. Sarah, and her grandson, Roger Anderton. She stipulated that the debts of Edward Eltonhead were to be paid. She did not name an executor. William Coursey and Katherine Coursey witnessed the will (MWB 1:94).
John Anderton patented several tracts of land in MD. In 1659 he patented 600 a. in TA Co., called Anderton (MPL 4:244, 381). The same year he patented 700 a. called Lostock (MPL 4:253, 411). In 1667 he patented another 100 a, in TA co. called Birchley (MPL 11:13, 61).
On 9 April 1664, John Anderton, aged 36, deposed that he had visited William Eltonhead, then in prison, and Eltonhead said that he left his land and personal estate to his wife (*ARMD* 49:206-207).
On 5 May 1675 John Anderton of CV Co., released his claim to 100 a. of Little Eltonhead Manor, which William Eltonhead had leased to John Anderton in 1654, to the Hon. Charles Calvert (*ARMD* 45:540-541).
John Anderton died in Liverpool and was buried there on 26 July 1675. His will was proved in Chester on 18 Aug 1675, and proved in MD on 31 Aug 1676. As John Anderton of Liverpool, merchant, he left his tobacco and other goods in Liverpool to his wife Gertrude and sons John and Francis. His wife and sons were also to have the arrears of an anuity of £10.0.0 granted by my late father by his will out of the demesne lands of

Birchley. His lands in MD were to go to his wife and two sons, who were never to go to MD to dispose of the lands, which could be sold by his executor, who was his wife Gertrude. Roger Anderton, William Gaudy, and George Barber witnessed the will (recorded in MD in MPL WRC#1:1, and posted by Alan Anderton of Bargo, NSW Australia, and by Anthony Anderson. On 15 Jan 1682 Gertrude, John, and Francis Anderton had evidently come to MD, when they conv. to Zorobabel Wells the tract Birchley on Second Creek.. Gertrude Anderton, a widow, had conv. a power of attorney to her son John (TALR 4:168). [Perhaps John did not mean to forbid his wife and sons to travel back to MD, but only meant they did not have to go the trouble—RWB].

John Anderton was the father of: JOHN; FRANCIS; and ROGER, may have d. before 1675 as he is not mentioned in his father's will.

5. JOHN ANDERTON, son of John (4) and Gertrude, was living in 1683 when he patented 50 a. Lostock's Addition in TA Co. (MPL 21:389, CB#3:382). He may have died without heirs, as this land seems to have come into the possession of his bro. Francis.

6. FRANCIS ANDERTON, son of John (4) and Gertrude, was in DO Co., MD, by 5 Nov 1700 when as Francis Anderton, Gent., and his wife Mary conv. To Ralph Dawson, Sr., of TA Co., 700 a. Lostock and 50 a. Lostock's Addition in TA Co., in exchange for three tracts in DO Co., 600 a. Cokiases Fields, and 450 a. Murphy's Addition and 200 a. Hemersley (TALR 9:22).

THE ANGE FAMILY

Refs.: A: *GAVN*:3 (cites *The VA Gazette*, 18 June 1767). B: Letter from V. L. Skinner, Jr., containing his findings on this family.

NB: Although the name may have eventually changed to Haines, the IGI lists many individuals named Ange in Stratford-on-Avon, Warwick. By 1761 the Ange/Haines Family had moved to Sussex county, DE (B).

1. JOHN ANGE of Stratford-on-Avon, Warwick, m. Eleanor [-?-]. They were the parents of (A): FRANCIS.

2. FRANCIS ANGE, son of John and Eleanor, was b. c1634 and d. about April 1767, aged 130 years old [*sic*] (A). He m. [-?-], a woman who was b. c1687 (A).

A gentleman of Maryland, hearing of Ange's great age, went to visit him and reported in a letter dated 9 Aug 1764 that Ange had told him his birthplace, the names of his parents, and that he could remember King Charles I being beheaded when he (Francis) was a "pretty big boy" (A).

Ange came to this country in a ship from Parkgate called *The Great Bengal*, and he served his time with one Nicholas Demar on Rappahannock (A).

He moved to SO Co., MD, and was found in Somerset County Tax Lists for 1734, 1736, 1738, 1739, perhaps in 1744 when Frank Hanes head of the household. In 1730, as Francis Haines, he had patented 50 a. Haines Grove (B).

In 1764 was described as having "scarce a wrinkle in his face, and thick black hair, with a very few gray hairs interspersed." His wife was then about 80, and had a son by him not older than 27 years old (A).

Francis Ange d. in SO Co. about two months ago at a very advanced age (A). Francis and his wife had at least one child: [-?-] (poss. DAVID), b. c1737.

3. DAVID ANGE (poss. son of Francis (2), whose son would have been born c1737), as David Ange or Hains, d. in SO Co., by May 1769. He m. Elizabeth [-?-]. Thomas Moor and Joseph Scrogin appraised the personal estate of David Hains or Ange on 8 May 1769, and valued it at £52.2.5. Martha Turner and Mary Williams signed as next of kin. Elizabeth Haines, admx., filed the inventory on 18 May 1769 (MINV 100:192).

Mrs. Elizabeth Haines or Unge, admx., with Levin and John Callaway, sureties, distributed a balance of £52.8.11 on 20 April 1770. The sum was divided among the widow and then the four children: Constant, Ephraim, Oratio, and James (BFD 5:401).

David and Elizabeth were the parents of: CONSTANT, EPHRAIM, [H]ORATIO, AND JAMES.

THE ANKETILL FAMILY
A Tentative Reconstruction

Refs.: A: "Anketill," *HSPV* 15:21. B: Historic St. Mary's Career Files, MSA, used with permission of the Historian. C: "Pedigree of Anketill of East-Almer and Stour-Preston," *Hutchins' Dorset*, 3rd ed., IV 513, cites Vis. of Dorset, 1623. D: "Anketill," *MGH*, 2nd ser. 2:267.

ARMS: Vert, a saltire ragule Argent. **CREST**: An oak tree proper, acorned Or (C).

Generations 1-5

1. WILLIAM ANKETILL of Shaftesbury m. Elizabeth, dau. of William Filoll of Woodlands, Co. Dorset. They were the parents of (C): WILLIAM; and JOHN.

2. WILLIAM ANKETILL of Lye, Dorset, son of William (1) and Elizabeth, m. Margaret Puncharton. They were the parents of (C): OLIVER; and THOMAS (m. and had issue).

3. OLIVER ANKETILL of Shaftesbury, son of William (2) and Margaret, m. and had at least one son (C): JOHN.

4. JOHN ANKETILL of Shaftesbury, son of Oliver (3), m. [-?-], dau. and heir of [-?-] Dawe of Sherbourne. They were the parents of (C): WILLIAM.

5. WILLIAM ANKETILL of Shaftesbury, son of John (4), m. Radegunde, dau. of John Poxwell. They were the parents of (C): THOMAS; WILLIAM; PETER; JANE; and ALICE.

Generations 6-10

6. THOMAS ANKETILL of Shaftesbury, Dorset, son of William (5) and Radegunde, m. Jane, dau. of [-?-] Gawen in Wilts. They were the parents of (A; C): GEORGE, of

Shaftesbury, m. and had issue; ANTHONY; CECILE, m. [-?-] Johnson; and EDITH, m. Robert Goodridge.

7. ANTHONY ANKETILL of Shafton, 2nd son of Thomas (6) and Jane, m. [-?-] and was the father of (A; D): JOHN.

8. JOHN ANKETILL of Shafton, son and heir of Anthony (7), d. in 1610. He m. Phill[ippa?], dau. of Thomas Grigg. John and Phill[ippa?] were the parents of (A; D): ANTHONY, of Bow Church Yard, London, b. 31 Aug 1590, m. Mary, dau. of Robert Bankworth; FRANCIS, b. 31 Dec 1591; PHILIPPA, b. 13 Nov 1594; KATHERINE, b. 3 Feb 1595, age 18 in 1623; JOHN, b. 20 Jan 1597; ELIZABETH, b. 7 Oct 1599; MARGARET, b. 13 Jan 1601; and HUMPHREY, b. 20 May 1610.

9. FRANCIS ANKETILL of Holborne, son of John (8) and Phillipa, was living in 1634. He m. Faith, dau. of George Arnold of Holborne.

As the second son of a second son, his arms were recorded in the Visitation of London (A) as: Vert, a saltire ragule Argent, in chief a crescent on a crescent.

Francis and Faith were the parents of (A): FRANCIS, son and heir; DOROTHY; MARY; ELIZABETH; and (prob.) JOHN (not shown in the Visitation).

10. FRANCIS ANKETILL, probably son of Francis and Faith, was b. c1622. He gave his age as c25 in 1647, and c39 in 1665 (*ARMD* 4:312, 49:500). He d. by Feb 1675. He m. 1st, Elizabeth [-?-], and 2nd, by 1654, Jane [-?-], who d. by 1673 (B).

He was in MD by 1640 when he sold a brown cow (*ARMD* 10:190). He was styled Gent., and had a brother John, a son George, and a daughter Faith, and so is tentatively placed as a son of Francis Anketill of Holborn by his wife Faith, dau. of George Arnold (B). It was not until 1659 that he claimed land for having immigrated with his wife Elizabeth, brother John, and servants John Hunt and Martyn Kingston (MPL R:162b).

On 27 Jan 1646, giving his age as c24, he testified he heard Leonard Calvert make a nuncupative will, appointing Margaret Brent as his extx. (*ARMD* 4:312; MWB 1:2).

On 6 March 1654 he witnessed the will of Cuthbert Fenwick of SM Co. (MCW 1:219 does not identify the source). In 1654 William Eltonhead leased land to Francis Anketill for the lifetimes of Francis, his wife Jane, and bro. John (PCLR WRC#1:360).

In April 1658 he recorded a cattle mark and mentioned a cow given to his daughter Faith (*ARMD* 41:56). On 8 Oct 1658 he was named Justice for CV Co. (B).

Francis Anketill of CH Co., Gent., about 1668 was mentioned as a brother of Francis Gumby, joiner (MPL 11:284)

Barnaby Jackson was transported c1638, claimed land for service in 1649, and m. Margaret, dau. of George Goodrick by 1659 (MPL ABH:37, 2:604, and 4:22). He died leaving a will dated 13 Feb, 1669, proved 28 May 1670. In his will he named his wife Margaret, and left personalty to Owen Guither, Constant Gunby, and Barnaby Anketill. Francis Anketill, Geo. Goodricke and Thos. Matthews witnessed the will (MWB 1:385).

Francis Anketill of CV Co., died leaving a will dated 2 Nov 1673, and proved 18 Feb 1675. He desired that the lease of 100 a. Anketill, held of Little Eltonhead Manor, should be renewed for the benefit of his three sons: Francis, George, and Barnaby and their heirs in natural succession. The lease was formerly held by the testator jointly with John and Jane Anketill, now both dec. He also left his three sons 500 a. at the mouth of Harris Creek, Little Choptank River. Sons were to be of age at 18. Gov. Charles Calvert was named executor. The will was witnessed by Spencer Hales and Luke Parkinson (MWB 2:398).

The personal property of Francis Anketill, Gent., was appraised by Christopher Rousby and George Thompson, and valued at 15680 lbs. tobacco (INAC 1:575).

Francis Anketill was the father of; FRANCIS; FAITH; GEORGE (mentioned in the will of his father, but there is no other record); BARNABY

Generation 11

11. JOHN ANKETILL, son of Francis (10) and bro. of Francis, d. before his brother. In 1654 William Eltonhead leased land to Francis Anketill for the lifetimes of Francis, his wife Jane, and bro. John. He was dead by the time his bro. made his will (B)

12. FRANCIS ANKETILL, Jr., son of Francis, Sr. (10), was under 18 in 1673, and d. c1686. He m. Elizabeth [-?-] who survived him.

He owned land on Choptank River. On 25 Nov 1685 he granted quitclaim of his right to land leased to his father by William Eltonhead in 1654 (PCLR WRC#1:360-361).

He d. by 20 Jan 1686 when an admin. bond on his estate was posted by widow Elizabeth. Capt. Thomas Courtney and Thomas Miles were appraisers (MDTP 13:438-9, 444). In 1687 his estate was appraised by Thomas Courtney and Thomas Miles and valued at £24.1.6 (INAC 9:329).

13. BARNABY ANKETILL, son of Francis, Sr. (10), was under 18 in 1673, d. 1733. He m. Elizabeth [-?-] who d. 1739 (B).

She may be the Elizabeth Ankatill named as one of the daughters of Lewis Evans in Evans' administration account. Evans' extx. married Christopher Vernon (MDTP 21:271).

On 13 Feb 1669 Barnaby Jackson left Barnaby Anketill a two year old heifer (MWB 8:48, 116). On 2 Nov 1673 Francis Anketill left him one-third of personalty and one-third and third choice of Choptank land (MWB 2:398).

Barnaby Anketill appraised estates in 1696, 1701/2, and 1709. He was called Gent in 1692 (B; INAC 14:31, 30:1).

William Hunt of AA Co. made his will on 4 March 1703, stating that if William Macclaman should die under age, Hunt's estate was to pass to Eliza Anctill (MWB 13:28).

On 15 Aug 1708 Anthony Semmes of CH Co. made his will stating that Barnaby Anctill was to have charge of the testator's children, Marmaduke, Mary, and Jane, during their minority (MWB 12:326).

Barnaby Anketill was one of several individuals left personalty in a codicil, dated 3 Jan 1711/2, to the will of Pain Turberville of SM Co. (MWB 13:391).

Barnaby Anketill was named as executor of the will of Edward Enloes of SM Co. on 21 April 1711 (MWB 13:216; INAC 33A:224, 36B:121, 38B:69).

On 4 Dec 1712 Barnaby and Eliza. "Auchill" witnessed the will of Constance Burgess of SM Co. (MWB 13:493).

In her will dated 14 Aug 1721, Margaret Butler, widow, of SM Co., directed that Mary Kelly was to have personalty at age 16, and was to serve the rest of her time with Barnaby "Anthile" (MWB 17;2).

On 29 Jan 1732 Barnaby "Anckel" received a payment from the estate of Jacob Booth of SM Co. (MDAD 11:581).

Barnaby Anctill of SM Co., died leaving a will dated 21 Feb 1732, and proved 12 April 1733. He left personalty to John Thompson at age 16, and left a competent living to cousin Jean Thompson during her widowhood. He named a godson Barnaby Angell, son of said Jean Thompson, and his own wife Elizabeth Anketill as extx. (MWB 20:635). His godson Barnaby Angell inherited his land.

Elizabeth "Antell" received a payment from the estate of Patrick Buly of SM Co. on 29 July 1734 (MDAD 12:356).

The estate of Barnaby "Amtell" was administered on 20 Aug 1734 by Elizabeth Amtell, the extx. An inventory of £141.19.6 was mentioned (MDAD 12:526).

Elizabeth Anktell of SM Co. died leaving a will dated 4 April 1737, proved 4 June 1739. She named her cousins Margaret Cavenough, Margaret Trippe, Francis Brian, and Barnabay Angell (the exec. And residuary legatee). Robert Senton, Anne Beaker, and John Dennis witnessed the will (MWB 22:82).

Barnaby Angell administered the estate of Elizabeth Anctell in Sep 1740. Assets of £149.5.6 were listed, and payments came to £7.7.11 (MDAD 18:57).

THE ATHY FAMILY

Refs.: A: Lawrence F. Athy, Jr. *Captain George Athy [of Galway and Maryland] And His Descendants: A Guide to the First 6th Generations of the Athy-Athey-Atha-Athon Family in America.* 3rd Edition. No place, no pub., 1999; B: John O'Hart. *The Irish and Anglo-Irish Landed Gentry* (1884). Repr.: Baltimore: Clearfield Co., Inc., 2000.

Sir WILLIAM DE ATHY served as a knight at Ardree near the town of Athy in the early fourteenth century and moved to Galway where he built the first stone residence, known as Athy Caste (A:3).

1. JOHN ATHY (possibly a descendant of Sir William, was living in Galway in 1577 when he built a stone house on the south side of St. Augustine St. (A:5).

Over the door of John Athy's house was a carving of the Athy coat of arms (A:5).

John Athy was the father of (A:5, 6): WALTER; and EDMOND (who had property in Galway and in Co. Mayo).

2. WALTER ATHY, son of John (1), was living as late as 1640. He may have married [-?-], dau. of Athy's business associate, Francis Martin (A:5).

Walter Athy was one of the "Forty-Nine" Officers, who served Charles I or Charles II in Ireland before 5 June 1649, and who were entitled to arrears [in pay] (B:372). Walter was the father of (A:5): FRANCIS.

3. FRANCIS ATHY, son of Walter (2), prob. d. by 1666, having m. [-?-], dau. of George Martin who had been Mayor of Galway in 1632. Francis and his wife had three sons (A:7): WALTER; GEORGE, b. c1642; and JOHN, b. c1644.

4. WALTER ATHY, son of Francis (3), m. Anne (poss. French). They were the parents of (A:7): MARY FRENCH, m. Walter Blake.

5. GEORGE ATHY, son of Francis (3), came to MD as an indentured servant (A:8).

He may be the George "Athley" who was transported c1662 (MPL 5:245). A George "Atte" of SM Co. completed his service about 1668 (MPL 11:543).

6. **JOHN ATHY**, son of Francis (3), came to MD as an indentured servant (A:8).

THE ATTWOOD FAMILY

Refs.: A: *BARD7*:10-11. B: "Petre." *Lawson*, pp. 38-ff. C: Digges of Warburton Papers. MS.246. MHS.

The Lineage According to Browning

1. **GEORGE ATTWOOD** "of Beverlyin" d. 1794. He m. Winifred Petre, dau. of Thomas (10) Petre and Ursula. She d. 1771. George and Winifred were the parents of (A): GEORGE.

2. **GEORGE ATTWOOD**, son of George and Winifred, d. at Warburton Manor in PG Co., MD, in 1744. He m. Anne Petre, and was the father of (A): ANNE, m. 3 June 1739, William Digges.

The Established Lineage

1. **GEORGE ATTWOOD** of Beverly, Co. Worcester, was b. c1637 and d. 17 Feb 1732 (not 1794), age 80. he is buried at Cloynes, Co. Worcester (B:41). He m. Winifred Petre, dau. of Thomas Petre and Ursula [-?-] [See The Petre Family elsewhere in this work]. She d. 14 Dec 1714 (not 1771) aged 77.

　　George and Winifred were the parents of (A:11; B:41):Dr. THOMAS of Worcester; PETER, b. 1682, d. 20 Dec 1734, aged 53; GEORGE; and WILLIAM.

2. **GEORGE ATTWOOD**, son of George (1) and Winifred (Petre), d. in PG Co. on 26 Sep 1744. Browning states that he m. Anne Petre (A:11).

　　On 30 Nov 1745 William Digges wrote to Dr. Attwood: "Mr. Attwood died on the 26th of September 1744 after 14 days' illness. He was attended by two doctors and a priest. He left two tracts of land: 1000 a. and 2800 a. [some of which seems to have been in VA] ..." (C).

　　He proved the will, dated 20 Aug 1709, proved 9 Oct 1710 [or 1720], of his uncle William Petre (B:41).

　　On 26 Nov 1732 John Bradford, Gent., conv. to George Attwood of AA Co., for £200, The Widow's Purchase, containing 1127 a. (PGLR Q:181). On 15 May 1731 George Attwood agreed that if Henry Witham, chirurgeon, and his wife Mary did not pay Francis Hall £10.0.0 annually for the support of Mary Witham, then Attwood would pay (PGLR Q:311).

　　Ann Attwood witnessed a deed on 25 July 1737 (PGLR T:493).

　　George Attwood witnessed a deed on 26 Sep 1739 (PGLR Y:95).

　　No record of any will, inventory, or account has been found for George Attwood.

　　George and Anne were the parents of (A:11): ANNE, m. on 3 June 1739, William Digges.

3. **ANNE ATTWOOD**, dau. of George (2), m. 3 June 1739 William Digges, son of Charles. She d. 14 Aug 1757 (C). He may be the William Digges who d. 28 March 1783.

On 22 Aug 1739 Charles Digges of PG Co. wrote to Dr. [Thomas] Attwood: "as an alliance is contracted between our familys [*sic*] by the marriage of my son to your niece ... " (C).

George Digges, exec., advertised he would admin. the estate of William Digges, late of Warburton (*MJBA* 1 July 1783).

William and Anne were the parents of the following children (Family record found in the Digges of Warburton Papers): CHARLES Attwood Digges, b. 17 May 1740, "son of William Digges of Warburton Manor, by Ann his wife, dau. of George, youngest son of George Attwood, late of Beverly in Co. Worcester, by Winifred his wife, dau. of Thomas Petre (son of William Petre, Baron Writtle and Lady Catherine, his wife, dau. of Edward Somerset, Earl of Worcester. Charles Digges d. 5 April 1769 (C). George Digges and Frank Leek, advertised they would admin. the estate (*AMG* 27 April 1769); FRANCES, b. 13 May 1741, d. 16 Nov 1748; THOMAS, b. 4 July 1742; GEORGE, b. 4 July 1743, d. 17 Nov 1792, age 49 years, 4 mos., 10 days. George Digges d. the night of 18 Nov 1792 at Warburton, PG Co. Notley Young, Clement Hill, and John Fitzgerald, execs., advertised they would settle the estate (*MJBA* 23 Nov 1792, 28 Dec 1792); THERESIA, b. 7 Oct 1744. Theresia Foster d. 11 Oct 1784; HENRY, b. 4 Feb 1746? [*sic*]; JOSEPH, b. 19 March 1746? [*sic*] Dr. Joseph Digges d. 13 Feb 1780 on the Island of Teneriffe; SUSANN, b. 28 May 1748, d. 21 Sep 1773; ANN, b. 1 June 1750; MARY, b. 23 Aug 1751, d. 23 June 1761; CHARLOTTE, b. 4 Aug 1753; and JANE, b. 18 Feb 1755.

THE AUCHTERLONEY/OUCHTERLONEY FAMILY

1. ALEXANDER AUCHTERLONEY, merchant of Dundee, was the father of at least two sons: JOHN; and PATRICK.

2. JOHN AUCHTERLONEY, son of Alexander (1) Auchterlony, merchant of Dundee, was living in MD in 1740. If he or any of his children are alive, they should contact the printer, to hear something greatly to their advantage (*AMG* 23 Aug 1764).

John Auchterlony was from Arbroath, Angus (*DSEW*:12).

John Auchterlony was living in PG Co., on 28 Jan 1740 when he witnessed the will of Richard Jones, Jr. (MWB 22:350).

John was the father of (*DSEW*:12): PATRICK, b. by 18 May 1753 when he was named in the will of his uncle Patrick; and JOHN.

3. PATRICK AUCHTERLONEY, mariner, son of Archibald (1), d. in CV Co., MD, by June 1754. He m. Elizabeth [-?-].

He resided at Abroath, Angus, and settled in CV. His will was proved in Edinburgh in 1758 (*SOCD*:120).

Patrick Ouchterloney [*sic*] d. leaving a will dated 18 May 1753, proved 28 June 1754, in which he named his wife Elizabeth, Patrick Ouchterloney, son of John Ouchterloney; the other children of Alexander Ouchterloney [his father?]; and an unborn child. His wife was to be extx. Ann Cockshutt, Metachi Foot, and David Arnold witnessed the will. On 28 June 1754 the widow Elizabeth said she would stand by the will (MWB 29:170).

On 10 Oct 1755 Charles Grahame and Edward Gantt appraised the personal property of Capt. Patrick Ouchterlony of CV Co. at £769.5.7. Ja. [John?] Ouchterlony and James John Mackall signed as next of kin, and Elizabeth Chesley, extx., filed the inventory of 29 March 1756 (MINV 60:621).

Elizabeth Ouchterlony, widow of Patrick Ouchterlony, mariner, in CV Co., sued David Mudie, writer [to the signet?] in Arbroath on 9 Feb 1758 (*DSAC*:60).

THE BARBER FAMILY

Dr. LUKE BARBER of Wickham Hall, England, d. by 1669 in SM Co. He m. in England Elizabeth Younge who m. 2nd on 25 Aug 1669 John Bloomfield of Saint Mary's City. Luke Barber came to MD in 1654 on the *Golden Fortune* (*SMMD*:15 cites *ARMD* 5:98, 102 and James Walter Thomas, *Chronicles of Colonial Maryland*, Eddy Press Corp.: Cumberland MD, 1913).

Dr. Barber was a servant in the household of Oliver Cromwell prior to 1654/5. After his arrival in MD he was a member of the Upper House of the Assembly in 1658 and 1659/60, and a member of the Council, 1656-1660, Justice of the Provincial Court, 1656-1660, and Deputy Governor 1657-1658 ("Luke Barber," *BDML* 1:114).

A letter from Lord Baltimore concerning Dr. Luke Barber dated 1658 is found in MPL 5:76, 77. Elizabeth Barber the Younger was transported by Luke Barber, Dr. in Physick, by 1659 (MPL 4:11). Edward "Barbier," bro. to Luke Barbier is mentioned in MPL WC#2:5).

William Catlyne or Cartlyne made his will on 1 Feb 1667. Among others he named Eliza "Barbier," Luke Barber, James Paddison and Joshua Guibert (MWB 1:343).

Luke Barber or Barbier of SM Co. d. leaving a will dated 31 July 1664 and proved 4 Jan 1674. He left his wife Eliza Michan [Wickham?] Hall for life. Then it was to pass in turn to his eldest son Luke and other sons Edward and Thomas. Son Edward was to have 500 a. Lukeland subject to entail, and son Thomas was to have Michan Hills subject to entail. If all three sons died without issue property was to pass to next of kin Barber vel Barber. Daus Eliza and Mary were to have personalty. Capt. Richard Banks and Randall Hinson were named execs. Walter Hall witnessed the will (MWB 1:534).

Henry Spink and James Patison appraised Dr. Luke Barber's estate at 13,617 lbs. tob. Joshua Guibert approved the inventory. (INAC 1:5).

Joachim [Joshua?] Guibert administered the estate of Dr. Luke "Barbier." A payment of 40,713 lbs. tob. was made to John Bloomfield who m. the decedent's widow (INAC 1:191).

Dr. Luke Barber was the father of (*BDML* 1:114): LUKE; EDWARD; THOMAS; ELIZABETH, m. Joshua Guibert; MARY; and ANNE.

THE BELT FAMILY
A Line Disproven

Refs.: A: "Belt of Overton." "Dugdale's Visitation of Yorkshire, with Additions." *The Gen.*, n.s., 16:170-174. B: Belt entries, IGI, 1988 ed. C: *YASP* 100. D: *YASP* 70. E:

YASP 1. F: Marion Nugent. *Cavaliers and Pioneers*. Vol. I. H: Stella Pickett Hardy. *Colonial Families of the United States.*

Stella Pickett Hardy, in *Colonial Families of the United States*, states that Humphrey Belt, emigrant to Virginia and ancestor of the Maryland Belts was a son of Sir Robert Belt and Grace Foxcroft. No documentary proof of Humphrey's parentage has been found, but the name Leonard appears in the Maryland generations.

Because there is a possibility that the Maryland Belts are connected somehow with the Yorkshire Belts, these notes are included.

Nevertheless, the connection between the English and Maryland Belts has yet to be proven. Humphrey Belt of VA and MD has not been placed in the Yorkshire Belt Family,

The Belts of Leake, Yorkshire (B):
Robert Belt was the father of: Mary, bapt. 7 March 1601 at Leake, Yorkshire; Anne, bapt. 10 May 1607 at Leake; Richard, bapt. 26 March 1609 at Leake; Margaret, bapt. 1 Sep 16 at Leake.

Unplaced Belts at All Saints, Pavement, York:
Mary Belt, bur. 14 Nov 1622 (C:100).
Jane Belt, bur. 20 June 1608 (C:1).
Anne Belt, bur. 27 July 1623 (C:1).
James Belt bur. 23 Oct 1623 (C:1).
Susanna Belt, bur. 27 May 1624 (C:1).
Mary Belt, dau. of Alderman Belt, bur. 11 April 1627 (C:2).
Henry Belt, bur. 24 Jan 1632 (C:4).

Unplaced Belts at St. Crux, York:
Margery Belt, bapt. 29 Aug 1556 (D:4).
Alice Belt, bapt. 27 June 1654 (D:9).
Ellen Belt, bapt. Aug 1576 (D:9).
Mary Belt, bapt. 18 Sep 1577 (D:11).
Elizabeth Belt, bapt. 2 Jan 1578/9 (D:11).
Jane Belt, bapt. 1 July 1584 (D:13).
William Belt bur. 26 Sep 1556 (D:60).
The wife of Mark Belt bur. 24 Aug 1590 (D:69).
Alice Belt m. James Boyes June 1593 (D:119).
Marye Belt bur. 11 Aug 1593 (D:69).

1. WILLIAM BELT m. Jennett Chapman on 3 June 1549 at St. Michael's Belfrey (E:114). They may have been the parents of the following, all married at St. Michael Belfrey (E:1116, 117): LEONARD, m. Marbelia Bekwith on 9 Sep 1573; MARK, m. Elizabeth Shaw on 28 Aug 1576); and HENRY, m. Agnes Watson on 20 Nov 1577.

2. LEONARD (or LANCELOT) BELT, son of William (1) and Jennett, was Town Clerk of the City of York, He was buried at St. Crux, Yorkshire, 5 Aug 1590 (D:69), leaving a will dated 11 April and proved at York 16 Dec 1590. He m. Mary, dau. of William Beckwith of York at St. Crux (or St. Michael Belfrey), on 9 Sep 1573 (E:116). They were the par. of (A): Sir ROBERT, bapt. 22 Feb 1575/6 (D:9); Sir WILLIAM, bapt. 27 March 1582 (D:); SARAH, m. 5 June 1599 at St. Crux, George Askwith; and LEONARD, bapt. and bur. 28 Dec 1588 at St. Crux, Yorkshire (B; D:14, 68).

3. Sir ROBERT BELT, son of Leonard (2) and Mary (Beckwith) was Alderman and Lord Mayor of the City of York. He was knighted 24 Aug 1640. He was bapt. 23 Feb 1575/6 at St. Crux, and d. 4 Sep 1656. He was buried at Bossall. He d. leaving a will dated 16 Dec 1652, proved 9 Oct 1656. He m. 1st, at St. Crux on 7 Feb 1602/3, Jane Hudson, who was bur. there on 29 June 1608 (C:1)). He m. 2nd, at Halifax, on 17 July 1609, Grace, dau. of Daniel Foxcroft. She d. 11 Aug 1664 and was buried at Bossall, leaving a will dated 24 April 1663.

Sir Robert was the father of the following children, bapt. at All Saints Pavement, York (A:172; B; C:37, 38, 40, 42, 44, 45, 47, 48, 116, 118) (by 1st wife): MARY. bapt. 20 Nov 1610, bur. 11 April 1627; (by 2nd wife): LEONARD, bapt. 1 April [16--?]; ROBERT, bapt. 24 July 1614, bur. 7 Jan 1614/5; DANIEL, bapt. 6 Aug 1615; GRACE, bapt. 17 Oct 1616; JOHN, bapt. at All Hallows, 8 May, bur. 9 May 1619; GRACE, bapt. 6 June 1620, m. Richard Nelson; SARAH, bapt. 10 Feb 1621, m. 1st, Joseph Oley of York, on 6 Feb 1648, and 2nd, Thomas Bawtry; ANN; bapt. 23 March 1622/3, bur. 1623; JOHN, bapt. 28 June 1624, bur. 31 July 1632; JASPER, bapt. 20 July 1625; WILLIAM, bapt. 22 Dec 1628; and ROBERT, bapt. 30 Nov 1630.

4. Sir WILLIAM BELT, son of Leonard (2) and Mary (Beckwith), was recorder of the City of York, and was admitted to Gray's Inn, 15 Nov 1598, and bur. at Belfreys, Yorkshire, on 11 Feb 1653/4 (E:232 states 11 Feb 1650/1). He d. leaving a will dated 9 Feb 1650/1, proved April 1651. He m. 1st, at St. Michael Belfreys, Yorkshire, on 24 Aug 1624, Susan Millington, widow (E:153). She was bur. on 26 Dec 1630 in the High Choir (E:170). He m. 2nd, at Carleton juxta Snaith, on 17 Feb 1631, Martha, dau. of Maximilian Waterhouse of Walling Wells, Co. Notts. (Lady Belt was bur. 26 Sep 1652: E:236).

Sir William was the father of (A:171; E:172, 179, 181, 183, 189, 194, 195) (by 2nd wife): WILLIAM, bapt. at Belfreys, 22 Feb 1631/2; RICHARD, bapt. 23 June 1634, bur. 31 July 1634 in the High Choir; MARTHA, bapt. 14 Jan 1635/6, m. Tobias Thurcrosse; ROBERT, bapt. 2 May 1637, bur. 22 July 1638 in the Low Cross Alley; and MARY, bapt. 24 April 1638, bur. 21 March 1638/9 in the High Choir.

The line breaks down here.

5. HUMPHREY BELT, age 20, is stated to have been a son of Sir Robert and Grace, but no documentary proof of his parentage has been found so far. His name does not appear in any of the Yorkshire Parish Registers examined to date.

Humphrey Belt was transported from London to Virginia in the *America*, William Barker, by certificate from the Minister of Gravesend, 23 June 1635

(*CBE1*:152). He seems to have still been in VA by 1652 when Thomas Cartwright was granted land in Lower Norfolk Co. adjacent Humph. Belt's (F:174). On 8 June 1654 he was granted 220 a. in Linhaven Parish, Lower Norfolk Co., for the transportation of 5 persons (F:289). Humphrey, Ann, John and Sarah Belt were transported to Maryland c1663 (MPL 5:373).

> Humphrey Belt died in AA Co. in 1698, aged 83 (H).
> He was prob. the father of: JOHN; SARAH; and ANN BELT.

BIGLAND, RALPH, of Whitehaven, Co. Cumberland, Eng., was in MD by 22 March 1749/50 when he m. Mary Kibble at Stepney Parish (*ESVR* 2:7).

Richard [sic] and Mary Bigland were the parents of (*ESVR* 3:42, 44, 45, 48): MARGARET, b. 26 Feb 1750/1; MARY, b. 15 Feb 1753; JOHN, b. 21 Feb 1756; ANNE, b. 16 Feb 1754; JOSEPH, b. 21 Feb 1756; WILLIAM, b. 19 Aug 1758; and ELEANOR, b. 14 June 1764.

Unplaced:

BIGLAND, ELIZABETH, m. Francis Maddux on 26 Aug 1757 (Register of Stepney Parish, Wicomico Co., at MSA, p. 76).

THE BILLINGSLEY FAMILY
A Line In Question

Refs.: A: Harry Alexander Davis. *The Billingsley Family [Billingsly-Billingslea] in America*. Washington: [The Author], 1936. B: Letter to the compiler from Dann Norton dated 15 August 2001

N.B.: The compiler is indebted to Dann Norton for bringing this new material to his attention.

Harry Davis and others have accepted the Billingsley pedigree in the Visitation of Shropshire as being the line of John, James, Thomas, Francis, and William Billingsley, 17th century immigrants to VA and MD. However, Research posted in 1998 and 1999 by Luke Potter show that John, son of Francis and Bridget was born in 1601 and died in London in 1655. (Davis had stated, without examining the parish registers of Asdtley Abbots, Shropshire, that John, son of Francis and Bridget, was born in 1587 and had married in 1612 (B).

Generations 1-5

1. ROGER BILLINGSLEY in Co. Salop, 20 Edward IV (1481), was the father of (A:7): ROGER.

2. ROGER BILLINGSLEY in Co. Salop, son of Roger, was the father of (A:7): ROGER.

3. ROGER BILLINGSLEY of Canterbury, Co. Kent, son of Roger (2), was the father of (A:7): ROGER; and WILLIAM.

4. ROGER BILLINGSLEY of Canterbury, Co. Kent, son of Roger (3), was the father of (A;7): WILLIAM.

5. WILLIAM BILLINGSLEY, son of Roger (3), was the father of (A:7): WILLIAM.

6. WILLIAM BILLINGSLEY, Citizen and Haberdasher of London, son of Roger (4), m. Elizabeth Harding. She m. 2nd, Sir Martin Bowes. William and Elizabeth were the parents of (A:7): WILLIAM; RICHARD; HENRY; CECILY, m. William Newce or Newer of Herts.; and MARTHA, m. John Robinson of London.

Generations 6-8

7. WILLIAM BILLINGSLEY, of Co. Salop, son of William (5), m. Cicely [-?-].

In the Visitation of Shropshire, 1623, he is listed as bearing **ARMS**: Argent, on a cross Sable voided of the field, five estoiles in cross between four lions rampant of the second (A:8).

William and Cecily were the parents of (A:8): JOHN; WILLIAM, m. and had a son Thomas; RICHARD; and JOAN, m. Hugh Chys.

8. HENRY BILLINGSLEY, son of William (6), was b. 153- and d. 22 Nov 1606 and is buried in the church of St. Catherine Coleman. He m. 1st, Elizabeth, dau. of Henry Bourne. She d. 29 July 1577, aged 36, and he m. 2nd, Katherine, widow of Robert Harding, and dau. of Sir John Cornwell. Katherine d. 1599, and Henry m. 3rd, Susanna, widow of Edward Barger, and dau. of [-?-] Tracey (A:8).

Henry was admitted a scholar of St. John's College in 1551, was apprenticed to a London haberdasher, and became a wealthy merchant. He translated Euclid with notes, and published his work in 1570. He was SheriFf and Alderman of London, and Lord Mayor of London elected 31 Dec 1596. He was knighted in 6 Feb 1586/7, and was M.P. for London (A:8).

Henry was the father of (A:8-9): HENRY; WILLIAM; THOMAS; RICHARD; and ELIZABETH.

9. JOHN BILLINGSLEY, of Astlewy, Co. Salop, son of William (7), was b. c1525. He m. Frances, dau. of William Acton of Aldenham. They were the parents of (A:9): FRANCIS, b. c1549; JENNE, m. Capt. Thomas Bailey; and CICELY.

10. FRANCIS BILLINGSLEY, of Astley, Salop, son of John (9), was living 1623. He m. by 1575 Bridget, dau. of Sir Thomas Vernon of Haslington, near Nantwich, Chester. Francis and Bridget were the parents of (A:9-10): DOROTHY; FRANCIS; MARY, m. Francis Rowley and had issue; FRANCES; JANNE; THOMAS; JOHN; MARGARET,

m. John Jeuan of Staffs.; JANE; WILLIAM; RACHEL; JUDITH; BENJAMIN; EDWARD; and BRIDGET.

11. FRANCIS BILLINGSLEY, of Abbott, Astley, Co. Salop, son and heir of Francis (10), was b. c1578, and m. by 1600, Eleanor, dau. of Thomas Kerrey of Bindweston, Salop. They were the parents of (A:10): FRANCIS, b. c1600; THOMAS; WALTER; JOHN; EDWARD; and DOROTHY.

12. JOHN BILLINGSLEY, son of Francis (10) and Bridget, was nopt b. in 1587 and m. in 1612 as Davis claimed , but was b. in 1601 and d. in London in 1655 (B).

The Line of "Dutch" John Billinglsey

1. JOHN BILLINGSLEY, may have been a son of William and Lucy [-?-] Billingsley of Hallon, Worfield, and grandson of William Billingsley, Lord of Astley Abbots who d. 1570, b. c1587 in Co. Salop, and m. Agatha [-?-], who was b. c1593 (B)..

John and Agatha became connected to the Quakers, and removed from England to Holland, where he d. by 1659. Agatha d. 1666 in Rotterdam (A:10).

John and Agatha were the parents of the following children, including **five sons who migrated to America** (A:10): JOHN; AGATHA, b. c1614; JAMES, b. 1616; THOMAS, b. 1618; FRANCIS, b. 1620; BRIDGET; FRANCES, b. c1624; JOANNE, b. 1626; WILLIAM, b. 1628; MARY; and WALTER.

2. JOHN BILLINGSLEY, son of John (1) and Agatha, moved to Nansemond Co., VA, and later to MD. He m. Eliza, poss. Cobreath, b. c1637, possibly a sister of John Cobreath, who deposed that in 1658/9 he carried letters from Billinglsey, living in Nansemond Co., VA, to his mother Agatha, living in Rotterdam, Holland (A:11-).

John Billingsley d. c1659, and his widow Eliza m. 2nd, by 1662, William Burgh. John and his wife were the parents of (A:13): HENRY, b. c1654; GEORGE, b. c1656; and JOHN, b. c1658/9, d. by Nov 1671.

3. JAMES BILLINGSLEY, son of John (1) and Agatha, was b. c1616, went to Holland with his parents, settled in VA with his bros. John and Francis by 1649, and c1656 was brought to CV Co. by his bro. Francis (A:14).

James m. 1st, [-?-], sister of Walter Carr, and 2nd, Susannah Ewen of CV Co. Susannah Ewen Billingsley d. testate by 9 Feb 1663/4. The couple had no children.

4. THOMAS BILLINGSLEY, son of John (1) and Agatha, was b. c1618, went to Holland with his parents, and later came to VA with his bro. William in 1650. He was brought to MD by his bro. Francis c1659. He m. Elizabeth [-?-] (A:16).

Billingsley d. leaving a will dated 26 March 1672 and proved March 1673. He was the father of (A:16-17): ELIZABETH; SARAH; MARY; and THOMAS.

5. FRANCIS BILLINGSLEY, son of John (1) and Agatha, was b. in England c1620, went to Holland, then VA, and settled in MD, where he d. intestate c1684. He m., prob. in Holland, Ann [-?-] (A:20).

Francis was the father of (A:22): JOHN, b. c1647; ANNE, b. c1650; FRANCIS, b. c1653; AGATHA, b. c1656, m. as his 2nd wife, Thomas Paget; EDWARD, b. 1658; and ANNE ELIZABETH, m. Thomas Sadler.

6. WILLIAM BILLINGSLEY, son of John (1) and Agatha, was b. c1628 in Co. Salop and d. Dec 1657. He moved to Holland, then to VA, and finally to MD. He m. c1651, Sarah Bowman, b. c1635 in Essex Co., VA (A:22).
William and Sarah were the parents of (A:23): SARAH ANN, b. 1652, m. her cousin John Billingsley; WILLIAM, b. c1655, d. in inf.; MARTHA AGATHA, b. 1658, d. age 13.

BIRCH, ANN, eld. dau. of Thomas Birch, chirurgeon and man midwife of the town of Warwick, Co. Warwick, England, m. Rev. Thomas Chase of St., Paul's Parish, BA Co. (MM1 cites St. Paul's Parish Register)

THE BIRNIE FAMILY

Refs.: A: Basil L. Crapster, "'In the Finest Cuntrey': A Baltimore Cooper at the End of the Revolution," *MHM* 72 (3) 413-418. B: Pender, Seamus, ed. *Census of Ireland circa 1659*. (1939). Repr.: Baltimore: Clearfield Co., Inc., 1997. C:. W. P. W. Phillimore, ed. *Indexes to Irish Wills* (1909-1920). Repr. Baltimore: Genealogical Publishing Co., Inc., 1997. D: Schlegel, Donald M. *Irish Genealogical Abstracts from the Londonderry Journal, 1772-1784*. Baltimore: Clearfield Co., Inc., 1990. E: *Index to the Act or Grant Books and to Original Wills of the Diocese of Dublin [c. 1638] to the Year 1800*. (1895), Repr.: Baltimore: Clearfield Co., Inc., 1997. F. P. Beryl Esutace, ed. *Registry of Deeds: Dublin: Abstracts of Wills. Vol. I 1708-1745. Vol. II 1746-1785* (1956), Repr. Baltimore: Clearfield Co., Inc., 1996. G: oseph Jackson Howard and Frederick Arthur Crisp, eds. *Visitation of Ireland.. Six Volumes in One*. Repr.: Baltimore: Clearfield Co., Inc.

Early Birnies and Clotworthys

JAMES CLOTWORTHY of Monnimoore, Londonderry, d. leaving an original will in 1659 (E:165).

PATRICK BIRNIE of Lurganagoose d. leaving a will probated in Derry in 1802 (C).

CHARLES BIRNIE of Coleraine, formerly of Strabane, d. leaving a will probated in Derry in 1836 (C).

JOHN BIRNIE of Templepatrick, Co. Antrim, d. leaving a will dated 6 Nov 1745, proved 7 March 1763. he named his sons William (eldest son), John, Alexander, and Samuel. He mentioned a freehold house and tenements, and 8 acres of land, the lease of a farm, and a bleach green and mill. William Livingston, of Cloghanduff, Antrim, linen draper, David Bell, linen draper, and William Bell, weaver, both of Templepatrick, witnessed the will (F: 2:150, will # 305).

The Maryland Family

1. CLOTWORTHY BIRNIE d. 1765. He m. Margaret Scott, b. 1717, d. 1803, dau. of Francis Scott (d. 1766) of Templepatrick, and sister of Dr. Upton Scott. Birnie was a tenant on the estate of the Upton family (Lord Templetown) near Templepatrick, Co. Antrim, Ireland.

Clotworthy and his wife had 11 children, including (A:413); HUGH, one of the elder children; JOHN, d. while a student at medical school; FRANCIS UPTON, d. at sea during the Revolutionary War; and CLOTWORTHY, II, emigrated to Big Pipe Creek in 1810.

2. HUGH BIRNIE, son of Clotworthy (1) and Margaret, was b. 1746 and d. 21 Aug 1822, age 76 years. In 1763 he moved to Philadelphia, and lived for a while in Baltimore (A:415-417). Unmarried, he d. at the estate of his brother, Clotworthy, II (A:418).

3. CLOTWORTHY BIRNIE, II, son of Clotworthy (1) and Margaret, moved to Big Pipe Creek area of MD c1819. Clotworthy Birnie, Jr., m. Harriot A. Worthington on 24 June 1828 at All Saints Parish. Their son, Clotworthy Worthington Birnie, was b. 10 inst., bapt. 16 March 1831 at All Saints Parish, Frederick Co. (*WMG* 6:10, 165).

THE BLAND FAMILY

Refs.: A: "Bland." *Familiae Minorum Gentium*, Vol. II. *HSPV* 38:421-426. B: *APPJ*.

1. ROGER BLAND of Orton, Westmorland, temp. Henry, VII was the father of (A): ADAM.

2. ADAM BLAND, of London, Skinner, son of Roger (1), m. Joan, dau. of William Atkins of St. Gregory's, London. She was buried there 10 July 1596 (A:421).

Adam was made free of his company 4 Edw. VI, 1549, and was Serjeant-Pelletier to Queen Elizabeth I, 1563. He and Joan were the parents of (A:421-422): WILLIAM, m. and had issue; PETER, m. and had issue; THOMAS, 3rd son, m. and had issue; JASPER, bapt. 1568, bur. 1596; GREGORY, bapt. 1567, settled in Ireland; FRANCIS, bapt. 1561, bur. 1566; RICHARD, bapt. 1562; JOHN, bur. 1564; WILLIAM, bapt. 1566; ELIZABETH, bapt. 12 May 1560, m. William Bury or Burle; MARY, bapt. 22 Jan 1569; and JOHN.

3. THOMAS BLAND, of London, Gent., Attorney, 3rd son of Adam (2), d. by May 1618. He m. 1st, Alice Garman, buried at St. Gregory's 12 July 1590; 2nd, Elizabeth, widow of William Yeardley, d. by July 1593, and 3rd, Mary, relict of Thomas Moody of London, grocer to Queen Elizabeth, and dau. of John Catcher, Esq. (A:422).

Elizabeth Bland "now wife of Thomas Bland of St. Martin's within Ludgate" d. leaving a will dated 19 July 1593 and proved 20 July 1593. She stated that she was late extx. of her mother Margaret Smith. She named the children of her late husband William Yeardley: Jasper, Margaret, Anne, Elizabeth, and Mary. She also mentioned the children of her brother Michael Harrison, her sister Sara Sawle, Alice Halwarde who had cared for her, and her aunt Alice Eccles. Her husband was to be sole exec. (*GGE* 1:812 cites PCC Nevell, 57).

Thomas Bland of Sundridge, Kent, d. leaving a will dated 18 Nov 1617 and proved 15 May 1618. He remembered the poor of Sundridge and of St. Bennet's near Paul's Cross. He mentioned the children of his brother John and of his brother Gregory, as well as those of his sister Elizabeth Bury, his god-dau. Judith Gilbie, and the children of his sister Gilbie; his god-dau. Joane Hope, his bro. Peter Bland and children, his dau.-in-law Ellen Lewis, Margaret Ball, and Emme Whitlatche; wife Mary, and son George and dau. Elizabeth. Son George to be exec., and sons-in-law William Ball, John Lewis, and John Bland to be overseers. He left property in Shoreditch to his son George and the latter's son Thomas. He mentioned the children of his son-in-law William Ball and his dau.-in-law Margaret Sale. He also named his son-in-law Jasper Yardley, and daus.-in-law Elizabeth Cooper and Mary Yardley. John Bland, Thomas Langhorne, Elizabeth Blande, Ralph Farrington and Sibbel Farrington witnessed the will (*GGE* 1:812 cites PCC Meade 47).

Thomas and Mary were the parents of (A:422): GEORGE, b. c1598; and ELIZABETH, b. c1601, m. Edward Holmwood at St. Antholin's on 26 Oct 1620.

4. GREGORY BLAND, son of Adam (2) and Joan, was bapt. at St. Gregory's on 22 April 1567, and settled in Ireland. He m. and had two daus. (A:422): JANE, settled in VA, m. 1st, her first cousin Edward Bland, and 2nd, John Holmwood; and FRANCES, settled in VA, m. John Coggan of Charles City Co., VA.

5. JOHN BLAND, of Sythe Lane in the parish of St. Antholine's and of Plastow, Essex, 5th son of Adam (2) and Joan Bland, was bapt. at St. Gregory's on 28 Sep 1572, and d. leaving a will dated 24 Sep 1627 and proved 20 April 1622 [sic], He m. Susanna Duclere, b. 1590 in Hamburgh, d. 1 Feb 1664 (B:95). She was a dau. of [-?-] and Marie du Dubleer [sic]. Susanna d. 1 feb 1664, and was buried with her husband (A:422).

John Bland was a "Hambro'" merchant, and of a free member of the Grocer's company and of the Merchant's Adventurers. He gave £5 to the daily morning lecture at St. Antholine's, in the vault of which church he was buried (A:422).

John and Susanna were the parents of the following children including three sons who came to VA (A:422 ff; B:96): MARY, bapt. 11 Nov 1607, m. 1st, Emanuel Proby, and 2nd, Thomas Nevile; SUSANNA, 2nd dau., m. Thomas Pierson of Wisbeach in the Isle of Ely, Gent; THOMAS, 1st son, m. twice, but d. s.p., JOHN, came to VA, but ret, to Eng., where he d. 1680; EDWARD, d. c1653, came to VA; ANNE, 3rd dau., bapt. 26 May 1619, m. Stephen Jackson of London, merchant; ELIZABETH, bapt. 30 Aug 1620, m. William Beare, Minister of Cowley near Colnbrook; HERBERT, d. young; ADAM, 5th son, d. unm. c1647 as he was about to embark for VA; ROBERT, 4th son, bapt. 22 Feb 1617, d. 1702, m. and had issue; WILLIAM, 6th son, bapt. 26 Dec 1622, d. unm., a merchant in Spain; ESTHER, b. 1623, d. 1625; RICHARD, bapt. 11

Feb 1624, m. and had issue; RACHEL, b. 1626, d. 1633; ARNOLD, 8th son, bapt. 1627, bur. 1634; THEODORICK, bapt. 16 Jan 1629, came to VA; and JOAN AMY, b. 1631, d. 1632.

6. GEORGE BLAND, son of Thomas (3), was b. c1598, age 4 in 1602. He was buried at St. Antholin's on 10 June 1648. He was the father of (A:422): THOMAS, named in his grandfather's will on 18 Nov 1617.

7. JOHN BLAND, of the Old Navy Office, Mark Lane, London, 2nd son of John (5) and Susanna, d. 8 June 1680, and was buried 12 June at St. Olave's, Hart St. He m. Sarah, dau. of Giles Green of Affington. She d. 4 March 1712 (A:423).

John Bland d. leaving a will dated 3 May 1680 and proved 23 June 1680, naming his wife and Thomas Povey as execs. He named his dau.-in-law Frances Bland and grandson John Bland (B:97 cites *GGE* 1:814).

John and Sarah were the parents of (A:423; b:96): JOHN, eldest son, d. 11 Jan 1659, age 13; GILES, settled on the James River in VA, m. and had issue; and THOMAS, bur. 21 Nov 1654, age 5.

8. EDWARD BLAND of Lion's Creek, James River, VA, son of John (5) and Susanna, d. c1653. He m. Jane, dau. of his uncle Gregory Bland. She m. 2nd, John Holmwood, and d. c1664. She was buried at Westover (A:423).

Edward lived some time in Spain before settling in VA, where his estate was called Kimages. He and Jane were the parents of (A:423): EDWARD, b. c1690, m. and had issue.

9. THEODORICK BLAND, 9th son of John (5) and Susanna, was bapt. 16 Jan 1629 at St. Antholine's, and d. 23 April 1671 at Westover, VA. He m. Anna, dau. of Col. Richard Bennet of Wyannock on James River. She m. as her 2nd husband Col. St. Leger Codd of "Wickacoma" [Wicomico?], and d. at Warton Creek in MD in Nov 1687 (A:424).

Theodorick Bland was a merchant at St. Lucar in Spain and later in VA, where he lived at Westover on the James River in Charles City Co. He was a member of the Council in Virginia (A:424).

Theodorick and Anne were the parents of (A:425): THEODORICK, b. Feb 1663 at Westover, where he d. Nov 1700, m. and had issue; RICHARD, b. at Berkeley's near Westover 11 Aug 1665, m. and had issue; JOHN, b. 8 Feb 1681 at Scarboro, d. 14 Nov 1787 at Ifford, Essex, m. and had issue.

10. THOMAS BLAND of London, Gent., almost certainly son of George (6), named in his grandfather's will on 18 Nov 1617 and d. by Jan 1674/5.

Thomas Bland d. leaving a will dated 30 Oct 1674 and proved 29 Jan 1674. He named his grandchildren, Jane and dau. Sarah Moyser, grandson Joseph Day, dau. Sarah wife of Joseph Day, and son Richard (*GGE* 1:814, cites PCC Dycer 2).

Thomas was the father of: RICHARD; SARAH, m. Joseph Day; and prob. THOMAS, who settled in MD.

11. THOMAS BLAND of London, merchant, is prob. a son of Thomas (10) as he named a sister Sarah Day in his will.

He is possibly the Thomas Bland who settled in MD. Thomas Bland of CV Co., Gent., immigrated c1672 (MPL 17:56). He m. as her third husband, Damaris [-?-], widow of Nicholas Wyatt. She was an approved midwife, and came to MD from VA with Wyatt and her dau. by a previous marriage (ARMD 66:xxiv).

He proved his rights to land in AA Co. in 1680 (MPL WC#2:310). He was in AA Co. by 12 June 1677 when he witnessed a deed (AALR IH#1:22). On 8 June 1697 he purchased 60 a. Crouch's Triangle from Joseph Crouch of AA Co. (AALR WT#1:18).

Thomas Bland d. leaving a will 25 Jan 1700 and proved 13 Jan 1701. He named his cousin Sarah, wife of Lawrence Pendrill, who were to inherit all his lands in AA Co., MD, and who were to be his execs. He named his sister Sarah Day, the two daus. of his bro., Sarah and Margaret Bland, and also Mary Kermish (or Keemish). Anthony Wells, Edward Grove, George Clinton, and Anthony Wells, Jr. witnessed the will (AWPL:75).

Unplaced:

BLAND, THOMAS, Citizen and Iron-Monger of London, d, leaving a will dated 28 July 1631 and proved 6 Sep 1631. He named his wife Rebecca, son John, brother John, and mother Mary Bland. He named his niece Abigail, dau. of his sister Joan, his kinsman Esdras Bland, his apprentice Robert Wakelyn, Rev. Mr. Shute, Mr. James the curate. He also named friend Robert Gosnold in Abchurch Lane, and the poor of All Saints Barking. His wife and son were residuary legatees, and his brother John was named exec. He also named his sister's children: Emanuel, Samuel, Hester, and Robert Demetrius. Richard Haten, Robert Waklinn, and John Heath, scrivener, witnessed the will (VGEW:257 cites [PCC?] St. John, 101).

THE FRANCIS BOARDMAN FAMILY

Boardman/Bordeman/Bordman/Bordmane Entries in the Parish Church of Gorton (*LPRS* 47). The entries were not strictly chronological.

Baptisms
Samuel, son of Hugh the Younger, 9 May 1641.
John, son of Hugh, 30 May 1652.
Thomas, son of Hugh of Openshaw, 23 Jan 1654/5.
Elizabeth, dau. of Hugh of Openshaw, 14 June 1659.
Mary, dau. of Hugh of Openshaw, 14 June 1659.
Sarah, dau. of John of Ardwick, 1 Jan 1659/60.
Mary, dau. of Samuel of Gorton, 16 June 1667.
[-?-], son of Samuel of Gorton, 25 June 1669.
Elizabeth, dau. of Thomas of Gorton, 1 Jan 1680.
Elizabeth, dau. of Thomas of Gorton, 1 Jan 1680/1.
Esther, dau. of Thomas of Gorton, 1 Feb 1686/7.

Robert, son of Thomas of Redish Greene, yeoman, 12 March 1686/7.
Elizabeth, dau. of Edward of Gorton, whitster, 3 April 1687.
Mary, dau. of Thomas of Gorton, yeoman, 24 Oct 1689.
Martha, dau. of Edward of Gorton, 29 May 1692.
Samuel, son of Samuel of Gorton, 14 March 1694.
Jenna, dau. of Samuel of Gorton, (b. 1673) bapt. 30 May 1695.
Francis, son of Samuel of Gorton, (b. 1675), bapt. 20 March 1695.
John, son of Thomas of Gorton, (b. 1676), bapt. 31 Dec 1696.
Elizabeth, dau. of Samuel of Gorton, (b. 1677), bapt. 20 May 1695.
Ann, dau. of Richard of Openshaw, 13 June 1697.
Martha, dau. of Richard of Openshaw, 5 March 1698/9.

Marriages
None found.

Burials
John, son of Hugh, 31 July 1650.
Hugh, son of Hugh, 1 Sep 1651.
[-?-], infant son of Hugh of Gorton, 7 June 1653.
Mary, wife of Hugh of Openshaw, 17 Nov 1657.
Elizabeth, wife of Hugh of Openshaw, 10 July 1658.
Michael of Gorton, 31 March 1664.
Margaret, wife of Edward of Falofelde, 19 Feb 1669.
Mary, dau. of Samuel of Openshaw, 3 May 1679.
Mary, dau. of Thomas, 29 Oct 1689.
Hugh of Gorton, 9 Aug 1694.
Samuel, of Gorton, 31 Dec 1697.
Anne, wife of Thomas, 10 Feb 1697.
Martha, dau. of Richard of Openshaw, 22 July 1701.

1. HUGH BOARDMAN, sometimes called the Younger, after 1653, called of Gorton, and later called of Openshaw, was bur. 9 Aug 1694. He m. 1st, Mary [-?-], buried 17 Nov 1657, and 2nd, Elizabeth [-?-], bur. 10 July 1658.
  Hugh was probably the father of (A): SAMUEL, bapt. 9 May 1641; JOHN, bur. 31 July 1650; HUGH, bur. 1 Sep 1651; JOHN, bapt. 30 May 1652 (perhaps the infant son bur. 7 June 1653); THOMAS, bapt. 23 Jan 1654/5; ELIZABETH (twin), bapt. 14 June 1659; and MARY (twin), bapt. 14 June 1659.

2. SAMUEL BOARDMAN, son of Hugh (1) of Gorton, was bapt. 9 May 1641, and was buried 31 Dec 1697. He was the father of: MARY, bapt. 6 June 1667, bur. 3 May 1679; [-?-], son, bapt. 25 June 1669; SAMUEL, bapt. 14 March 1694.; JENNA, b. 1673, bapt. 30 May 1695; FRANCIS, b. 1675, bapt. 20 March 1695; and ELIZABETH, b. 1677, bapt. 20 May 1695.

3. THOMAS BOARDMAN, of Gorton, and Redish Greene, son of Hugh (1) of Gorton, was bapt. 23 Jan 1654/5. He m. Anne [-?-], who was buried 10 Feb 1697.

Thomas was probably the father of: ELIZABETH, bapt. 1 Jan 1680; ELIZABETH, bapt. 1 Jan 1680/1; ESTHER, bapt. 1 Feb 1686/7; and ROBERT, bapt. 12 March 1686/7; MARY, bapt. 24 Oct 1689, bur. 29 Oct 1689.; and JOHN, b. 1676, bapt. 31 Dec 1696.

4. FRANCIS BOARDMAN, son of Samuel (2), was b. 1675 and bapt. 20 March 1695 in Gorton, Lancs. He d. by Aug 1727 in SO Co., MD. He m. Sarah [-?-].

On 24 Oct 1699, Francis Boardman, age 21 and 4 mos., was bound to Henry Brown, master of the *Loyalty*, which was headed for VA or MD (*PTAT*:192).

In 1722 Graves Jarrett willed Hoggs Down to his wife Mary, and then to Graves Boardman, son of Francis Boardman (*WILR*:203).

Ja. Mackmorie and Thomas Collier appraised the goods and chattels of Francis Boardman on 30 Aug 1727, stating they were worth £48.14.5. Giles Bashshaw and Thomas Bashshaw signed as next of kin. Sarah Boardman, admx., filed the inventory on the same day (MINV 13:338).

Sarah Boardman, admx., filed an account of Francis Boardman's estate on 22 Dec 1728. An inventory of £48.14.5 was cited, and payments came to £7.10.6 (MDAD 9:306).

Francis was the heir to property in England, according to a notice was published some years after his death. "Francis Boardman, son of Samuel Boardman of Gorton, Lancs., came to MD, several years ago, married and had children. He has inherited a considerable estate in England, and should apply to John Eden of SM Co." (*AMG* 14 July 1768).

Francis and Sarah were the parents of (*ESVR* 1:164; *WILR*:247): GRAVES, b. by 1722; SAMUEL, d. intestate by Jan 1746; and SARAH, b. 6 Oct 1725 in Stepney Parish, WI Co.

5. GRAVES BOARDMAN, son of Francis (4), m. Susannah [-?-].

On 24 May 1745 Graves Boardman and his wife Susannah sold 50 a. Hogg's Down to David Polk.

On 27 Jan 1746 Graves Boardman sold to John Williams 80 a. of Little Belean, which Benjamin Tull had sold in 1729 to Samuel Boardman; Samuel Boardman had since d. intestate (*WILR*:246-247).

On 13 Jan 1747 he sold 50 a. of Hogg's Down, now called Goslee's Content, to Thomas Gosley (*WILR*:204).

THE ROBERT BONE FAMILY

Refs.: A: Data generously mader available by Greg Burton. B: Register of Saint Bridget Beckermet, Cumberland, England, FHC Film 0090563.

1. ROBERT BONE was born in Sella Fields, Co. Cumberland. He married Ann Fletcher on 11 June 1783 in Saint James, Whitehaven, Cumberland, England (B).

Robert and Anne were the parents of (A): JOSEPH, bapt. 26 Dec 1785; ROBERT, bapt. 18 Nov 1787; ANN, b., 6 Sep 1789; FLETCHER, twin, b. 28 Oct 1791; JOHN, twin, b. 28 Oct 1791; WILLIAM, b. 12 March 1795; and JANE, b. 28 Dec 1789.

2. FLETCHER BONE, son of Robert (1) and Anne, was born 28 Oct 1791 in Sella Fields, Co. Cumberland, and d. 23 Sep 1859 in BA Co., MD (B: Sun, obit). He m. Isabella [-?-], b. in Eng., d. 1873. Both are buried at Waugh Church, Long Green Pike, BA Co.

Their tombstones at Waugh Church read: "In Memory of Fletcher Bone Died Sep. 23, 1859 aged 65 years and 11 months "Dear wife, weep not for me For all your tears are vain Prepare to meet your God That we meet again." "Isabella wife of Fletcher Bone born in England died in Baltimore 1873."

Fletcher and Isabella were the parents of (A): MARY JANE, b. 9 Feb 1826, d. 5 Feb 1912, at Notchcliff, BA Co.; WILLIAM, b. c1829, d. 20 Oct 1888; FLETCHER, Jr., b. c1831; AGNES REBECCA, b. 1835, m. [-?-] Langley; ELIZABETH, d. after 1868, m. John H. Durham on 17 July 1846; and ANN, d. after 1888, m. [-?-] Durham.

3. WILLIAM BONE, son of Robert (1), was born on 12 March 1795 in England, Cumberland County, Sella Fields (B). He m. Jane Thorton on 4 Dec 1819 in BA Co., MD.

William and Jane (Thorton) were the parents of: ROBERT, b. 7 June 1820, bapt. 13 Oct 1821 at St. John's & St. George's Parish; ANN, b. 21 Aug 1822., bapt 3 June 1823 at St. Paul's Episcopal Chruch, Baltimore; and ELIZABETH, b. 27 May 1824.

THE BOOTH FAMILY

Refs.: A: Llewellyn A. Digges. "The Pye Line of Descent." Typescript, MHS.

1. Major JOHN BOOTH of Brienton, Co. Hereford, d. 1690. He m. Catherine Broughton, d. 1693. Both are buried east of the vestry in the church yard of St. Michael Brienton. They were the parents of (A): Capt. EDWARD RUDHALL, d. 29 Oct 1685; CHARLES; and JAMES.

2. CHARLES BOOTH, son of Major John (1) and Catherine, m. 3 Feb 1701, at St. Gervais, France (where many English Catholics had fled), Barbara Symes, dau. of Jacques Symes of St. Margaret's, Westminster, and his wife Elizabeth Neville (dau. of William Neville).

Two sons of Charles and Barbara, James and Edward, provided for their nephew Edward H. Pye, son of Charles Pye of Glymont, CH Co., MD (A).

Charles and Barbara were the parents of eight children, including (A): MARY ELIZABETH, b. 20 Dec 1701, m. **Charles Pye of MD** (See **The Pye Family** in *British Roots*, vol. 1); JAMES, d. March 1774; WILLIAM, d. c1794; BARBARA, d. 19 May 1799; EDWARD RUDHALL, d. 1800.

THE BOWDLE FAMILY
A Tentative Reconstruction

Refs.: A; Ivor J. Sanders. *English Baronies*. New York: Oxford University Press, 1960. B: Transcript of will of John Bowdler, C: *HSPV* 28:63. D: Gordon Gyll, Esq. "Notes on the Surname of Bowdler." *The Gen.* 1:279-285. E: Bowdle/Bowdler Chart compiled by Thomas N. Bowdle of Walnut Creek, based on: a) "Bowdler of Shrewsbury" *HSPV* ? (1623):58, 59, 61, 62; b) John Bowdler, Esq. *The Bowdler Family of Shrewsbury*, and item D above.

NB: Early Generations from Visitation pedigrees, which usually contain no dates or citations, must be supported with documentary evidence.

Generations 1-5

1. BALDWIN, Castellan of Montgomery, Lieutenant of Roger of Montgomery, Earl of Shrewsbury, was the father of (E): BALDWIN de BOLLERS; and ODE de HODENEL.

2. BALDWIN de BOLLERS, son of Baldwin (1), was said to be a Baron in 1165 (but he is not listed as such in A). He m. Sybilla de Falaise, niece of Henry I (E). Nothing is known of her ancestry, but she was probably not a dau. of William de Falaise, Lord of Stogursey, Somerset (A:22).

      Baldwin and Sybilla were the parents of (A:22; X): ROBERT; BALDWIN, d. 1209; and MAUD, m. Richard Fitz-Urse.

3. ROBERT de BOLLERS, Baron of Montgomery, son of Baldwin (2) and Sybilla, d. 1203. He m. Hillaria de Trussbot, living 1219. Sanders states that Robert d. s.p. 1203, and Hillaria d. s.p. 1241. Nevertheless, they are stated to have been the parents of (E): PHILIP; WILLIAM; ROBERT of Smethcote; and RICHARD.

4. RICHARD de WILDERLEY, son of Robert (3) and Hillaria, was the father of (E): Sir STEPHEN.

5. Sir STEPHEN BOWDLER, Kt., of Hope Bowdler, son of Richard (4), as Stephen de Hope called Stephen de Bullers, conformed the grant made by his father Richard de Wildredeley [*sic*] (E: cites C:50-51). Sir Stephen was the father of (E): JANE, m. Richard Higgins of Stretton; JOHN; and HUGH, living 1308.

Generations 6-10

6. JOHN BOWDLER of Hope Bowdler, son of Sir Stephen (5), was the father of (E): JOHN.

7. JOHN BOWDLER of Hope Bowdler, son of John (6), was the father of (E): STEPHEN.

8. STEPHEN BOWDLER, of Hope Bowdler, son of John (7), was the father of (E): Sir WILLIAM.

9. Sir WILLIAM BOWDLER, Kt., of Hope Bowdler, son of Stephen (8), m. Anne, dau. of Sir Philip Grant, Kt. They were the parents of (E): Sir STEPHEN, m. Joanne, dau. of Sir Nicholas Brinsbow, Kt.; and poss. THOMAS.

10. THOMAS BOWDLER of Hope Bowdler, poss. son of Sir William (9), is not shown in the Visitation, but is shown in the pedigree prepared for John Bowdler (E). He was the father of WILLIAM.

Generations 11-15

11. WILLIAM BOWDLER of Hope Bowdler, son of Thomas (10), was the father of (E): HUGH; and JANE, m. John Botfield, who took the name of Thyn.

12. HUGH BOWDLER of Hope Bowdler, son of William (11), was the father of (D:279): WILLIAM.

13. JANE BOWDLER, dau. of William (11), m. John Botfield, who took the name of Thyn. They were the parents of (E): THOMAS, m. Jane, dau. of John Hygons-Stretton; and RALPH, d. 1515.

14. WILLIAM BOWDLER of Wolstason, son of Hugh (12), m. Ann Thyn, dau. of Ralph Thyn. They were the parents of (D:279): THOMAS; and ROGER.

15. RALPH THYN, son of John and Jane (13) Bowdler, D. 1515. He was the father of (D): WILLIAM, Lancaster Herald in 1602 (D); THOMAS, d. 1546; and ANN, m. William Bowdler (14 above), her first cousin once removed.

16. ROGER BOWDLER of Wolstason, son of William (14) and Ann, m. Jane, dau. of Thomas Haynes of Stretton. They were the parents of (D:279-280; X): WILLIAM, m. Eliz. Gease and had issue; THOMAS, m. Catherine Brown; RICHARD, m. and had issue; and JOHN.

17. JOHN BOWDLER of Shrewsbury, son of Roger (16) and Jane, d. by 1594. He m. 1st, Catherine, dau. of Thomas Montgomery of Shrewsbury, and 2nd, Elizabeth, dau. of Adam Waring of Charlton, Shrewsbury (E). Elizabeth was the sister of Richard Waring, whose son Basil who had a son **Sampson Waring, who came to MD**. Sampson Waring and Thomas Bowdle, son of Andrew (see below), are second cousins.

John Bowdler of Shrewsbury, d. leaving a will dated 23 May 30 Elizabeth, and proved 16 Feb 1594. He named his son Samuel, wife Elizabeth, his daus. Susan and Mary, not yet 20, son Andrew ("if he take good ways, and be ruled by his good friends and brothers"), not yet 20, son Roger, not yet 20, son William, Anne (dau. of son Thomas), the children of son William, Margery Hughes, and cousins Richard Harding and Johan Tibbey, and the children of the testator's brother Richard. Sons William and

Samuel were to be executors. Friends and kinsmen John Brooke, Esq., Roger Pope, Esq., and Richard Waring, Gent., to be overseers. George Phes [*sic*] the elder, Thomas Browne, draper, William Montgomery, and Edward Phillips witnessed the will. A codicil dated 14 Oct 159-? names a son Adam (B).

By Catherine, John was the father of (D:280): WILLIAM, m. Elis. Meighman.

By Elizabeth, John was the father of (D:280): MARY, m. Thomas Hunt of Newcastle; SAMUEL, d. July 1631, m. and had issue; ROGER, m. [-?-] Lloyd; ANDREW; and SUSAN, m. [-?-] Langley; THOMAS (had a dau. Anne); and ADAM.

Generation 16

18. ANDREW BOWDLER, son of John (17) and Elizabeth, went to Co. Kerry, Ireland (C:280). He m., perhaps in 1599, Joan, dau. of John Bury of Ballybegan, Ireland. Andrew was a High Sheriff., tax collector and leaseholder in Co. Kerry from 1610 to 1612.

Andrew and Joan were the parents of (D:280; X): THOMAS; and JOHN.

Generation 17

19. THOMAS BOWDLE, son of Andrew (18) and Joan, may be the Thomas Bowdle who dropped the final R from his name and came to MD c1658, and settled in TA Co., MD.

Francis Armstrong entered rights for transporting Thomas Bowdlell [*sic*] and others on 21 April 1662 (MPL 5:64).

He m. by 1666 Jone, widow of Dr. Stephen Clifton of CV Co., and dau. of William Turner of CV Co. Other sources state that he m. 1st, Joanna Loftus, and 2nd, Phoebe Loftus. He received two land grants from Lord Baltimore: Bowdle's Chance and Bowdle's Choice (E).

THE BRANTHWAYT FAMILY

Refs.: A: "Branthwayt of Carlinghill." *CWFO*:16. B: *AWLH*.

The William Branthwayt Family

ARMS: Or, on a bend Sable, three lions passant guardant of the field. **CREST**: On a rock, an eagle rising, all proper. (Respite given for proof of these arms, but no proof made) (A). However, the arms were registered at the College of Arms in 1632 with a label of three points and the eagle in the crest tinctured Argent (B:49-50).

1. EDWARD BRANTHWAYT of Carlinghill, Westmorland, d. 1629. He m. [-?-], dau. of [-?-] Calvert of Kiplin, Co. Ebor [York]. He and his wife had at least one son (A): ROBERT.

2. ROBERT BRANTHWAYT, son of Edward (1), d. 1645. His first wife was [-?-] Poultney, and his second was Anne, dau. of William Carter of St. Martin's in the Fields "in the suburb's of London" (A).

Robert was a Gentleman Jailer of the Tower of London, temp. James I, and Secretary to Sir Richard Weston, K.G., Lord Treasurer of England for the Irish Affairs. Branthwayt also served as constable of Dublin Castle (A; B).

Robert and Anne were the parents of (A): ROBERT; OLIVER, d. unm.; WILLIAM, "died beyond sea;" ELEANOR, d. young; and PHILADELPHIA, d. young.

3. ROBERT BRANTHWAYT of Carlinghill, Westmorland, son of Robert (2) and Anne, was b. c1624, and was age 40 on 22 March 1664. He m. Elizabeth, dau. of Richard Burton, and sister of Sir Thomas Burton of Brampton. They were the parents of (A); ANNE, b. c1663, age 1 year and 3 mos. on 22 March 1664.

4. WILLIAM BRANTHWAYT, son of Robert (2) and Anne, is stated in Foster to have "died beyond sea (A)." Actually he came to MD. See his entry in the *BDML*.

THE BRITTON FAMILY

1. NICHOLAS BRITTON of Thost, Co. Devon, on 9 Sep 1700 bound himself to serve Edward Eaton of Ratorios Tower, as a servant for 4 years on Eaton's Plantation in MD (AALR WT#2:71). He is prob. the Nicholas "Bratten [*sic*]" who m. Mary Wood on 21 Feb 1709 in All Hallows Parish, AA Co. (*AACR*:25).

In 1699 he gave a power of attorney to Isaac Winchester of TA Co. to collect debts for goods Britton sold for Charles Jones and Co. transported on the *Resolution* (AALR WT#1:108).

He had no land in AA Co. and left no estate in MD.

2. NICHOLAS BRITTAIN, relationship to Nicholas (1) not established, was b. c1735. He gave his age as 27, when he deposed on 10 Sep 1762 (BAEJ: Charles Ridgely, Ridgely's Goodwill).

He m. by 20 Feb 1761, Alathea, widow of James Finley of BA Co. (MDAD 47:155).

On 12 March 1763: Avarilla Boring, widow, conv. to Nicholas Britton her right of dower, 1/3 interest in Boring's Forest, Boring's Gift and Cuckoldmaker's Hazard (BALR B#L:116).

THE BROOKES FAMILY

Refs.: A: "Brook." *Familiae Minorum Gentium.* III 919.

1. PERCIVAL BROOKES of York, merchant, d. leaving a will dated 28 Feb 1616, proved 9 Nov 1629. He was the father of (A): JAMES; BENJAMIN; LEONARD; FRANCIS; WILLIAM; CHRISTOPHER; THOMAS; MARY, m. [-?-] Jacques; ELIZABETH, m. William Nicholson; and SARAH.

2. JAMES BROOKES of York, merchant, son of Percival (1), died 1675, age 81, and was buried at Aldborough. He m. Priscilla Jackson, who survived him, and resided at Howgrave, where she made her will on 11 Dec 1691 (A).

James Brookes was Alderman and Lord Mayor of York in 1651, He bought Ellenthorpe (A).

James and Priscilla were the parents of (A): Sir JOHN, Bart., d. 1691; and ANNE, m. Sir William Wyvill (ancestors of **William Wyvil who settled in MD**. See The Wyvil Family in vol. 1 of British Roots).

THE DAVID BROWN FAMILY

1. [-?-] BROWN was the father of: DAVID; JANET, m. Archibald Erskine; ELIZA; and poss. JAMES; JOHN; and ALEXANDER.

2. DAVID BROWN of SO Co., bro. of Janet and Eliza, d. in SO Co. by Sep 1697.

As Col. David Brown, he and Roger Woolford were named overseers of the will of Owen Maragh of SO Co. on 18 March 1681/2 (MWB 6:45).

David Brown d. leaving a will dated 19 July 1697 and proved 17 Sep 1697. He named Thomas Wilson; the College at Glasgow (to have money to support any of his relations to be educated therein); James Browne; Margaret and Mary Erskine daus. of his sister; sister Eliza; John Brown; Alexander Brown (to have 80 a. The Meadows, 600 a. Thornton, 300 a. Hachita, and Jeshimon. If Alexander Brown failed to cultivate the land, it was to go to Ephraim Wilson. Abraham Wilson, Thomas Wilson, Jr., and Margaret and Mary Erskine were named execs. (MWB 6:150).

3. JANET BROWN, sister of Col. David and Eliza, m. Archibald Erskine who d. by May 1687.

On 7 Jan 1686/7 Archibald Erskine of Snow Hill, SO Co. made his will, naming his wife Janet as sole legatee, and appointing his brother David Brown as exec. (MWB 4:256).

Archibald and Janet were the parents of: MARGARET; and MARY.

4. MARY ERSKINE, dau. of Archibald and Janet (3), and niece of Col. David Brown, m. [-?-] Brown, and was the mother of: GEORGE Brown of Edinburgh (PCLR DD#4:631).

THE JOHN BROWN FAMILY
A Tentative Reconstruction

Refs.: A: Evelyn Ballenger. *Warfield Records*. Annapolis: Thomas Ord Warfield, 1970. B: James Wade Emison, *1962 Supplement to the Emison Families Revised (1954)*. Vincennes: The Author, 1962. C: IGI International Genealogy Index, 1988 ed. D: George Sherwood, *American Colonists in English Records*.

Generation 1

1. JOHN BROWN of London is stated by Emison to have been the father of four sons who grew to maturity (C): THOMAS, bapt. 10 Sep 1622 at St. Margaret's, Westminster); poss. JOHN, bapt. 20 Jan 1625 at St. Margaret's Westminster, prob. d. young; Capt. JOHN of London, mariner, bapt. 16 April 1626 at St. Margaret's Westminster); Capt. PEREGRINE; and JAMES "FRISTRE? [or FRISBIE?]."

Generation 2

2. THOMAS BROWN, son of John (1), was bapt. 10 Sep 1622 at St. Margaret's, Westminster, and d. in Md. His widow m. 2nd, William Hopkins.

On 20 Feb 1659 Thomas Browne was granted 100 a. called Brownston on the north side of Severn (AALR IH#2:212).

William Hopkins d. in AA Co., MD, leaving a will dated 26 July 1702 and proved 6 Aug 1702. He named his wife's eldest son and her grandsons William and Henry Lewis. He also named Thomas, Eliza, John, and William Hopkins Jobson, children of John and Ann Jobson, Ann Jobson was to be extx. Patrick Ogilvie, Jas. Barley, Geo. Hodges, and A. Cockett witnessed the will (MWB 11:212).

Thomas Brown had at least one son: THOMAS.

3. Capt. JOHN BROWN, mariner, son of John (1), of London, was bapt. 16 April 1626 at St. Margaret's Westminster, Mddx (C).

Ballenger cites the *Archives of Md.* to show that he and Capt. Peregrine Brown were brothers.

John "Browne" of AA Co. d. leaving a will dated 31 March 1688 and proved 19 Jan 1689. He named his wife Mary as extx. She was to have his estate real and personal but if she remarried, she was to have one-half, and the rest was to go to William Hopkins in trust for William Green, son of testator's dau. Mary Green. If Mary and William Green both died without issue, the land was to descend to his cousin Thomas Browne. William Hopkins, Edward Branch and Thomas Brown witnessed the will (MWB 1:320).

John Brown is stated by Emison to have been the father of at least two daughters: MARY, m. [-?-] and had a son: William Green; and ELINOR, m. Capt. Richard Warfield.

4. PEREGRINE BROWN, son of John (1), is probably the Peregrine Brown who m. Sarah [-?-].

Peregrine and Sarah were the parents of the following children, bapt. at St. Dunstan's, Stepney (LDS Controlled Extraction Programs of St. Dunstan's Parish Records CO55766, 55767, 55768): ELIZABETH, bapt. 4 Oct 1640; RICHARD, bapt. 8 Dec 1642; MARTHA, bapt. 21 Jan 1649; PEREGRINE, bapt. 8 May 1651; PEREGRINE, bapt. 9 Dec 1652; JAMES, bapt. 29 July 1655; and MARY, bapt. 23 July 1657.

Generation 3

5. THOMAS BROWN, son of Thomas (2), m. Katherine (poss. Summerland), although Emison states he m. Katherine Harris, dau of William. Even so, his will mentions a brother-in-law John Summerland (B:164).

On 26 Feb 1674 Thomas Brown, son of Thomas, for a valuable consideration, released and forever quitclaimed to his father-in-law William Hopkins any part of the estate of Brown's father, Thomas Brown, dec. (AALR IH#2:216). On 9 March 1674 Thomas Brown, son of Thomas, dec., conv. 100 a. Brownston to William Hopkins (AALR IH#2:212).

On 20 June 1686 Thomas "Browne" of Severn River and William Hopkins witnessed the will of John Summerland of Severn River, AA Co., who named among other children, a dau. Katherine Brown (MWB 4:234).

On 4 Aug 1692 Thomas Browne conv. 98 a. Brown's Chance (patented by Brown on 1 Oct 1687) to Daniel McComas. Brown's wife Katherine released her right of dower (AALR IH#2:98).

On 13 Sep 1692 Thomas Brown conv. to Michael Taylor 100 a. Friendship originally granted to Thomas Brown and William Hopkins on 10 Aug 1683 and conv. by deed of gift from William Hopkins to Brown. Thomas Brown's wife Katherine released her right of dower (AALR IH#2:43).

Thomas and Katherine were the parents of (B:164-165): THOMAS; JOHN, m. Rebecca Yieldhall; VALENTINE, m. Elizabeth Pierpoint; HANNAH; and JOSHUA, m. Margaret Chew.

6. PEREGRINE BROWNE son of Peregrine (4), was bapt. 9 Dec 1652 at St, Dunstan's, Stepney. He is almost certainly the Peregrine Brown who d. by Aug 1713. He m. 1st, Mary, probably sister of James Frisby, and 2nd, Margaret Brock, on 25 Dec 1692 at St. Dunstan's. Stepney (*STDU* 2:193). Margaret was a dau. of Joseph Brock.

Peregrine Brown of St. Catherine Creechurch, on 8 Dec 1703 deposed that having m. a sister of James Frisby of CE Co. who died leaving a will dated 10 Sep 1702, and arranged for the education of Frisby's sons Thomas, James, and Peregrine, he could attest to Frisby's signature on the will (*AWPL*:83).

On 22 April 17--, John Cary of London, merchant, John Burridge of Lyme Regis, Dorset, and George Cole of London, merchant, conv. 600 a. Chilbury to Peregrine Brown of London, merchant (BALR TR#RA:436).

Peregrine Browne of the City of London, merchant, d. leaving a will dated 23 Feb 1711/2, proved 10 Aug 1713. He left all his plantations in MD called Turkey Point and Ratcliffe Cross to his wife Margaret, and named his children Peregrine, Joseph, John, and Margaret Brown, and Elizabeth Duddlestone. His father-in-law, Joseph Brocke, was to be overseer. The will was witnessed by Wh. Kennett, John Nottingham, and Tho. Kilner (D:167).

On 30 Sep 1712 Peregrine Browne, Sr., was granted admin. of the goods of Peregrine Brown, Jr., who d. in MD, a bachelor. On 17 Oct 1713, administration on the estate of Peregrine, Jr. was granted to Margaret, the widow and extx. of Peregrine Brown, Sr. (*AWAP*:42)

Peregrine Brown was the father of the following children, all bapt. at St. Dunstan's, Stepney (Controlled Extraction Programs of St. Dunstan's, Stepney, Mddx 55:768, 55:771): (by Mary), JAMES, bapt. 22 March 1681; MARY, bapt. 27 Feb 1683; FRISBY, bapt. 6 Feb 1688; PEREGRINE, bapt. 30 April 1689; and JOHN, bapt. 8 Oct 1690; (by Margaret Brock), JOSEPH, bapt. 20 Sep 1694; ELIZABETH, bapt. 1 Jan 1695; and MARGARET, bapt. 14 July 1697.

Generation 4

7. PEREGRINE BROWN, son of Peregrine (6) Brown and his first wife Mary was bapt. 30 April 1689. (He was bur. in St. Paul's Parish, KE Co., MD, on 14 Feb 1711 (*ESVR* 1:15). He probably d. in MD a bachelor. In Sep 1712 admin. was granted to his father Peregrine Brown, but the elder Peregrine Brown died, and in Oct 1713, admin. was granted to Margaret, widow of the father of Peregrine, Jr. (*AWAP*:42). Peregrine Brown, Jr.'s estate was admin. on 19 April 1713 by Col. Thomas Smith, of KE Co., and Richard Bennett, of QA Co. (INAC 36A:187). His estate was admin. again c1717 by the same admins. (INAC 38B:112).

8. JOHN BROWN, son of Peregrine (6) Brown and his first wife Mary, was bapt. 8 Oct 1690, and stated he was "of the Kingdom of England," when he m. in Shrewsbury Parish, KE Co., Mrs. Rachel Scott, widow of Col. Edward Scott, on 28 Oct 1726 (*ESVR* 2:2). He d. in Shrewsbury Parish, KE Co., on 9 Jan 1728/9.

John Brown's estate was inventoried on 3 June 1729. Next of kin were James Cruckshank and Gideon Pearce. Rachel Brown, admx., filed the inventory on 13 Aug 1729 (MINV 15:158).

On 15 Dec 1729 Rachel Brown of KE Co., widow, conv. to Samuell Wright, the dower or third part of a tract left by Col. Edward Scott in his last will to his son William Scott called Stepney Heath Manner, and Samuell Wright the possessor of the other 2/3 parts, as it was allotted by Edward Scott admin. of the sd. Col. Edward Scott to the afsd. Rachel Brown (KELR JS#X:399).

On 28 Oct 1730 Rachel Brown of KE Co., widow, John Tilden, Gent., and his wife Katherine, and Isabella Blay, spinster, conv. to William Pearce, Gent., land which William Blay, late of afsd. county, Gent., had owned at the time of his death: Blays Parke resurveyed as William..., Howells Addition and James' Inspection, 880 a., and one other tract in BA Co., called Dale Town, 300 a. and including within the survey 400 a. out of a patent formerly surveyed by Thomas Howell called Howells Out Lands of 700 a., ... and other land (KELR JS#16:73).

On 15 Nov 1731 Henry Knock of KE Co., and his wife Susanna, conv. to Mrs. Rachel Brown of the same county, widow, 11 a. of a tract formerly called Bennetts Hope, now called Rachel's Farm, part of a tract called Childs Harber but now called Hamshore, 11 a. (KELR JS#16:185).

On 23 June 1732 Aquilla Paca of BA Co., Gent., and his wife Rachel, conv. to Peregrine Brown, son of the same Rachel by her late husband John Brown, late of SO Co., Esq., dec., a tract called Bennets Hope and now upon a resurvey thereof in the name of the same Rachel called Rachel Farm, 345 a.; also a tract called Blays Range, 100 a.; also part of a tract called Childs Harbour now Hampshire which the same Rachel purchased of Henry Knock; also the tract called Philips Neglect, 400 a., excepting 89 a. sold to Henry Knock out of the tract called Rachels Farm (KELR JS#16:237).

John and Rachel were the parents of: PEREGRINE, b. 1 Oct 1727.

9. JOSEPH BROWN, son of Peregrine (6) and Margaret (Brock), was bapt. 20 Sep 1694 in London, and was in Philadelphia by 1731.

On 14 Oct 1717 Maurice Burchfield, Surveyor General of His Majesty's Customs in the Southern District of America, and Joseph Brown, late of London, merchant, son and heir of Peregrine Brown, late of London, dec., conv. 400 a. to James Phillips; the deed stated that Peregrine Brown made a will naming wife Margaret as extx.; the following tracts in Maryland were owned by Peregrine Brown at the time of his death: Addition, 400 a.; Bachelor's Addition, 50 a.; Bachelor's Hope, 400 a.; Chilbury, 250 a.; Waters' Neck 100 a. The Maryland Court of Chancery decreed that these tracts should be held to satisfy the debts of Browne (BALR TR#A:485).

On 22 May 1718 Maurice Burchfield, Surveyor General of His Majesty's Customs, and Joseph Browne, late of the City of London, son and heir of Peregrine Brown, late of the City of London, merchant, conv. to Thomas Smith of Chester River 500 a. called Ratcliffe Cross (KELR BC#1:295).

On 3 March 1731 Jos. Brown of the City of Philadelphia, Gent., to Nicholas Riley of KE Co., the sd. Jos. Browne as heir-at-law to his father Peregrine Browne, late of the City of London, merchant, agent to Mrs. Margt. Brown of London, relict and extx. of said Peregrine Brown, a tract called Plum Park (KELR JS#16:235).

THE WESTON BROWNE FAMILY

Refs.: A: "Browne (No. 4)," *HSPV* 13:165-167

Generations 1-5

1. ROBERT BROWNE "in occidentalibus Angliae partibus" married and was the father of at least two children (A:166): RICHARD of Wakefield, Yorks (m. Agnes, dau. and coheir of William Welles, and had one dau. Agnes, who m. William Gargrave, Esq.); and THOMAS.

2. THOMAS BROWNE of Abbotts Rooding, Essex, 2nd son of Robert (1), m. Joanne, sister of John Kirkham of Devonshire, They were the parents of (A:166): THOMAS.

3. THOMAS BROWNE of Langhowse in Abbotts Rooding, son of Thomas (2) and Joanne, m. Mary Carleton, dau. and heiress of Thomas Carleton. They were the parents of (A:166): Sir WESTON; and Sir HUMPHREY, Justice of the Court of Common Pleas, temp Henry VIII.

4. Sir WESTON BROWN of Abbotts Rooding, son of Thomas (3) and Mary, was knighted by the King of Aragon, temp Henry VII. He m. Maude Mordant, dau. of Sir William Mordant of Turvey in Co. Bedford (A:166).

Sir Weston and Maude were the parents of (A:166): JOHN; Sir ANTHONY, m. twice but died s.p.; [-?-], m. John Prior, son of Sir Andrew Prior, Kt.; [-?-], m. [-?-] Smith of Lincolnshire; [-?-], m. [-?-] Cutts of Debden; and [-?-], m. [-?-] Knighton of Suffolk.

5. JOHN BROWNE of Abbotts Rooding, Esq., son of Sir Weston (4) and Maude, m. Etheldred Vere, dau. and coheiress of Henry Vere of Addington, Esq. They were the parents of (A:166): GEORGE; and HENRY, of London, d. 1558, m. and had issue.

Generation 6

6. GEORGE BROWNE of Clovills Hall in Abbots Rooding, Co. Essex, son of John (5) and Ethelred, m. 1st, Elizabeth Leventhorpe, dau. of John Leventhorpe, and 2nd, [-?-] Wilford (A:166).

George and Elizabeth were the parents of (A:166-167): WESTON; JOHN of Wickham Hall, Esq.; ANN, m. Rowland Elliot of Stortford, in Essex or Herts.; ELIZABETH, m. Henry Jernegan, 4th son of Sir George Jernegan of Somerleton, Suffolk.

Generation 7

7. WESTON BROWNE of Rookeswood in Essex, Esq., son of George (6) and Elizabeth, d. 1580. He m. 1st, Mary, dau. of Sir Edward Capell of Hadham. She d. s.p., and he m. 2nd Elizabeth Pawlett, dau. of Giles Pawlett (A:167).

Weston and Elizabeth were the parents of (A:167): ANTHONY, d. s.p.; CATHERINE, m. Nicholas Waldegrave, son of Edward Waldegrave of Borley, Co. Essex (Nicholas and Catherine were the parents of: Frances, d. by 5 April 1641, m. by 1605, Sir Richard Weston, Earl of Portland, from whom descend **Jerome and Frances White** of MD); and JAYNE, m. 1st, Edward Wyatt of Tillingham, Essex, and 2nd, Sir Gamaliel Capell, Kt. (by whom she was the mother of Alice Capell, m. Robert Wiseman, **Passenger on the Ark and the Dove**, and whose descendants settled in MD).

THE BRUCE FAMILY

Refs.: A: Query from Mrs. Nancy J. Ellis of Corona del Mar, CA, in *The Scottish Genealogist*. B: *SOCD*. C: Nancy Jones Ellis, *Norman, Andrew, and Selkirk Bruce in Maryland: Their Ancestors in Scotland and Their Descendants in America*. Laguna Niguel: Royal Literary Publications, 1993.

1. NORMAND BRUCE, mason and burgess of Edinburgh, was b. c1650 and d. betw. 1714 and 1718 in Edinburgh. He m. 1st, Janet Anderson, in Canongate, 1672. He m. 2nd, Christian Law on 29 Nov 1678 in Edinburgh, and 3rd, Elizabeth Gilmore on 17 July 1687 in Edinburgh (C:6).

By Janet Anderson he was the father of (A); WILLIAM, b. 21 July 1672; ELIZABETH, b. 5 April 1674; and MARIA, b. 17 Jan 1678.

Normand and Christian were the parents of (A:7): JOHN, b. 16 Sep 1679; ALEXANDER, b. 28 June 1681; JANET, b. 24 Aug 1683; and CHARLES (or NORMAND), b. 6 Dec 1685.

2. CHARLES BRUCE, glazier, son of Norman (1), d. 1768 in Edinburgh. He m. 3rd, in Edinburgh in 1727, Helen Cleland, dau. of James Cleland, Dean of the Merchant Guild in Edinburgh, and his wife Helen Selkirk, a dau. of James Selkirk, merchant of Edinburgh.

Charles and Helen were the parents of (A): NORMAND, b. 1733; MARGARET, b. 1737, m. Robert Brymer, in 1756; KATHERINE, b. 1740, m. Thomas Herriot in 1762; Capt. JAMES, b. 1742, m. Eupham Spence in 1768; ANDREW, b. 1744; CHARLES, b. 1745; SELKRIG, b. 1751; and (poss.) WILLIAM (in B).

3. NORMAND BRUCE, son of Charles (2) and Helen (Cleland), was b. 1733 in Edinburgh, and came to MD, where he m. Susannah Key.

He was in MD by 2 Nov 1757 when he was listed as a creditor in the estate of Thomas Mattingly of SM Co. (MDAD 41:252). He settled in Washington Co., MD (B).

4. ANDREW BRUCE, son of Charles (2) and Helen (Cleland), was b. 1744 in Edinburgh, came to MD where he m. Barbara Murdoch. He settled in AL Co., MD c1795 (B).

5. SELKRIG BRUCE, dau. of Charles (2) and Helen (Cleland), was b. 1751, m. c1774 in Edinburgh, Robert Dods; later came to MD (A). She d. 24 April 1825 in New Windsor, MD (B).

5. WILLIAM BRUCE, son of Charles (2) of Edinburgh, settled in WA Co., MD, by 1785 (B).

THE WILLIAM BRYAN FAMILY

1. TIMOTHY BRYAN, on 7 Jan 1773, wrote to his son William, saying he had received William's letter of last 18 Feb. Timothy said, in part, "I am glad you are in a good situation, but you are ungrateful and disobedient for traveling without my consent, like a poor man's son. But it's only a trick of yours, so I forgive you. I leave all my property to you. I hope you return soon. Don't overthrow yourself. Property deserves a good settlement. Your mother and family join me ..." Signed, Timothy O'Bryan. Witnessed by Robert Barrett Knight, James Nash, atty., and Richard Barrey. The letter was recorded 2 March 1774 (BACT 4:94-96).

Timothy was the father of: WILLIAM.

2. WILLIAM BRYAN, of Baltimore Town, stationer and book binder, son of Timothy (1), on 3 Oct 1774, conv. prop. to John Merryman (BACT 4:125).

THE BURCH FAMILY

Refs.: A: Burch data compiled by Fredric Z. Saunders, 5186 S. Cobble Creek Rd. # 6K, Salt Lake City, UT 84117-6723; e mail at fzasaund@ix.netcom.com. web site: http://pweb.netcom.com/~fzsaud/ B: John Francis Haswell, Transc. *The Register of St. Andrew's Parish Church, Penrith, 1556-1812.* The Cumberland and Westmorland Antiquarian and Archaeological Society, Parish Register Section, Volumes 26-30.

Mr. Saunders compared the published parish registers with the original parish register, FHL microfilm 147202. He notes that the name was often spelled Britch.

1. OLIVER BRITCH, householder, was bur. at St. Andrew's, Penrith, on 15 April 1642. He m. 1st, Margaret Walleis on 27 Oct 1611. She was bur. on 16 Feb 1617/8, and he m. 2nd, Ales Readhead on 30 Nov 1619. She was bur. 26 March 1660 (A).

By his second wife, Oliver was the father of the following children, all of whom were baptized at Penrith (A): DOROTHY, bapt. 24 Sep 1620, m. Christofer Simson on 19 Jan 1646/7; THOMAS, bapt. 18 June 1622; ALES, bapt. 24 June 1624, buried 11 Aug 1641; and MARIE, bapt. 23 June 1629, bur. 8 July 1631.

2. THOMAS BRICH/NIRCH/BURCH, son of Oliver (1) and Ales, was bapt. 18 June 1622 at Penrith. He married Annas [-?-]. She was buried at Penrith 17 June 1660 (A). Saunders suggests that because the deaths of Thomas and his eldest sons Oliver and Edward are not recorded at Penrith, he is probably the Thomas who settled in MD.

Thomas Birch was in CV Co. by 6 July 1665 when he assigned 50 a. of land in MD to John Richardson. On 21 Nov 1665 Henry Hare of CV Co. sold 200 a. of land called Harefield, described as being in TA Co., but actually in KE Co., to Burch (See *ARMD* 57:102-103, 169, 186, 187, 197, 207).

Thomas and Ales were the parents of the following children, bapt. at Penrith (A): AYLES, bur. 19 Nov 1646; OLIVER, bapt. 30 Oct 1647; EDWARD. bapt. 1 Feb 1649/50; DOROTHY, bapt. 16 Nov 1652, bur. 20 July 1656, from smallpox; GEORGE, bapt. 12 Oct 1656, bur. 22 Oct 1662; ANN, twin, bapt. 12 June 1660, bur. 30 June 1662; and GRACE, twin, bapt. 12 June 1660, bur. 20 Oct 1662.

3. OLIVER BURCH, son of Thomas (2) and Ales, was bapt. 30 Oct 1647 at Penrith, Eng., and d. by May 1729 in CH Co. He m., Barbara Tennison who was b. c1663 in Northumberland Co., VA. Some researchers have believed that Barbara was a Scott because Thomas Burch, son of Oliver and Barbara, deposed in Oct 1763 mentioning his "uncle John Scott." Thomas' mother Barbara had a sister Katherine who m. John Scott (A).

Oliver Burch settled in MD, where he patented a tract of land called Penray [*sic*] in CH Co. on 1 June 1698 (MPL 38:139). In his will Burch called the tract Penrick, but there is enough similarity in names Penrick and Penrith to support the theory that the Maryland inhabitant was the Oliver bapt. 1647 at Penrith.

Oliver Burch d. leaving a will dated 15 feb 1726/7 and proved 27 May 1729.

Oliver and Barbara were the parents of (A): JUSTINIAN, b. c1680/2, m. Susanna Davis; THOMAS, b. c1684, d. by Oct 1765; KATHERINE, m. Thomas Swan;

ANN, m. Samuel Swann; JOHN, d. by March 1734, m. Mary [-?-]; ELIZABETH, m. 1st, John Cade, 2nd, Thomas Owen; BARBARA, m. 1st, Thomas Allanson, and 2nd, William Colier; EDWARD, b. c1700, m. Mary Anderson; BENJAMIN, b. c1703, m. Winifred; ELINOR; and JONATHAN, b. c1708.

THE BURGESS FAMILY OF MARLBOROUGH, WILTS
by Fredric Z. Saunders

Refs.: A: Fredric Z. Saunders, "Burgess Family of Marlborough, Wilts." Fredric Z. Saunders can be reached at 5186 S. Cobble Creek Rd. # 6K, Salt Lake City, UT 84117-6723; e mail at fzasaund@ix.netcom.com; web site: http://pweb.netcom.com/~fzsaud/ B: *Marriages of St. Peter's, Marlborough, Wiltshire.* Wiltshire Parish Registers, London: Phillimore Co. C: *Marriages of St. Mary the Virgin, Marlborough, Wiltshire.* Wiltshire Parish Registers, London: Phillimore Co.

1. WILLIAM BURGESS of Marlborough, Wilts, d. by Nov 1641. He m. Alice [-?-].

    William Burgis of Marlborough, Wilts, d. leaving a will dated 14 June 1640 and proved 6 Nov 1641 (PCC Wills, (1641), 129 Evelyn, FHL microfilm 092151). In this will he named his wife Alice Burges; dau. Mary the wife of Edward Puttman; dau. Martha wife of Edward Hutchins; dau. Elizabeth Burgis, his youngest daughter, who was to have for her marriage portion the bond of 100 pounds due unto him from Mr. Christopher Fowles, and also bequeathed her additional sums of money; son Isacke Burgis; Mary and Elizabeth Burgis daughters of Joseph Burgis, deceased; the lease he bought in Gloucestershire and made over to his son Joseph, deceased, to be held by his daughter-in-law Elizabeth Burgis and her mother during their lives; residue to son Daniel who was made executor. His bro.-in-law William Blissett and very good friends, Thomas Hunt, and William Barnes were named overseers. Nicholas Proffitt, William Blissett, Jr., and George Thomas witnessed the will.

    William Burgess was the father of: JOSEPH, dec.; ISAAC; DANIEL; MARY, m. Edward Puttman; MARTHA, m. Edward Hutchins; and ELIZABETH.

2. JOSEPH BURGESS, of Almondsbury, Glos., son of William (1), d. leaving a will dated 22 March 1638 and proved 25 Nov 1639 (PCC Wills (1639) 178 Harvey, FHL microfilm 92145). Joseph had two daus.: MARY; and ELIZABETH.

3. ISAAC BURGESS, son of William, was b. c1615, and was buried on 10 Oct 1668. He m. Anne York on 13 Aug 1640, by lic., at St. Peter's, Marlborough (B:11). She m. 2nd, John Keynes on 17 Jan 1669/70 at St. Peter and Paul, Marlborough (B:18).

    Isaac Burgess was High Sheriff of Wiltshire.

    On 30 Nov 1672 John Keynes of Marlborough, Wilts, produced a deed to Benjamin Lawrence of Marlborough, chandler, for the sale of land in Anne Arundel Co., MD, and a letter of attorney to William Burges, Thomas Taylor, Nathaniel Heathwicke, and George Puddington so that Keynes could enter the land and give possession to

Lawrence (Peter Wilson Coldham, *Lord Mayor's Court of London Depositions Relating to Americans*, 1980).

Mr. John Keynes was buried 13 Dec 1675. He left a will written 1 Jan 1674 and proved 20 March 1675. He named his wife Anne Keynes and made numerous bequests to children and grandchildren from a prior marriage, and other relatives. He also made bequests to his wife's son Isaack Burges, his wife's son Daniel Burges, his wife's daughter Parke, his wife's son William Burges, his wife's son Samuell Burges at 21, his wife's son Jeremy Burges at 22, his wife's daughter Anne, and his wife's daughter Mary at 18. Also mentioned was his "brother-in-law" Mr. Daniel Burgess (PCC Wills 31 Bench, (1676), FHL microfilm 092316)

Isaac and Anne (York) Burgess were the parents of (A: cites the records of St. Peter and Paul, Wilts.): WILLIAM, poss. bapt. 2 July 1626; ISAAC, bapt. 7 Jan. 1641; bur. 15 Apr. 1679; ANNE, 20 Nov. 1642; JOSEPH, b. c1644, d. 1672 AA Co., MD; DANIEL, b. c1646; ELIZABETH, b. c1648, m. Mr. [-?-] Parke or Parker; MARY, bapt. 1 Sep 1654, bur. Dec 1654; SAMUEL, bapt. 25 Jan 1656; JEREMIAH, bapt. 17 July 1658; and MARY, bapt. 12 Oct 1660.

4. DANIEL BURGESS, son of William (1) and Anne, was b. c1612 (B), matriculated at New Inn Hall, Oxford, 11 July 1634, age 18. He held the livings of Staines, Mddx., and Sutton Magna, Wiltshire. He was later appointed Rector of Colingbourne Ducis, Wilts., but was ejected in 1662. He d. June 1679, leaving at least one son (B; See also *VHC Wilts.* 3:105, 107): DANIEL.

5. JOSEPH BURGES, of Wilts., Eng., and AA Co., MD, son of Isaac (3), was transported to Md. c1668, but returned to Wiltshire (MPL 12:591).

He died leaving a will dated 22 Oct 1672, proved 27 Nov 1672. He named his mother, then the wife of John Keynes of Marlborough, and brothers and sisters Isaac, Daniel, Elizabeth, William, Samuel, Jeremia, Anne, and Mary (*GGE* 2:1085).

6. WILLIAM BURGESS, son of Isaac (3) and Anne, and bro. of Joseph, was bapt. 2 July 1626 at St. Peter and Paul, Marlborough, Wiltshire, and d. 1687/8 in Md. He m. 1st, Elizabeth, dau. of Edward Robins; 2nd, Sophia, widow of Richard Ewen, and 3rd, Ursula [-?-], who later m. Dr. Richard Moore (*BDML* 1:182).

William immigrated to MD c1650 (MPL Q:403). On 30 Nov 1672 John Keynes of Marlborough, Wilts., Gent., attested that William Burgess, Thomas Taylor, Nathaniel Heathwick and George Puddington have been appointed as attorneys to secure possession of land in AA Co. which had been assigned to Benjamin Lawrence of Marlborough, chandler (*CBE* 2:207).

William Burgess of South River, AA Co., died leaving a will dated 11 July 1685, proved 19 Feb 1686/7. He named his children Edward (and his children William and Elizabeth), George, William, John, Joseph, Benjamin, Charles, Elizabeth, Ann, and Susanna (wife of Nicholas Sewell and mother of Charles and Jane). Wife Ursula was to be executrix (MWB 4:242).

Unplaced:

BURGESS, JEREMIAH, m. Susanna Hill on 28 March 1676 at St. Peter's, Marlborough, Wilts (B:19).

BURGESS, OBADIAH, m. Susanna Dyer on 30 Nov 1671 at St. Peter's, Marlborough, Wilts (B:18).

BURGESS, THOMAS, m. Alice Cheney on 7 Aug 1617 at St. Peter's, Marlborough, Wilts (B:2).

BURGESS, THOMAS, m. Margery Smith on 26 March 1618 at St. Peter's, Marlborough, Wilts (B:3).

BURGESS, WILLIAM, of Burbidge, m. Rose Merriman on 11 May 1634 at St. Peter's, Marlborough, Wilts (B:8).

BURGESS, WILLIAM, m. Rebeckah Wallis on 23 April 1660 at St. Mary the Virgin, Marlborough (C:83).

THE BYSSHE FAMILY

Refs.: A: "Bysshe," *SUBE*:198-199. B: "Ancestors of Wallace Joseph Jenkins," web site on FamilyTreeMaker. C: "Bysshe," *Visitation of Surrey, HSPV* 43:103-104. D: *HSPV* 8:135. E: Bysshe data posted by Ruby Mc (contact RubyMcH@home.net)

ARMS: Or, a chevron between three roses Gules. **CREST**: A hind (*biche*) trippant Argent (A).

Generations 1-5

1. JOHN BYSSHE was living 45 Edw. III. He married Isabella, dau. and heir of William, brother of John who was son and heir of John [-?-] of Barstowe, Co. Surrey. John and Isabella were the parents of (A): Sir THOMAS, Kt.; WILLIAM; and MICHAEL.

2. WILLIAM de la BYSSHE, second son of John (1) and Isabella, was living 15 Rich. II. He married Mary, dau. and heir of Geffery Edmonds of Barstowe, Co. Surrey. William and Mary were the parents of (A): Sir WILLIAM.

3. Sir WILLIAM de la BYSSHE, son of William (2) and Mary, was living 14 Hen. V and 36 Hen. VI. He married Elizabeth Wokindon of Co. Essex. They were the parents of (A): JOHN; and RICHARD, Clerk; Rector of Burstowe, Co. Surrey.

4. JOHN BYSSHE, the Elder, son of Sir William (3) and Elizabeth, was living 38 Hen.

VI, and d. by 1494, when his will was proved (E: cites PCC 15 Vox). He married Joan Zouche, dau. of Sir Oliver Zouche. John and Joan were the parents of (A): JOHN; and WILLIAM.

5. JOHN BYSSHE, Esq., of Burstowe, Co. Surrey, son and heir of John (4) and Joan, died by 1522, when his will was proved (B; E: cites PCC 15 Maynwaryng). He married Joan Redingers, dau. of John Redingers als Redinghurst of Redinghurst, Co. Surrey. John and Joan were the parents of (A): WILLIAM, Esq.

6. WILLIAM BYSSHE, second son of John (4) and Joan, m. [-?-] Slifield, dau. of Thomas Slifield, Esq. William and his wife were the parents of (A: B; C): ROBERT.

Generation 6

7. WILLIAM BYSSHE, Esq., of Burstowe, son of John (5) and Joan, was living 26 Hen. VIII. He m. Sarah (A); or Jane (B; E) Wintershull, dau. of Robert Wintershull, Esq., of Wintershull, Surrey.

William and Sarah/Jane were the parents of (A; B; C; E): JOHN, Esq.

8. ROBERT BYSSHE of Worthe, Co. Sussex, son of William (6), m. [-?-] Bostock. They were the parents of (A: B; C): JOHN, Sr., d. by 1582.

Generation 7

9. JOHN BYSSHE, Esq., of Burstowe, son of William (7) and Jane, d. 1568, when his will was proved (E: cites PCC 20 Babington). He married Mary Courthop, dau. of John Courthop of Co. Kent (A).

John and Mary were the parents of (A: B; C): MERCY, m. John Bysshe, Jr.; RICHARD, d. unm.; THOMAS, m. Anna Bysshe; JOHN; WALTER, m. Margaret Matthew; ERASMUS, b. 1623 in Reigate, Co. Surrey, m. Juliana Alchin; CATHERINE; JOANNA; ANNA, m. Tobias Kemp; and URSULA, married John Cudginton.

10. JOHN BYSSHE, Sr., of Worth, Co. Sussex, son of Robert (8), d. by 1582, when an Inq. P. M. was held and his will was proved (E: cites Chancy 197.77, and PCC 34 Tirwhite). He m. Mercy Glymin, dau. of Thomas Glymin, Esq., of Burstowe, Co. Surrey (A).

John and Mercy were the parents of (A: B): JOHN, Jr., b. c1554; MATTHEW, Gent., died between 22 Sep 1624 and 1 Feb 1624/5; MERCY, m. John Bysshe (12); and ANNA, m. Thomas Bysshe.

Generation 8

11. THOMAS BYSSHE, of Burstowe, Co. Surrey, son of John (9) and Mary, m. his cousin, Anna, dau. of John (10) Bysshe of Worth, Co. Sussex.

Thomas and Anna were the parents of (A): EDWARD; THOMAS, d. s.p.; DAVID, d. s.p.; WILLIAM, d. s.p.; MARTHA, m. Anthon. Emery of Co. Surrey; THOMAS, d. unm. in 1633; and JOHN, m. Margaret Killingbeck of York.

12. JOHN BYSSHE, Jr., son of John (10) and Mercy, was born c1554 (he was age 28 in 1582) in Worth, Co. Sussex, and died by 1626, when his will was proved (E: cites PCC 54 Hele). He married his third cousin, Mercy Bysshe, dau. of John Bysshe, Esq. (10), and Mary.

John and Mercy were the parents of (B): WILLIAM; and HESTER, b. by 1626, m. Edward Alfrey who was b. by 22 Oct 1528 in Gullege, East Grinstead, Co. Sussex, and d. 21 April 1642.

Generation 9

13. EDWARD BYSSHE, Esq., of Burstowe, Co. Surrey, son of Thomas (11) and Anna, died 1655. He m. Mary, dau. of John Turner of Ham, Co. Surrey. They were the parents of (A): THOMAS; JOHN; **Sir EDWARD, Garter King of Arms**, m. [-?-] Green; MARIA; SARAH; ANNE; and JANE.

14. WILLIAM BYSSHE, son of John (12) and Mercy, was b. in Worth, Co. Sussex, and d. 24 April 1638. He m. 1st, Margaret James, b. by 27 June 1596, dau. of Roger and sister of Sir James of Reigate, Co. Surrey. He married 2nd, Joan [-?-], who was named as her husband's extx. (E).

William Bysshe left a will proved 29 May 1638. An Inq. P. M. was held at Westerham on 21 May 1638. His will was proved 29 May 1638 (E: cites PCC 52 Lee).

William and Margaret were the parents of (B): URSULA, died by 1702; ROGER, born c1623 in Worth, m. 1st, Ann Jermyn, and 2nd, Ellen Parr (by whom he was the ancestor of the **poet Percy Bysshe Shelley**) MARGARET; and SARAH.

Generation 10

15. Sir EDWARD BYSSHE, Clarenceux and Garter King of Arms, son of Edward (13) and Mary (Turner). Edward Bysshe, Gent., bachelor, age 25, and Margaret Greene of St. Olave, Old Jewry, spinster, 18, dau. of John Greene, Esq., of the same place, who gave his consent, were granted a license on 4 Nov 1635 to marry at St. Olave, Old Jewry (*FOLO*). Margaret was a dau. of John Green of Boys Hall, Essex, Serjeant-at-Law. She survived Sir Edward, and died and was buried at Burstow (D).

16. URSULA BYSSHE, dau. of William (14) and Margaret, died by 1702 in Northumberland Co., VA. She married 1st, Richard Thompson of Maryland, who was born 1613 in Norwich, Co. Norfolk, and died between 1644 and 1647, Ursula Bysshe Thompson married 2nd, in 1647, Col. John Mottrom, and 3rd, on 25 Feb 1655/6, Major George Colclough. (She did not marry Col. Isaac Allerton, Jr., c1659).

Richard and Ursula (Bysshe) Thompson were the parents of (WJJ): ELIZABETH, b. c1642 in Northumberland Co., VA, d. by 25 May 1697, m. Col. Peter Presly, Gent.; BISH, d. after 1663; RICHARD, Jr., b. c1646; and SARAH, d. 1673 in Kiccowtan Parish, m. Lt.-Col. Thomas Willoughby II, in 1657.

CAMPBELL, JAMES, b. 16 March 1748, son of John and Jane Campbell of Smiths-borough, Co. Monaghan, m. Sarah Rutter on 11 Jan 1764 in St. Mary Ann's Parish, CE Co. (Barnes, *Md. Marr. 1634-1777*).

THE CAPELL FAMILY

Refs.: A: "The Wiseman Family," *British Roots...* . B: "Capell," *The Visitation of Essex, 1612, HSPV* 13:171. C: "Browne (No. 4)," *The Visitation of Essex, 1612, HSPV* 13:165-167. D: "Rutland," *Burke's Peerage and Baronetage*, 1970 ed. E: "Essex," *Burke's Peerage and Baronetage*, 1970 ed. F: *PASC*. X: Undocumented Pedigree Chart of Gamaliel Capell from the Ancestral File of the LDS Church.

ARMS: Gules, a lion rampant between three cross crosslets fitchee Or (B).

1. JOHN CAPELL of Stoke Neyland, Suffolk, m. Joane [-?-]. They were the parents of (E): Sir WILLIAM.

2. Sir WILLIAM CAPEL of London, Kt., second son of John (1), was poss. b. 1426, d. 6 Feb 1515 (X). Twice Lord Mayor of London, 1508, 1509, and Knighted by Henry VII, he was buried in a "stately chapel," built by him in St. Bartholomew's Church by the Exchange (C:171). He m. Margaret Arundell, d. after 8 Dec 1519 (C:171; X). She was a dau. of Sir Thomas and Catherine (Chiddock) Arundell.

Sir William and Margaret were the parents of (*RD500*:241; *PASC*:282; *WAR7*: Line 214; X): ELIZABETH, b. c1451; MARY, b. c1453; Sir GILES, b. c1455; DOROTHY, b. c1457, m. John La Zouche of Haryngworth; ELIZABETH, b. c1480, d. 25 Dec 1555, m. William Pawlett, Marquess of Winchester (They were the ancestors of **Philip Carteret of NJ and NC**, **Philip Dumaresq** of MA, and **Thomas Wingfield of VA**); and poss. HENRY, b. c1505.

3. Sir GILES CAPELL of Hadham, Herts. (C:171), Sheriff of Essex, son of Sir William (2) and Margaret, was b. c1455. He m. Isabel Newton, of Wake, Co. Somerset, dau. and coheiress of Sir John and Ellen (Daubeny) Newton (C:171). She was b. c1489 (C:171; E; X).

Sir Giles and Isabel were the parents of (X): Sir EDWARD; and MARGARET, b. c1486.

4. Sir EDWARD CAPELL of Hadham, Herts. (C:171), son of Sir Giles (3) and Isabel, was b. c1484 and d. 19 May 1577 (X). He m. Ann Pelham, b. c1492, of Laughton (X). She was a dau. of Sir William Pelham and his wife Mary Carew.

Sir Edward and Ann were the parents of (X): Sir HENRY, b. c1514; GYLES, b. c1516, d. c1618; WILLIAM, b. c1518; ELIZABETH, b. c1520; ANNE, b. c1522; MARY, b. c1524; and GRACE, b. c1526.

5. Sir HENRY CAPELL, Kt., of Raynes, Co. Essex (B), son of Sir Edward (4) and Ann, was born c1514 and died 25 June 1588. On 16 Aug 1543 he m. Lady Catherine

Manners (B), d. 9 March 1572 (X). She was a dau. of Sir Thomas Manners, K.G., Earl of Rutland. For her Royal Descent see *RD500*:40-41.

Sir Henry and Catherine were the parents of (*RD500*:41; *PASC*:282; X): Sir ARTHUR, b. c1544, d. 11 April 1632, m. Margaret Grey (They were the ancestors of **Edward Hyde, 3rd Earl of Clarendon, Colonial Governor of NY and NJ**); WILLIAM, b. 1556, d. 1583; EDWARD, b. c1558; JOHN, b. 2 June 1560; Sir GAMALIEL; AGNES, b. c1562; FRANCES, b. 18 March 1564, m. 1st, on 14 Sep 1585, John Shurley, and 2nd, John Trayton; ANNE, b. 8 June 1566, m. R. Chester; ROBERT, b. 19 Feb 1567; and MARY, b. 26 Jan 1569.

6. Sir GAMALIEL CAPELL, of Raynes, Co. Essex, 4th son of Sir Henry (5), was age 4 in 1570 [b. 2 Jan 1561?] and d. 10 Nov 1633 (X). He was knighted in 1603 (B). He m. Jayne Brown, 2nd dau. of Weston and Elizabeth (Pawlett) Browne Jayne had m. 1st, Edward Wyatt of Tillingham, Essex) (B).

Sir Gamaliel and Jayne were the parents of: ALICE, m. Robert Wiseman, **Passenger on the Ark and the Dove** (A).

THE CARLYLE FAMILY

Refs.: A: Richard Henry Spencer, "The Carlyle Family," *GVFWMG* 1:564-588.

Generations 1-5

1. HILDRED de CAERLEOL or de **KARLEOL**, fl. c1066-1130 [A 64 year life span seems a bit long--RWB]. He is said to have m. a granddau. of Waltheof, Earl of Northumberland. He acquired the Manor of Newbie on the Moor, and was the father of (A:564): ODARD.

2. ODARD de KARLEOL, son of Hildred (1), d. by 1177. He is said to have been in the service of King Henry I at the Castle of Carlisle when it was besieged by King William of Scotland in 1174. He left two sons (A:565); ROBERT; and RICHARD.

3. ROBERT de KARLEOL, son of Odard (2), was b. c1139 and d. 1209. He held the lands of Lockerbie in Annandale, Dumfrieshire. After 1194 he witnessed several charters of William de Brus. He left two sons (A:565): ADAM; and ODARD.

4. ADAM de KARLEOL, son of Robert (3), d. c1213. He is the first to have a clearly established connection with Scotland, and was the first to hold Kinmount. He m. Matilda [-?-], and left one son (A: EUDO.

5. EUDO de CAERLEOL, son of Adam (4), d. c1230. In 1217 he sided with Alexander II, King of Scots, against Henry III of England, who ordered that Adam's lands in Norfolk be confiscated and given to Robert de Vaux. Eudo left one son (A:566): WILLIAM.

Generations 6-10

6. Sir WILLIAM de CAERLEOL, son of Eudo, was knighted by 1245. Some time before 1252 as Sir William, son of Eudo de Carleol, he granted an annual rent from lands to a relative, Adam, son of Roger de Carliol. He left two sons (A:566): WILLIAM; and EUDO.

7. WILLIAM de CARLEIL, the Younger, son of William (6), d. by 25 June 1274, having m. Sapentia [-?-], and leaving a son (A:566): WILLIAM.

8. WILLIAM de CARLEIL, son of William the Younger (7), succeeded his grandfather, and was knighted some time before Jan 1304. He m. Lady Margaret Bruce, dau. of the Earl of Carrick, and sister of King Robert the Bruce. He d. by March 1329, leaving two sons (A:566): WILLIAM, d. by 1347 leaving his estates to his nephew William; and JOHN.

9. JOHN de CARLEIL, son of William (8), is said to have been at the Battle of Halidon Hill, and to have d. by 1347, leaving one son (A:566): WILLIAM.

10. WILLIAM de CARLEIL, son of John (9), inherited the estates of both his father and uncle. He left a son (A:567): JOHN.

Generations 11-15

11. JOHN de CARLEIL, son of William (10), first appeared in 1398 as one of the conservators of a truce with England. He d. c1433, leaving a son (A:567): WILLIAM.

12. Sir WILLIAM de CARLEIL of Torthorwald, son of John (11), was one of the numerous band of Knights, Esquires, and Archers, who attended Princess Margaret, dau. of James I of Scotland, when she m. the Dauphin, later Louis XI of France, on 24 June 1436. He m. Elizabeth, dau. of Sir Duncan Kirkpatrick who d. by 1436. In 1443 William was styled Lord of Kinmount of Torthorwald, and died before Nov 1463, leaving issue (A:568): JOHN (Ancestor of the Lords Carleil); ADAM (inherited Bridekirk); JAMES, Rector of Kirkpatrick; and MARGARET, m. Sir William Douglas, 3rd Marquess of Queensberry.

13. ADAM de CARLEIL, son of Sir William (12), inherited Bridekirk, and died by 1500, leaving one son (A:569); ADAM.

14. ADAM de CARLEIL, son of Adam (13), is mentioned in various documents in 1499, 1500, and 1516, and d. 1581. He had a Papal dispensation dated 17 Feb 1502 to marry Ellen, dau. of Simon Carruthers of Mouswald and his wife Catherine Carleil. Adam and Ellen had several sons, the eldest of whom was (A:569): ALEXANDER.

15. ALEXANDER CARLEIL, Laird of Brydekirk, son of Adam (14) and Ellen, was living in 1547. He and his son Adam, "the young Laird," were mentioned by Sir Thomas

Carleton, English Warden of the Borders in 1547 as being the only gentry in Annandale, Liddlesdale, and Nithsdale, who never submitted to the English, except for Douglas of Drumlanrig. Alexander was the father of (A:569); ALEXANDER, d. 1593, s.p.; HERBERT, b. 1558, d. 1632, m. Margaret Cunningham; and EDWARD, of Lymekilns.

Generations 16-20

16. EDWARD CARLILE of Lymekilns, son of Alexander (15), d. by 1615. He m. Grace Irving of Bonshaw, and left two sons (A:570): ADAM; and ALEXANDER of Munaythwaite, living in 1647.

17. ADAM CARLILE of Lymekilns, eldest son of Edward (16), d. by 1637. he m. 1637, leaving three sons (A:570): EDWARD of Lymekilns; ADAM, b. 1634, d. 1685, m. Janet Muirhead; and JOHN.

18. EDWARD CARLILE of Lymekilns, son of Adam (17), d. by 1699. He m. Margaret, dau. of Gavin Young, Minister of Ruthwell. Her monumental inscriptions read "Here lies Margaret Young, spouse of Edward Carlsle of Limekilns, deceased May 14, 1665, of her age 48." Edward and Margaret were the parents of (A:57): ADAM.

19. ADAM CARLILE of Limekilns, son of Edward and Margaret, was b. in 1638. He m. Grizel Menzies of Culteraws, by whom he was the father of (A:571); JOHN, of Limekilns; ALEXANDER; MARY, m. David Murray of Beltriding; MARGARET, m. Christopher Carruthers of Hardrigg; and WILLIAM, surgeon, b. 1685, d. 3 July 1744, m. Rachel Murray of Murraythwaite.

20. ALEXANDER CARLISLE, son of Adam (19), migrated to SO Co., MD, where he d. in 1726. On 6 Sep 1720 he m. Margaret McAllister of that county. He left two sons (A:571): ADAM, b. 13 Feb 1724/5; and JOHN, b. 28 Feb 1725/6, d. s.p.

21. WILLIAM CARLILE, surgeon, son of Adam (19), was b. 1685 and d. 3 July 1744. He m. Rachel Murray of Murraythwaite. They left two sons (A:571): GEORGE; and JOHN.

Generation 21

22. ADAM CARLILE, son of Alexander (20), was b. 13 Feb 1724/5. After the death of his mother he went to Scotland to live, and m. Philadelphia Carruthers of Holmains. When his uncle John died he inherited Limekilns, but was ruined when a bank in Ayr collapsed in 1766. He left six sons, who may have d. s.p. (A:571): ALEXANDER; ADAM; JOHN; JAMES; GEORGE; and WILLIAM.

23. JOHN CARLYLE, second son of William (21) and Rachel, was b. 6 Feb 1720, and came to America about 1740. He settled first at Dumfries, VA, and then at Belhaven, on the Potomac River. In 1754 Lieut. Gov. Robert Dinwiddie appointed him Major and

Commissary of the Virginia forces. In 1748 he married 1st, Sarah Fairfax, dau. of William and Sarah Fairfax and later, 2nd, Sybil West. He died leaving issue (A:574-ff.)

Unplaced:

CARLISLE, Dr. JOHN, of the Island of Jamaica, married last evening, Betsy, eld. dau. of the late Capt. Richard Lane of Baltimore (*MJBA* 19 Feb 1790).

THE CARUS FAMILY

Refs. A: Nicholson and Burn, *History and Antiquities of the Counties of Westmorland and Cumberland*, I 244-245. B: Boumphery et al., *An Armorial for Westmorland and Lonsdale* (1975). C: Hudleston et al., *Cumberland Families and Heraldry* (1978). D: "Carus of Asthwaite, 1615," *CWFO*:25.

ARMS: Azure, on a chevron between ten cinquefoils Argent, three mullets Gules. **CREST**: A falcon with wings expanded Sable, charged on the breast with a cinquefoil Argent (D).

1. RICHARD CARUS fl. temp Henry VIII, was granted the manor of Kirby-Lonsdale after the dissolution of the monasteries. He was the father of at least two children (A): THOMAS; and CATHERINE, m. Rowland Philipson (They may have been the ancestors of Ann who m. 2nd, Thomas, Baron Arundell of Wardour Castle; Thomas and Ann were the parents of Ann, who m. **Cecil Calvert, 2nd Baron of Baltimore**).

2. THOMAS CARUS, son of Richard (1), m. Margaret, dau. of William Wilson of Stavely, Gent.

Thomas and Margaret were the parents of (A; D): WILLIAM; and CHRISTOPHER.

Thomas was also the father of an illegitimate son (D): ROBERT, ancestor of the family of Carus, Tredaugh, Ireland.

3. WILLIAM CARUS, son of Thomas (2) and Margaret, m. Isabel, dau. of Thomas Leyburne of Cunswick (A: D).

William and Isabel were the parents of (A; D): THOMAS; ADAM; ROBERT; CHRISTOPHER; RICHARD; ELIZABETH, m. Roger Smith of Kendall; MARGARET, m. Christopher Sandis of Furness, Lancs.; ANNE, m. Christopher Nicholson of Crook, Westmorland; HELEN (or ELLEN), m. Randall Washington of Shap, Westmorland; and JANE, m. Jo. Sawrey of Plompton.

4. CHRISTOPHER CARUS, second son of Thomas (2) and Margaret, m. and was the father of (D): NICHOLAS.

5. THOMAS CARUS, of Highton, Lancs., son of William (3) and Isabel, d. 3 July 1571. He m. Catherine, dau. of Thomas Preston of Preston Patrick by his wife Anne, the dau. of William Thornborough of Hampsfield (A: 1:240; D).

Thomas was Justice of the King's Bench (D), and it may be he who acquired the manor of Kirby Lonsdale (B).

Thomas and Catherine were the parents of (A; D): THOMAS, m. Anne Preston and had issue; RICHARD; Sir CHRISTOPHER; WILLIAM; MARY, m. 1st, Edward Middleton of Middleton Hall, and 2nd, Sir Henry Kighley of Inskip, Lancs.; ETHELDRED, m. William Thornborough of Hampsfield (ancestors of the **Thornborough Family of MD**); ISABEL, twin; ANNE, twin; and GRISOLD.

6. NICHOLAS CARUS, of Kendall, Westmorland, son of Christopher (4), m. and was the father of (D): KATHERINE, dau. and sole heir, m. Rowland Philipson of Calgarth.

THE CAVE FAMILY EXPANDED

Refs.: A: "Cave-Browne-Cave," *Burke's Peerage, Baronetage, and Knightage*, 1956 ed., pp. 402-405 [The early generations require documentation]. B: "Cave," *Burke's Dictionary of the Peerage and Baronetage of the British Empire*, 1853 ed., pp. 179-181. C: *HSPV 2* (various pedigrees of Babington and Cave).

Generations 1-5

1. JORDAN de CAVE, was the father of (A): BRIAN.

2. BRIAN de CAVE, son of Jordan (1), was the father of (A): ROBERT.

3. ROBERT de CAVE, son of Brian (2), m. a dau. of Thomas de Metnam and was the father of (A): THOMAS.

4. THOMAS de CAVE, son of Robert (3), m. Joyce, dau. of William St. Quintin, Lord of Brayns Burton, and was the father of (A): GEOFFREY.

5. GEOFFREY de CAVE, son of Thomas (4), m. Mabel, dau. of Robert de Talso. He was the father of two sons (A): ALEXANDER, Dean of Durham, and PETER.

Generations 6-10

6. PETER de CAVE, son of Geoffrey (5), m. the dau. and heir of Sir Thomas de Bromflete, and had three daus., and two sons, including (A; B:179): ALEXANDER; and THOMAS, ancestor of the Caves of Finton; KATHERINE, m. John Tiplingham; JANE, m. John Dawney of Sesay, York; and BEATRIX, m. Philip de Woldby.

7. Sir ALEXANDER de CAVE, son of Peter (6), was living in 1275, and m. the dau. of Peter de Malden, Lord of Mulgrave, and was the father of (A): PETER; JANE, m. Thomas Skelton of Skelton; URSULA, m. Sir John Ella; JOYCE, m. Sir Thomas Pollington; and MARGARET, m. Ralph Andleby.

8. PETER CAVE, son of Sir Alexander (7), m. Anne, dau. of Sir Simon Ward. They were the parents of (A; B:179): Sir ALEXANDER; MARY, Prioress of Walton; and ELIZABETH, m. John Middleton of Middleton-super-Wold.

9. Sir ALEXANDER CAVE, son of Peter (8), m. Amphelicia, dau. of Sir Jeffrey Hotham. They were the parents of (A): Sir JOHN; MARGARET, m. Ansel de St. Quintin; JANE, m. Sir Roger Keike; MARY, m. Sir John Risby; and ELIZABETH, m. William Ellerker.

10. Sir JOHN CAVE, son of Sir Alexander (9), m. the dau. and heir of Peter Genille. They were the parents of (A): Sir ALEXANDER.

Generations 11-15

11. Sir ALEXANDER CAVE, Kt., son of Sir John (10), m. Katherine Somerville, dau. of Roger Somerville of Grindall, Co. York. He and his wife were the parents of (A:403): Sir PETER; Sir ALEXANDER; GRACE; KATHERINE, m. Sir John Markenfeld; and ANNE, m. Gilbert Stapleton of Boyton, Co. York.

12. Sir PETER CAVE, son of Sir Alexander (11), m. Anne Ingleby, dau. of Ralph Ingleby. He and his wife were the father of three sons, the eldest of whom was (A:403; B:179): PETER; JOHN, Abbot of Selby; and ALEXANDER.

13. PETER CAVE, son of Sir Peter (12), m. Mary Burdett of Rothwell, Co. Northampton. Peter was succeeded by his eldest son (A:403): THOMAS.

14. THOMAS CAVE, son of Peter (13), m. Thomasine Passamer, of Essex. They were the parents of (A:403; b:179): RICHARD; and JOHN, great-grandfather of Francis Cave of Sinecross, Leics.; HENRY, m. [-?-] Belgrave; WILLIAM; and CHRISTOPHER.

15. RICHARD CAVE of Stanford, Northants., son of Thomas (14), m. 1st, Elizabeth Marvyn (by whom he had a son and a dau.), and 2nd Margaret Saxby.

     Richard and Elizabeth were the parents of (A; B:179): EDWARD of Wenwick, Northants.; and MARGARET, m. Thomas Saunders of Harington.

     Richard and Margaret were the parents of (A:403): Sir THOMAS; ANTHONY of Chicheley, Bucks (d. leaving four daus.); Sir AMBROSE, Chancellor of the Duchy of Lancaster; FRANCIS, ancestor of the Caves of Baggrave; RICHARD of Pickwell, Leics., ancestor of the Caves of Yately, Hunts.; BRIAN of Ingarsby, Leics.; and BRIDGET, m. Francis Tanfield of Gayton, Co. Northampton (Their dau. Ann Tanfield m. Clement Vincent of Harpole, Co. Northampton, and they were the ancestors of **The Randolph Family** of VA (*PASC*:236).

Generation 16

16. Sir THOMAS CAVE of Stanford, Co. Northants., son of Richard (15), m. Elizabeth Danvers (dau. and coheir of Sir John Danvers, Kt., of Waterstock, Oxford. They were the parents of (A:403; B:179): ROGER; AMICIA, m. John Hunt; MARY, m. William Skeffington; MARGARET, m. Sir William Meringe, Kt.; and ELIZABETH, m. Sir Humphrey Stafford, Kt., of Blatherwick, Co. Northants.

17. FRANCIS CAVE of Baggrave, Leics., son of Richard (15), was a Doctor of Civil Laws. He m. Margaret, dau. of Thomas Lisle of Co. Surrey. Francis and Margaret were the parents of (C:120): THOMAS; ANTHONY; BRIAN; HENRY, of Barrow; LISLEY; MARGARET, m. Humphrey Babington; and DOROTHY.

18. ANTHONY CAVE of Chicheley, Bucks., son of Richard (15) and Margaret, was a merchant. He m. Elizabeth, dau. of Thomas Lovat of Astwell. He was the father of (C:126; *PASC*:65): JUDITH, m. Sir William Chester (ancestors of **William Throop** who settled in Marshfield, MA); ANNA, m. Griffith Hampden; MARTHA, m. John Newdigate, and MARY, m. Sir Jerome Weston (Their daughter Mary was bapt. at Rothwell, Essex, on 26 April 1579, and on 10 Feb 1598/9 m. William Clerke, by whom she was the mother of **Jeremy Clerke** settled at Newport, RI (*PASC*:65)).

19. BRIAN CAVE of Ingarsby, 8th son of Richard (15) and Margaret, m. Margaret, dau of Sir George Throckmorton, Kt. They were the parents of (C:128): EDWARD, m. Barbara, dau. of Sir William Devereux; FRANCES; MARIA; and HENRY.

Generation 17

20. ROGER CAVE of Stanford, Co. Northants., son of Sir Thomas (16), d. 26 July 1586. He m. Margaret Cecil, sister of William Cecil, 1st Baron Burleigh, minister of Elizabeth I.
      Roger and Margaret were the parents of (A:403; B:180): THOMAS; Sir WILLIAM; CECIL; JOHN, d. unm.; ELIZABETH, m. Walter Bagot; MARGARET, d. 1594, m. Sir William Skipwith (They were ancestors of **The Skipwith Family** of VA and possibly of MD); and FRANCES, m. Sir Edmond Bussey, Kt.

21. MARGARET CAVE, dau. of Francis (17) and Margaret, m. Humphrey Babington. They were the parents of (C:206; See also "Babington," in *British Roots*, vol. I): THOMAS; EDWARD, of London; Rev. ADRIAN; and WILLIAM, of the Inner Temple.

22. HENRY CAVE of Barrow, son of Francis (17) and Margaret, m. Philippa, only dau. and heiress of Robert Braham of Barrow supre Sore. They were the parents of (C:120): MARGARET, m. her first cousin Rev. Adrian Babington, Rector of Cossington; THEOPHILUS, age 34 in 1619; WILLIAM, age 24; EDWARD, age 23; THOMAS, age 20; HENRY, age 17; ANNA, m. William King of Edmondthorpe, Leics.; and KATHERINE, unm. in 1619.

23. HENRY CAVE of Ingarsby, Leics., son of Brian (19) and Margaret, m. Elizabeth, dau. of George [or Gregory] Isham of Pitchley, Northants. (C:128). He was the father of (C:120, 133): ELIZABETH, m. Thomas Marbury of Warden, co. Bedford (either Elizabeth, or her sister Margaret may well have been the grandmother of **Francis Marbury** of CH Co., MD); EUSEBIUS; FRANCIS; BRIAN, m. Frances, dau. of Sir Erasmus Dryden of Canons Ashby, Bart.; MARGARET, b. c1583, giving her age as "four score" in a deposition made in 1663, m. Rev. Edward Marbury (bapt. 24 Sep 1581, Parson of St. James, Garlick Hithe, and St. Peter's Paul's Wharf); ANNA; BARBARA; and MARY.

Generation 18

24. THOMAS BABINGTON, of Temple Rodeley, son of Humphrey and Margaret (21) (Cave), m. Catherine Kendall, dau. of George Kendall of Smithesby of Co. Derby. They were the parents of (C:206): THOMAS; and others.

25. Rev. ADRIAN BABINGTON, son of Humphrey and Margaret (21) (Cave), m. Margaret Cave, dau. of Henry (22) Cave of Barrow-upon-Soar, Leics. KATHERINE, bapt. 25 March 1613, m. 1st, Arthur Storer, and 2nd, Mr. Clarke. By Arthur Storer, Katherine Babington was the mother of **Anne Storer** who m. 1st, Dr. Truman of Maryland, and 2nd, Robert Skinner, and had issue by both husbands.

Generation 19

25. THOMAS BABINGTON, son of Thomas (24) and Catherine (Kendall), was b. 11 Aug 1615, and died in 1680. He m. Catherine, dau. of Sir Cornelius Vermuyden. They were the parents of, among others, (A:54: B): ELIZABETH (not mentioned in Burke), m. **Andrew Cooke** of London, who came to MD. c1661.

Unplaced:

CAVE, [-?-], m. by 2 Feb 1698 Agnes, sister of Robert Morley, whose will made that date and proved 16 Oct 1602 named many people including his sister Agnes Cave and her children Agnes, Anthony (1st son), Thomas (2nd son), William (3rd son), and Robert Cave (youngest son, under 15) (*GGE*:899).

THE CECIL FAMILY

Refs.: A; Anthony Wagner. *Pedigrees and Progress*. London: Phillimore and Co., 1975.

1. DAVID CECIL d. 1536. He was admitted a freeman of Stamford, Lincs., in 1494. He was the father of (A): RICHARD; and JOAN, m. by 1525 Edmund Browne, Alderman of Stamford.

2. RICHARD CECIL, of Burleigh, Northants., son of David (1), d. 1553. he was the father of (A; *MCS5:*Line 21): Sir WILLIAM CECIL, Baron Burleigh, d. 1598, Secretary of State to Queen Elizabeth I; MARGARET, m. Roger Cave, from whom descends **The Skipwith Family** of VA (See **The Cave Family** elsewhere in this work); and ELIZABETH, bur. 6 dec 1611, m. Sir Robert Wingfield (ancestors of **Thomas Wingfield of New Kent Co., VA**).

THE CHALMERS FAMILY (1)

Refs.: A: PCLR DD#3:60. B: *AACR*.

1. [-?-] CHALMERS was the father of at least three sons (A): ROBERT; WALTER; and JAMES.

2. ROBERT CHALMERS, bro. of Walter and James, was a merchant in Leith, and was living on 23 April 1763. He m. Ann, dau. of William Boog. They had a son (A): PATRICK.

3. WALTER CHALMERS, brother of Robert and James, was b. c1717. He gave his age as c34 in a dep. made 23 April 1751 (MCHR 8:906). He settled in AA Co., MD, as Rector of Westminster Parish (A). The Rev. Walter Chalmers d. 27 Dec 1759. He was buried in Severn Church (B:139; *AMG* 3 Jan 1760).

Robert Swan, admin., advertised he would settle the estate (*AMG* 7 Feb 1760).

4. JAMES CHALMERS, bro. of Robert and Walter, was postmaster of Fockaden, Scotland, and had a son (A): GEORGE, b. before 23 April 1763.

THE CHALMERS FAMILY (2)

N.B.: This line needs more work. There seems to be no connection with the family of James Chalmers, Annapolis Silversmith, who m. Sarah Ridgeway.

Refs.: A: Elizabeth Bordley Gibson. *Biographical Sketches of the Bordley Family of Maryland For Their Descendants.* Philadelphia: Henry B. Ashmead, 1865. B: "Chalmers, George," *DNB* 3:1354-1355. C: *Shippen and Other Families*, 1855

1. [-?-] CHALMERS was the father of at least two sons: [-?-], who settled in MD; and Col. CHARLES, who m. Margaret Jekyll.

2. [-?-] CHALMERS, son of [-?-], and bro. of Col. CHARLES Chalmers, settled in MD c1763. He might be the James Chalmers, Capt. of a Maryland Loyalist Regiment in 1777, b. Scotland in 1727, d. in London, 4 Oct 1806. Loyalist James m. 1763 Arianna Margaretta Jekyll, and is credited by some with being the author of "Plain Truth." (See *Gentlemen's Magazine*, 76 (2) 986, and *MHM* 18:300).

3. Col. CHARLES CHALMERS, son of [-?-], m. Margaret Jekyll, dau. of John and Margaret (Shippen) Jekyll (she d. c1750), granddau. of Edward (1677/8-1712) and Anna Francina (Van der Heyden) Shippen, and great-granddau. of Matthias and [-?-] (Herrman) Van der Heyden. Col. Chalmers took his wife to England where she died (A:22; D:xix-xx).

      Col. and Mrs. Chalmers had at least one son (A:22): GEORGE.

4. GEORGE CHALMERS, son of Col. Charles and Margaret (Jekyll) Chalmers, was b. c1742 at Fochabers in Moray, d. 31 May 1825, a descendant of the Chalmers Family of Pitensear. He studied law in Edinburgh, and at the age of 21 accompanied his uncle to Maryland, where he practiced law at Baltimore. With the outbreak of the Revolutionary War he returned to Great Britain (B).

CHANDLEE, WILLIAM, son of William, of Kilmore, Co. Kildare, Ireland, m. Sarah Cotty on 25 d. 1 mo., 1710 in Nottingham MM (Barnes, *Md. Marr. 1634-1777*).

THE CHENEY FAMILY

Refs.: A: P. Beryl Eustace, ed. *Registry of Deeds: Dublin: Abstracts of Wills. Vol. I 1708-1745. Vol. II 1746-1785* (1956). Repr. Baltimore: Clearfield Co., Inc., 1996. B: *Index to the Act or Grant Books and to Original Wills of the Diocese of Dublin [c. 1638] to the Year 1800.* (1895), Repr.: Baltimore: Clearfield Co., Inc., 1997. C: John P. Prendergast. *The Cromwellian Settlement of Ireland.* (1922). Repr.: Baltimore: Clearfield Co., Inc., 1999.

ARMS: (of Cheney of Chesham Boys, Bucks): Chequy Or and Azure, a fess Gules, fretted Argent (*Burke's General Armory*).

1. FRANCIS CHENEY of Chesham Boyes [Bucks], Esq., some time between 1650 and 1660 subscribed £600 pounds to take part in the Cromwellian Settlement of Ireland (C:423). He may have been the ancestor of the Cheneys of Mount Cheney, Co. Cork.

2. [-?-] CHENEY was the father of: JAMES; ANDREW, d. by Jan 1775; CATHERINE, m. Vincent Bradston by marriage license dated 1730 (B:971); MARY; and ELIZABETH.

3. JAMES CHENEY of Mount Cheney, Co. Cork, Ireland, son of [-?-] (2), d. by May 1780.

      James d. leaving a will dated 9 Jan 1775 and proved 20 May 1780. He named his four sons, Dr. Andrew Francis, Oliver, James, and Bradston Cheney. He named his sisters Catherine Bradston otherwise Cheney, Mary Cheney and Elizabeth Cheney. To his daughters Helena and Elizabeth he left £800.0.0 each on their days of marriage. To his granddaughter Elizabeth Cheney, dau. of son Oliver, he left £400.0.0 on her marriage. He named a deceased brother Andrew. His son James and Thomas Lucas of

Richardfordstown, Co. Cork were named executors. He mentioned lands in Macetown, Painstown, Polenewtown, Riggins, and Corballis, Co. Meath, and town and lands of Mount Cheney otherwise Cloghanaspig and Knockstondon, Barony of Ibane and Barryroe, Co. Cork. John Jervois, Esq., and Arthur Jervois, Esq., both of Cork, and Jonas Travers of Dublin, Gent., witnessed the will. Thomas Spring, Dublin, Gent., and John McGee, of Dublin, writing clerk, witnessed the memorial (A:2:305, will # 617).

James was the father of: ANDREW FRANCIS; OLIVER; JAMES; BRADSTON; HELENA; and ELIZABETH.

4. ANDREW FRANCIS CHENEY, chirurgeon, son of James (3), settled in MD by 1755, and d. in SO Co. 28 Feb 1790. On 15 July 1755 as Andrew Francis Cheney, chirurgeon, son of James Cheney, of Mount Cheney, Co. Cork, Ireland, he m. Mary Day Scott, dau. of Day Scott, in Stepney Parish, Wicomico Co. (Barnes, *Md. Marr. 1634-1777*; *ESVR* 3:42; **NB**: *TMFO*:41, mistakenly describes the marriage as taking place in St. Mary Anne's Parish, CE Co.).

Tubman Lowes of SO Co., in his will dated 31 Dec 1758, proved 29 April 1761, left 6 guineas to each of his godsons, sons of Dr. Andrew Francis "Chesney" [Cheney] (MWB 31:384).

Dr. Andrew Francis Cheney died 28 Feb 1790 in SO Co. at an advanced age (*MJBA* 23 March 1790). He does not seem to have left a will.

On 15 Nov 1796 George Day Scott made a will naming several relatives including his sister Mary Cheney, nephew Dr. Ware Cheney (who was named co-exec. and was to have lands), and nephew Francis Tubman Cheney. He also named his niece Esther, wife of Ware (SOWB EB#7:568).

Andrew Francis and Mary (Scott) Cheney were the parents of at least two sons: FRANCIS TUBMAN; and WARE.

CLARK, JANE, of the Island of Barbados, died in CE Co. by Feb 1737 when her estate was admin. by Thomas Boulding. She had three daughters (MDAD 16:69): HANNAH, living in Barbados in Feb 1737; FRANCINA, living in Great Britain in 1737; and ANN, m. in St. Stephen's Parish, CE Co., on 29 Jan 1733/4 Thomas Boulding of CE Co. (*CECH*:6).

THE CLIFTON FAMILY EXPANDED

Refs.: A: "Clifton of Clifton and Lytham," *Burke's Commoners*, II, 54-57. B: "Clifton of Clifton, Westby, ... ," *LAFO*. C: "Clifton of Clifton," *CS* 84:86-87.

ARMS: Sable, on a bend Argent, three mullets Gules. **CREST**: An arm in armour embowed, the hand grasping a sword (C:86).

1. WILLIAM CLIFTON m. Isabel Thornborough, dau. of William Thornborough of Hampsfield. They were the parents of (A: B): THOMAS.

2. THOMAS CLIFTON of Westby, son of William (1), m. Ellen Osbaldeston. They were the parents of (A: B): CUTHBERT.

3. CUTHBERT CLIFTON of Westby, son of Thomas (2), d. 1596. He m. Catherine Hoghton, dau. of Sir Richard Hoghton. Cuthbert and Catherine were the parents of (A: B): THOMAS.

4. THOMAS CLIFTON of Westby, son of Cuthbert (3), m. Mary Norris, dau. of Sir Edward Norris of the Speke, Lancs. Thomas and Mary were the parents of (A: B): Sir CUTHBERT.

5. Sir CUTHBERT CLIFTON of Westby, son of Thomas (4), d. 1634. he m. 1st, Ann Tildesley, dau. of Thomas Tildesley of Morley, Lancs. He m. 2nd, Dorothy, dau. of Sir Thomas Smith, Kt., one of the honorable family of the present Lord Carrington (C:86).

      Sir Cuthbert and Anne were the parents of (A: B; C:86): THOMAS; CUTHBERT; and ELIZABETH, m. Sir William Gerard of Brynne and Garswood, Kt. and Baronet (His brother Richard Gerard was a passenger to Maryland on *The Ark* and *The Dove* expedition).

      By Dorothy Smith, Sir Cuthbert was the father of: LAWRENCE; FRANCIS; and JOHN (all three of whom were slain in HM service in the late rebellion); GERVASE, m. Dorothy, dau. of Richard Mascy of Rixton, Sr.; ANNE, m. Richard Norris; ALICE, m. Richard Mascy of Rixton, Jr.; JANE, m. Thomas Eccleston of Eccleston; DOROTHY, a nun at Paris; KATHERINE, a nun at Antwerp; and MARY, m. William Lathom of Mosborow, Lancs.

6. THOMAS CLIFTON of Westby, son of Sir Cuthbert (5), d. 16 Dec 1657. He m. Anne Halsall, dau. and coheir of Sir Cuthbert Halsall and his wife Dorothy (a natural dau. of the Earl of Derby).

      Thomas and Anne were the parents of (A: B; C:87): CUTHBERT, m. Margaret, dau. and sole heir of George Ireland of Southworth, and d. s.p.; Sir THOMAS, b. c1628, m. twice and had issue; JOHN, m. [-?-], widow of George Parkinson, and dau. of Thomas Blackburne; WILLIAM; RICHARD; JAMES; ANNE, d. unm.; ELIZABETH, a nun at Gravelkin; ALICE, m, (without the consent of her parents) Alexander Rigby, son of Joseph Rigby of Aspull, Lancs.; BRIDGET, m. Thomas Westby of Malbreck; FRANCES, m. [-?-] Holgate of London; MARGARET, a nun at Gravelin; and ANNE, a nun at Gravelin.

7. JAMES CLIFTON, son of Thomas (6) and Anne, and "nephew of Margaret Brent," immigrated to MD between 1660 and 1663 with his wife Anne (A; MPL AA:324). James m. by 1674, Ann, sister of George Brent, Gent. Her Royal Descent is given in *PASC*:36. (MPL 6:26, 19:382). James may have moved to VA when the Brents left MD.

THE CONEY FAMILY

Refs.: A: "Cony of Bassingthorpe." *HSPV* 50:259-263. B: Research by the late Richard T.

Foose of Kissimmee, FL, and generously made available to the compiler by Mr. Foose. C: "Sutton," *Visitations of the County of Nottingham, 1569 and 1614 (HSPV* 4:143).

NB: The account published in Lincolnshire Pedigrees differs somewhat from the material compiled by Richard T. Foose, and published in Vol. I of this work.

ARMS: Sable, on a fess cotised Or, between three conies Argent, as many escallops of the field (A:259).

1. GEOFFREY CONY m. Elizabeth, dau. of William Copledike. They were the parents of (A:259): ANTHONY, m. and had descendants; WILLIAM; and ROBERT of Yaxley, Hunts, ancestor of the Conys of Yaxley.

2. WILLIAM CONY, son of Geoffrey (1) and Elizabeth, was a Merchant of the Staple. He m. [-?-], dau. of [-?-] Bell of Fishtoft. They were the parents of (A:260): RICHARD of Bassingthorpe; and THOMAS of Hanthorpe, m. and had issue.

3. RICHARD CONY of Bassingthorpe, Merchant of the Staple of Calais, son of William (2), was buried at Bassingthorpe on 12 April 1545. He m. Jane Ellis, dau. of Thomas Ellis of Paunton. She was buried at Bassingthorpe on 5 July 1649.

 Richard and Jane were the parents of (A:260); THOMAS; WILLIAM, bur. 20 May 1558 at Bassingthorpe; GODFREY, bur. 22 Sep 1542 at Bassingthorpe; EDMUND, bapt. 26 May 1543, bur. 6 Feb 1543/4; and ELIZABETH, m. 1st, Richard Thorold of Morton, and 2nd, George Cradock of Stafford.

4. THOMAS CONY of Basingthorpe Hall, son of Richard (4) and Jane, was age 16 in 1545, and was bur. at Bassingthorpe on 15 Oct 1611. He m. Alice, dau. of Sir Thomas Leigh, Kt., Lord Mayor of London in 1556. Alice d. by 1621 (A:260).

 Thomas d. leaving a will dated 22 May 1611 and confirmed by sentence on 3 Dec 1621. Admin. was granted to his son Sir Thomas Cony, Kt.; a second admin. was granted 6 June 1633 (A:260-263).

 Thomas and Alice were the parents of (B): Sir THOMAS, bapt, 15 Sep 1561; MARY, bapt. 21 July 1566, bur. 13 Jan 1566/7; SUSAN, bapt. 1 May 1568 at Bassingthorpe, m. Sir William Sutton on 10 Nov 1584; PEREGRINE. bapt. 30 Oct 1569 at Bassingthorpe, m. and had issue; ROSE, bapt. 14 June 1573, m. 16 April 1595, Thomas Butler of Paunton; FRANCES, bapt. 1 March 1574/5 at Bassingthorpe, m. 22 Jan 1599/1600 Augustine Earle of Stragglethorpe; and ARTHUR, bapt. 30 June 1577 at Bassingthorpe, m. and had issue.

5. Sir THOMAS CONEY, Kt., of Basingthorpe Hall, son of Thomas (4) and Alice, was bapt. at Old Jewry, London, on 15 Sep 1561 and was buried at Bassingthorpe on 22 Nov 1637. He m. 1st, Elizabeth Patten (dau. of William and Anne (Johnson) Patten). His 2nd wife whom he m. at Northoline on 13 March 1591/2, was Anne, widow of William Tundall, and dau. of Hanmon Upton, (descended from Suttons of Washingborough, Lincoln). His 3rd wife was Mary Snelling. She m. on 18 Jan 1637/8, Edward Armstrong of Corby (A:261).

 He was knighted at Whitehall on 23 Sep 1603. He left a will dated 26 Oct 1637, and proved 9 Jan 1637/8 (A:261).

By Elizabeth Patten, Sir Thomas was the father of (A:269): Sir SUTTON, knighted at Welbeck on 10 Aug 1619, m. and had issue; ELIZABETH, m. after 1611, John Osborne of Thorpe-by-Water, Co. Rutland (Query if she m. 2nd, William Sharpe); ANNE, m. John Dalton of Scredington; and SUSAN.

By his second wife, Sir Thomas was the father of (A:161): THOMAS.

By Mary Snelling, Sir Thomas was the father of (A:261; B): RICHARD, bapt. 23 May 1632, Major in the Army; and MARY, bapt. 27 May 1634 at Corby.

6. SUSAN CONY, dau. of Thomas (4) and Alice, was bapt. 1 May 1568 at Bassingthorpe, m. Sir William Sutton of Averham, Notts, on 10 Nov 1584. He was 14 years old in 1575 (C:143).

Sir William and Susan (Cony) Sutton were the parents of (C:143): ROBERT, m. Elizabeth Manners; RICHARD; HENRY; ALICE, m,. Thomas Simcock; SUSAN, m. William Oglethorpe of Oglethorpe, Yorkshire; MARY; ELIZABETH; and GERVASE.

7. SUSAN SUTTON, dau. of Sir William and Susan (6) cony) Sutton, m. William Oglethorpe of Oglethorpe, Yorks. They were the ancestors of (*RD500*:289-290): **James Edward Oglethorpe**, 1696-1785, the founder of Georgia, and also **Victor Emanuel II**, 1829-1878, King of Sardinia and 1st King of a United Italy.

THE CONN FAMILY

Refs.: A: Gerald R. Tudor. "Descendants of Hugh Conn." Electronic genealogy posted on www.FamilyTreeMaker.com. B: *Indexes to Irish Wills*. Ed. by W. P. W. Phillimore. (1909-1920). Repr. Baltimore: Genealogical Publishing Co., Inc., 1997. C: David Dobson. *Scots-Irish Links, 1675-1725*. Two Parts in One (1994, 1995). Repr.: Baltimore: Clearfield Co., Inc., 1999. Provides clues to Irishmen in Scotland, and Scots in Ireland.

NB: Mr. Tudor writes: "We cannot confirm the parentage of Hugh Conn, but there are leads in Northern Ireland."

1. THOMAS CONN, d. c1626. He came from Kirkcudbrightshire, Scotland, to Northern Ireland, c1611/6. Thomas Conne left a will in the Diocese of Derry, Ireland, in 1626 (B: 5:24).

He is believed to have been the father of (A): THOMAS.

2. THOMAS CONN, poss. son of Thomas (1), was b. c1620, is stated to have been the father of (A): JOHN.

3. JOHN CONN, son of Thomas (2), was listed on the Muster Rolls of Limavady in 1666. He is stated to have been the father of (A): HUGH.

4. HUGH CONN, son of John (3), was b. c1685 in Macgillighan, Ireland, and d. 28 June 1752 in MD. He m. 1st, Elizabeth Todd, who d. c1717, and 2nd, c1722, Jean [-?-], b. c1702, d. 4 March 1747/8.

Hugh Conn studied at the School in Foghanveil (Faughanville), and graduated from the University of Glasgow (A). Hugh Conn was described as a Scotch-Irish student at Glasgow University (C: Part Two:6).

THE RANDALL-COOKE CONNECTION

Refs.: A: KELR JS#W:562. B: KELR JS#X:420. C: MWB 13:485.

1. BENJAMIN RANDALL of KE Co. immigrated by 1680 (MPL WC#2: 156, 157). On 7 April 1680 he purchased from John Wedge and wife Susanna tract Mount Pleasant, 350 a. granted by patent dated 5 Sept 1679 to the said John Wedge of KE Co. (A). On 30 May 1680 Elis Humphries and his wife Sarah, of KE Co. conv. to Benjamin Randall of the same Co., land in Langford Bay, 200 a., known as Jamaica (KELR B:21). Benjamin Randall died and the tract Mount Pleasant descended to his son Benjamin (A). Benjamin was the father of: BENJAMIN, Jr.; and ANN.

2. BENJAMIN RANDALL, son of Benjamin (1), inherited the tract Mount Pleasant, and by his will of 1716 left it to his cousin Thomas Cooke. (A) Benjamin Randall, by his last will dated 1 Dec 1716, recorded in the Prerogative Office of Canterbury, devised to his cousin Thomas Cook all his several tracts in Maryland. (KELR JS#23:270)

3. ANN RANDALL, dau. of Benjamin (1), m. 1st Henry Staples, 2nd, Robert Burman, and 3rd, Edward Blay. Henry Staples of KE Co. at the time of his death owned a 200 a. tract called Killey Langford surveyed for him on 3 June 1685 on w. side of the main branch of Langford's Bay. Staples died leaving a will proved 3 Oct 1686 leaving the residue of his estate to his wife Ann Staples. She m. 2nd, Robert Burman, Gent., and 3rd Colonel Edward Blay late of KE Co., deceased. Ann Randall Staples Burman Blay died about Aug 1712 leaving her brother the said Mr. Benjamin Randall, Jr. (B) Actually the will of Ann Blay, wife of Edward Blay, Fent., of CE Co., dated 18 Feb 1705/6, proved 28 Aug 1712, named William Blay, son of her husband Edward Blay, who was to have 210 a. part of Little Grove in KE Co., and 200 a. part of The Grove. Her husband Edward Blay was to be exec. (C)

4. THOMAS COOKE of the Parish of Waltham Holy Cross in the County of Essex, Kingdom of England, heir at law of Benjamin Randall, late of London, Gent., who was the only son and heir of Benjamin Randall late of KE Co., Maryland, Gent., on 1 Jan 1724 conv. to James Cruckshanks of said KE Co., Maryland, chirurgeon, the tract Mount Pleasant. (A) On 23 Dec 1728 Thomas Cook of Waltham Holy Cross in the county of Essex and Gent., heir and devisee of Mr. Benjamin Randall late of London, Gent., to James Cruckshank of KE Co., chirurgeon, 200 acres Killey Langford. (B)

     Thomas Cooke of the parish of Waltham Holy Cross in the county of Essex, Kingdom of England, Gent., heir at law of Benjamin Randall late of London, Gent., who was the only son and heir of Benjamin Randall late of KE Co., Maryland, on 1 Jan 1724 conv. to James Cruckshanks of KE Co., Maryland, chirurgeon. Whereas by letters patent dated 4 Aug 1679 a patent was granted to Ellis Humphreys of KE Co. afsd. a parcel called Jamaica, 200 acres. On 31 May 1680 Ellis Humphreys and his wife Sarah conveyed same to said Benjamin Randall of KE Co. (KELR JS#X:1)

THE COPE FAMILY

Refs.: A: *PASC*:185. B: "Cope of Hanwell," *Burke's Peerage*, 1956 ed., pp. 510-511. C: "Pedigree of the Family of Cope," *MGH*, ser. 3, 4:208 ff. D: Gary Boyd Roberts. *Ancestors of American Presidents*. Santa Clarita: Carl Boyer, 3rd, 1995. E: Gary Boyd Roberts. *Royal Descents of 500 Immigrants to the American Colonies or the United States*. GPC, 1993. F: *PECD: Pedigrees of Some of the Emperor Charlemagne's Descendants*. 3 vols. Repr.: GPC, 1988. G: James Anderson Winn. *John Dryden and His World*. New Haven: Yale University Press, 1087. Chart betw. pp. 12 and 13.

NB: Charles M. Hanson, writing in *TAG* 70 (3) 156-161, refutes the descent of Oliver Cope of PA as given in *RD500* (E). Oliver was a son of John Cope of Hesleden, Wilts, yeoman and Elizabeth [-?-], living in Avebury, Wilts, but he does not have the descent from Sir Anthony Cope as falsified by Walter Ellis, Heraldic Engraver from England.

NB: James Anderson Winn states that he relied on Walter C. Metcalfe's Visitation of Northamptonshire made in 1564 and 1618-9 (Mitchell and Hughes, 1887) and the Histories of Northamptonshire by Bridges and Baker. Winn verified the information wherever possible by checking original wills (G:515).

Generations 1-5

1. JOHN COPE of Dinshanger, Northants. M.P., and High Sheriff of that county, d. 1414. He m. Elizabeth, dau. and heiress of John Newenham (B).

John Cope was described as a "very important person" in the reigns of Richard II and Henry IV (B).

John and Elizabeth were the parents of (B): WILLIAM.

2. WILLIAM COPE, son of John (1) and Elizabeth, m. the dau. and heir of William Gossage of Spratton, Northants. They were the parents of (B): STEPHEN.

3. STEPHEN COPE, son of William (2) was the father of (B): WILLIAM.

4. WILLIAM COPE, Esq., of Banbury, Co. Oxford, and Hanwell, Cofferer to King Henry VII and Keeper of Porchester Castle, son of Stephen (3), was b. c1450 and d. 1513. His will is filed PCC 12 Fetiplace (G:chart, 515). He is said to have m. 1st, Agnes, dau. of Stephen Harcourt of Stanton Harcourt; however Winn states that he m. 1st, Barbara, dau. of George Quarles of Ufford, Northamptonshire (G:chart). William m. 2nd, by 1496, Jane, dau. and heir of John Spencer, Gent., of Hodnell Co. Warwick (B; G). Jane m. 2nd, William Saunders of Banbury. Her will is in PCC 7 Porch (G:515).

William received a great gilt standing cup with branches from King James [IV?] of Scotland. The cup is mentioned in the will of his son John (G:515).

According to Winn, William and Barbara were the parents of STEPHEN.

According to the account in Burke, William and Agnes were the parents of (B): HENRY, m. Ann Saunders; and STEPHEN, Serjeant of the Poultry to Henry VIII, and was ancestor of the Copes in America.

William and Jane were the parents of (A; B; G; chart): Sir ANTHONY, d. 1551; EDWYN, d. by 1526; WILLIAM, d. s.p.; and Sir JOHN, d. 1558.

5. STEPHEN COPE of Bedhampton, son of Sir William (4) and Barbara (G) or Agnes (B) was b. 1473, and m. Anne Saunders, dau. and coheir of William Saunders of Oxford (C).

He is not traced in Winn. Stephen and Anne were the parents of (C): Sir ANTHONY, d. 1586.

6. Sir ANTHONY COPE, son of Sir William (4) and Jane (Spencer), d. 1551. His will is in PCC 30 Bucke. He m. Jane Crews, dau. of Matthew Crews of Oynne, Devon (B), d. 1570. Her will is in PCC 23 Lyon (G:chart, 515).

Sir Anthony was the author of *The Historie of ... Annibal and Scipio* (1554), and *A Godly Meditacion upon XX Select and Chosen Psalmes* (1547). He was knighted in 1 Edw. VI and was Sheriff for Oxfordshire and Berks (B).

Sir Anthony and Jane were the parents of (A; D:239; G:chart): EDWARD; and ANNE, m. Sir Kenelm Digby of Drystoke, Rutland.

7. EDWYN COPE, son of William (4) and Jane, d. by 1526. He m. Anne [-?-]. Edwyn and Anne are not mentioned in any printed genealogies, but they appear in the wills of their parents. Edward was dead by the time his mother died in 1526 (G:515).

Edwyn and Anne had one son (G:chart): WILLIAM.

8. Sir JOHN COPE, of Canons Ashby, Northants, Sheriff of Northants, and M.P., son of Sir William (4) and Jane, d. 1558. He m. 1st, Bridget Raleigh, dau. of Edward and Anne (Chamberlain) Raleigh. For the Royal Descent of Bridget Raleigh, See *PASC*:184-185.

In his will, PCC 25 Noodes, Sir John left the great gilt cup to his grandson Edward, and a silver basin to his son George, to whom he has already given houses and land. He also named his dau. Elizabeth Dryden (G:515).

Sir John m. 2nd, Mary Mallory and 3rd, Margaret (Tame) Stafford, but he had no issue by his 2nd and 3rd wives (A; G:chart).

Sir John and Bridget were the parents of (A; G): ERASMUS, d. 1558, m. Mary Heneage and had issue; GEORGE, d. 1572, m. Dorothy Spencer and had issue; ANTHONY of Adston, d. 1558 (his will is in PCC 18 Welles), m. Eleanor Stafford; JOAN, m. Stephen Boyle; and ELIZABETH, m. John Dryden (They were the ancestors of **The Cheseldyne Family** of Maryland, and **The Marbury Family** of New England; through the Marbury family, John and Elizabeth were the ancestors of Presidents Franklin Delano Roosevelt and George Herbert Walker Bush).

Generation 6

9. Sir ANTHONY COPE, son of Stephen (5), d. 1586. He was a Recusant in 1569. He m. Anne Stafford, dau. of Sir Humphrey Stafford of Blathewyde. [Note that Winn states that Anthony Cope of Adston m. Eleanor, dau. of Sir Humphrey Stafford of Blatherwick].

Sir Anthony and Anne were the parents of (C): EDWARD, d. by 1634; and poss. others.

10. EDWARD COPE, son of Sir Anthony (6) and Jane (Crews), was b. 1517 and d. 20 June 1557. He m. Elizabeth Mohun, dau. and Heiress of Wollaston, Northants. She m. 2nd, George Carleton (B).

Edward and Elizabeth were the parents of (B; D:239; G:chart): WILLIAM, b. 1544, d. 1606; Sir ANTHONY of Banbury, b. 1548, d. 1614 (imprisoned for his Puritan activities, he left a will, PCC 22 Cope), m. and had issue; Sir WALTER, d. 1614, m. and had issue; and URSULA, m. John D'Oyly (John and Ursula were the ancestors of **President Calvin Coolidge**).

Generation 7

11. EDWARD COPE, son of Sir Anthony (9), d. by 1634. He married Maud [-?-]. They were the parents of (C; E:325): JOHN, of Mardonl; and **EDWARD, "went to America."**

12. Sir ANTHONY COPE, 1st Bart., son of Edward (10) and Elizabeth, was b. 1549 and was bur. 23 July 1615. He was knighted by Queen Elizabeth and created a Baronet in 1611.

He m. 1st, Frances Lytton, dau. of Rowland Lytton. She was buried 13 Jan 1600/1, and Sir Anthony m. 2nd, in 1605, Anne, dau. of William Paston. By his first wife he was the father of (B): Sir WILLIAM, 2nd Bart., whose son was Sir John, 3rd Bart.; RICHARD, settled in Ireland; JOHN, b. 1590, d. unm.; ANTHONY, settled in Ireland; and ELIZABETH, m. Sir Richard Cecil.

Generation 8

13. JOHN COPE, son of Edward (11) and Maud, m. Margaret [-?-]. John and Margaret were the parents of (E:325): JOHN.

14. RICHARD COPE, son of Sir Anthony (12) and Frances, d. 1628. He settled in Ireland and m. Anne, sister of Sir William Walter of Wimbledon, Surrey. Richard and Anne were the parents of (B): WALTER; WILLIAM of Icombe, Glouc.; and ANTHONY.

Generation 9

15. JOHN COPE, son of John (13) and Margaret, m. Elizabeth [-?-]. They were the parents of (E:325): **Oliver Cope**, who settled in PA, and m. Rebecca [-?-].

16. WILLIAM COPE, Esq., of Icombe, Co. Gloucester, son of Richard (14) and Anne, m. Elizabeth, widow of Sir John Cope, 3rd Bart. of Hanwell (B:511), and dau. of Francis Fane, 1st Earl of Westmorland by his wife Mary Mildmay. William and Elizabeth were the parents of (E:42; F: 1:209): RACHEL ELIZABETH.

Generation 10

17. RACHEL ELIZABETH COPE, dau. of William (16) and Elizabeth (Fane), m. Thomas Geers. Their dau. Elizabeth Geers m. William Gregory and had a dau. Elizabeth who m. John

Nourse; John and Elizabeth (Gregory) Nourse were the parents of **James Nourse of PA and MD** who m. Sarah Faunce [actually Fouace] (E:42; F: 1:209).

THE CORNISH FAMILY REVISED
Contributed by Fredric Z. Saunders

Refs.: A: Fredric Z. Saunders (5186 S. Cobble Creek Rd. # 6K, Salt Lake City, UT 84117-6723; e mail at fzasaund@ix.netcom.com. web site: http://pweb.netcom.com/~fzsaud), "Genealogy of the Cornish Family of Tiverton, Devon, England," (available at his web site). B: Fredric Z. Saunders. "Edward Robins, Corrections to His English Ancestry, and Identification of His Wife Jane Skinner," *MGSB* 37 (2) 169-186. C: "Alice Skinner and Elizabeth Read: Two Ridgely Wives," by Richard T. Foose, *MGSB* 29 (1) 60-66. D: *Marriage Licenses of the Diocese of Exeter.* Ed. by J. L. Vivian. E: Tiverton Bishops Transcripts 1605-1742, Church of England. E: Fredric Z. Saunders, "The Cornish Family of Tiverton, England," *MGSB* 42 (1) 51-101. F: "Cornish," *Visitation of London; HSPV* 15:191.

ARMS: Sable, a chevron embattled Or, between three roses Argent. **CREST**: A Cornish cvhough ppr. (F).

1. WALTER CORNISH of Tiverton, Devon, possibly a descendant of the Cornish Family of Cornish Hall, Cornwall. He may have m. Margaret [-?-], who was buried 14 Jan 1559/60 at Tiverton (A).

Walter Cornish was the father of (A): GEORGE, b. c1549; EDMOND, b. c1542, bur. 24 April 1603, m. on 15 Sep 1565 Alice Coram; and RALPH/RAFE, b. c1544, bur. 27 June 1602 at tiverton, m. in Dec 1570, Margaret [-?-].

2. GEORGE CORNISH, son of Walter (1), was b. c1549, and was bur. 6 Feb 1607/8. He m. Maria/Mary Lawrence who was bur. 15 Sep 1622 at Tiverton (A).

George and Maria/Mary were the parents of the following children, whose baptisms when indicated, were at Tiverton (A): ALICE, b. c1564, m. Robert Read on 5 Nov 1591; PRUDENCE, b. c1566, m. 1st, John Goddard on 27 April 1594, and 2nd, [-?-] Isaac on 16 Jan 1606/7; JAMES, b. c1568, m. as his 1st wife, [-?-] [-?-], and 2nd, Sarah Beryman on 26 Dec 1611; ANNE, bapt. 28 Sep 1570,. m. James Ottway; THOMAS, bapt. 4 March 1571/2, d. between 1619 and 1641; JOHN, bapt. 14 Nov 1573, d. young; MARGARET, bapt. 9 Jan 1574/5, m. 1st, John Middleton on 18 Nov 1601, and 2nd, [-?-] Levitt or Libbett; ELLEN/ELINOR, bapt. 12 April 1577, m. Humfry Morgan on 3 Oct 1603; RICHARD, bapt. 25 Jan 1578/9; and GEORGE, bapt. 18 April 1581, bur. 12 Oct 1655 at St. Mary Magdalen Milk St., London, m. Isabel Roberts by license dated 6 May 1611.

3. JAMES CORNISH of Tiverton, Co. Somerset, son of George (2), was b. c1568 and d. by Nov 1635. He m. 1st [-?-] [-?-], and 2nd, Sarah Beryman, who d. testate in 1641, leaving a will proved in the Archdeaconry Court of Exeter (B:173).

James Cornish left a will dated the last day of August 1633, and proved 12 Nov 1635. He stated that he wanted to be buried in the churchyard of the parish church of Tiverton aforesaid as close as possible to the place where his first wife was buried. He made bequests to his wife Sarah, sons George (the ygst. son), and John, daus. Sara, Mary, Agnes, and Isabell (the ygst. dau.), all the previous six unmarried. He mentioned what he had given his dau. Dinah Chilcott at her marriage, and dau. Alice Skynner. Wife Sarah was extx., and sons James Cornish, John Cornish, and George Cornish and son-in-law Aquila Skinner were named overseers. Signed James Cornish Senior. Wit: Henry Crosman, John Jennings, and Henry [-?-]. As James Cornish the elder, clother, he added a codicil on 3 June 1635, naming sons James and John Cornish, sons-in-law Aquila Skinner and Richard Crudge, "all his grandchildren" (unnamed), and brother George Cornish of London and his wife (unnamed). He also named Andrew Speed, Sr. and his wife (unnamed), John Cornish the elder, George Cornish the elder, Mary Hollings the wife of (Mark?) Hollings, Richard More, (Amy?) Horsey wife of Stephan Horsey, Dorothie Alred wife of Thomas Alred, Jaine Hagley. The codicil was witnessed by James Cornish, Jr., Aquila Skynner, John (Funse?), and William Skynner (B: cites PCC 116 Sadler).

James Cornish was the father of (B:181; C; D): (poss.) JANE; (and definitely): ELIZABETH, bapt. 8 March 1613/4; JAMES; JOHN; GEORGE; SARA; MARY; AGNES, bapt. 29 Oct 1617; DINAH, m. [-?-] Chilcott; ALICE, m. Aquila Skinner (Their dau. Alice m. **Henry Ridgely of MD**); and ISABEL (ygst. dau.), bapt. 8 Nov 1625.

4. RICHARD CORNISH, son of George (2) and Maria/Mary, was bapt. 25 Jan 1578/9 and was bur. 29 Sep 1625. On 27 June 1604 he m. Grace Gooding. She m. as her 2nd husband Richard Honniwell on 24 April 1628 (A).

Richard and Grace were the parents of the following children, bapt. at Tiverton (A): JANE, bapt. 6 Jan 1606/7, bur. 28 Oct 1608; JOHN, bapt. 14 March 1609/10; JANE, bapt. 15 Aug 1612 as "Jone", m. 1st, by license dated 16 April 1630 Edward Robins (C:1111), and 2nd, George Puddington, came to live in AA Co., MD, by 1674; ALICE, bapt. 28 Aug 1614 at Tiverton; THOMAS, b. c1616, m. Agnes Puddington on 13 Jan 1634/5; and GRACE, bapt. 14 Feb 1618/9, m. George Drew on 2 May 1639.

THE CRACKWELL FAMILY

1. RICHARD CRACKWELL of Burrowgreene, Cambridgeshire, was the father of: JOHN, b. c1663.

2. JOHN CRACKWELL, age 21, from Burrowgreene, Co. Cambridgeshire, son of Richard Crackwell (1), on 26 Aug 1684 bound himself to John Bright of London, to serve for four years in MD (*SEEA*:89).

In Nov 1703 Walter Meakes of KE Co. conveyed 100 a., part of the Forest of Deane, to John Cracknell (CELR 1:237). [Despite the apparent differences in spelling, this is probably the same individual who signed the indenture in 1684--ED].

He is probably the John Cracknell of CE Co. who died leaving a will dated 12 Nov 1705 and proved 12 March 1706/7. He left his eldest son John 100 a., Forest of Danes. Sons William and Thomas were to have personalty. Wife Elizabeth was named extx. and residuary legatee. Michael Bellikin, Thomas Smith, and Eliza Furaner witnessed the will (MWB 12:170).

John was the father of: JOHN; WILLIAM; and THOMAS.

THE CROMWELL FAMILY
Some inconclusive notes.

Refs.: A: Francis B. Culver. "Cromwell Family: A Possible Cromwell Clue." *MG* 1:339-356.

Entries in Malmesbury Abbey Church Registers (A:355).
Cromwell, John, son of Philip and Margaret, bapt. 11 July 1634.
Cromwell, Margaret, wife of Philip, bur. 15 July 1634.
Cromwell, John, son of Philip and Margaret, buried last July 1634.
Cromwell, Philip, m. Elinor Cooper 22 Jan 1634/5.
Cromwell, John, son of Philip and Eleanor, bapt. 26 June 1635.
Cromwell, Idith, dau. of Philip and Eleanor, bapt. 9 July 1637.
Cromwell, John, of this town, one of the chief Burgesses, buried 27 Dec 1639.
Cromwell, Mary, dau. of Richard and Elizabeth, bapt. 24 Jan 1641/2.
Cromwell, Edith, dau. of Eleanor, bur. 8 Jan 1643.
Baynam, Martha, sister of Richard Crumwell's wife, bur. 10 Dec 1642.
Cromwell, Edith, dau. of Thomas and Anne, bapt. 8 Jan 1643/4.
Cromwell, Edith, dau. of Thomas and Anne of this town, bur. 2 Feb 1643/4.
Cromwell, Thomas, son of Thomas and Anne of this town, bapt. 16 Sep 1645.
Cromwell, Agnis, dau. of Thomas and Agnis [*sic*] of this town, bapt. 18 March 1646/7.
Cromwell, Jane, dau. of Thomas and Anne, bapt. 4 July 1649.
Cromwell, [-?-], dau. of Thomas and Anne, bapt. 18 July 1651.
Cromwell, Milicent, wife of John Cromwell of Malmesbury, dec. 23 May and was bur. 25 May 1656.

Cromwell Extracts from the Registers of Great Somerford, Wilts. (Taken from the Bishop's Transcripts at Salisbury Registrar's Office) (A:356).
Cromwell, William, son of John, bapt. 20 Oct 1605.
Cromwell, Mary, dau. of Richard, bapt. 4 May 1619.
Cromwell, Mary, dau. of Richard, bapt. 1 Jan 1620/1.
Cromwell, Richard, son of Richard, buried 24 June 1620.
Cromwell, John, bur. 10 Dec 1669.
Cromwell, Ann, m. Richard Freeth 24 June 1700.

THE JOHN CROMWELL FAMILY of WILTS

1. JOHN CROMWELL d. c25 Dec 1639. He m. Edith [-?-].
   John Cromwell d. leaving a will dated 23 Dec 1639 and proved at Great Somerford on 19 Feb 1639/40. He asked to be buried in the churchyard of St., Paul's, Malmesbury, and named his wife Edith, son Philip and the latter's children John and Edith, his own son Richard. Robert Arche, Gent., and Thomas Burgess, yeoman were named overseers. Roger Jarrett, Thomas Burgess, and William Smith were witnesses.
   The inventory of John Cromwell's estate was taken 20 Jan 1639/40, and amounted to £204.16.4 (A:350 cites Archdeaconry of Wilts, filed Wills, 1639, old No. 53).
   John and Edith were the parents of (A:351): WILLIAM, poss. bapt. 20 Oct 1605 at Great Somerford; **PHILIP, b. 1610 or 1612 at Malmesbury, Wilts., d. 20 March 1693 at**

Salem, MA (his descendants are traced in A:351-353); RICHARD, m. Elizabeth [-?-], sister of Margaret Baynam, leaving a dau. Mary, bapt. 23 Jan 1641/2 at Malmesbury; and **THOMAS, b. c1617 at Malmesbury, d. 17 March 1686 at Salem, MA** (His family is traced in A:353).

THE CROMWELL FAMILY OF MARYLAND

Culver discusses the legend that William, John, Richard, and Edith Cromwell of Maryland were children of Henry Cromwell, and grandchildren of Sir Oliver Cromwell of Hichen Brook, Kt., an uncle of Oliver Cromwell the Lord Protector of England, but he states there is no proof to the legend (A:339).

Culver goes on to suggest that there is an equal possibility that the Maryland Cromwells may be related to the Cromwells of Wiltshire, discussed above, because of the recurrence of the names William, John, Richard, Edith, and Philip (A::339-340).

THE CUNNINGHAM FAMILY

Refs.: A: "Cunynghame," *Burke's Peerage*, 1956 ed., pp. 573-574.

1. WILLIAM CUNYNGHAME of Polquhairn was living in 1585. He married 1st, Janet McAdam, and 2nd, Agnes Muir. He was the father of (A): WILLIAM.

2. WILLIAM CUNYNGHAME, 1st of Milncraig, in Colyton, co. Ayr, son of William (1), acquired Milncraig by his marriage with the dau. of William Cathcart of Corbleston. He was the father of (A): WILLIAM.

3. WILLIAM CUNYNGHAME of Milncraig, son of William (2), married the dau. of David Crawford of Kerse, Co. Ayr. He was the father of (A): DAVID.

4. DAVID CUNYNGHAME of Milncraig, son of William (3), died in Dec 1659. He married Margaret, dau. of John Mason, Burgh Clerk of Ayr. They were the parents of: Sir DAVID, 1st Bart. of Milncraig.

5. Sir DAVID CUNYNGHAME, 1st Bart. of Milncraig, son of David (4), died 28 Jan 1708. He married 1st, Isabel, youngest dau. of the 1st Viscount Stair, and 2nd, on 16 March 1698, Elizabeth, dau. of Sir Robert Baird, 1st Bart. of Saughton Hall.

He acquired Robertland from Sir Alexander Cuningham, 3rd Bart. of Robertland ("Fairlie-Cunginhame of Robertland," *Burke's Peerage*, 1956 ed., p. 569).

Sir David was the father of at least two sons (A): Sir JAMES, 2nd Bart.; and Sir DAVID, 3rd Bart.

6. Sir JOHN CUNNINGHAM of Robertland, relationship to the above not determined, was the father of: DAVID.

7. DAVID CUNNINGHAM, second son of Sir John (6) Cunningham of Robertland, Scotland, came to VA or MD about 22 years ago (c1729). He is asked to contact Robert Peter, merchant, or William Cunninghame, merchant, at the Falls of Rappahannock in VA, for good news (*AMG* 16 Oct 1751).

A William Cunningham died by Jan 1797 when his admx. Elizabeth Cunningham of Norfolk advertised she would settle his estate (*GAVN*:82 cites *The Norfolk Herald and Public Advertiser* 5 Jan 1797).

NB: See the "Fairlie-Cunninghame of Robertland [Co. Ayr] in *Burke's Peerage*, 1956 ed., pp. 569-570.

THE DALYZELL FAMILY

Refs.: A: Deposition of Robert Montgomerie, M. A. of the Town of Kilmarnock, Scotland, made 28 March 1752, recorded in FRLR E:150-155. B: Deposition of John Hopkins, Merchant of Kilmarnock, made 28 March 1752, recorded in FRLR E:150-155. C: Extracts from the Parish Registers of Kilmarnock, recorded in FRLR E:150-155. D: Power of Attorney by Anna Dalzell Hopkins, made 7 April 1752, recorded in FRLR E:150-155.

1. JAMES DELAZEEL [sic], late bailee of the Burgh of Dumfries, was the father of: ANN, m. Robert Hopkins.

2. ANNA DELAZEEL or DALZELL, dau. of James, m. on 26 April 1710, Robert Hopkins, son of Matthew of the Town of Kilmarnock, who died there in March 1719 (C).

Ann Dalzell Hopkins was still living on 7 April 1752 when she made her son James Hopkins, now of London, her attorney, to recover her share of her son Matthew's estate (D).

Robert and Ann had four children (A; C): MATTHEW, b. 3 Sep 1711; ELIZABETH, b. 8 May 1713, d. c1718; JAMES, b. 2 Dec 1714; and JOHN, b. 25 Sep 1715, d. c1718.

3. MATTHEW HOPKINS son of Robert and Anna (2), was born March 1719 in Kilmarnock, Scotland, settled in MD, and d. there in or about the month of Jan 1751 (A). He died intestate and his widow Mary Brown m. Henry Threlkeld (D; see "The Threlkeld Family," in *British Roots of Maryland Families* (Baltimore: Genealogical Publishing Co., Inc., 1999), pp. 422-423).

Matthew Hopkins left a personal estate worth £1875.13.6, as appraised by Alexander Beall on and John Needham on in March 1750. John Dalyzell, minor, signed as next of kin. [-?-] Hopkins, admx., filed the inventory on 6 May 1751 (MINV 45:115).

4. JAMES HOPKINS, son of Robert and Anna (2), was b. 2 Dec 1714, and given a power of attorney by his mother in 1752. He was a chirurgeon living in London (FRLR E:180).

5. JOHN DALYZELL, degree of relationship to above not known, minor, signed the inventory of Matthew Hopkins in March 1750 as next of kin (MINV 45:115). He m. Eleanor [-?-].

He is almost certainly the John Dalyell from Colvend, Kirkcudbrightshire, and nephew of John Dalyell of Fairgirth who had d. in 1764 (*DSSB*:39). John came to FR Co., MD before 1760 (*DSEW*:91).

On 15 June 1756 John Dalyzell and his wife Eleanor, in consideration of the love they had for their son Archibald Offutt, conveyed him one-half of Cool Spring Level, cont. 296 a. (FRLR E:1077).

THE DANBY FAMILY

Refs.: A: "Danby." *HSPV* 16:88-89. B: *PASC2*.

ARMS: Argent, per chief, in chief three mullets Sable (*PASC*:30).

1, Sir ROBERT DANBY of Thorpe m. Elizabeth, dau. and one of the heirs of Aslaby. They were the parents of (A): Sir JAMES.

2. Sir JAMES DANBY, son of Sir Robert (1) and Elizabeth, m. Agnes, dau. and heir of Sir John Langton. They were the parents of (A): Sir CHRISTOPHER.

3. Sir CHRISTOPHER DANBY, son of Sir James (2) and Agnes, m. Margery, dau. and co-heir of Thomas le Scrope, 5th Lord Scrope of Masham (B:109; *PASC*:29-30). They were the parents of (A): Sir CHRISTOPHER.

4. Sir CHRISTOPHER DANBY, son of Sir Christopher (3) and Margery, was b. c1505 and d. 14 June 1571. He m. Elizabeth, b. 25 April 1500, dau. of Richard Neville, Lord Latimer (descendant of King Edward III), and his wife Anne Stafford (*PASC*:29).

Sir Christopher and Elizabeth were the parents of (A): Sir THOMAS, m. Mary, dau. of Ralph, Earl of Westmorland; CHRISTOPHER; JOHN; JAMES; MARMADUKE; WILLIAM; DOROTHY, m. John Nevill of Leversedge; MARY, m. Sir Edward Mauleverer (ancestors of **Anne Mauleverer, wife of John Abbott of Burlington Co., NJ**); JANE, m. Roger Meynell; MARGARET, m. Christopher Hopton of Arnely Hall; ANN, m. Walter Calverley; ELIZABETH, m. Thomas Wentworth of Ashby; MADALYN, m. Marmaduke Wyvill (ancestors of **Marmaduke Wyvill of MD**; see *British Roots*, vol. 1, p. 480); and MARGERY, m. Christopher Mallory.

THE DORSEY-DARCY FAMILY
A Line Still Unproven

Refs.: A: "D'Arcy-Barons D'Arcy, Earls of Holderness," *BDEP*. B: *RD500*:176. C: *WAR7*. D: "Identity of Edward Dorsey I: A New Approach to an Old Problem," by Caroline Kemper Bulkley, *MG* 1:377-406. E: "Edward Dorsey: A Review and A Questtion," by Nellie Owings Chaney, *MGSB* 38 (2) 210-215. [This last article has generated a great deal of controversy. The line is not proven, but is included because of possible leads.] F: Ancestry of Edward Dorsey of AA Co., MD, from the Ancestral file of the LDS. G:*PASC2*.

ARMS: Azure, semee of crosses-crosslet and three cinquefoils Argent (A:159).

Generations 1-6

1. Sir JOHN D'ARCY, Baron of Knayth, Lincs., m. Emmeline, dau. of Walter Heron of Hedlestone, Northumberland. They were the parents of (C:Line 88): Sir JOHN.

2. Sir JOHN D'ARCY, 2nd Baron D'Arcy of Knayth, son of Sir John (1), was b. 1317, and slain at the Battle of Crecy, 5 March 1355/6. He m. 1st, by July 1332, Alianore, dau. of Sir Robert de Holand. Sir John m. 2nd, on 7 Jan 1344/5, Elizabeth de Mainill, b. 15 Oct 1331, d. 1368. She m. 2nd, Sir Piers de Mauley.
Sir John and Elizabeth were the parents of (C:Line 88): Sir PHILIP.

3. Sir PHILIP D'ARCY, Lord D'Arcy of Knayth, son of Sir John (2), was b. 21 May 1352, and d. 24 April 1399. He m. Elizabeth Gray, d. Aug 1412, dau. of Sir Thomas and Margaret (de Presfen) Gray of Heton. Sir Philip and Elizabeth were the parents of (C:Line 88): JOHN.

4. JOHN D'ARCY, 5th Baron D'Arcy, son of Sir Philip (3), was b. c1377/6, and d. 9 Dec 1411. He m. Margaret de Grey, d. 1 June 1454, dau. of Henry, Lord Grey of Wilton, by his wife Elizabeth Talbot (**Descendant of Edward I**) (G:110).
Lord John and Margaret were the parents of (C:Lines 13, 88): PHILIP; and JOHN.

5. Sir PHILIP D'ARCY, son of and heir of John (4) and Margaret, was b. c1398 and d. aged 28 by 18 Feb 1426/7, without male issue. He m. by 1412 Alianor Fitzhugh, dau. of Henry Fitzhugh, 3rd Lord Fitzhugh, by his wife Elizabeth (de Grey). Alianore m. 2nd, by 18 Feb 1426/7, to Sir Thomas Tunstall, and 3rd, to Sir Henry Bromflete (G:110-111).
Sir Philip and Alianor were the parents of (G:111): ELIZABETH, m. James Strangeways; and MARGARET, born posthumously, m. John Conyers (ancestors of **George and Nehemiah Blakiston of MD**)

6. JOHN D'ARCY, 7th Baron D'Arcy, son of John (4), was b. c1400, and d. 1458. He m. Joan Greystoke, dau. of John, Lord Greystoke, by Elizabeth, Lady of Wem (**Descendant of Edward III**) (B; C: Line 13; G:209).
John and Joan were the parents of (B; G:209): RICHARD; and four other sons and four daus.

Generations 6-10

7. RICHARD D'ARCY, son of John (6), was b. c1424 and d. by 1458. He m. Eleanor Scrope, dau. of Sir John Scrope, Lord Scrope of Upsal, and was the father of (B; C:Line 13; G:211): Sir WILLIAM.

8. Sir WILLIAM D'ARCY, 8th Baron D'Arcy, son of Richard (7), was b. 1443 and d. 1488. He m. Eupheme Langton, by whom he was the father of (B; C:Line 13; G:210): Sir THOMAS.

9. Sir THOMAS D'ARCY, K.G., 1st Baron D'Arcy of D'Arcy, son of Sir William (8), was b. c1467, and was beheaded at Tower Hill on 20 June 1537, and buried at St. Botolph's, Aldgate. He was created Baron D'Arcy of D'Arcy in 1509. He m. 1st, Dowsabel Tempest, dau. of Sir Richard and Mabel (Strickland). He m. 2nd, Edith Sandys, widow of Ralph Neville, and dau. of Sir William Sandys, Kt., of the Vyne (G:210).

    Sir Thomas and Dowsabel were the parents of (B; C:Line 13; G:210): Sir ARTHUR.

10. Sir ARTHUR D'ARCY, son of Sir Thomas (9) and Dowsabel, was b. c1505 or 1516 at Brimham, Yorkshire (F), and d. 3 April 1560 (F) or 1561 (E).

    By his wife Mary, b. c1520 at Beddington, dau. and coheir of Sir Nicholas Carew of Beddington, Surrey, he was the father of several children, including (A:158; C:Line 13; G:210): THOMAS; Sir HENRY, d. without male issue; and SIR EDWARD, m. Elizabeth Astley and was the grandfather of **Mary Launce** of MA, who m. **Rev. John Sherman** (B:176).

11. THOMAS D'ARCY, son of Sir Arthur (10), was b. at Hornby Castle, Yorks. (F). The birth date of 1565 given in F is not possible because his father d. in 1560, and Thomas' first wife died in 1572 and he m. 2nd, c1573, He d. 6 Nov 1605. He m. 1st, Elizabeth, dau. and coheir of John, 3rd Baron Conyers. She d. 6 June 1572. He m. 2nd, c1573, Collubia [-?-]; he m. 3rd, by 20 April 1583, Mary Kitson (F). Thomas became the head of the family on the death of his older brother, Sir Henry.

    Mary Kitson is stated to have been born c1567 at Hengrave, and to have d. 28 June 1644 at Colchester, England (F). If this is true, Thomas could not have m. 3rd, c1594 Elizabeth as given in F.

    Thomas and Elizabeth Conyers had issue (A:158): Sir CONYERS.

    Thomas and Mary (Kitson) are alleged to have been the parents of (F): ELIZABETH, Countess Rivers, b. 1584, d. 9 March 1650, m., 14 May 1602, Thomas Savage, Viscount Savage; THOMAS, b. c1586, m. c1606 Mary Fitz; MARY, b. c1588, d. 1627, m. c1606 Roger Manwood, and 2nd, c1615, Sir Thomas Maples; SUSAN, b. 1590, d. 1612; EDWARD, b. c1590; and PENELOPE, b. 1593, d. by 2 July 1661, m. 1st, 28 June 1611, Sir John Gage, Bart., 2nd, in 1612 Sir William Hervey; and 3rd, Sir George Trenchard.

Generation 11

12. Sir CONYERS D'ARCY, Kt., of Hornby, son of Thomas (11) and Elizabeth (Conyers), d. 3 March 1653. He m. Dorothy, dau. of Sir Henry Bellasyse, Bart.

By Letters Patent dated 10 Aug 1641, King Charles I conferred upon Conyers D'Arcy the title of Baron D'Arcy. Sir Conyers and Dorothy were the parents of several children, including (A:158): CONYERS; and poss. (D): EDWARD, b. 1619/20, "said by some to have died the same year."

13. EDWARD DARCY, son of Thomas (11) and Mary (Kitson), was b. c1590. He is alleged to have been the father of (F): EDWARD.

Generation 12

14. CONYERS D'ARCY, son of Sir Conyers (12) and Dorothy, d. 14 June 1689. He m. Grace, dau. and heiress of Thomas Rokeby. He was created Earl of Holderness by Letters Patent dated 5 Dec 1682.

Conyers and Grace had several children including (A:159): CONYERS, 2nd Earl of Holderness; URSULA, m. Christopher Wyvil (Their great-grandson **William Wyvil** settled in MD; See **The Wyvil Family** in *British Roots of Maryland Families*, Volume I); ELIZABETH, m. Sir Henry Stapleton, Bart.; GRACE, m. Sir John Legard, Bart.; and MARGARET, m. Sir Henry Marwood, Bart.

15. EDWARD D'ARCY or DORSEY, possibly son of Sir Conyers (12), is identified by Bulkley as one of seven possible Edward Dorseys who came to Maryland. Bulkley and Chaney cite Dugdale's *Visitation of York* (Ed. by J. W. Clay. vol. 2, 1907, pp. 80-81), which stated that Edward was bapt. at Hornby 27 Jan 1620 and died the same year. However a search of Hornby records has failed to reveal any such child (D:382; E:12).

Chaney feels that such a definite date of baptism must have had its basis in fact, while the fact that the Hornby Registers do not show any child Edward, may mean that the record was deliberately removed.

Joshua Dorsey, the Settler's son, used a seal bearing the D'Arcy cinquefoils (E:213).

In 1632 an "Edward Darcie aged 13," was licensed to go to Bergen with his master Richard Ghips or Gibbs (D:383-384, cites *The Genealogist*. 23:125).

It is possible that if Edward, son of Conyers, became a member of the non-conformist sect, that a member of his family may have removed the page from the parish register in anger, just as Victorian fathers are said to have obliterated the names of erring children from the Family Bible.

Nevertheless, in spite of the reasoning done by Bulkley and Chaney, this compiler feels that the question of Edward Dorsey's ancestry has not been settled beyond reasonable doubt. As a Dorsey descendant himself, he wishes it had been so settled!

16. EDWARD DORSEY, son of Edward (13), is stated to have been born c1619, settled in AA Co., MD, where he d. on 2 Aug 1659. He m. Anne [-?-]. The contributors to the ancestral file state, without any documentation, that he m. 1st, in 1638, Anne Howard; 2nd, [-?-], and 3rd Anne [-?-].

THE DRUNCKORD FAMILY

1. ANTHONY DRUNCKORD, reedmaker of Quaker St., Spitalfields, Mddx., m. Susanna [-?-]. Both were living in Sep 1685.

They were the parents of at least one son (*LEMG*:25): JAMES.

2. JAMES DRUNCKORD, son of Anthony and Susanna, on 14 Sep 1685 was bound to Samuel Roberts to serve him for seven years in MD. Both his parents witnessed the indenture (*LEMG*:25).

He settled in BA Co., MD, and prob. m. Mary, dau. of Thomas Greenfield, whose will, dated 8 Jan 1704, named several children including a dau. Mary "Drunkord" (MWB 3:470).

James Ines [Ives?] of BA Co. made a will on 4 March 1703/4, and among other bequests left personalty to James "Drunkword" and heirs (MWB 3;4).

On 20 June 1704 Drunckord was listed as a debtor in the inventory of James Frisby, Esq., of CE Co. (INAC 30:368).

James Drunkcord d. by 12 March 1705, when as James "Dunckard" his estate was appraised at £55.9.0 (including 4,250 lbs. tob.) by Thomas Edmonds and John Kemball (INAC 25:104).

On 3 March 1707 his estate was admin. by John Debruler. An inventory of £55.9.0 was cited and payments came to 18,134 lbs. tob. (INAC 28:79).

No record of any descendants has been found, but Samuel Merryman acquired 308 a. called Drunkord's Hall. The bequest of James Ines [Ives] cited above suggests that Drunckord left heirs. It is possible, but by no means proven, that Merryman's wife Mary, who had been the widow of Thomas Eager, was a dau. or widow of James Drunckord, and not the dau. of Humphrey Boone, as suggested by Francis B. Culver in "The Merryman Family," *MG* 2:213-214.

THE DUNBARR FAMILY

1. JOHN DUNBARR was the father of: JOHN.

2. JOHN DUNBARR, age c22, tailor, son of John Dunbar, from Glasgow, Scotland, on 21 July 1684 bound himself to Francis Partis of London, to serve for four years in MD as a tailor (*SEEA*:52).

John Dunbar of SM Co. died leaving a will dated 22 March 1708/9 and proved 30 April 1709. He left his dwelling plantation to his two sons and three daus. Son William and wife were to have the tanyards. His eldest dau. Mary, and dau. Sarah were left personalty. His wife and son William were joint execs. Timothy Swillivant, Anne Merrell, and Thomas Underwood were named execs. (MWB 12, Part 2:54).

John Dunbar was the father of: WILLIAM; MARY; SARAH; and one other son and one other dau.

THE EBURNATHY FAMILY

1. JOHN EBURNATHY of Grange Oneland, Co. Armagh, was the father of the following sons (according to depositions of James Delap of Ballihaden and Alenander Gray Drummanon in Co. Armagh) (CHLR O#2:66): JOHN, Jr; THOMAS; JAMES; and WILLIAM.

2. JOHN EBURNATHY, son of John (1), d. by April 1733, He m. Ann [-?-] who d. by March 1742.

John Abernathy d. leaving a will dated 11 March 1733 and proved 21 Nov 1734. He left one-half of his real estate to his wife Anne, and the other half to his father John living in or near Armagh in the Kingdom of Ireland. He mentioned his bros. Thomas, James, and William, living in or near Armagh. Wife Ann and Robert Hanson were named execs (MWB 20:608).

The inventory of his personal estate was taken on 4 May 1733 by Thomas Hawkins and Ignatius Luckett, and filed 27 Nov 1733 by the execs. His personal property was appraised at £4040.3.11 (MINV 17:578; see also CHLR O#2:64). His widow Ann was living on 12 March 1734/5 (CHLR O#2:90).

Anne Ebernethy left a will dated 23 Dec 1737 and proved 11 Sep 1742. She named her grandson Peter White, son of her dau., Sarah wife of Francis Ware, Mary Manarel wife of John, Susannah, Sarah, and Elizabeth, daus. of Francis Ware, Frances, Sarah, and Mary Brown, daus. of Dr. Brown, grandson Thomas Ryan, and J. Doncastle. Execs. were Francis Ware and Jno. Doncastle (MWB 22:455).

3. THOMAS EBERNATHY (or ABERNATHY), son of John (1), settled in CH Co., prior to 21 Nov 1734 when he recorded a p/a from his father (CHLR O#2:66).

4. JAMES EBERNATHY, son of John (1), settled in CH Co. prior to 21 Nov 1734 when he recorded a power of attorney from his bro. William Abernathy (CHLR O#2:67).

THE EDGAR FAMILY

1. RICHARD EDGAR of Mddx., was the father of: RICHARD, b. c1657.

2. RICHARD EDGAR, age 27, son of Richard (1) Edgar from Co. Mddx., on 24 July 1684 bound himself to Edward Burford of London, to serve as a ropemaker for four years in MD (*SEEA*:80).

On 13 Sep 1692 Richard Edgar witnessed a deed in CH Co. (CHLR R:466). He was alive on 21 Oct 1715 when he witnessed another deed (CHLR F#2:76).

Richard Edgar married Joanna [-?-]. They were the parents of (CHLR Q:19, 26): WILLIAM, b. 24 June 1693; JOHN, b. 30 Aug 1699; and SARAH, twin, and ELIZABETH, twin, b. 28 Oct 1706.

THE EYRE/EURE FAMILY

Refs.: A: *HSPV n. s., Vol. 8*:89-90.

ARMS: Quarterly, 1: Argent, on a chevron Sable, three quatrefoils Or. 2: Or, three pairs of barbacles Sable (Padley); 3: Argent, a greyhound courant Sable, on a chief dancetty of the last three bezants (Blackwall); 4: Or, a chevron Gules between three martlets Sable, a crescent for difference (Stafford); On an excutcheon of pretense: Two Bars and a canton charged with a chaplet (untinctured) (Hulme). **CREST**: An armed leg couped et the thigh quarterly Or and Gules (A).

1. STEPHEN EYRE of Hassop m. Anne, dau. and heir of Thomas Blackwall of Shirley. They were the parents of (A): RAPH.

2. RAPH EYRE, son of Stephen (1), m. Gertrude, dau and coheir of Humphrey Stafford of Eyham, Co. Derby, and had issue (A): THOMAS (m. and had issue); GERVASE, d. unm.; ADAM; ROGER; GEORGE; ROWLAND, Groom of the Presence Chamber to James I; and JANE, m. Christopher Pegg.

3. ADAM EYRE of Bradway in the Parish of Notton, Co. Derby, son of Raph (2), d. Nov 1634. He m. Eliz., dau. of Thomas Barlow. They were the parents of (A): ROULAND; FRANCIS, **now residing in Maryland**; AGATHA, m. Francis Stevenson of Ounston, Derby; and GERTRUDE, m. William Strelley of Beauchief, Co. Derby.

THE FAIRFAX FAMILY

Refs.: A: *MCS5*:Line 76. B: "Fairfax," *HSPV* 40;1295.

1. Sir THOMAS FAIRFAX of Cameron, 1st Lord Fairfax, was the father of (A): Rev. HENRY.

2. Rev. HENRY FAIRFAX, son of Sir Thomas (1), was born 14 Jan 1588 at Denton, Yorks., died 6 April 1665, of Oglethorpe, Rector of Bolton-Percy, Yorks. He married Mary Cholmley of Whitby, born 1593, died 8 Jan 1649/50, age 56, buried at Bolton-Percy. She was a dau. of Sir Henry Cholmley of **Magna Charta Descent** and his wife Margaret Babthorpe (See RD500:40-42 for her Royal Descent from Edward III).

Rev. Henry and Mary were the parents of (A): HENRY.

3. HENRY FAIRFAX, 4th Lord Fairfax of Cameron, son of Rev. Henry (2) and Mary, was bapt. 20 April 1631 at Ashton-under-Lyme, and died 9 April 1688. He married Frances, died 14 Feb 1683/4, daughter of Sir Robert Barwick of Tolston, Yorks (A: cites *NCP* 5:231).

Henry Fairfax was an M.P. for the County of York in 1678. He and his wife were the parents of (A; B): THOMAS, 5th Lord Fairfax; HENRY; BARWICK, d. unm. in 1712; and [-?-], dau.

4. THOMAS FAIRFAX, 5th Lord Fairfax, son of Henry (3) and Frances, died in 1710. He married Catherine, daughter and heiress of Thomas, Lord Colepeper. Thomas and Catherine were the parents of (B): THOMAS, 6th Lord Fairfax; HENRY COLEPEPER, d. unm.; ROBERT, 7th Lord Fairfax, d. unm.; MARGARET; CATHERINE; FRANCES; and MARY.

5. HENRY FAIRFAX of Tolston Lodge, Yorks., son of Henry (3) and Frances, was born 20 April 1659 at Bolton-Percy, and died 1708, of Denton and Tolston. He married Anne, dau. of Richard Harrison of Cave (A).

Henry Fairfax was High Sheriff of Yorkshire in 1691. He and his wife were the parents of (A; B): HENRY, d. unm. in 1759; Hon. WILLIAM; BRYAN; DOROTHY; and ANN.

6. THOMAS FAIRFAX, 6th Lord Fairfax, and Proprietor of the Northern Neck of VA, son of Lord Thomas (4) and Catherine, **settled in VA**, where he died at Greenway Court, Frederick Co., VA on 11 Dec 1788 (A; *GAVN*:119).

7. Hon. WILLIAM FAIRFAX, President of the Council of VA, son of Henry (5) and Anne, was bapt. 30 Oct 1691 at Newton-Kyme, and died 3 Sep 1757, having settled in VA. He was married twice and had issue by both wives (A; B).

THE FILMER FAMILY

Refs.; A: "Filmer," *HSPV* 42:16.

ARMS: Sable, three bars and in chief as many cinquefoils Or. **CREST**: On a ruined tower Or, a falcon [Argent], wings expanded proper [beaked and belled Or] (A).

1. JAMES FILMER of Otterden, Kent, m. Margery, dau. of Robert Reyner. They were the parents of (A): ROBERT.

2. ROBERT FILMER, of East Sutton, son of James (1), d. 1585, age 60. He m. Frances, dau. of Sir Robert Chester of Royston, Herts. Robert and Frances were the parents of (A; *PECD* 2:28): Sir EDWARD; CATHARINE, m. Thomas Gilbert of Sandwich; AFFRA, d. s.p.; MARIA, m. John Meriwether of Eithorne, Kent; ROBERT; HENRY; and ANTHONY.

3. Sir EDWARD FILMER of East Sutton, Kt., son of Robert (2) and Frances, d. 2 Nov 1629. He m. Elizabeth Argall, d. 9 Aug 1638. Both are buried in the church at East Sutton. Elizabeth Argall was a dau. of Richard Argall and Mary Scott (A descendant of Edward I) (*PASC*:111-112; *PECD* 2:38; *RD500*:242).

Sir Edward and Elizabeth were the parents of (A; *PECD* 2:38, 133): Major HENRY; Sir ROBERT (political writer, author of *Patriarcha*); KATHERINE, m. after 1619, Robert Barham, Jr. (They were the parents of **Capt. Charles Barham** of Surry

Co., VA); MARY, m. John Knatchbull; ELIZA; SARAH; ROBERT; EDWARD; JOHN; REGINALD; RICHARD; and AUGUSTINE.

4. Major HENRY FILMER, son of Sir Edward (3) and Elizabeth, was b. at East Sutton and moved to VA where he was a Member of the House of Burgesses for James City Co., 1642/3, and Warwick Co., 1666/7.

He m. in England, Elizabeth [-?-], by whom he was the father of (*PECD* 2:133): MARTHA, m. Thomas Green, Jr.

Unplaced:

FILMER, EDWARD, Dr. of Laws, of East Sutton, Kent, bachelor, age 30, and Archibella Clinkard, spinster, dau. of Archibald Clinkard of Sutton Valence of Kent, who consents, m. by allegation dated 29 Jan 1686/7, at East Sutton (*HSPV* 24:184).

FILMER, ROBERT, of East Sutton, Kent, Esq., m. by allegation dated 8 Aug 1618, Ann Heaton of Westminster, spinster, at St. Leonard's in the precinct of St. Martin le Grand (*HSPV* 23:75).

FILMER, THOMAS, of the Inner Temple, Bachelor, age 23, and Susan Fiennes of St. Giles in the Fields, Mddx., spinster, age 23, at her own dispose, were m. by allegation date 7 Nov 1683 at St. Giles in the Fields, afsd. (*HSPV* 24:168).

THE FRISBY FAMILY

Refs.: A: Francis B. Culver, "Frisby Family," *MG* 1:451-467. B: *HSPR* 68:64. C: *TMFO*. D: *AWPL*. E: *HSPR* 38. F: *BDML*. G: Wilmer H. Sanner. *The Frisby and Sanner Families of Maryland*. Sanner. Baltimore: Optic Bindery, 1976. H: *HSPR* 41.

1. WILLIAM FRISBY, dyer, married Christian [-?-]. They were the parents of the following children, baptized at St. Peter's, Paul's Wharf, London (E:161, 162, 163, 164, 166, 168): WILLIAM, bapt. 9 March 1623, buried in the churchyard of St. Peter's, "coffined" (H:210); SUSANNA, bapt. 26 May 1624; JOHN, buried 14 Dec 1724 in the churchyard of St. Peter, toward the farther end, coffined (H:211); JOHN, bapt. 25 Oct 1625, buried 5 Nov 1625 close to the wall near the cloister door of St. Peter's (H:214); JAMES, bapt. 5 Nov 1626; JUDITH, bapt. 28 Nov 1627, buried 3 Nov 1627 in a box close to Mr. Leonard's wall in St. Peter's churchyard (H:215); JOHN, bapt. 30 March 1630, buried 22 May 1632 at St. Peter's (H:216); [-?-], bapt. 1 Sep 1633; and THOMAS, bapt. 25 Dec 1634.

2. JAMES FRISBY, son of William (1) and Christian, was bapt. 5 Nov 1626, and m. Mary, dau. of John Maddox of London, citizen and Barber-Chirurgeon of London in the Strand, Parish of St. Martin's in the Fields (C).

In Nov 1651 Robert Nicholson, son of Francis, of London, left a legacy to James Frisby and others in VA (C). James Frisby immigrated to Maryland c1665, bringing with him his wife Mary and children James, Thomas, Mary and William (MPL 8:130).

Sanner concurs that James Frisby was in VA by 1654, and that he m. Mary [-?-]. He moved to CE Co., MD, and acquired land by 1663 (G:5). He was a Commissioner of Kent Island in June 1665 (*ARMD* 3:529).

Frisby d. leaving a will dated 22 Dec 1673, and proved 12 Oct 1674. He named his wife Mary and children James, William, Thomas, and Mary. His wife Mary and son James were named as execs. Abraham Stran and Nich. Dorrell witnessed the will (G:5; MWB 2:11).

James and Mary were the parent of (G:5): JAMES, bapt. 29 March 1650 at St. Martin Orgar and St. Clement Eastcheap; WILLIAM, b. by 1664; MARY (almost certainly the sister of James the testator of 1702: who m. Peregrine Brown); THOMAS, d. 1685 s.p.; WILLIAM (all b. before the family arrived in Md.); and JONAS.

3. JAMES FRISBY, son of James (2), was bapt. 29 March 1650 at St. Martin Orgar and St. Clement Eastcheap. In 1691 he instituted action in chancery for claims on the estate of his maternal grandfather, John Maddocks (B:64; C).

He died leaving a will dated 10 Sep 1702, proved in England on 3 Dec 1703, and in CE Co., MD on 19 June 1704 (MWB 3:268).

On 8 Dec 1703 James Frisby of Whitechapel, Mddx., merchant, deposed he was a son of the testator, who d. in Oct 1702, and Peregrine Brown of St. Catherine Cree Church, London, deposed he had married the testator's sister (D:83-84).

In Dec 1703 probate of the estate of James Frisby of CE Co., MD, was granted to James Frisby, son of the dec., with similar powers reserved to Thomas and Peregrine Frisby. In Dec 1706 double probate was granted to sons Thomas and Peregrine Frisby (AWAP:115).

James was the father of (A:454): JAMES, b. 1676, d. young; MARY, b. 1678/9, d. unm.; SARAH, m. 1st, Thomas Robinson, and 2nd, Stephen Knight; THOMAS, b. 1681, d. 1715/6; JAMES, b. 1684, d. 1719; PEREGRINE, b. 1688, d. 1738; MARY, b. 1690, d. unm.; JACOB, b. 1694; FRANCES, b. 1696; FRANCIS, bapt. 1696; and WILLIAM, b. 1699, d. 1724.

Unplaced:

FRISBY, JOHN, of the Parish of St. John's, Hackney, Mddx, late of MD, was dead by Dec 1740 (PCLR EI#5:168).

FRISBIE, RICHARD was b. 1668, and m. Margaret Emerson on 30 Nov 1618. He came to VA on the *Jonathan* in 1619. Sanner suggests he may be the ancestors of the later Frisby Family of Maryland (G:3). However, no proof of the relationship has been found.

THE GODBY FAMILY

Refs.: A: Peter Wilson Coldham, "Jasper Godby of Baltimore County, MD., 1756," *NGSQ* 65 (4) 267.

1. JASPER GODBY, in 1756 was living in Old Street Square near St. Luke's Church in London. He was married and had at least three children (A): JASPER; EDWARD; WILLIAM (was m. by 1756).

2. JASPER GODBY, son of Jasper, was sentenced to transportation to the colonies in Jan 1746 and Sep 1747 in London, and was transported to MD in Jan 1746 on the *Plain Dealer*, Capt. James Dobbin. His name also appears in a list of passengers transported to MD from London in Jan 1748, by the *St. George*, Capt. James Dobbins, and registered in KE Co. (*KPMV*:110, 114). As Jasper "Goodbie," he m. Ann Bosell on 25 May 1755 (SJSG:212).

     In Sep 1756 he was living in BA Co., when he wrote to his parents in London, asking them not to think ill of him for not coming home, but making no mention of his marriage. In his letter he did not mention his marriage, but he did name his brother Edward, and mentioned the wife of his brother William (A; *KMPV*:308).

     It is possible that he returned to England, for in Jan 1774 Ann, wife of Jasper Godby, was transported from Middlesex to VA by the *Justita*, Capt. Finlay Gray (*KPMV*:245).

THE GOODHAND FAMILY

Refs.: A: Robert W. Barnes and F. Edward Wright. *Colonial Families of the Eastern Shore*. Westminster: Family Line Publications, 1996. 2:147-148. B: "Goodhand of Kirmond-le-Mire." *Lincolnshire Pedigrees. HSPV* 51:412-413.

ARMS: Chequy Argent and Gules, on a fess Azure, three left hand gauntlets of the first (B).

1. ANDREW GOODHAND, the earliest known member of the family, m. Margaret, dau. of John Thoresby. They were the parents of at least one son (B:412): THOMAS.

2. THOMAS GOODHAND, son of Andrew (1), m. Jane, dau. and coheir of [-?-] Harvy of Clee. Thomas and Jane were the parents of (B:412): CHARLES; and THOMAS.

3. CHARLES GOODHAND, son of Thomas (2) and Jane, m. Jane Fotherby, of Newmanby. Charles and Jane were the parents of (B:412): JOHN.

4. JOHN GOODHAND of Kirkland-le-Mire and Market Rasen, son of Charles (3) and Jane, was buried at Rasen on 8 Sep 1590. He m. 1st, Magdalen, dau. of Robert

Plumpton of Plumpton, Co. York. He m. 2nd, at Market Rasen on 10 June 1568, Isabella [-?-]. She m. 2nd, at Market Rasen on 27 Nov 1591, William Patrick.

John and Magdalen were the parents of (B:412): WILLIAM.

John and Isabella were the parents of (B:412): ANNE, bapt. 3 Feb 1568/9 at Market Rasen, m. on 21 Oct 1585 Henry Hooke, D.D.; and JOHN, bapt. 25 Nov 1571, m. Ellen Sim.

5. WILLIAM GOODHAND of Kirmond and Binbrook, son of John (4) and Magdalen, d. leaving a will dated 12 aug 1616 and proved 26 May 1617. He m. 1st, Anne, dau. of Augustine Waterton of Messingham, age 10 in 8 Elizabeth. William m. 2nd, Anne or Agnes, dau. of George Gilby of Stainton-le-Hole. She was extx. of her husband's estate, and d. leaving a will dated 23 Nov 1617 and proved 23 March 1617/8 (B:412).

William and Anne (Waterton) were the parents of (B:412): CHARLES; MAGDALEN, m. at Walesby on 9 July 1617 Anthony Micklethwaite; and MARGARET, m. [-?-] Broke.

William and Anne or Agnes Gilby were the parents of (B:413): WILLIAM; GEORGE, m. Mary Micklethwaite; EDWARD; JOHN; NICHOLAS; and [-?-], m. Roger Banister.

6. WILLIAM GOODHAND, 2nd son of William (5) and Anne or Agnes (Gilby), was living in 1616. By license dated 3 Oct 1604, he m. Faith, dau. of John Micklethweaite of Kirmond.

William and Faith were the parents of (B:412): ANDREW, 1st son, age 29 in 1634; THOMAS; WILLIAM; JOHN, m. Lucilla Roper; and others.

7. WILLIAM GOODHAND, 3rd son of William (6) and Faith, m. Elizabeth, dau. and heiress of John Winche of London. They were the parents of the following children, whose baptisms and/or burials took place at Hawerby [Hawerby-cum-Beesby, Lincs] (B:413): FRANCIS, bapt. 8 Feb 1638/9; CHARLES, 2nd son; MARMADUKE, 3rd son, bur. 8 May 1649; CHRISTOPHER, 4th son; ELIZABETH, bapt. at 20 Oct 1640; WILLIAM, bapt. 11 Nov 1642; JANE, bapt. 20 Nov 1644; MARGARET, bapt. 24 Nov 1648; MARMADUKE, bapt. 8 May 1650; and JOHN, bapt. 13 Nov 1654.

8. CHRISTOPHER GOODHAND, 4th son of William (7) and Elizabeth, is placed as the Christopher who was on Kent Island, MD, by 1672 when he claimed land for service because (1) he was of the appropriate age, (2) as a fourth son he would have little prospects of inheritance, and (3) his son was named Marmaduke, possibly after his brother in England (MPL 15:379). He m. Hannah, dau. of Sarah Harris.

Goodhand was in KE Co. by 16 June 1674 when he witnessed the will of William Head (MWB 2:29). On 16 May 1681 Sarah Harris, widow of Kent Island made her will, and named her son-in-law Christopher Goodhand and his wife Hannah. Sarah Harris also named a grandson John Ingram and a dau. Sarah Browne (MWB 4:157).

Christopher d. leaving a will dated 3 May 1704 and proved 4 Oct 1704. To dau. Elizabeth, he left 300 a. Poplar Neck, provided she married with mother's consent, otherwise tract to pass to son Marmaduke. No exec. was named (MWB 3:654).

His estate was inventoried on 15 May 1705, by J. Winchester and Benjamin Wickes, who valued his personal property at £64.6.10 (INAC 26:224). A second inventory, worth £568.7.8, was filed on 14 May 1707 by Hannah Goodhand, the extx (INAC 26:326).

Hannah Goodhand of Kent Island, died leaving a will dated 17 April 1719 and proved 20 April 1721. The heirs named were grandson Peasly Ingram, £5. To grand-dau. Hannah Goodhand and hrs., 100 a., Pipers; should she die without issue, sd. land to pass to male issue of son Marmaduke, exec., and Sarah, his wife. Failing such issue to female issue of afsd. son and dau.; and personalty; they were to receive estate at age of 18. To granddaus. Eliza and Sarah, Mary, wife of Thos. Hampton, and Saml., son of Benja. Wickes, dec., personalty. The will was witnessed by Ben. Ball, Alexandr. Ogston and Robert Porter. A deposition shows that Robert Porter had d. before the date of probate (MWB 16:318).

The estate of Hannah Goodhand was appraised on 18 Aug 1721 by Valentine Carter and George Cummerford, and valued at £511.16.6. Joseph Wickes and Samuel Wickes approved the inventory (MINV 6:52).

Hannah Goodhand's estate was admin. by Marmaduke Goodhand on 27 July 1726. An inventory of £511.16.5 was mentioned (MDAD 7:485).

Christopher was the father of: ELIZABETH, may have m. [-?-] Ingram; and MARMADUKE.

9. MARMADUKE GOODHAND, son of Christopher (8), was named in his father's will. He d. by June 1762. He m. 1st, Sarah [-?-], and 2nd, Letitia, widow of [-?-] Brown.

On 27 Feb 1718, Hannah Goodhand, seamstress, Marmaduke Goodhand and his wife Sarah, of QA Co., Gent., conv. to Nathaniel Pearce of KE Co., Gent., a tract called Stonetone, 500 a. KELR JS#W:6).

Marmaduke Goodhand d. leaving a will dated 6 Nov 1756 and proved 10 June 1762. To son Marmaduke Goodhan [sic] he devised his plant. and adj. tract, being part of one moiety of the tract Point Love, and moiety of another tract called Silley, both making up the home plantation. Sons Marmaduke and Jonas Goodhand to have the land equally divided between them. Mentioned were daus.: Cozby Goodhan [sic], Elizabeth Horn and Sarah Goodman; grandchildren: Nathaniel Brown Goodhand, Hannah Goodhand. Wife Letitia was extx. The will was witnessed by Mary Barnes, Thomas Barnes, Sr. and Jo. Smyth (MWB 31:656).

The personal estate of Marmaduke Goodhand of Kent Island was appraised on 13 Sep 1762 by Samuel Blunt and Emory Sudler. Marmaduke and Jonas Goodhand signed the inventory as next of kin. Letitia Goodhand, extx., filed the inventory on 16 June 1763 (MINV 60:459).

On 28 Oct 1762 Letitia Goodhand of Kent Island, widow, gave to her son, Aquila Brown of Kent Island, 400 a., her moiety of Woodyard Thickett, granted to Phillip Conner by patent on 1 June 1670 (QALR RTF:273).

Marmaduke Goodhand was the father of: MARMADUKE; JONAS; COSBY (dau.); ELIZABETH, m. [-?-] Horn; SARAH, m. [-?-] Goodman.

10. JONAS GOODHAND, son of Marmaduke (9), m. by 29 Dec 1766, Mary Ann, dau. of John Wilson of Kent Island, QA Co. (MWB 35:482).

THE GEORGE GORDON FAMILY

1. Rev. CHARLES GORDON, of Ashkirk, Roxburgh, was the father of (*DSSA*:78): Capt. GEORGE.

2. Capt. GEORGE GORDON, son of Rev. Charles, was a merchant, and settled in MD where he died by 1748 (*DSSA*:78).

GORDON, ALEXANDER, tenant of David Lumsden of Cushnie, was forced into the Rebellion of 1715 by the Earl of Mar. He was transported on 24 May 1716 in *The Friendship*, and landed in MD in Aug 1716 (*JANE* 1:18).

GORDON, ROBERT, of Patapsco River, BA Co., on 15 Oct 1719 was given a power of atty. by "his good friend" William Gordon of St. Michael's Parish, Barbados. (Source?)

THE GORSUCH DESCENT FROM CHARLEMAGNE

Refs.: A: *PECD* Vol. 3.

1. CHARLEMAGNE, King of the Franks, Emperor of the West, b. 2 April 742, d. 28 Jan 813/4; m. 3rd, c771, Hildegarde of Swabia, b. c758, d. 30 April 783 (A:34). They had: PEPIN.

2. PEPIN, son of Charlemagne (1), was King of Italy, 781-810, and consecrated King of Lombardy in 781. He was b. April 777, d. at Milan, 8 July 810 (A:34). He was the father of: BERNARD.

3. BERNARD, son of Pepin (2), was King of Italy 813-817. He was b. 797, and d. at Milan, 17 April 818; m. Cunnigunde [-?-], who d. c835 (A:34). They were the parents of (A:34): PEPIN.

4. PEPIN, son of Bernard (3), was Count of Senlis, Peronne, and St. Quentin. He was b. c815, and d. after 840. He was the father of (A:34): HERBERT.

5. HERBERT I, son of Pepin (4), was Count of Vermandois, Siegneur de Senlis, Peronne, and St. Quentin. He was b. c840, and was murdered c902. He was the father of (A:34): BEATRIX.

6. BEATRIX de VERMANDOIS, dau. of Herbert I (5); m. Robert I, Duke of France, Marquis of Neustria, and King of the West Franks. Robert died 15 June 923. They were the parents of (A:34): HUGH MAGNUS.

7. HUGH MAGNUS, son of Robert and Beatrix (6), was Count of Paris. He d. in June 956, having m. as his 3rd wife, Hedwig, Princess of Germany, dau. of Henry I, the Fowler, Emperor of Germany. They were the parents of (A:34): HUGH.

8. HUGH CAPET, son of Hugh Magnus (7), was King of France, 987-996. He was b. after 939, and d. 24 Oct 996. He m. by 969, Adelaide of Poitou, b. c945/50, d. 1004, dau. of William I, Count of Poitou, and Adele, dau. of Rollo, Duke of Normandy. They were the parents of (A:34): ROBERT II.

9. ROBERT II, son of Hugh Capet (8) and Adelaide of Poitou, was King of France, 988-1031. He was b. 970 at Orleans and d. 20 July 1031. His 2nd wife was Constance of Toulouse, d. 1033. Robert and Constance were the parents of (A:34): HENRY I.

10. HENRY I, King of France, 1031-1060, son of Robert II (9) and Constance of Toulouse, was b. c1005/11, and d. Aug 1060. He m. Anne of Russia, d. 1074/5, dau. of Jaroslav I, Grand Prince of Kiev, d. 20 Feb 1053/4, by his 2nd wife Ingigarde, dau. of Olaf, first Christian King of Sweden. Henry and Anne were the parents of (A:35): HUGH MAGNUS.

11. HUGH MAGNUS, Duke of France, son of Henry I (10) and Anne of Russia, was b. 1101, and was a Leader of the First Crusade. He m. Adelaide de Vermandois, d. c1120, dau. of Heribert IV, Count of Vermandois and Vexin by his wife Adele de Vexin, dau. of Raoul III the Great, Count of Valois and Vexin. Hugh and Adelaide were the parents of (A:35): ISABEL.

12. ISABEL de VERMANDOIS, Countess of Leicester, dau. of Duke Hugh Magnus (11) and Adelaide de Vermandois, d. by July 1147. She m. 1st, Robert de Beaumont, b. c1046, d. 5 June 1118, Siegneur de Beaumont, Pont Audemer, Brionne and Vatteville in Normandy, and Count of Meulan in the French Vexin, Earl of Leicester, son of Roger de Beaumont. Robert and Isabel were the parents of (A:35, 163): ISABEL (ELIZABETH).

13. ISABEL (ELIZABETH) de BEAUMONT, living in 1172, dau. of Robert de Beaumont and Isabel de Vermandois (12), Mistress of Henry I of England; m. Gilbert de Clare, 1st Earl of Pembroke, buried at Tintern Abbey, 14 Sep 1148. Gilbert and Isabel were the parents of (A:163): RICHARD de CLARE.

14. RICHARD de CLARE, "Strongbow," 2nd Earl of Pembroke and Viceroy of Ireland, son of Gilbert and Isabel (13) (de Beaumont) Clare, was b. c1130, d. 5 April 1176 at Dublin. He m. on 11 Aug 1171, Eva of Leinster, d. 1177, dau. of Dermat MacMurrough, King of Leinster, and his wife More O'Toole. Richard and Eva were the parents of (A:163): ISABEL.

15. ISABEL De CLARE, *sine jure* Countess of Pembroke, dau. of Richard (14) and Eva (of Leinster) de Clare, was b. 1172, buried 1220 at Tintern Abbey. She m. in Aug 1189 at London, Sir William Marshall, 3rd Earl of Pembroke, Marshal of England, and Regent of the Kingdom, 1216-1219. He was b. 1146 and d. 14 May 1219, and was buried in the Knights Templar's Church in London. William and Isabel were the parents of (A:163): SYBIL.

16. SIBYL MARSHALL, dau. of Sir William (15) and Isabel (de Clare), m. by 14 May 1219, William de Ferrers, 5th Earl of Derby, who d. at Evington, near Leicester, March 1254. William and Sibyl were the parents of (A:163): MAUD.

17. MAUD de FERRERS, dau. of William and Sibyl (16) (Marshall) Ferrers, d. 12 March 1298/9, having m. William de Vivonia, d. 22 May 1298/9, son of Hugh de Vivonia, and [-?-] Malet, whose father William Malet was a Magna Charta Surety. William and Maud were the parents of (A:163): CECILY.

18. CECILY de VIVONIA, dau. of Hugh and Maud (17) (de Ferrers) de Vivonia, was b. 1257, and d. 10 Jan 1320/1 at Stoke-under-Hamden. She m. John Beauchamp of Hatch, Co. Somerset, b. by 1249, d. at Hatch, 24 Oct 1283, son of Robert IV de Beauchamp and Alice de Mohun. John and Cecily were the parents of (A:164): Sir JOHN.

19. Sir JOHN BEAUCHAMP of Hatch, 1st Lord Beauchamp and Governor of Bridgewater Castle, 1325, son of John and Cecily (18) (de Vivonia) Beauchamp, d. after 20 Oct 1336; m. 1301 Joan Chenduit, d. 9 Feb 1372. Sir John and Joan were the parents of (A:164): WILLIAM.

20. WILLIAM BEAUCHAMP of Wellington, Co. Somerset, son of Sir John (19) and Joan (Chenduit) Beauchamp, was b. c1302, and d. before the death of his father in 1336. William was the father of (A:164): MARY.

21. MARY BEAUCHAMP, dau. of William (20) Beauchamp, m. John Bodulgate. John and Mary had (A:164): ELIZABETH (MARY).

22. ELIZABETH (MARY) BODULGATE, dau. of John and Mary (21) (Beauchamp) Bodulgate, m. Richard Wydeville of Grafton (son of John Wydville of Grafton), Seneschal of Normandy, 1426, Constable of the Tower of London, 1424, and Lieutenant of Calais, 1426, Sheriff of Northampton 1437, he died leaving a will dated 29 Nov 1441. Richard and Elizabeth were the parents of (A:164): JOAN.

23. JOAN WYDEVILLE, dau. of Richard and Elizabeth (Mary) (22) (Bodulgate) Wydeville, d. by 1462, (sister of Richard Wydeville, Earl Rivers), m. as his second wife at Calais, 1429, William Haut of Bishop's Bourne, Co. Kent. He was b. 1390, d. between 30 Sep 1462, and 4 Oct 1462, and was buried in the Abbey of St. Augustine at Canterbury. William and Joan were the parents of (A;164): Sir WILLIAM.

24. Sir WILLIAM HAUT, son of William and Joan (23) (Wydeville), was b. c1430, d. 2 July 1497; m. Johanna Horne [or Heron], dau. of Henry Horne [or Heron] of Heron, by whom he was the father of (A:164): Sir THOMAS.

25. Sir THOMAS HAUT, K. B., 1501, Justice of the Peace, son of William (24) and Johanna (Heron), was b. c1466, d. 28 Nov 1502; he m. c1485, Isabel or Elizabeth Frowick, dau. of Sir Thomas Frowick of London and Ealing, Co. Middlesex, and Joan Sturgeon. Sir Thomas and Isabel were the parents of (A:164): JANE.

26. JANE HAUT, dau. of Sir Thomas (25) and Elizabeth (Frowick), was b. c1486. She m. 2nd, Robert Wroth of Enfield, Mddx, who d. between 8 May 1535 and 26 May 1536, son of John and Margaret (Newdigate) Wroth. Robert and Jane were the parents of (A:164): Sir THOMAS.

27. Sir THOMAS WROTH, Kt., son of Robert and Jane (26) (Haut) Wroth, was a resident of Enfield, Co. Mddx, was b. 1516, d. between 9 Oct 1573 and 16 April 1575. He m. c1539/40, Mary Rich, dau. of Sir Richard Rich, 1st Lord Rich, Lord Chancellor of England and his wife Elizabeth Jenks. Thomas and Mary were the parents of (A:164): MABEL.

28. MABEL WROTH, dau. of Sir Thomas (27) and Mary (Rich) Wroth, was b. c1542, and was bur. at Bishop's Bourne Church in 1596. She m. 1st, on 10 June 1560, Edward Aucher of Bishop's Bourne, Co. Kent, b. c1540, d. 14 Feb 1567/8, son of Anthony Aucher of Ottringden and Affra Cornwallis. Edward and Mabel were the parents of (A:165): ELIZABETH.

29. ELIZABETH AUCHER, dau. of Edward and Mabel (28) (Wroth) Aucher, was b. c1561/2, and was buried at Canterbury Cathedral, 3 Dec 1627; m. c1580/1, Sir William Lovelace, the Elder, bapt. at St. Alphege, Canterbury, 30 Sep 1561, d. at Canterbury between 6 and 19 Oct 1629, son of William and Anne (Lewis) Lovelace. Sir William and Elizabeth were the parents of (A:165): Sir WILLIAM.

30. Sir WILLIAM LOVELACE, the Younger, son of Sir William and Elizabeth (29) (Aucher) Lovelace, was bapt. at St. Alphege, Canterbury, on 12 Feb 1583/4, d. 12 Aug 1627 at Groll, Holland; m. as her 1st husband, in 1610, Anne Barne, b. betw. 1587-92, d. at London betw. 15 May 1632 and 22 May 1633, dau. of Sir William and Anne (Sandys) Barne. Sir William and Anne were the parents of (A:165); ANNE.

31. ANNE LOVELACE, dau. of Sir William (30) and Anne (Barnes) was b. in Co. Kent, Eng., c1610, d. in "parts beyond the seas" (Virginia) early in 1652; m. c1628, Rev. John Gorsuch, Rector of Walkern, Co. Herts., b. c1600/9, d. betw. 1647/51 (A:165). See **The Gorsuch Family** in *British Roots*, Vol. 1.

THE GRAZEBROOK FAMILY

Refs.: A: George Grazebrook. "Pedigree of the Family of Grazebrook." *MGH* Ser. 3, Vol. III, pp. 117-ff. B: "Grazebrook of Shenston and Middleton." *BLG* 1906 ed., p. 714.

This family has not been found to have imperial, royal, or baronial connections, and so has not figured in the writings of Weis, Sheppard, Faris, or Roberts.

1. BARTHOLOMEW de GRAZEBROOK, d. by 1268. He m. Edith [-?-]. A younger son, he left Yorkshire, and settled in Shenston, Staffs. About 1204-1214 he was granted the manor house of de Brays by Robert de Grendon. At his death he was survived by his widow and two sons (A): ADAM, d. s.p., by Jan 1294; and ROBERT.

2. ROBERT de GRAZEBROOK, son of Bartholomew (1), d. by Jan 1293/4 (B) or 1305 (A), leaving a son (A): ROBERT.

3. ROBERT de GRAZEBROOK, son of Robert (2), was living in 1305, when, with Ralph de Pype, he condoned a felony [*sic*]. He was the father of (A): ROBERT.

4. ROBERT de GRAZEBROOK, son of Robert, in 1345 was styled *miles* or Knight. He was living in 1348. He left two sons (A): WILLIAM; and JOHN, alive in 1346.

5. WILLIAM de GRAZEBROOK, son of Robert (4), inherited Gresbroke Hall, and purchased Swetewallemore in Shenton. He was the father of (A): JOHN; and WILLIAM, who "set out for foreign parts."

6. JOHN de GRAZEBROOK, son of William (5), was one of the Collectors of the Subsidy for Shenston in 1377. He was living in 1383, and was the father of (A): JOHN.

7. JOHN de GRAZEBROOK, son of John (6), inherited his father's estate after 1383. He d. by 1410, leaving a son (A): JOHN.

8. JOHN de GRAZEBROOK, son of John (7), was living in 1445. He left a son (A): JOHN.

9. JOHN de GRAZEBROOK, son of John (8), inherited Gresbrooke Hall, and some other estates. He is stated in B:714 to have been 11th in descent from Bartholomew. He was living temp Henry VII. He was the father of two sons, both named John (A): JOHN "Senior," inherited Gresbroke Hall and the Shenston estates; and JOHN, "Junior," inherited the estate and Stoke Hall in Middleton.

10. JOHN de GRAZEBROOK, "Junior," son of John (9), inherited Stoke Hall, Middleton, Warwick. He left a will dated 26 May 1540, proved at Lichfield in 1542. He m. Isabel [-?-], whose will was dated 15 March 1550/1 and proved at Lichfield on 25 Jan 1554/5 (B).

     John and Isabel were the parents of (A): JOHN; ALVERY; ROBERT, buried 6 Jan 1588/9; HENRY; HUGH; MARGARET, m. [-?-] Shurrock; and ELIZABETH, m. [-?-] Hylley.

11. ALVERY DE GRAZEBROOK, son of John (10) and Isabel, d. leaving a will dated 24 Sep 1575, proved 7 March 1576 (B). He m. Margaret, dau. of Thomas Keene of Sutton Coldfield, Co. Warwick, by his wife [-?-], the eldest dau. of William Gibbons of Little Sutton.

Alvery and Margaret left four daus. (A): MARGARET, b. c1556, d. 1629, m. Henry Seawell (ancestors of **Henry Sewell of MD**); ANNE, m. Thomas Roper; PRUDENCE; and MARY.

THE GUTTERIDGE FAMILY

Refs.: A: Peter Wilson Coldham. "Genealogical Gleanings." *NGSQ* 65 (4) 267.

1. JOHN GUTTERIDGE of Waltham Abbey, Essex, was the father of (A): EDWARD.

2. EDWARD GUTTERIDGE, son of John (1), m. Mary Scarf on 24 Oct 1759 in St. John's Parish (SJSG).

Gutteridge was in BA Co., MD by Oct 1756 when he wrote a letter to his father thanking him for sending clothes and asking for a violin and music books. He mentioned his brothers and sisters (A).

Edward refused to take the Oath of Fidelity in 1778 but he did sign in 1781 (*BARP*).

As Edward Gutherey he was listed in Gunpowder Upper Hundred in 1783 as owning 42 a. Enloes Desire, 17 a. Guthereys Chance, and Enloes Shift (1783 Assessment List for BA Co.: MSA S 1161-2-8).

THE HALFORD FAMILY EXPANDED

Refs.: A: *HSPV* 3:35. B: *HSPV* 73:29. C: *HSPV* 50-51:438-439. D: Justin Simpson, "Extracts from the Registers of Edith Weston Parish, Co. Rutland," *The Gen.* 1:292, 334-336, 362-3.

ARMS: Argent, a greyhound passant Sable, on a chief Azure, three fleurs-de-lis Or.

1. WILLIAM HALFORD was the father of (A: C): ROGER.

2. ROGER HALFORD, son of William (1), m. Grace, dau. of [-?-] Brodgate. They were the parents of (A: C): WILLIAM, of Welham, Leics., m. and had issue; RICHARD; and [-?-], dau., m. [-?-] Brendwood of Co. Warwick.

3. RICHARD HALFORD, 2nd son of Roger (2), settled in Edith Weston, Rutland, and d. 1627. He m. Dorothy, dau. of [-?-] Moore of Weld (or the Weale), Co. Bucks. Mrs. Dorothy Halford was buried at Hambleton on 14 Jan 1676 (D).

Richard and Dorothy were the parents of (A: C; D): RICHARD, age 21 in 1618, m. twice and had issue; THOMAS, bapt. 7 Dec 1600, Parson of the Church of Edith Weston; ROGER, bapt. 13 Dec 1601, merchant of London, d. unm.; DOROTHY, bapt. 9 Oct 1603 m. Jno. Cooper; MARY, bapt. 19 Sep 1605. d. young; ELIZABETH, bapt. 28 Oct 1606, prob. d. young; ELIZABETH, b. 15 Nov, bapt. 19 Nov 1611, bur. 11 1627, Dec, unm.; JOHN, bur. 22 Dec 1605, d. s.p.; WILLIAM, d. s.p.; JANE, married

William Burton of Brenston; GRACE, m. James Oliver of Norton, Co. Leics.; and SUSAN, m. Francis Roos.

4. THOMAS HALFORD, son of Richard (3) and Dorothy (Moore), was Rector of Edith Weston, was bapt. 7 Dec 1600 and d. 1648 (D). He m. Catherine, dau. of William Dowman of Uffington, Lincs., on 21 Feb 1629/30 at Uffington. (D).

Thomas and Catherine were the parents of (A: C; D): THOMAS, bur. 15 April 1640; JANE, bapt. 12 Oct 1630, m. Richard Barr of Dowsby, Co. Lincoln; RICHARD, bapt. Sep 1631/2; CATHERINE, bapt. 7 Dec 1631, m. Richard Clamp of Lynn Regis; and ANNE, bapt. 1 Dec 1644, m. Robert Wilson, Rector of Edith Weston (They were the ancestors of the **Peale Family** of MD).

THE HARDESTY FAMILY

Refs.: A: Hamilton and Ina Cross. *Hardesty Genealogy, 1600-1986*. Oregon [IL]: The Authors, Rev. 1985. B: Francis Collins. *Registers of Hampsthwaite, Co. York*. Yorkshire Parish Register Society, 1902. Vol. 13.

1. WILLIAM HARDESTY, d. by 1661. He m. Anne [-?-]. William Hardesty d. leaving a will dated 4 March 1661, in which he named three children, and dau.-in-law Dorothie, wife of his son Arthur. William and Ann were the parents of (A:4): ARTHUR; and (poss.) WILLIAM; and ROBERT.

2. ARTHUR HARDESTY, son of William (1) and Ann, was b. c1600/3 in Hampsthwaite, York. He d. before his father, and was buried 14 Sep 1658. He m. Dorothy [-?-].

Arthur left a will dated 2 Aug 1658 and proved 1 Feb 1659. He named his "brothers-in-law" William and Robert Hardesty; his wife Dorothy; his children Thomas, Sarah, Marie wife of Joseph Ibbison, Anne wife of John Wright, eldest son William, and grandchildren. Wife Dorothy was to be extx. Chris. Spence, Fras. Browne, Geo. Cocke witnessed the will (*Knaresborough Wills*. Vol. II, p. 241. Pub. for the Surtees Society).

Arthur and Dorothy were the parents of the following children, baptized at Hampsthwaite, Yorkshire (A:4; B:25, 27, 28, 30, 33, 35): MARY, bapt. 6 Oct 1631/2, m. Joseph Ibbeson; ANN, bapt. 3 Oct 1633, m. John Wright; WILLIAM, bapt. 6 March 1635/6; JOHN, bapt. 9 Aug 1639; THOMAS, bapt. 4 Sep 1641/2; and SARAH, bapt. 14 Sep 1645.

3. THOMAS HARDESTY, son of Arthur (2) and Dorothy, was bapt. 4 Sep 1643 at Hampsthwaite (B:33). He moved to Hollins, York, and m. Mary Favill (bapt. 29 June 1633 at Burnsall, Yorks.) at Hampsthwaite on 4 May 1665.

Thomas and Mary were the parents of the following children, bapt. at Hampsthwaite, Yorks (A:4, 7; B:82); DOROTHY, bapt. 6 Oct 1666; ARTHUR, bapt. 23 June 1668, prob. d. young; FRANCIS, bapt; 10 March 1671; ARTHUR, bapt. 5 Dec 1675; ELIZABETH, bapt. 2 Nov 1678, d. 22 Nov 1678; SUZANNA, bapt. 2 Nov

1680[?]; ELIZABETH, bapt. 5 Nov 1681; CHARLES, bapt. 6 Nov 1695; PAUL, bapt. 13 Feb 1698; and MARY, bapt. 17 March 1699.

4. FRANCIS HARDESTY, son of Thomas (3), was bapt. 10 March 1671 at Hollins, Yorks. He migrated to AA Co., MD, where he d. 1734. He m. 1st, on 3 Jan 1703, Ruth Morley Gaither, who was bur. 2 Oct 1719 (*AACR*:18, 200), and 2nd, on 4 Dec 1719, Dorcas Linthicum. He had children by both wives (A:4, 7).

By Ruth Morley he was the father of (*AACR*:26): FRANCIS, b. 27 Feb 1707 at All Hallows Parish, m. Alice Brown.

By Dorcas Linthicum, Francis was the father of (*AACR*:37, 41): DEBORAH, b. 8 Dec 1720; THOMAS, b. 6 March 1721, bapt. 23 Oct 1723; PETER, b. 19 Sep 1723, d. 1766; JOHN, b. 29 Jan 1727; ROBERT, b. 23 Oct 1730, d. 1790; and (poss.) FRANCIS, b. 26 Dec 1734, m. Susannah Denune.

THE HARDY FAMILY

1. HENRY HARDY d. in CH Co. by Sep 1714. He may have m. on 21 Aug 1694 Elinor Compton, dau. of John Compton of SM Co. (CHLR Q:23). At the time of his death he was m. to Ann [-?-], poss. widow of [-?-] Ashman. She m. 3rd, William Foster, and d. by Dec 1717.

Henry Hardy d. leaving a will dated 21 Dec 1705, proved 20 Sep 1714. He named his wife Ann extx., and left her 1/3 of his personal estate. Dau. Ann was to have all land, Hardy's Purchase, and 1/3 of his personalty at age 18. The residue of his personal estate was to go to his kinsman Henry, son of George Hardy of Loughborough, Leics., and if he died without issue, the property was to go to Henry's brother George. Philip Briscoe and his son John were named execs. Walter Story was named overseer. Richard Coe, Richard Beaumont, Magius Sinclair and Mary Sinclair witnessed the will (MWB 13:733).

The estate of Henry Hardy was administered on 29 Sep 1716 by the admx. Ann Hardy, who listed an two inventories worth £93.0.7 and £10.5.0. Payments came to 25,993 lbs. tob. Payments were made to John Richard and Allward Hardy (or to John, Richard, and Allward Hardy), William Compton, and Richard Ashman, among others (INAC 37A:21).

On 30 Jan 1717 William Compton and George Brett appraised another inventory of Henry Hardy's personal property. It came to £34.16.8 (INAC 39A:35).

Ann Foster, widow of CH Co., d. leaving a will dated 10 Oct 1717 and proved 13 Dec 1717. She named her son John Ashman, and dau. Mary, wife of Richard Ankrum, her dec. husband William Foster, son Richard Ashman and granddau. Ann Oliver and James Penny. Ann Foster directed that whatever was due Henry Hardy, a legatee in the will of her former husband, Henry Hardy, was remain in the hands of her son Richard Ashman until called for (MWB 14:424).

On 26 Jan 1717 Richard Ashman, administrator de bonis non, settled Hardy's estate and made payments coming to £20.16.6 to John Perry, admin. of Cornelius White, and to the unnamed residuary legatee, living in Great Britain (INAC 39C:128; see also MDAD 4:229).

In an account filed 4 Aug 1718, Ann Hardy, admx. of Henry Hardy, received a payment from the estate of John Killingsworth of CH Co. (MDAD 1:85).

Henry and Ann were the parents of: ANN.

2. GEORGE HARDY of Loughborough, Leics., was named as kinsman in the will of Henry Hardy of CH Co., as were George's two sons (mwb 13:733): HENRY; and GEORGE

3. ANN HARDY, dau. of Henry (1), was named in her father's will, but research to date has failed to show whether she died or married.

THE HARRINGTON FAMILY

Refs.: A: Boumphrey, at al. *An Armorial for Westmorland and Lonsdale.* B: "Harington--Barons Harington," *Burke's Dormant and Extinct Peerages.* C: "Harington--Barons Harington of Exton, Co. Rutland," *Burke's Dormant and Extinct Peerages.*

1. OSULF or ACULF of Flemingby, was the father of (A): ROBERT of Harrington.

2. ROBERT of HARRINGTON in Cumberland, son of Osulf or Aculf, was the ancestor of (A): Sir ROBERT.

Proven Generation 1

3. Sir ROBERT de HARRINGTON or HAVERINGTON of Harrington, Cumberland, descendant of Robert (2), d. 1297, having m. Agnes, Lady of Aldingham who d. 1293, daughter of Sir Richard Cancefield of Cancefield and Farleton, Cumberland, by his wife Eleanor (or Alicia), Lady of Aldingham who was the daughter of William le Fleming of Aldingham (*WAR7*:Line 34, cites *NCP* 6:314).

Sir Robert had two sons named in the Inq. Post Mortem, held 12 Edward II [c1319], of Annora, wife of John de Lancaster (*Cal. of Inq. P. M.*, vol. 8, # 172): MICHAEL, d. c1307; and Sir JOHN.

Generation 2

4. Sir JOHN de HARRINGTON, 1st Lord Harrington, son of Sir Robert (3) and Agnes, was heir to his brother Michael, and gave his age as 41 in 1319. He was knighted 22 May 1306, and d. 2 July 1347. He was First Lord Harrington, and M.P., 1326-1347. He m. Joan (possibly Dacre) (*WAR7*:Line 34).

He held the manors of Aldingham, Thurnham and Ulverston in Lancashire, Witherslack and Hutton Roof in Westmoreland, and Austwick and Harrington in Cumberland (*NCP* 6:314-315; *VHC Lancs.*, 8:202, and *Cal. Inq. P. M.* 9: # 30).

Sir John's wife is placed as a member of the Dacre family because Sir John's guardian was a Dacre, and the Dacre arms are on a tomb believed to be that of John and Joan in Cartmel Church (Proc. of the Cumb. and Westm. Antiq. and Arch. Soc., 5:109).

Burke says that this Sir John was one of the "stout young men" summoned in 34 Edward I to attend the King to Scotland, and was knighted with Prince Edward. In 4 Edward II he was summoned to the Scottish Wars. In 14 Edward III he was given a license to impark 600 acres of wood, moor and marsh within the precincts of Aldingham. Burke also says he m. Margaret, dau. of Sir Richard Barlingham (C).

Sir John and his wife (probably Joan) were the parents of at least two sons (B): Sir ROBERT; and Sir JOHN.

Generation 3

5. Sir ROBERT de HARRINGTON, Kt., son of Sir John (4) and Joan, was knighted in 1331, and died in Ireland in 1334. He m. Elizabeth de Multon, daughter of Thomas and Eleanor (de Burgh) de Multon. After Sir Robert's death she m. 2nd Walter de Birmingham (*MCS4*:Line 15).

Sir Robert and Elizabeth were the parents of (B): Sir JOHN, b. c1328; ROBERT, ancestor of the Lords Harrington of Exton (see below); and SIMON, ancestor of the Harringtons of Bishton.

6. Sir JOHN de HARRINGTON, son of Sir John (4) and Joan, held Farleton in Melling Parish, Lancs. He m. Katherine, daughter of Sir Adam de Banastre by his wife Margaret de Holand. Katherine died a week after her husband.

In Sep 1352 Henry, Duke of Lancaster, granted John de Harrington a lease of the manor of Hornby. He also held the Manors of Bolton-le-Moors, Chorley and Aighton. In 1358 he went to London on the King's Service (*WAR7*:Line 34).

Sir John and Katherine (de Banastre) were the parents of the following children (*MCS4*:Line 15; (*WAR7*:Line 34; D): ROBERT, of full age, d. 35 Edward III [c1362] beyond the seas; THOMAS, may have also died beyond the seas; and Sir NICHOLAS.

Generation 4

7. Sir JOHN de HARRINGTON, 2nd Lord Harrington of Aldingham, son of Sir Robert (5) and Elizabeth (de Multon), was b. c1328 (age 19 on 2 July 1347), and d. at Gleaston Castle on 28 May 1363. He m. 1st, Elizabeth, widow of Walter de Birmingham the Elder, and 2nd, Joan, daughter of Walter de Birmingham (*MCS4*:Line 15).

With his first wife Elizabeth he was enfeoffed by Robert de Clipston of the Manor of Grandon, Northampton (*Cal. Fine Rolls*, 8:399). He was an M.P., 1347-1349 (*NCP* 6:316).

Sir John was the father of (B; D): SIR ROBERT, age 6 in 1364; AMY, m. John Carnell; ISABEL, m. Hugh Fairfax; and ALICE.

8. Sir NICHOLAS de HARRINGTON, son of Sir John (6) and Katherine, was born in 1345 and was alive in 1397. He married by 20 May 1379, Isabel English, dau. of Sir William English (or Lengleys) of Cumberland (*Calendar of Fine Rolls*, 9:137). [If the line of Sir William L'English or Lengleys carried the Arms of the elder line, Sable, three lions rampant argent, these arms could be quartered by this line of Harrington descendants].

Sir Nicholas and his wife had issue (*WAR7*:Line 34): Sir JAMES, Kt.; Sir WILLIAM; (probably) ISABEL, m. Sir Thomas Tunstall. In 1397 she was named when the Chantry of Thurland Castle was founded (See Chippindall's article on the Tunstalls); and NICHOLAS, of Huyton.

Generation 5

9. Sir ROBERT de HARRINGTON, K.B., 3rd Lord Harrington of Gleaston Castle, 28 March 1356, was a son of Sir John (7) and Joan (de Birmingham). He was knighted at the Coronation of Richard II. He was summoned to Parliament from 1377 to the end of his life (C).

He died at Aldingham, 21 May 1406, having m. (as his 2nd wife) Isabel Loring, widow of Sir William Cogan of Huntsfield, and daughter of Sir Nele Loring, K. G. She died in 1386.

Sir Robert and Isabel were the parents of (*MCS4*:Line 103; B; D): Sir JOHN, 4th Baron; and Sir WILLIAM of Hornby, 5th Baron; and ISABEL, m. Sir John Stanley.

10. Sir JAMES de HARRINGTON, of Blackrod, Justice of the Peace, son of Sir Nicholas (8), was a soldier at Agincourt in 1415. He married Ellen, dau. of Thomas Urswick of Urswick. (*WAR7*:Line 34: cites *VHC Lancs*. III, 424, V, 300; *Richmondshire*, by Whitaker, II, 251).

Sir James and Ellen were the parents of (*WAR7*:Line 34): Sir RICHARD.

11. Sir WILLIAM HARRINGTON, K.G., son of Sir Nicholas (8) and Isabel, held Farleton and Chorley, and d. 22 Feb 1439/40. He was a standard bearer at Agincourt in 1415 and was wounded at the Siege of Rouen in 1419. He married Margaret Neville, b. by 1387, dau. of Sir Robert and Margaret (de la Pole) Neville.

Sir William and Margaret were the parents of (*RD500*:331, 440, 441; *WAR7*:Line 35): AGNES, d. 1490, m. Sir Alexander Radcliffe of Ordsall; ISABEL, d. 1441, m. in 1411 Sir John Boteler of Bewsey, Kt. (They were ancestors of **Col. John Waller of VA**); and MARGARET, m. Richard Braddyll (They were the ancestors of **George Talbot, Jr.**, known as **Peter Talbot** of **MA**).

12. NICHOLAS HARRINGTON of Huyton, son of Sir Nicholas (8) and Isabel, m. Margaret Lathom. They were the parents of (*RD500*:348): [-?-], dau., m. Nicholas Eltonhead (from whom descend the **Eltonhead** families of VA and MD, including: **Jane Eltonhead** who m. 1st, Robert Moryson, and 2nd, Cuthbert Fenwick of MD).

Generation 6

13. Sir WILLIAM HARRINGTON, son of Sir Robert (9), d. 1457. He m. Elizabeth, sister of Hugh Courtenay, Earl of Devon. He was summoned to Parliament from 26 Feb 1421 to 6 Sep 1439, and was Sheriff of Yorkshire, and Governor of the Castle of York. .

He served in the wars in France in the reigns of Kings Henry V and Henry VI.

Sir William was the father of (B): ELIZABETH, m. William Lord Bonville.

14. Sir RICHARD HARRINGTON, son of Sir James (10) and Ellen (Urswick) Harrington, d. 1466/7, married Elizabeth Bradshagh, b. 1402, dau. of Sir William Bradshagh who d. in 1415, and granddau. of Sir Hugh Bradshagh and Margaret de Verdon (dau. of Sir John de Verdon. Margaret m. 2nd Sir John Pilkington).

Sir Richard may have married an earlier wife if he was the Sir Richard whose daughter Eleanor, b. c1400/5, married John de Pickering.

Sir Richard may be tentatively placed as the father of (*WAR7*:Line 34): ISABEL, m. John de Pickering; (by Elizabeth Bradshagh): Sir WILLIAM, d. 1488; m. Elizabeth Pilkington; and MARGARET, m. Sir Thomas Pilkington, who was slain in 1437.

Generation 7

15. Sir WILLIAM HARRINGTON, son of Sir Richard (14), d. 12 Aug 1488. He m. in 1442 Elizabeth Pilkington, dau. of Edmund and Elizabeth (Booth) Pilkington, and a descendant of Sir John Verdon.

Sir William and Elizabeth were the parents of (*WAR7*:Line 34): Sir JAMES.

Generation 8

16. Sir JAMES HARRINGTON, son of Sir William (15), was b. 1448 (age 40 in 1488). He m. Isabella Radcliffe, d. 20 June 1497, dau. of Sir Alexander Radcliffe of Ordsall.

Sir James and Isabella were the parents of (*WAR7*:Line 34): ALICE, m. Ralph Standish.

THE HARINGTONS OF EXTON

Generations 1-5

1. ROBERT HARINGTON, ancestor of the Lords Harington of Exton, son of Sir Robert (#5 above) and Elizabeth (Multon), m. and was the father of (C): JOHN.

2. JOHN de HARINGTON, son of Robert (1), d. 1421. He m. Agnes, dau. of Lawrence Flete, of Flete, Lincs., and was the father of (C): ROBERT.

3. ROBERT de HARINGTON, son of John (2), m. one of the daus. of John de la Laund, and was succeeded by his son (C): JOHN.

4. JOHN de HARINGTON, son of Robert (3), m. Catherine, dau. and heir of Sir Thomas Colepeper, thus acquiring the Manor of Exton, in Rutland. John and Catherine were the parents of (C): ROBERT.

5. ROBERT HARINGTON, son of John (4) and Catherine, d. 1501. He was Sheriff of Rutland in 1492 and 1498. He m. Maud, dau. of Sir John Prisett, Chief Justice of the Court of Common Pleas. Robert and Maud were the parents of (C): Sir JOHN.

Generation 6

6. Sir JOHN HARINGTON of Exton, Sheriff of Rutland, son of Robert (5), m. Alice, dau. of Henry Southill. They were the parents of (C): Sir JOHN.

Generation 7

7. Sir JOHN HARINGTON, son of John (6) and Alice, was Sheriff of Rutland, and Treasurer to the Army to Henry VIII at Boulogne. He m. Elizabeth, dau. and heir of Robert Moton of Peckleston, Co. Leicester. They were the parents of (C): Sir JAMES.

Generation 8

8. Sir JAMES HARINGTON, son of Sir John (7) and Elizabeth, d. 1592. He m. Lucy Sidney, dau. of Sir William and Anne (Pagenham) Sidney, and a descendant of Edward I of England. Sir James and Lucy were the parents of (*RD500*:262; C): JOHN; Sir HENRY; JAMES; MABEL, m. Sir A. Noel; and FRANCES, m. Sir William Leigh (They were ancestors of **Mary Newdigate** who m. William Stephens, Colonial Governor of Georgia).

Generation 9

9. Sir HENRY HARINGTON, son of Sir James (8) and Lucy, m. 1st, Cecilia Agar, and 2nd, Ruth Pilkington.

Sir Henry and Ruth were the parents of (*RD500*:262): ELIZABETH, m. Richard Moryson (Their son **Francis Moryson**, was deputy and acting colonial Governor of Virginia).

Unplaced:

HARINGTON, EDITH, d. 1353. She m. Gilbert Culwen. They were the ancestors of **Capt. George Curwen of Salem, MA** (*WAR7*:Line 37).

HARRINGTON, JOHN, son of Sir James Harrington of Merton, Oxford (who had been knighted at Whitehall on 23 Dec. 1628), came to Md. in 1659, and was a brother-in-law of John Norwood (Newman, To Maryland, cites *MGH* 4th ser., 2:175.

HARINGTON, MARGARET, m. Thomas Lumley, 2nd Baron Lumley. They were the ancestors of **Cuthbert Fenwick of MD** (*RD500*:354).

THE HEUGH FAMILY

Refs.: A: Register of Prince George's (Rock Creek) Parish, MO Co., 1711-1798, MSA. B: Register of Prince George's (Rock Creek) Parish, MO Co., 1791-1845, MSA.

1. THOMAS HEUGH, merchant of Falkirk, Stirlingshire, was the father of (DSSD:159): ANDREW; and CHARLES, d. unm.

2. ANDREW HEUGH, son of Thomas, d. 6 Jan 1771 in FR (later MO) Co., MD. He was in MD by 14 Oct 1751 when he was m. by Moses Tabbs, to Sarah Needham in Prince George Parish, MO Co. (A:280).

Although no will was recorded in the Prerogative Court of MD, a testament was made and given up by James Dennistoun the Younger of Colgrain, Dunbartonshire, on behalf of John Heugh, eldest son of the deceased. There were references to Thomas Heugh, merchant of Falkirk, his [Andrew's] wife Sarah, and children: Elizabeth, Ann, Jean, John, Sarah, Mary, Andrew, Harriet, Christian, Martha, and Margaret. Also mentioned were James Heugh of Broomage, Nathan Claggar [Clagett], Frederick Wedsell, and Robert Tilley, all of MO Co., and Samuel Turner of MO Co. William Wilson, Writer [to the Signet?] in Edinburgh, was cautioner. The testament was registered 22 June 1791 (*DSSD*:159).

Andrew and Sarah were the parents of (A:280, 281; B:99, 100): ELIZABETH, b. 27 Oct 1754; ANNA, b. 28 June 1758; SARAH, b. 30 June 1756 (poss. the Sarah who was bur. 31 Oct 1800); MARGARET, b. 16 June 1760; JOHN; ANDREW, Jr., bur. 14 June 1796; and JEAN; MARY; HARRIET; CHRISTIAN, and MARTHA.

3. JOHN HEUGH, son of Andrew (2), was living on 6 March 1789.

On 6 March 1789, John Heugh of MO Co., MD, eldest son of Andrew Heugh of Leek Forest, MO Co., dec., and Sarah, dau. of John Needham, merchant, of Leek, Staffordshire, appointed James Dennistoun the younger, of Colgrain, Dunbartonshire, his atty.in Great Britain. John Heugh named his grandfather Thomas Heugh, merchant in Falkirk, Stirlingshire, and Charles Heugh, second son of Thomas. He also mentioned property in Baxter's Wynd, Falkirk, Stirlingshire, which his father Andrew had purchased from William Johnston, late smith in MO Co. William Needham was one of the witnesses (*DSSF*:61).

THE EDWARD HICKMAN FAMILY

1. EDWARD HICKMAN, cornchandler, m. Ann Rigsby on 6 Feb 1661 at Newport Pagnell, Bucks., England. He seems to have died before 1685 and his widow m. John Wilson. Edward and Ann (Rigsby) had at least one son (IGI, 1988 ed.): EDWARD, bapt. 22 March 1665 at Newport Pagnell.

2. EDWARD HICKMAN, son of Edward and Ann, was bapt. 22 March 1665 at Newport Pagnell. On 21 Aug 1685, at age 21 he was bound to Thomas Newbold for 5 years' service in MD. Edward's father-in-law, John Wilson. of Little Old Bailey, London, cutler, witnessed the indenture (*LEMG*:43; *CBEB*:539).

THE HICKS FAMILY

1. THOMAS HICKS, b. 1659 at Whitehaven, Cumberland, Eng., settled in MD c1671, and d. 1722 in DO Co., MD. He m. c1679 Sarah, dau. of Levin Denwood of Northampton Co., VA (*BAF*:2739).

Thomas Hicks of DO Co., d. leaving a will dated 24 July 1720 and proved 6 Aug 1722. He named his children Levin, Thomas, and Ann Rider, his son-in-law John Rider, and his grandchildren Ann (eld. dau. of son Levin), Sarah (dau. of son Thomas), and John Rider and Sarah Rider. His wife Sarah was named extx. Maj. Henry Ennalls, John Leme, Mary Leme, and Phill. Feddeman witnessed the will (MWB 17:310).

Thomas and Sarah had issue (A): THOMAS, b. 1687; LEVIN; and ANN, m. John Rider.

2. THOMAS HICKS, son of Thomas and Sarah, was b. 1687, and d. 1722, having m. Elizabeth, dau. of Col. Roger Woolford of SO Co. (*BAF*:2738).

Unplaced:

HICKS, Capt. JOHN, d. c1749/53, came to SM Co., Md., from Whitehaven, Cumberland, Eng.; m. Anne; had issue: GEORGE; WILLIAM; MARY, m. William Hennor or Kennor of Northumberland Co., VA; and ELIZABETH (*BDML* 1:440).

THE CLEMENT HILL FAMILY
A Tentative Reconstruction

Refs.: X: Undocumented material from an LDS Ancestral File.

1. RICHARD HILL, was b. c1580 at Compton Bassett, Wilts, England, where he died on 25 June 1645. It was there, on 8 May 1606, that he m. Marie Seager, b. 28 Sep 1583, also at Compton Bassett.

Richard and Marie were the parents of (X): RICHARD, b. 30 Aug 1607.

2. RICHARD HILL, son of Richard (1) and Marie (Seager) Hill, was b. 30 Aug 1607 at Calne, Wilts. he m. on 27 April 1630 at Compton Bassett Joane Breache, b. 3 Oct 1605, d. 1 March 1678/9, all at Compton Bassett.

Richard and Joane were the parents of the following children, who d. at Compton Bassett unless otherwise noted (X): RICHARD, b. c1630, d. 24 May 1631; RICHARD, b. 3 March 1632/3, d. 16 Nov 1710; ANDREW, b. 3 Dec 1636, d. 28 Feb 1636/7; MARIE, b. 19 March 1637/8 at Compton Bassett; BRIDGET, b. 18 March 1637/8, d. 26 March 1640; EDWARD, b. 28 June 1640 at Calne, Wilts; CLEMENT, b.

12 May 1641 at Compton Bassett; JOHN, b. 13 April 1644 at Compton Bassett; and WILLIAM, b. 26 Nov 1646 at Compton Bassett.

3. CLEMENT HILL, son of Richard (2) and Joane, was b. 12 May 1641 at Compton Bassett, Wilts. He d. 1708 in SM Co.

Clement Hill immigrated to MD by 1675 with Elizabeth Gibbs (MPL 18:312). On 8 Jan 1675 Eliza Moy, widow of Richard Moy, named him as one of the executors of her will and one of the guardians of her children (MWB 2:396).

Clement Hill d. leaving a will dated 17 Nov 1702 and proved 26 Nov 1708. He left land in BA and PG Cos. to his nephew Clement Hill, Jr. He also named his godson Thomas Cooper, and Luke and John Gardiner, Jr., sons of Richard Gardiner. John Marrott, John Bullock, and Jno. Attaway witnessed the will (MWB 12:252).

4. JOHN HILL, son of Richard (2) and Joane, was b. 13 April 1644 at Compton Bassett, and d. there on 8 Nov 1721. About 1674 he m. Millicent [-?-], b. c1646 and d. 11 Oct 1691, all at Compton Bassett. They were the parents of (X): CLEMENT, b. 4 April 1670.

5. CLEMENT HILL, son of John (4) and Millicent, was b. 4 April 1670 at Compton Bassett, Wilts. He came to MD, and settled in PG Co., where he d. 1743. He m. and had children.

Clement Hill, Jr., was in PG Co. by 1 June 1700 when he patented 740 a. Compton Bassett (MPL 34:261, 38:161).

THE HONYWOOD FAMILY, Part 1

Refs.: A: *SUBE*:37-38.

Generations 1-6

1. WILLIAM de HONYWOOD of Posting, Co. Kent, was living in the reign of Henry I and died in the reign of Henry II. He was the father of (A): THOMAS.

2. THOMAS de HONYWOOD, son of William (1) was the father of (A): EDWIN.

3. EDWIN de HONYWOOD, son of Thomas (2), m. Mabilia, dau. of Nicholas de Handle. They were the parents of (A): PAGAN.

4. PAGAN de HONYWOOD, son of Edwin (3) and Mabilia was the father of (A): ALAN.

5. ALAN de HONYWOOD, son of Pagan (4), was living in the reign of Edward III. He was the father of (A): WILLIAM.

Generations 6-9

6. WILLIAM de HONYWOOD, son of Alan (5), m. Catherine, dau. and heir of Thomas Caseborne of Caseborne in Cheriton. They were the parents of (A): ALLAN.

7. ALLAN de HONYWOOD, son of William (6) and Catherine, was the father of (A): THOMAS.

8. THOMAS de HONYWOOD, son of Allan (7), served in Parliament for Hythe, Co. Kent, 20 Hen. VI, and died in the next reign. He m. Mary, dau. of William Lovelace de Bethersden (A).

Thomas and Mary were the parents of (A): JOHN; ROBERT, LL.D., d. 1522, Canon of Windsor and buried in St. George's Chapel; three sons; and two daus.

9. JOHN de HONYWOOD, son of Thomas (8) and Mary, m. 1st, Agnes, dau. and heir of Henry Martin; and 2nd, Alice Barnes of Wye.

John and Agnes were the parents of (A): JOHN, d. 1557; BENNET, m. [-?-] Dryland; ISABEL, m. [-?-] Latchford; MARY, m. 1st, [-?-] Biys, and 2nd, [-?-] Gay; and JANE, m. [-?-] Ferrers.

John and Alice were the parents of (A:38): ROBERT, whose descendants are traced below in **The Honywood Family, Part 2**.

THE HONYWOOD FAMILY. Part 2

Refs.: (New as of 3 February 2001): A: "The Posterity of Mary Honywood at her Death in 1620," *The Topographer and Genealogist* 1 (1846): 397-411). B: "Honywood Evidences," hereafter cited as "Evidences," *The Topographer and Genealogist* 1:568-576. 2:169-192, 256-269, 312-337, 433-446). C: Sir Alexander Croke. *The Genealogical History of The Croke Family, Originally Named Le Blount.* Oxford: Printed by W. Baxter for John Murray ... and Joseph Parker, 1823, hereafter cited as Croke. published in 1823 in 2 volumes. D: Joseph Hunter. *Familiae Minorum Gentium.* London: The Harleian Society Publications, Visitation Series, vol. 40, 1896). E: *PASC.* F: *Visitation of Kent, 1592.* G: "Honywood," from "Berry's Essex Pedigrees," in Appendix. *HSPV* 14:733. H: "Honywood," *Visitation of Essex, HSPV* 13:424. I: "Poyntz, of Cowdray Park," *Burke's Commoners* 3:540. J: James Renat Scott. *Memorials of the Family of Scott, of Scot's-Hall in the County of Kent.* London: 1876. K: "Heneage of Hinton," *Burke's Commoners* 4:104. L: "Walker-Heneage of Compton Bassett," *Burke's Commoners* 4:369. M: William Berry. *County Genealogies: Pedigrees of the Families in the County of Sussex.* London: Sherwood Gilbert and Piper, 1830. N: *Visitation of Kent, 1619. HSPV* 42. O: "Croke of Studley," *Burke's Commoners.* P: "Thomson." *Visitation of Kent, 1619. HSPV* 42:10. Q: "Moody of Aspley," *Burke's Commoners,* 2:563. R: "Denne of Kent and Sussex," *Burke's Commoners* 3:21. S: "Sayer of Pett," *Burke's Commoners,* 3:505. T: "Sayer," *Visitation of Essex. HSPV* 13:485. U: "Sayer of Pett Place," *Burke's Landed Gentry* 1906, p. 1484. V: "Fleete," in D:1297. W: "Tithables of Lancaster Co., Virginia, 1654," *VMHB* 5:254. X: Undocumented Descendancy from the

Ancestral File of the LDS [all such material must be accepted with extreme caution]. Y: Christopher Johnston. "The Brooke Family," *Maryland Genealogies* (Baltimore: Genealogical Publishing Co., Inc., 1980), vol. 1. Z: Joseph Foster, Ed. *London Marriage Licenses, 1501-1869*. London: Bernard Quarritch, 1887. AA: William Berry, *County Genealogies, Pedigrees of Hertfordshire Families*. London: John Russell Smith, 1844. AB: Same Reference as "L." AC: John Brooks Threlfall. "An Extension of the Sheafe Family." *English Origins of New Eng. Families, 2nd ser*, (Baltimore: Genealogical Publishing Co., Inc.) 3. AD: Walter K. Watkins. "Some Guilford, Conn., Settlers and Their Relationship, or the Sheafe Family in England and New England," *English Origins of New Eng. Families, 2nd ser*, (Baltimore: Genealogical Publishing Co., Inc.), 3. AE: Mrs. Wirt Johnson Carrington, "Bacon Family," *GVFWMQ* 1:200. AF: Christopher Johnston, "Tilghman Family," *Maryland Genealogies* (Baltimore: Genealogical Publishing Co., Inc., 1980), vol. 2.

NB: All pedigrees taken from heraldic visitations should be regarded as tentative as little or no documentation in provided.

This compilation has two goals: first, to determine just how many children, grandchildren, great-grandchildren, and great-great-grandchildren Robert and Mary (Atwater) Honywood actually had, and second, to identify the American settlers who descend from this couple.

When Mary Honywood, sister and coheir of Robert Waters, of Lenham, Co. Kent, wife of Robert Honywood, died at Markeshall in the 93rd year of her age and 44th year of her widowhood on 16 May 1620, her epitaph (cited below) stated that she "had at her death lawfully descended from her 367 children:" 16 of her own body, 114 grandchildren, 228 in the 3rd degree [great-grandchildren], and 9 in the 4 degree [great-great-grandchildren].

Research to date has found 18 children, six of whom died young, unmarried, or without children. Some of the following may have been born after Mary's death, or died before she did. I have identified or found mention of: 107 grandchildren, 267 great-grandchildren, and 57 great-great-grandchildren.

More importantly Robert and Mary (Atwater) Honywood were the ancestors of several families that settled in the American colonies. **Mary Baker, was the first wife of Robert Brooke**, who settled in Maryland. **Samuel Tilghman, mariner, was commissioned "Admiral" of the Maryland fleet. Capt. Henry Fleete of Maryland and Virginia**, a passenger on the *Ark* and *Dove* expedition to Maryland. **Capt. George Lyddall** and **Thomas Willis** came to VA, and **Sir Philip Honywood**, the Royalist Officer came to VA in 1649, but returned to England. **Anthony Thompson** and **William Read** settled in Connecticut. **John Read**, brother of William, settled in MA.

This account is based on several major sources. The first is a MS. of about 20 leaves, now part of the MS. Lansdowne 658. In 1727 it belonged to Peter Le Neve, who added this title: "An Account of the Mariages [*sic*] and Issues of Robert Honywood and Mary his Wife, 1620." Le Neve, who was Rouge Croix Pursuivant, on 7 March 1692 stated that he compared his account with an old book in the hands of a Mr. Sadleir of Bassinghall Street, London, and that the two accounts agreed (Peter Le Neve's account is contained in A).

The second source was a MS of some 147 leaves written prior to 1620 entirely by Robert Honywood, eldest son of Robert and Mary (Atwater) Honywood, and contains original notes and evidences of relating to the Honywood Family of Charing and Markshall, including a detailed register of the births, baptisms, and sponsors of his family as well as other source materials. Compiled in 1612 it was brought down to 1622. It is more detailed than Le Neve's work, and differs from LeNeve's work in the sequence of some descents (B).

The third source was by Sir Alexander Croke (C). Other sources used for additional documentation are cited in the text.

This is not the first attempt to compile the descendants of Robert and Mary (Atwater) Honywood. Joseph Hunter, compiled such a record (D). Hunter wrote that the pedigrees he included in pp. 1296-1301 were "intended to shew the 367 children ... born before her [Mary Atwater Honywood's] decease, as mentioned in her epitaph." He cited her monumental inscription in Fuller's "Worthies," Kent, p. 85. The pedigrees were copied from Lansdowne MS.685. Peter LeNeve stated he had compared the account there with a MS. belonging to a Mr. Sadler of Basinghall Street, London, 7 March 1692. Hunter concluded that there were however, not many more than 300.

The Descendants of Robert and Mary (Atwater) Honywood

Generation 1

1. ROBERT HONYWOOD of Charing, Kent, and Mark's Hall, Essex, son of John and Alice (Barnes) Honywood, was b. 1525 at Henewood, Postling, Kent, and d. on 22 April 1576 at Pette in Charing (B:568). In Feb 1543, he m. Mary Atwater, dau. and coheir of Robert Atwater or Waters of Lenham and Royton, Co. Essex. She was b. 1527 at Royton, Lenham, Essex, and d. on 16 May 1620, aged 93. She was buried in 1620 at Markshall, Essex (A:397; B: 1:568).

Robert Atwater or Waters of Royton, Parish of Lenham, Essex, had two daughters, the elder of whom, Joyce, m. Humphrey Hales of the Dungeon, in Canterbury. Mary, the younger, brought the estate at Royton, another at Charing, and other property to her husband (B: 2:397).

The epitaph of Mary Atwater Honywood, in the church of Markeshall, Essex, bears this inscription: "Here lieth the body of Mary Waters, the daughter and coheire [*sic*] of Robert Waters of Lenham, in Kent., Esquire, wife of Robert Honywood of Charing, in Kent, only husband who had at her deceased lawfully descended 367 children, 16 of her own body, 114 grandchildren, 228 in the third generation, and nine in the fourth, She lived a most pious life, and in a Christian manner, d. here at Markishall in 93 yeare of her age, and 44 of her widowhood, 11 May 1620 (A:410).

Robert and Mary were the parents of the following 18 children (A:398; E:112; F; G; H; "Honeywood," D:1296-1297): ROBERT, b. 27 Sep 1545 at Charing, Kent (B: 1:569); KATHARINE, bapt. 19 Dec 1546, at Charing, Kent; PRISCILLA, b. c1548 Charing, Kent, England, m. Thomas Engham; ANTHONY, b, c1550, at Charing, Kent, m. Anne Tofts, widow of Francis Gibson, b. c1550/5 in Kent, and d. s.p. (B: 1:570); MARY, d. young; THOMAS, b. 1551 at Petts, Co. Kent; MARY, b. c1552 at Charing,

Kent, m. George Morton; ANNE, b. c1555 at Charing, Kent, m. Sir Charles Hales of
Thanington, Gent.; GRACE, b. 1556 at Charing, Kent, m. Michael Heneage of London,
Gent.; ARTHUR, d. young; WALTER, b. c1559 at Charing, Kent, d. unm.;
ELIZABETH, b. 2 Dec 1561, of Markeshall, Essex, m. George Woodward of Lee,
Bucks; RICHARD (omitted in A); ARTHUR, b. 19 Feb 1563 at Charing, Kent, m.
Elizabeth Spencer; SUSAN, bapt. 20 March 1564 at Charing, Kent, m. Richard
Renchinge of Norfolk; BENNETT, b. 22 June 1567 at Charing, Kent, m. Henry Croke
(or Crooke) of Oxfordshire, bro. of William; DOROTHY, b. 30 July 1569 at Charing,
Kent, m. William Croke; and ISAACK, bapt. 30 Nov 1570 at Charing, Kent, killed at
the Battle of Newport, d. s.p.

Generation 2

2. ROBERT HONYWOOD, son of Robert (1), was b. on 18 Sep 1545 at Charing,
Kent. He m. 1st, at age 24, on 3 July 1569, Dorothy Croke (or Crooke), who was b.
1549 in London or Middlesex, sole dau. of John Croke, Doctor of Civil Laws by his
wife Dorothy Theobalds (A:399). She d. 16 Dec 1580 giving birth to her dau. Susan (B:
1:569, 2:170).

Robert m. 2nd, on 9 July 1584, at Black Friars, London, Elizabeth Browne,
2nd dau. of Sir Thomas and Mabel (Fitz Williams) Browne, of Beechworth Castle (B:
2:170-171). She was b. on 26 June 1579 (I; "Honywood," D:1296-1297).

ARMS: of Robert Honywood, son of Robert and Mary (Atwater) Honywood:
Quarterly: 1 and 4: Argent, a chevron between three falcons' heads erased Azure; 2 and
3: Sable and fess wavy Argent, charged with two bars wavy Azure, between three swans
of the second, beaked Gules. **CREST:** A wolf's head couped Ermine (F).

Robert and Dorothy were the parents of seven children (B: 2:170; F; G;
"Honywood," D:1296-1297): DOROTHY, m. Henry Thompson, Gent.; Sir ROBERT, b.
6 Feb 1574, at Great St. Bartholomew's, London; ROGER, b. 20 Sep 1575 at Great St.
Bartholomew's, London, d. 29 Oct 1580; MARY, b. 20 Sep 1576 at St. Stephen's, near
Canterbury, m. John Moyle; JOYCE, b. 10 Jan 1577/8 at Great St. Bartholomew's,
London, m. Richard Sadler; ELIZABETH, b. 26 June 1579 at Pett, in Charing, Kent,
and d. at Roton in Oct 1579[?]; and SUSAN, b. 15 Dec 1580 at Pett, in Charing, m.
Thomas Denne, b. c1580 at London.

Robert and Elizabeth were the parents of ten children (B: 2:171-172;
"Honywood," in D:1296): [THOMAS?], b. 1585 at Beechworth Castle, d. before
baptism; THOMAS, b. 15 Jan 1586/7 at Beechworth Castle, Surrey, England;
MATTHEW, b. 21 Dec 1587 at BeecHworth Castle; ANN, b. 26 Dec 1588 at Pett in
Charing, m. Sir John Wilde of Canterbury; PETER, 11 Dec 1589 at Pett in Charing, d.
by 15 Dec 1685 (Peter Honywood of London and West Hawkes, Kingsnorth, Co. Kent,
was sole exec. of the will of his bro. Henry. Peter d. leaving a will dated 5 July 1682
and proved in London on 15 Dec 1685); HESTER, b. 13 Jan 1591/2 at Great St. Helen's,
London, m. John Sayer of Boucher's Hall; HENRY, b. 14 July 1593 at Pett in Charing,
d. leaving a will dated 18 Nov 1662, proved in London in Nov 1663; MABEL, b. 15
March 1594/5 at Pett; MICHAEL, Clerk, Dean of Lincoln, b. 1 Oct 1596 at great St.
Helen's, London, d. leaving a will dated 28 May and proved in London on 21 Sep 1681
(He founded the Cathedral Library at Lincoln, where his portrait hangs (A)); and

ISAACK, b. 17 Feb 1600/1 at Hoxton in Lady Bond's House, m. Mary Atwater (or Waters).

3. KATHERINE HONYWOOD, dau. of Robert (1) and Mary, was bapt. 19 Dec 1546 at Charing, Kent, Eng., and m. 1st, William Fleete, Gent., who was b. in 1544, and was living 27 Dec 1584. She m. 2nd, (marriage settlement dated 20 April 1586), William Henmarsh, who was b. c1541 (B: 1:570; "Fleete," D:1297).

Katherine and William Fleet had 12 children, including (A:399; D:1297; E:112): ROBERT, b. 1568; WILLIAM, b. c1570; PRISCILLA, b. 1572, m. John Seaman; MARY, b. 1574, prob. d. young; KATHERINE, b. 1576, m. John Parkehurst; MARY, b. c1578, m. George Strode; ANN, b. c1580; JOHN, b. c1582; THOMAS, b. c1584, drowned at Horton River (B: 1:570); MARGARET, b. c1586, m. Francis Tooke of Goddington; JOYCE, b. c1588, m. John Roberts of Hertford; and one other.

Katherine and William Henmarsh were the parents of three children (A:400; "Fleete," in D:1297): WILLIAM; JANE, m. Richard Willis of Cambridge; and THOMAS.

4. PRISCILLA HONYWOOD, dau. of Robert (1) and Mary, was b. c1548. She m. Sir Thomas Engham of Goodneston, Kent (marriage settlement dated 31 Oct 1567). Sir Thomas was b. in 1546 (B:1:570; *HSPV* 42:50; "Additional Pedigrees," F:126).

Thomas and Priscilla were the parents of eleven children ("Engham" D:1298; J): MARIA, b. c1570; VINCENT, b. c1572. d. s.p.; EDWARD, b. c1574; MARY, d. young; MARY, d. young; MARY, m. Thomas Baker of Battell, Sussex; DOROTHEA, m. 1st, Thomas Kenne of Co. Somerset, and 2nd, Richard Crackenthorpe, D.D.; WILLIAM, b. c1586 at London, d. s.p.; ROWLAND, b. c1588 at London; ELIZA, m. Charles Evers of Malton, bro. of Rudolph, Baron Evers; and JANE, m. William Rufford of Butler, Co. Berks.

5. MARY HONYWOOD, dau. of Robert (1) and Mary, was b. c1552 at Charing, Kent, England. She m. (marriage settlement dated 27 Jan 1573) George Morton, Esq., who was b. 1551, at Charing, Kent, England (B: 1:570).

George and Mary were the parents of six children, b. at Charing ("Morton," D:1298): ROBERT; HELEN; WILLIAM; ELIZABETH; THOMAS; and ALBERT, b. c1585.

6. ANNE HONYWOOD, dau. of Robert (1) and Mary, was b. c1555, at Charing, Kent. She m. (marriage settlement dated 10 May 1573), Charles Hales, Esq., of Tharrington, Kent, b. 1553. He was a son and heir of Thomas Hales (B: 1:570).

Charles and Anne were the parents of thirteen children, b. at Charing, Kent (A:400; "Hales," D:1298-9): ROBERT; JOAN; THOMAS, m. Ann Peyton; MARY, m. Thomas Moninges; JOICE; DOROTHY, m. Richard Shrubsole; CHARLES, m. Margaret Finch; JOHN, m. Bennet Finch; ALICE; JAMES; JOAN, m. Thomas Tooke; FRANCIS, m. Margaret Bingham; and STEPHEN.

7. GRACE HONYWOOD, dau. of Robert (1) and Mary, was b. 1556 at Charing, Kent. She m. on 12 Aug 1577 at Bowchurch, London (marriage settlement dated 20

April 1578) Michael Heneage of London, Gent. He d. 30 Dec 1600 (B: 1:570, 2:172).

Michael Heneage, younger son of Robert and Lucy (Buckton) Heneage, was appointed Keeper of the Records in the Tower of London in 1581, and was buried in the Cathedral Church of St. Paul's (K; L).

Michael and Grace (Honywood) were the parents of the following eleven children, whose dates of birth were found in a book written in Michael Heneage's own hand and dated 2 April 1601 (Some of the entries were in Latin) (A:400-401; B: 1:570, 2:172-173; "Heneage," D:1299): ANN, b. 10 Oct 1579, m. Ralph Gill; THOMAS, b. 21 Jan 1581/2; ROBERT, b. 28 Feb 1583/4, d. young; JOHN, b. 7 Dec 1585, d. young; LUCY, b. 24 Feb 1586/7, m. William Read of Canterbury; CATHERINE, b. 30 April 1588; MICHAEL, b. 20 Sep 1589; ROBERT, b. 3 Aug 1591, may have d young; JOHN, b. 25 March 1594/5; MARY; and (poss.) WILLIAM (omitted in A:400-401).

8. ELIZABETH HONYWOOD, dau. of Robert (1) and Mary (Atwater) Honywood, was b. 2 Dec 1561 at Markeshall, Essex, England, m. [as his second wife] (marriage settlement dated 18 Dec 1574) George Woodward, Esq., b. 10 April 1549 of Burgate, Suffolk, England. He d. at Lee on 26 Jan 1597 (A:570).

George and Elizabeth were the parents of thirteen children (A:401): ANN, b. 28 Oct 1582, of Upton, Bucks, England, m. as his 2nd wife, Rev. Thomas Sheafe; ELIZABETH, b. c1583, m. Thomas St. Nicholas; HENRY, b. c1587; SARAH, b. 2 Feb 1588, m. John Agard; ROBERT, b. c1589; BRIDGET, b. c1590, m. 1st, Thomas Lyddall, b. 1612, may have m. 2nd, Thomas Heneage, Esq., b. 21 Jan 1581 St. Katherine Coleman, London; she may have m. 3rd, George Liddall, Esq., b. c1595, of Upton, Bucks; ISAACKE, b. c1591; MARGARET, b. 9 Feb 1591, m. Sir John Ashburnham, Kt., b. c1603, of Upton, Bucks; MARY, b. 1592, m. Thomas Egleston, b. c1588; REBECCA, b. 19 July 1593, m. Thomas (Nicholas) Weston; RACHEL, m. Charles Pulton and had issue; GEORGE; and MARTHA, m. 1st, Rev. James Bacon, and 2nd, Rev. Robert Peck.

9. RICHARD HONYWOOD, of Horsham, Sussex, son of Robert (1) and Mary, was omitted in "Posterity." He is tentatively placed between Elizabeth, b. 1561, and Arthur, b. 1563. He d. 12 Feb 1613, and was buried 17 Feb 1613 at Horsham. On 4 May 1583 he m., at Horsham, Sussex, Elizabeth, dau. and heiress of J. Monk, Gent., of Nuthurst, Sussex.

Richard and Elizabeth were the parents of five children (M:30-39): ROBERT, b. 1 Feb 1584, d. May 1669; ELIZABETH, b. 10 Nov 1588, d. s.p., m. John Shurley; JEREMY, b. 2 March 1599, d. at Horsham, age 49; JAMES, b. 10 Jan 1606, d. age 22; and JOHN, b. 9 Aug 1611, d. age 34.

10. ARTHUR HONYWOOD, son of Robert (1) and Mary (Atwater) was b. on 19 Feb 1563 at Charing, Kent. He m. Mrs. Elizabeth Spencer, b. c1568, of Chard juxta Sutton, Kent, England.

ARMS: of Arthur Honywood, son of Robert and Mary (Atwater) Honywood: Quarterly: 1: Argent, a chevron between three falcons' [hawks'?] heads erased Azure, a crescent charged with a mullet for difference; 2: Argent, on a chevron Gules, three talbots statant Or; 3: [Sable], three covered cups within a bordure Or; 4: Sable, two bars

Or, a chief Argent. **CREST**: A wolf's head couped Ermine, on the neck a crescent charged with a mullet for difference (H).

Arthur and Elizabeth were the parents of the following twelve children, who were possibly b. at Chard, Kent ("Honywood," D:1296-1297; N:47): ROBERT, b. c1589, d. young; ANTHONY, b. c1591, but elsewhere his age was given as 19 in 1619; MARY, b. c1593, m. James Watts and had issue (B: 1:576); SUSAN, b. c1595; HENRY, b. c1597 (age 14 in 1619); DOROTHY, b. c1599, m. [-?-] Denne and had issue (B: 1:576); RACHEL, b. c1601; KATHERINE, b. c1603; JOHN, b. c1605 (age 8 in 1619); JANE, b. c1607; MARGARET, b. c1609; and ROBERT, b. c1611.

11. SUSAN HONYWOOD, dau. of Robert (1) and Mary, was bapt. 20 March 1564 at Charing, Kent, m. Richard Renching of Norfolk. He d. April 1598 (B: 1:571).

Richard and Susan (Honywood) Renching were the parents of four children (A:401): HELEN, m. Whetenhall Tilghman; THOMAS; SUSAN, m. Edward Boghurst; and NATHANIEL.

12. BENNET HONYWOOD, dau. of Robert (1) and Mary, was buried Waterstock, Co. Oxford, on 27 Oct 1638. She m. (marriage settlement dated 11 June 1586) Henry Croke (or Crooke), Esq., barrister-at-law, second son of Sir John Croke, of Chilton, Bucks, and bro. of William (B: 1:571). Henry d. before 1607.

Henry and Bennett were the parents of seven children (A: 402; "Crooke," *Visitation of Essex," HSPV* 13.:517; O: 1:357): Rev. HENRY, D.D.; ANNE, m. William Walton; DOROTHY, prob. d. young; ELIZABETH, m. Thomas St. Nicholas, barrister, at St. Dusntan's, Fleet St., on 17 Feb 1624 (A:402, cites *Collectanea Topograhica et Genealogica*, 5:217); DOROTHY; KATHERINE; and NATHANIEL.

13. DOROTHY HONYWOOD, dau. of Robert (1) and Mary, was b. 30 July 1569 at Charing, Kent. She m. (marriage settlement dated 30 Jan 1591) William Croke, Esq., of Chilton, Bucks, son of John Croke.

William and Dorothy were the parents of at least five children (A:402, which errs in stating she also married as a second husband Henry Thompson; this was her niece Dorothy; D:1301; O: 1:358): ALEXANDER, b. 23 Feb 1594, m. and had issue; ELIZABETH, b. 21 June 1597, m. John Keling, Esq.; CATHERINE, b. 12 Oct 1598, m. Richard Davis; EDWARD, b. 11 Feb 1602, d. young (Le Neve states that he m. Susan Coo and had issue); and FRANCIS, of Steeple Aston, Oxfordshire, b. 6 Sep 1605, d. 1672, having m. Alicia Castle, and leaving children (Le Neve omits Francis).

Generation 3

14. DOROTHY HONYWOOD, dau. of Robert (2) and Dorothy, m. on 27 Feb 1586/7 at Dorking, Henry Thompson, b. 1569 at Royton, Lenham, Kent (B: 1:571, 2:172; O: 1:358).

Henry and Dorothy were the parents of the following ten children, who were b. at Lenham, Kent ("Honywood," D:1296-1297; P; Note that A:402 incorrectly assigns these children to Dorothy (13), dau. of Robert (1) and Mary): ROBERT, b. 2 March 1594; MARY, b. 14 Oct 1598; JUDITH, b. 11 Aug 1602; JOHN, b. 18 Nov 1604, prob.

d. young; PETER, b. c1606, perhaps at Charing; ELIZABETH, b. 20 Sep 1607; WILLIAM, b. c1609 (not in P); CHARLES, b. c1610, perhaps at Charing; ANTHONY, b. 30 Aug 1612; and JOHN, b. c1614.

15. Sir ROBERT HONYWOOD, son of Robert (2) and Dorothy (Croke), was b. 6 Sep 1574, at Great St. Bartholomew's, London. He m. on 4 Dec 1598 at Alderman Barnham's House, Alice Barnham, dau. of Sir Martin Barnham, of Hollingbourne, Kent. She was b. c1569 (B: 1:572; D:1296-1297).

Sir Robert and Alice were the parents of twenty children, b. between 1599 and 1622 (A:403; B: 1:571-573; D:1296-1297): MARTIN, b. 12 Dec 1599 at Hollingbourne, d. young; ROBERT, b. 3 Aug 1601 at Hollingbourne; JUDITH, b. 5 July 1602 at Hollingbourne, m. John Sherley; JOHN, b. 28 Sep 1603 at Charing; ELIZABETH, b. 11 Sep 1604 at Charing, d. young; THOMAS, b. 29 Sep 1605 at Hollingbourne; MARTIN, b. 9 Feb 1606 at Hollingbourne; MARY, b. 29 July 1608 at Charing; ANNA, b. 31 July 1609 at Charing; FRANCIS, b. 17 Aug 1610 at Charing; DOROTHY, b. 30 Aug 1611 at Charing; ALICE, b. 10 Jan 1612/3 at Charing; ISAACK, b. 15 Feb 1613/4 at Charing; BENEDICT, b. 7 Feb 1614/5 at Charing; PHILIP, b. 26 Dec 1616 at Charing; MARGARET, b. 18 March 1617/8 at Charing; JANE, b. 14 April 1619 at Charing; PRISCILLA, b. 6 May 1620 at Charing; and ELIZABETH, b. c1621 at Charing; and VICESSIMUS, b. c1622 at Charing.

16. MARY HONYWOOD, dau. of Robert (2) and Dorothy, was b. 20 Sep 1576 at St. Stephen's, near Canterbury, and d. 7 Jan 1613/4. She m. at Charing Church on 11 July 1593, John Moyle, Esq., b. poss. c1576 at Buckwell, Kent, d. 2 Jan 1613/4, son of Robert Moyle (B: 1:573).

John and Mary were the parents of (A:403; B: 1:573): ROBERT; DOROTHY; MARY; ANN (or AMY); JOHN; THOMAS; DOROTHY; WALTER; MARTIN, d. at Markeshall on 18 Jan 1615; ANTHONY; and RICHARD.

17. JOYCE HONYWOOD, dau. of Robert (2) and Dorothy, was b. 10 Jan 1577/8 at Great St. Bartholomew's, London. She m. Richard Sadler, Esq., b. c1578 at Sopwell, Hertfordshire. Richard was the son of Edward and Anne (Leigh) Sadler of Temple Dinsley, Herts.

Richard and Joyce were the parents of ten children, b. in London or Middlesex, and from whom descend the Sadleirs of Sopwell, Ireland (A:403; D:1296-1297; Q:563): ROBERT, b. c1602; MARY, b. c1604; RAPHAEL, b. c1606; RICHARD, b. c1608; DOROTHY, b. c1610; MARGARET, b. c1612; THOMAS, b. c1614; EDWARD, b. c1616; BLUNT, b. c1618; and HENRY, b. c1620.

18. SUSAN HONYWOOD, dau. of Robert (2) and Dorothy, was b. 15 Dec 1580 at Pett, in Charing (B: 2:170). She m. Thomas Denne, b. c1580 at London. He was a son of Vincent Denne, LL.D., and his wife Joan Kettell.

Thomas and Susan were the parents of four children (R:21): VINCENT, Sergeant-at-Law, M. P.; WILLIAM, living in 1663; JOHN, living in 1663; and ELIZABETH, m. her cousin Vincent Nethersole of Nethersole House, Kent.

19. Sir THOMAS HONYWOOD, of Mark's Hall, Essex, son of Robert (2) and Elizabeth, was b. 15 Jan 1586/87 and d. leaving a will dated 24 May 1666 and proved in London on 7 Aug 1666. On 10 May 1634 a license to marry at All Hallows in the Wall or St. Leonard's Shoreditch, was granted to Sir Thomas Honywood. Kt., of Markeshall, Essex, bachelor, age 47, and Hester Manning of St. Bartholomew near the Exchange, widow of John Manning. Elsewhere her name is given as Hester Lamotte, b. c1609, of London, Middlesex, England (G:734; Foster:705; *HSPV* 26:217).

In his will he left all the land he had by the will of his late bro. Matthew to his son John Lamotte Honywood (G:733-734):

Sir Thomas and Hester were the parents of two children: JOHN LAMOTTE, b. c1635, of Mark's Hall, Essex; and ELIZABETH, bapt. 20 Aug 1637, m. Sir John Cotton, Bart.

20. MATTHEW HONYWOOD, son of Robert (2) and Elizabeth, was b. c1575, poss. at Beechworth Castle, Surrey, and d. by Oct 1638. He m. Elizabeth Rivers, b. c1600, dau. of Sir George Rivers of Chafford, Co. Kent. Bart. She was pregnant when her husband made his will.

Matthew Honywood of Charing Cross d. leaving a will dated 18 Sep 1638 and proved in London 26 Oct 1638.

Matthew and Elizabeth were the parents of at least one son, b. after his great-grandmother's death (G:733-734): MATTHEW, b. c1637 at Charing, Kent.

21. ANN HONYWOOD, dau. of Robert (2) and Elizabeth, was b. 26 Dec 1588 at Pett in Charing. She m. Sir John Wilde, b. c1575.

Sir John and Ann were the parents of seven children, two of whom probably d. before their great-grandmother's death ((A:403-404; B: 1:573-574; *HSPV* 42:18): ROBERT, b. c1599 at Markeshall; ANN, b. c1601 at Markeshall; ELIZABETH, b. c1605 at the Archdeacon's House in Canterbury; FRANCIS, b. c1609 at St. Martin's Hill; DUDLEY, b. c1611 at Christ Church, Canterbury (not in the Visitation, may have d. young); JOHN, b. 8 Aug 1612 at Markeshall; HESTER, b. c1613 at Mystoole, Chatham, near Canterbury (not in the Visitation, may have d. young); HELLEN (or ELEANORA), b. 26 Oct 1615 at St. Martin's Hill; and DOROTHY, b. at Mystoole, near Canterbury.

22. HESTER/ESTHER HONYWOOD, of Robert (2) and Elizabeth, was b. 13 Jan 1591/2 at Great St. Helen's, London. She m. on 7 Aug 1610, John Sayer, Esq., who was M.P. for Colchester in 1645. He was b. c1579, at Bourchier Hall, Essex, the son of Sir George and Dorothy (Higham) Sayer. He d. 1658, and was buried at Aldham, Essex (B: 1:574; S).

John Sayer was a very active committee-man during the Commonwealth (S).

John and Hester/Esther were the parents of seven children ((A:404; B: 1:574; D:1296-1297; S [which names only three children]; T; U): DOROTHY, b. 2 Jan 1613/4, m. John Barnaby of Colchester; ELIZABETH; Sir GEORGE, b. c1615 (age 19 in 1634), knighted in 1640, and d. 11 July 1650, leaving issue; HESTER, b. at Wm. Higham's House, in Suffolk, prob. d. young; ANN; Sir JOHN; and HESTER.

23. WILLIAM FLEETE of Chatham, Kent, and Gray's Inn, London, son of William and Katherine (3), m. Deborah Scott, dau. of Charles and Jane (Wyatt) Scott. William Fleete was a member of the Virginia Company.

Deborah Scott Fleete, d. leaving a will dated 27 March 1651 and proved 23 Jan 1651/2. She left all her goods to her cousins Sir Robert and Sir Edward Filmer, who were to be repaid for the sums they had lent her for the recovering of her son Henry from a great illness, and for furnishing him with the provisions necessary for his last voyage to VA. Henry Frenoham, Thomas Davy witnessed the will. The will was proved on 23 Jan 1651/2 by Sir Robert Filmer, Kt., one of the executors, with power reserved for Sir Edward Filmer, the other executor (*VGEW*:567 cited PCC Bowyer, 5; *PASC*:112).

William and Deborah were the parents of fourteen children (A:404 [which gives the order of birth of the first twelve children]; B: 1:574 [which does not add the last two children]; V): CHARLES; GEORGE; THOMAS; KATHERINE; ELIZABETH, prob. d. young; WILLIAM; Capt. HENRY; BRIAN; FRANCIS; [-?-], dau.; EDWARD; ELIZABETH; REGINALD; and JOHN.

24. PRISCILLA FLEETE, dau. of William and Katherine (3), was b. 1572 at Charing, Kent, England. She m. John Seaman, b. c1570. They were the parents of two children (A:404; V): KATHERINE, b. 1594; and JOHN, b. 1596.

25. KATHERINE FLEETE, dau. of William and Katherine (3), was b. 1576 at Charing, Kent, England; she m. John Parkehurst, b. c1574. They were the parents of three children (A:405; "Fleete," D:1297): KATHERINE, b. c1598; DOROTHY, b. c1600; and ELIZA, b. c1602.

26. MARY FLEETE, dau. of William and Katherine (3), was b. c1578 at Charing, Kent, England. She m. George Strode, b. c1576, in Dorsetshire.

George and Mary were the parents of thirteen children, two of whom were b. after the death of their great-grandmother (A:405; "Fleete," D:1297): ELIZABETH, b. c1600; JOHN, b. c1602, prob. d. young; [-?-], b. c1604; MARY, b. c1606; JOHN, b. c1608, prob. d. young; ISAAC, b. c1610; JACOB, b. c1612; ABRAHAM, b. c1614; JANE, b. c1616; MARTHA, b. c1618; NAOMI, b. c1620; JOHN, b. c1622; and [-?-], b. c1624.

27. MARGARET FLEETE, dau. of William and Katherine (3), was b. c1586 at Charing, Kent, England. She m. Francis Tooke, b. c1584 at Goddington, Kent, England.

Francis and Margaret were the parents of at least six children, b. at Goddington, Kent (A:405; "Fleete," D:1297): JOHN, b. 1608; RICHARD, b. 1610; ANTHONY, b. 1612; NICHOLAS, b. 1614; MARY, b. 1616; and FRANCIS, b. 1618.

28. JOYCE FLEETE, dau. of William and Katherine (3), was b. c1588 at Charing, Kent, England. She m. John Roberts, b. c1586, of the town of Hertford. They were the parents of five children (A:405; B: 1:574, which gives the dates of birth): AVICE, b. 9 Sep 1616; JOHN, b. 30 Dec 1617; WILLIAM, b. 10 Nov 1619; FRANCIS, b. 17 Sep 1621; and JAMES, b. 26 Dec 1622.

29. JANE HENMARSH, dau. of William and Katherine (3), m. Richard Willis of Co. Cambridge. Jane and her husband were the parents of four children (A:405; "Fleete," D:1297): THOMAS, d. by 1670 in Lancaster Co., VA (W); RICHARD; WILLIAM; and ELIZABETH.

30. EDWARD (EDWIN) ENGHAM, son of Thomas and Priscilla (4), was b. c1574 at London, Middlesex, England. The "Additional Pedigrees" in *The Visitation of Kent*, 1592, states that he m. (1st) Philippa, dau. and heir of Gibbons of Rownden, and 2nd Eliza Evelin or Euelin, who was b. c1576.

By Philippa, Edward was the father of five children (A:405): WILLIAM; THOMAS, d. s.p; PRISCILLA, unm. in 1591; KATHERINE, unm. in 1592; and MARY, unm. in 1592.

Edward and Eliza (Evelyn) were the parents of seven children (X): THOMAS, b. c1600; EDWARD, b. c1602; MARY, b. c1604; ELIZABETH, b. c1606; JOHN, b. c1608; ISAACKE, b. c1610; and an unnamed child, [-?-], b. c1612.

31. MARY ENGHAM, dau. of Thomas and Priscilla (4), was b. 1578, in London or Middlesex, England. She m. Thomas Baker, second son of John and Elizabeth [-?-] Baker of Battell, Sussex. He was b. 1574, and was barrister.

Thomas and Mary (Engham) Baker were the parents of twelve children, possibly b. at either Goodneston, Kent, or Battell, Sussex (A:406; B: 1:574-575; Y:92): THOMAS, prob. d. young; JOHN, d. s.p.; [-?-], d. before baptism; MICHAEL; GEORGE; THOMAS; PRISCILLA; MARY, prob. d. young; ELIZABETH, prob. d. young; ELIZABETH; [-?-], d. before baptism; and MARY, b. 25 Feb 1627, of Battell, Sussex, m. **Robert Brooke who settled in MD.**

32. DOROTHY ENGHAM, dau. of Thomas and Priscilla (4), was b. c1584 poss. at London. She m. 1st Thomas Kenne, Esq., b. 1582, in Gloucestershire, and 2nd, Richard Crakenthorpe, D.D., of Black Nolley, Essex ("Engham," D:1298).

By Thomas Kenne she was the mother of the following four children (A:406; B: 1:575; "Engham," D:1298): PRISCILLA; GEORGE; THOMAS; and [-?-].

Richard Crakenthorpe and Dorothy were the parents of three children (A:406; Engham," D:1298): DOROTHY; JOHN; and ELIZABETH.

33. ELIZABETH ENGHAM, dau. of Thomas and Priscilla (4), was b. c1590 at London, Middlesex, England. She m. Charles Evers, Esq., b. c1588 at Malton, Yorkshire, bro. of Rudolph, Baron Evers.

Charles and Elizabeth were the parents of four children only two of whom have been identified (A:406; B: 1:575): [-?-]; PRISCILLA; THOMAS; and [-?-].

34. JANE ENGHAM, dau. of Sir Thomas and Priscilla (4), m. William Rufford of Butler, Co. Berks. William and Jane were the parents of (A:406; "Engham," D:1298): THOMAS; WILLIAM; ENGHAM; JANE; and [-?-].

35. ROBERT MORTON, son of George and Mary (5) (Honywood) Morton, was b. c1575, poss. at Charing, Kent, England. He m. Ann Finch, b. c1577, dau. of Sir Henry Finch, and widow of Levin Palmer.

Robert and Ann were the parents of three children (A:407; B: 1:575): GEORGE; MARY; and ALBERT.

36. THOMAS HALES, son of Charles and Anne (6) (Honywood), m. Ann Peyton, dau. of Thomas Peyton of Knowlton, Kent., Esq.

Thomas and Ann were the parents of nineteen children, of whom six have not been identified by name (A:407; "Hales," D:1298): THOMAS; ANN; LUKE; ELIZABETH; CHARLES; ROBERT; SAMUEL; STEPHEN; CHARLES; JOHN; MARY; DOROTHY; FRANCIS; and six others whose names are not known.

37. MARY HALES, dau. of Charles and Anne (6) (Honywood) Hales, m. by license granted 12 May 1595 Thomas Moninges, of Canterbury, Gent. (T:933).

Thomas and Mary (Hales) Moninges were the parents of eleven children (A:407; "Hales," D:1298): THOMAS; CHARLES, d. young; CHARLES; MARY; ANN; JANE; DOROTHY; STEPHEN; THOMAS; WILLIAM; and RICHARD.

38. DOROTHY HALES, dau. of Charles and Anne (6) (Honywood) Hales, m. Richard Shrubsole, Gent.

Richard and Dorothy were the parents of four children (A:407; "Hales," D:1298): ANN, b. c1609; CHARLES; SUSAN; and THOMAS.

39. CHARLES HALES, son of Charles and Anne (6) (Honywood) Hales, m. Margaret Finch, by whom he was the father of five children (A:408; "Hales," D:1298): CHARLES; BENNETT; FRANCIS; THOMAS; and ELIZABETH.

40. JOHN HALES, son of Charles and Anne (6) (Honywood) Hales, was b. c1591 at Charing, Kent, England. He m. Bennett Finch, b. c1593, dau. of William and Bennetta (Honywood) Finch (N:80).

John and Bennett were the parents of four children (A:408; "Hales," D:1298): ANN; CHARLES; ANN; and JOHN, b. c1623.

41. JOAN HALES, dau. of Charles Hales and Anne (6) (Honywood) Hales, m. Thomas Tooke of Beere, Kent

Thomas and Joan were the parents of five stillborn children, and the seven listed below (A:408; "Hales," D:1298; N:154; "Padwick of Horsham," *BLG* 1906 ed., p. 1276): CHARLES; JOHN; ANN; MARY; MARGARET; THOMAS; and DOROTHY.

42. FRANCIS HALES, son of Charles Hales and Anne (6) (Honywood) Hales, m. Margaret Bingham (B: 1:575).

Francis and Margaret were the parents of at least one child (A:408; "Hales," D:1298): GRACE; and perhaps others.

43. ANN HENEAGE, dau. of Michael and Grace (7) Honywood, was b. 10 Oct 1579 (B: 2:172), and was buried 23 March 1609. On 22 May 1596 a license to marry was issued to Anne Heneage of St. Catherine Cree Church, London, spinster, dau. of Michael Heneage of the same, Gent., and Ralph Gill of St. Peter ad Vinicula in the Tower of London, Gent. (Z:548). Gill d. 12 Feb 1620 and was buried at St. Peter's in the Tower, He left a will proved 3 March 1621, and an Inquisition Post Mortem was held 17 Oct 19 James I. Like his father before him, Ralph Gill was Lion Keeper at the Tower of London (AA:68).

They were the parents of seven children (A:408; "Heneage." D:1298): THOMAS, prob. d. young; ROBERT, m. Mrs. Anne Dormer; WILLIAM; THOMAS; ELIZABETH, m. [-?-] Gregory; GRACE; and MARY.

44. THOMAS HENEAGE, of Battersea, Co. Surrey, eldest son of Michael and Grace (7) (Honywood), was b. 21 Jan 1581 at St. Katherine Coleman, London and d. at Battersea on 9 Aug 1641. He m. Bridget, relict of Sir Thomas Lyddall, and dau. of George Woodward (AB):

Thomas and Bridget were the parents of at least two children: Sir MICHAEL; and ELIZABETH, m. as his first wife, Edward Mainwaring, by whom she had 10 children.

45. LUCY HENEAGE, dau. of Michael and Grace (7) Honywood, m. William Read of Canterbury, who was b. 1565 and d. 24 April 1621.

William and Lucy were the parents of four children (A:409; "Heneage." D:1292): JOHN, b. 1604; WILLIAM, b. 1605; ANNE; and (poss.) REBECCA, b. c1615, Rebecca Read of East Barnett, Herts, spinster, age 17, dau. of William Read of Canterbury (and her marriage at the disposal of Thomas Heneage of East Barnett), and William Wandesford of St. Gregory's London, merchant tailor, bachelor, age 26, on 26 July 1632 were granted a license to marry at East Barnett (*HSPV* 26:207).

46. ANN WOODWARD, dau. of George and Elizabeth (8) (Honywood) Woodward, was b. 28 Oct 1582, at Upton, Bucks., and was buried 30 Sep 1614 at Welford, Berks. (I:161). She m., as his 2nd wife, Thomas Sheafe, bapt 10 Oct 1562 at Cranbrook, Kent, and died in childbirth. Thomas Sheafe d. at his home in Wickham, Welford, Berks. leaving a will dated 4 June 1639, and proved 2 March 1639/40 (B: 1:575; AC:168)

Thomas Sheafe held a doctor of divinity degree from King's College, Cambridge, and was rector of Welford, Berks., and later a canon of St. George's Chapel, Windsor (AC:167, 168).

Thomas and Ann were the parents of one child (AC:167; AD:161): EDWARD, b. c1607.

47. ELIZABETH WOODWARD, dau. of George and Elizabeth (8) (Honywood) Woodward, was b. c1583 at Upton, Bucks. She m. on Monday, -- Jan 1609, Thomas St. Nicholas, b. c1581 (B: 1:575).

Thomas and Elizabeth were the parents of four children (A:409): ELIZABETH; TIMOTHY, prob. d. young; SAMUEL; and TIMOTHY.

48. SARAH WOODWARD, dau. of George and Elizabeth (8) (Honywood) Woodward, was b. 2 Feb 1588, poss. at Upton, Bucks. She m. John Agard, b. c1593, of Upton, Bucks.

John and Sarah were the parents of one dau. (A:409): MARY, b. c1617.

49. BRIDGET WOODWARD, dau. of George and Elizabeth (8) (Honywood) Woodward, was b. c1590. She m. 1st, Sir Thomas Lyddall, b. 1612 (AF). She m. 2nd, Thomas Heneage, Esq. (44 above), b. 21 Jan 1581 St. Katherine Coleman, London; she may have m. 3rd?, George Liddall, Esq., b. c1595, of Upton, Bucks.

Sir Thomas and Bridget were the parents of at least one child: Capt. GEORGE.

50. REBECCA WOODWARD, dau. of George and Elizabeth (8) (Honywood) Woodward, was b. 19 July 1593 at Upton, Bucks. On 18 Sep 1616 a license to marry at St. Margaret's, Westminster, was granted to Thomas Weston, b. c1599, of St. Giles-in-the Fields, and Rebecca Honywood of Westminster, spinster (Z).

Thomas and Rebecca were the parents of two daus (A:409): BRIDGET, b. c1623; and RACHEL, b. c1625.

51. MARTHA WOODWARD, dau. of George and Elizabeth (8) (Honywood) Woodward, m. 1st, Rev. James Bacon, Rector of Burgate, Suffolk, and 2nd, Rev. Robert Pecke of Hingham, Norfolk. Rev. Pecke went to New England, but returned to England. The will of Rev. Robert Peck was dated 24 July 1651 and proved 10 April 1658 (PCC Wootton, 153) (*GGE*:93-94).

Martha Honywood and Rev. James Bacon may have been the parents of: NATHANIEL BACON, **Councillor and Acting Governor of VA** (*Eng. Orig. of New Eng. Fam.* 3:556); and MARTHA BACON, b. c1634 in Burgate, Suffolk, England, **m. by 1656 in Carter Creek, Gloucester Co., VA, Anthony Smith, who d. c1662/7 in VA.**

52. SUSAN HONYWOOD, dau. of Arthur (10), was b. c1595 at Chard, Kent, England. She may have m. Thomas Denne of Canterbury.

Their four children, listed in "Denne, of Kent and Susssex." *Burke's Commoners*, 3:21, were: VINCENT, Sergeant-at-law, M.P., m. and had issue; WILLIAM, living 1663; CHARLES, living 1663; and ELIZABETH, m. her cousin Vincent Nethersole of Nethersole House, Kent.

53. HELEN RENCHINGE, dau. of Richard and Susan (11) (Honywood), was buried 30 Dec 1632, prob. at the birth of her son Benjamin. She m. Whetenhall Tilghman, b. 1576, son of William and Susanna (Whetenhall) Tilghman (AF:445).

Whetenhall Tilghman was the uncle of Dr. Richard Tilghman, b. 1626, d. 1675, who settled in MD in 1661.

Whetenhall and Helen (Renchinge) Tilghman were the parents of eight children (A:409; AF: cites the 1619 Visitation of Kent, the Parish Register of Snodland, and *HSPV* 40:1300): SAMUEL, d. young; MARY, bapt. 11 Dec 1608; ISAAC, b. 1615, d. 21 Dec 1644; NATHANIEL, b. 1616; SAMUEL, b. 1618 (He is probably the Samuel

Tilghman, who had long commanded a vessel trading to MD, and in July 1658 was commissioned "Admiral" of the Maryland fleet; AF:447); JOSEPH, bapt. 2 Jan 1625; SUSAN; and BENJAMIN, bapt. 25 Jan 1633.

54. SUSAN RENCHINGE, dau. of Richard and Susan (11) (Honywood), m. Edward Boghurst (or Boggas). They were the parents of one child (A:409; B: 1:575): MARY.

55. REV. HENRY CROKE (or CROOKE), D.D., Clerk in holy orders, son of Henry and Bennett (12) Honywood, d. 1642. He m. Sarah, dau. of Rev. Henry Wilkinson, Rector of Waddesden (O: 1:357).

Rev. Henry inherited the house and estate of Waterstock from his uncle Sir George Croke.

Rev. Henry and Sarah were the parents of (O: 1:357-358): Sir GEORGE of Waterstock (He m. Jane, dau. of Sir Richard Onslow, and left two daughters, one of who m. Sir Thomas Wyndham; ELIZABETH; SARAH; JOHN, Gent. of the Bed Chamber to Charles II, d. 1670; HENRY, a linen-draper in the Hay Market; and SAMUEL.

56. ANNE CROKE (or CROOKE), dau. of Henry and Bennet (12) (Honywood), m. William Walton of Little Burstead, Essex, Freeman of the Clothworkers of London in 1634.

William and Anne were the parents of two children ("Walton," Visitation of Essex." *HSPV* 13:517): GEORGE, age 18 in 1634; and SUSAN.

57. CATHERINE CROKE, dau. of William and Dorothy (13) Honywood, was b. 12 Oct 1598. She m. Richard Davis *als* Puleston of London, merchant, and had four children (A:402; B: 1:576): SAMUEL; JOHN; and two unnamed twins.

Generation 4

58. ROBERT THOMPSON, son of Henry and Dorothy (14) (Honywood) Thompson, was b. on Shrove Tuesday, 2 March 1594 Lenham Chapel, Royton House, Kent (B: 2:172). He m. Dorothy Swann, b. c1596 at Lenham Chapel, Royton House, Kent, dau. and coheir of Thomas Swann, Gent., dec.

Robert and Dorothy were the parents of four children (B: 2:575-576; N): MARY, d. young before 1620; ELIZABETH, d. young before 1620; DOROTHY, d. young before 1620; and DOROTHY, bapt. 30 Sep 1621 at Shepherd's Well, Kent, England (she m. 1st, Edward Merriweather, b. 1598 at Barfreston, Kent, England, and 2nd John Moyle, b. c1617 at Shepherd's Well, Kent, England).

59. MARY THOMPSON, dau. of Henry and Dorothy (14) (Honywood) Thompson, was b. 14 Oct 1598 at Royton, Lancs. She m. George Hussey, bapt. 27 April 1597 at Salehurst, Sussex, England.

George and Mary were the parents of four children (B: 1:576, which names only son Henry.): HENRY, m. [-?-] Lamb; (poss.) MARY; (poss.) DOROTHY, may have m. [-?-] Harington, b. c1628 at Slinfold, Sussex, England; and JUDITH, of

Slinfold, Essex, spinster, age c26, and John Evans of Bletchingley, Surrey, bachelor, age c30, on 3 July 1663 were granted a license to marry at Ivell, Sussex, or Horley, Surrey, with the consent of Judith's father, George Hussey (*HSPV* 23:90).

60. JUDITH THOMPSON, dau. of Henry and Dorothy (14) (Honywood) Thompson, was b. 11 Aug 1602, Lenham, Kent, England, m. Thomas Scott, bapt. 5 April 1605 at Godmersham, Kent, England.

Thomas and Judith are stated to have been the parents of four children (X): CHARLES, bapt. 21 June 1627 St. Alphage, Canterbury, Kent [and prob. d. young]; DOROTHEA, bapt. 30 Jan 1629 at St. Alphage, Canterbury, m. Daniel Gotherson, who had been bapt. 27 Sep 1618 St. George Southwark, Surrey; CHARLES, b. c1631, at St. Alphage, Canterbury; and THOMAS, bapt. 10 May 1632 St. Alphage, Canterbury.

61. ANTHONY THOMPSON, son of Henry and Dorothy (14) (Honywood) Thompson, was b. 30 Aug 1612 Lenham, Kent, England, m. Mirable Fitch b. c1614 Lenham, Kent, England. **By 1634 the family seems to have settled in CT**.

Anthony and Mirable are stated to have been the parents of five children (X): BRIDGET, b. c1630 at Lenham (m. 1st, Rev. John Bowers, b. 1629/1630 Derby, New Haven, CT, and 2nd, William Hoadle, b. c1636 at Lenham, Kent); ANTHONY, b. Dec 1634 New Haven, New Haven, CT; HANNAH ANNA, b. 8 June 1645 at Stonington, New London, CT (m. Capt. John Stanton. b. 1641/1643 Stonington, New London, CT); LYDIA, b. 16 July, bapt. 25 July 1647 at New Haven, New Haven, CT (m. 1st, Isaac Crittenden, b. 1643 Guilford, New Haven, CT, 2nd, John Crittenden, b. c1643, of New Haven, Connecticut, m. 3rd, John Meigs, b. 28 Feb 1641 at Rehoboth, Bristol, MA) and EBENEZER, b. 15 Oct 1648 at Guilford, New Haven, Connecticut (m. 1st, Deborah Dudley, b. 20 Sep 1647 at Guilford, New Haven, CT, and m. 2nd, Mary Welbe, b. c1616, at Lenham, Kent, England).

62. JUDITH HONYWOOD, dau. of Sir Robert (15), was b. 5 July 1602 at Hollingbourne, Kent. She m. 1st, John Sherley, of Lewes, Sussex, and 2nd, Sir Thomas Pelham, Bart., b. 1597, at Halland, Laughton, Sussex.

John Sherley and Judith had three children (A:410; B: 1:575): FRANCIS, b. 8 June 1620 at Lewes; JOHN, b. 1622; and FRANCIS.

63. Sir PHILIP HONYWOOD, son of Sir Robert (15) and Alice, was b. 26 Dec 1616 at Charing, Kent. On 18 Dec 1667 a license to marry at St. Dunstan's in the West, or at Lincoln's Inn Fields was granted to Sir Philip Honywood, Kt., of Portsmouth, Co. Southampton, and Frances Neale of St.-Giles-in-the-Fields, Mddx., spinster, age 20, whose father was dead, and who[se marriage] was at the disposal of [-?-] Neale of St. Giles-in-the Fields (Z:705).

He is prob. the Col., later Sir Philip Honywood, Royalist officer, who **went to VA in 1649** (*VGEW*:568).

Sir Philip Honywood, of Charing, Co. Kent, d. leaving a will dated 14 Dec 1684 and proved 12 May 1686. He mentioned a wife, and named his sister Priscilla and sister Wilkinson, his nephew Charles, Dr. Jacob, Sir Robert Haywood, sister Knatchbull, and his only dau. Frances, who was to be sole executrix and legatee.

On 28 Feb 1684 a commission was issued to William Jacob, M.D., and John Wilkinson, Esq., as guardians of Frances Honywood, minor dau. of Sir Philip, to administer his estate during the minority of his dau.

On 12 May 1686, Frances Sayers als. Honywood, now wife of George Sayers, proved the will (*Virginia Wills* (Baltimore: Genealogical Publishing Co., Inc), p. 761.

Sir Philip was the father of: FRANCES, a minor in 1684, and wife of George Sayer by May 1686.

64. ROBERT MOYLE, son of John and Mary (16) (Honywood) Moyle, m. Priscilla Fotherby, dau. of Dr. Fotherby, Dean of Canterbury.

Robert and Priscilla were the parents of four children, two of whom were born in the lifetime of Mary (Atwater) Honywood (A:576): CECILY; and three others whose names are not known.

65. MARY MOYLE, dau. of John and Mary (16) (Honywood) Moyle, m. [-?-] Godfrey. They were the parents of five children (A:576): ROBERT, b. 11 Aug 1616, prob. d. young; ANN, b. 26 April 1618, prob. d. young; ELIZABETH, b. 31 July 1619; MARY, b. 19 Jan 1620/1; [-?-], b. 25 June 1622.

66. ROBERT SADLER, of Sopwell, Herts., son of Richard and Joyce (17) (Honywood), was b. c1602 at London, Middlesex, England. Robert m. Ellen, dau. of Thomas Bancroft, and left an only dau. and heiress ((D:1296-1297; Q): ELLEN, m. Thomas Saunders of Beechwood.

67. ELIZABETH HONYWOOD, dau. of Sir Thomas (19) and Hester, was bapt. 20 Aug 1637 at Mark's Hall, Essex, England. She m. as his second wife, Sir John Cotton, Bart., b. 1621, of Connington, Hunts.

Sir John and Elizabeth were the parents of several children, only three of whom survived ("Cotton of Connington," *BEDB*: 138): Sir ROBERT, 5th Bart., b. 1669, of Gidding, Hunts. (m. 1st, Elizabeth Wigston, b. c1682, and 2nd, Sarah Morton, b. c1673); ELIZABETH (m. 1st, Lyonel Walden, Esq., of Huntingdon, and 2nd, [-?-] Smith, Esq., of Westminster); MARY, d. s.p., having m. Dr. Roger Kenyon.

68. Sir GEORGE SAYER, son of John and Hester (22) (Honywood), was b. c1615 (age 19 in 1634), was knighted in 1640, and d. 11 July 1650. By his wife Jane [-?-], he left a posthumous daughter (S):
ESTHER, b. Sep 1650 (On 13 March 1675, Hester Sayer of Boucer's Hall, Essex, spinster, age 22, dau. of Sir George Sayer, dec., with the consent of her mother was granted a license to marry either at St. Andrew Undershaft or St. Katherine Cree Church. John Marsham, of Coxton, Co. Kent, Esq. {later Sir John Marsham, Bart.}, widower) (Z:893).

69. Sir JOHN SAYER, son of John and Hester (22) (Honywood), d. on 4 Sep 1667. He was buried at St. Margaret's Westminster. He m. Katherine, dau. of John Van Hossen Van Piershill, of Zealand.

He was a page to the Prince of Orange, and a colonel of the Foot.

Sir John and Katherine were the parents of five children (S): GEORGE, Vice Chamberlain to Queen Catherine, consort of Charles II, and also to Queen Mary II, who made him sub-governor and gentleman of the bedchamber to William, Duke of Gloucester. He m. Frances, dau. of Sir Philip Honywood; ROBERT; JOHN; CHARLES; and ADOLPHUS.

70. Capt. HENRY FLEETE, son of William (23) and Deborah, was b. at Chatham, Kent, Eng. He m. Sarah Burden, b. c1595 at Chatham, Kent. Eng.

Capt. Henry Fleete settled in VA, and came to MD as a passenger on the Ark and the Dove.

Henry and Sarah were the parents of two children (*PASC*:112): SARAH, b. c1640, m. Edwin Conway, b. c1644; and HENRY, b. 1655 Lancaster City, King and Queen Co., VA, m. Elizabeth Wildey, b. 1655 Lunenberg, Co. VA.

71. THOMAS WILLIS, son of Richard and Jane (29) (Henmarsh), d. by 1670, He m. Mary [-?-], and may have had a daughter: ELEANOR who m. **Robert Alden who settled in VA;** this couple had a daughter Mary, b. 1681 in Middlesex County, VA, and m. Martin Nalle.

72. MARY BAKER, dau. of Thomas and Maria (31) (Engham) Baker, was b. 25 Feb 1627 at Battell, Sussex, England. She m. as his 1st wife, Gov. Robert Brooke, b. 3 June 1602, Whitemarsh, Southampton Co., England.

Mary Baker Brooke d. before her husband settled in MD.

Robert and Mary were the parents of four children (Y): Col. BAKER, b. 16 Nov 1628 at Battell, Sussex, Eng.; MARY, b. 19 Feb 1630 at Battle, Sussex; Major THOMAS, b. 23 June 1632 at Battell, Sussex; and BARBARA, b. 1634 at Wickham, Kent.

73. CHARLES TOOKE, of Bere, son of Thomas and Joane (Hales) (41), was b. 1611 and d. 1664. He m. Bridget, 2nd dau. and coheir of Nicholas Toke of Godington.

Charles and Bridget had several children, including ("Padwick of Horsham," *Burke's Land Gentry* 1906 ed., p. 1276): THOMAS, b. 1644, d. 1697, m. 1st, in 1665, Catherine Hales, dau. of Sir Robert Hales of Beakesbourne, and had children by her. He m. 2nd, Elizabeth, dau. of Mathew Babington of Rothley Temple, Co. Leicester.

74. ROBERT GILL, Lion Keeper at the Tower of London, son of Ralph, and Ann (43) (Heneage), d. leaving a will dated 26 Feb 1672 and proved 19 July 1673. He is buried at St. Peter's in the Tower of London. He m. Anne Dormer, who is also buried in the Tower. She was a dau. of William and Anne (Dowhurst) Dormer of London.

Robert and Ann were the parents of (A: 410; *Collectanea Topographica et Geenalogica* 8:280; "Herts.," pp. 67-68): ROBERT, d. s.p.; WILLIAM, buried 10 Sep 1686 as "Capt. William Gill" at the Tower (He m. and had two children); ANNE; MARY; and KATHERINE.

75. ELIZABETH GILL, dau. of Ralph and Ann (43) (Heneage) Gill, m. [-?-] Gregory.
Elizabeth and her husband were the parents of (A:410): WILLIAM; GRACE; and ELIZABETH.

76. Sir MICHAEL HENEAGE, Kt., of Gray's Inn, son of Thomas (44) and Bridget, d. December 1711. A marriage license was granted on 1 Sep 1662 to Michael Heneage, of Gray's Inn, bachelor, age about 30, and Phebe Foot, spinster, of St. Mary Aldermanbury, age abut 19, with the consent of her father Samuel Foote (*HSPV* 23:75; *GGE*:1283). Phebe Foote Heneage d. by Oct 1705 ("Walker-Heneage of Compton Bassett," *Burke's Commoners* 4:369).
Samuel Foote, London merchant, left a will dated 17 Oct 1705 and proved 16 March 1710. He named nephews and nieces, Cecil Walker (and her son Heneage Walker), and Charles, Phebe, Grace, and Bridget Heneage, sons and daughters of my late dear sister, the Lady Phebe Heneage (*GGE*:1282-1283, cites PCC Young, 55).
Sir Michael and Phebe were the parents of: CHARLES, d. 1738, leaving two daughters, who d. unm.; CECIL, m. John Walker of the Inner Temple and Hadley, Mddx., by whom she had a son Heneage Walker; PHEBE; GRACE; and BRIDGET.

77. ELIZABETH HENEAGE, dau. of Thomas (44) and Bridget, d. 13 May 1676. She m. as his first wife, Edward Mainwaring of Whitmore, son of Edward and Anne (Lomax). Edward was bapt. 7 April 1635 and d. 1704, leaving a will dated 17 Feb 1702 and proved 26 Jan 1704 ("Cavenagh-Mainwaring of Whitmore," *BLG* 1906:1109).
Edward Mainwaring m. 2nd, on 29 July 1679, Bridget, dau. of Sir Thomas Trollope, and had children by her.
Edward and Elizabeth had 10 children including: BRIDGET, m. Thomas Key of Islington; ANNE, m. Rev. John Taylor; ELIZABETH, d. unm.; and seven others.

78. Capt. GEORGE LYDDALL, son of Sir George and Bridget (49) (Woodward), **settled in VA** and patented land on the Pamunkey River in 1654. He also commanded a fort on the Mattaponi in 1679. He is said to have been the father of (AE:200): ANN, m. Capt. Edmund Bacon.

79. VINCENT DENNE, Sergeant-at-Law, M. P., son of Thomas and Susan (52) Honywood, m. his cousin Mary Denne, dau. of Thomas Denne, Recorder of Canterbury and his wife, Dorothy Tanfield.
Vincent and Mary (Denne) Denne were the parents of four children ("Denne," *Burke's Commoners* 1:20-21): DOROTHY, m. Thomas Girder, Esq.; MARY, m. Thomas Nethersole, Esq., of Nethersole; HONEYWOOD, m. Gilbert Knowles, Esq.; and BRIDGET, m. Robert Beake, Gent.

Unplaced:

HENEAGE, CATHERINE, m. Edward Stoughton (*Eng Orig. of New Eng. Fam.*, 6:369).

THE HORNE FAMILY

Refs.: A: Christopher Johnston. "Sewall Family." *MG* II, 318-323. B: Robert Barnes. "The Darrell Family." *British Roots of Maryland Families.* GPC, 1999. C: "Horne," *Visitation of Warwickshire, 1618,* in *HSPV* 12:343.

1. JOHN HORNE, married Margery Morton. They were the parents of: REGINALD.

2. REGINALD HORNE of Pikesley, Co. Shropshire, son of John (1) and Margery, married Margery Lee. They were the parents of (A:318; C): MATILDA, who m. by 1544 William Sewell from which marriage descended **Charles Pye of MD** and of **Henry Sewall of MD)**; WINIFRED, m. Matthew Dorrington; JOHN; and ELENA, m. Robert Cooke.

3. JOHN HORNE of Childes Areole, Co. Salop, son of Reginald (2), married Jane, dau. of Thomas Morton of Ingleton, Staffs. They were the parents of (C): MARGARET, m. John [Ulnett?] of London; MARIA, m. Henry Crowder of Stoke *juxta* Coventry; REGINALD; JOHANNES; THOMAS; and ALICIA, m. Richard Holland of Sadlington, Co. Leic., clerk.

4. REGINALD HORNE of Stoke infra lib'ttaes of Coventry, son and heir of John (3), married Anne, dau. of Thomas Pachet of Harwell, Leics. Reginald and Anne were the parents of (C): HENRY, age 31 in 1619; JOHN, of London, married Martina Frowicke of Germania Inferiori; FRANCIS; REGINALD; ANNA; and JOHANNA.

5. HENRY HORNE, son and heir of Reginald (4) and Anne, was age 31 in 1619. He married Cassandra, dau. of Christopher Randall of Stoke. Henry and Cassandra were the parents of (C): ANNA, b. by 1619.

THE JAMES HORNE FAMILY

1. JAMES HORNE of Bethersden, Kent (B), m. [-?-] Betenham, by whom he had: ELIZABETH.

2. ELIZABETH HORNE, dau. of James, m. Thomas Darrell of Scotney (B). They were the ancestors of **Gov. Thomas Greene of MD**.

Unplaced:

HORNE, AVICIA, dau. of [-?-] of Appledore, m. William Engham of Engham. They were the parents of: VINCENT ENGHAM of Goodneston, Kent, who m. 1st: Editha Goodneston. They were the ancestors of Mary Baker who m. **Robert Brooke of MD**.

HORNE, JOAN, dau. of Henry Horne of Heron, m. Sir William Haute, d. 1497. Sir William was knighted in 1465 at the coronation of Queen Elizabeth Wydeville. Sir

William and Joan were the parents of *(MCS5*:Line 153A; *PECD* 3:164): Sir THOMAS, d. 1502, m. Isabel Frowick (from whom descends the **Gorsuch Family of MD**).

THE MICHAEL HOWARD FAMILY

Refs.: A: *TMFO*:96. B: *SSLM*:422.

1. [-?-] HOWARD of Dublin, was the father of (A): MICHAEL; ADAM; FRANCIS; MATTHEW; ANNE, m. [-?-] Plunkett; ROSE, m. [-?-] Wilson.

2. MICHAEL HOWARD, son of [-?-] and bro. of Adam, Francis, and Matthew, came to MD some time before he was admitted to the practice of law in various courts in 1717 (B:422). He never married and at his death, left a will dated 1 Feb 1734, proved 30 Aug 1737. He mentioned but did not name his parents, and mentioned his nephew Michael William, now living with him, son of his brother Matthew, late of the City of Dublin, dec., who also left a widow Sarah and a dau. Elizabeth; he mentioned the two sons of his bro. Adam of the Co. of West Meath, Ireland, and his bro. Francis, and sisters Ann Plunkett and Rose Wilson (MWB 21:779).

In May 1738 probate was granted to the brother Francis Howard, with similar powers reserved to Samuel and Herbert Hyde and to Adam and Michael William Howard. By Aug 1757 Francis Howard had died intestate and admin. was granted to Christopher Plunkett, son of Ann Plunkett, widow. Samuel Hyde had renounced and Herbert Hyde and Adam and Michael William Howard, Daniel Delany and Walter Carmichael had died (*AWAP*:157).

3. MATTHEW HOWARD, son of [-?-] (1), and bro. of Michael, Adam, and Francis, died in Dublin before 1 Feb 1734, having m. Sarah, and leaving issue (MWB 21:779): MICHAEL WILLIAM; and ELIZABETH.

THE HUETT FAMILY

NB: There are several conflicting accounts of the Huett family, and they need to be reconciled and confirmed from contemporary documents.

Refs.: A: *BDML*. B: *TMFO*. C. *The DNB*. D: *ALCA*.

The first possible Line of Descent

1. THOMAS HUETT, clothworker of Eccles, Lancashire, married and was the father of (B; *ALCA*): Rev. JOHN.

2. Rev. JOHN HUETT, son of Thomas (1), was b. Sep 1614, and attended Pembroke College, Cambridge and Oxford Universities, D.D., was minister of St. Gregory's by St. Paul's, was executed in 1658 for his part in an unsuccessful pro-Stuart uprising.

Although he performed the marriage of Cromwell's daughter to Lord Falconridge, he was such as staunch Royalist that he occasionally took an offering for the exiled King Charles [II], urging his congregation to remember a "distressed friend." He m. 1st a daughter of Robert Skinner, merchant tailor of London, and 2nd, Mary, daughter of Robert Bertie, 1st Earl of Lindsay. He had three children by his 1st wife and 2 daughters by his second wife (C).

Rev. John had at least one son (A): JOHN, b. c1640.

3. JOHN HUETT, son of Rev. John (2), was b. c1640, and d. 1698. He m. c1686 Rachel (Battian?) who later m. Col. Nicholas Evans (A).

John Huett immigrated to MD in 1677 as a free adult from England. After the Stuart Restoration he received an annuity of £100 in appreciation of his father's loyalty. He may have returned to England where he was ordained in 1682 by the Bishop of London.

When he came back to MD, he was minister of Stepney, Somerset, and Dorchester Parishes, as well as delegate to the Lower House from Somerset County, 1692. He was discharged because as an ordained minister he was not eligible to serve in the Assembly (A).

John and Rachel were the parents of (A): ANNE, m. 1st Matthew Nutter, and 2nd Alexander Leckie; and SUSANNA, m. Joseph Johnson.

The second possible Line of Descent

1. Dr. JOHN HEWETT, was the father of (D): JOHN.

2. JOHN HEWETT, Gent., son of Dr. John Hewett, d. 1668. He was the father of (D): JOHN.

3. JOHN HEWETT, son of John Hewett, Gent. (2), was admitted pensioner at age 18 at St. John's, 5 Aug 1682. he was born in Surrey and migrated to Oxford. He kept school at Leytonstone, Yorkshire, and had was the father of (D):

4. JOHN HEWETT, admitted at Magdalen Hall, Oxford, 1709. [If this line is true, then the immigrant to Maryland could not be the son of Rev. Dr. JOHN HUETT, the Royalist]

THE HURST FAMILY

Refs.: A: Hobart Key, Jr. *By My Strong Hand: The Key Family of Texas and Prince George's County, Maryland*. Marshall [TX]:" Port Caddo Press, 1965.

1. JOANNES HIRST, wright, was the father of (A:116): THOMAS; ELIZABETH, m. 11 Sep 1539, Roger Key (from whom descend **Philip, and possibly Wlliam and Henry Key** of MD, and **William Lenman** of MD); WILLIAM.

2. THOMAS HIRST, of Marton, at Poynton, Prestbury Parish, Lancs., son of Joannes (1), m. in 1539, Margery, dau. of Olive Ward of Prestbury. They had several children, including (A:116): RICHARD.

3. WILLIAM HIRST, son of Joannes (1), was an inhabitant of Great Marsden, Lancs., when he appeared in several court proceedings in 1531, 1541 and 1545 (at the latter he was styled "William Hirst, greave, of Colne") (A:116).

4. RICHARD HIRST, son of Thomas (2) and Margery, m. Ellen Cottrell, and had several children, baptized at Prestbury. Their youngest son was: JOHN, b. 1591.

5. JOHN HIRST or HURST, son of Richard (4) and Ellen, was b. 1591, and in 1624 he m. Dorothy Robinson of Little Marsden, and appears there in a Lancashire Royalist Composition Paper, in a petition, dated 2 Feb 1651, from Ann Blundell, wife of Robert (A:116).

John and Dorothy were the parents of: GEORGE; RICHARD; and ANDREW.

6. GEORGE HURST, son of John (5) and Dorothy, m. Elizabeth Field, and had at least two sons (A:116): SAMUEL (For the descendants of a Samuel Hurst of George, see *British Roots of Maryland Families*, vol. I); and JOHN.

7. RICHARD HURST, son of John (5) and Dorothy, was transported to MD in 1662 (A:116; MPL 11:582).

In 1675 William Hurst had a grant from William Hooke of Great Marsden, of one messuage late in the occupation of Andrew and Richard Hurst, who "did longe since departe out of thys country" (A:116).

8. ANDREW HURST, son of John (5) and Dorothy, was transported to MD in 1673 (A:116; MPL 17:463).

9. JOHN HURST, son of George (6) and Elizabeth, m. Elizabeth Wilson in 1685, and in 1689 he and his wife and two sons immigrated to AA Co., MD, where he bought land called Luffman's Division (A:176-117).

John Hurst was in AA Co. by 22 April 1692 when he witnessed the will of John Ray (MWB 7:76).

John and Elizabeth may have been the parents of the following children, born in St. Margaret's Parish, Westminster, AA Co (AACR:103): ISAAC, b. 15 Sep 1687; ELIZABETH, b. 27 Feb 1680 [1690?]; and JOHN, Jr., b. 2 Feb 1697.

THE HENRY HYDE FAMILY EXPANDED

Refs.: A. "Hyde of Hyde and Norbury." *ECEA*:44-46

ARMS: Azure, a chevron between three lozenges Or. CREST: An eagle with wings elevated Sable (*NERA* 6:413).

Generations 1-5

1. MATTHEW de HYDE was living in the reign of Henry III, c1220. He was the father of (A:44): ROBERT; and RICHARD (whose son Thomas de Hyde was living c1290).

2. ROBERT de HYDE, son of Matthew (1), about 1220 was granted Norbury, Newton, Shalcrosse, and Fernilee. He was called "Lord of Norbury" in 1255. He m. [-?-], heiress of Thomas de Norbury, in whose right he held Norbury. Robert and his wife were the parents of (A:44): Sir ROBERT; RICHARD; and HUGH (had lands in Dene, Norbury, from his father, and took the name Dene).

3. Sir ROBERT de HYDE, son of Robert (2), was so called c1260, and d. c1290. He m. Margery, dau. of Robert de StoKeport, by whom he was the father of (A:44): JOHN; and ALEXANDER (Ancestor of the Hydes of Denton, Lancs.)

4. JOHN de HYDE, son of Sir Roger (3), was living in 1270 and 1317. He m. Isabella, dau. and coheir of Sir William de Baggilegh, with whom John had half the Manor of Hyde. John and Isabella were the parents of (A:44): Sir JOHN; and RICHARD (had lands in Hurdsfield in 1317).

5. Sir JOHN de HYDE, son of John (4) and Isabella, was living in 1344 (when he was called "John, son of John" and in 1364. He m. 1st, Margaret, dau. of Sir John Davenport of Wheltrough, Chester, and 2nd, c1361, Alice [-?-] who was living in 1364.

Sir John and Margaret were the parents of (A:44): ROGER, d. s.p.; WILLIAM, d. s.p.; ROBERT; RALPH (Ancestor of the Hydes of Urmston, Lancs.); HUGH, living 1401; and MARGERY.

Sir John and Alice were the parents of (A:44): THOMAS (had lands in Knutsford, 1380).

Generations 6-10

6. ROBERT de HYDE, son of Sir John (5) and Margaret, was living in 1403. He m. [-?-], dau. of Robert de Staveley of Staveley, They were the parents of (A:44): ROBERT; WILLIAM; RICHARD; and JOHN.

7. ROBERT de HYDE, of Norbury and Hyde, son of Robert (6), was living in 1403, 1416, and 1460. He was the father of (A:44-45): JOHN.

8. JOHN de HYDE, son of Robert (7), d. before his father, in 1460. He m. Matilda, dau. of Hamo Massie of Rixton, Lancs. John and Matilda were the parents of (A:45): HAMNET.

9. HAMNET HYDE, of Norbury and Hyde, son of John (8) and Matilda, d. in 1476. He m. 1st, by 1441, Margaret, dau. of Thomas Davenport of Henbury. He m. 2nd, c1463, Joan [-?-], who was a widow in 1466.

Hamnet and Margaret were the parents of (A:45): JOHN, d. s.p.; and THOMAS.

Hamnet and Joan were the parents of (A:45): PETER; and AGNES, m. Edmond Berdsey.

10. THOMAS HYDE of Norbury and Hyde, son of Hamnet (9) and Margaret, was living in 1523, He m. a dau. of Knivetson, of Underwood, Co. Derby. Thomas and his wife were the parents of (A:45): ROBERT; [-?-], m. Nicholas Massie; [-?-], m. Thomas Massie; [-?-], m. [-?-] Bardsley; [-?-], m. Robert Tatton; ELLEN, m. John Newton; and GILES.

Generations 11-15

11. ROBERT HYDE of Norbury and Hyde, son of Thomas (10), succeeded his father in 1524 and was called "lately dead" in Dec 1528. An *Inq. P.M.* was said to be dated 1530-1. He m. 1st, by 1492, Margaret, dau. of Richard Holland of Denton. He m., 2nd, [-?-] Skargill; and 3rd, [-?-], dau. of Sir John Boydell.

Robert and Margaret were the parents of (A:45): HAMNET; JOHN; and ANNE, or AGNES, m. John Arderne of Harden (Ancestors of **Humphrey Warren of MD**).

Robert and his 3rd wife were the parents of (A:45): LAWRENCE (Ancestor of the Hydes, Earls of Clarendon, and the Hydes of Berkshire.

12. HAMNET HYDE, son of Robert (11) and Margaret, was living in 1526 and is said to have d. before his father.

Hamnet Hyde m. Margaret, dau. of Lawrence Warren of Poynton, by whom he was the father of (A:45): ROBERT; LAWRENCE; and KATHERINE, m. [-?-] Strangeways of Strangewais.

13. ROBERT HYDE of Norbury and Chester, son of Hamnet (12) and Margaret, was living in 1541 and d. on 17 Jan 1570/1. An *Inq. P. M.* was held in 1571. Robert m. 1st, Catherine, dau. of John Dunkenfield. He m..2nd, Jane, dau. of William Davenport; 3rd, [-?-] Sneyd; 4th, [-?-], widow of [-?-] Prestland, and dau. of Sir Hugh Cholmondley. Robert Hyde m. 5th, [-?-], widow of John Legh of Boothes, and dau. of [-?-] Spurtsall.

By Jane Davenport, Robert Hyde was the father of (A:46): ROBERT; HAMNET; WILLIAM; EDWARD; THOMAS (called Thomas Hyde, D.D., living at Salisbury, 1630); RICHARD, bur. 14 Sep 1627; RANDLE (Keeper of Cawood Castle, York, 1630); DOROTHY, m. William Davenport of Woodford, Esq.; ELLEN, m. Thomas Unwin of Sussex, Gent.; and ANN, m. John Higham of Higham in Worneth, Gent.

14. ROBERT HYDE of Norbury and Hyde, son of Robert (13) and Jane, was age 28 in 1571, and died at Norbury on 22 March 1614, and was buried at Stockport on 5 April. His Inq. P. M. was held in 1620. He m. Beatrix, daughter of Sir William Calverly of Calverly, Co. York. She was buried at Stockport on 21 Dec 1624.

Robert and Beatrix were the parents of (A): HAMNET; ROBERT; THOMAS; WILLIAM, b. c1597/1600 at Stockport; URIAN; JOHN, bur. 16 June 1605; ELIZABETH, m. Francis Gore of Tupton, Co. Derby; ALICE, m. Richard Joy; JANE, m. Edward Vawdrey of the Riddings, Co. Chester; MARGARET, m. George Hulton; BEATRIX, m. John Frodsham; ANNE, m. Richard Risley; MARY, m. c1608 John Nuttall of Cattonhall, Chester (probably kinsman of John Nuthall of Maryland); and CATHERINE, m. 1st William Hulton; 2nd, Roger Nowell of Reade, Lancs.; and 3rd Saville Radcliffe of Todmorden.

15. HAMNET HYDE, son of Robert (14) and Beatrix, was age 17 in 1580 and d. in May 1643, In 1583, he m. Mary, dau. of John Warren of Poynton. She was bur. 28 March 1639. Hamnet and Mary were the parents of (A:46): ROBERT.

16. WILLIAM HYDE, son of Robert (14) and Beatrix, was b. c1597/1600 at Stockport. He may be the William Hyde who d. 6 Jan 1681 at Norwich, CT. He m. Ellen Stubbs, and they were the ancestors of at least one son: SAMUEL, b. c1636 at Hartford, CT.

Generation 16

17. ROBERT HYDE, son of Hamnet (15) and Mary (Warren) d. in his father's lifetime before 1642. He m. 1st, Margaret, daughter and coheir of Thomas Fitton, 2nd son of Sir Edward Fitton. She died c1618 having given her husband 10 children. Robert m. 2nd, Anne, daughter of Robert Hyde of Hatch, Co. Wilts. She was buried at Stockport on 15 Nov 1638.

Robert and Anne had 12 children. Robert was the father of (A): (by 1st wife): ROBERT, d. s.p.; THOMAS, d. s.p.; EDWARD, m. and had issue; WILLIAM, Citizen of London; HAMNET, d. 1656, unm.; PHILIP, d. 1631, unm.; BEATRICE, m. Thomas Gerard of the Riddings; MARY, m. Edward Rigby; ANNE; and LUCY; (by 2nd wife); ROBERT; LAWRENCE; THOMAS; CHARLES; HENRY; PETER, d. 1624/5; THOMAS, d. 1624; FRANCES, d. 1624; MARGARET, m. [-?-] Jeffrays of London; ANNE, d. 1632; ELIZABETH, d. 1624; and ANNE, d. 1636.

Generation 17

18. HENRY HYDE, son of Robert (17) and Anne (Hyde) Hyde, was described in the Visitation of Cheshire of 1663 as being **"now in Maryland, America."** Henry Hyde immigrated c1656 (MPL 5:516). He m. Frances, evidently daughter of John and Joan Wachope. He died in SM Co. leaving a will dated 29 Oct 1675, proved 6 Nov 1675. His will named his wife Frances, "brother" Thomas Hatton, daughter Ann (grand-daughter of John and Joan Wachope), dau. Margaret, and son Robert (MWB 2:361).

Henry and Frances (Wachope) had issue: ROBERT; ANNE; and MARGARET.

THE INCH FAMILY

1. [-?-] INCH, prob. of Kidderminster, Worcs., was the father of two sons: JOHN, settled in MD; and WILLIAM.

2. JOHN INCH, son of [-?-] (1), settled in KE Co., MD, where he d. by April 1735.

John Inch m. Hannah, widow of Jonathan Woodland. On 27 April 1730 Blackledge Woodland of KE Co., planter and his wife Christiann and John Inch of said county, planter, and his wife Hannah, conv. to Jonathan Woodland of the afsd. county, cordwainer, their right to a plantation, which William Woodland of KE Co., dec., by his last will dated 6 Nov 1708 desired that his house and dwelling plantation be divided in two equal parts and that his wife Hannah have one part during her life and that after her decease it be given to his son Blackledge Woodland (KELR JS#16:21).

Hannah Inch, age c44, dep. on 16 Sep 1735 regarding the bounds of a tract called Orchard Neck; when she was 8 or 9 years old her uncle James Galloway told her ... (KELR JS#18:203).

Inch d. leaving a will dated 7 March 1734/5 and proved 11 April 1735, leaving the tract New York to a son Benjamin. If Benjamin died under age 21, the property was to go to the testator's brother William Inch in Kidderminster, Worcestershire. Inch named his wife Hannah as extx. (MWB 21:415).

3. BENJAMIN INCH of Steele Pone [Still Pond?], KE Co., d. by March 1747.

Benjamin left a will dated 15 Dec 1746 and proved 28 March 1747. He left 50 a. to Benjamin Woodland, and named his brothers Blackledge [Woodland] and William Jones (who was named exec). Andrew Devine, Ann Flanigan?, and Michael Bryan witnessed the will (MWB 25:79).

THE IRELAND FAMILY

Refs.: A: Nancy Moler Poeter. *The Comegys Family.* Baltimore: Gateway Press, 1982.

1. JOSEPH IRELAND of Halifax, Yorks., m. Deborah [-?-], by whom he was the father of (A:22): JOSEPH, b. 17 June 1727.

2. JOSEPH IRELAND, son of Joseph (1) and Deborah, was born 17 June 1727, near Halifax, Yorkshire, Eng. (A:22). He d. in KE Co., MD, prior to Dec

1773. He m. Alethea Comegys, dau. of William and Ann Comegys. She m. 2nd, Jonathan Worth.

On 17 Dec 1773, Ebenezer Reyner and James Black appraised the personal estate of Joseph Ireland at £393.14.7. Alethea Ireland, admx., filed the inventory on 27 Sep 1774 (MINV 118:237). As Alethea, wife of Jonathan Worth she filed a list of debts worth £539.11.7, and a list of accounts worth £440.4.6 (MINV 122:405, 411).

Alethea, wife of Jonathan Worth, administered the estate of Joseph Ireland on 24 April 1776. She cited an inventory of £593.14.7, and listed payments of £771.15.3 (MDAD 73:299).

Joseph and Alethea were the parents of (A:22-23): WILLIAM, born 28 June 1762, married Julia H. McMichael; JOSEPH, b. 8 March 1765; JOHN, b. 28 April 1767; and ALPHONSO COSDEN, b. 3 Nov 1771.

THE ISHAM FAMILY

Refs.: A: "Isham," *Burke's Peerage, Baronetage, and Knightage*, 1956 ed., pp. 1173-1174.

ARMS: Gules, a fess wavy, and in chief, three piles, also wavy, points meeting in fesse Argent. **CREST**: A demi-swan with wings displayed Argent, beaked Sable.

1. HENRY ISHAM was the father of (A): ROBERT.

2. ROBERT ISHAM, son of Henry (1), was the father of (A): ROBERT.

3. ROBERT ISHAM of Pytchley, son of Robert (2), d. 31 March 1424. He was Escheator of Northampton, 1391-1392, and in 1403, was granted custody of the Manor of Cranford by King Henry IV.

Robert was the father of (A): ROBERT.

4. ROBERT ISHAM of Pytchley, son of Robert (3), was also Escheator of Northampton, 1438-1439. He was b. c1402, and d. 1475. He m. Margaret, dau. and heiress of Aston of Knuston, in Northampton. He served as Solicitor to Elizabeth Woodville, wife of King Edward IV (A).

Robert and Margaret had four sons, including (A): WILLIAM.

5. WILLIAM ISHAM of Pytchley, eldest son of Robert (4) and Margaret, d. 13 June 1510. He m. Elizabeth Braunspath, d. 20 Sep 1478. She was a dau. of Thomas Braunspath of Glooston, Leicestershire (A).

William and Elizabeth were the parents of (A): THOMAS ISHAM, b. c1456.

6. THOMAS ISHAM of Pytchley, son of William (5), was b. c1456. He m. c1485, Ellen, dau. of Richard Vere of Addington and Thrapston, Northampton (A).

Thomas and Ellen were the parents of (A): EUSEBY; and JOHN.

7. EUSEBY ISHAM of Pytchley, son of Thomas (6), d. leaving a will proved 11 Dec 1546. He m. Anne, eldest dau. of Giles Pulton (A).

Euseby and Anne were the parents of twenty children, including (A): GYLES, d. 1559; ROBERT; GREGORY; and JOHN.

8. GREGORY ISHAM, of Braunston, Northampton, and one-time Merchant of London, son of Euseby (7) and Anne, d. 4 Sep 1558, age 38. He m. Elizabeth, dau. of Matthew Dale of Bristol. She m. 2nd, William Rosewell of Ford Abbey (A).

Gregory Isham was a Freeman of the Mercer's Company, and became a landowner of some consideration in Northampton (A).

Gregory and Elizabeth had two sons and two daus., including (A): EUSEBY (EUSEBIUS); and ELIZABETH, m. Henry Cave (from whom may descend **Francis Marbury of MD**).

9. Sir EUSEBIUS ISHAM, son of Gregory (8), d. 11 June 1626. He m. Anne Borlase, dau. of Sir John Borlase, and a descendant of William I, the Lion, King of Scotland (A; *RD500*:338).

Sir Eusebius was knighted by James I on 11 May 1603. He was High Sheriff of Northampton in 1584, and built the house at Pytchley (A).

Sir Eusebius and Anne were the parents of (A): JOHN; and WILLIAM.

10. WILLIAM ISHAM, son of Sir Eusebius (9) and Anne (Borlase) m. Mary Brett, dau. of William Brett of Toddington (*RD500*:338; *PECD* 2:166).

William and Anne were the parents of: HENRY.

11. HENRY ISHAM, son of William (10) and Mary Brett, settled in VA, and m. Mrs. Katherine Banks Royall (*RD500*:338, 399; *PECD* 2;166).

Henry and Katherine were the parents of: MARY, m. William Randolph and ANNE, m. Francis Epes, III.

THE ISRAEL FAMILY

Refs.: A: Data supplied by J. Robert Israel of Fairview, NC. B: Merchant Taylor's Company Records, searched by Peter Wilson Coldham. B: *HSPR* 76. C: *HSPR* 80-81.

NB: J. Robert Israel warns that the connections between the early generations are tenuous at best. Mr. Israel's notes are based on research by Peter Wilson Coldham and William M. Mann, Jr.

1. JOHN ISRAEL (also written as ISULL, IZSALL, ISALLE or IZARELL) of St. Giles Without Cripplegate, m. Elizabeth Whittington of Shadwell at St. Dunstan's Stepney, on 13 July 1608. Israel may have been quite young as the birth of his dau. Anne in 1610 describes her as the dau. of "John Iszall, maryed boy in Rosemary Lane") (A).

John may have been related to the following: Elizabeth Israel, bapt. 1594 at St. Helen's Bishopsgate, and Ales (or Alice) Israel, m. Danile Thorn in 1619 at St. Katherine by the Tower (A).

In 1615 he was described as a silk weaver; in 1618 as a carman (A). On 1 Sep 13 James I (1615) a true bill was issued stating that "at East Smithfield, Mddx., John Israell, late of East Smithfield, assaulted, struck, beat and wounded John Willis so that his life was despaired of." On 5 & 6 Oct 1615 John Israel and Richard Israel, barber, both of East Smithfield, were prosecuted for assault and battery on John Wills of Rosemary Lane (A: cites Middlesex Sessions Records).

John Israel may have d. by 1638 since Elizabeth Whittington Israel may be the "Widow Israel" listed with two tithes on p. 369 of *Inhabitants of London in 1638*. On p. 219 of the same book she was listed as living in East Smithfield in the parish of St. Botolph Aldgate (A).

John and Elizabeth were the parents of the following children, baptized at St. Botolph Without Aldgate (A): ANNE (ISZALL), bapt. 9 Dec 1610; ROGER (ISRAEL), bapt. 20 Aug 1615; HENRY (ISALLE), bapt. 25 Oct 1618; and (prob.) SARAH, m. Thomas Webster of St. Botolph without Aldgate in 1635.

2. ROGER ISRAEL, son of John (1), silk weaver, was bapt. 20 Aug 1615 at St. Botolph without Aldgate. He m. Isabel [-?-], and had several children bapt. at St. Botolph without Aldgate. His estate was administered in 1665, the year of the Great Plague, which killed some 70,000 inhabitants of London (A).

3. HENRY ISRAEL, son of John (1), was bapt. 25 Oct 1618 at St. Botolph without Aldgate. On 13 Sep 1636 Henry Israel m. Tace (Beatrice) LaCrowe by. St. Gregory by St. Paul (A). Tace was the widow of John La Crowe who on 1 March

1629/30 was admitted as "foreign brother" of the Weavers' Guild., He lived in the parish of St. Botolph Aldgate.

Henry was the first of three generations of Israels to be styled "Gent." On 6 Dec 1638 Henry Israel was admitted as a "foreign brother" to the Weavers' Guild. He probably did not come from across the sea, but he may have been called "foreign brother" because of his residence at Sandwich, Kent (A).

Henry Israel, Gent., d. and was buried on 18 Dec 1652 (B:164).

Henry and Beatrice were the parents of (A): JASPER, bapt. 29 Sep 1638 at St. Mary Whitechapel; WILLIAM, bapt. April 1643 at St. Botolph Aldgate (He may have been the William Israel who was sentenced to transportation and reprieved in 1669); JOHN, bapt. 18 June 1647 at St. Botolph Aldgate; and GRACE, bapt. Oct 1647 [*sic*] at St. Botolph Aldgate.

4. JOHN ISRAEL, son of Henry (3), was bapt. 18 June 1647 at St. Botolph Aldgate, London, and d. intestate in Oct 1689 (A). He m. Mary Crawley, dau. of Robert Crawley, grocer of Friday St., London.

On 29 July 1663 as John Israel, son of Henry Israel, late of Sandwich, Kent., dec., was bound for seven years to Edward Holding of Tower Street, panner (B: Apprenticeship Bindings, MF 314, fol. 214). On 8 Dec 1670 John Israel, by servitude to Edward Holding, was admitted as a member of the Merchant Taylor's Company (B: Freedom Admissions, MF 324).

John Israel, of St. Botolph Aldgate, London, Citizen, merchant taylor, bachelor, aged about 24, and Mary Crawley of St. Matthew, Friday St., London, spinster, age about 24 and at her own dispose, were granted a license to marry on 28 July 1671 at either St, Bardolph [*sic*] [Botolph], Aldersgate, or Islington, Mddx. (*HSPV* 23:191).

Israel was styled a Norway Merchant of London.

On 9 Nov 1689 administration on his estate was granted to Mary Israel, widow and relict of John Israel, formerly of St. Botolph Aldgate, in the County of Middlesex (A).

John and Mary (Crawley) were the parents of the following children, bapt. at St. Katherine by the Tower (unless otherwise noted) (A; C:24, 29, 35): MARY, bapt. 16 May 1672, may have m. Robert Vincent, shipwright; **JOHN, bapt. 18 June 1674, immigrated to MD**; ANNE, bapt. June 1676, d. testate and unm. by Jan 1746; ELIZABETH, bapt. June 1676, a spinster age 30, on 18 Dec 1709 at St. Katherine Creechurch, she m. Peter Williams, a widower; PETER, bapt. May 1678 at St. Botolph Aldgate, d. 7 Sep 1689; JACOB, bapt. at St. Botolph Aldgate, d. 1 Sep 1689; and SARAH, bapt. 13 Dec 1683 at St. Peter Aldgate, m. Moses Wheeler at St. Katherine by the Tower on 19 Dec 1703.

5. JOHN ISRAEL, son of John (4) and Mary, was bapt. at St. Katherine's by the Tower, 18 June 1674, and is probably the Immigrant to MD. John Israel, formerly of London, now residing in MD, merchant, on 19 Oct 1701, appointed Thomas Besson of London, Jr., of AA Co. his attorney (AALR WT#1:210).

John Israel, Gent., and Merchant Taylor, was the father of (A): JOHN LACON, b. 1717, m. Joanna Dorsey; ROBERT, b. 1719, d. 1795, m. Priscilla Baker; MARY; and SARAH.

Unplaced:

ISRAEL, DANIEL, was buried at St. Katherine's by the Tower on 9 Nov 1661 (B:174).

THE KING FAMILY

Refs.: A: *ESVR* 1:27. B: Ilfracombe, Devon, Parish Register, abstracted in the International Genealogy Index.

1. MILES KING of Ilfracombe, Devon, son of Martha, was bapt. 23 June 1608 at Ilfracombe, where he m. Joan Harris on 15 Aug 1627. They were the parents of the following children, bapt. at Ilfracombe (B): JOAN, bapt. 10 Feb 1627/8; CATHERINE, bapt. 10 May 1629; SUSANNA, bapt. 20 Jan 1632; MARTHA, bapt. 9 Nov 1637; MYLES, bapt. 6 April 1635; MATTHEW, bapt. 5 Feb 1638; JONE, bapt. 22 Dec 1644; and ELIAS, bapt. 18 June 1648.

2. MYLES KING, son of Miles (1) and Joan, was bapt. 6 April 1635 at Ilfracombe. He m. Mary [-?-]. They were the parents of at least one son, bapt. at Ilfracombe (B): MYLES, bapt. 24 Jan 1660.

3. MATTHEW KING, son of Miles (1) and Joan, was bapt. 5 Feb 1638 at Ilfracombe, where he m. Mary Harris on 17 Sep 1667 (B). Matthew and Mary were the parents of the following, all bapt. at Ilfracombe (B): MARY, bapt. 18 Jan 1668; WILLIAM. bapt. 5 Oct 1671; DORCAS, bapt. 27 Sep 1674; and ELIZABETH, bapt. 11 Sep 1677.

4. ELIAS KING, son of Miles (1) and Joan, was bapt. 18 June 1640 at Ilfracombe (B). He was in MD by 20 Jan 1684 when he wit. the will of Edward Mullins (MWB 4:81). On 24 Dec 1699 he m. Mary Tilden. Mary King was bur. 25 Oct 1702, and Elias King was bur. 13 Feb 1706 (A: cites St. Paul's Parish, Kent Co., MD).

Elias King d. leaving a will dated 2 Feb 1706, proved 21 Feb 1706, naming partners Robert Dunckley and Edward Scott, and the children of Charles Tilden who were to have his plantation and personalty. Thomas Ringgold and Edward Scott were execs. Edw. Worrell, Evan Evans, and Thomas Williams were witnesses. At his death, he owned lands in KE, QA and BA Counties (MWB 12:83).

On 15 Jan 1757, his heirs in England were two great nieces: Mary, wife of Nicholas Watters of Ilfordcombe, and Sarah Andrews, widow, also of Ilfordcome. On 15 Jan 1757, Mary and Sarah appointed Richard Lovering and Thomas Lovering of Tamstock [?], Co. Devon, their attorneys (PCLR BT#1:91).

5. MYLES KING, son of Miles (2) and Mary, was bapt. 24 Jan. 1660 at Ilfracombe. He m. Sarah [-?-]. They were the parents of definitely one and probably two daughters (B): (prob.)

MARY, m. Nicholas Waters on 18 May 1719 at Ilfracombe, Devon (B).; (def.) SARAH, bapt. 5 Oct. 1706 at Ilfracombe, where she m. on 26 March 1727 William Andrews.

Other King entries from Ilfracombe Parish Register (B)
Miles, m. 19 April Ann Aye.
Miles, m. 2 July 1658 Mary King
Matthew, son of Miles and Mary, was bapt. 23 April 1659.

THE KIRKBRIDE FAMILY

Refs.: A: *RD500*. B: "Kirkbride of Ellerton." *CWFO*:70. C: "Kirkbride." *CWFO*:69. D: "Kirkbride." *CFAH*:190-191.

ARMS (of Kirkbride): Argent, a saltire engrailed Vert (C).
ARMS (of Kirkbride of Ellerton): Argent, a cross engrailed Sable, a label of three points for difference (B).

Generations 1-5

1. Sir RICHARD KIRKBRIDE, Kt., was the father of (C): RICHARD; JOHN; and ELIZABETH.

2. JOHN KIRKBRIDE, 2nd son of Sir Richard, was the father of: GEORGE; MARY, m. [-?-] Lowther; AGNES, m. Richard Barnes; ELIZABETH, m. Robert Blenkinsop; MARGARET, m. John Coldall; ELEANOR, m. William Osmotherley; CYSSLEY, m. Thomas Hewett; RICHARD, m. [-?-] Whitfield; and JOHN.

3. GEORGE KIRKBRIDE, son and heir of John (2), d. 1511 (D). He m. [-?-] Therkel. They were the parents of (C; D): RICHARD; CHRISTOPHER; ROBERT; and JAMES (these four all d. s.p.); ELIZABETH, b. c1478, m. John Dalston of Dalston; ISABEL. b. c1482, m. 1st, Thomas Beauchamp, and 2nd, Gilbert Weddale; and EMON [EMMOTTE], b. 1490, m. Robert Clyborne (Her son Edmond was the father of Eleanor Clyborne who m. her 3rd cousin Richard Kirkbride).

4. RICHARD KIRKBRIDE, 2nd son of John (2) m. Christina Whytfeld of Cumberland (D). They were the parents of (C): RICHARD, d. without surviving issue; WALTER; PERCIVAL; THOMAS, d. s.p.; CYSSLEY; and ANNE.

5. PERCIVAL KIRKBRIDE, 3rd son of Richard (4), m. [-?-] Sewell, by whom he was the father of (C): 5 other sons; and RICHARD.

6. RICHARD KIRKBRIDE, 6th son of Percival (5), was living in 1564. He m. [-?-] Monkers, by whom he was the father of (C): RICHARD.

Generations 6-10

7. RICHARD KIRKBRIDE of Ellerton, Co. Cumberland, son of Richard (6), m. Eleanor, dau. of Edmund Cliburne of Cliburne, Co. Westmorland, his 6th cousin (B; C). They were the parents of (C): BERNARD; and RANDLE of New-Biggin, Cumberland.

8. BERNARD KIRKBRIDE, Esq., of Ellerton, son of Richard (7) and Eleanor, d. c1622. He m. Dorothy Dudley, dau. of Edmund and Catherine (Hutton) Dudley, of Yanwith, Westmorland (B). Dorothy was a descendant of Edward III (A:130).

     Bernard and Dorothy were the parents of (B): RICHARD; CHRISTOPHER, d. unm.; CLIBURNE, a merchant in Newcastle-upon-Tyne, d. s.p.; and ISABEL, m. John Saunderson of Newcastle-upon-Tyne.

9. RICHARD KIRKBRIDE, Esq., of Ellerton, son of Bernard (8) and Catherine, d. 28 Sep 1659. He m. Bridget Maplate, dau. of Edward Maplate, Vicar of Addingham, and a Prebend of the Church of Carlisle (B; D).

     Richard Kirkbride was a Col. of a Regiment of Foot in the Army of King Charles I, under the command of William, Marquess of Newcastle (B).

     Richard and Bridget were the parents of: BERNARD; MARY, m. William Graham of Nunnery, Cumb.; and BARBARA, m. Leonard Barrow of Anstable, Cumb.

10. BERNARD KIRKBRIDE, Esq., of Ellerton, son of Richard (9) and Bridget, was b. 27 March 1629. He m. Jane Featherstonehaugh, dau. of Sir Timothy Featherstonehaugh of Kirk Oswald, Cumberland, a Royalist and a descendant of Edward III, by his wife Bridget Patrickson (A:130; B).

     Bernard was a lieut.-col. to Sir Henry Fetherston [*sic*]. Kt., in the service of King Charles I (B).

     Bernard is stated to have been the last male heir of the family (D). Nevertheless, Roberts states that Bernard and Jane were the parents of (A, but he cites *LDBR* 3:210-213): MATTHEW.

11. MATTHEW KIRKBRIDE, son of Bernard (10) and Jane (A), m. Magdalen Dalston. They were the parents of (A:130): JOSEPH.

Generation 11

12. JOSEPH KIRKBRIDE, son of Matthew (11) and Magdalen, settled in PA, and m. 1st, Phebe Buckshaw; 2nd, Sarah Stacy; and 3rd, Mrs. Mary Fletcher Yardley (A:130).

THE LAKING FAMILY

Refs.: A: Roy Victor Harrington, "Family History of Catherine Elizabeth Weise," unpub. ms. generously made available to the compiler. B: David Agricola, M.D., *The Lakin Family* (Amundsen Press, 1989). C: Rev. Henry Sanders, *History and Antiquities of*

Shenstone (Bibliotecha Topographia Britannica, 1794). D: *Tamworth Parish Registers, 1558-1614*. Staffordshire Parish Register Society: 1917.

NB: The compiler is indebted to Roy Victor Harrington for generously sharing his research.

1. JOHN LAKIN (LAWKIN?), was b. c1604 in Tamworth, Stafford (IGI?). If the birth date is correct, he could not be the John Lakin who m. c1610 Penelope [-?-].

John and Penelope were the parents of (A): EDWARD, b. c1611; WILLIAM, b. 1615; MARYE, b. c1619; ROBERT, b. c1622; ANNE, b. 1625, d. 1626; THOMAS, b c1628; ANNE, b. c1630; and ELIZABETH, b. c1632.

2. WILLIAM LAKIN, poss. son of John (1) and Penelope, was bapt. 9 Feb 1615 in Mancetter Parish, Warwickshire. He m. Alice Rowell, bapt. 27 Feb 1619 in Mancetter Parish, dau. of Thomas and Alice (Milner) Rowell (A).

William and Alice were the parents of (A): GEORGE, b. c1642; and WILLIAM, b. 1644.

3. WILLIAM LAKIN, son of William (2) and Alice, was b. 1644 in Shenstone Parish, Staffordshire, and bapt. 15 Sep 1644 in Mancetter Parish, Warwickshire, although he, or more likely another William was bapt. 3 June 1655 in Shenstone Parish. He d. 29 July 1708, age 64, intestate, in Shenstone (A).

On 2 May 1671, when he was 27, William m. Elizabeth Symons in Shenstone Parish Church. She was bapt. 28 March 1647 in Mancetter Parish (A).

William and Elizabeth were the parents of the following children (A): ELIZABETH, b. 1672; SARAH, b. c1673; ABRAHAM, b. c1675/7; DEBORAH, b. 1683; and JOSEPH, b. 1685.

4. ABRAHAM LAKIN, son of William (3) and Elizabeth, was b. c1675/7 in Shenstone, and is placed by Victor Harrington as the immigrant in Maryland.

Abraham was listed as a servant in the inventory, dated c1702/3, of Joseph Hanslap, Gent., of AA Co. (INAC 23:196).

On 6 March 1712 Abraham "Lacany" was a debtor in the admin. acct. of William Greenhap of Prince George's Co. (INAC 34:147).

Abraham Laking and "Martin" [Martha] Lee were married in Queen Anne's Parish, Prince George's Co., on 10 October 1717 (Marriage Register of Queen Anne's Parish, Prince George's Co., p. 1).

Abraham Laking died in PG Co., leaving a will dated 25 November 1744 and proved 16 December 1744. he left 102 a. on the west side of Kitoctin Mt. to his sons Abraham and Joseph. His son Benjamin was to have the 100 a. dwelling plantation Joseph and Margaret's Rest, at the death of the testator's wife Martha, who was to be extx. Thomas Mackee, Jane Mackee, and Robert Lyth witnessed the will (MWB 23:289).

John Dickeson and Larkin Pierpoint appraised the estate of Abraham Laking on 13 May 1745, and assigned a value of £192.13.7 to his personal property. Abraham and Joseph Lakin signed as next of kin. Martha Laking, extx., filed the inventory on 13 May 1745 (MINV 30:376).

Martha Laking filed an administration account on 14 May 1745. Payments came to £34.14.8. Those receiving payments included Abraham, son of the deceased, dau. Martha wife of Isaac Plummer, and dau. Sarah wife of Robert Lyeth. The deceased left four young children, unnamed.

Abraham Laking was the father of: ABRAHAM; JOSEPH; BENJAMIN; MARTHA, married Isaac Plummer, and SARAH, married Robert Lyeth.

Selected Entries in Tamworth Parish Register:
Lawkin, Thomas, son of Henry, bapt. 17 Nov 1568 (D:7).
Lawken, John, m. Dorothy Sawbridge, 5 Dec 1568 (D:28).
Lawkyn, William, of William, bapt. 18 Feb 1570/1 (D:36).
Lawkyn, Margaret, of William, bapt. 12 Sep 1573 (D:45).
Lawkyn, Thomas, of Ammington, buried 26 Nov 1576 (D:55).
Lawkyn, Marie, m. Robert Gryndon, 26 Nov 1579 (D:71).
Lawkin, Dorothy, dau. of Thomas of Wilncott, bapt. 22 March 1581 (D).
Lawkins, Agnes, wife of Thomas, buried 21 May 1587 (D:109).
Lawkin, Thomas, of Wilncott, buried 24 Nov 1587 (D:111).

THE LAMPHIER-GOINGS FAMILIES

Refs.: A: Deposition of Elizabeth Lamphier, widow, age 63, made 8 Aug 1767 (PGLR BB#2:42-44). B: J. Estelle Stewart King. *Abstracts of Wills and Inventories of Fairfax Co., VA, 1742-1801*. Privately printed, 1936.

N.B. I am indebted to Henry C. Peden, Jr., for bringing Elizabeth Lamphier's deposition to my attention in his book *Maryland Deponents, Volume 3* (Westminster: Willow Bend Books, 2000).

1. THOMAS LAMPHIRE, d. in Coreigheen in August before the deponent left Ireland. He m. Elizabeth Kyle, who survived him. They were the parents of four sons and three daus.(A): ELIZABETH, m. John Burgess; WILLIAM, m. 1st, Elizabeth, dau. of Ambrose Lane of Lane's Park, and 2nd, [-?-] Evans; MARY, m. Joseph Tinson of Orchard Town near Clonmell (After her death Tinson m. 2nd, Garter Hunt, dau. of John Hunt of Clonag); JOSEPH, m. Elizabeth, dau. of Robert Bradshaw of Co. Limerick; **THOMAS, settled in MD**; JOHN, unm.; and SARAH, d. of smallpox before the deponent left Ireland.

2. ELIZABETH LAMPHIER, dau. of Thomas (1) and Elizabeth (Kyle), m. John Burgess. They were the parents of (A): **HENRY BURGESS, came to America.**

3. THOMAS LAMPHIER, son of Thomas (1) and Elizabeth (Kyle) Lamphier, lived at Coreigheen, Ireland, and settled in MD and d. by Aug 1767. He m. at Leieskeveeen, Co. Tipperary, Ireland, Elizabeth Going, b. c1703, dau. of Robert and Mary (Rowe) Going.

Elizabeth Going Lamphier was living as a widow in PG Co., in Aug 1767 when she made a deposition about her husband's family, and her own family (A).

On 7 May 1744 Thomas Lamphier, John Muchette of Charles Town, and Ralph Falkner executed a deed [or contract] stating they wanted to build a "manufactory of matting and brewing on the lot of John Muchette in Charles Town, CH Co. (CHLR :X#2141).

Thomas Lamphier d. in CH Co., MD prior to 23 March 1747 when his personal estate was appraised by William Neale and Roger Smith at £37.2.7. Going Lamphier and Elizabeth Lamphier signed as next of kin. John Muskat filed the inventory on 6 June 1748 (MINV 36:126).

Thomas and Elizabeth (Going) Lamphier were the parents of (A): GOING, who lived in Fairfax Co., VA; SUSANNA, m. John Patterson, living in MD; and VENUS, living in MD according to her mother's deposition, but as Venus Lamphier of PG Co., MD, she d. testate, leaving a will dated 14 Feb 1768 and proved on 24 Nov 1769 in Fairfax C., VA. She left her niece Betty Patterson 100 pds, Irish money, and named her nephews William and Thomas Patterson, her bro. Going Lamphier, and sister Susanna Patterson (B:28 cites Fairfax Co., Will Book C).

4. HENRY BURGESS, son of John and Elizabeth (2) (Lamphier) Burgess, was a clothier by trade, who came to America with his uncle Thomas, husband of the deponent. Henry m. Elizabeth Lamphier, dau. of Thomas Lamphier, Sr. Henry Burgess d. a few years ago, as notified in a letter to the deponent by John Patterson (her son-in-law). Henry left six children, three by a former wife (A).

5. GOING LAMPHIER, son of Thomas (3) and Elizabeth, was living in CH Co., by 2 Dec 1751 when he was listed as a creditor of Rev. Henry Ogle of CH Co. (MDAD 32:24). By 1767 he was living in Fairfax Co., VA (A).

6. SUSANNA LAMPHIER, dau. of Thomas (3) and Elizabeth, m. John Patterson. They were described in Elizabeth Lamphier's petition as living in MD, but they seemed to have moved to Fairfax Co., VA, where John Patterson's will, dated 6 Oct 1765, was filed for probate on 13 Aug 1768. He named his wife Susanna, and children William, Thomas, and Betty. James Conwell and Going Lamphier witnessed the will (B:26 cites Fairfax Co. Will Book C).

The Going Family

1. [-?-] GOING was the father of three sons and one dau. (A): ROBERT; RICHARD, m. and lived in Bristol; MARY, m. E. White; and JAMES.

2. ROBERT GOING, son of [-?-] (1), d. by Aug 1767. He may be, or be related to the Robert Going of Crannagh, Co. Tipperary who left a will dated 1732 (*Index to Irish Wills, Volume II, Calendar of Wills in the Diocese of Cashel and Emly, 1618-1800* {GPC}, p. 13).

He m. Mary Rowe, d. by Aug 1767, dau. of Gregory Rowe. They were the parents of (A): JOHN, left Ireland when his sister Elizabeth was a child, returned, some years later and then went to Eng., m. at Plymouth, and had children; PHILIP, m. 1st, Sarah Pike, 2nd, Mary Knight, and 3rd Susanna Godding; JAMES, m. 1st Dorothy Tyeney, and 2nd, Elizabeth Kyle; MARY, m. James Walpoole; ROBERT, m. Jane Johnston; SARAH, m. Richard Franklin, attorney; ELIZABETH, the deponent, m. Thomas Lamphier (See above).

3. JAMES GOING, son of [-?-] (1), lived in Clonmel, where he served as Mayor. He m. and was the father of (A): MARY, m. {-?-] [-?-]; REBECCA, m. {-?-] [-?-]; SUSANNA, unm.; RICHARD, Mayor of Clonmel.

THE LAYFIELD FAMILY REEXAMINED

Refs.: A: Clayton Torrence. *Old Somerset on the Eastern Shore of Maryland.* (1935). Repr.: FLP, 1992. B: Letter dated 24 June 1999 from Victoria Lane, The Goldsmith's Company (Goldsmith's Hall, Foster Lane, London, EC2V 6BN) to Jane West of La Plata, MD, who has generously shared its contents with the compiler. C: Letter dated 18 May 1999 from the Corporation of London records office (PO Box 270, Guildhall, London EC2P 2FJ) to Jane West of La Plata, MD, who has generously shared its contents with the compiler. D: *HSPR 7: The Parish Registers of St. Michael's, Cornhill, London, Containing Marriages, Baptisms, and Burials from 1546 to 1754.* Ed. by Joseph Lemuel Chester. London: the Harleian Society, 1882. E: *HSPV 30.* F: *HSPV 33.* G: *IL (The Index Library of the British Record Society,* various volumes). H: Joseph L. Foster. *London Marriage Licenses, 1521-1869.* London. Bernard Quarritch, 1887. I: "John Layfield." *DNB.* J: Records of St. Clement Dane's, London, extracted in the "Controlled Extraction" program of the LDS and available on the IGI. X: Undocumented material from the LDS "Ancestor Search."

NB: The compiler is indebted to Jane Thorsell West for making available her abstracts of the PCC Wills cited below. Most wills proved before 1858 are in the records of the PCC (Prerogative Court of Canterbury), held by the Public Record Office.

1. JOHN LAYFIELD was b. c1560, possibly at St. Mary's, Reading, Berks., and d. 6 Nov 1617. John Layfield m. c1590 Bridget Robinson (mother of Anne Snow), b. 1563, dau. of Christopher Robinson (b. c1529 at "Reading, Leicestershire") who m. 20 Jan 1549/50 at Reading, Berks, Lucy Webbe, (b. c1526 at Reading, Berks) (X). A bachelor, and parson of St. Clement Dane's, aged 40, he was granted a license by the Bishop of London on 22 Jan 1602/3 to marry Elizabeth, age 30, of St. Ethelburga's, widow of John Brichett who had been deceased about 12 months; to marry at St. Mary's Whitechapel (H; J:62;7).

John Layfield matriculated at Oxford a pensioner from Trinity College in Lent 1577/8. He took his B.A. in 1581/2, his M.A. in 1585 and his D.D. in 1603. He was a Fellow from 1585 to 1603. He was admitted at the Inner Temple in 1606. He was Rector at Aldwinkle St. Peter's, Northants., 1598-1602 and Rector of St. Clement Dane's, London, from 1602 to 1617. He was one of the first Fellows of Chelsea College in 1610 (*ALOX*).

He was possibly the "chaplain and attendant" of George Clifford, 3rd Earl of Cumberland, during his expedition to the West Indies in 1598 (I).

In 1606 his name was on the list of "Revisers of *The Bible*." With other clergymen he sat at Westminster and revised the books of *The Bible* from *Genesis* to *2nd Kings* (I).

John Layfield, D.D., Parson of St. Clement Dane's, Mddx., d. testate in 1617 (G:43:217 cites PCC 123 Welden). John Layfield, Doctor of Divinity, Parson of St. Clements died leaving a will dated ... and proved ... . He left all his lands and tenements in the Parish of old Hoo in Somersetshire and the Parish of Royston to his wife Bridget and then to his oldest son Edward. He also named his son Thomas and dau., Denny. He gave £20 to his wife's oldest dau. Anne Snow, another £20 to Bennet [-?-], and £10 to the Parish of St. Clements. He named his old servant goodwife Janis [-?-] and John Bowls. He named his cousin [-?-] Fowle executor. William Robinson, John Snow, and Thomas Suliboro witnessed the will. In a "post script item" Layfield named his wife's brother D. Robinson and his cousin Nicholas Carone as overseers

Bridget Layfield of the Parish of St. Swithin's, London, widow, late wife, and administrator of all the goods, chattels, and rights of John Layfield, died leaving a will dated 1628 and proved 1629. She named her grandchildren Bridget, Anna and Nathaniel Snow, children of her daughter Anna Snow £5 each to be paid to her son-in-law John Snow. She named her son-in-law Edward Batty and his son John Batty, sister Amy [-?-], and the children by her late husband John Layfield: Edward, Thomas, and Denny, now the wife of Edward Batty. She named her sons-in-law John Snow and Edward Batty and friends Thomas Smith and wife of London as executors. [-?-] Smart, John Linofuid, and Charles Bragg, Sr., witnessed the will (G:44 cites PCC 60:Ridley).

John Layfield was the father of three children baptized at St. Clement Dane's in London (J): EDWARD, b. 8 Jan 1604/5; THOMAS, bapt. 3 Sep 1605; and (dau.) DENNY, m. by 1628 Edward Batty.

2. EDWARD LAYFIELD, son of John (1), was b. 8 Jan 1604/5, and was buried at All Hallows Barking on 10 Aug 1680 (*ALOX; ALCA*).

Foster places him as a son of Edmund[?] (*ALOX*), but he is more likely to be the son of John, the Rector of St. Clement Dane's. He was admitted to the Merchant Taylor's School in 1617. As "*cler. fil.*" [son of a clergyman], he matriculated at St. John's College on 28 June 1620, age 16. He took his B.A. in April 1624, and was incorporated at Cambridge in 1625. He took his M.A. on 13 May 1626, and was incorporated at Cambridge in 1633. He received a D.D. He held a number of ecclesiastical appointments, including: Rector of Ibstock, Leicester (1632), Canon Residentiary at St. Paul's (1633), Archdeacon of Essex (1634), Vicar of All Hallow's Barking (1635), Rector of East Horsley, Surrey (1637), Rector of Wrotham, Kent (1638), Rector of Chiddingfield, Surrey (1640, until he was sequestered by the Westminster Assembly of 1635), Rector of Colne Wakes, Surrey (1640-1666), and Rector of Barnes, Surrey (1663-1680) (*ALOX*).

Edward Layfield, D.D., Prebendary Residentiary of St. Paul's, d. testate in 1680 (G:71 cites PCC 1680:108). In his will, dated 1 June 1680, he named his youngest son Charles as exec. and mentioned the Parishes of Barking and Bannes [Barnes?]. John

Bobbs, Bridget Hawksworth, Molion Polo, and Gawen (X) Robinson witnessed the will (PCC 1680:108).

Edward was the father of: CHARLES; prob. others.

3. THOMAS LAYFIELD, son of John (1), was bapt. 3 Sep 1605 at St. Clement Dane's, London (J). Could he be the Thomas Layfield, Gent., who d. by 18 Nov 1659?

* * * * *

1. THOMAS LAYFIELD, Gent., from Sutton Coldfield, Warwick, relation to the above not proven, d. by 18 Nov 1659 (B). Thomas Layfield of Sutton Coldfield, Warwick, d. testate in 1658 (*IL* 61 cites PCC 1658, fol. 358).

Thomas, probably of London, married Margaret [-?-], who m. 2nd, by 1709 [-?-] Nottle. Mr. Layfield and wife Margaret were the parents of at least three children: GEORGE; THOMAS, b. c1641; and SAMUEL, b. c1646.

2. GEORGE LAYFIELD, son of Thomas (1) and Margaret, settled in SO Co., where he d. by March 1703. Layfield m. 1st, c1690/2, Elizabeth, widow of Col. William Stevens. They had no children, and he married 2nd, in Oct 1697, Priscilla, daughter of John and Sarah (Keyser) White, and niece of his first wife. Priscilla White Layfield m. as her 2nd husband, Capt. John Watts of Accomack Co. (A:376).

Layfield held a number of offices: Revenue Collector for Pocomoke District, Customs Official, and Deputy Notary (A: 375).

A resident of Pocomoke, SO Co., Layfield d. leaving a will dated 27 March 1703, proved 26 March 1703, naming daughter Eliza (who was to have tracts Conveniency, Hog Quarter, and Miller's Lot), wife Priscilla (to have Newport, a parcel of land given her by her father John White, also Creadwell and 500 a. Poplar's Point). He also named kinswoman Rose Thorogood and brothers Francis Thorogood and William and Stevens White. William Miskill, Francis Brown, Magdalen Bonson, and Francis Thorogood witnessed the will (MWB 3:497).

On 1 July 1703 his estate was appraised by William Powell and Henry Scholfield at a value of £357.18.6 (INAC 24:109). His estate was administered on 18 July 1706 by his extx., Priscilla, now wife of John Watts. The account mentioned an inventory of £364.11.6, and named a Mr. Samuel Layfield (INAC 26:73).

On 19 June 1728 Peter Collier and his wife Elizabeth (daughter of George Layfield), and Priscilla Watts of Accomac Co., VA, relict of George Layfield (who was a brother of Samuel Layfield), sold 150 acres Convenience to Mary Hampton and Robert King. (In 1703 this tract had been willed by George Layfield to his wife Priscilla, daughter of John White) (WOLR:134).

George and Priscilla (White) Layfield were the parents of:
ELIZABETH, m. Peter Collier.

3. THOMAS LAYFIELD, son of Thomas (1) and Margaret, was b. c1641, and m. Elizabeth Stirhop in Jan 1667/8.

He was apprenticed to George Courthopp of the Goldsmith's Company in 1654, and gained his freedom on 5 July 1661 (B).

Thomas Layfield of St. Martin's in the Field, Middlesex, Goldsmith, bachelor, age c26, m. by license dated 24 Jan 1667/8 Elizabeth Stirhop of St. Giles, Cripplegate, London, spinster, age c20, with consent of her mother; alleged by Mr. Robert Barecroft of St. Martin's aforesaid, Gent; m. at St. Clement Dane's, Middlesex (F:229).

4. SAMUEL LAYFIELD, son of Thomas (1) and Margaret Layfield, was b. c1646 in England and d. by Aug 1709 in MD. He m. 1st, on 9 Jan 1685 at St. James, Duke Place (X), Mary Oliver, who was buried 21 March 1687/8 at St. Michael's, Cornhill, in the Lower Vault on the South Aisle (D:270). He m. 2nd, Sarah [-?-], and prob. 3rd, Mary [-?-], his wife at the time of his death.

He may be the Samuel Layfield of St. Bride's, London, age c34, widower, who m. by license dated 14 July 1680, Anne Moore of St. Clement Dane's, spinster, age c18, with the consent of her father Ellis Moore; m. at Barnes, or Putney, Surrey (E:36).

Samuel Layfield m. Anne King on 5 June 1690 at St. James, Duke Place, London (X).

Samuel Layfield of St. Michael's, Cornhill, London, goldsmith, age c40, husband of Mary Oliver (niece of James Hall of St. Clement's East Cheap, citizen and grocer of London, whose will was dated 16 Nov 1665 and proved 19 Nov 1686) appeared 8 Sep 1686 and deposed that he was present when James Hall died 10 or 11 Aug 1686. (See *GGE* 684-686 for more data on the Halls and Olivers).

Samuel Layfield was mentioned in the will, signed 13 April 1691 and proved 6 May 1691, of John Hall of London, goldsmith (*GGE* 1:683).

Samuel was a goldsmith of the City of London. Samuel Layfield, son of Thomas Layfield, Gent., of Sutton Coldfield, was apprenticed to Robert Fowlse on 18 Nov 1659 (Apprentice Book 2:106). He gained his freedom on 29 Nov 1671 and became a liveryman in 1674. He went on to be a Warden of the Company, and between 1672 and 1691, had six apprentices (B).

Samuel did not register a maker's mark at Goldsmith's hall, but Hilton Price, in his *A Handbook of London Bankers*, and Ambrose Heal in *London Goldsmiths, 1200-1800*, recorded that he was in a list of bankers, and he was at the King's Head in the Royal Exchange, Cornhill, in 1685, and was then at the White Horse in Lombard St. in 1694-1697 [*sic*] (B).

In 1692 Samuel Layfield was living in Cornhill Ward occupying property valued at £70 rent per annum. His household consisted of a wife, one child, and one male and one female servant (C).

Samuel came to SO Co., MD c1706 (A: 376). A resident of Hogg Quarter, SO Co., Samuel died leaving a will dated 25 May 1709, and proved 30 Aug 1709. He named his
wife Mary, children Thomas and Mary, his mother Margaret Nottle (who was to be maintained by estate during her life), and asked that the debts of his brother [-?-] Layfield be paid. John Allmery, Patrick Guthrie, and Joseph Taylor witnessed the will (MWB 12, part 2: 176).

Francis Thorowgood and Pierce Bray appraised Samuel Layfield's estate on 10 Sep 1709, and valued it at £322.3.4. A Mr. Thomas Layefield was mentioned (INAC 31:3). The same two appraisers prepared an additional inventory, worth £9.5.10 on 16 March 1711. Thomas and Mary Layfield signed as next of kin (INAC 33A:212).

Samuel Layfield was the father of (D:153, 270, 273) (by Mary): JOHN, bapt. 9 April 1686 at St. Michael's, Cornhill; SAMUEL, buried at St. Michael's (in the Lower Vault in the South Aisle) on 7 Oct 1687; (by Sarah): DAVID, bur. at St. Michael's, Cornhill (in the Lower Vault) on 4 April 1692; (poss. by 3rd wife Mary): THOMAS; and MARY.

5. THOMAS LAYFIELD, son of Samuel (4), was living on 30 June 1724 when he answered the bill of complaint of Henry Darnall. concerning the Elizabeth, relict of [-?-] Stevens who m. George Layfield, long since dec., uncle of the respondent. The said Elizabeth died, and then George m. Priscilla White by whom he had one daughter. The widow is living in VA, and the dau. m. Peter Collier of SO Co. Layfield also stated that after the death of George Layfield, Samuel Layfield, father of the respondent, made a will and left the greater part of his estate to his widow, since dec., and to the sister of the respondent, now living near Bury St. Edmonds, Co. Suffolk, now m. to John Barlow (MCHR 5:65 ff.).

Unplaced:

LAYFIELD, BRIDGET, widow, of St. Swithin's, London, d. testate in 1629 (*IL* 44 cites PCC 60-Ridley).

LAYFIELD, ROBERT, was in SO Co. by 3 Dec 1710 when he was listed as a creditor to the estate of Nathaniel Cottman of SO Co. (INAC 32B:125).

He d. by 19 Nov 1716 when Richard Chambers and Mercy Fountain appraised his personal estate at £40.18.8. William Skinner and William Planner approved the inventory (INAC 37B:199).

THE LEWGER/LEWGAR FAMILY

Refs.: A: "Lewgar," *HSPV* 32:188-189; B: "Lewger, John," *BDML 2:533;* X: Undocumented material in the Ancestral File of the LDS.

1. WILLIAM LEWGAR of Clopton in Suffolk was the father of (A): GREGORY; THOMAS; and ELIZABETH, m. [-?-] Brooke of Essex.

2. GREGORY [or GEORGE] LEWGAR of Ipswich, son of William (1), was married twice. His first wife has not been identified. He m. 2nd, Ann, dau. of Edward Latymer of Freston, Suffolk. By his first wife he was the father of (A): GREGORY; by his second wife he was the father of (A): THOMAS; and ELIZABETH.

3. GREGORY LEWGAR of Hasted, Essex, son of Gregory (2), m. Joane, dau. and co-heir of John Freeman of Hadley, Suffolk. They were the parents of (A; X, provides approximate dates of birth): PHILIP, b. c1598; THOMAS, b. c1600; Rev. JOHN, b. c1602; and (dau.) BENNETT, b. c1604.

4. PHLIP LEWGAR of Barton, Co. Norfolk, son of Gregory (3), m. Winifred, dau. of Robert Berney of Gunton, Norfolk. They had at least one dau. (A): ELIZABETH.

5. Rev. JOHN LEWGAR, son of Gregory (3) and Joane, was b. c1602 at Hasted, and d. of the Plague c1665 in London (B). He m. Anne [-?-], b. c1606, d. c1642 in MD.

John was admitted to Trinity College in 1616 and received his B.A. in 1619. An Anglican minister, he converted to Roman Catholicism, and by 1647 was a Catholic priest (B).

John Lewger immigrated in 1638 with his wife Ann, son John and others. He was a Member of the Governor's Council, and also served as Secretary of the Province (MPL 1:13, 15, 17, 19). He was granted 1000 a. in 1659 for ten years of service (MPL R:9a).

John and Ann were the parents of (B; X): JOHN, b. c1628; poss. ANN, b. c1630, m. William Tattershall; and poss. CECILY, b. c1632.

6. JOHN LEWGAR, son of John (5) and Ann, was b. c1628 in London, and d. c1669 in CH Co., MD. About 1660 he m. Martha [-?-], who m. 2nd, by c1674, John Galsey (MPL ABH:150, 12:502, and Prov. Court MM:508).

John Lewger was transported in 1637 at the age of 9 (MPL 1:17, 19).

John Lewger d. leaving a will dated 26 Nov 1669 and proved 9 Dec 1669. He left St. Barbara's Manor to his sons John and Thomas jointly. Dau. Elizabeth was to have 300 a. adjoining the Manor. Wife Martha was residuary legatee. No exec. was named. Thomas Galley and Gep. Lodge witnessed the will.

John and Martha were the parents of at least three children, b. in CH Co., MD (MWB 5:281; X): THOMAS, b. c1655; JOHN, b. c1657, and ELIZABETH, b. c1659, m. 1st, by c1676, Richard Midgely, and 2nd, c1677 John Wright.

7. ANN LEWGAR, dau. of John (5), was transported c1658 (MPL 4:568). She m. William Tattershall and had a special warrant from Lord Baltimore in 1661 for 50 a. (MPL 4:618).

THE THOMAS LLOYD FAMILY

Refs.: A: "Lloyd of Dolobran." *BLG* 1906 ed. pp. 1024-1026. B: *RD500*. C: *PASC*:170.

ARMS: Azure, a chevron between three cocks Argent, armed, crested and wattled Or. **CREST**: In front of a fern brake a goat salient Argent, horned and unguled Or, gorged with a flory counter-flory Sable. **MOTTO**: *Esto vigilans* (A).

NB: The early generations must be accepted only tentatively.

Generations 1-5

1. IVAN *Teg*, or *The Handsome*, of Dolobran, Co. Montgomery, ap David, *ap* Jenkin, *ap* Llewellyn, *ap* Einion of Lloydiarth, *ap* Celynyn, m. Mawd, dau. of Evan Blaney of

Tregynon and Castle Blaney, Co. Monaghan, Ireland. Ivan and Mawd were the parents of (A): OWEN.

2. OWEN LLOYD, son of Ivan (1) and Mawd, was the first of his family to assume the name Lloyd c1476. He m. Catherine, dau. of Reynault, son of Sir Griffith Vaughan, Knight Banneret. They were the parents of (A): EVAN; DAVID of Rhosvawr; and MARGARET, m. John Grey, Lord of Powys.

3. EVAN LLOYD of Dolobran, son of Owen (2) and Catherine, m. Gwenhafar, dau. of Meredith Lloyd of Melvod. They were the parents of (A): DAVID; and JOHN.

4. DAVID LLOYD of Dolobran, J.P., son of Evan (3) and Gwenhafar, was b. 1523. He m. 1st, Eva, dau. of Edward Price of Eglusig, by whom he had no issue. He m. 2nd, Eva, dau. of David Goch, son of Jenkin Vaughan of Bodoach. David and his 2nd wife Eva were the parents of (A): DAVID.

5. JOHN LLOYD, son of Evan (3) and Gwenhafar, m. Margaret, sister of Sir Roger Kynaston of Hordley. Her Royal Descent from Henry IV is given in B:82. John and Margaret had at least one son (A): HUMPHREY of Dyffryn, assumed the name WYNNE.

6. DAVID LLOYD of Dolobran, J.P., son of David (4) and Eva, was b. 1549. He m. Ales, dau. of David Lloyd of Llanarmon-Mynydd-Maur. They were the parents of (A): JOHN.

7. HUMPHREY WYNNE, son of John Lloyd (5) and Margaret, assumed the name Wynne. He m. Mawd, *ferch* Oliver *ap* Thomas Pryce. Humphrey and Mawd had at least one dau (B:82): CATRIN or KATHERINE, m. her cousin John Lloyd.

Generations 6-9

8. JOHN LLOYD of Dolobran, J.P., son of David (6) and Ales, was b. 1575. He m. his cousin, Catrin or Katherine, dau. and coheiress of Humphrey (7) Wynne of Duffryn. John and Catrin were the parents of (A): CHARLES.

9. CHARLES LLOYD of Dolobran, J.P., son of John (8) and Catrin, was b. 1597. He m. Elizabeth, dau. of Thomas Stanley, son of Sir Edward Stanley, grandson of Sir Foulk Stanley, and great-grandson of Sir Piers Stanley, whose father, Sir Rowland, was a brother of Lord Strange of Knockyn, Salop.

Charles and Elizabeth were the parents of (A): CHARLES; JOHN, b. 1638, one of the Six Clerks in Chancery, m. and had issue; THOMAS, b. 17 Feb 1640; and ELIZABETH, m. Sir Henry Parry of Penamser, Merioneth.

10. CHARLES LLOYD of Dolobran, J.P., son of Charles (9) and Elizabeth, was b. 9 Dec 1637 and d. 26 Sep 1698. He m. 1st, on 11 Nov 1661, Elizabeth, dau. of Sampson

Lord of Stackpole Court, Salop, and 2nd, on 8 Feb 1686, Ann Lawrence of Lea. Co. Hereford.

Charles Lloyd joined the Society of Friends in 1662 and suffered much persecution (A).

Charles and Elizabeth were the parents of (A): CHARLES; and SAMPSON.

11. THOMAS LLOYD, son of Charles (9) and Elizabeth, was b. 17 Feb 1640, and d. 10 Sep 1694. He m. 1st, Mary Jones (for her Royal Descent see *RD500*:277), and 2nd, Patience Gardiner Story. He was a member of the Society of Friends, and he resided in Merion Twp., PA. **He was Deputy Governor and President of the Provincial Council of PA** (C).

Thomas Lloyd was the father of (C); HANNAH, b. 1666, m. 1st, John Delaval, and 2nd Richard Hill; MORDECAI, b. 1669, d. s.p.; JOHN, b. 1671, d. s.p.; MARY, b. 1674, m. Isaac Norris; THOMAS, b. 1675, m. and had issue; ELIZABETH, b. 1677, m. Daniel Zachary and had issue; MARGARET, b. 1685, d. 1693; DEBORAH, b. 1682, m. Dr. Mordecai Moore; and SAMUEL, b 1684, d. in infancy.

12. SAMPSON LLOYD, son of Charles (10) and Elizabeth, was b. 26 Feb 1684. He m. 1st, Elizabeth, dau. of Sybil Good. Elizabeth d. 10 April 1692 and he m. 2nd, in 1695, Mary, dau. of Ambrose Crowley (A).

Sampson and Elizabeth were the parents of (A): ELIZABETH; SARAH, m. John Gulson of Coventry; ANNE, m. B. Stretch of Bristol; and MARY, d. 1731.

Sampson and Mary were the parents of (A): CHARLES, b. 31 Dec 1696; AMBROSE, b. 1698, d. 1742; and SAMPSON, b. 15 May 1699, m. and had issue.

Generation 10

13. CHARLES LLOYD, son of Sampson (12) and Mary, was b. 31 Dec 1696 and d. 12 Feb 1741. He m. Sarah, dau. of Benjamin Careless by whom he had four sons and three daus., including (A): **THOMAS, b. 2 Oct 1731, d. in America.**

14. SAMPSON LLOYD, a banker in Birmingham, son of Sampson (12) and Mary, was b. 15 May 1699. He m. 1st, on 26 Sep 1717, Sarah Parkes, and 2nd, 17 Sep 1727, Rachel, dau. of Nehemiah Champion. Sampson had one son by his first wife and several children by his second wife including (A): CHARLES.

Generation 11

15. CHARLES LLOYD of Bingley Hall, Northants, son of Sampson (14) and Rachel, was b. 22 Aug 1748. In 1774 he m. Mary Farmer of Bingley House, Warwick. They were the parents of a number of children, including (A): ANNA, m. Isaac Braithaite of Kendal (Their son Joseph Bevan Braithwaite m. Martha Gillett and was the father of: **Anna Lloyd Braithwaite of MD**, m. Richard Henry Thomas, b. 1854, d. 1905, physician and Quaker minister: B:82).

THE LOWE FAMILY OF ST. MARY'S CO.

Refs.: A: Data provided by William W. Lowe, 304 N. Pitt St., Alexandria, VA. B: Henry F. Waters. *Genealogical Gleanings in England.* 2 vols. 1901. Repr. GPC, 1969. C: *HSPR 5: Register of St. Mary Aldemary, London, ... , 1558 to 1754.* Edited by Joseph Lemuel Chester. London: The Society, 1880. D: *HSPR 73. The Registers of St. Michael Basishaw, Part II.* Trans. and ed. by A. W. Hughes Clark. London: the Society, 1943

A. ROBERT LOWE within the Brode Yard, Bow Lane, may be the Robert Lowe, merchant taylor, who was buried 5 April 1631 (C:166). Mrs. Low, widow in Bow Lane, was buried 13 Nov 1647 (C:175).

Since Robert of Bow Lane was a merchant taylor, and Robert Lowe, factor, was a member of the Clothworker's Company, there may be a connection between the two families.

Robert Lowe was the father of the following children, whose births and deaths are recorded at St. Mary Aldemary, London (C:69, 71, 73, 74, 154, 156, 157): JOHN, buried 10 May 1607; ROBERT, bapt. 22 April 1606, bur. 23 Dec 1612 in St. Mary Aldemary Church; ABRAHAM, bapt. 4 June 1609, bur. 10 Sep 1609; THOMAS, bapt. 23 Sep 1610; ROBERT, bapt. 12 Sep 1613. He may be the Robert Lowe, son of Robert of Basing Lane, buried 3 Dec 1614; and WILLIAM, bapt. 7 July 1616.

1. ROBERT LOWE, possibly a relative of Robert (A), was born c1604 and died c1653. On 3 Nov 1634 he married 1st, at Hayes, Kent, Ann Allott, who was born 13 Dec 1612 and died between 11 Nov 1642 and 15 Feb 1643. Robert Lowe married 2nd, on 15 Feb 1643 at St. Mary Aldemary, Ann Green, of this parish, by license (C:19).

Robert Lowe was made a free member of the Company of Clothworkers in 1625 (A).

William Allot of St. Mary Abchurch in his will dated 10 Nov 1634 gave his son-in-law Robert Lowe and his wife each £5.0.0, and no more because his dau. was fully endowed (A).

Robert Lowe, factor, citizen and clothworker of St. Michael Basishaw, died leaving a will dated 1653 (PCC 223) (A: cites *Boyd's Inhabitants of London, 1635-1653,* p. 41041). He named his wife Anne and children, John, Elizabeth, Anne, Robert, and Thomas Low. His brother-in-law John Short of Candlewood St., London, woolen draper, was named executor.

Robert Lowe, factor, and Ann were the parents of several children, all but the first baptized at St. Michael Basishaw (A; D:9, 10, 11, 12, 13, 95. 98): ANNE, bapt. 13 Dec 1635 at St. Mary Abchurch, buried 23 April 1638 in St. Michael Basishaw Church (A); SARAH, bapt, 25 April 1637, bur. 29 Sep 1641 in St. Michael Basishaw Church; JOHN, bapt. 10 Sep 1638; ELIZABETH, bapt. 9 May 1640; ROBERT, bapt. 11 Nov 1642.

By his second wife Robert was the father of: THOMAS, bapt. 1 March 1644 at Hayes, Kent.

2. JOHN LOWE, possibly the son of Robert (1) and Ann (Allott) Lowe who was bapt. 10 Sep 1638 at St. Michael Bassishaw, London, died on or before 14 July 1701 in SM Co. He married, possibly 29 April 1679 in North Ormsby, Lincs., Rebecca (poss. Moody), widow of [-?-] Wright, who died c1709 in MD. She married 3rd, Thomas Mudd (A). Rebecca, late Rebecca Wright, extx. of Major John Lowe, and wife of Thomas Mudd, died between 5 July 1706 and 5 April 1709 (INAC 29:17).

On 10 April 1696 William Hutchinson of CH Co. conv. The Garden to John Lowe and George Dent of SM Co., carpenters. The deed stated that the tract bordered on Oxon Run (PGLR A:6).

The marriage of Rebecca Lowe to Thomas Mudd is cited by Fresco as having been taken from St. Mary's County Rent Roll, published in *The Chronicles of St. Mary's*, vol. 25, nos. 11 and 12, Nov and Dec 1977.

In Maryland Major John Lowe patented: (1) Inclosure, 75 a. in SM Co. on 1 June 1700 (MPL WD:232, DD#5:6). The Rent roll states that this tract was in St. George's Hundred, and by 1707, Thomas Mudd held it by [virtue of] his marriage to the widow (B; D:19); (2) The Garden: On 10 April 1696 William Hutchison conveyed this tract, in CH Co., to George Dent and John Lowe of SM Co. (PGLR A:6). NB: An undated deed (c1688) shows that John Lowe, William Hatton, and Robert Hopkins witnessed a deed of division of the tract Gisborough between Peter Dent, now age 21, and his brother George Dent, now 14, sons of Thomas Dent, late of St. George's Hundred, SM Co. (CHLR P:89); and (3) The Brothers: On 8 May 1712, William Hatton, Gent., of PG Co., and Thomas Dent., Gent., of CH Co., conv. 236 a. of The Brothers to John Lowe, planter of PG Co., for only 5 shillings and other good causes (PGLR F:184). The low purchase price indicates a possible family relationship.

John Lowe left a will dated 30 May 1698. He named a kinsman Marshall Lowe (A).

On 28 Nov 1689 as John Loe he signed the address of the Inhabitants of SM Co. to King William (*ARMD* 8:147).

On 24 Feb 1693/4 a special commission for the Court of Oyer and Terminer was issued to Samuel Holdsworth, Nathaniel Dare, John Bayne, JOHN LOWE, and John Watson, Gents., Commissioners and Justices for the trial of the said ship, the *Margaret* of London (*ARMD* 20:42).

In 1698 the sheriffs of the Province made a report to the governor and council, for what ships and vessels trading to sea, and what sloops and shallops there were. In SM Co. John Lowe had the only ship in the county, the *Planter*, now belonging to Liverpool. He had three ships and one shallop (*ARMD* 25:597).

On 8 May 1700 John Low surveyed 75 a. Inclosure in St. George's Hundred. By 1707 it was held by Thomas Mudd who had married the widow of the deceased (Rent roll). The tract was patented 1 June 1700 (MPL 14:232).

On 16 July 1701 William Watts, Adam Bell, and Thomas Lowe appraised the inventory of Major John Lowe of SM Co., and valued his personal estate at £446.18.2 (INAC 21:208). [It is most likely that Thomas Lowe signed the inventory as approving it--RWB].

Mrs. Lowe, extx. of John Lowe of SM Co. received a payment from the estate of James Tarleton on 22 July 1703 (INAC 24:9).

The estate of Major John Lowe was administered on 5 April 1709. His wife Rebecca, late Rebecca Wright, and now wife of Thomas Mudd, had died. The inventory of £446.18.2 was cited and payments of £489.4.3 were listed. Robert Crane and Thomas Ray were mentioned (INAC 29:177). Another account was filed on 20 May 1709. The extx. was dead, and distribution was to Elizabeth Mudd, dau. of the deceased (INAC 29:300).

He was the father of the following children, named in his will A): JOHN, b. possibly 12 Aug 1683 in Eng., d. by 3 June 1774, m. c1711/6, Mary (Holmes) Hawkins; ELIZABETH, b. between 13 May 1683 and 1690, m. by 1702/3, Henry Mudd, brother of her mother's second husband; ALICE; ELEANOR; and REBECCA.

3. ROBERT LOWE, son of Robert (1) and Anne (Allott) Lowe, was bapt. 11 Nov 1642. He is probably the Robert Lowe of St. Michael le Quern, Gent., and bachelor, married Elizabeth Baker on 21 May 1666, with the consent of her guardian, John Short (A).

He is probably the Robert Lowe of All Hallows, Lombard St., widower and clothworker, aged about 23, who married Mrs. Mary Middleton, of Poplar, Mddx., aged about 25 at St. Barthlomew the Less, London, on 18 May 1676 (A).

Robert Lowe was made free as a full member of the Clothworker's company on 13 June 1666 (A). Robert Lowe died leaving a will dated 14 Nov 1680, in wh ich he described himself as a citizen and clothworker of London and named his wife Mary, son Robert, daughters Elizabeth Lowe, Hannah Lowe, Elizabeth Middleton and Sarah Middleton (A).

Robert and Elizabeth were the parents of (A): (poss.) ELIZABETH.

Robert and Mary (Middleton) Lowe were the parents of (A): HANNAH, bapt. 2 April 1677 at St. Dunstan, Stepney; poss. ROBERT, bapt. 4 April 1678 at St. Giles Cripplegate; and poss. REBECCA, bapt. 12 April 1679 at St. Giles, Cripplegate.

4. THOMAS LOWE, possibly son of Robert (1) by his second wife, was bapt. 1 May 1644 at Hayes, Kent. On 21 Dec 1666 Thomas Lowe married Frances Rutland at St. Bartholomew's the Less, London, (A).

On 28 Nov 1689 as Thomas Low he signed the address of the Inhabitants of SM Co. to King William (*ARMD* 8:146). He witnessed the will of Major John Lowe (A).

Thomas Lowe was in SM Co. by 11 May 1698 when he witnessed the will of Richard Walker of SM Co. (MWB 7:385).

Thomas Love (or Lowe) patented the following tracts of land: (1) on 5 March 1688: Freestone Point, 250 a., SM Co.; surveyed on 5 March 1687 by William Watson and Thomas Lowe (MPL 25:350, 33:324, 700; D:117); (2) on 5 Oct 1695: Partnership, 260 a., SM Co., surveyed on 25 July 1694 for William Watson and Edward Barber's land; patented by Love/Lowe and Watson; Margaret Watson later held 130 a. (MPL 40:63; D:52). The Rent Roll shows that the two men surveyed this tract in Chaptico Hundred on 25 July 1694. By 1707, 130 a. was held by Margaret Watson (B). (3) on 10 Nov 1695: Love's Adventure, 136 a., SM Co., tract was indicated as being "formerly" in SM Co. (MPL 40:125; D). A search of CHLR through 1722 failed to reveal any data; and (4) on 10 Nov 1695: Love's Enjoyment, 311 a., SM Co. (MPL 40:133).

Thomas Lowe d. by 22 June 1705 when Frances Lowe posted bond to administer the estate of Thomas Lowe (A). On 22 May 1706 Frances Lowe admin. the estate of Thomas Lowe. She cited an inventory of £105.8.2 and listed payments of £22.19.3 (INAC 26:155).

Thomas and Frances were the parents of (A): THOMAS, bapt. 13 Aug 1669 at St. John's Hackney.

THE MAGRUDER FAMILY

Refs.: A: *RD500* (cites *Yearbook of the Clan Gregor Society* 52 (1978) 55-63, 53 (1979): 53-71. X: Undocumented Magruder Ancestor Chart in LDS Ancestral File, which must be used with care.

1. JAMES MAGRUDER was b. in 1519 and d. in 1592. He was the father of (X): JOHN.

2. JOHN MAGRUDER, son of James (1), was b. in 1544 at Craugnech, Perthshire, Scotland, and d. in 1600. He m. Margaret Murray, b. by 1555, dau. of James Murray. John and Margaret were the parents of (X): ALEXANDER I.

3. ALEXANDER MAGRUDER I, son of John (2) and Margaret, was b. in 1569 and d. on 1 May 1617 in Perthshire, Scotland. On 28 March 1605 he m. Margaret Drummond Campbell of Glenorchy, Scotland, who was b. in 1571 and d. on 8 Sep 1598 (A).

Margaret was the dau. of Nicholas Campbell, b. c1517/22, d. on 2 Aug 1587, and his wife Katherine Drummond, b. c1545, d. in 1704 at Benduchy. Her Royal Descent from Robert II of Scotland is given in A:99. Alexander and Margaret (Campbell) Magruder were the parents of (*DSEW*:284): ALEXANDER II; and JOHN.

4. ALEXANDER MAGRUDER II, son of Alexander I (3) and Margaret, was b. in 1610 at Calmaclone, Scotland and d. 25 July 1677 in CV Co., MD. He m. 1st, Sarah [-?-], and 2nd, about 1648, Eliza [Hawkins], b. 1627 (A:99; *DSEW*:284).

Alexander Magruder d. leaving a will dated 20 Feb 1676 and proved 25 July 1677. He named his wife Eliza, and the three children he had had by her, who were to have the home plantation. Sons Alexander and Nathaniel were to have the plantation after the death of his wife. Sons James and John were to have 900 a, in two tracts, Alexandria and Dumblain. Son Samuel was to have 500 a. Good Luck. Dau. Eliza, not yet 14, was to have 200 a. Crainagh [named for his grandfather's home]. Wife Eliza and sons James and Samuel were to be executors. James Magruder, Jno. Lane, Jno. Johnson, Jas. Soulivant, and Jas. Guthrey witnessed the will. In a codicil dated 12 March 1677 the testator named his three eldest sons: James, Samuel, and John, and his three youngest children, Alexander, Nathaniel, and Eliza (MWB 5:261).

Alexander and Sarah were the parents of: JAMES; SAMUEL; and JOHN.

Alexander and Eliza were the parents of (*DSEW*:284): ALEXANDER, b. 1672, d. 1746; NATHANIEL; and ELIZA.

5. JOHN MAGRUDER, son of Alexander I (3) and Margaret, was b. c1651 and came to MD c1651 (*DSEW*:284).

THE MANNERS FAMILY

Refs.: A: "Rutland." *Burke's Peerage and Barontage.* 1970 ed.

1. Sir JOHN MANNERS, Kt., of Etal, m. Anne, dau. of Sir John Middleton of East Swinburne (A: *PASC*:207). Sir John and Anne were the parents of: Sir ROBERT.

2. Sir ROBERT MANNERS, Kt., of Etal, and Sheriff of Northumberland, son of Sir John (1) and Anne (Middleton), was b. c1430 and d. 1461. He m. Joan, dau. of Sir Robert and Maud (Grey) Ogle, and a descendant of King Edward I (A; *PASC:*207).
　　　　Sir Robert and Joan were the parents of: Sir ROBERT.

3. Sir ROBERT MANNERS, Kt., Sheriff of Northumberland, M.P., son of Sir Robert (2) and Joan, d. 1495. He m., by license dated 13 June 1469, Eleanor de Ros, sister and coheir of the 11th Baron Ros Hamlake, and dau. of Thomas de Ros, 9th Lord Ros (thus with **Royal Descent from Edward I**), by his wife Philippa de Tiptoft (A; *PASC*:206, 207).
　　　　Sir Robert and Eleanor were the parents of: ELIZABETH, b. c1461, m. Sir William Fairfax; and Sir GEORGE, b. c1465.

4. Sir GEORGE MANNERS, 12TH Baron Ros, son of Sir Robert (3) and Eleanor (de Ros), was b. c1465 and d. 23 Oct 1513 (A). He m. Lady Anne St. Leger, b. c1466, d. 21 April 1526, dau. and heiress of Sir Thomas St. Leger, Kt., by his wife Anne Plantagenet, **sister of King Edward IV** (A). Sir George and Anne were buried in St. George's Chapel, Windsor Castle.
　　　　Sir George and Anne were the parents of: Sir THOMAS (See *RD500*:40 for his descendants); ANNE, b. c1488; RICHARD, b. c1490, m. Margaret Dymock; ELIZABETH, b. c1492; ANTHONY, b. c1494; CECILY, b. c1496; Sir OLIVER, b. c1500; JOHN, b. c1504; ELEANOR, b. c1505, bur 16 Sep 1547, m. John Bourchier, Earl of Bath; MARGARET, b. c1505, d. between 27 Jan 1558 and 12 June 1599, m. 1st, Henry Strangeways, and 2nd, Robert Heneage of Yorkshire; KATHERINE, b. c1511, m. Sir Robert Constable, Kt. (They were the ancestors of Dorothy Stapleton, who m. **Thomas Nelson of New England**; they were also ancestors of **Marmaduke Wyvill of MD**).

5. Sir THOMAS MANNERS, K.G., Earl of Rutland, son of Sir George (4) ands Anne (St. Leger), poss. by 1488, d. 20 Sep 1543. He m. Eleanor Paston, b. by 1496, d. 1551, dau. of Sir William and Bridget (Heyden) Paston, of Wiverton, Eng. Sir Thomas was buried at Bottesford, Leics., and Lady Eleanor was buried at St. Leonard's, Shoreditch (A).
　　　　Sir Thomas and Eleanor were the parents of: ELIZABETH, m. Sir John Savage; ANNE FRANCIS, b. 1524, d. after 27 June 1549, m,. 3 July 1536, Henry

Neville, Earl of Westmorland; HENRY, Earl of Rutland, b. 23 Sep 1526, m. Margaret Neville; Sir JOHN, b. c1528, m. Dorothy Vernon; FRANCES, b. c1532, m. Henry Neville, Baron Abergavenny; GERTRUDE, b. c1535, d. 1556, m. Sir George, 6th Earl of Talbot; and CATHERINE, b. c1537.

6. Lady CATHERINE MANNERS, dau. of Sir Thomas (5) and Eleanor (Paston), was b. c1537, and d.9 March 1572. She m. on 16 Aug 1543 Sir Henry Capell, Kt., of Raynes, Essex (A), who was poss. .b. c1514, d. 25 June 1558. They were the ancestors *(RD500*:40): of Alice Capell who m. **Robert Wiseman**, passenger on the *Ark* and *Dove* expedition to MD; and also of **Edward Hyde, 3rd Earl of Clarendon, and Governor of NY**.

THE MARBURY FAMILY
A Tentative Reconstruction

Refs.: A: Meredith B. Colket, Jr. *The Marbury Ancestry*. Philadelphia: The Magee Press, 1936. B: Ms. Notes on the Marbury ancestry, author and provenance unknown. C: "Old Warden Parish." *Bedfordshire Parish Registers*. Ed. by F. G. Emmison. Bedford: County Record Office, 1935. D: Entry from St. Margaret Patten's Church, London, transcribed for the IGI in a controlled extraction program (CO21661).

The compiler is deeply indebted to Betty deKeyser of Pasadena, MD, for generously sharing the results of her Marbury research.

Old Warden Parish (C).

Baptisms: (It should be noted that at this time the New Year began on 25 March),
Marbury, Thomas, son of John, 20 Jan 1576.
Marbury, John, son of John, Esq., 15 Nov 1577.
Marbury, Edw., son of John, Esq., 24 Sep 1581.
Marbury, Dorothy, dau. of John, Esq., 3 Jan 1582.
Marbury, Eliz., dau. of John, 22 Dec 1583.
Marbury, Robert, 1 April 1585.
Marbury, Richard, son of John, Gent., 10 July 1586.
Marbury, Henry, son of John, Esq., 6 Sep 1588.
Marbury, Ann, dau. of John, Esq., 15 Nov 1590.
Marbury, Martha, dau. of John, 10 Oct 1591.
Marbury, Grissell, dau., of John, Esq., 25 April 1593.
Marbury, Magdalene, dau. of John, 21 Jan 1597.
Marbury, Thomas, son of Thos., 26 Sep 1602.
Marbury, Magdalen, dau. of Mr.Thomas, 15 Jan 1603.
Marbury, Eusebius, son of Thomas, Gent., 17 May 1605.
Marbury, Edward, son of Thomas, Gent., 16 Oct 1606.
Marbury, Eliz., dau. of Mr.Thomas, 15 Oct 1607.
Marbury, Judith, dau. of Mr. Thomas, 2 May 1609.

Marbury, Steward, son of Mr. Thomas, 24 Sep 1610.
Marbury, Anne, dau. Mr. Thomas, 19 Dec 1611.
Marbury, Chas., son of Mr. Thomas, 29 April 1613.
Marbury, Dorothy, dau. of Thomas, Gent., 30 Aug 1614.
Marbury, Robert, son of Mr. Thomas, 14 Dec 1615.
Marbury, Mary, dau. of Mr. Thomas, 4 March 1616.
Marbury, Barbara, dau. of Mr. Thomas, 27 Aug 1617.
Marbury, Margaret, dau. of Mr. Thomas, 2 Dec 1619.
Marbury, Hen., son of Mr. Thomas, 1 Feb 1620.
Marbury, Eliz., dau. of Thomas, Esq., 9 Oct 1627.

Marriages:
Marbury, John, and Ann Summerland, 23 April 1576.
Marbury, Edward, and Shakbridge Kinge, 12 Oct 1579.

Burials:
Marbury, Thomas, son of John, 16 Nov 1577.
Marbury, Thomas, Esq., "Sergeant of the Queen's Pantry," 15 July 1590.
Marbury, Mrs. Eliz., widow, 23 April 1591.
Marbury, John, Esq., 20 Aug 1615.
Marbury, Robert, son of Mr.Thomas, 1 May 1621.
Marbury, Mrs. Elizabeth, dau. of Thomas, 12 July 1627.

1. THOMAS MARBURY of Hougton-Conquest, and Old Warden, Co. Bedford, was buried in the latter place on 15 July 1590 (C). He m. Elizabeth [-?-] who was buried on 23 April 1592 (A:48).

Thomas was described as "Sergeant of the Queen's Pantry." In 1562 he, his wife Elizabeth, and his son John leased Brome Close, Old Warden, Beds., for 80 years (Wixamtree Hundred, *VHC Bedfordshire*:255. He d. leaving a will dated 13 Dec 1587, stating he wished to be buried in the parish church of Ampthill. He named his wife Elizabeth, and Elizabeth, dau. of his dau. Anne Conquest (A:48).

Thomas was the father of (A:48; C; Betty deKeyser's search of the parish records of Houghton Conquest): JOHN, b. 1540; (prob.) EDWARD, m. Shakbridge Kinge on 12 Oct 1579 at Old Warden; and ANNE, m. [prob. George] Conquest.

2. JOHN MARBURY of Old Warden, son of Thomas (1), was buried at Warden on 5 Sep 1615. His unknown first wife d. in 1578, and he m 2nd, on 23 April 1579 at Old Warden, Anne Summerland. He m. 3rd, Dorothy [-?-], who was buried 22 Oct 1623 at Old Warden.

He is prob. the John Marbury who matriculated pensioner at St. John's Cambridge, in 1570, and was admitted to Gray's Inn in 1573 (*ALCA*).

John was the father of (A:48; C; English Chancery Court Depositions supplied by Betty de Keyser): (by his first wife): THOMAS, bapt. 20 Jan 1576, JOHN, bapt. 15 Nov and bur. 16 Nov 1577; JOHN, bapt. 23 Nov 1578; (by second wife): ANN, bapt. 18

Oct 1579; LEWIS, bapt. 30 Oct 1580;[1] EDWARD, bapt. 24 Sep 1581; DOROTHY, bapt. 3 Jan 1582; ELIZABETH, bapt. 23 Dec 1583, d. 1659, buried at Oakington, Cambs., having m. Robert Audley (1589-1654); ROBERT, bapt. 1 April 1585; RICHARD, bapt. 10 July 1586, d. by Jan 1639/40;[2] HENRY, bapt. 6 Sep 1588; ANN, bapt. 15 Nov 1590; MARTHA, bapt. 10 Oct 1591; GRISSELL (dau.), bapt. 25 April 1593; MAGDALENE, bapt. 21 Jan 1597; GEORGE, m. Anne [-?-] (they had a son Richard, b. 2 Jan 1623); and ANTHONY, settled in St. Kitts where he d. testate and unm. between 1638 and 1641, naming his brothers Thomas and Edward as execs.

3. THOMAS MARBURY of Old Warden, Beds., son of John (2), was bapt. 20 Jan 1576 at Old Warden, and d. c1640, according to a deposition made by his widow. He m. c1600 Elizabeth Cave, sister of Eusebius Cave, and dau. of Henry Cave of Ingarsby, Leics., and his wife Elizabeth, dau. of Gregory Isham. Elizabeth Isham was a sister of Euseby Isham (A:49, 52). Elizabeth Cave's bro., Brian Cave, m. Frances Dryden, niece of Bridget Dryden who m. Rev. Francis Marbury (of a different family).

Thomas Marbury was admitted to Gray's Inn, London, on 1 May 1595. In 1609, he and Richard Cartwright were granted Walford and Harwood, and in 1617 they were granted Houghton Regis in Bedfordshire (A:49):

Thomas and Elizabeth (Cave) Marbury were the parents of (A:49; C): THOMAS, bapt. 26 Sep 1602; MAGDALINE, bapt. 17 May 1603; EUSEBIUS, bapt. 17 May 1605; EDWARD, bapt. 16 Oct 1606; ELIZABETH, bapt. 15 Oct 1607, and as "Mrs." Elizabeth, was buried on 12 July 1627; JUDITH, bapt. 2 May 1609; STEWARD, bapt. 24 Sep 1610; ANNE, bapt. 19 Dec 1611; CHARLES, bapt. 29 April 1613; DOROTHY, bapt, 30 Aug 1614; ROBERT, bapt. 14 Dec 1615, bur. 1 May 1621; MARY, bapt. 4 March 1616; BARBARA, bapt. 27 Aug 1617; MARGARET, bapt. 2 Dec 1619; HENRY, bapt. 1 Feb 1620, bur. 8 Feb 1620; and ELIZABETH, bapt. 9 Oct 1627.

4. EDWARD MARBURY, son of John (2) and Anne (Summerland) Marbury, was bapt. 24 Sep 1581. He was Parson of St. James, Garlick Hithe, and St. Peter's, Paul's Wharf (A).

---

[1]Research by Betty deKeyser shows that Lewis Marbury of Clifford's Inn m. Persis (Haydock) Knight, widow, on 14 Feb 1632, at St. Mary Abchurch, London. He was buried on 4 May 1633 at St. Mary Woolchurch Haw. His will in 1633 (PCC [-?-] 43) names his relict Persis, a stepson, Isaac Knight, and a dau. Rebecca. Persis Marbury was buried on 13 Nov 1646. The IGI states that Lewis and Persis were the parents of: ANNE, b. 24 Sep 1626; and REBECCA, b. 9 Sep 1627.
[2]Richard called himself a barber chirurgeon in two depositions, and his wife Cisley also deposed. Both were of St. Sepulchre's, London, and Cisley gave her age as 29 in 1628. She was able to sign her name. She is probably the Cicely Marbury, widow, aged 36, of St. Sepulchre's, London, who, with John Tingle of the same parish, innholder, bachelor, were granted a license to marry at St. Sepulchre's, on 20 Jan 1639/40 (*HSPV* 26:248).

Edward Marbury, clerk, parson of St. James, Garlick Hithe, bachelor, ag~ 32, and Margaret Cave, now of the same parish, age c20, dau. of Henry Cave, late of Ingersby, Leics., with the consent of her mother Elizabeth Cave, widow, were granted a license to marry at St. James afsd., on 10 Nov 1617; attested by Lewis Marbury, of Clifford's Inn, Gent. (*HSPV* 26:55).

5. EUSEBIUS MARBURY, son of Thomas Marbury (3), and nephew of Rev. Edward Marbury, was bapt. 17 May 1605 at Old Warden (A:51). Manuscript notes of an unknown provenance suggest he may have gone to MD, but it is more likely that he stayed in England as his son Edward was born in London.

As Eusebius Marbury, Gent., of St. James, Garlick Hithe, bachelor, he m. by license issued 25 April 1636, Frances Quarles of Catford, Kent. The license, attested by Charles Marbury of Deptford, Kent, stated they were to be married at St. Peter's, Paul's Wharf, or St. James' Clerkenwell (A:51; *HSPV* 26:226).

Manuscript notes suggest that Eusebius was the father of (B): **EUSEBIUS, Jr., b. c1637, went to VA; ELIZABETH, b. c1638, came to MD in 1659; m. 1st, Dr. Luke Barber, and 2nd, John Blomfield;** EDWARD, bapt. 5 May 1643 at St. Margaret.Patten's, London; and **MARTIN, in CH Co., MD in 1664** (when he conveyed land to William Love. See CHLR B#1:195).

6. EDWARD MARBURY, son of Thomas (3), was bapt. 16 Oct 1606 at Old Warden. He might be the Edward Marbury, Gent., of St. Ives, Huntingdon, bachelor, age 25, who was granted a license on 25 Feb 1632/3 to marry at St. Bride's Catherine Audley, of the same parish, spinster, age 22 or 23, dau. of Robert Audley, Esq., who consented, as attested by Francis Dorrington, of the same parish, Gent.(*HSPV* 26:210).

7. EUSEBIUS MARBURY, supposed son of Eusebius (5) and Frances, was b. c1637, prob. in England. **He is stated to have settled in SM Co., MD**, and to have been the father of (B): FRANCIS, b. c1660 in SM Co., and CORNELIUS, b. c1662 in SM Co., MD; on 13 April 1715 Cornelius Marbury, age 53, deposed concerning a property belonging to Luke Barber and his wife, Elizabeth (Chancery Record PL#3:239).

8. ELIZABETH MARBURY, supposed dau. of Eusebius (5) and Frances, is said to have some to MD c1659, and to have m. 1st, Luke Barber, and 2nd, John Blomfield.

Luke Barber, d. by 9 March 1674 when his estate was admin. by Joachim Guibert. Payments were made to Barber's unnamed relict who m. John Blomfield (INAC 1:191).

9. FRANCIS MARBURY, supposed son of Eusebius (7), was b. c1660/3 in England or SM Co. He gave his age as 50 or so in March 1713 (A). He d. by 22 Jan 1733. He m. Mary, dau. of Leonard Greene of CH Co., and granddau. of Gov. Thomas Greene (A:50-51). Supporting the theory that he was the son of Eusebius is the fact that one of his sons was named Eusebius, and the name Eusebius is found in no other branch of the Marbury family.

Unplaced

MARBURY, KATHERINE, was buried 19 May 1628 at St. James Clerkenwell (*HSPR* 17:192).

THE M'CUBBIN FAMILY
A Tentative Reconstruction

1. Sir JOHN MacCUBBIN of Knockdolian, Ayrshire, is said to have been the father of (*SOCD*:91): JOHN, b. c1630.

2. JOHN MacCUBBIN, poss. son of Sir John (1), was b. 1630, and d. Sep 1685 in AA Co., MD, where he migrated c1659. He m. 1st, Catherine Howard, and 2nd, Elinor Carroll (*DSS5*:153; *SOCD*:91; *DSEW*:258).

John MacCubbin was the father of (*SOCD*:91): JOHN; SAMUEL; WILLIAM; ZACHARIAH; MOSES; AND ELIZABETH.

THE MacPHERSON FAMILY

1. JAMES MacPHERSON of Culloden, Invernessshire, was the father of (*DSSA*:181; *DSEW*:335A): DONALD.

2. DONALD MacPHERSON, son of James, was b. c1708 in Culloden, and came to Port Tobacco, MD, c1727, where he was an indentured servant of John Baynes (*DSSA*:181; *SOCD*:194 cites *MHM* 1:347).

Daniel and William McPherson witnessed the will of John Nally of CH Co. on 6 Feb 1732 (MWB 20:578).

Is it possible he was the "Daniel" McPherson who d. in CH Co. leaving a will dated 22 May 1740, proved 1 Oct 1740, naming wife Elizabeth, extx., and sons Richard, Basil, and Alexander (not yet 18), and daus. Mary and Elizabeth. Francis Ignatius Boarman, William McPherson, Jr., and Susanna Malley (or Nalley) witnessed the will (MWB 22:275).

THE MERRIKEN FAMILY

1. JOHN MERRIKEN, of Ratcliffe in parish of St. Dunstan's Stepney, als Stebenheath, Mddx, m. Christian [-?-].

In an undated deposition, Edward Smith of Baltimore County deposed that some 50 years earlier John Merriken purchased New Scotland. Smith knew old John Merriken as he was in his house often (AALR IT#5:44).

John and Christian were the parents of (*TMFO*: cites *ARMD* 20:541, 23:20, and Newman's *Mareen Duvall of Middle Plantation*; IGI): HUGH, b. c1656; JOSHUA; and JOHN.

2. HUGH MERRIKEN, son of John (1), came to Maryland, but returned to Eng., where he died intestate. Hugh Merriken, of MD, d. by Feb 1698 when admin. was granted by the PCC, to the widow Anne Merriken (*AWAP*:210).

Hugh Merriken of AA Co., boatwright, purchased from Thomas Lightfoot of Baltimore Co., smith, 100 a. of Best Success, now called Merriken's Purchase (AALR WH#4:125).

On 28 Feb 1700, his widow Ann lived in Raleigh Inn, Parish of Stepney, Mddx, with an infant child Eliza. On the latter date she appointed Giles Bond of London, mariner, now bound for Maryland, to be her attorney (AALR WT#1:262).

In an undated deposition, Mary Eagle declared that she knew three brothers, John, Hugh, and Joshua, very well, and that John lived on New Scotland, and after his death the two surviving brothers, Hugh and Joshua, lived together for four or five years, then married and parted. One lived on one side of the creek and the other on the other side until Hugh Merriken returned to England (AALR IT#5:44).

Hugh and Anne were the parents of: JOSHUA; and ELIZA, bapt. 14 Sep 1698 at St. Dunstan, Stepney.

3. JOSHUA MERRIKEN, son of John (1), was described in an undated petition of Joshua Merriken of Hugh (2), as having served as attorney in fact to Hugh Merriken (2) after the latter's return to England. After Hugh Merriken died, Joshua the brother, held the property, New Scotland, in right of Hugh's son Joshua, the petitioner, but after the county records burned c1704, Joshua took possession in his own right (AALR IT#5:44).

Mary Eagle deposed that after Hugh Merriken returned to England and died. his brother Joshua, uncle of the petitioner, took possession of the land [New Scotland] and remained there until his death. This is the land where Joshua's son John now lived (AALR IT#5:44).

Joshua Merriken was the father of: JOHN.

4. JOHN MERRIKEN, son of John (1), was described in an undated deposition (post 1704) of Robert Eagle, age 71, as being uncle to Joshua Merriken, the petitioner, as having lived on part of New Scotland, but Eagle always understood the land was in the right of Hugh Merriken (2) (AALR IT#5:44).

5. JOSHUA MERRIKEN, son of Hugh (2), returned to Maryland, m. and had issue (*BCF*).

Joshua Merriken petitioned that his uncle Joshua (3), son of John, took possession of New Scotland, but the land rightfully belonged to his father, Hugh Merriken. Margaret Todd, Nathan Linthicum, David Rablin, and Joshua Jones all made depositions supporting Joshua's claim (AALR IT#5:44-51).

THE MORAUNT-PECKHAM-HAUTE FAMILY

Refs.: A. W. G. Davis. *The Ancestry of Mary Isaac*. 1955.

1. THOMAS MORAUNT was the father of (A:140): Sir WILLIAM.

2. Sir WILLIAM MORAUNT, son of Thomas (1), m. Joan, dau. of William and Isabel Apuldrefeld. Joan and her sister Denise, who m. Stephen Everard, were sisters and coheirs of their bro. John who d. s.p. Joan held ½ of ¼ of a manor, and advowson (A:140).

Sir William and Joan were the parents of (A:140): Sir THOMAS; WILLIAM; and ROBERT.

3. Sir THOMAS MORAUNT, son of Sir William (2) and Joan, was seized in fee tail of a portion (perhaps ½) of a manor in 12 Edward III. He was the father of a dau. (A:140): LORA.

4. LORA MORAUNT, dau. of Sir Thomas (3) m. 1st, Sir Thomas Coven, and 2nd, James Peckham.

Lora was seized in fee tail of ½ of a manor, and advowson, She presented Robert Lambourn [to the living?] temp. Richard II. James Peckham presented William Hacche [to the living?] temp Richard II (A:140).

By Sir Thomas Coven, Lora was the mother of three children (A:140): ROBERT, d. s.p; THOMAS, d. in infancy; and ALICE, m. Sir Nicholas Haute.

By James Peckham, Lora was the mother of (A:140): REYNOLD.

5. ALICE COVEN, dau. of Thomas and Lora (4) (Moraunt) Coven, m. Sir Nicholas Haute, # 8 in "The Hawte Family" in *British Roots of Maryland Families*, vol. 1, p. 238. The maiden name of his wife is not shown, and only two children are named.

Sir Nicholas and Alice were the parents of four children (A:1409): WILLIAM, who sued John Uvedale c1418 over the right to present [a clergyman] to the church at Warehorn (He was the ancestor of **The Wroth Family**, from whom several Maryland families descend); THOMAS, d. s.p.; EDMOND; and NICHOLAS.

THE MUSGRAVE FAMILY

Refs.: A: "Musgrave." *The New Complete Peerage.* B: *RD500*:174. C: "Musgrave of Hartley Castle." *Burke's Peerage and Baronetage.* 1956 ed. pp. 1585-1586. D: *MCS5*. E: "Musgrave of Hartley, 1615." *CWFO*:91. F: "Musgrave of Eden Hall," *CWFO*:92-93. G: *CFAH*:238-239.

Generations 1-5

1. THOMAS de MUSGAVE, d. c1246. In 1235 he bargained for rights of pasturage for his tenants in Murton. He was probably the same Thomas de Musgrave who was amerced at the Cumberland Assizes in 1242. He m. Alice, dau. and heir of William Sandford.

Thomas and Alice were the parents of (A): Sir THOMAS; RICHARD; and HUGH.

2. Sir THOMAS de MUSGRAVE, son of Thomas (1), d. c1287. He m. Sybil [-?-] who was alive in 1272 (A).

About 1246 he made a grant of land in Brampton. In 1256 he was included in a list of yeomen, all of full age, and holding 20 librates of land, but not a whole knight's fee (A).

In 1265 he was a knight, and he granted his brother Richard a share of the manor of Orton, and in 1273 settled the manors of Musgrave, Sandford and Murton on Richard and another brother Hugh, if he himself should not have any male heirs (A).

In 1269 he was a steward to Roger de Leyburn, and in 1278 he and Ranulph de Dacre were granted [the right to hold] a market and fair at Orton (A).

Thomas and Sybil had one dau. (A): AVICE, m. by Oct 1289 Thomas de Hellebeck, when she acknowledged her uncle's succession to Musgrave (Avice and Thomas had two daughters and coheirs: Isabel, m. Richard de Blenkinsopp; and Margaret, m. Robert de Swinburne).

3. RICHARD de MUSGRAVE, son of Thomas (1), d. by Jan 1301. Richard m. 1st, [-?-] [-?-], and 2nd, by 1292, Christian [-?-], who survived him (A).

In 1297 he was appointed joint collector in Cumberland of the 8th [a share of taxes] granted to the king, but was declared too old to carry out the office of coroner for Westmorland (A).

Richard was the father of (A): (by his first wife): ALICE, m. Thomas de Newton; (by second wife): THOMAS, d. 1314; and RICHARD.

4. THOMAS de MUSGRAVE, son of Richard (3), d. by 21 Aug 1314. He m. in or before 1301, Sarah, sister of Sir Andrew de Harcla; she m. 2nd, Robert de Leyburn, Sheriff of Lancs. (A).

Thomas was a minor when his father died, but by 1307 was a commissioner to send men to Carlisle (A).

Thomas and Sarah were the parents of (A): THOMAS.

5. Lord THOMAS de MUSGRAVE, son of Thomas (4), d. by 1385. He m. 1st, Margaret, dau. and coheir of William de Ros, and 2nd, by 9 June 1345, Isabel, widow of Robert de Clifford, Lord Clifford, and dau. of Maurice de Berkeley, Lord Berkeley, by his wife, Eve la Zouche (A; C).

Thomas de Musgrave held a number of public offices including: deputy sheriff of Westmorland, Member of Parliament for Westmorland, and Keeper of the Town of Berwick. Between 1350 and 1373 he was summoned to Parliament as Lord Musgrave (but his descendants were not summoned) (A).

By his 1st wife, Thomas was the father of (A; E): Sir THOMAS.

6. Sir THOMAS de MUSGRAVE, son of Lord Thomas (5) and Margaret, was age 8 in 1345, and d. in his father's lifetime, in 1372. He m. Elizabeth, dau. of William Fitzwilliam of Sprotborough (E).

Little is known of him except that he was knighted by 1372, and that he appears to have inherited the manor of South Holme from his mother (A).

Sir Thomas had one son (A; E): THOMAS.

Generations 6-10

7. Sir THOMAS de MUSGRAVE, son of Sir Thomas (6), was his grandfather's heir (A). However, Burke states that he was a son of Thomas (5) and Isabel (C:1585). He d. c1409. There is some confusion over the name of his wife. He may have m. 1st, by 1372, Mary, dau. of Alan de Strother. He may have m. 2nd [-?-], mother of his heir (A). His 2nd wife may have been a dau. of Lord Dacre (See Visitation of The North, 1489-1500, in *Surtees Society*, 144:15). About 1388 he may have m. [-?-], dau. and heir of Alice, wife of John Westwood (See *Calendar of Inquisitiones Miscellaneous*, 6:90).

   Foster states that Sir Thomas m. Alice, dau. of Richard Plantagenet, Earl of Cambridge, by Maud, dau. of Thomas, Lord Clifford. Earl Richard gave his dau. Alice the manors of Crosby and Morton in Westmorland (E).

   Among the offices Sir Thomas held were: Justice of the Peace for Westmorland, 1390; Sheriff of Cumberland, 1391/2; and member of the King's Council, summoned 1401 (A).

   Sir Thomas was the father of (A; E): Sir RICHARD; and ELIZABETH, m. Henry Wharton.

8. Sir RICHARD, son of Sir Thomas (7), is stated by Burke to have m. Elizabeth [-?-]. Foster states that he m. Elizabeth, dau. of Sir Thomas Beetham, and sister of Sir Edward (E). She predeceased him, and both are buried in Kirkby Stephen Church (A).

   Richard was fined in 1410/11 for not taking up knighthood (A).

   Sir Richard and Elizabeth (Beetham) were the parents of (C:1585; E): THOMAS; RICHARD; ELIZABETH, m. Thomas Garth; ISABELL/MABEL, m. Thomas Middleton (ancestors of **The Thornborough Family of MD**); ELEANOR, m. Roland Thornborough (also ancestors of **The Thornborough Family of MD**); MARY, m. Thomalin Warcop; AGNES, m. Robert Warcop; and MARGARET, m. Thomas Elderton.

9. THOMAS de MUSGRAVE, son of Sir Richard (8) and Elizabeth, d. in 1447. He m. Joan, dau. and coheir of Sir William Stapleton of Edenhall (E).

   Sir Thomas and Joan were the parents of (C:1585; D:Line 113; E): Sir RICHARD; Sir JOHN (ancestor of the Musgraves of Musgrave Hall); NICHOLAS (ancestor of the Musgraves of Haydon Castle); WILLIAM (ancestor of the Musgraves of Crockdale in Cumberland); MARGARET, m. John Sandford; ELIZABETH, m. Christopher Lancaster; and MARY, m. Nicholas Ridley.

10. RICHARD MUSGRAVE, son of Sir Richard (8) and Elizabeth, m. the dau. and coheir of William Stapleton, by whom he was the father of (E): MARY, m. Richard Ridley.

11. Sir RICHARD de MUSGRAVE, son of Sir Thomas (9) and Joan, m. Joan, dau. of Thomas Lord Clifford.

   Sir Richard and Joan were the parents of (C:1585; D:Line 113: E): Sir EDWARD; MARGARET, m. John Heron; THOMAS; JOHN; MARY, m. George Martindale; and JANE.

12. NICHOLAS MUSGRAVE, son of Sir Thomas (9) and Joan, m. Margaret, dau. and heir of William Filliol. They were the parents of (E): THOMAS.

13. Sir EDWARD MUSGRAVE, son of Sir Richard (11) and Joan, d. 23 May 1542. He m. 1st, Alice, dau. of Thomas Radcliffe, and 2nd, Joan, dau. of Sir Christopher Ward of Givendale (F).

      Sir Edward was knighted at Flodden Field in 1513. Sir Edward and Joane were the parents of (D:Line 113; F): Sir WILLIAM; and SIMON.

14. THOMAS MUSGRAVE, son of Nicholas (12) and Margaret, was the father of (E): WILLIAM.

Generation 11

15. Sir WILLIAM MUSGRAVE, son of Sir Edward (13) and Joan, d. 18 Oct 1544. He m. Elizabeth, dau. of Sir Thomas Curwen of Workington. He was knighted at Jedburgh, 25 Sep 1523. Sir William and Elizabeth were the parents of (D:Line 113): Sir RICHARD.

16. Sir SIMON MUSGRAVE, son of Sir Edward (13) and Joan, m. Juliana, dau. of [William] Ellerker of Yorkshire.

      Sir Simon and Juliana were the parents of (F): CHRISTOPHER; THOMAS; RICHARD; JOHN; and ANNA, m. Sir Nicholas Curwen of Workington.

17. WILLIAM MUSGRAVE, of Johnby Hall, son of Thomas (14), was b. 1518 and d. 1596. He m. Isabel, dau. and heir of James Martindale (G).

      William was Sheriff of Cumberland in 1573 and 1592 (G).

      William and Isabel were the parents of (G): THOMAS (d. v.p. leaving a dau. Isabella who m. 1st, her cousin John Musgrave of Catterlen, and 2nd, John Vaux of Catterlen); and Sir EDWARD.

Generation 12

18. CHRISTOPHER MUSGRAVE, son of Simon (16) and Juliana, died in his father's lifetime. He m. Jane, dau. of Sir Henry Curwen of Workington (F).

      Christopher and Jane were the parents of (F): Sir RICHARD; JULIANA, m. John Skelton of Armathwaite; MARY, d. unm.; and MARGARET, m. Francis Whitfield of Whitfield.

19. Sir EDWARD MUSGRAVE, son of William (17) and Isabel, was living in 1628 and bought Scaleby Castle. He m. Catherine Penruddock, and they were the parents of (G): WILLIAM.

Generation 13

20. Sir RICHARD MUSGRAVE, K.B., 1st Bart., son of Christopher (18) and Jane, m. Frances Wharton, dau. of Philip, 3rd Baron Wharton and his wife Frances Clifford.

Sir Richard and his wife were the parents of (B; F): Sir PHILIP, 2nd Bt.; and MARY, d. unm., buried at Canterbury.

21. WILLIAM MUSGRAVE, son of Sir Edward (19) and Catherine, m. Catherine, dau. of Hugh Sherburne of Esholt and Guiseley. They were the parents of (G): Sir EDWARD.

Generation 14

22. Sir PHILIP MUSGRAVE, 2nd Bart., son of Sir Richard (20) and Frances, m. Juliana Hutton, dau. of Richard Hutton of Goldsborough, Yorkshire (F).

Sir Philip and Juliana were the parents of (B; F): Sir CHRISTOPHER, 4th Bt.; RICHARD; PHILIP; WILLIAM; SIMON; THOMAS, Archdeacon of Carlisle; and FRANCES, m. Edward Hutchinson of Wickham Abbey.

23. Sir EDWARD MUSGRAVE, Bart., son of William (21) and Catherine, was b. 1621 and d. 1673. He was created a Baronet in 1638 and was later fined £960 for his loyalty to the Royalist cause.

Sir Edward was the father of (G): Sir RICHARD, Bart.; and JANE, m. Sir Wilfride Lawson, Bart. (Their dau., Frances Lawson, m. Henry Tolson, and they were the parents of **Francis Tolson of PG Co., MD**).

Generation 15

24. Sir CHRISTOPHER MUSGRAVE, 4th Bart., son of Sir Philip (22) and Juliana, m. 1st, Mary Cogan, dau of Andrew Cogan of Greenwich, Kent, and 2nd, Elizabeth, dau. of John Frankland of Ware, Mddx., Bart. (F).

Sir Christopher and Mary were the parents of (B; F): PHILIP; CHRISTOPHER; and MARIA.

Sir Christopher and Elizabeth were the parents of (F): JOHN.

Generation 16

25. PHILIP MUSGRAVE, son of Sir Christopher (24) and Mary, m. Mary Legge. They were the parents of (B): Sir CHRISTOPHER, 5th Bart.

Generation 17

26. Sir CHRISTOPHER MUSGRAVE, 5th Bart., son of Philip (25) and Mary, m. Julia Chardin. They were the parents of (B): ANNA, m. Henry Aglionby. They were the grandparents of **John Yates** of VA (B)

THE KNEVETT/NEVITT FAMILY

The compiler is indebted to Vickie S. Connor for sharing unpublished materials in her possession. These materials, compiled some time ago by a Catholic priest, refer to medieval fine, patent, and close rolls, *inquisiitones post mortem*, and the *Victoria Histories of the Counties of England.*

Refs.: A: Nevitt History from England to Maryland. unpub. [anonymous] ms. generously made available to the compiler by Vickie S. Conner. B: J. B. M. Untitled notes on the Knevett/Neviit Family, in the possession of the compiler. C: *WAR7*. D: *MCS5*. E: Roger Virgoe. "The Earlier Knyvetts: The Rise of a Norfolk Gentry Family, Part I. *Norfolk Archaeology* XL (1990) 1-14. F: -----. -----. Part II. *Norfolk Archaeology*. XLI (1992) 249-178. G: David F. H. Kelley, "A Royal Line from Edward I to Dorothy May Bradford of Plymouth, Mass.," *TAG* 46 (2) 117-118, 47 (2) 87.

ARMS: Argent, a bend engrailed Sable, within a bordure of the Same (E:2).

1. Sir JOHN KNYVETT, first definitely established ancestor of the family, held property in Southwick, Northants, in 1316. He was with Edward I beyond the seas in 1286. He held estates in Cambridgeshire in 1315 (B:5; E:2).

     Sir John was the father of (B:5; E:2): RICHARD.

2. RICHARD KNYVETT, son of Sir John (1), d. 1352. He m. Joan, dau. of Sir John Worth in 1304 (E:2). Richard obtained his wife's lands, and became Keeper of the Forest of Clive in 1324 (B:5).

     Richard and Joan were the parents of (B:5; E:2): Sir JOHN, Chancellor of England.

3. Sir JOHN KNYVETT of Southwick, Co. Northampton, Chief Justice of the King's Bench, and Lord Chancellor of England, son of Richard (2) and Joan, died in 1381 having m. Alianore Basset, dau. of Ralph and Joan Basset (For her Magna Charta descent, see C: Line 288).

     Sir John became Chief Justice and Chancellor under John of Gaunt 1372-1376, and was executor of the will of Edward III. While he was Chancellor he summoned the Good Parliament, where the first Speaker of the House of Commons was elected by two knights from each shire and representatives from each borough (B:5).

     Sir John and Alianore were the parents of (B: 5; C:Line 188; E:2-3): Sir JOHN; ROBERT; RICHARD; HENRY; RALPH; and MARGERY.

4. Sir JOHN KNYVETT, M.P. for Huntingfield, 1397/8, son of Sir John (3) and Eleanor, d. in 1418. He m. Joan Botetourt, dau. and heiress of Sir John Botetourt of Mendlesham, Suffolk (C: Line 216A; G:117). By this marriage he acquired Mendlesham, Hamerton, Hunts., and Winwick and Turning (B:5; C: Lines 188, 238. cites *NCP* II 13; e:2-3).

John and Joan were the parents of (B:5; G:117): Sir JOHN; MARGARET, m. 1st, Sir Robert Ty, who d. s.p., and 2nd, Sir Thomas Echyngham (the ancestors of **Dorothy May**, who m. Gov. William Bradford of MA; KATHERINE; and ELIZABETH, m. 1st, Sir John Radcliffe of Chaderton (by whom she had a son Edmund Ratcliffe); 2nd, [-?-] Morley; and 3rd, Edmund Stapleton.

5. ROBERT KNYVETT, son of Sir John (3) and Eleanor, d. 10 Jan 1418/9. He m. 1st, by 1382, Joan, dau. and heiress of John Chastelyn by Isolde, coheiress of Belhouse, and 2nd, Elena Fitzwater who d. 1436 (E:10).

By Joan, Robert was the father of (E:10; G:117): THOMAS of Stanway.

By Elena, Robert was the father of (E:10): JOHN, of Shenfield, d. 1450, m. Margaret; JOAN; and ROBERT.

6. Sir JOHN KNYVETT, Sheriff of Northants., 1427, son of Sir John (4) and Joan, d. in 1446. He m. Elizabeth Clifton, b. c1392, heir of Sir Constantine Clifton, 2nd Baron de Clifton (C: Line 218; E: 2). By this marriage, Buckenham Castle came into the family's possession (B:6; C: Line 238, cites *NCP* III 308). Sir John sold Southwick Manor in 1442 to John Lynne, who m. his dau. Joan (B:5; G:117).

Sir John and Elizabeth were the parents of (B:6; C: Lines 188 and 238; E:3): Sir JOHN; MARGARET, b. c1412, may have m. Richard Chamberlaine of Tilsworth, Beds. (They were the ancestors of **The Marbury Family** of New Eng.); JOAN, m. 1st, Robert Toppes of Norwich, and 2nd, Richard Roos; RICHARD, d. s.p.; MARGARET; and ANNE.

7. THOMAS KNYVETT of Stanway, Essex, son of Robert (5) and Joan, d. 1458. He m. 1st, Eleanor, dau. of John Dorward, and 2nd, by 1454, Margaret [-?-]. By his first wife he was the father of (E:10; G:117): THOMAS; JOHN; RICHARD; and ROBERT.

8. Sir JOHN KNYVETT, son of Sir John (6) and Elizabeth, was b. c1416, and d. 1491. He m. Alice, dau. of William Lynne of Bassingbourne, Cambridgeshire and of London (E:3).

Sir John and his son William fought for the future Edward IV under Richard Neville, Earl of Warwick (B:6).

Sir John and Alice were the parents of (B:6, 8; C: Line 188, cites *Surtees Soc. Pub.* 144:10, 155): Sir WILLIAM, b. 1440; CHRISTINA, may have m. Sir Henry Colet, Mayor of London; ELIZABETH, d. unm. in 1482; and MARGERY.

9. JOHN KNYVETT of Stanway, Essex, son of Thomas (7) and Eleanor, d. 1481. He m. c1443 Margaret Baynard, by whom he was the father of (E:10; G:117): THOMAS, b. c1447; JOHN; RICHARD; and ROBERT.

10. Sir WILLIAM KNYVETT, Knight of the Shire, son of Sir John (12) and Alice, was b. 1440, and d. 1515. He was knighted in 1475. He m. 1st, Alice Grey, dau. of Sir John Grey and granddau. of Reginald, Lord Grey of Ruthin (For her Royal Descent from Edward III, see *RD500:* 161).

Sir William m. 2nd, Joan Stafford, dau. of Humphrey Stafford, 1st Duke of Buckingham (B:6; C:Line 93B). He m. 3rd, Joan Courtenay, sister and heir of Thomas, 6th Earl of Devon.

He took part in an uprising against Richard III. He lost Buckenham, and was attainted for the rest of Richard's reign. After the Battle of Bosworth in 1485 Sir William petitioned Henry VII for reversal of the attainder and return of his properties.

Sir William was made Councillor and Chancellor to Edward, 3rd Duke of Buckingham (B:7).

Sir William and Alice were the parents of (B:6, 8; C: Line 188; E:3): Sir HENRY, Ambassador, with Bishop Gardiner, to the Emperor Charles V, and to France; EDMUND, m. Eleanor Tyrrell; and ALICE, m. John Thwaites (They were ancestors of **The Lowe Family** of Maryland).

Sir William and Joan were the parents of (B:7): EDWARD, heir of his father's manors and titles; CHARLES, Collector for the Duke of Norfolk; ANNE, m. Charles Clifford; and ELIZABETH.

11. Sir THOMAS KNYVETT, son of John (9) and Joan, was b. 1447, and d. 1479. In 1460 he m. Elizabeth, dau. of William Lunsford of Battell, Sussex and great-granddau. of Thomas and Margaret (Knyvett) Echyngham (G:117).

Sir Thomas and Eleanor were the parents of (E:10; G:117-118): EDWARD of Stanway, b. 1466, d. 1501, m. three times; MARGARET, m. John Roydon (her dau. Elizabeth m. John Clopton); and THOMASINE, m. as his 3rd wife, Sir William Clopton, d. 1530 (They were ancestors of **Walter Clopton of New Eng.**, **Mary Clopton of New Eng.**, wife of Thomas Daggett of Boxted, Suffolk, and of **Dorothy May of MA**, wife of Gov. William Bradford.

12. EDMUND KNYVETT, son of Sir William (10) and Alice, m. Eleanor, sister of Sir James Tyrrell, who held the Tower of London.

Edmund and Eleanor were the parents of (B:8; C:Lines 4, 188; F:260): Sir THOMAS (continued the Buckenham line); and Sir EDMUND; CHRISTOPHER, d. 1520; JAMES, d. unm.; Sir ANTHONY, d. 1549, m. twice; WILLIAM, d. after 1546; MARGARET; DOROTHY; and ANNE, m. George St. Leger.

13. CHARLES KNYVETT, son of Sir William (10) and Joan, was b. c1480, and d. c1526. He m. 1st, Agnes, dau. of John Calthrope, and widow of William Curson, and 2nd, Anne, dau. of William Lacy of London (F:260). Charles was given the manors of Hamerton and Winwick. He also held properties near Penehurst, Kent.

Charles was the father of (B:13-14; F:260): ANTHONY, a member of the Royal Household, he was pardoned by Mary in 1553, but executed and attainted in 1554 (B:14); RICHARD; ROBERT, d. s.p; and ELIZABETH.

14. Sir THOMAS KNYVETT, son of Edmund (12), d. Aug 1512. He m. Muriel Howard, dau. of Thomas Howard, 2nd Duke of Norfolk (B:8).

Knyvett was a friend of Henry VIII. He d. as commander of the *Regent*, which sank with all hands lost after a battle with a French warship (B:8).

Sir Thomas was the father of (B:8; F:260): EDMUND (ancestor of the Knyvetts of Buckenham); Sir HENRY, m. and had two sons who d. s.p.; ANNE, m. Thomas Thursby; and CATHERINE, m. 1st, William Fermor; and 2nd, Nicholas Mynne.

15. Sir EDMUND KNYVET, of Ashwellthorpe, Co. Norfolk, son of Edmund (12) and Eleanor, was b. 1490, and d. 1 May 1539, leaving a will dated 24 June 1537, proved 1546. He m. Jane (Joan) Bourchier, who died 17 Feb 1561/2.

Sir Edmund and Jane were the parents of (C:Line 4, 188; *RD500*:146): JOHN (ancestor of the Knyvetts of Ashwellthorpe); WILLIAM of Fundenhall; EDMUND; ELIZABETH, m. Francis Bohun (ancestors of **Edmund Bohun, Chief Justice of SC**); and poss. other daus.

16. RICHARD KNYVETT, son of Charles (13), d. 1559 at Westminster. He m. Hellen, dau. of William Harding, a wealthy London mercer and Surrey landowner (B:14).

Richard was a messenger and envoy from 1541 under his half-cousin, Sir Henry Knyvett. He remained on the continent during the final years of the reign of Henry VIII (B:14). Knyvett was evidently out of favor with the Duke of Somerset, protector of the realm during the minority of Edward VI. Somerset sold Knyvett's house in London as part of crown collections. Richard and his brother Anthony received pardons during the reign of Mary (B:14).

Richard Knyvett purchased the manor of Radford Semele, east of Warwick, from Thomas, Lord Darcy of Chiche, Essex, in 1556 (B:14).

Richard and Hellen were the parents of (B:14; *HSPV* 24:100): MARY, spinster of St. Anne's Blackfriars, on 13 Feb 1580/1, was granted a license to marry Henry North, 2nd son of Roger, Lord North in 1581; and HENRY, b. c1559, aged 7 mos. at his father's death.

17. EDMUND KNYVETT, son of Sir Thomas (14) and Muriel, in 1517 was made a ward of Charles Brandon, Duke of Suffolk, who had m. Mary Tudor, sister of Henry VIII.

In 1533, when he was 25, he gained control of the Buckenham lands. By the laws of primogeniture he was the heir to Buckenham Castle, and other lands.

18. JOHN KNYVETT, of Plumstead, Norfolk, son of Sir Edmund (15) and Jane, was living in 1543, but died in his mother's lifetime. He m. (settlement dated 28 Feb 1513) Agnes Harcourt, dau. of Sir John Harcourt of Stanton-Harcourt, Knt.

John and Agnes were the parents of (C:Line 4): Sir THOMAS; and ABIGAIL, m. Sir Martin Sedley (ancestors of **Elizabeth Sedley who m. [-?-] Macdonald**, and came to MD, and of **Muriel Gurdon who m. Maj. Richard Saltonstall of New Eng.**; See **The Sedley Family** elsewhere in this volume).

19. HENRY KNYVETT, son of Richard (16) and Helen (Harding) was born c1559 in Radford Semele, Warwickshire, Eng. and died after 1589. He married Magdalen Ford (A).

Elizabeth I gave the wardship of Henry Knevet at age 3, for upbringing and for conformity, to Sir William More, her agent and sheriff in Surrey who had helped to eliminate the Roman Catholic presence south of London late in her reign. Sir William had just completed his new manor house at Losely just south of Guilford in 1569 when Elizabeth visited, accompanied by Thomas Howard, 4th Duke of Norfolk. Norfolk met the children at Losely and bought the wardship of Henry Knevit then age eleven (A).

Henry entered Magdalen College at Oxford in 1571 at the actual age of 13, a somewhat common occurrence at the time. The alumni records of Oxford and Cambridge confuse Henry Knevit of the Radford Semele manor of Warwickshire with Henry Knyvet of Ashwellthrop, Norfolk (A).

Henry Knevit next appears listed in the ciphers found at the Norfolk House (Charterhouse) in 1572 at the time of the Duke's trial and execution. He had apparently been a messenger for Norfolk for two years (A).

After Oxford it is possible that Henry Knevit entered the Inns of Court since there was an appreciable recusant contingent there over the years but this conjecture is not certain. Henry was sent to the continent by Walsingham, the vigilant conformer, as a carrier and cipher expert in 1577-78. This shows how much confidence Elizabeth and her agents had in their program of educating the children of known recusants (A).

In 1589 Henry Knevit sold Radford Semele to John Browne of Barnham, Sussex, grandson of his mother Helen or Ellen Harding, by Sir Thomas Browne of Betchworth Castle (B:15).

Henry and Magdalen were the parents of: HENRY, Jr., b. c1590; and ROBERT.

20. Sir THOMAS KNYVETT, Lord Berners and Sheriff of Norfolk, son of John (18) and Agnes, was b. c1539, and d. 9 Feb 1617/8. He m. Muriel Parry, d. 25 April 1616, dau. of Sir Thomas Parry (D: Line 18).

21. HENRY KNYVETT, Jr., Naval Captain, son of Henry (19) and Magdalen, was born c1590, and resided in northwest London. As Henry Knyvett of the precinct of St. Martin le Grand, on 30 December 1618, he was granted a license to marry at St. Leonard's in St. Martin's le Grand, Alice Armistead of St. Michael le Quern, spinster, in St. Leonards, St. Martin-le-Grand. (*HSPV* 23:25).

Henry and Alice were the parents of (B): RICHARD, b. c1619 in Eng., d. c1652 in MD.

22. RICHARD NEVITT, son of Henry (21) and Alice, was b. c1619, and a ward of John Saunders of Peter and Paul's Wharf. Saunders and Thomas Cornwallis owned one-fourth of a 50 ton small pinnace, *The Dove*. Lord Baltimore, Jerome Hawley, Richard Gerard, and Frederick Wintour owned the remaining shares (*NFMP*:48).

John Saunders and his ward Richard Nevitt signed on for the voyage to Maryland, where Richard Nevitt m. and had children (B:15).

THE HUGH NEVITT FAMILY

Refs.: A: *LMCD*.

1. [-?-] NEVITT was the father of the following children, named in the will, dated 27 July 1673, proved 5 Oct. 1680, of his son Hugh: HUGH; WILLIAM; RICHARD; ARTHUR.

2. HUGH NEVITT, son of [-?-], died in VA, leaving a will dated 27 July 1673, proved 5 Oct. 1680. On 6 Sept. 1664 Hugh Nevitt was granted 400 a. on the north side of Mattapony? River at head of Fornham Creek (A:31). On 1 Feb. 1666: Hugh Nevitt and George Seaton, merchants of VA, were appointed attorneys to recover a debt owed by Thomas Godlington of London, to Richard Sherhood of Thames St., St. Mary at Hill.

In his will, dated 27 July 1673, proved 5 Oct. 1680, he named John Nevett, son of Richard Nevett, to be executor, bro. William and his daus.; bro. Richard, and his daughters, and bro. Arthur, who was sent for to come to VA. Admin. with will annexed was granted on 5 Oct. 1680 to nephew John Nevett.

3. WILLIAM NEVITT, Citizen and Haberdasher of the City of London, son of [-?-], was the father of (A:42): JOHN NEVETT, age 23, in 1672, son of William Nevett, signed a deposition stating that his father had sent goods to Hugh Nevitt in VA, and that he was sent to VA with the goods (A:48); JANE; ANNE; and SUSANNAH.

4. RICHARD NEVETT of Whitchurch, Salop, turner, son of [-?-], on 17 Nov. 1673: had a son: John, who on that day assigned to Jane, Anne, and Susanna Nevitt, daughters of William Nevett of London, merchant, all the legacies he had from his (John's) uncle Hugh Nevett of VA, dec. (A:49); also several daus.

5. ARTHUR NEVETT, son of [-?-], is named in the will of his bro. HUGH.

Unplaced:

KNYVET, JOHN, Sr., of Norfolk, m. Joan, widow of Sir Robert de Tye of Barsham. John and Joan were the parents of (C:Line 59; D: Lines 88, 88A): MARGARET, alive in 1467, m. c1415-24, Sir Thomas de Echyngham.

THE NICHOLSON FAMILY (1) EXPANDED

Refs.: A: *MGH* 4th ser., 2:110. B: PCLR EI#9:509. C: *SSLM*:542. D; *BDML*. E: Nigel Nicholson, *Nicholson: Being a Compilation of Family Trees of Nicolson-Nicholson* (1996), data made available to the author by Bruce L. Nicholson, University of Maine.

1. GEORGE NICHOLSON of Loanend, Durham, died 21 April 1665. He married Eleanor [-?-] who was buried 19 March 1690 (E).

George and Eleanor were the parents of at least two sons (E): WILLIAM, d. 1690; and GEORGE.

2. WILLIAM NICHOLSON, son of George (1), was buried at Berwick on Tweed, on 4 May 1690. He married Ann [-?-] who was buried 2 Nov 1691 "in linen, contrary to the act."

William and Anne were the parents of (A): ANTHONY, bapt. 20 Oct 1641; WILLIAM, bapt. 1656, bur. Oct 1656; WILLIAM, b. and d. 1663/4; WILLIAM, bapt. 22 Feb 1665/6; JOSEPH, b. 1669, d. 1671; and several daus., including ELINOR, m. [-?-] Foster; ANNE; and ELIZABETH.

3. GEORGE NICHOLSON, son of George (1) and Eleanor, was the father (or grandfather) of (E): JAMES.

4. WILLIAM NICHOLSON, son of William (2) and Ann, was bapt. 22 Feb 1665/6 and died in MD in 1719. In his will, dated 25 Sep and proved 19 Oct 1719, he named his sisters Mrs. Elinor Foster, Anne Nicholson and Elizabeth Nicholson, and William Hunt to be the executors of his estate in England (MWB 15:325).

William had at least three sons living in March 1754 (B): JOSEPH, living at Chestertown, KE Co., MD, m. Hannah [-?-]; BENJAMIN, living at Berwick on Tweed, m. Margaret [-?-]; SAMUEL, of Stockton-upon-Tees, Co. Durham, Dr. of Physic; m. Elizabeth [-?-].

5. JAMES NICHOLSON, son or grandson of George (3), settled in AA Co. Nigel Nicholson, in his book refers to letters in Berwick-on-Tweed from this James Nicholson.

James Nicholson married Rebecca Ward in All Hallow's Parish, AA Co., on 4 Oct 1722 (*AACR*:34). They were the parents of (*AACR*:37, 41): JAMES, b. 16 Sep 1723, bapt. 18 Oct 1723; and ALICE, b. 26 Aug 1726, bapt. 19 Sep 1726.

6. JOSEPH NICHOLSON, son of William (4), married and had several children including (C; D): JOSEPH, Jr.; BENJAMIN, d. 1792 in BA Co., m. Mary, dau. of John Ridgely and had issue (C:541).

7. JOSEPH NICHOLSON, Jr., son of Joseph (6), died in 1786. He was admitted to practice law in several courts beginning in Jan 1755. In July 1757 he m. Elizabeth, dau. of Major Hopper of QA Co. (C).

NOBLE, WILLIAM, of Snaith, Yorks., m. by 7 Sep 1728, Mary, sister of Thomas Wainwright, who on that day, conveyed personal property to his niece Ellen Noble (AALR RD#1:44).

William was the father of the following children, whose baptisms at the parish church of Snaith, and whose recognition as nephew and niece by Thomas Wainwright were recorded in AALR TI#1:53): JOHN, bapt. 17 Sep 1700; and ELLEN, bapt. 31 March 1703.

THE NORRIS FAMILY
A Tentative Reconstruction

Refs.: A: "Norris of Wood Norton Hall." *BLG* 1906. pp. 1241-1242. B: Harry Alexander Davis. "The Norris Family." Typescript, Rare Book Room Library of Congress.

The Line in England

1. GEOFFREY NORRIS, of Tilney, was party to a fine of property in Lynn in 1363, and brought land in Tilney in 1382. He was the father of (A): GEOFFREY.

2. GEOFFREY NORRIS, son of Geoffrey (1), was b. c1370, and had two sons (A): GEOFFREY; and JOHN, stated in Burke to have been Vicar of South Lynn in 1444, and d. 1504.

3. GEOFFREY NORRIS, Lord of Monpinzoms Manor, in West Bliney, Norfolk, son of Geoffrey (2), d. in 1464. He m. Margery [-?-], by whom he was the father of (A): JOHN, b. c1425.

4. JOHN NORRIS, of West Bliney, Norfolk, son of Geoffrey (3), was b. c1425 (B), and was the father of (A; B): ROBERT, b. c1460.

5. ROBERT NORRIS of West Bliney, son of John (4), was b. c1460, and was the father of (A; B): GEOFFREY.

6. GEOFFREY NORRIS, son of Robert (5), was under age in 1504. He was the father of (A: B): JOHN.

7. JOHN NORRIS, of Congham, son of Geoffrey (6), was living in 1566. He m. [-?-], dau. of [-?-] Might of Gunthorpe, Norfolk, and was the father of (A; B): THOMAS; GEOFFREY; and CUTHBERT, D.D., Archdeacon of Sudbury.

8. THOMAS NORRIS, son of John (7), was b. 1549, and was the patron of the living of Anmere. He was the father of (A): THOMAS, of Anmere; and ROBERT, of Congham (His line is traced in Burke).

9. GEOFFREY NORRIS, is placed by Davis as a son of John (7), and to have been the father of (B): THOMAS.

The Line in Maryland.

10. THOMAS NORRIS, is placed by Davis as the son of Geoffrey. He is said to have been born in Congham, Norfolk, in 1608, and to have d. in 1679. In 1637 he m. Anne Hynson (B).

     He settled in Nansemond Co., VA, in 1631 and in SM Co. in 1637. Davis states that there were several Norris families living in Co. Norfolk, but the names

Cuthbert and Geoffrey (found in the descendants of Thomas of Maryland) appear only in the Congham branch (B).

Norris was a follower of William Claiborne. After arriving in MD, he was associated with his brother-in-law Daniel Glover, and he may have been associated with his father-in-law in Nansemond Co., VA (B).

Thomas and Anne (Hynson) Norris were the parents of (B; see also KELR GL#1:108/132): THOMAS, b. c1638; EDWARD, b. Oct 1639; GEOFFREY, d. age 2 or 3 years; DANIEL, b. April 1643 in Nansemond Co., VA; CUTHBERT, b. Aug 1645, d. age 23, having drowned at sea; ROBERT, b. Dec 1647; ANN, b. c1650,; and JOHN, b. 1652.

11. DANIEL NORRIS, son of Thomas (10), and brother of Anne and Thomas, d. in KE Co.by 12 March 1707. He was in KE Co. by 28 June 1684 when he stated he was formerly an inhabitant in the City of London, England, but now was an inhabitant of KE Co., MD (KELR K:91). He described the family of his eldest sister (KELR GL#1:108/132).

A statement by Daniell Norris of KE Co., age c64, was recorded cJune 1706. In it he declared that his eldest sister, Ann Norris married William Woodroofe at a village called Cowley in Glo[uce]stershire in England who was eldest brother of Thomas Woodroofe who came to a place or towne called Salem in the Province of West New Jersey in America and there inhabiting near 30 years, died. Norris also stated that Joseph Woodroofe, eldest son and heir of said dec'd. Thomas in the lifetime of said Thomas came from said Salem to visit the deponent at his dwelling house in KE Co. Maryland; that he was well acquainted with Thomas and Joseph in London before any of them came to America, and that said William Woodroofe had in his lifetime issue several sons by the said Ann this deponent's sister, viz., John, William, Francis and Thomas and two daus., viz., Mary and Ann, which this deponent was well acquainted in England, some of which may yet be alive there. He knows of no one in America now alive so nearly related to the deceased Thomas Woodroofe and Joseph Woodroofe his son who died at Salem as afsd. as he, the deponent, is (KELR GL#1:108/132).

Daniel Norris died in KE Co. leaving a will dated 13 Jan. 1706, proved 23 March 1707. He named his son-in-law William Bentley and the latter's daus. Mary and Patience. He also named his son Daniel, daughter Eliza, and brother Thomas Norris. He mentioned three tracts and 120 acres left to testator by his bro. Thomas Norris; land bought of Richd. Tighlman, and land bought of Michael Miller. If the children of his sister should arrive from England, their passage was to be paid for by his devisees. Finally he was to be buried beside his deceased wife Elizabeth. He named William Trew, Sr., and Henry Hosier as execs. (MWB 12:242).

His estate was inventoried on 4 May 1707 by Thomas Piner and Arthur Miller, and valued at £65.5.0 (INAC 28:186). See also INAC 30:178, 31:60, 32C:20.

Daniel Norris was the father of several children, including: ELIZABETH, m. William Bentley; and DANIEL.

12. ANN NORRIS, dau. of Thomas (10), and sister of Daniel and Thomas, was stated by the said Daniel to have married William Woodroofe at a village called Cowley in Glostershire in England.

William was the eldest brother of Thomas Woodroofe who came to a place or towne called Salem in the Province of West New Jersey in America and there inhabiting near 30 years, died, leaving a son Joseph.

Norris added that the said William Woodroofe had in his lifetime issue several children by the said Ann this deponent's sister, with whom he was well acquainted in England, some of which may yet be alive there (B).

William and Ann (Norris) Woodroff were the parents of (B): JOHN; WILLIAM; FRANCIS; THOMAS; MARY; and ANN WOODRUFF.

13. ELIZABETH NORRIS, dau. of Daniel (11), m. William Bentley. She stated that she knew her cousin Francis Woodroofe who was William Woodroofe's son; that he dwelt sometime in her father's Daniell's house in London and called her father uncle and her mother aunt (KELR GL#1:110/134)

THE OFFLEY FAMILY EXPANDED

Refs.: A: G. C. Brewer and H. W. F. Harwood. "Pedigree of Offley." pub. serially in *The Genealogist*, n.s., 19:217 ff. B: *APPL*. C: *Offley Family Papers*. Ed. and comp. by John Brockenbrough Offley. Williamsburg [VA]: 1975.

Generation 1

1. JOHN OFFLEY of Stafford, was b. c1440, and m. Margery [-?-], who m. 2nd [-?-] Dillarne of Stafford. John Offley is called Richard in a grant of arms made Feb 1654 by Ryley, Norroy King of Arms, to his great-grandson Francis Offley of Ebbing. John and Margery had (A; C): WILLIAM.

Generation 2

2. WILLIAM OFFLEY, son of John (1) and Margery, was b. c1480 and d. 1560. He was buried in St. Peter's Church, Stafford (C), was twice Mayor of Stafford, and later moved to Chester, where he was sheriff in 1517. He m., 1st, [-?-], dau. of Dorrington, Co. Stafford (her sister m. a Mr. Craddock). He m., 2nd, prob. Elizabeth, widow or daughter of William Rogerson of Chester (C: states she was Anne Rogerson).

William had five children by his 1st wife and seven by his 2nd (A; C): Sir THOMAS, b. 1500 at Stafford; JOHN, Sheriff of Chester, 1544 and Mayor 1553; m. and had issue; MARGARET, m. 1st John Nichols and 2nd, Stephen Kerton; ELIZABETH or ISABEL, m. 1st, Thomas Blower, and 2nd, [-?-] Amcottes; MARGERY, m. 1st Thomas Michell, and 2nd, James Lawson; (by 2nd wife): ROBERT, bur. 29 April 1596; THOMAS, bur. 1 Feb 1588/9 at St. Andrew Undershaft; RICHARD, d. by 28 Dec 1582; m. and had issue; WILLIAM, bur. 7 Jan 1600/1; HUGH; KATHERINE, m. by 1 Feb 1551/2 Robert or William Bowyer; and [-?-], dau., m. Gyles Jacob.

Generation 3

3. Sir THOMAS OFFLEY of Madeley Manor, Staffs, son of William (2) and his first wife, was b. at Stafford, c1500, and d. 29 Aug 1582. and was buried at St. Andrew's Undershaft, London on 17 Sep following. He m. Joane Nechells, dau. and heiress of John Nechells (C).

Thomas was sent to London at the age of 12, and educated at the Jesus School of St. Paul's Churchyard. Later he was a member of the Merchant Taylor's Guild and served as its Master in 1547. He served as Alderman of Potsoken Ward up to 1550. He moved to Aldergate Ward where he was Alderman from 1580 until 1592. He was Sheriff of London in 1553, and led the London militia against the forces of Sir Thomas Wyatt. In 1556 he was knighted by Queen Mary, and was Lord Mayor of London (C).

Sir Thomas and Joane were the parents of (C): HENRY; ROBERT; and [-?-], a son who d. in infancy.

4. ROBERT OFFLEY, son of William (2) and Elizabeth, d. 1596. A merchant of London, he m. Rose, widow of [-?-] Brakun. They were the parents of (A; B:255): ROBERT.

5. RICHARD OFFLEY, son of William (2), and Elizabeth, was born at Chester, and died by 28 Dec 1582. He m. Jane, dau. of Sir William Chester, Kt., Lord Mayor of London when St. Paul's Steeple was on fire (1561). She was buried 29 Feb 1611/2 at St. Mary's Woolnoth (A:20:49).

Richard Offley was a Merchant Taylor and Master of the Company, 1572 and 1582. He was also a Merchant of the Staple, and a Factor for Sir Thomas Offley at Callice, and died within 6 mos. of Sir Thomas. Richard's estate was administered (P.C.C. admons.) on 28 dec 1582 and 28 Nov 1583 (A:20:49).

Richard and Jane were the parents of (A:20:49-50): MARTIN, bapt. at St. Mary's Woolnoth on 19 March 1579/80; FRANCIS, bur. 15 Aug 1581 at St. Mary's Woolnoth; HUGH, 1581-1582; THOMAS, d. by 21 May 1612; RICHARD, Citizen and Merchant Taylor of London, d. by 2 Jan 1643/4; ROBERT, bur. 30 Dec 1610 at St. Mary's Woolnoth; WILLIAM, m. Jane [-?-]; ELIZABETH, bur. 20 Aug 1691 at St. Mary's Woolnoth, m. by license. granted 1 Feb 1591/2, Richard Beney of St. Mary's Woolnoth, London, goldmith *(HSPV* 25:196) (They were possibly the ancestors of **Richard Cheney of AA Co., MD**; for whose ancestry, see *British Roots of Maryland Families*, vol. 1); KATHERINE, m. Edward Delves of St. Mary's Woolnoth, goldsmith.

6. HUGH OFFLEY, son of William (2) and Elizabeth, was b. at Chester, d. at London and was bur. 17 Dec 1594 at St. Andrew Undershaft. He was made a Freeman of the Company of Leathersellers, and became Alderman, and later Sheriff in 1588. He m., 1st, Anne, dau. of Alderman Robert Harding (whose will was printed in *The Genealogist*, n.s., 16:267-269). Anne d. 14 Nov 1588, and he m. 2nd, on 25 March 1589 at St. Mildred Poultry/St. Mary Colechurch, London, Dorothy, widow of John Weld, and dau. of Roger Greswold (A).

One of Hugh's grandsons, David Offley of New Southampton Buildings in the Parish of St. Giles-in-the-Fields, London, may be the **David Offley** who moved to

Boston, MA, by 1638 where he was a member of the Ancient and Honourable Artillery Company (C).

Hugh had eight children by his 1st wife, and one by his 2nd (A): ROBERT, bapt. 29 June 1563, bur. 1565; THOMAS; ROBERT, d. 4 Nov 1631; WILLIAM; SYMON; HUGH, bapt. 24 Aug 1578 at St. Andrew Undershaft, London; ELIZABETH, bapt. 8 Dec 1566; m. Sir James Deane of London; and MARGARET, d. in inf.; and (by 2nd w.): SUSANNA, bapt. 28 June 1590, m. Philip Giffard.

Generation 4

7. HENRY OFFLEY of Madeley Manor, Staffs, son of Sir Thomas (3) and Joane, was b. c1535 and d. in London on 3 Sep 1613. On 7 July 1567, he m. Mary, dau. of Sir John White, who had been Lord Mayor London in 1563).

Henry and Mary were the parents of (C): THOMAS; HENRY; MARY; and Sir JOHN.

8. ROBERT OFFLEY, son of Robert (4), was a member of the Virginia Company. On 3 Feb 1588/9 he m. at St. Dionis Backchurch, Ann Osborne, dau. of Sir Edward Osborne, Sheriff and Lord Mayor of London.

Robert and Ann were the parents of (B:256): SARAH, m. 1st, Capt. Adam Thoroughgood, and 2nd, John Gookin, and 3rd, Col. Francis Yardley.

9. THOMAS OFFLEY, of London, son of Hugh (6) and Ann (Harding), was bapt. 10 Dec 1564 at St. Lawrence Poultney, d. in London, 23 Aug 1630; soon after 20 Dec 1592 he m. Anne, dau. of Henry Clitherow of London; she d. by 14 Sep 1638;

Thomas and Anne were the par. of: HUGH, bapt. 10 Nov 1594 at St. Andrew Undershaft, London, d. 1595; son, d. 1654; CHRISTOPHER, age 30 in 1633/4; THOMAS, d. beyond the seas, 12 Dec 1627; JUSTINIAN, d. in the East Indies by 10 May 1629; FRANCIS, b. 1611 at Wilbing in Prussia, and had a confirmation of his arms in 1654; CATHERINE, m. 1st [-?-] Brewster; 2nd, Rev. Philip Edelen of Middlesex and Alverstoke, Hants (See **The Edelen Family**, in *British Roots of Maryland Families*, Vol. I); ANNE; and BRIDGET, m. Edward Draxe (A).

Generation 5

10. Sir JOHN OFFLEY, Kt., of Madeley Manor, Staffs, son of Henry (7) and Mary, was b. c1586, and d. June 1647. He m. Anne Fuller, dau. of Nicholas Fuller of Chamber House, Berks (C).

Sir John was knighted by James I at Theobald's on 25 April 1615. He was High Sheriff of Staffs in 1616, and an M.P. for Staffs in 1625 and 1628. Sir John was also a Gentleman of the Bedchamber to King James I (C).

Sir John and Anne were the parents of (C): JOHN; ELIZABETH; ANNE; KATHERINE (Katherine Offley, of St. Martin's in the Fields, spinster, age 21, dau. of Sir John Offley, who gave his consent, and Thomas Wyllys, of St. Andrew's Holborn, bachelor, age 26, were granted a license to marry on 16 March 1643/4; marriage to take place at either St. Andrew's Holborn, or St. Mary Magdalen, Old Fish St: *HSPV* 26:273); and SARAH.

Generation 6

11. JOHN OFFLEY, Esq., of Madeley Manor, Staffs, of Sir John (10) and Anne, was b. c1619, and d. 1658. As John Offley, Esq., of Middle Temple, bachelor, age 24, he m 1st, by license granted 13 July 1641, Dorothy Lidcott, spinster, also aged about 24, dau. of Sir John Lidcott (who gave his consent) of Mousley, Surrey (*HSPV* 26:259). John Offley m. 2nd, in March 1647/8, Mary Broughton, dau. of Thomas Broughton of Broughton Hall, Staffs (C).

John Offley entered Trinity College, Oxford, in Oct 1635. He was Sheriff of Staffs in 1649. In May 1650 he was committed to the Tower of London, for his alleged conspiracy in support of King Charles I. Izaak Walton dedicated his work, *The Compleat Angler*, to him in 1653.

John Offley and Dorothy were the parents of (C): MICHAEL.

John and his 2nd wife Mary were the parents of (C): JOHN, b. at Madeley, in 1651. He m. Anne Crewe, dau. of John Crewe of Crewe Hall, Cheshire (Their son, John Offley, adopted the surname Crewe by Act of Parliament in 1708 so he could inherit the Crewe estate. He was the ancestor of the Marquess of Crewe (C)).

Generation 7

12. MICHAEL OFFLEY, of Madeley Manor, son of John (11) and Dorothy, was b. c1638, and was bapt. at Newport, Staffs, on 12 Aug 1638 (C). In 1658 he emigrated to AA Co., MD (MPL 5:247, 9:478, and 15:300). He then established an estate in CE Co., MD. In May 1679 Lord Baltimore granted him 800 a. called Hugh Offley in CE Co. In 1681 the Duke of York granted him 600 a. in New Castle Co., DE, where his descendants settled (C).

Michael Offley was the father of (C): CALEB, settled in PA, but his son Michael later returned to KE Co., MD; HASADIAH; BENONA; and [-?-], dau., m. Thomas Shaw (by whom she had a child, Hazadiah Shaw).

Unplaced:

OFFLEY, EDWARD, of KE Co. and his wife Elizabeth, c1698 granted to James Mitchel of England, mariner, their right to a sum of money in the hands of Richard Thomas of Hartford in England (KELR M:78A). On 23 April 1698 Edward Offley witnessed the will of Thomas Collins who directed that his own mother Offley was to be maintained from his (Collins') estate for her life (MWB 6:118}

OFFLEY, JOHN, d. in TA Co. by 10 Nov 1685 when his personal estate was valued at £52.0.1 by Robert Smith and William Sparks (INAC 8:487).

THE PAYNE FAMILY

The compiler is indebted to Harry Meixell of Gettysburg, PA and Norman Payne of Livingstone, TX for generously allowing the results of their research to be included in this work.

Refs.: A: Registers of St. Mary Magdalen, Old Fish Street, London.

1. THOMAS PAYNE m. Elizabeth [-?-]. They were the parents of (A): MARY, bapt. 10 March 1694; FLAYLE, bapt. 29 Nov 1696; THOMAS, bapt. 10 July 1698, prob. d. young; THOMAS, bapt. 10 July 1700, prob. d, young; JOHN, bapt. 27 Oct 1702; and THOMAS, bapt. 1 Oct 1704.

2. FLAYLE PAYNE, son of Thomas (1) and Elizabeth, was bapt. 29 Nov 1696 at St. Mary Magdalen, Old Fish Street, London (A). He settled in MD.

Payne was in PG Co. by 8 March 1735 when John Abington, with the consent of his wife Mary, conveyed 100 a,. Paine's Delight, to Flayle Paine (PGLR T:243).

THE PENRUDDOCK FAMILY

1. [-?-] PENRUDDOCK was the father of: ANTHONY; and ELIZA, m. Mr. [-?-] Seaborne.

2. ANTHONY PENRUDDOCK, brother of Eliza Seaborne, is not listed in Skordas, but evidently acquired land in MD. He d. by May 1642, having married [-?-].

He d. leaving a will dated 29 Dec 1641 and proved 2 May 1642. To his wife he left his personal estate and anything he might inherit from Lord Windsor, lately dec., or from Lord Herbert, son and heir of the Earl of Worcester; he named his daus. Jane and Lucy; cousins George and Edward Penruddocke, niece Lady Jane FitzWilliam and her husband Col. Fitzwilliam; his sister Mrs. Eliza Seaborne; and cousin John Penruddock. He stated he lived and died a Roman Catholic (Withington. "Maryland Gleanings in England." *MHM* 3:194).

Anthony Penruddock was the father of: JANE; and LUCY.

3. EDWARD PENRUDDOCK was named as a cousin in the 1641 will of Anthony Penruddock. In Jan 1656 Edward Penruddock and George Duke, prisoners at Exeter, petitioned that they might be transported to VA instead of Barbadoes, to which they had been ordered (*CBE1*:308).

THE PETRE FAMILY

Refs.: A: "Petre." *Burke's Peerage*, 1956 ed. p. 1722. B: "Petre." *Lawson*, pp. 38-ff.

Generations 1-5

1. JOHN PETYR, m. Alice [-?-]. She d. 6 Dec 14 Edw. IV, having m. as her 2nd husband, John Storke. John and Alice were the parents of (B): JOHN; and poss. NICHOLAS (said to have inherited Bakebear in Co. Dorset from his mother).

2. JOHN PETYR, son of John (1) and Alice, d. by 1472, He was the father of (B): WILLIAM.

3. WILLIAM PETYR of Torbrian, Co. Devon, son of John (2), was age 24 in 1475. He m. Joan [-?-], and they were the parents of (B): JOHN; and WILLIAM, m. Joan, dau. and heir of Roger Arundell of Calwoodley, and had issue.

4. JOHN PETER/PETRE of Torbrian, son of William (3) and Joan, m. Alice, dau. of John Colling of Woodlands, Parish of Ipplepen, Devon. Lawson mentions a document dated 1 Oct 1554 from the Mayor of Exeter to John Petre, "Citizen," his wife Alice, and William her son (B).

       John and Alice were the parents of (B): Sir WILLIAM; JOHN, 2nd son, d. 7 July 1568, m. and had issue; JOHN, 3rd son, d. 12 Feb 1570; RICHARD, Chancellor of Exeter; WYLLMOT, m. John Petre; ROBERT, Auditor of the Exchequer, m. Margaret Tyrrel; ALICE, m. Thomas Reade of Uplowman, Devon; and THOMASINE, m. William Parkin of Parkins.

5. Sir WILLIAM PETRE, Kt., LL.D., Chancellor of the Order of the Garter, son of John (4) and Alice, was b. 1500, and d. at Ingatestone on 13 Jan 1571/2. He m. 1st, Gertrude, dau. of Sir John Tyrrell of Warley, Essex. She d. 28 May 1541 and Sir William m. 2nd in 1541, Anne, widow of Sir Thomas Tyrrell of Heron Place, Essex, and dau. of Sir William Browne, Lord Mayor of London (by his wife Alice Keble. Sir William and Alice were also ancestors of **The Gorsuch Family of MD**). Anne Brown Petre d. at Ingatestone on 10 March 1581 (B).

       Sir William was a person of great learning, and was one of the principal Secretaries of State during the reigns of Henry VIII, Edward VI, Mary, and Elizabeth (A).

       By Gertrude Tyrrell, he was the father of (A; B): JOHN, d.s.p; DOROTHEA, b. 1535, m. Nicholas Wadham of Merrifield, Soms.; and ELIZABETH, m. John Gostwick of Willington.

       By Anne Browne, Sir William was the father of (A): EDWARD, d. s.p.; KATHERINE, m. John Talbot of Grafton; Sir JOHN, b. 1549; THOMASIN, b. 7 April 1543, m. Ludovick Greville; WILLIAM; JOHN; and ANNE.

Generation 6

6. KATHERINE PETRE, dau. of Sir William (5) and Anne, was b. 25 April 1545 at Ingatestone. On 18 Aug 1561 she m. John Talbot of Grafton, Co. Worcester. They were the parents of (B:50): GERTRUDE, b. 22 March 1562; ANNE, b. 3 June 1564;

GEORGE, b. 19 Dec 1566, Earl of Shrewsbury, d. unm.; MARY, b. 21 March 1567; and JOHN, b. 10 Feb 1570.

7. Sir JOHN PETRE, 1st Baron Petre, son of Sir William (5) and Anne, M.P. for Essex, d. 11 Oct 1613. He m. Mary, dau. of Sir Edward Waldegrave, Kt., of Borley, Essex (by his wife Frances Neville). Sir John was elevated to the peerage as Baron Petre of Writtle, Essex, on 21 July 1603.

Sir John and Mary were the parents of (A): WILLIAM, 2nd Baron Petre; EDWARD, b. 1577, d.1577/8; MARY; ELIZABETH; MARGARET; ANNE, b. 1592, d. 1583; KATHERINE; JOHN, m. Dorothy [-?-]; THOMAS, m. Elizabeth Baskerville; and ROBERT, b. 1587, d. 1590.

Generation 7

8. JOHN TALBOT, son of John and Katherine (6) Petre, was b. 20 Feb 1570. He m. Eleanor Baskerville. They were the parents of: JOHN, 10th Earl of Shrewsbury (#3 in *British Roots of Maryland Families* (1999), p. 418, and ancestor of Anne Talbot who m. **Henry Darnall of MD**).

9. WILLIAM PETRE, 2nd Baron Petre, son of Sir John (7) and Mary, was b. 24 June 1575 and d. 5 May 1627. He m. on 8 Nov 1596, Lady Catherine Somerset, dau. of Sir Edward, Earl of Worcester. William and Catherine were the parents of (A; *BARD7*: 10-11; additional children found in the Ancestral File of LDS): ELIZABETH, b. 25 Sep 1597, m. William Sheldon; JOHN, b. 23 Oct 1598, d. 1604; ROBERT, 3rd Lord Petre, b. 22 Sep 1599; MARY, b. 23 Dec 1600, m. John Roper, Baron Teynham; WILLIAM, b. 28 July 1602, m. Lucy Fermor; EDWARD, b. 21 Aug 1603; THOMAS, b. 10 May 1606; CATHERINE, b. 10 June 1697, m. John Caryll, and 2nd, Baron Writtle; ANN, b. 1609, d. 1610; HENRY, b. 27 March 1611, m. Anne Gage; and GEORGE, b. 15 Aug 1613, m. Anne Fox.

Generation 8

10. THOMAS PETRE, son of William (9) and Catherine, was b. at Westhorndon on 10 May 1606 (B:51). He m. Ursula, dau. of Richard (or Walter) Brooke of Lapsley Hall, Suffolk.

Thomas and Ursula were the parents of (B:41; *BARD7*:11): WILLIAM, d. 1709; ANNE, d. leaving a will dated 15 Feb 1706/7, proved 17 April 1707 (naming her sister Winifred wife of George Attwood as sister and extx., and also naming her nephews Dr. Thomas and George Attwood: B:76); MARY; WALTER; THOMAS; FRANCIS; and WINIFRED, b. c1637, d. 14 Dec 1714, aged 77 (not 1771), m. George Attwood of Beverly, Co. Worcester (See **The Attwood Family** elsewhere in this work).

THE PHILIPSON FAMILY

Refs.: A: "Philipson of Thwatterden Hall, Westmorland, 1615, and of Conishead, Co. Lanc." *CWFO*:104. B: "Philipson." *AWLH*:231-232.

ARMS: Quarterly 1 and 4: Gules, a chevron between three boars' heads couped Ermine. 2: Or, a fesse dancettee between three cross-crosslets fitchee Gules (Sandys), 3: Per fesse Azure and Gules, a castle Argent (Rawson) (A).

1. ROBERT PHILIPSON of Hallinghall, Co. Westmorland, m. [-?-], dau. of [-?-] Dockwray of Dockwray Hall, near Kendall. They were the parents of at least one son (A): ROWLAND.

2. ROWLAND PHILIPSON, of Hallinghall, son of Robert (1), d. 30 Aug 1516. He m. Katherine, dau. of Richard Carus of Staveley. They were the parents of (A): ROBERT.

3. ROBERT PHILIPSON, of Hallinghall, son of Rowland (2), d. 22 Dec 1539. By his wife Jennet, dau. of Thomas Laybourne of Cunswick, Westmorland, Esq., he was the father of (A): CHRISTOPHER.

4. CHRISTOPHER PHILIPSON, of Calgarth in Westmorland, son of Robert (3) and Jennet, d. 21 Aug 1566, He m. Elizabeth, dau. of Robert Briggs of Helsfell Hall, Westmorland (A).

　　　　Christopher was Receiver to Edward VI for his revenues in Westmorland (A). He bought Calgarth in 1565 (B).

　　　　Christopher and Elizabeth were the parents of (A): ROWLAND; NICHOLAS, d. s.p.; FRANCIS, d. s.p.; ROBERT of the Middle Temple, d. s.p.; MILES; ANNE, m. 1st, Christopher Carus of Staveley, and 2nd, John Richardson of Rampside Hall, Lancs.; and JENNET, m. Thomas Ward of Rigmayden in Westmorland.

5. ROWLAND PHILIPSON alias THIRWALL, of Calgarth, Esq., Justice of the Peace, son of Christopher (4) and Elizabeth, m. Katherine, dau. and sole heir of Nicholas Carus of Kendal.

　　　　He was granted arms in 1581: Gules a chevron between three boars' heads couped Ermine, tusked Or. Crest: Five ostrich feathers three Argent, two Gules, set in a mural crown Or (B).

6. MILES PHILIPSON of Thwatterden Hall, Westmorland, Justice of the Peace, son of Christopher (4) and Elizabeth, m. Barbara, sister and coheir of Francis Sandys of Consihead, Lancs. By this marriage the Sandys and Rawson quarterings were brought into the Phulipson arms (A).

　　　　Miles Philipson was granted arms: Gules a chevron between three boars' heads couped Ermine, tusked Or, within a bordure of the third. Crest; Five ostrich feathers, three Gules, two Argent. Mantling: Gules, doubled Or, lined white (B).

　　　　Miles and Barbara were the parents of (A): ROBERT, m. Anne Latus and had issue; FRANCIS, d. s.p.; ELIZABETH, d. s.p.; JANE, d. s.p.; CHRISTOPHER, m.

Bridget Kirkby and had issue; THOMAS, d. s.p.; JOHN, Bachelor of Civil Law, and Fellow of Merton College, Oxford; Capt. MILES, m. Mary Wharton; MARY, m. Samuel Knipe; and ANNE.

7. ANNE PHILIPSON, dau. of Miles (6) and Barbara, m. Thomas, Baron Arundell of Wardour Castle, Wilts., and Count of the Holy Roman Empire. They were the parents of (among others): Lady ANNE, d. 23 July 1649 in her 33rd year, m. (settlement dated 20 March 1627/8, **Cecil Calvert, 2nd Baron Baltimore** (*MCS5*: Line 63); and MARY, m. Sir John Somerset (They were ancestors of **Maria Johanna Somerset** who m. Richard Smith of MD).

THE PILKINGTON FAMILY

Refs.: A: Lieut.-Col. John Pilkington. *History of the Pilkington Family of Lancashire and Its Branches from 1066 to 1600*. Liverpool: Privately printed for the author by C. Tingling and Co., 1912. B: "Milborne-Swinnerton-Pilkington," *Burke's Peerage, Baronetage, and Knightage*, 1956 ed., pp. 1733-1734.

ARMS: Argent, a cross flory voided Gules. CREST: A mower with his scythe, Ppr., habited per pale Argent and Sable (B:1734).

Generations 1-5

1. ALEXANDER PILKINGTON, b. c1110, d. 1180, is the first individual for whom existing records can document a place in the pedigree of Pilkington progeny. The Lancashire Pipe Roll of 31 Henry II (1184-1185) mentions Alexander of Alexander and William of Alexander, both of Salford Hundred. They are believed to be members of the family. The above Alexander appears to have had at least three children (A:23-24), and his wife may have been a member of the de Rivington family.

Alexander was the father of: ALEXANDER, who assumed "de Pilkington" as a surname; WILLIAM, who was a party to a final concord of 4 John (1202), along with his brother Alexander and his sister Alice; this William probably died between 1210 and 1213); and ALICE, was living in 1202.

2. ALEXANDER PILKINGTON, son of Alexander (1) and [-?-] (poss. de Rivington), held the manor of Pilkington during the reign of King John, and may have been in possession as early as Henry II. He was alive in 1185, and may have lived as late as 1231. In the Great Inquest of 1212 concerning service due to the King, he was one of the 17 "trusty Knights" who were appointed commissioners. He may have married Ursula, daughter of Gerard de Workedlegh, but no proof has been found.

He probably died after 1231 when he witnessed one of the Lord Ellesmere Deeds, and prior to 1242 when Sir Roger de Pilkington held the manor of Pilkington. The second Alexander de Pilkington may have been the father of (A:24-27): ROGER; ROBERT ("of Alexander de Pilkington," is mentioned in a quit claim of 21 Sep 1247;

he is believed to have had two sons: a) Robert, killed in 1291 by an arrow shot by Nicholas de Dogwero in Salford; and b) Adam, who fell from an oak in Pilkington, and was killed); and JOHN.

3. ROGER PILKINGTON, son of Alexander (2) de Pilkington, was lord of the Manor of Pilkington as early as 1242. He also inherited the 6 oxgangs in Rivington which had been held by his ancestors. In 1221 he was a witness to a charter of Gilbert de Notton. He probably died by 1270 for shortly after that date his son Alexander held the manor (A:27-28). He had at least one son:
ALEXANDER.

4. JOHN PILKINGTON, son of Alexander (2), or of the latter's brother William above. He was the father of: ALEXANDER de Pilkington (pardoned for the death of Adam del Wode because he had killed del Wode in self-defence. Later one Henry del Wode was tried for fatally wounding Alexander Pilkington. Alexander was believed to have had a son: Richard, mentioned in a deed as having married Joan, widow of Adam de Pennington, shortly after the latter's death in 1309).

5. ALEXANDER PILKINGTON, presumed to be the son of Sir Roger (3) Pilkington, was born c1225 and died c1291. Between 1270 and 1291 he added to his Rivington estates, and eventually his family became the owners of seven-eighths of the entire township.
         Just before his death he conveyed all of his lands in Rivington to his second son Richard who had just married Ellen, daughter of William de Anderton of Rumworth and Anderton.
         He died by 1291 when his eldest son was in possession of the Manor of Pilkington. The Plea Rolls indicate that Alexander's wife was named Alice, and she may have been a daughter of Henry de Chetham, and sister of Sir Geoffrey de Chetham. This assumption is based on the fact that the manors of Chetham and Crompton (formerly held by Sir Geoffrey de Chetham) were lately held by members of the Pilkington family. His widow Alice was named in the Plea rolls of 1301 and 1309.
         Sir Alexander was the father of four sons: Sir ROGER; RICHARD, the second son, was ancestor of the Rivington branch; Sir JOHN, b. c1265, and was M.P. for Lancashire in 1316; he married Margery, dau. of William de Anderton of Anderton and Rumworth. He may have been the father of three sons (a. John; b. Thomas; and c. Henry, who held three burgages of land in Salford in 1330); and ADAM, married Matilda (Maud), daughter of Elias de Penulbury, Lord of Wickelswick and Pendlebury.

6. Sir ROGER PILKINGTON, son of Alexander (5) and Alice (de Chetham) Pilkington, was b. c1255, and d. 1322. He succeeded to the manors of Pilkington, Chetham and Crompton in 1291. He may have had three wives: 1st, Amery, daughter and coheir of Sir Gilbert de Barton. This connection is made because after the death of Amery, c1294/5, Roger became possessed of one-sixth of the manor of Barton, "by the Courtesy of England," which said that a man and his issue became entitled to the inheritance of his deceased wife, *if there were children by the marriage.* The sons by this marriage were Roger and William.

Sir Roger married as his second wife Alice, daughter of Sir Ralph de Otteby, who settled on the couple the manor of Otteby in Co. Lincoln. There was one son, Alexander, by this marriage.

About 1310 Sir Roger married as his third wife Margery, probably a Middleton. By 1323 his widow Margery was m. to Sir Adam de Swillington. Their were two sons, Richard and Adam, by this marriage.

An extant armorial seal of Sir Roger shows a shield charged with a cross patonce voided, the shield surmounted by the device of a squirrel on a tree branch.

Sir Roger was the father of (A:31-38; B:1733): (by Amery): ROGER; and WILLIAM, living in 1344; (by Alice): ALEXANDER, finally inherited the Manor of Otteby by 1346, but may have died without issue as the manor was later held by John Laverton; (by Margery): RICHARD (was mentioned in a suit in 1332) and ADAM (was tried with others in 1337 for entering the Free Chase of Queen Isabella, and carrying away the deer, etc).

Generations 6-10

7. Sir ROGER PILKINGTON, son of Sir Roger (6) and Amery (de Barton), was b. c1291 and d. 1343. On 7 Jan 1325, Sir Roger was summoned to perform military service in Guienne. Under the Privy Seal, King Edward III granted him exemption from Knight service for life on 16 May 1341. He died in 1343, the year in which his eldest son, being then under age, was fined for not taking a knighthood.

Sir Roger m. Alicia, sister of Henry de Bury, Jr., and daughter of Henry de Bury, Lord of Bury, by his wife Margery, dau. of Richard de Radcliffe of Radcliffe. Alicia brought the manor of Bury into the family. Alicia died intestate about 1374, and her eldest son was appointed administrator.

Sir Roger and Alice (de Bury) were the parents of four sons and three daughters (A:38-43): ROGER; ROBERT, b. 1329, died in or after 1399; HENRY (died after 1374, and left two sons: John, and Richard); RICHARD, Rector of Prestwich in 1361, d. 1400; JANE, m. John del More of Liverpool; MARGARET, m. Sir John de Arderne, son of Sir Thomas (They had only one daughter: Matilda, m. 1st, Thomas, 3rd son of Sir John de Stanley of Lathom, and 2nd, Sir Robert Babthorp); and ISABEL, m. Nicholas de Prestwich.

8. Sir ROGER PILKINGTON, son of Sir Roger (7) and Alice (de Bury) Pilkington, was born about 1325, and died 2 Jan 1406. His wife has not been identified. From his father he inherited the manors of Pilkington, Cheetham and Crompton, and from his mother the manor of Bury.

In 1343, while under age, he was fined for not undertaking knighthood. He was fined again in 1345. He was appointed to the Commission of Peace for Lancs. in 1350. On six occasions he was returned as Knight of the Shire for Lancashire, 1363, 1364-5, 1368, 1376-7, 1382, and 1384. In the great heraldic controversy, *Scrope vs. Grosvenor*, he was one of four Pilkingtons who were summoned to give evidence before the court of chivalry.

He died on 2 Jan 1406/7 and his inquisition post mortem was dated 11 Aug 1407. He left issue (A:43-4): Sir JOHN; ISABEL, m. 1st, Thomas de Lathom, son of Sir

Thomas de Lathom, and 2nd, Sir John de Dalton; and LORA, m. 1398 Laurence de Standish of Standish (*MCS4*:Line 116).

9. Sir JOHN PILKINGTON, son of Sir Roger (8) de Pilkington, was b. c1363/4 (37 Edward III), and died 16 Feb 1420/1. Although his age was given as 34 or more at his father's Inquisition he was probably closer to 44. In 1383 when about 20, he married Margaret, daughter and heiress of Sir John de Verdon. Margaret was the widow of Hugh de Bradshagh, by whom she had one son Sir William de Bradshagh, who in turn had an only daughter, Elizabeth who married Sir Richard Harrington.

 Dame Margaret was a daughter of Sir John de Verdon, d. 1392, and his first wife Maud. His daughter became his sole heiress after the death of his second wife. She was a ward of the Duke of Lancaster, and since Sir John de Pilkington married her without obtaining the Duke's consent, he had to pay 20 marks for a pardon. By this marriage Sir John obtained the manors of Stagenhoe (Herts.), Brixworth, Clipsworth and Kelmarsh (Northants.), Bressingham (Norf.), and of Stanstead and Chedburg (Suff.).

 Sir John and his son, John Pilkington, Jr., fought at Agincourt, and Sir John supplied a quota of three esquires, ten lances, and forty archers. In 1419 he was appointed sheriff of Northamptonshire.

 Sir John died 16 Feb 1420/1 and his wife died 24 Nov 1436. By their marriage they had five sons and four daughters. (A:44-47; B:1733). The children were: Sir JOHN, d. s.p.; EDMUND, whose son succeeded to the Pilkington estates of his uncle; ROBERT (ancestor of the Yorkshire branch); HENRY, d. young; ROGER, d. s.p.; KATHERINE, m. Sir Henry Scarisbrick of Scarisbrick Hall, Co. Lancs.; ELIZABETH, m. Sir William Atherton; MARGARET, m. 1st Nicholas Griffin, d. 12 Oct 1436 (They were the ancestors of **Simon Lynde of MA**: *RD500*:371); *MCS4*:Line 55); m. 2nd Sir Thomas Savile. and HANNAH, m. Sir Francis Bernard of Acorn Bank, Westmorland.

10. EDMUND PILKINGTON, son of Sir John (9) and Margaret (de Verdon), m. Elizabeth, dau. of Sir Thomas Booth (*WAR7*:Line 34).

 Edmund and Elizabeth were the parents of (*WAR7*:Line 34): ELIZABETH, m. Sir William Harington (They were the parents of (*MCS4*:Line 129): Sir JAMES HARINGTON, m. Isabella Radcliffe and had a dau.: Alice, who m. Ralph Standish).

11. ROBERT PILKINGTON, of Bury, Lancs., and later of Sowerby, York, son of Sir John (9) and Margaret (de Verdon) Pilkington, was b. c1398. In 1434 he and fifty-five others had to take an oath that they would not maintain peacebreakers.

 After the death of his mother in 1436 he succeeded to the Manor of Chedburgh, Suffolk.

 He married Joan (possibly Rawson), by whom he was the father of (A:68-70; B:1733): Sir JOHN; HENRY; CHARLES; GEORGE; THOMAS; EDMUND; ROBERT; RICHARD; ELIZABETH, m. by 1456 Edmund Greenhalgh of Brandlesome, Lancs.; and MARGARET, m. Nicholas Tempest of Bracewell.

12. Sir JOHN PILKINGTON, son of Robert (11) and Joan, was b. c1420. He m. Joan [-?-] who m. 2nd, Sir Thomas Wortley.

Sir John was knighted in 1471 and made a K.B. in 1475. He was Constable of Chester Castle for life. He held Pilkington Hall, Wakefield. He was appointed Chamberlain of the Exchequer by Edward IV (B:1733).

By Elizabeth Lever he had an illegitimate son (B:1733): ROBERT.

13. Sir CHARLES PILKINGTON, 3rd son of Robert (11) and his wife Joan [-?-], of Worksop, Co. Notts., was b. c1423, and d. by June 1485. He m. Elizabeth, dau. of James Gateford, of Gateford, by whom he acquired the estates in the counties of Nottingham, Derby and Warwick.

In 1479 he was appointed one of the Gentlemen ushers of the King's Chamber, and in 1480 was placed on the Commission of Array for defense against the Scots. That same year he was appointed High Sheriff of Nottingham and Derby. In 1483 he was one of the attendant Knights at the Coronation of King Richard III.

Sir Charles made his will on 3 July, 2 Rich. III (1484); it was proved 24 June 1485. He left bequests to his wife Elizabeth, and then to his lawful son, Edward.

The children of Sir Charles and Elizabeth (Gateford) Pilkington were (A:79-80): EDWARD, m. Margaret Caser of Newark; and ISABEL, b. 1473, d. 1522; m. John Towneley, son of Richard Towneley.

Generations 11-15

14. ROBERT PILKINGTON, of Bradley Manor, Nether Bradley, York, son of Sir John (12) and Elizabeth Lever, d. 31 Jan 1497/8. He m. 1st, Alice Burell, and 2nd, Alice, dau. and heiress of William Bernard of Knaresborough. Robert was a Freeman of the City of York (B:1733).

Robert and Alice (Bernard) were the parents of (B:1734): ARTHUR, b. 1482.

15. ARTHUR PILKINGTON, son of Robert (14) and Alice, was b. 1482, and d. by 29 June 1537 when administration on his estate was granted. He m. Alice, dau. of Nicholas Savile, of Newhall, York. Arthur and Alice were the parents of (B:1734): ROBERT, b. c1514.

16. ROBERT PILKINGTON of Bradley, son of Arthur (15) and Alice, was b. c1514, and d. 1541. He m. Rosamond Waterton, dau. of Sir Thomas Waterton of Walton. Robert and Rosamund were the parents of (B:1734): THOMAS.

17. THOMAS PILKINGTON, son of Robert (16) and Rosamund, d. 1565. He m. Barbara Reresby, dau. of Lionel and Anne (Swift) Reresby. Thomas was Bowbearer to Queen Elizabeth. Thomas and Barbara were the parents of (B:1734): FREDERICK.

18. FREDERICK PILKINGTON of Nether Bradley, son of Thomas (17) and Barbara, m. Frances Rodes, dau. of Francis Rodes, of Barlborough, Derby, Justice of the Court of Common Pleas. Frederick and Frances were the parents of (B:1734): Sir ARTHUR.

Generation 16

19. Sir ARTHUR PILKINGTON, Bart., of Stanley, York, son of Frederick (18) and Frances, m. Ellen Lyon, dau. of Henry Lyon of Roxbury, Lincs. Sir Arthur and Ellen were the parents of (among others): CATHERINE, m. John Lowe, son of Vincent and Anne (Cavendish) Lowe (Her sons **Nicholas and Henry Lowe** settled in MD: *RD500*:161).

Unplaced:

PILKINGTON, JAMES, Bishop of Durham, m. Alice Kingsmill, dau. of Sir John and Constance (Goring) Kingsmill. Their dau. Deborah Pilkington m. Walter Dunch, and they were the parents of **Deborah Dunch, Lady Deborah Moody, founder of a colony at Gravesend, LI**, m. Sir Henry Moody, 1st Bart. (*RD500*:383).

PILKINGTON, RUTH, m. Sir Henry Harington, son of Sir James and Lucy (Sidney) Harrington. Sir Henry and Ruth were the parents of: ELIZABETH, m. Sir Richard Moryson (They were the parents of (*RD500:*262); **Francis Moryson**, colonial Governor of VA).

THE PRIESTLEY FAMILY

Refs.: "Priestley." Joseph Hunter. *Familiae Minorum Gentium. HSPV* 37:95-96.

1. JOSEPH PRIESTLEY, of Birstall Field-Head, Yorkshire, was b. 1661 and d. 2 Aug 1745, aged 84. He m. Sarah Hayley, b. 1660, d. 29 Dec 1728, aged 68. Both are buried at Birstall (A:95).

Joseph was a maker and draper of woollen cloth. Sarah Hayley Priestley introduced Non-Conformist principles into the family (A:95).

Joseph and Sarah were the parents of (A:95): JOHN, m. Phoebe Webster in 1721 (His descendants are traced in A:8); JONAS, b. 1700; SARAH, m. John Keighley of Heckmonwyke on 6 Oct 1725; and [-?-] (dau.), m. William Ash of Heckmonwyke.

2. JONAS PRIESTLEY of Birstall Field-Head, youngest son of Joseph (1) and Sarah, was b. in 1700, and d. 18 Feb 1779. He m. 1st, Mary, dau. and heir of Joseph Swift of Shafton, Co. York. She d. 28 Dec 1739, at the birth of her fifth child. Jonas m. 2nd, Hannah Holdsworth of Wakefield, widow of [-?-] Wilson.

Jonas and his first wife are buried at Birstall. His second wife was housekeeper to Dr. Doddridge at the time of her marriage to Jonas Priestley (A:95).

Jonas and Mary were the parents of (A:95): JOSEPH, b. 13 March 1733; JOSHUA, m. Mary Drake, b. c1735, d. 17 Dec 1823, age 88; TIMOTHY of London and Manchester, V.D.M., m. and had at least one son; JAMES, went abroad at 19, and "was never heard of afterwards;" and MARTHA, m. John Crouch of London, and in 1809 was a widow, when she communicated the details of this pedigree.

3. JOSEPH PRIESTLEY, LL.D. and F.R.S, son of Jonas (2) and Mary, was b. 13 March 1733 at Field Head and d. in Pennsylvania on 6 Feb 1804. He m. at Wrexham in 1762, Mary, dau. of Isaac Wilkinson, ironmaster.

Dr. Joseph Priestley died 6 Feb 1804. He would have been 71 next 24 March (*BT* 18 Feb 1804, cites the *Pa. Argus*).

Mrs. [Mary], wife of Dr. Joseph Priestley, d. at Northumberland, PA, on 21st inst. (*BFG* 6 Oct 1796).

Joseph and Mary were the parents of (A:95-96): JOSEPH, b. at Leeds, lived in America, but by 1820 had returned to England, m. twice and had issue; WILLIAM; HENRY, d. young; and SARAH, b. at Warrington, m. William Finch of Heath Forge near Dudley.

Unplaced:

PRIESTLEY, [-?-] [poss. JAMES] , d. c1790. He m. Mary Ann [-?-] who d. 30 March 1835.

Mrs. Mary Ann, died Mon., 30th ult., in her 86th year, mother of Edward Priestley. Formerly a resident of Annapolis, for many years she had been a resident of Baltimore (*AMG* 2 April 1835).

[-?-] and Mary Ann were the parents of: EDWARD, b. c1779.

PRIESTLEY, EDWARD, son of [-?-] and Mary Ann, was b. c1779. A cabinet-maker, he d. Sunday morning last, in his 59th year. He was a native of Annapolis, and came to Baltimore about 1790, a friendless orphan with a helpless mother. He leaves two sons. Long obit is given (*AMG* 16 March 1837 cites the *BA*).

He left a will, and names a niece named Durding.

PRIESTLY, ELIZA, m. John Bowers by AAML dated 3 Dec 1810.

PRIESTLEY, WILLIAM, of TA Co. d. by 11 May 1772 when D. Sherwood and John Sherwood appraised his personal estate at £9.15.8. David Priestley and Perry Priestley signed as next of kin. Pollard Edmondson, admin., filed the inventory on 5 April 1774 (MINV 117:322).

THE PRITCHETT FAMILY

1. MICHAEL PRITCHETT married Margaret Smith on 5 Nov 1678 in Harborne, Staffordshire (IGI, 1988 ed.). They were the parents of: JOHN.

2. JOHN PRITCHETT, son of Michael (1), was a native of Harburne Parish, Staffs. He came to PG Co., MD, where he married on 2 March 1701 Eliza Bener, a native of Stepney Parish, Mddx. (PGKG:239).

John and Elizabeth were the parents of (PGKG:239): WILLIAM, b. 2 Oct 1703; JOHN, b. 11 Sep 1707; MARY, b. 12 March 1708; and THOMAS, b. 15 March 1710.

THE RERESBY FAMILY

Refs.: A: "Phipps-Reresby," *Familiae Minorum Gentium, HSPV* 40:1288.

1. GEORGE RERESBY of Thriberg, was the father of at least two sons (A): FRANCIS, of Todwick, whose will was dated 1690; and LEONARD.

2. LEONARD RERESBY, of Ecclesfield, Gent., son of George (1), was buried 14 Sep 1678. He m. Emote Wilson, widow of [-?-] Hobson and dau. of Thomas Wilson of Ecclesfield, who left a will [dated?] 10 May 1679.

     Leonard and Emote were the parents of (A): FRANCIS; and MARY, bapt. 21 April 1670, m. 21 Sep 1692 William Sitwell of Sheffield, Attorney.

3. FRANCIS RERESBY, of Ecclesfield, son of Leonard (2) and Emote, was bapt. 1 May 1673 and buried 10 June 1722. He m. Alice, dau. of Nicholas Hacket of Auston. She was buried 25 Sep 1726 (A).

     Francis and Alice were the parents of (A): MARY, bapt. 27 March 1695, buried 12 Sep 1769, having m. George Phipps on 18 April 1718; and JOHN, bapt. 12 Jan 1698/9.

4. JOHN RERESBY, son of Francis (3) and Alice, was bapt. 12 Jan 1698/9, and was buried 25 Sep 1752. He m. Hannah Johnson of Bawtry (A).

     John and Hannah were the parents of (A): ANNE, b. c1724, was 14 in 1738 and was living unm. in 1777; JOHN, b. 13 Sep 1728; and WILLIAM, b. 14 Jan 1729, d. a minor and unm.

5. JOHN RERESBY, son of John (4) and Hannah, was b. 13 Sep 1728, and was "supposed to be living in MD in 1777" (A).

     John Reresby, exec., advertised he would settle the estate of Mrs. Rachel Gladman of Annapolis (*AMG* 12 Sep 1765). He filed an account of her estate on 26 Feb 1767 (MDAD 55:342).

     John Reresby may have left the Province, or died as no other record of him in MD has been found.

THE REYNOLDS FAMILY

Refs.: A: S. F. Tillman. *Christopher Reynolds and His Descendants*. Washington: The Goetz Co., 1959. B: Robert Davis Hughes. *The Reynolds Family of Dayton*. Dayton; The Reynolds & Reynolds Family, 1949.

1. CHRISTOPHER REYNOLDS was b. c1530 in Kent, Eng. He settled in London where he engaged in trade. He may have had a brother Nathaniel, and a sister Dorothy, d. 21 Nov 1572, who m. William Tilghman, son of Richard and Juliana [Newman] Tilghman (See **The Tilghman Family** in Volume 1 of *British Roots of Maryland Families*) (A:1).

Reynold's wife has not been identified, but he was the father of (A:1; B:11-12): GEORGE, b. c1555; CHRISTOPHER; MARY, d. young; JOHN; THOMAS; CORNELIUS; RICHARD, b. 1575; ROBERT; WILLIAM; and several daus.

2. RICHARD REYNOLDS, son of Christopher (1), was b. c1575. He m. Ann Harrison in 1605 and settled in Sussex, Eng. Richard became the head of a vast shipping and commercial business. He is said to have died in York Co., but Tillman states it is unknown whether it was Co. York, Eng., or York Co., VA (A:1).

Richard and Ann were the parents of (A:1; B:12): WILLIAM, b. 1606 (twin); ROBERT, b. 1606 (twin); EDWARD; NICHOLAS; JOHN, b. 1612; JAMES; GILBERT; CHRISTOPHER; and several daus..

3. WILLIAM REYNOLDS, son of Richard (2) and Ann, was b. c1606 in Kent, Eng., and settled for a while in Sussex, and in August 1636 arrived in Plymouth Colony, MA. William m. Margaret Exton. (A:1; B::12).

William and his wife made several trips to England, and some of their children were born there. He died in England while on such a trip (A:1).

William and his wife had seven daus. and the following sons, five of whom settled in Chester Co., PA (A:12); JAMES; ROBERT HENRY; JOHN, b. 1650; WILLIAM; FRANCIS; HENRY, b. 1 May 1655; JOSEPH; and THOMAS.

4. HENRY REYNOLDS, son of William (3) and Margaret, was b. 1 May 1655, perhaps at Chichester, Sussex, Eng., and d. 7 Aug 1724. He landed in 1661, 1671, or 1678, in Burlington Co., NJ (A:22).

Henry m., on 10 Nov 1678, Prudence Clayton (who d. 4 Feb 1728). Henry and Prudence settled in Chester Co., PA. They were the parents of (A:22; B:12): MARGARET, b. 23 May 1680, m. [-?-] Maulder or Moulder; MARY, b. 13 Sep 1682; FRANCIS, b. 15 Aug 1684; PRUDENCE, b. 20 March 1687; DEBORAH, b. 16 April 1689; WILLIAM, b. 30 May 1691 [and may have d. young]; HENRY, b. 16 Aug 1693; JOHN, b. 21 Dec 1695; HANNAH, b. 11 Nov 1697, d. 13 March 1726, m. Richard Brown on 30 Aug 1717; and WILLIAM, b. 5 July 1701.

5. HENRY REYNOLDS, son of Henry (4) and Prudence, was b. 16 Aug 1693 in Chester Co., PA, and d. 17 Dec 1779 in CE Co., MD. In 1717 he m. 1st, Hannah Brown, b. 31 Oct 1707 and d. 12 Dec 1731. He m. 2nd, on 23 March 1733, Mrs. Ann Howell. She d. 16 June 1741; Henry m. 3rd, 23 April 1743, Mary, widow of Jacob Haines (A:26).

Henry and Hannah were the parents of (A:26; B:12). RACHEL JANE, b. 6 Nov 1717, m. 1st, John Piggott, 2nd, Jacob Dingee; and 3rd, [-?-] Churchman; WILLIAM, b. 22 Jan 1721; SAMUEL, b. 26 Aug 1723; HENRY, b. 1 Feb 1725; JACOB, b. 14 Sep 1728; and JOSEPH, b. 30 June 1730.

Henry and Mary were the parents of (A:26): BENJAMIN, b. 30 Nov 1743; JOHN, b. 20 May 1745 (twin); ISAAC, b. 20 May 1745 (twin); JESSE, b. 22 Aug 1747; DAVID, b. 27 March 1750; and ELISHA, b. 2 Feb 1752.

Henry Reynolds may have also been the father of (A:26): STEPHEN; REUBEN; EBENEZER (who settled in KE Co., MD); MARIE, m. [-?-] Peeples; and SARAH, m. [-?-] Phillips.

THE RICH FAMILY

Refs.: A: J. Hall Pleasants. "The Gorsuch and Lovelace Families." Reprinted in *GVFV* III. B: "Rich." *NCP*. C: Brice McAdoo Clagett, "The Ancestry of Capt. James Neale," *MGSB* 31 (2) 137-153.

1. RICHARD RICH, son of John le Rich who fl. 1412, of Rich's Place, Hants., was Sheriff of London, 1441, was a member of the Mercer's Company. He is said to have d. c1469 (A:504; B: cites Morant's *Hist. Essex* 2:101; C:144, 146). Richard was the father of (C:142): THOMAS; and KATHERINE, fl. 1466, m. William Marrow (c1410-1464), Master of the Grocer's Company and Alderman, Sheriff and Lord Mayor of London (William and Katherine were the ancestors of **Capt. James Neale of MD**) (C:142).

2. THOMAS RICH of London, son of Richard (1), was the father of (A:504, B): RICHARD.

3. RICHARD RICH of London, son of Thomas, m. Joan Dingley. They were the parents of (A:503, 504): RICHARD.

4. RICHARD RICH, Baron Rich of Leez, Lord Chancellor of England, son of Richard (3) and Joan, was b. c1496 in the Parish of St. Lawrence, Jewry, London, and d. 12 June 1567 at Rochford (A:502-505). He m. c1535 Elizabeth Jenks, dau. of William Jenks, Grocer, of London. Elizabeth d. at St. Bartholomew's, London, and was buried at Rochford, Essex on 18 Dec 1558 (A:504; B).

He assisted at the judicial murders of Fisher and Sir Thomas More (B). On 16 Feb 1546/7 he was created Baron Rich. He declared for Queen Mary, and was a Commissioner of Claims for her Coronation on 28 Aug 1553 (B).

Richard and Mary were the parents of (B; *PASC*:132): HUGH, m. but d. s.p. in his father's lifetime; ROBERT, 2nd Baron Rich; MARY, m. c1539/40 Sir Thomas Wroth, b. 1516, d. by 16 April 1575; Member of Parliament (See **The Wroth Family** in *British Roots of Maryland Families*, GPC, 1999); and ELIZABETH, m. by 1557, Robert Peyton, Esq., of Ishleham, Cambridge (ancestors of **Major Robert Peyton of VA**).

Richard Rich also had an illegitimate son (*WAR7*:line 230B): NICHOLAS.

5. ROBERT RICH, 2nd Baron Rich, son of Richard (4) and Mary, was b. c1537 and d. 27 Feb 1580/1. He was buried at Felstead. He m. by 25 Nov 1554, Elizabeth, dau. and heir of George Baldry, Lord Mayor of London. She m. 2nd, Robert Forth, and was buried 19 Dec 1591 at St. Gregory's by St. Paul's, London (B).

Robert and Elizabeth were the parents of (B): RICHARD, m. Catherine, dau. of Sir Thomas Knyvett, but d. s.p.; and ROBERT, 3rd Baron Rich and Earl of Warwick.

6. NICHOLAS BROWN, illegitimate son of Richard Rich (4), Baron Rich, was Sheriff of London, m. Anne Machell (*WAR7*:Line 230B cites *TAG* 22:27-29, 158, 60:91).

Nicholas and Ann were the parents of: ANNE, m. Percy Browne (parents of **Nathaniel Browne of Middletown, CT**).

7. ROBERT RICH, 3rd Baron Rich, son of Robert (5) and Elizabeth, was b. c1560. He m. Penelope Devereux, dau. of Walter Devereux, 1st Earl of Essex and Lettice Knollys (*RD500*:45).

> On 6 Aug 1618 he was created Earl of Warwick (B).
> Robert and Penelope were the parents of (*RD500*:46): ROBERT.

8. ROBERT RICH, 2nd Earl of Warwick, son of Robert (7) and Penelope, m. Frances Hatton. They were the parents of (RD500:46): ANNE, m. Edward Montagu, 2nd Earl of Manchester (ancestors of **Lord Charles Greville Montagu, Colonial Gov. of SC**).

THE ROBERTS FAMILY OF WOOLSTONE, GLOUCESTERSHIRE TO LONDON TO CHARLES CO., MD
Contributed by Fredric Z. Saunders

Refs.: A: Fredric Z. Saunders. "The Roberts Family of Woolstone, Gloucestershire, to London to Charles Co., Maryland." Posted at his web site fzsaund@ix.netcom.com. (Used with permission).

NB: Fredric Z. Saunders can be reached at 5186 S. Cobble Creek Rd. # 6K, Salt Lake City, UT 84117-6723; His e mail address is fzasaund@ix.netcom.com. Web site: http://pweb.netcom.com/~fzsaud.

1. THOMAS ROBERTS was b. c1500 and d. by April 1557 at Woolstone, Gloucs. He m. Elizabeth [-?-], who was living in 1580.

Roberts d. leaving a will dated 7 May 1556 and proved 8 April 1557. Although only an abstract of the will is given here, the full text of Thomas Roberts' will, a list of his debts, and an inventory can be accessed at "http:// www1.netcom.com/ bin/page_counter?/~fzsaund/robertswill1.html.".

Roberts, a husbandman of the town of Woolstone, directed that he be buried in the churchyard of Wolston. He named his dau. Elizabeth, Elizabeth Roberts the dau. of William, the children of Thomas Jones, Nicholas and Margery Kent, his son John, his wife Elizabeth, the latter two to be execs. Thomas Bate and Richard Davis were named overseers. Thomas Pyrange, Richard Davis, and William Roberts witnessed the will.

Thomas and Elizabeth were the parents of (A): WILLIAM, b. c1529, m. Maude Manninge, and d. between 3 Feb 1560 and 31 Dec 1561 at Woolstone; [-?-] (dau.), b. c1531, m. Thomas Jones; [-?-] (dau.), b. c1533, m. Mr. Kente; JOHN. b. c1535; and ELIZABETH, b. before 1556, m. Thomas Woode on 21 Oct 1574.

2. JOHN ROBERTS, son of Thomas (1) and Elizabeth. was b. c1535 and d. by Dec 1581 at Woolstone. He m. Elizabeth [-?-].

John Roberts d. leaving a will dated 21 Dec 1580 and proved 31 Dec 1581 Woolstone. Only an abstract is given here (The full text of his will and a list of his debts can be accessed at "http://www2.netcom.com/~fzsaund/robertswill2.html."). Roberts directed that he be buried in the churchyard of Woolston. He remembered the poor of the parish of Woolstone. He named his sons John, Edward, Richard (not yet 21), and

George (not yet 21). He named his daus. Jane, Anne, Elizabeth, Mary (all under the age of 18). His wife Elizabeth and son Edward were named execs. They were to keep and find the testator's mother honestly while she was alive. Nicholas Banar? and Thomas Wodde were named overseers. Daniell Dawkes, Thomas Fynche, and Pinle? Jinnon? witnessed the will.

John and Elizabeth were the parents of (A): JOHN, b. c1555, d. shortly before 29 Nov 1615; EDWARD, b. c1557, m. Ann [-?-]. and d. between 2 June 1616 and 7 May 1617 at Woolstone; RICHARD, b. after 1559 (under age 21 in 1580); JONE (JANE?), b. after 1562 (under age 18 in 1580); ANNE, b. after 1562 (under age 18 in 1580); ELIZABETH, b. after 1562 (under age 18 in 1580); MARY, b. after 1562 (under age 18 in 1580); and GEORGE, bapt. 11 Apr. 1574 and was living 1616.

3. JOHN ROBERTS, son of John (2) and Elizabeth, was b. c1555 and d. shortly before 29 Nov 1615 at Woolstone. He m. Margaret [-?-].

John and Margaret were the parents of (A): NICHOLAS, bapt. Jan 1600; and GEORGE, bapt. 15 Jan 1600/1.

4. GEORGE ROBERTS, son of John (3) and Margaret bapt. 15 Jan. 1600/1, and was bur. 29 March 1654 at St. Andrew Holborn, Mddx. He m. 1st [-?-] [-?-]; and 2nd, by license dated 9 Sep 1634 Anne Reade (A).

George Roberts, son of John Roberts of "Wolstone," Gloucs. was bound apprentice in London as a draper in 1617 to Richard Kemble, and granted his freedom in 1625 (A).

He d. leaving a will dated 18 Feb 1653 and proved at Westminster 12 April 1654. An abstract is given here (The full text of the will is posted by Mr. Saunders at the website: http://www2.netcom.com/~fzsaund/robertswill3.html). As George Roberts of Saint Andrew's, Holborne, in the County of Middlesex, Draper, he named his children, none of whom were yet 24 years old: eldest son George, his eldest dau. Sibella, son Edward, and daus. Mary, Elizabeth, and Susanna. Wife Anne was named sole extx. John Reade and Willmson [Williamson?] witnessed the will.

George and Anne were the parents of (A): SIBELLA, living 1654 (may be a child of first wife); ANN. bapt. 3 June 1638, bur. 21 Sep 1641; all at St. Bartholomew the Great, London; DYNAH, bapt. 19 Jan 1639/40, bur. 21 Jan 1641/2, all at St. Bartholomew the Great, London; GEORGE, bapt. 17 Aug 1645 at St. Bartholomew the Great, living 1693; MARY, bapt. 25 Jan 1645/6 at St. Bartholomew the Great, m. by lic. dated 16 Sep 1662 Thomas Allanson, and **d. CH Co., MD**; EDWARD, bapt. 31 Oct 1647, **d. unm. betw. 15 Jan 1676 and 22 Nov 1677 at CH Co., MD**; ELIZABETH, bapt. 5 July 1649 at St. Andrew Holborn, Mddx, living 1654; ANN, bap. 1 April 1651 and bur. 6 March 1652/3, all at St. Andrew Holborn, Mddx; and SUSANNA, living 1654.

THE WILLIAM ROBERTS FAMILY
A Tentative Reconstruction

Refs.: A: "Roberts of Glassenbury." *BEDB*: 444-446. B: *BEKE*: 177-178. X: Undocumented chart of the Roberts Family in the possession of Mrs. Robert Ware of Sudlersville, MD, who has generously made it available to the compiler.

ARMS: Azure, on a chevron Argent, three mullets Sable (A).

1. WILLIAM ROBERTS of Cranbrook, Kent, is stated by Berry to have been the son of William, of Stephen, or Robert, of William Roberts, alias de Goodhurst, and to have been the father of (B:177): ROBERT.

2. ROBERT ROBERTS of Cranbrook, son of William (1), was the father of (B:177): RICHARD; STEPHEN; and JOHN.

3. STEPHEN ROBERTS, son of Robert (2), was the father of (B:177): JOHN.

4. JOHN ROBERTS, son of Stephen (3), m. Agnes [-?-], and was the father of (B:177): STEPHEN, d. s.p.; WALTER; ANN, m. [-?-] Selwyn of Co. Sussex; and SARAH, m. as her first husband, [-?-] Bates, and as her second, [-?-] Ashbur... .

5. WALTER ROBERTS, son of John (4), d. c1520. He m. 1st, 23 Oct 1463, Margaret, dau. of John Penn, Esq. She d. 6 May 1480, and he m. 2nd, Isabel, dau. of Sir John Culpeper, Kt., and 3rd, Alice, widow of Lord Abergavenny, and dau. of Richard Nayler (B:177).

 Walter is the first definite progenitor given in the account in Burke (A). He inherited his estate by the death without issue of his brother Stephen. An adherent of the Lancastrian cause he was attainted of treason by Richard III, but had his property restored with the accession of Henry VIII. By his three wives he is said to have had 30 children! (A).

 Walter Roberts was sheriff of Kent 5 Henry VII, and built the moated house in the Valley of Glassenbury (B:177).

 Walter and Margaret were the parents of (B:177): JOHN; MARY, m. 1st, Simon Linche, and 2nd, [-?-] St. Nicholas; ELIZABETH, m. Gervaise Hendley; and JANE, m. [-?-] Exhurst of Horden.

 Walter and Isabel were the parents of (B:177): MARTIN, who became a priest.

 By Alice, Walter Roberts was father of (B:177); THOMAS; and WILLIAM of Battell, Co. Sussex.

6. THOMAS ROBERTS of Glassenbury, Esq., son and heir of Walter (5), was b. 21 Sep 1494, and was buried at Cranbrook in 1557, age c63. He m. Elizabeth, dau. of Sir James Frammingham of Suffolk, Kt. She was buried age c60 at Cranbrook (B:177).

 Thomas Roberts was Sheriff of Kent 25 Hen. VIII (A; B:177).

 Thomas and Elizabeth were the parents of (X): WALTER; THOMAS, b. 31

Oct 1523, d. 1567; JOHN, of Borzell, b. 6 Aug 1531, m. Elizabeth Pigott and was ancestor of the Roberts of Borzell Ticehurst, and Stone House, Warbleton, Sussex; MARY, m. Thomas Cheney of Woodley; and JANE, m. 1st. Richard Burston, and 2nd, Richard Love.

7. WALTER ROBERTS of Glassenbury, son of Thomas (6) and Elizabeth, m. 1st, on 22 Jan 1555, Catherine, dau. of George Fane (not listed in Burke: A), and 2nd, Frances, dau. and heir of Mr. Alderman John Maynard of London (A; B:177).

    Walter and Catherine were the parents of (B:177): ELIZABETH, m. George Colepeper.

    Walter and Frances were the parents of (B:178): Sir THOMAS; EDWARD, 2nd son, m. Judith, dau. of William Bird, and had issue; ALEXANDER of Thorpe, near London, d. 1649, m. [-?-], dau. of Thomas Culwich, and has issue; JOHN, d. April 1582, age 11; GRISELDA, d. April 1571, age between 4 and 5.

8. Sir THOMAS ROBERTS, Bart., of Glassenbury, son of Walter (7), was buried 23 Feb 1627, age 67. He m. Frances, dau. of Martin James, Esq., of Smarden, Kent. She d. Feb 1648 (B:178).

    Sir Thomas was knighted 23 July 1603, and created a Baronet in July 1620. He was Sheriff of Kent in 1623. He was described as "hospitable without excess and charitable without ostentation" (A).

    Sir Thomas and Frances were the parents of (A; B:178): Sir WALTER; THOMAS, d. unm.; JOHN, d. unm. ; WILLIAM; FRANCES, m. 1st, John Hooper of Stockberry, and 2nd, Henry Crisp; ELIZABETH, m. Sir Alexander Culpeper, Kt., of Bedgbury; and ANNE, m. Thomas Crisp, Esq., of Goudhurst.

9. WILLIAM ROBERTS, son of Sir Thomas (8) and Frances, is stated by Burke to have d. unmarried (A). He is not named at all by Berry (B:178) The compiler of the chart states that **he came into KE Co., MD, c1665**. He m. Elizabeth [-?-] in England. She d. some time after 1665 (X).

    No documentary proof of William Roberts' parentage has been found to date.

    William and Elizabeth were the parents of (X): JAMES, d. c1718 in CV Co.; ISAAC; and WILLIAM, d. 1722 in KE Co., MD.

A SECOND WILLIAM ROBERTS FAMILY

1. WILLIAM ROBERTS of Saint Botolph Without Aldersgate, London, died by 1684. He married Mary [-?-].

    William and Mary were the parents of (IGI): EDWARD, bapt. 25 March 1666 ; STEPHEN, bapt. 5 Jan 1670; and WILLIAM, bapt. 13 Aug 1673.

2. WILLIAM ROBERTS, son of William and Mary, was bapt. 13 Aug 1673 at St. Botolph without Aldersgate. As William, son of William Roberts, dec., on 1 Aug 1684, he was bound to William Frisby for 12 years service in Maryland *(LEMG)*.

THE ROBINS FAMILY REVISED
Contributed by Fredric Z. Saunders.

Refs.: A: Fredric Z. Saunders. "The Robins family." posted at fzsaund@ix.netcom.com.
B: Diocese of Exeter Marriage Bonds and Allegations (FHL MF 916997).

NB: Mr. Saunders can be reached at 5186 S. Cobble Creek Rd. # 6K, Salt Lake City, UT 84117-6723; e mail at fzasaund@ix.netcom.com.
web site: http://pweb.netcom.com/~fzsaud.

1. THOMAS ROBINS was b. c1480 and living in Jan 1531 at Holdenby, Northants., Eng. He m. Joan [-?-], b. c1486; living 1535 at Holdenby.

Thomas and Joan were the parents of (A): WILLIAM, living 1535; RICHARD, b. c1508 (had two children in 1535), bur. 22 June 1584 Long Buckby; JOHN, living 1531; JOYS, b. c1512 (had two children in 1535), m. Thomas Hoggies; JOAN, living 1531; THOMAS, living 1546; HENRIE, m. Ales (Butlyn?), d. between 8 Oct 1569 and 2 March 1569/70 at Holdenby; and EDWARD, b. c1520 (had one child in 1546), m. Margaret [-?-], and d. betw. 8 Oct and 13 Dec 1546 at Upton, Northants.

2. RICHARD ROBINS, son of Thomas (1) and Joan, was b. c1508 (had two children in 1535), and was bur. 22 June 1584 at Long Buckby.

Richard Robins, yeoman, of Long Bagby, Northants, d. leaving a will dated 20 Oct 1582 and proved 4 Nov 1584. Only an abstract is given here (he full text of the will is posted at Mr. Saunders website:"http://www1.netcom.com/bin/page_counter?/~fzsaund/robinswill3.html).
Robins directed that he be buried in the north aisle within the parish church of Longbubgy aforesaid. He left Mother Church of Petersborough four pence, and left 20s to the poor of his parish. He named his grandchildren Richard, William, Edward (not yet 21), Thomas (not yet 21), Jone (not yet 21), John (not yet 21), children of his son Thomas, his dau. Elizabeth, the children of William Wylles, which he had by the testator's dau. Alice, the children of Henry Alman of Mares Ashby which he had by the testator's dau. Jone Three, his dau. Alice Willis, dau. Creaton. Son Thomas was to be exec. William Willes and John Creaton were to be supervisors of the will. John Woodworth scriptoreus [scribe?]. John Andrew and Henry Collman [were witnesses].

Richard was the father of (A): THOMAS, b. c1535; ELIZABETH, living 1582; ALICE, m. William Willes in May 1568 and was bur. 16 April 1626 at Long Buckby; JONE, m. Henry Alman and was living 1582; and ISABELL, m. 1st, John Draper in Jan. 1569, m. 2nd John Creaton.

3. THOMAS ROBINS, son of Richard (2), was b. c1535, and was bur. 8 Aug 1606 at Long Buckey, Northants. He m. c1563 Elizabeth Pawmer (or poss. Parker or Parish).

There are different opinions on the surname of Thomas' wife Elizabeth. A 1939 manuscript by Thomas Robins listed her name as Parkes or Parker. A book published in 1971 by Greenall, abstracting the Long Buckby parish records listed the spelling as Pamer. A County Archivist at the Northamptonshire Record Office in 1996 stated it was very difficult to read, but thought it looked very much like parish. The record is available on FHL microfiche 6127993.

Saunders believes that the name resembles the name which appears a few entries away in the marriage records, and is more readable as Pawmer. As the surname Pamer/Pawmer/Palmer is one that occurs in the parish and neighboring ones, he is more inclined to believe that is the correct surname.

Thomas and Elizabeth were the parents of (A): RICHARD, b. c1566; WILLIAM, b. c1569, living 1609; EDWARD, b. c1572, living 1582; THOMAS, b. c1575, living 1582; JONE, b. c1578, m. William Wills on 11 March 1594; JOHN, b. c1581, living 1582; HENRY, b. c1584, bur. 7 Dec 1584 at Long Buckby; and SAMUEL, bapt. 20 June 1587 at Long Buckby.

4. RICHARD ROBINS, son of Thomas (3) and Elizabeth, was b. c1566, and was bur. 19 May 1634 at Long Buckby. He m. Dorothy Goodman on 21 June 1597.

Richard Robins d. leaving a will dated 1 March 1633. Only an abstract is given here (The full text of the will can be accessed at http://www2. netcom. com/~fzsaund/robins.html). Richard named John Thorneton of Broackall Esq. and William Cartwright of Northants., Gent, to have a sum for the use of the poor of [Long] Buckby. His son and heir was to provide for the testator's wife Dorothy, his sons Obedience and Edward, son John, son Thomas, his two youngest children Lemuell and Mary, daus. Sara, and Contenew. He mentioned his grandchildren and his three brothers. Son Richard was to be the sole exec. Wm Cartwright and Richard Carvel (his mark) and Valentine Robinson (his mark) witnessed the will.

Richard and Dorothy were the parents of the following children, baptized at Long Buckby, Northants (A): CONTINIC, bapt. 2 April 1598, m. John Eyre, living 1634; RICHARD, bapt. 10 Dec 1599, m. Alice [-?-], and d. betw. 27 May 1674 and 3 Jan 1678; **OBEDIENCE, bapt. 26 April 1601, m. Grace O'Neil Waters, and d. 1662 at Northampton Co., VA**; JOHN, b. 25 Sep 1602; **EDWARD, bapt. 26 Aug 1604, and d. by May 1641 in Accomac Co., VA**; SARAH, bapt. 1 Sep 1606; THOMAS, bapt. 3 April 1608; DOROTHY, bapt. 23 Dec 1610, bur. 1 Nov 1624 at Long Buckby; LEMUELL/LAMUELL, m. Richard Marriatt; and MARY.

5. EDWARD ROBINS, son of Richard (4) and Dorothy, was bap. 26 Aug 1604 at Long Buckby and d. between 1 Feb. and 17 May 1641 in Accomac Co., VA. He m. Jane Cornish on or about 16 April 1630 (B).

Jane Cornish was not a dau. of James Cornish, nor was she the Jane Cornish, dau. of Richard, bapt. 6 Jan 1606/7. She may have been a relative of James Cornish's brother George, who attended the church of St. Mary Magdalen Milk Street, London. This is the same church where some of the children of Edward and Jane were baptized (A).

Edward and Jane were the parents of the following children, bapt. at St. Mary Magdalen Milk St. unless otherwise noted (A): **RACHEL, bapt. 20 Nov 1631, m. Richard Beard** by 1649 and had descendants in MD; WILLIAM, bapt. 4 June and bur. 10 June 1633; CHRISTIAN (dau.), bapt. 4 May 1634; **ELIZABETH, bapt. 20 May 1635, m. William Burgess and had descendants in MD**; SARAH, bapt. 25 July 1636 at St. Dunstan's in the East, London; RICHARD, bapt. 31 June and bur. 29 Aug. 1637 at St. Dunstan's; and RACHEL, bapt. 3 Oct 1638 at St. Dunstan's in the East.

THE ROS FAMILY

Refs.: A: Hedley. B: S. N. Smith, "Sir William de Ros of Ingmanthorpe," *MGH*, 5th ser., 10:20. C: *MCS5*. D: *WAR7*. E: *PASC*.

Generations 1-5

1. PIERS de ROS, d. by 1130. He m. Adeline, dau. of William Spec of Wardon, Beds.

Adeline's brother, Walter Espec, d. 1153. He had been Baron of Wark and Helmsley. When he died without surviving issue, his Barony of Old Wardon in Bedfordshire was divided between the heirs of his sisters Helwise and Albreda, and the Barony of Helmsley in Yorkshire went to the heirs of his youngest sister Adeline (A:225-226).

Piers de Ros is stated to have probably taken his name from Rots in Calvados, but other sources say he took his name from Roos in Holderness, a manor long held by the Ros family of Helmsley (A:226).

Piers and Adeline were the parents of (A:225): EVERARD, Baron of Wark and Helmsley, of age in 1130, d. by 1153, m. Eustache [-?-]; and ROBERT.

2. ROBERT de ROS, son of Piers (1) and Adeline, d. c1162/3, having m. Sybil de Valoines. She m. 2nd, William de Percy, Lord of Topcliffe, and 3rd, Ralph d'Aubigny (A:225).

In 3 Henry II, Robert paid 1,000 marks for livery of the lands inherited by his mother from her brother Walter Espec. He was a generous benefactor to the Knights Templar. Some time between 1147 and 1153 he confirmed a gift to Rievaulx for masses to be said for the souls of his uncle, father, and his brother Everard (A:226).

Robert and Sybil were the parents of (A:225; D: line 215): EVERARD, Baron of Wark and Helmsley, d. 1183; WALTER; PIERS, Archdeacon of Carlisle, d. 1196; and JOAN, m. as 2nd wife Sir John Lovel, Kt.

3. EVERARD de ROS, son of Robert (2) and Sybil, was still a minor in 1166, and died in 1183. He m. Roese, dau. of William Trusesbutt, and sister and coheir of Robert Trussebutt, Lord of Warter and Hunsingore, Yorks (A:225). Roese d. c1195.

In 1176, Everard paid £528 as a fine for his lands, and in 1180 he paid £100 to possess the lands formerly held of the Earl of Albemarle.

About 1246, (28 Feb, 31 Henry III), an inquest was held on the estates of Agatha Trussebut, who held the manor of Dicton, Yorks, and also lands in Bucks. Her heir was William de Ros (*Calendar of Inq. P. M.*, Vol. 1, No. 97).

Everard and Roese were the parents of (A:225): ROBERT, Baron of Ros and Helmsley; PIERS; and JOAN, m. Stephen de Mainil.

4. ROBERT de ROS, Baron of Wark and Helmsley, son of Everard (3) and Roese, was aged 13 in 1185. He d. in 1226, having m. in 1191 Isabel, widow of Robert de Brus, and illegitimate dau. of William, King of Scots (A:225).

Richard I imprisoned Robert in Normandy for some unknown offense. In 14 John, Robert assumed the habit of a monk, and his lands were placed in charge of Philip d'Ulcote, but the following year Ros was Sheriff of Cumberland. During the Baron's struggle with John, at first he sided with John, but later took the Barons' part, and was a surety for the Magna Charta. Later he was a Knight Templar.

Robert was the founder of Helmsley Castle in Yorks., and of Werks Castle in Northumberland. The former went to his elder son, and the latter to his younger son.

Robert bore **ARMS**: Gules, three water bougets (three, or trois bots, a pun on his mother's name) (*HSPV* 113-114:47).

Robert and Isabel were the parents of: Sir WILLIAM, Baron of Helmsley, d. 1264; and Sir ROBERT, Baron of Wark, d. c1269/70.

5. Sir WILLIAM de ROS, Baron of Helmsley, son of Robert (4) and Isabel, d. 1264. He m. Lucia, dau. of Reginald Fitz-Piers, son of Piers of Blain Llyfni, Wales (A:225. but *WAR7*:Line 89, gives a different lineage for Lucia).

Sir William was one of the Barons who attested the confirmation of Magna Charta in Jan 1235/6. He bore **ARMS**: Gules, three water bougets Argent (*HSPV* 113-114:127).

Sir William and Lucia were the parents of (A:225): Sir ROBERT, Baron of Helmsley; Sir WILLIAM of Ingmanthorpe; Sir ALEXANDER of Haltwhistle; Sir HERBERT; Sir JOHN; PIERS; LUCY, m. Robert de Plumpton; and ALICE, m. Sir John Comyn.

6. Sir ROBERT de ROS, Baron of Wark, son of Robert (4) and Isabel, d. c1269/70. He m. 2nd, Christian, dau. of Sir Roger Bertram and Ida (C: line 118, cites *NCP* 11:119-121).

Sir Robert was Chief Justice of the King's Bench in 1234, and Chief Justice of the Forests north of Trent, 1236. He bore **ARMS**: Or, three water bougets Sable ("Glover's Roll," *HSPV* 113-114:148).

Sir Robert was the father of (A:225): WILLIAM of Mindrum; ROBERT, Baron of Wark, d. 1274, m. Margaret, dau. of Piers de Brus, and sister and coheir of Piers de Brus of Kendal; IDA, m. Roger Bertram, Baron of Mitford; and [ISABEL?], m. Sir Roger de Merley, Baron of Morpeth.

Generations 6-10

7. Sir ROBERT de ROS, Baron of Helmsley, son of Sir William (5) and Lucia, d. 17 May 1285. He m. Isabel, dau. and heir of William d'Aubigny, Lord of Belvoir. She d. 15 June 1301 (A:225).

He sided with Simon de Montfort and was summoned to Parliament in 1264. On 28 June 1283 he was summoned to the Assembly at Shrewsbury, as was a William de Ros, probably his brother (A:229).

A writ for the *inquisition post mortem* on his estate was issued 4 June, 13 Edward I, and was held some time later. It showed that he held numerous parcels of land. His son William was aged 30 or more at the time, and his wife Isabel was named a dau. and heir of William de "Aubeny" (*Cal. Inq. P. M.*, Vol. II, no 580).

Sir Robert bore **ARMS**: Gules, three water bougets Argent, a label Azure. The arms of Belvoir/d'Aubigny were: Or, two chevrons Gules, a bordure of the second ("Glover's Roll," *HSPV* 113-114:127).

Sir Robert and Isabel were the parents of; WILLIAM, Lord of Helmsley, d. 1316; ROBERT, Constable of Wark; JOHN; NICHOLAS; ISABEL, m. Walter, Lord Fauconberg; and MARY, m. William, Lord Brewes.

8. Sir WILLIAM ROS of Ingmanthorpe, son of Sir William (5) and Lucia, d. by May 1310. He m. Eustache, dau. and heir of Ralph, son of Hugh de Greasley, and widow of Sir Nicholas de Cantelo (B:20).

Sir William inherited Ingmanthorpe from his father, to whom it passed after the death of Agatha de Trussebut, sister of Roese, wife of Everard de Ros (B:20).

He bore **ARMS**: Azure, three water bougets Or ("Walford's Roll," *HSPV* 113-114:182).

Sir William d. shortly before 28 May 1310, and was buried in the Church of the Gray Friars, Yorks., beside his wife, who predeceased him. His wife, whom he m. before 16 Jan, 21 Edward I, was the heir of Peter de la Hays (*Cal. Inq. P. M.*, Vol. III, # 95). The writ for Sir William's *inq. p. m.* was issued 28 May, 3 Edw. III. He held the Manor of Illesdon, Co. Derby "by the courtesy of England" (as survivor of his wife), by the inheritance of Eustache, his "sometime wife." Her next heir was William de Cantalo, age 18, son of William de Cantelo (*Cal. Inq. P. M.*, Vol. V, # 173).

Sir William and Eustache were the parents of (A:230): Sir WILLIAM, d. by 12 Nov 1334; THOMAS, of Dowsby, Lincs.; MARGARET; MARY, Prioress of Rosedale, d. 1310; LUCY, m. Sir Robert Plumpton; ISABEL, m. Marmaduke de Thweng; and JUETTA, m. Sir Geoffrey Scrope.

9. Sir ALEXANDER de ROS of Haltwhistle, son of Sir William (5) and Lucia, d. by 1306. He inherited the Manor of Haltwhistle, which came into the family when his grandfather Robert m. Isabel of Scotland (A:231).

Sir Alexander had one son: WILLIAM of Yalton.

10. ROBERT de ROS, Baron of Wark, younger son of Robert (6) and Christian, d. by 20 April 1274. He m. Margaret, dau. of Piers de Brus, and sister and coheir of Piers de Brus of Kendal. She d. by 30 Jan 1306/7. She divided her estate (one-fourth of her brother's estate, including the Barony of Kendal), between her son William and her nephew Marmaduke de Thweng (C: line 118, cites *NCP* 11:120-121, and Sanders, *English Baronies*).

Robert and Margaret were the parents of: WILLIAM of Kendal Castle.

11. WILLIAM de ROS, 1st Lord Ros of Helmsley, and M.P., son of Sir Robert (7) and Isabel, was b. c1255, and d. prob. by 16 Aug 1316. He m. by 1287 Maude de Vaux, dau. of John de Vaux. William and Maude were the parents of (C:Lines 1 and 2, cites *NCP*

11:96, and Saunders, *English Baronies*): WILLIAM; and AGNES, d. by 1328, m. Payne de Tibetot.

12. WILLIAM de ROS of Yalton, son of Sir Alexander of Haltwhistle, d. by 30 Jan, 19 Edw. III, when the writ for his *inq. p. m.*, was issued. He held the manor of Yelton jointly with his wife Elizabeth, who survived.

William was the father of: JOAN, age 36 at her father's death, m. John de Ellerker; and MARGARET, d. before her father, having m. Thomas Musgrave and leaving a son Thomas Musgrave, age 8 (*Cal. Inq. P. M.*, Vol. VIII, # 599).

13. WILLIAM de ROS of Kendal Castle, son of Robert (10) and Margaret, d. by 9 May 1310 (C: line 118). He was the father of: Sir THOMAS.

14. WILLIAM de ROS, 2nd Lord Ros of Helmsley and M.P., son of William (11) and Maude, was of age in 1316, and d., in Brittany cAug 1369. He m. [c1325] Margery de Badlesmere, dau. of Bartholomew de Badlesmere and Margaret de Clare, by whom he was the father of (C:Lines 1, 33, 79; E:277): THOMAS; ALICE, d. by 1344, m. Sir Nicholas de Meinill; ELIZABETH, m. William la Zouche, 1st Lord Zouche; and (prob.) MAUD, m. John de Welles, 3rd Lord Welles (They were ancestors of **Elizabeth Tudor**, Queen of England, and of colonial settlers **Anne Humphrey**, **Herbert Pelham**, and **John West**).

15. Sir THOMAS de ROS of Kendal, son of William (13), was b. c1307, and d. c1390/1. He m. a dau. of Sir John Preston of Westmorland. They were the parents of (C:Line 118): JOHN.

16. THOMAS de ROS, 4th Lord Ros, and M.P., 3rd son of William (14) and Margery, was b 13 Jan 1336/7 at Stoke Albany, and d. at Uffington on 8 June 1384. He m. by license dated 1 Jan 1358/9, Beatrice de Stafford, dau. of Sir Ralph Stafford, K.G., and Margaret de Audley.

Thomas and Beatrice were the parents of (C:Line 1; D:Line 94; E:242): Sir WILLIAM, K.G; MARGARET, d. 1384, m. Sir Reynold Grey; and ELIZABETH, m. Thomas de Clifford.

17. JOHN de ROS of Kendal, son of Sir Thomas (15), d. 1358. He m. Catherine, dau. of Sir Thomas Latimer. They were the parents of (C:Line 118): ELIZABETH, b. 1356, m. in 1383, Sir William Parr, Kt. of Parr and Kendal, d. 4 Oct 1405.

18. Sir WILLIAM de ROS, K.G., 6th Lord Ros of Helmsley, son of Thomas (16) and Beatrice, was b. c1368, and d. testate at Belvoir on 1 Sep 1414. He m. Margaret de Arundel (**descendant of Henry III**), d. 3 July 1438, dau. of Sir John and Elizabeth (DeSpencer) Arundel (C:Lines 1, 121).

Sir William was an M.P., 1394-1413 and Treasurer of England, 1403-1404.

Sir William and Margaret were the parents of five sons and four daus., including (C: line 1; E:242): JOHN, 7th Lord Ros; Sir THOMAS, 8th Lord Ros; and

MARGARET, m. c1415, James Tuchet, Lord Audley (ancestors of **The Molyneux Family** of Sefton).

Generation 11

19. Sir THOMAS de ROS, 8th Lord Ros, younger son of Sir William (18) and Margaret, was b. 26 Sep 1406, and d. 18 Aug 1430, "in the King's Wars in France." He m. Alianor de Beauchamp, dau. of Richard Beauchamp, Earl of Warwick, by his wife Elizabeth Berkeley. Alianor m. 2nd, Edmund Beaufort, Duke of Somerset (E:243).

Sir Thomas and Alianor were the parents of (E:31, 243): THOMAS; and MARGARET, m. 1458, William de Botreaux.

Generation 12

20. THOMAS de ROS, 9th Lord Ros, son of Sir Thomas (19) and Alianor, was b. 9 Sep 1427, and was beheaded at Newcastle on 17 May 1464. He m. Philippa de Tiptoft, dau. of John Tiptoft, Lord Tiptoft, by Joyce Cherleton. Phillipa m. 2nd, Thomas Wingfield (E:243).

Thomas de Ros was a loyal adherent to the Lancastrian cause, and after the rout at Towton in 1461, he fled abroad, but returned to England (E:243).

Thomas and Philippa had two sons and four daus., including (E:243): MARGARET, m. Sir Thomas Burgh, Kt.; and ALIANOR, m. Robert Manners of Etal (They were ancestors of **Philip and Thomas Nelson** of New England, and of Alice Capell who m. **Robert Wiseman** of the *Ark* and the *Dove* Expedition to MD, and whose descendants settled in MD).

THE ROUS FAMILY

Refs.: A: *HSPV 13 n.s.*

ARMS: Sable, two bars engrailed Argent. **CREST**: A man's head Argent, beard, hair, and whiskers Sable, wearing a cap of the last tied with ribbons of the first (A).

1. [-?-] ROUS of Stewkley m. and had issue (A): JOHN; EDMUND (Minister of Huntington, d. c1676, m. and had issue); GERVASE (Commissary to the Earl of Mulgrave's Regt.); and THOMAS (Citizen and Barber Chirurgeon of London, d. s.p.).

2. JOHN ROUS of Stewkley, son of [-?-] (1), d. c1660 age 50 or more. He m. Isabella, dau. and coheiress of Sir Thomas Maples of Stow. John and Isabella were the parents of (A): THOMAS, d. unm. c1677 age 48; Capt. EDMUND (m. but has no issue); JOHN (m. and had issue); AUGUSTINE (m. and had issue); HENRY; ROBERT; ISABELL; **ANNE, m. [-?-] Thompson in Maryland in the West Indies**; MARY, m. her cousin John Rous, son of Rev. Edmund; and JANE, m. Rev. Gervase Fuller of Huntington.

3. **ANN ROUS**, dau of John (2) and Isabella, was listed in the 1684 Visitation of Huntington as having m. [-?-] **Thompson, and "living in Maryland in the West Indies"** (A). Anne "Rowse" was transported to MD by 1673 (MPL 17:531).

THE SAVORY FAMILY

Refs.: A: "William Savory: William Savory's Visits to Ireland," *PHSL* 17:380-387; B: *PHSL* 18:33-48. C. Records of Philadelphia Monthly Meeting, in Hinshaw's *Encyclopedia of American Quaker Genealogy*. Vol. II

While checking the Huguenot Society of London Proceedings for another family, I stumbled across an account of the Savory Family of Kent County, Maryland.

1. **JOSEPH SAVORY** was b. 1646 in Montpelier, France. In 1685 he left for England with his sons, including a William and a Moses, and settled at Wandsworth, Surrey. He was the father of: WILLIAM; MOSES; and perhaps others.

2. **WILLIAM SAVORY**, son of Joseph, was b. by 1685, and d. 1739 in KE Co., MD. He m. at Wandsworth, Surrey, Eng., on 2 April 1706, Dorothy Sessions.

    William Savory, Sr., was listed in the KE Co. Debt Books between 1733 and 1752 as owning several tracts of land: Probus, Galloway's Chance, Pope's Forest, Cornwallis Choice, Carola, and Locust Point (*INKE*:32).

    He settled in KE Co., MD, where he is said to have died in 1739. He died intestate but left an inventory appraised on 22 June 1739 at £301.14.1 by Samuel Groome and William Graves. Thomas Williams, Jr., signed as creditor, and Nathaniel Ricketts and Esther Salter signed as next of kin. William Savory, admin., filed the inventory on 23 June 1739. An additional inventory worth £39.19.8 was filed by the administrator on 5 May 1741 (MINV 24:277, 25:431).

    William had at least one son: WILLIAM.

3. **WILLIAM SAVORY**, son of William (2) and Dorothy, was a cabinet maker who settled in Philadelphia, where he d. in 1787. William was buried 28 da., 5 mo., 1787, age 65. He may have m. 1st, Penelope [-?-]. He definitely m. [perhaps as his 2nd wife] on 19 April 1746, Mary, dau. of Rees Peters. Mary was bur. 26 da., 7 mo., 1804, age 82 (C:417).

    William Savory of Kent Co., planter and his wife Penelope, on 19 March 1733, conv., to Joseph Everett of KE Co., carpenter, the upper part of a tract called Galloways Chance on the e. side of Worton Branch, 100 acres (KELR JS#16:439).

    He may be the William Savory who patented 210 a. known as Savory's Farm, in 1743 (*INKE*:66).

    William and Mary were the parents of (C:417): SARAH, d. 21 da., 5 mo. 1748; ELIZABETH, b. 30 da., 5 mo., 1747; WILLIAM, b. 14 da., 7 mo., 1750; THOMAS, b. 13 day., 10 mo., 1751, m. and issue (traced in C:417); JOSEPH, b. 14 da., 2 mo., 1753, d. 16 da., 2 mo., 1757; MARY, b. 27 da., 1 mo., 1755, d. 9 da., 9 mo., 1775, age 20; ELIZABETH, b. 24 da., 12 mo., 1756; JOSEPH, b. 18 da., 3 mo., 1759, d. 16 da., 8 mo., 1770, age 11; JOHN, b. 21 da., 11 mo., 1760, d. 5 da., 9 mo., 1761; ANN, b. 21 da., 12 mo., 1762, marr. at Philadelphia MM, on 1 da., 11 mo., 1781, John

Poultney (C:643); BENJAMIN (twin), b. 22 da., 1 mo., 1765, d. 4 da., 5 mol, 1765, age 3 mos.; and RACHEL (twin), b. 22 da., 1 mo., 1765, d. 29 da., 8 mo., 1766, age 19 mos.

Unplaced:

SAVORY, WILLIAM, of BA Co., Gent., on 19 Aug 1742, purchased from Caleb Beck of KE Co., planter, and his wife Mary, part of a tract called Long Compton, cont. 12 acres (KELR JS#24:5).

THE ABRAHAM SCOTT FAMILY

Refs.: A: "Robert Scott Family (Western Run)," FCA, MHS. B: *QRNM.* C: Henry Chandlee Forman. *Tidewater Maryland Architecture and Gardens.* New York: Bonanza Books, 1956. X: Undocumented material in the Ancestral File of LDS.

1. JOSEPH SCOTT of Lower Ancholm, Eng., was b. c1606, and had at least one son (X): ROBERT, b. c1632.

2. ROBERT SCOTT, of Lesson Hall, Woodhall, Co. Cumberland, Eng., son of Joseph (1), was b. 1632 at Lowerancholm, Cumberland, and d. 27 March 1705. He was buried at Tiffinthwaite. He m. Mary Hammond, dau. of John and Rebecca (Berrie) Hammond on 6 Nov 1657 at Holme Meeting, Soc. of Friends (A: X). The family resided at Lesson Hall, Cumberland (X).

    Robert and Mary were the parents of (A; C:1655; X): JOHN, b. 9 Dec 1653; RUTH, b. 1660, m. Thomas Scott on 9 May 1688; MARY, b. 15 Jan 1661, bur. 10 April 1717, m. William Wright on 15 Aug 1684; ESTHER, b. 1664, d. 23 Dec 17611; JANE, b. 1666, d. 1715; MOSES, b. 22 Oct 1667, m. Rebecca Drewry on 23 Sep 1711; SARAH, b. 1668, m. 23 Sep 1711, John Key; ABRAHAM, b. 1669, m. Elizabeth Harrison on 6 Oct 1664; and JOSHUA, b. 1672, d. 7 May 1674.

3. JOHN SCOTT, son of Robert (2) and Mary, was b. 9 Dec 1653, and on 30 Sep 1687 he m. Elizabeth Cupe. They were the parents of (A; C:165): RUTH, m. William Park; ABRAHAM; and poss. others.

4. ABRAHAM SCOTT, son of John (3) and Elizabeth, brought a Certificate of Removal to PA (Forman states he brought his certificate from Woodhall to Gunpowder Meeting: C:165). He m. Elizabeth Dyer, whose family owned a number of mills.
    Abraham and Elizabeth were the parents of (A): ABRAHAM.

5. ABRAHAM SCOTT, son of Abraham (4) and Elizabeth, m. in 1751, Elizabeth Rossiter. **He settled in BA Co., MD**.
    On 26 d., 2 m., 1772, Abraham Scott, his wife Elizabeth, and children Rachel, Amos, Jesse, Rossiter, Heather, and Thomas, were received into Gunpowder MM by certificate of removal from Rights Town (Wrightstown) MM (B:62).
    They were the parents of (A; B:18, 180): RACHEL, m. James Mason; ROSSITER, b. 8 d., 12 m., 1756, m. 1789 Edith Lukens; AMOS, b. 26 d., 9 m., 1759;

THOMAS, m. 1793, Elizabeth Matthews; and JESSE, m. 1787, Rebecca Johns; and poss. others.

THE SCOTT FAMILY of CO. KENT

Refs.: A. James Renat Scott. *Memorials of the Family of Scott, of Scot's-Hall in the County of Kent*. London: 1876.

1. Sir WILLIAM SCOTT of Scott's Hall, Smeeth, Kent, son of Sir John and Agnes Beaufitz, m. Sibyl, dau. of Sir John Lewknor of Goring and West Dean, Sussex.

Sir William and Sybil were the parents of (A:254-255; *PASC*:111): Sir JOHN; EDWARD, of the Mote, Iden, m. Alice Fogge; ANNE, m. Sir Edward Boughton; CATHERINE; and ELIZABETH.

2. Sir JOHN SCOTT of Scott's Hall, Kent, son of Sir William (1) and Sybil, d. by 1534. He m. Anne (or Amy) Pympe, dau. of Reynold and Elizabeth (Pashley) Pympe, and a descendant of Edward I. Sir John was Sheriff of Kent.

Sir John and Anne/Amy were the parents of four sons and seven daus., including (A:254-255; *PASC*:111): Sir REYNOLD; Sir JOHN; WILLIAM, m. Anne Fogge (she m. 2nd, Henry Isham); Richard, m. Mary Whetenhall; MILDRED, m. 1st, John Digges, and 2nd, Richard Keyes; CATHERINE, m. Sir Henry Crispe; ISABELLA, m. Richard Adams; ALICE; MARY, m. Nicholas Ballard; ELIZABETH, m. Stephen Whitfield; SYBIL, m. Richard Hynde; ANNE, m. Sir [-?-] Pollard; GEORGE; and PASHLEY.

3. Sir REYNOLD SCOTT, son of Sir John (2) and Anne/Amy, d. testate on 16 Dec 1554. He m. 1st, Emelyn Kempe, dau. of William and Eleanor (Browne) Kempe. They had one son and two daus. Sir Reynold m. 2nd, Mary Tuke, dau. of Sir Bryan Tuke, of Layer Marney, Essex, Secretary to Cardinal Wolsey. Sir Reynold and Mary had five sons and four daus. (*PASC*:111).

Sir Reynold was Captain of Calais, and Sheriff of Kent. His will was dated 4 Sep 1544 and proved 13 Feb 1554/5. Mary Tuke Scott was still alive in 1555 (*PASC*:111).

By Emelyn Kempe, Sir Reynold was the father of (A:254-255; *PASC*:111): Sir THOMAS SCOTT; CATHERINE, m. John Baker; and ANNE, m. Walter Mayney.

By Mary Tuke, Sir Reynold was the father of: CHARLES; and MARY, m. Richard Argall (They were the ancestors of **Charles Barham of Surry Co., VA**).

4. Sir THOMAS SCOTT of Scott's Hall, son of Sir Reynold (3) and Emelyn Kempe, d. testate 30 Dec 1594. He m. 1st, Elizabeth Baker, d. 17 Nov 1593, dau. of Sir John Baker of Sissinghurst Castle, Cranbrook, Kent, by his wife Elizabeth Dinley. Sir Thomas m. 2nd, 1583, Elizabeth Heyman, d. 29 June 1595; and 3rd [sic], Dorothy Bere, widow of John Heyes, Edward Scott, and George Fynche (*PASC*:111).

Sir Thomas and Elizabeth (Baker) were the parents of (A:254-255; *PASC*:111-112): Sir EDWARD; THOMAS, m. 1st, Mary Knatchbull, and 2nd, Elizabeth Honywood; Sir JOHN, of Nettlested; CHARLES; RICHARD, m. Catherine Heyward; ROBERT of Mersham; ELIZABETH, m. 1st, John Knatchbull, and 2nd, Sir Richard Smythe; EMELINE, m. Robert Edolphe; ANNE, m. 1st, Richard Knatchbull, and 2nd, Sir Henry Bromley; MARY, m. 1st, Anthony St. Leger, and 2nd, Alexander Culpeper

(She was the ancestor of **Col. Warham Horsmanden of Charles City Co., VA; Ann Culpeper Danby of VA; Frances Culpeper Stephens Berkeley of VA; Capt. Alexander Culpeper of VA; John Culpeper of NC and SC; and Col. St. Leger Codd of MD**); REGINALD; Sir WILLIAM; JOSEPH; ANTHONY; and BENJAMIN.

5. CHARLES SCOTT, of Egerton, Godmerhsam, Kent, son of Sir Reynold Scott (3) and his second wife Mary Tuke, d. 1617. He m. Jane Wyatt, dau. of Thomas Wyatt of Allington Castle, Kent.   Charles and Jane were the parents of two sons and two daus. including (*PASC*:112): THOMAS; and DEBORAH, m. William Fleete of Chatham, Kent (Her son Capt. **Henry Fleete, settled in MD and VA**).

6. THOMAS SCOTT, son of Charles (5) and Jane, was b. at Egerton House, Kent, in 1567, and d. there on 31 March 1635. He m. 2nd, 1604, Mary Knatchbull, b. at Mersham, Kent, d. at Egerton House, Kent, on 1 March 1616.

Thomas and Mary were the parents of (*PECD* II, 240): **DOROTHEA, settled Oyster Bay, L. I., NY**, and bapt. 22 Sep 1611, m. 1st, Daniel Gotherson, and 2nd, Joseph Hogben.

THE SEDLEY FAMILY

Refs.: A: "Sedley," *HSPV* 86:196-197. B: *MCS5*; Line 18. C: Sedley data posted by Joyce Ream, `reamjp@compusmart.ab.ca`, who has been of great help. See also <reamjp@mail.interbaun.com>

ARMS: Azure, a fess wavy between three goats' heads erased Argent, a crescent for difference. **CREST**: Out of a ducal coronet Or, a goat's head erased Argent, charged with a crescent for difference.

N.B.: For earlier generations, see *HSPV* 32:243.

1. JOHN SEDLEY was Lord of the Manor of Southfleet, Kent, and Auditor of the Exchequer to King Henry VII. He was married three times. He married 1st, Elizabeth Jenks, daughter and co-heir of Roger Jenks of London. She died without issue. He married 2nd, Elizabeth Cotton, of Hamstall Ridware, Staffordshire. John Sedley and Elizabeth Cotton had three known children. John Sedley married 3rd, Agnes Wyborne, daughter of John Wyborne of Hakewell, Kent. She died without issue (C).

John and Elizabeth (Cotton) were the parents of (C): WILLIAM, m, Anne Grove, the daughter and heir of Roger Grove of London. William was High Sheriff of Kent in 1547; MARTIN, who married Elizabeth Monteney; and DOROTHY, who became a Nun at Dartford, Kent.

2. MARTIN SEDLEY, son of John (1) and Elizabeth, was buried at Morley St. Peter, Norfolk, on 28 Jan 1571/2. He m. as her 3nd husband, Elizabeth Monteney at Morley St. Botolph, Norfolk, in March 1548. She was the dau. of John Monteney of Mountnessing, Essex, and had previously been m. to Thomas Sexton (C).

Martin Sedley purchased Morley, Norfolk, about 1545 (C).

Martin Sedley and Elizabeth (Monteney) were the parents of (C): MARTIN, who married first Ann Shelton and second Abigail Knyvett

3. MARTIN SEDLEY, son of Martin (2) and Elizabeth, was buried at Morley St. Peter, Norfolk, on 10 Feb 1609/10. He m. 1st, Ann Shelton, daughter of Roger Shelton of Depham, Norfolk. He m. 2nd, Abigail Knyvett, dau. of John Knyvett of Ashwellthorpe, Norfolk, and Agnes Harcourt (C).

Abigail Knyvett was b. at Ashwellthorpe and d. at Wacton, Norfolk, on 15 Dec 1623. A Monumental Brass in Wacton Church recorded the death on that date of Abigail Sedley, daughter of John Knyvett of Ashwellthorpe, and late wife of Martin Sedley.

The will of Martin Sedley of Morley, Gentleman, dated 12 May 1608, confirmed 11 Oct 1609, ratified 17 Jan 1609/10, and proved 5 March 1609/10, mentioned his sons, Martin, Robert, and "Raffe" (now Sir Raffe Sedley, Knight), and his wife, Abigail, his sole executrix (C).

The will of Abigail Sedley of Barford, widow, dated 21 July 1620 and proved 22 Dec 1623, mentioned her son, Martin Sedley as sole executor, her daughter-in-law, Bridget Sedley, her brother, Edmund Knyvett, and "my sonne Gurdon my daughter" and their children (C).

Some pedigrees erroneously have Abigail as the daughter of Sir Thomas Knyvett, but he was actually her brother. Sir Thomas Knyvett and his wife, Muriel Parry, did have a daughter named Abigail, who married Edmund Mundford, and it is she who has been confused with the Abigail who married Martin Sedley. However, as Sir Thomas Knyvett's daughter, Abigail, was born on September 6th, 1576, and the first of Martin and Abigail Sedley's children was baptized on May 18th, 1578, at Morley St. Botolph, Norfolk, it could not have been Sir Thomas Knyvett's daughter who married Martin Sedley. There is also the indisputable evidence of the wording on Abigail Sedley's Monumental Brass in Wacton Church, mentioned above (C).

Martin Sedley and Ann (Shelton) were the parents of (C): AMY (m. 1st, Robert Yarham, and 2nd, John Smyth of Corton, Suffolk; she was mentioned on a plaque for Martin Sedley in Morley St. Peter Church); EDMOND (bapt. at Morley St. Peter on 24 March 1565/6, and was living in 1589; d. s.p.); Sir ROGER, bapt. at Morley St. Peter on 2 Oct 1568; he was referred to as "Ralphe" on a plaque for Martin Sedley in Morley St. Peter, and as "Raffe" in his father's Will); and ELIZABETH, bapt. 27 June 1571 at Morley St. Peter, d. young; she was not mentioned on a plaque for Martin Sedley in Morley St. Peter Church (Ream).

Martin Sedley and Abigail Knyvett had four children (Ream): ROBERT, bapt. 18 May 1578 at Morley St. Botolph, Norfolk, d. s.p. in 1613, and was buried at Barford, Norfolk; ABIGAIL, bapt. 31 Dec 1579, at Morley St. Botolph, Norfolk, d. unm., and was buried in 1610, at St. George Tombland, Norwich; MARTIN, bapt. 1 Oct 1581 at Morley St. Botolph, Norfolk; and MURIEL, bapt, 20 April 1583 at Morley St. Botolph, Norfolk, m. as his 2nd wife, Brampton Gurdon of Assington, Suffolk, at Morley St. Peter, on 8 July 1606, she d. 22 Aug 1661, and was buried at Southburgh, Norfolk.

4. MARTIN SEDLEY, son of Martin (3) and Abigail, was bapt. 1 Oct 1581 at Morley St. Botolph, and d. on 23 Jan 1652/3, and he was buried at Barford, Norfolk. He m. Bridget Pettus at Barkway, Hertfordshire, on 22 May 1608. She was the dau. of Sir John Pettus and Bridget Curtis (C).

Bridget Pettus was baptized at St. Simon and St. Jude, Norwich, on 29 Nov 1588, and d. on 28 Oct 1652, and was buried at Barford (C).

Martin Sedley of Morley St. Peter and Barford d. leaving a will dated 10 Jan 1652/3, and proved 20 May 1653, mentioned his sons, Thomas, Charles, John, Isaac, Anthony, and Robert, his daughters and sons-in-law, Bridget and John Sheppard, Muriel and William Reymes, Ann and Samuel Fawether, and Abigail and Thomas Talbot, his grandson, William Sedley, his sister, Muriel Gurdon, and his nephew, Brampton Gurdon, the executor being his son, John (C).

Martin Sedley and Bridget (Pettus) had 15 children (C): BRIDGET, bapt. 20 April 1609 at St. Simon and St. Jude, Norwich, and m. John Sheppard of Mendlesham, Suffolk; ABIGAIL, who was baptized 26 Dec 1609 at St. Simon and St. Jude, where she was bur. 29 Dec 1610; JOHN, bapt. 18 April 1611 at St. Simon and St. Jude, m. Elizabeth Spring; MARTIN, bapt. 6 May 1612 at St. Simon and St. Jude; THOMAS, bapt. 17 Aug 1613 at Morley St. Peter; MURIEL, bapt. 1 Dec 1614 at Morley St. Peter, m. William Reymes; ANN, bapt. 10 March 1615/6 at Morley St. Peter, m. Samuel Fawether of Halesworth, Suffolk; MARTIN, bapt. 11 May 1617 at Morley St. Peter; HENRY, bapt. 6 Aug 1618 at Morley St. Peter; WILLIAM, bapt. 6 Aug 1618 at Morley St. Peter; ABIGAIL, bapt. 15 Dec 1619 at Morley St. Peter, m. Thomas Talbot; ROBERT, bapt. 1 Jan 1621/2 at Morley St. Peter; ANTHONY, bapt. 11 April 1624 at Morley St. Peter; CHARLES, bapt. 5 July 1628 at Morley St. Peter, Norfolk; and ISAAC, d. s.p., c1675, his will being proved on 23 June 1675.

5. MERIELL/MURIEL SEDLEY, dau. of Martin (3) and Abigail, was bapt. 20 April 1583 at Morley St. Botolph, Norfolk, and m. as his 2nd wife, Brampton Gurdon of Assington, Suffolk, at Morley St. Peter, on 8 July 1606. She d. 22 Aug 1661, and was buried at Southburgh, Norfolk

Brampton Gurdon, son of John and Amy (Brampton) Guredon, was M.P., 1620, and Sheriff of Suffolk, 1625-1629, who d. 1649 (B).

By Brampton Gurdon, Muriel was the mother of: MURIEL, m. June 1663, **Major Richard Saltonstall, Esg., of Watertown, MA** (*MCS5*:Line 44).

6. JOHN SEDLEY, son of Martin (4) and Bridget, was bapt. 18 April 1611 at St. Simon and St. Jude, Norwich, and d. on 28 Sep 1681, aged 71, according to the Barford Monumental Inscriptions. He m. Elizabeth Spring at Pakenham on 21 Nov 1639.

Elizabeth was the dau. of Sir William Spring and Elizabeth Smith of Pakenham, Suffolk, and was bapt. 2 May 1621 at Pakenham. She d. on 24 Nov 1679 and was buried at Barford, Norfolk.

John Sedley of Barford was High Sheriff of Norfolk in 1658. The Will of John Sedley of Barford, Gent., dated 10 Sep 1680, and proved 19 Nov 1681, mentioned his sons, John (his executor), William, Isaac, and Martin, and his daughter, Bridget Sedley, the witnesses being Oliver St. John, Sedley Reymes, and John Pitcher.

John Sedley and Elizabeth (Spring) had nine children (C): WILLIAM, b. at Morley St. Peter, Norfolk, and baptized at Pakenham on 22 Sep 1640, m. Ann Witherick; MARTIN, was of Barford, which he sold and moved from Norfolk; ELIZABETH, who was bapt. 18 Nov 1646 at Morley St. Peter, m. Thomas Weld at Wymondham, Norfolk, on 20 Oct 1664; JOHN, bapt. 28 Aug 1649 at Morley St. Peter, where he was bur. 7 Nov 1711, m. Ann [-?-]; ISAAC, bapt. 24 Feb 1655/6 at Morley St. Peter; BRIDGET, bapt. 15 Dec 1657 at Morley St. Peter, bur. at Barford on 26 Dec 1657 (but her burial was recorded at Morley St. Peter); KATHARINE, bapt. 25 Dec 1657, bur. at Barford on 8 April 1659 (but her burial was recorded at Morley St. Peter); BRIDGET, bapt. 20 April 1659 at Morley St. Peter; and ANN.

7. **WILLIAM SEDLEY**, son of John (6) and Elizabeth, was b. at Morley St. Peter, Norfolk, and was baptized at Pakenham, Suffolk, on 22 Sep 1640. He was buried at Morley St. Peter on 17 Oct 1704 (A: C). He m. Ann Witherick, daughter and heiress of Peter Witherick and Ann Boreman (C).

Ann Witherick was also coheiress of her grandfather, Edmund Boreman, an Alderman of Norwich, Norfolk. She was baptized at St. Michael at Plea, Norwich, on January 2nd, 1640/1641, and she was buried at Morley St. Peter on November 11th, 1709 (C).

The will of Ann Witherick Sedley, dated 26 Oct 1709, and proved 24 Nov 1709, mentioned her four daughters, Elizabeth Needham (her sole executrix), Ann, Katherine, and Bridget, and her son John.

An administration for William Sedley, late of Morley, dated 26 Oct 1704, was signed by his son, John Sedley of Morley, John Sedley (his nephew?), and his nephew, Edward Sedley of the Parish of St. Andrew, Holborn, Mddx.

William Sedley and Ann Witherick had 10 children, all bapt. at Morley St. Peter (A: C): MARTIN, bapt. 16 May 1661; JOHN, bapt. 27 Jan 1662/3, d. s.p. leaving a will proved 13 Aug 1715, first mentioned Elizabeth Stone, the older daughter of Robert Stone of Wymondham, Norfolk, gentleman, and Elizabeth Stone's daughter, Elizabeth, and, later in the Will, his cousin, Edward Sedley of St. Andrew, Holborn, Mddx., oilman, his cousin, John Sedley, Edward's brother, his cousin, Martin Sedley, son of Martin Sedley, deceased, late brother of Edward and John, his sister, Katherine Gurney, and his brother-in-law, William Tench, the executors being Edward Sedley and William Balye; EDMUND, bapt. 10 May 1664, d. leaving a will dated 15 Nov 1707 and proved 15 Oct 1709, naming his sisters, Ann, wife of John Brandon, Clerk, and Elizabeth Needham, widow, and Elizabeth Needham's children, Charles, Thomas, Robert, Elizabeth, Mary, and Ann. He requested that he be buried in the Chancel of the Church at Barford, Norfolk; ELIZABETH, bapt. 16 April 1666, m. Charles Needham at Old Buckenham, Norfolk, on 6 Oct 1688; ANN, bapt. 8 Oct 1667, m. Rev. John Brandon; BRIDGET, bapt. 19 April 1670, m. William Tench of Norwich at St. Stephen's Church, Norwich, on 3 Jan 1709/10; WILLIAM, bapt. 19 March 1672/3, and who, it was noted "and buried not long after;" KATHERINE, bapt. 4 June 1674, m. John Gurney of Tasburgh, Norfolk, and d. s.p.; ABIGAIL, bapt. 22 Aug 1678, d. unm., and was bur. at Morley St. Peter on 21 Aug 1709.; WILLIAM, bapt. 24 Sep 1679, and was bur. on 26 Nov 1697 at Morley St. Peter.

8. **MARTIN SEDLEY** of Barford, 2nd son of John (6) and Elizabeth, m. and was the father of the following children (A): EDWARD, of Morley St. Peter, d. s.p., leaving a will proved 2 Oct 1728 (PCC Brook, 304), m. Mary, dau. of Henry Somner of Dunton, Bucks; JOHN; MARTIN, m. and had issue; CATHERINE, m. James Somner; and **ELIZABETH, m. [-?-] Macdonald, now in Maryland.**

9. **EDWARD SEDLEY**, son of Martin (8), d. leaving a will dated 2 March 1727/8, with a codicil dated 10 April 1728, and two codicils dated 18 July 1728. It was proved 2 Oct 1728. It mentioned his brother, John, his sisters, Catharine Somner, and **Elizabeth Macdonald, now in Maryland**, his brother-in-law, James Somner, his nieces, Elizabeth Somner, eldest daughter of his sister, Catharine, Mary, wife of (blank) Hussey, and second daughter of his sister, Catharine, and Sarah Somner, another daughter of his sister, Catharine, his nephews, Loftus Wharton Somner (who died between the date of the will and the July 18th, 1728, codicil), and Henry Somner, his cousins, Elizabeth Needham, widow, Bridget Tench, wife of William Tench, Katherine

Gurney (with a reference to John Gurney, her husband), his late cousin, Ann Brandon, her (unnamed) daughter, and her husband, John Brandon, other cousins and kinsmen, Edward Weld, James Weld, Samuel Weld, Thomas Weld, Thomas Needham, and Charles Needham, and a friend, William Horne of the Middle Temple, London, and William's wife, Elizabeth. The joint executors were James Somner and Edward Weld (C).

THE SHARPE FAMILY

Refs.: A: Sharpe Family Data compiled by James W. Ridgway of Olympia, WA, who cited three sources for his information: (1) The Farnes-Shackleton Association (located in Salt Lake), which has done considerable research on the Isaac family; (2) Research by Richard T. Foose of Kissimmee, FL.; and (3) the Isaac Family Association.

1. RICHARD SHARPE m. Jane [-?-]. They were the parents of (A): WILLIAM.

2. WILLIAM SHARPE, son of Richard (1) and Jane, was b. 31 Jan 1589 and d. c1615, when his estate was administered. William married 3 Nov 1612 in South Stoke, Lincolnshire to Elizabeth Coney, b. at Bassingthorpe on 1 Feb 1592 (A).

Sharpe lived at or near Great Gonerby, Lincolnshire, England.

William and Elizabeth had at least two children (Research made available to the compiler by the late Richard T. Foose of Kissimmee, FL): ELIZABETH, bapt. 23 Feb 1612, m. 1632, Richard Isaacke of Fulbeck, Lincs.; and ANN, bapt, 14 May 1615.

THE SHOWEL FAMILY

THOMAS ROADES SHOWEL, was in BA Co. by Aug 1756 when he wrote a letter to his grandfather Thomas Roades of Without Lawfords Gate, Bristol, and enclosing a letter to his mother. He asked his grandfather and uncle to send money for his passage back to England, and mentioned his sister. He evidently stayed in Maryland since he married Phyllis Anna Baxter on 29 Dec 1760 in St. Thomas Parish (Coldham, "Gen. Gleanings," *NGSQ* 65 (4) 266). She was born 26 Feb 1743, daughter of John and Mary Baxter (*BATH*:18, 35).

Thomas and Phyllis Anna were the parents of (*BATH*:15): ELIZABETH, b. 6 Nov 1761.

THE ROBERT SMITH FAMILY

Refs.: A: *SSLM*:634. B:"Robert Smith." *BDML* 2:748.

1. [-?-] SMITH of Penryn, Cornwall, had at least two sons (A: B): RENATUS, d. 1719; and ROBERT, d. 1706/7.

2. ROBERT SMITH, probably from Penryn, Cornwall, son of [-?-] (1), and bro. of Renatus, d. by March 1706/7. Robert m. c1680, probably Anne Gaines, widow of Thomas Hynson (B).

Robert immigrated by 1677 and in Nov. 1677 was admitted to practice law in Kent Co. (A). He was a member of the Associator's Convention, 1689-1692 from TA Co., and represented that county in the Lower House of the Assembly, 1692-1693.

On 22 June 1697 Robert Smith of TA Co., and his wife Anne, conv. to Thomas Usher of Kent Co., a parcel of land called New Harbour, 100 acres (KELR M:66a). On the same day Robert Smith and his wife Anne, of TA Co., conv. to Marcy Sedley of Kent Co., and her heirs, 100 acres, part of Mount Pleasure (KELR M:66b).

Robert and Anne were the parents of (B): ANNE, d. by 1724, m. Anthony Ivy (d. 1714).

THE SMITHSON FAMILY

Refs.: A: "Thomas Smithson." *BDML* 2:753.

1. CHRISTOPHER SMITHSON of Moulton, Yorks., d. 1650. He m. Dorothy, dau. of Leonard Calvert of Kipling, and sister of George Calvert, 1st Lord Baltimore (A).

Christopher and Dorothy were the parents of (A): GEORGE; and THOMAS.

2. GEORGE SMITHSON, son of Christopher (1) and Dorothy, was b. 1620, and d. c1667/8. He prob. m. Eleanor, dau. of Col. Charles Fairfax (A).

George Smithson was a Justice of the North Riding of Yorkshire, 1654-1660 and 1665-1667/8, and a member of Parliament for the North Riding in 1654, and for the Borough of Northallerton, 1658. He was a Major in the army of the Parliament during the Commonwealth, and a Col. in 1660 (A).

George and Eleanor were the parents of (A): THOMAS, d. 1713/4, s.p., Speaker of the Maryland Assembly, 1701-1704; GEORGE, b. 1653; WILLIAM, clerk of DO Co., 1677/8-1681; CHARLES; JOHN; CHRISTOPHER, b. 1670; DOROTHY, m. Michael Fletcher of Richmond, Yorks; ELEANOR; MARY.

3. THOMAS SMITHSON, son of Christopher (1) and Dorothy, was b. c1625 and d. 1695. He was clerk of DO Co., MD, 1681-87 (A).

THE SOMERSET FAMILY

Refs.: A: The Marquis of Ruvigny. *Plantagenet Roll of the Blood Royal: The Clarence Volume*. 1905. B: *TMFO*. C: *PRHE*.

Generations 1-5

1. JOHN OF GAUNT, Duke of Lancaster, K.G., son of King Edward III and Philippa of Hainault, was b. 1340 and d. 1399. He m. his 3rd wife Katherine Roet Swynford in 1397.

ARMS (used on a seal in 1363):Quarterly France ancient [Azure semy de lis Or] and England [Gules, three lions passant guardant Or], a label of three points ermine (C:77).

John and Katherine had had a number of children born before their marriage, but after their marriage, John of Gaunt had them made legitimate by Act of Parliament in 1397 (A: Table I; C:78; *PASC*:15): JOHN of BEAUFORT, Marquis of Dorset, b.

c1372; HENRY BEAUFORT, Cardinal of Winchester; THOMAS, K.G., b. c1400, Earl of Dorset, m. and had one son who d. young; and Lady JOAN, m. 1st, Robert de Ferrers and 2nd, Ralph Neville, 1st Earl of Westmorland.

2. JOHN BEAUFORT, K.G., Earl and Marquis of Somerset, son of John (1) of Gaunt, was b. c1370 and d. 16 March 1409/10. He m. by 28 Sep 1397, Margaret de Holand, dau. of Sir Thomas and Alice (Fitz-Alan) de Holand (*MCS5*: Line 90; *PASC*:17).

ARMS (before legitimation): Party per pale Argent and Azure, over all, on a bend Gules, three lions passant guardant Or, and a label of three points France. (after legitimization): Quarterly France ancient and England, within a bordure componee Argent and Azure (C:81).

John and Margaret were the parents of (*PASC*:17; *WAR7*:Line 252): HENRY, 2nd Earl of Worcester, d. s.p.; JOHN, K.G., Duke of Somerset; THOMAS, Earl of Perche, d. unm. 1432; EDMUND; JOAN, m. 1st, James I, King of Scotland (ancestors of **Robert and John Barclay of NJ**); and 2nd, Sir James Stewart, "the Black Knight of Lorne;" and MARGARET, m. Thomas Courtenay, 5th Earl of Devon.

3. JOHN BEAUFORT, K.G., 1st Duke of Somerset, son of John (2) and Margaret, was b. by 25 March 1404 and d. 27 May 1444. He m. c1442 Margaret Beauchamp, d. by 3 June 1482, dau. of Sir John Beauchamp of Bletsoe. Margaret m. 1st, Sir Oliver St. John (*PASC*:17)

John and Margaret were the parents of two daus. (*PASC*:17): MARGARET, m. 1st, John de la Pole, 3nd Duke of Suffolk, 2nd, Edmund Tudor, Earl of Richmond (by whom she was the mother of **King Henry VII**, 3rd, by 1464, Henry Stafford, and 4th, Thomas Stanley, Earl of Derby.

John Beaufort also had an illegitimate dau.: THOMASINE, m. Reynold Grey, Lord Wilton.

4. EDMUND BEAUFORT, Duke of Somerset, son of John (2) and Margaret (de Holand), was b. c1406 and was killed at the Battle of St. Albans on 22 May 1455. He m. c1436, Eleanor (Beauchamp) Ros (*MCS5*: Line 90).

Edmund and Eleanor were the parents of (*PASC*:18; *WAR7*: Line 1): HENRY; EDMUND, Duke of Somerset, killed at Tewkesbury, s.p.; JOHN, Earl of Dorset, d. s.p; THOMAS, d. by 1463; MARGARET, m. Humphrey de Stafford; ALIANOR, m. 1st, James Butler, Earl of Ormond and Wiltshire (ancestors of **Sir Herbert Pelham of New England**), and 2nd, Robert Spencer; ANNE, m. Sir William Paston; JOAN?, m. 1st, Sir Robert St. Lawrence, and 2nd, Sir Richard Fry; ELIZABETH, d. by 1492, m. Sir Henry Lewes; and MARY, m. [-?-] Burgh.

5. HENRY BEAUFORT, Duke of Somerset, son of Edmund (4) and Margaret, was b. c1436 and was beheaded at Hexham on 15 May 1464. He was Constable of Dover Castle and Warden of the Cinque Ports in 1459, but was attainted in 1464 (*NCP* XII (1) 54-57).

By Joan Hill, Henry Beaufort was the father of an illegitimate son (*MCS5*: Line 90): CHARLES, Earl of Worcester.

6. CHARLES SOMERSET, K.G., created 1st Earl of Worcester on 1 Feb 1513/4, illegitimate son of Henry Beaufort (5), Duke of Somerset, was b. c1460 and d. 15 April 1526. He m. 1st, Elizabeth Herbert. He m. 2nd, Elizabeth, dau. of Thomas West, Lord la Warre (*MCS5*: line 79A). He m. 3rd, Eleanor Sutton, dau. of Edward Sutton, 2nd Lord Dudley (*PASC*:19).

Charles and Elizabeth (Herbert) were the parents of (*MCS5*: Line 32, cites *NCP* XII (2), 851): Sir HENRY.

Charles and Elizabeth (West) were the parents of three children, including (*MCS5*: Line 79A; *PASC*:19): MARY, m. William Grey, K.G., XIII Lord Grey of Wilton.

Generations 6-10

7. Sir HENRY SOMERSET, K.G., Earl of Worcester, son of Charles (6) and Elizabeth (Herbert), d. 26 Nov 1549. Sir Henry m. 1st, with papal dispensation, Margaret Courtenay, dau. of William Courtenay and Katherine (dau. of King Edward IV). She d. s.p., and he m. 2nd, Elizabeth Browne, dau. of Sir Anthony and Lucy (de Neville) Browne (*PASC*:19).

Sir Henry and Elizabeth were the parents of (*MCS5*: Line 32; *PASC*:19) WILLIAM; ELIZABETH (if she did m. Sir Roger Vaughan, she may have been an ancestor of **Sir Jeffrey Jeffreys of VA**, but the linkages are by no means proven).

8. WILLIAM SOMERSET, K.B., K.G., Earl of Worcester, son of Sir Henry (7) and Elizabeth, was b. c1527, and d. 21 Feb 1588/9. He m. 1st, by 29 Jan 1549/50 Christian North, dau. of Edward, 1st Lord North by Alice Squire. Christian was living in March 1563.4. William m. 2nd, Theophila Newton, dau. of Sir John Newton (*PASC*:19).

William and Christian were the parents of: EDWARD.

9. EDWARD, 4th Earl of Worcester, K.G., son of William (8) and Christian, was b. c1550, and d. on 3 March 1627/1628. About 1575 he married Lady Elizabeth Hastings, d. 1621 (a descendant of George, Duke of Clarence, K.G., bro. of Edward IV (A: Table II; *PASC*:255).

Edward and Elizabeth were the parents of several children, including eight sons (A: Table XXXV); HENRY, Marquis of Worcester; Hon. CHARLES, m. Elizabeth Powell; ELIZABETH, m. Sir Henry Guildford; CATHERINE, m. William, Lord Petre (See **The Petre Family** elsewhere in this work); ANNE, m. Sir Thomas Wintour of Lidney, Gloucs.; FRANCES, m. William Morgan; BLANCHE, b. c1583, d. 1649, m. 1607, Thomas, 2nd Lord Arundell of Wardour (c1575-1643, brother of Anne Arundel who married Cecil Calvert, 2nd Lord Baltimore).

10. HENRY, Marquis of Worcester, son of Edward (9) and Elizabeth, was b. c1577, and d. 18 Dec 1646. About 1600 he m. the Hon. Anne Russell who d. 1639. Anne Russell was the dau. of John Russell, Lord Russell, and Elizabeth Cook (*PASC*:255).

Henry and Anne were the parents of several children including (A: Table XXXV): Lord JOHN SOMERSET.

11. ANNE SOMERSET, dau. of Edward (9) and Elizabeth,, is stated by Ruvigny, to have m. Sir Thomas Wintour of Lidney, Gloucs. However, she may have m. Sir Edward Wintour of Sydney [*sic*], Gloucs., and to have been the mother of at least four sons ("Robert Wintour." *BDML* 2:905): Sir JOHN, Secretary to Queen Henrietta Maria; **EDWARD, came to MD in 1634**; **FREDERICK, came to MD in 1634**; and **ROBERT, arrived in MD in 1637** and d. 1638 (the latter three seem to have d. s.p.).

12. Lord JOHN SOMERSET, 2nd son of Henry (10), Marquis of Worcester, m. the Hon. Mary Arundell. They were the parents of (A: Table XXXV): HENRY, of Penthy Court, Co. Gloucester; THOMAS; and CHARLES.

Generation 11

13. CHARLES SOMERSET, son of Lord John (12) and Mary (Arundell) Somerset, m. 1st, Jane Thomas, dau. of Walter Thomas. He m. 2nd, Catherine Sawyer, nee Baskerville, dau. of Walter and Alice (Goodyer) Baskervile (*PASC*:256).

Charles and Catherine were the parents of four children (A: Table XXXV): CHARLES; HENRY; MARY JOHANNA; and ELIZABETH.

Generation 12

14. MARY JOHANNA SOMERSET, dau. of Charles (13) and Catherine, m. 1st, Col. John Lowther of the English Army, and 2nd, c1697 in CV Co., as his 3rd wife, Capt. Richard Smith of CV Co. (B: cites *The Complete Peerage*, and Chancery Liber 3:849-850).

THE SORRELL FAMILY

Refs.: A: Robert J. C. K. Lewis. *Lewis Patriarchs of Early Virginia & Maryland, With Some Arms and Origins*. No place: the Author, 1989. B: "Sorrell (No. 1)." *HSPV* 13:490. C: "Sorrell (No. 2)." *HSPV* 13:491.

ARMS of Sorrell of Great Waltham, Essex: Gules, two leopards (or lions passant guardant) ermine, a crescent for difference. (B).

NB: Visitation pedigrees must always be used with care.

The William Sorrell Family

Generations 1-5

1. WILLIAM SORRELL of High Eston, Essex, was the father of (A:); THOMAS, b. 1510; and ROBERT of High Eston (for his descendants see *HSPV* 13:490-491).

2. THOMAS SORRELL, son of William (1) was b. 1510 at Much Waltham. He was the father of (A): JOHN, b. 1530 at Great Waltham; and ROBERT.

3. ROBERT SORRELL, of High Eston (or High Easter), son of William (1), m. Clement [-?-], who m 2nd, Thomas Wiseman. Robert and his wife were the parents of (A: B; C): THOMAS of High Eston.

4. JOHN SORRELL of Much Waltham, Co. Essex, son of Thomas (2), m. Alice Tendring. They were the parents of (A: B): ROBERT, b. 1550.

5. THOMAS SORRELL of High Eston, son of Robert (3), was the father of (C): JOHN of Stebbing Parsonage.

6. ROBERT SORRELL, son of John (4), was b. 1550 at Great Waltham. About 1570 he m. Margery, dau. of John Frank of Tarling, Essex. They were the parents of at least two sons, both born at Great Waltham (A; B): ROBERT, b. 1572; and JOHN, b. 1575, d. s.p.

7. JOHN SORRELL of Stebbing Parsonage, Essex, clerk of the Assizes, son of Thomas (5), m. Margery, widow of Robert Bernard. and dau. of Robert Sorrell (poss. # 6) of Waltham. John and Margery were the parents of (C): THOMAS; and SUSAN, b. 1591, m. John Litle of Halsted (Her children are shown in *HSPV* 13:435).

8. ROBERT SORRELL, son of Robert (6) and Margery, was b. 1572 at Great Waltham, and resided at Writtle. On 1 Nov 1593 he m. Mary or Maria, dau. of Thomas Everard, Esq., of Great Waltham (A).

Robert and Maria were the parents of (A who gives dates of birth; B): MARY, b. 1598, m. William Conier of Chelmsford; ANN, b. 1596; MARJORY, b. 1601, m. Nicholas Conier of Mountnessing; THOMAS, b. [1613?]; JOHN, b. [1604?]; and ROBERT, b. 1615.

9. JOHN SORRELL, son of Robert (6) and Margery, was b. 1575 at Great Waltham. According to Lewis he was the father of THOMAS (11 below), but the 1634 Visitation of Essex states that he d. s.p (B).

10. THOMAS SORRELL of Stebbing Parsonage, son of John (7) and Margery, was living in 1634. He m. Susan, dau. of John Caley of Colchester. They were the parents of (C): JOHN; THOMAS; WILLIAM; MARGARET; SUSAN; and ALICE

Generation 6

11. THOMAS SORRELL, according to Lewis, a son of John (9), but according to the 1634 Visitation, the first son of Robert (8) was b. 1613 at Great Waltham. No family is listed for him in the Visitation (B), but Lewis states that he m. Susan [-?-].

In 1616 he witnessed the will of Richard Everard of Great Waltham (See *VGEW*: 451-2).

Thomas and Susan were the parents of the following children (A): JOHN, b. 2 April 1612, may have gone to VA; THOMAS, b. 11 April 1614; SUSANNA, b. 1 April 1616; ROBERT, b. 21 May 1618, may have gone to VA; RICHARD, b. 1 May 1620, may have gone to VA; and TIMOTHY, b. 8 Oct 1622, may have gone to VA.

12. JOHN SORRELL of Waltham Parsonage, son of Robert (8) and Mary, m. Mary, dau. of Thomas and [-?-] (Thorogood) Aylett of Coggeshall, Essex. John and Mary were the parents of (B): MARY, age 5 in 1634.

Generation 7

13. JOHN SORRELL, son of Thomas (11) and Susan, was b. 2 April 1612, and may have come to VA c1635. He was the father of (A): THOMAS, b. c1633 in England, and came to Rapphannock Co., VA c1678, m. and had issue.

14. ROBERT SORRELL, son of Thomas (11) and Susan, was b. c1618, and came to VA c1637, but returned to England c1642. He m. Rebecca Woodward c1643, and returned to VA c1647, and d. 1676. Rebecca was a dau. of John Woodward who was a brother of Thomas Woodward, Mint Master (A).

Robert and Rebecca were the parents of (A): ROBERT, Jr., b. c1644; THOMAS, b. 1647; JOHN, settled in Essex Co., VA, and d. 1700, m. Dorcas White and had issue; and EDWARD, settled in Essex Co., VA.

15. RICHARD SORRELL, son of Thomas (11) and Susan, was b. 1620, and came to VA c1640. He m. Ann [-?-] (poss. George), and was the father of (A): GEORGE; ANN; and FRAN.

The John Sorrell Family

1. JOHN SORRELL of Stebbing, Essex, may have been a son of John (12) and Mary (Aylett). He m. Dorothy [-?-]. They were the parents of (MDTP 22:338-342; PCLR TP#4:364): RICHARD; and JOHN of Great Baddow, Essex.

2. RICHARD SORRELL, son of John Sorrell (1) and wife Dorothy of Stebbing, Essex, settled in Anne Arundel Co., where he d. by 4 Dec 1713. He m. 1st, Eliza, dau. of Edward and Alice Skidmore.

By 4 Dec 1713 his widow and admx. had m. 2nd, Thomas Robinson. Sorrell left one bro.: John, of Great Baddowe, Essex, dec., who left a widow Sarah, a son Thomas (who m. Mary [-?-], and a sister Sarah wife of John Gardner (PCLR TP#4:364).

Administration of his large estate was granted to Thomas Robinson and wife Rachel of AA Co. Edward Skidmore of KE Co. claimed that Sorrell had married his sister.

On 4 Dec 1713 Sarah Sorrell, widow of John Sorrell of Great Baddow, Co. Essex (said John was the youngest bro. of Richard Sorrell of AA Co.). Thomas Sorrell, only son of said John Sorrell, and Thomas' wife Mary, and Thomas's sister Sarah wife of John Gardner, all appointed John Bond of parish of St. Mary Magdalene, Bermondsey, Surrey, mariner, their atty. to receive from said Thomas Robinson and wife Rachel all land and property due them as heirs at law and next of kin of said Richard Sorrell (PCLR TP#4:364; MDTP 22:338; and INAC 33B:144).

3. JOHN SORRELL, of Great Baddow, Essex, son of John and Dorothy, was a brother of Richard, who settled in AA Co., MD. John died by 1713, leaving two children (MDTP 22:338-342): THOMAS, bapt. 30 Sep 1679; and SARAH, bapt. 10 May 1683, m. John Gardner.

4. THOMAS SORRELL, son of John (3) was bapt. 30 Sep 1679. He m. Mary [-?-] (MDTP 22:338-342).

THE SPARKS FAMILY

1. JOHN SPARKS died leaving a will dated 2 Sep 1699, and proved 3 Jan 1701 in KE Co., MD. In it he left to his sons John and George, 100 acres called Buckslide. His wife Ellinor was made extx., and was to have personal estate. John Salter, Eliza Robinson, and Thos. Prestige witnessed the will (MWB 12:154).

John and Eleanor were the parents of: JOHN, Jr.; and GEORGE.

2. JOHN SPARKS of the Burrough of Christchurch, Twyneham in the county of Southton in the Kingdom of England, butcher, eldest son and heir and devisee of John Sparks (1), late of Chester River in Kent Co., Maryland, dec'd. and George Sparks of the Borough of Christchurch Twynehan afsd. glover, one other of the sons and devisees of the said John Sparks, dec'd., on 23 Oct 1716 stated that whereas the said John Sparks and George Sparks are or one of them is lawfully entitled to 100 acres called Buckhill, they have appointed Hugh Arbuthnott(?) of Weymouth in the county of ... England, mariner, their attorney (KELR BC#1:181).

Unplaced:

SPARKS, GEORGE, was in KE Co. by 25 July 1750 when he witnessed the will of Arthur Miller (KEWB 3:130).

THE SPRIGG FAMILY
A Tentative Reconstruction

Refs.: A: Henry F. Waters. *Genealogical Gleanings in England*. 2 vols. 1901. Repr. GPC, 1969. B: Beverly Fleet. *Virginia Colonial Abstracts*. Repr. in 3 vols. GPC. C: Jennings Cropper Wise. *Ye Kingdome of Accawmacke or The Eastern Shore of Virginia in the Seventeenth Century*. 1911. Repr.; Baltimore: Clearfield Co., Inc., 1990. D: Peter Wilson Coldham. *American Wills and Administrations in the Prerogative Court of Canterbury, 1610-1857*. GPC, 1989. E: *Genealogies of Virginia Families from the Virginia Magazine of History and Biography*. 5 vols. GPC, 1981. F: Annie Lash Jester. *Adventurers of Purse and Person, 1607-1625*. Sponsored by the Order of First Families of Virginia, 1956. G: Katherine Beall Adams. *A Maryland Heritage*. X: Undocumented Ancestral File in the LDS Family History Center.

ARMS: Chequy Or and Azure, a fess Ermine. CREST: A laurel branch Vert. Thomas Sprigg of MD used these arms on a seal when he signed the inventory of Martin Falkner in PG Co., in 1698 (G:274, cites *Heraldic Marylandiana*, by Harry Wright Newman).

1. THOMAS SPRIGGS, of Banbury, Northamptonshire, was b. 1604, and d. c1678/9 in London, Eng. He m. in 1629 Katherine or Anne Griffin, who was b. 1610 in Kettering, Northamptonshire, and d. after 17 Aug 1661 (poss. in MD). She was a dau. of George Griffin of Kettering, "b. 1594, said to have m. in 1587" (why we cannot trust undocumented material in the Ancestral File).

John Andrews, now residing in the Island of Barbados left a will dated 30 Nov 1648 and proved 11 Feb 1649. He left 1,000 lbs. good Muscovado sugar or £30 to Thomas Sprigg and £5 to his wife Maudlin to buy a ring. If Andrews' bro. Samuel, his executor, should die before he reaches the age of 21, then Sprigg and his wife should have an additional £100 and £20 respectively (A:603-604 cites PCC Pembroke, 20). In Feb 1650 admin. of his estate granted to William Creeke in March 1649 was revoked and granted to Samuel Wild during the minority of brother Samuel Andrews and the absence abroad of Morgan Powell and Thomas Sprigg (D:7).

Thomas Sprigg of London, merchant, d. leaving a will dated 19 May 1675, proved 14 Jan 1678. He appointed Mr. Maurice Thomson, Col. George Thomson, Sir William Thomson, and Major Robert Thomson his executors and trustees (A:66 cites PCC King, 10).

David Griffin of Bassinghall Street, London, citizen and tallow chandler, d. leaving a will dated 11 Nov 1679 and proved 12 Dec 1679. Among other bequests he left his sister Katherine Sprigg, widow, the rent of a house and an orchard at Stratford Bridge, Clos., for her life. He also named her four children: Thomas, Abraham, Katherine, and Joane (A:1075 cites PCC King, 61).

Lieut. Col. Samuel Griffin was living in Northumberland Co., VA when he made his will on 2 Feb 1703. He made a bequest to Katherine, dau. of the testator's sister Kath: Sprigg, dec. (B: 1:536 cites Northumberland Co. Record Book 17:213-215).

Thomas and Katherine/Anne were said to have been the parents of (X): Lieut. THOMAS, b. c1628/30 at Kettering; ABRAHAM; KATHERINE (mentioned in the will of her uncle Samuel Griffin of Northumberland Co., VA; and JOANE (and poss.) NATHANIEL.

2. Lieut. THOMAS SPRIGG, poss. son of Thomas (1) and Katherine/Anne, was b. c1628/30 at Kettering, and d. 29 Dec 1704 in CV Co., MD. Thomas Sprigg age 35, deposed in 1665 (*ARMD* 49:501-502). In 1694 he gave his age as 64 (MPL WRC#1:696).

Thomas Sprigg m. 1st, after 1650, Katherine Graves, dau. of Thomas Graves. She was the widow of Capt. William Roper, Burgess from Accomack Co., in 1636 (F:190). The Ancestral File states that he m. in [by] 1668 Eleanor Nuthall, b. c1645/6, d. c1694/1704. In 1668 the Council of Maryland issued an order dividing the estate of John Nuthall, dec., among his three children, John and James Nuthall, and Eleanor wife of Thomas Sprigg (*ARMD* 5:34; X).

Thomas "Sprigge" was in Accomack Co., VA, on 25 March 1651 when he took an Oath of Fidelity to the "Commonwealth of England as it is now established without Kings or House of Lords" (C:135).

Thomas Sprigg immigrated to MD by 1658 with his wife Catherine and Verlinda Roper, Edward Bushell, Nathaniel Sprigg, and Hugh Johnson (MPL Q:208, 309). He was in MD by 1657 when he sued John Neville (*ARMD* 10:546).

On 18 Jan 1658 he patented 600 a. called Sprigley, which he received for transporting himself, his wife Catherine, her dau. Verlinda Roper, Edward Bushell, Nathaniel Sprigge, and Hugh Johnson. This land was located on the Chester River which divides Kent and Queen Anne's Co. Thomas and Catherine sold the land to Simon Carpenter on 17 Aug 1661 (G:274, cites *MHM* 8:74, 75).

He patented 325 a. in CV Co. called Kettering, on 8 Sep 1685 (MPL 25:179, 32:342). On 1 Aug 1698 he patented 500 a. in Prince George's Co. called Sprigg's Request (MPL 39:46). He also patented a tract called Northampton (G:274).

On 16 March 1700 Thomas Sprigg for love and affection conv. 200 a., part of the 1000 a. called Northampton and the 325 a. called Kettering, to his eldest dau. Sarah Pearce and to his grandson John Pearce. The 200 a. had recently been owned by John Sprigg, dec. If John Pearce died without heirs, the land was to go to Sarah Pearce's dau. Sarah Bell, wife of James Bell (PGLR A:361).

Thomas Sprigg held a number of offices in colonial Maryland. He was Justice of CV Co., and Justice of the Quorum in 1658, 1661, 1667, 1669-1670 and 1670 (*ARMD* 3:424, 5:147). He was High Sheriff of CV Co. in 1664-1665 (*ARMD* 3:490-491, 520).

Thomas Sprigg d. leaving a will dated 9 May 1704, proved 29 Dec 1704. He stated he was to be buried beside his wife and children Mary, John, and Elias, who had predeceased him. He left various bequests to children Sarah Pearce, Thomas, Martha Prather, Eleanor Nuthall, Elizabeth Wade, and Ann Gittings. He also named friends Samuel Magruder, Edward Willett, and John Smith, sons-in-law Thomas Stockett, Robert Wade, Philip Gittings, and Thomas Prather, and granddau. Eleanor Stockett, grandson Thomas Stockett. Son Thomas was executor (G:276 cites *MHM* 8:75).

Samuel Magruder and Edward Willett appraised the personal estate of Thomas Sprigg, Sr., on 28 Jan 1704. They assigned a value of £311.11.0 to the property (MWB 3:571).

Evidently Thomas Sprigg, Jr., declined to act as executor of his father's estate. On 6 Aug 1706 Mr. Robert Wade, Mr. Philip Gittings, and Thomas Prather filed an account. Out of assets of £311.11.0, payments of £8.6.8 were made (INAC 26:72).

Thomas and Katherine (Graves Roper) Sprigg were the parents of (F:190): SARAH, b. c1658, d. 1736, m. 1st, 1676 John Peerce, b. c1650/5, d. c1687/1700, and 2nd, Enoch Combes; and THOMAS, b. c1670, d. after 1736, m. Margaret Mariarte.

Thomas and Eleanor (Nuthall) Sprigg were the parents of (G:275-276): CATHERINE; JOHN, d. c1700, unmarried; ELLEN (See *MHM* 8:75); MARTHA, m. Thomas Prather; ELEANOR, m. 1st, Thomas Hilleary, who d. 1697, and 2nd, John Nuthall, III (her cousin); ELIZABETH, m. Robert Wade; ANN, m. Philip Gittings; and MARY, d. 27 Jan 1694, m. 12 March 1689, Thomas Stockett.

3. NATHANIEL SPRIGG, poss. son of Thomas (1) and Katherine, was transported to MD by 1658 by Lieut. Thomas Sprigg (MPL Q:208).

Nathaniel was living on 21 Nov 1676 when he was listed as a debtor in the inventory of Guy White (INAC 3:111). On 20 Jan 1678 Thomas and Nathaniel Sprigg were listed as debtors in the inventory of James Pennington (INAC 6:59).

Nathaniel Sprigg and John Nuthall appraised the estate of John Clark of CV Co. on 3 Feb 1684 (INAC 8:321).

THE STEUART FAMILY

Refs.: A: Gladys P. K. Nelker. *The Clan Steuart-Stewart-Stuart, 800-1970 A.D.* No place: no pub., 1970. B: John Stewart of Ardvorlich, "The Stewarts of Annat, Ballachallan, and Craigton," *The Stewart Society Magazine* (reprinted in A:110-114). C: John Stewart of Ardvorlich, "Stewarts of Ballachallan," *The Stewart Society Magazine* (reprinted in A:114-116). Note the variations in spelling.

1. ALEXANDER STEWART (of the 28th generation of descendants of Alpin, King of Scots), son of John, was b. c1581 and d. 14 Jan 1647 at the age of 76. He m. [-?-], dau. of McNab of Aucbarn. They were the parents of (A:20): JOHN, of Annat; WALTER; ANDREW; JAMES (ancestor of Maj.-Gen. Robert Stewart of Rait); and ARCHIBALD of Glassingall, Sterling.

2. JOHN STEWART of Annat, son of Alexander (1), d. 1650. He m. 1st, Janet Graham, dau. of Jasper or Gespard Graham of Gartur; and 2nd, Elizabeth, dau. of John Campbell of Kinloch.

John and Janet (Graham) Stewart were the parents of (A:20-21): ALEX-ANDER of Annat; DUNCAN; and GEORGE.

John and Elizabeth (Campbell) Stewart were the parents of: WILLIAM; JAMES of Edinburgh; CHARLES; Capt. HENRY; JANET; and JEAN.

John Stewart may have had a natural son named John Dow.

3. DUNCAN STEWART, second son of John (2), d. 1670. He purchased Ballachallam. He was the father of (A:21): GEORGE; and perhaps others.

4. GEORGE STEWART, son of Duncan (3), d. by 1751. He m. Mary Hume, dau. and eventual heiress of Harry Hume of Argaty, Perthshire (C:114).

In 1751 Mary Home Stewart, widow, succeeded her brother George Home of Agarty, and David Home Stewart, son of George and Mary, was served heir to his grandfather (C:114).

George and Mary were the parents of (A:21): DAVID HOME of Ballachallam, d. 1768 (he had no legitimate issue, but he had a natural son Duncan); **Dr. GEORGE HUME, came to MD**; JAMES; **WILLIAM, may have come to MD**; JANET, m. Walter Grahame of Nether Glenny; and other daus.

5. Dr. GEORGE HUME STEUART, son of George (4) and Mary (Hume), was b. c1700, and d. 1784 in Scotland. He is buried at Kilmadock, Perthshire, Scotland. George Hume Steuart came to MD c1722/3, and m. Anne Digges in 1744 (*SOCD*:149). She was b. 22 Nov 1721 in PG Co., the dau. of George Digges, and d. 20 Sep 1814. She is buried at Doden, AA Co. (A).

Dr. George Hume Steuart returned to Scotland after his brother's death (C:115-116). He died in Scotland (A:24).

On 5 April 1788 Ann Stewart of Annapolis, MD, widow of George Home Stewart, who had died in Perthshire, appointed her son David her attorney in matters concerning her husband's estate. William Stewart was a witness (*DSSF*:110).

George and Anne (Digges) Steuart were the parents of (A:24-32): GEORGE HUME, b. 1747 (changed his name to Hume in order to inherit an estate); SUSANA, b. 1749, m. Judge James Tilghman; Dr. CHARLES, b. 1750, m. Elizabeth Calvert; DAVID, b. 1751, d. unm.; WILLIAM, b. 1754; Dr. JAMES, b. 1755; ANNE, b. 1757, d. 1767; MARY, b. 1759, d. 1776; and JEAN, b. 1761, d. 1778.

THE TALBOT/TARBURT FAMILY
A tentative reconstruction.

Refs.: X: Undocumented material in the LDS Ancestral File and the International Genealogy Index.

1. ROBERT TALBOTT was b. c1600 at Waplington, Yorkshire, and was buried 22 May 1646 at Allerthorpe. He m. on 3 Feb 1629 at Allerthorpe by Pocklington Ellis [-?-]. They were the parents of (X): PAUL, bapt. 30 Jan 1640

2. PAUL TALBOTT/TALBURT, son of Robert (1) and Ellis, was bapt. 30 Jan 1640 at Allerthorpe, where he was buried 4 Nov 1714. His wife has not been identified, but he was the father of (X): JOHN, b. 1671 at Waplington.

3. JOHN TALBOTT/TALBURT, son of Paul (2), was b. 1671 at Waplington (X), came to Md., and settled in PG Co., MD, where he d. 25 May 1735. He m. Sarah Lockyear, dau. of Thomas, on 2 Feb 1696 in St. John's Piscataway Parish, PG Co. (PGKG:244, 253).

On 28 Oct 1699, Thomas Locker of PG Co., for the fatherly love he bore his dau. Sarah, now wife of John "Talbutt," conveyed her 88 acres, being one-half of 170 a. Langley now in PG Co., but formerly in CH Co. (PGLR A:195)

John and Sarah were the parents of (PGKG:244): PAUL, b. 18 Dec 1697; THOMAS, b. 3 Sep 1699, may have d. young; JOHN, b. 23 Feb 1700; ALICE, b. 31 Aug 1703; BENJAMIN, b. 8 April 1705; OSBURN, b. 8 July 1708; WILLIAM, b. 13 Jan 1715; ANN, b. 3 May 1712; SARAH, b. 18 Jan 1718; and THOMAS, b. 20 Dec 1720.

THE MICHAEL TAYLOR FAMILY

1. THOMAS TAYLOR of Witton Gilbert, Co. Durham, married Alice, and had issue (PCLR TL#2:397): MICHAEL; STEPHEN, died s.p.; ELEANOR, m. by 18 Dec 1697 Hugh Shield of Witton Gilbert; and ALICE, d. s.p.

2. MICHAEL TAYLOR, son of Thomas (1) and Alice went to MD about 13 years ago (before Dec 1697), returned to Witton Gilbert about 12 years ago, and then went back to MD. Hugh and Eleanor Shield claim to be his heirs (PCLR TL#2:397).

THE PHILIP TAYLOR FAMILY
A Tentative Reconstruction

Refs.: A: Emerson B. Roberts. "Captain Philip Taylor and Some of His Descendants." *MG* 2:427-440. B: A. Russell Slagle. "Captain Philip Taylor and Some of His Descendants: A Correction." *MG* 2:441-442. X: Undocumented Taylor Ancestry in LDS Ancestral File.

1. THOMAS TAYLOR was b. 1560, and was the father of (X): PHILIP.

2. PHILIP TAYLOR, son of Thomas (1), was b. 1585 at Marden, Herefordshire, and m. [-?-] [-?-] on 20 Feb 1616 at Llangenuth, G, Wales. His unidentified wife was b. 1580 (X).

Perhaps by a previous marriage, Philip was the father of (A:427, X): PHILIP, b. 1610.

3. PHILIP TAYLOR, son of Philip (2), was b. 1610 at Marden, and d. 1648 in MD. He m. 1st, Jane [-?-], and 2nd, Jane Fenwick, possibly a sister of Cuthbert Fenwick. She m. 1st, Capt. Thomas Smith, and 3rd, William Eltonhead (A:430). She d. at SM Co., MD, testate, in 1659 (A:431).

Taylor came to VA in the *Africa* and was in Accomac Co., VA, by 1637, when he brought his wife (A:427). In 1642/3 he was Burgess for Northampton Co., VA. He went to MD with William Claiborne and was engaged in the battle at the mouth of Wicomico River (A:428).

Philip and Jane (Fenwick) were the parents of (A): THOMAS, b. c1643; and SARAH, m. 1st, William Anderton, and 2nd, Thomas Courtney.

4. THOMAS TAYLOR, son of Philip (3) and Jane (Fenwick), was b. c1643 and d. c1696 in DO Co. (B:441). Thomas Taylor, age 16, deposed in Feb 1659, chose his mother Jane, relict of William Eltonhead, as his guardian (*ARMD* 41:447). Thomas Taylor, son of Philip and Jane, m. by 20 March 1669, Frances [-?-] (B:441 cites Warrants 12:206). Frances, b. c1648, is stated to have been the dau. of John Yardley of Flintshire, Wales (X).

On 27 Feb 1669, with consent of his wife Frances, Thomas conv. 1200 a. Taylor's Inheritance to Arthur Wright (DOLR 1 Old:4). On 28 Feb 1669 Thomas and Frances conv. 50 a. Musketta Quart[er?] to Robt. Seale (DOLR 1 Old:5).

As High Sheriff, on 1 March 1669, he conv. 220 a. Taylor's Island to Daniel Holland. Wife Frances consented (DOLR 1 Old:15). On the same day, he conv. 80 a. St. John's Island, to Daniel Holland; wife Frances consented (DOLR 1 Old:17; see also 1 Old 134, 147, 153, 160, 161, 3 Old:18, 247, 4 Old:28, (DOLR 3 Old:10).

On 10 Oct 1694 Major Thomas Taylor patented 400 a. Welchman's Kindness (MPL 37:272).

On 2 Oct 1696 Thomas Taylor of DO Co., Gent., conv. all his property to his four sons: John, Thomas, Philip, and Peter Taylor, provided they would provide maintenance for their parents, Thomas and Frances Taylor, and for their two youngest sisters, Frances and Mary Taylor. They were also to make over to their sister Aloysia Taylor 400 a. on Hunting Creek if she should require it (DOLR 5 Old:85).

Thomas and Frances were the parents of: JOHN; THOMAS; PETER; PHILIP; FRANCES; MARY; and ALOYSIA.

THE CHRISTOPHER THOMAS FAMILY

Refs.: A: Richard Henry Spencer. *The Thomas Family of Talbot County, Maryland, and Allied Families*. Baltimore: William N. Wilkins, 1914. B: "Thomas, Christopher." *BDML*, 2:813. C. Eleanor Pratt Covington McSwain. *My Folk: The First Three hundred Years*. The [North Carolina?] Historical Society, 1972. D: Caroline V. Sudler. "The Thomas Line of Talbot County, Maryland." Typescript, a copy of which was generously made available to the compiler by William Pennington of Chevy Chase, MD.

1. The Rev. TRISTRAM THOMAS, Rector of Alford Parish, Surrey, was b. c1522. He was the father of (C:170): JOHN, b. c1548, of Chevening, Kent, England; EDMOND, b. c1550; and RICHARD, b. c1552 at Sevenoaks, Kent, Eng.

2. EDMOND THOMAS, son of Rev. Tristram (1), m. and was the father of (C:170): TRISTRAM, b. c1579.

3. TRISTRAM THOMAS, son of Edmond (2), was b. c1579, and d. at Sundridge, Co. Kent, d. by Feb 1640. He m. Elizabeth Marsh of Westerham, Kent (a few miles south of Sundridge and Sevenoaks), sister of Raph Marsh (C:170).

In his will dated 21 March 1639 and proved 2 Feb 1640 he mentioned land bought of Christopher Emerson, called Dryhill Farm. He named his wife Elizabeth, son Richard, son Tristram, and son Christopher. He named John, Peter, Elizabeth, Johan and Austyn, the five children of his dau. Elizabeth Austen. His estate "Pollard" was already in the hands of his son Edmond, who had two sons Tristram and Edmund. He named his son Leonard, and his youngest son Edward His son Christopher had already been given his inheritance. He also named his brother-in-law Raph Marsh of Westerham and his daus. Marie and Sarah Thomas (C:170; D).

Tristram and Elizabeth were the parents of (A; C:170): RICHARD; TRISTRAM; CHRISTOPHER; ELIZABETH, m. [-?-] Austen (and had five children: John, Peter, Johan, Elizabeth, and Ausytn) and EDMOND (who had two sons Tristram and Edmund); LEONARD; EDWARD; MARIE; and SARAH.

4. CHRISTOPHER THOMAS, son of Tristram (3), was b. c1609 and d. March 1670. He m. 2nd, Mrs. Elizabeth Higgins, who later m. Matthew Smith (C:172)

Christopher sailed for Virginia in 1635, and he moved to MD, where he was a Burgess for the Isle of Kent, MD (A; C:170-171).

Christopher Thomas immigrated in the mid-1630s to MD, perhaps as an indentured servant, and in 1637/8 represented Kent Island in the Assembly. No mention is made of any relations (B).

On 19 Nov 1679 Elizabeth Smith, wife of Matthew Smith, and former wife of Christopher Thomas conveyed to Tristram Thomas her quit claim to 350 a. called Barbadoes Hall, patented in 1665 by Christopher Thomas (TALR 3:315).

Christopher was the father of (A; C:172): TRISTRAM.

5. TRISTRAM THOMAS, son of Christopher (4), was bapt. 20 Sep 1629 at Orpington, Kent, and d. May 1686 in MD. He m. Anne Coursey some time before 10 Nov 1670 when William Coursey conveyed his brother-in-law Tristram Thomas, Gent., 400 a. on Wye River called Trustram (TALR 1:126).

Tristram Thomas, his wife Anne, and their sons Thomas, Christopher, and Tristram, were brought to MD in 1665 by William Coursey (MPL 9:327).

Tristram Thomas was in TA Co. by 4 May 1671 when as "Trustam" Thomas he witnessed the will of Robert Smith (MWB 1:466).

It was as Trustam Thomas that he d. leaving an undated will proved 22 May 1686. He named Christopher, William, Stephen, Trustam, and Thomas Thomas. He does not name them as sons, but that relationship may be inferred from reading the will. Mrs. Anne Thomas was named extx. John Stephens, Thomas Gough, and John Glendenning witnessed the will (MWB 4:226)

Tristram and Ann were the parents of (B; C:173): TRISTRAM, b. c1666, d. Feb 1745/6; and WILLIAM, b. 1669, d. 1740.

THE THORNBOROUGH FAMILY

A number of conflicting accounts of the Thornborough family exist. Many years of working on this family, using printed abstracts of primary sources at the George Peabody Library, and the work of the late Dr. Terrence Fahy and Cynthia Snider of Beltsville, have made it necessary to reconcile the conflicting statements. The descent given below is the result. Although the works of numerous authors and researchers have been consulted, the final decisions have been the compiler's, and the errors in interpretation may be laid at his door.

Refs.: A: Delmar Leon Thornbury. "Original Source Records Relating to the Thornbury Family." Washington: 1933. Typescript at the Library of Congress. B: *Record Society*. C: *Transactions of the Cumberland and Westmoreland Antiquarian and Archaeological Society (CWAA)*. D: William Farrar. *Records Relating to the Barony of Kendale*. Ed. by John Curwen. Volume I. Cumb. and Westm. Antiq. and Arch. Soc. Record Series, IV. Kendal: Titus Wilson and Sons, 1923. Volume II. Cumb. and Westm. Antiq. and Arch. Soc. Record Series, V. Kendal: Titus Wilson and Sons., 1924. Volume III. Cumb. and

Westm. Antiq. and Arch. Soc. Record Series, VI. Kendal: Titus Wilson and Sons, 1926. E. Cheshire and Lancashire Record Society. F: Frederick W. Ragg. "Shap, Rosgille and Some Early Owners ... ." *CWAA*, new ser. Vol. 14. G: Research by the late Dr. Terrence Fahy of Martin, SD, and graciously made available to the compiler by Cynthia Snider of Beltsville, MD. H: Undocumented Thornborough Descendancy Chart, in Ancestral File of the Church of Jesus Christ of Latter Day Saints (must be used with care). I: Antiquary on Horseback: The First Collections of the Rev. Thos. Machell, Chaplain of King Charles II, Towards a History of the Barony of Kendal. Transc. and edited by Jane M. Ewbank. J: John Curwen. Later Records Relating to North Westmorland and the Barony of Appleby. Cumberland and Westmorland Antiquarian and Archaeological Society, Record Series. VIII. Kendal: 1932. K: Frederick W. Ragg. "de Lancastre ... ." CWAA, new series 10:428.

ARMS: Ermine, fretty Gules, a chief of the last.

Generations 1-5

1. WALTER (son of Peter, son of Robert, of Orm, of Ketel of Eldred) is designated as being of the 6th generation because he is 6th in descent from Eldred. Walter took the name of Thornborough (A).

Walter was the father of: NICHOLAS; and (possibly) WILLIAM who m. Margaret and was mentioned as being sued in 1246 by the Chaplain of Whixley.

2. NICHOLAS de THORNBOROUGH, son of Walter (1), was the father of at least one son (A): ROLAND.

3. ROLAND de THORNBOROUGH, son of Nicholas (2), was prob. b. c1240, d. c1307. He m. c1269 Alice Lascelles, daughter of William de Lascelles by his wife Amice, daughter of Rowland de Renegill or Rosgille (G) (son of Peter and brother of Walter (#1) above).

Between 1260 and 1270 Roland was granted land in Sleddale Brunolf, Westmoreland, by his mother-in-law Alice (de Renegill or Rosgill) Lascelles, dau. of Roland de Rosgill and widow of William de Lascelles (D:1:300; F:14:19-20).

Between 1260 and 1275 Roland witnessed various documents. In 1272 he was one of the jurors on the Inquisition post mortem of William de Lindesay, and in 1280 he was a witness. (A: cites D: 2:181, 182; B: 48:236, 253).

Between 1272 and 1283, the Canons of Hepp granted to Roland de Thornburgh a messuage in Kirkeby in Kendale. (D:1:10). In 1278 Roland held lands in Reagill and Meaburn Maud of the Abbey of Hepp (F:14:60).

In 1280 Amice, daughter of Roland de Renegill, granted to Roland 5 acres, with 1 acre meadow, with buildings and one toft in the dale of Sleddale Brunhof, which she had by inheritance from her father Roland (D:1:301).

In 1283 Roland de Thornborough stated at the Inq. post mortem that Roland de Renegill held land in Sledale and Tyrehger, and that Matthew de Redman held Selside (A: cites B: 48:253).

About 1291 or 1292 William, son and heir of William de Lascelles, granted to Roland de Thornborough and his wife Alice, his rights to certain lands and tenements which he had by inheritance from his mother Amice, daughter and heir of Roland de "Revegyle [sic]" (D:1:301; F:14:19-20). In 1295 William Lascelles of Eskerigg released Roland de Thornborough from payment of mark rent (A; D: 1:301).

In 1298 Roland, son of Nicholas witnessed a deed in Sleddale and the same year he sued Henry de Hayburgh (A: cites D: 1:301; G).

Roland and Alice were the parents of: WILLIAM, b. c1274.

4. WILLIAM de THORNBOROUGH, son of Roland (3) and Alice, was b. c1274, and d. by 1350. He married c1314 Elena de Culwen, who survived him (A; G).

On 22 Sep 1285 William de Thornborough appeared as the representative of Henry le Boteler, son of Richard, in a case against Nicholas le Boteler, son of William in Assize Mort d'Ancestor at Whittington, Lancs., (A: cites Lancaster Assize Rolls, in E: 49:217).

In 1300 William was bailiff (lawyer) for Nicholas de Leyburn in a legal proceeding (A: cites Assize Rolls 990). In 1310 William de Thornburgh was in Ireland (A), and in 1311 he signed as a member of the jury at the Inquisition Post Mortem of John de Bellewe (Bella Aqua) (B: 48:309). In 1338 William held land in Strickland Ketel (A: cites Assize Rolls 1425). In 1343 a deed of entail settled lands on the heirs of William de Rosgill, then to William de Thornburgh, then to the latter's sons Roland, William, and Robert, and then to the "right heirs of William de Thornburgh." (A; F:14:61).

William died by 1350 when an order was issued to choose his successor as Coroner for Westmorland (A).

A writ for an inquisition post mortem was issued 16 May 34 Edward III (1361). He died the Tuesday before St. Wilfred, 23 Edward III (1350), and was found to have given Sleddale in Westmorland to his son Roland and Roland's wife Alice. He held Selset, Whynfell, and Sklemiser in Westmorland. His next heir was his son Roland, age 35 or more (Calendar of Inquisitones Post Mortem X: Edward III, no. 605).

William and Elena were the parents of (G): ROLAND; WILLIAM, poss. chaplain, in 1347 was released from a bond of 100 shillings by John de Egglesfield, Lord Muncaster (A: cites Mss. 18); and ROBERT.

5. ROLAND de THORNBOROUGH, son of William (4) and Elena, was b. c1314, and was alive as late as 1377 (A; G). He m. 1st, Alice L'Engleys, and 2nd, (poss.) [-?-] de Sandford (G).

In 1341 William (4 above) enfeoffed his son Roland, and Roland's wife Alice [Lengleys], with half a slate quarry in Sleddale (G: cites Cal. Inq. Misc. File 180 [7]). In 1375 the minor children of Roland Thornborough and his second wife were legatees of William de Sandford, when the executors of William de Sandford gave land to Roland de Thornborough for the use of his minor children: Roland, John, Robert, Margaret, Isabel, and Idonea (G).

Roland and his mother Elena, widow of William, were in a case brought against them by William de Culwen, uncle of the said Elena (F:14:16-20, 61).

In 1353 Roland had a suit against John and Christian de Rosgill, but the case was not prosecuted (A: cites Assize Roll 1453). On 13 Aug 1358 Roland, son of William de Thornburgh released to Joan and Christiana, daughters of Robert de Rosgille, his claim to a yearly rent of 40 marks granted to Roland and his father William by their father Robert (F:14:37-38, 61).

In 1364 William, son of Roland Thornborough was granted lands and tenements in Sleddale with the right to make a mill (A). In 1369 Roland was present at the Inq. P. M. on the estate of Robert de Clifford (C: 22:339). In 1374 Roland witnessed various deeds and was at the Inq. P. M. held on the estate of Marmaduke de Thweng (D:2:184, 185).

Roland was the father of (G): (by 1st wife): WILLIAM, b. c1340, of age in 1364; THOMAS, b. after 1340; (by 2nd wife; all children were minors in 1375): ROLAND; ROBERT, m. by 1388, Isabel, dau. of Thomas de Warcop; JOHN; MARGARET; ISABEL; and IDONEA.

Generations 6-10

6. WILLIAM de THORNBOROUGH, son of Roland (5) and Alice (L'Engleys), was b. c1340, and probably died c1417, age c75 (A; G). His wife has not been positively identified. He may have m. the heiress of the Manor of Ashby. On the other hand, the *VHC Lancs.* VIII 279 states that as the grandfather of William who m. Eleanor Musgrave (See below), he m. Eleanor Shelford. However, Fahy suggests his wife may have been a member of the de Patton Family (G).

In 1374 William and Roland were Knights of the Shire for Westmoreland; in 1391 William de Thornburgh and William de Curwen were members of Parliament for Westmoreland, and in 1392 William was Escheator for the County of Northumberland (A).

William was the father of (A: D:2:248; G): ROLAND, b. c1365; WILLIAM, b. by 1366; MARGARET, m. by marriage settlement dated April 1397, William Machell; and JOAN, b. c1382, m. Richard de Roos.

7. ROLAND de THORNBOROUGH, son of William (6), was living in 1402 and d. by 1422. About 1390 he m. Katherine [-?-], who m. 2nd, Sir John Lancaster (G).

In 1404 Roland de Thornborough, at the instigation of Thomas de Warcop, Under Sheriff, forcibly carried away Margaret, aged 9, dau,. and coheiress of Robert de Sandford, and married her to Thomas de Warcop, son of the aforesaid Under Sheriff (J:130).

In 1413 and 1415 he was Knight of the Shire for Westmoreland (D:1:311). He died by 27 July 1421, and by 1422 his widow had m. Sir John Lancaster (G). In 1421 Sir John Lancaster petitioned Parliament that on 27 July 1421 he was at Mauds Meaburn at the house of Katherine, formerly wife of Roland de Thornburgh, when John, Thomas, Roger, Robert, and Oliver Thornburgh, with the assent of William their father, attacked him (G). In 1439 Elizabeth Crackenthorpe complained that William de Thornburgh of Selside, and his brothers Edward, Leonard, and Roland, were involved in the death of her husband, Robert Crackenthorpe (A).

In 1447 Margaret, sister of William, Roland, Edward and Leonard, and wife of Henry Threlkeld, had died, and there was an agreement between the brothers and the Threlkelds (A).

Roland and Katherine were the parents of (G): WILLIAM; ROLAND, b. c1395; EDWARD, b. after 1396; LEONARD, b. post 1397; MARGARET, b. c1400, d. by 1447 having m. Henry Threlkeld; and ELIZABETH, b. c1401, m. by 1426 Robert Sandford.

8. WILLIAM de THORNBURGH, son of William (6), was b. c1366. Fahy suggests that it is possible it was he and not his nephew who m. Eleanor, dau. of Sir Richard Musgrave (G). However, the *VHC Lancs* VIII states that he m. Margaret, dau. of John Washington.

Information about him and his family is derived from: an accusation made in 1410 by Sir Thomas Tunstall against him and his four sons, a petition made in 1421 by Sir John Lancaster, and a complaint made by Elizabeth Crackenthorpe.

William was the father of (G): JOHN, b. c1396 (in 1410 was accused by Sir Thomas Tunstall of hunting without leave in Kendal Park (G:L cites De Banco Rolls, Trinity, 11 Henry IV); in 1421 he murderously attacked Sir Thomas Lancaster; in 1439 he was involved in the death of Robert Crackenthorpe); THOMAS, b. c1397 (was involved in 1410, 1421, and 1439); ROGER, b. c1398 (was involved in 1410 and 1421 but not 1439); and OLIVER, b. c1400 (in 1439, was accused by Elizabeth Crackenthorpe of murdering her husband).

9. WILLIAM de THORNBOROUGH, was b. c1394/1406 (G) and d. between 1456 and 1459, and held Hampsfield. He is placed as a son of Roland (7) and Katherine by Fahy (as will be seen below), even though the *VHC Lancs VIII* states that he was son of William (8) and Margaret. He m. c1427 Eleanor, dau. of Sir Richard Musgrave (G).

In 6 Henry VI (1427) William de Thornborough, son of Roland, and William's wife Eleanor petitioned and John de Lancaster and wife Katrine, "de forciantes," stating that messuages (properties) and land in Strickland Ketel, Bamton Cundale, Kellet, and Brougham should be entailed on the heirs of William and Eleanor, and failing heirs male, on the brothers of William, and then on the right heirs of William de Thornborough the Elder [prob. the father of Roland] (K).

In 1432 William and Oliver de Thornborough were jurors on the Inq. Post Mortem of William Stapleton (A). He was escheator in 1436, and in 1438, as William de Thornburgh, King's Esquire, was granted an Island in Windermere Lake (A; D: 2:70).

William and Eleanor were the parents of (G): ROLAND, b. c1427; GILES; [-?-], dau., m. [-?-] Bellingham; [-?-], dau., m. [-?-] Duckett; and DOROTHY, m. Richard Gilpin.

10. ROLAND de THORNBURGH, son of William (9) and Eleanor, was b. c1427, and d. by 8 Jan 1480/1. He m. an unidentified wife c1451.

On 8 July 1471 he was granted for life the office of Porter of the King's Castle at Carlisle. On 26 Feb 1474 he was granted all the messuages, houses, shops, etc., in the town and lordship of Penrith, Cumberland, formerly held by John Clifford, Lord Clifford, who had been attainted for high treason. In 1473 and again in 1475 he was Justice of the Peace for Cumberland (G; *Patent Rolls, Edward IV and Henry VI, 1467-1477*, pp. 264, 424, 610).

Roland had one son (G): WILLIAM.

11. WILLIAM de THORNBOROUGH, son of Roland (10), son of William (9) and Eleanor, d. 19 Dec 1521. He m. by 1481 Elizabeth Broughton, daughter and heiress of Sir Thomas Broughton. Elizabeth brought to the Thornboroughs the lands of the Copelands (G).

On 20 June 1480 William Thornburgh was named commissioner of array for Westmorland (*Patent Rolls, 1476-1586*, p. 214). On 20 July 1486 he was ordered arrested for disobedience, and was pardoned on 17 Aug 1486. He was to take the Oath of Allegiance to King Henry VII (*Patent Rolls, 1485-1494*, pp. 119, 132, 133).

By 31 May 1487 he was Gentleman Usher of the King's Chamber, and was granted an annuity of £20 from the Lordship of Penrith, Cumberland. On 22 Aug 1490 he was granted an annuity of £20 from the issues of the King's Towns of Lanhumby and Gamolesby, if he would give up the earlier annuity (*Patent Rolls, 1485-1494*, pp. 173, 331).

In 1523 an inquisition post mortem was held on the estate of William Thornborough who d. 19 Dec 13 Henry VIII (1521). William possessed the manor of Selsett and half the lordship of Whynfel! in the vill of Strickland Ketyll in Kendall, which he held of the heirs of Edward Redmayne, also lately dec. William also held the lordship of Patton by the yearly rent of one red rose if demanded; half the lordship of Langlesdale; one tenement in Skelsmesser, and 2 tenements in Crosthwayte. William left a son and heir Roland, aged 24 (D: 1:241).

William and Elizabeth (Broughton) were the parents of (A; G): ROLAND, b. c1496; NICHOLAS, b. c1498; THOMAS, prob. d. in inf.; ANNE, m. by 4 Aug 1512, Thomas Preston; ELIZABETH, m. by settlement dated 19 May 1507 William Kirkby; ELLINOR, m. by settlement dated 1496/7 Richard Curwen, son of John; and ISABEL, m. by settlement dated 28 Aug 1517 William Clifton of Westby.

Generations 11-15

12. ROLAND THORNBOROUGH, son of William (11) and Elizabeth, was b. 1496, and d. before 11 Jan 1535. About 1517 he m. Margaret Middleton, dau. of Sir Geoffrey Middleton of Middleton Hall. Margaret survived him and m. 2nd, Robert Curwen (G). In 1517 Sir Thomas Parr, Kt., of Kendall [father of Katherine Parr who m. Henry VIII], made his will. He left to his servant Roland Thornborough, son of William, the [post of master forester] of the old park at Kendal, after the death of William *(Surtees Society*, 87:116).

Roland and Margaret were the parents of: WILLIAM, b. 1518; ROLAND, b. c1519/34, bur. 19 May 1599 at Kendal unm. and childless; ELIZABETH, m. Thomas Warcop; ANN, m. Thomas Ross; ELIANOR, m. Robert Beck; ALICE, m. John or Thomas Kellett; and AGNES, m. Robert Curwen.

13. NICHOLAS THORNBOROROUGH, son of William (11) and Elizabeth, d. 1570, m. and had (possibly): NICHOLAS.

14. WILLIAM THORNBOROUGH, son of Roland (12) and Margaret (Middleton), was b. c1518, and d. 1552, and m. Thomasine Bellingham, dau. of Sir Robert Bellingham. She d. 11 Aug 1582 and is buried in the Bellingham Chapel at Kendal Church (G; I:96).

William Thornborough died 18 Nov 6 Edward VI (1552). At an inquisition post mortem taken at Kirkeby in Kendal on 4 Jan 6 Edward VI (1552/3), he was recorded as holding the manor and capital messuage of Haverbreke Hall in Bethuim, a moiety of a water mill, the manor or lordship of Patttob, a moiety of the manor or lordship of Whynfell, six messuages of Selside and a messuage in Skelsmesser. The inquisition stated that as William Thornborough in 1547 he had granted to Nicholas Thornborough and others the house and site of his manor of Selsed in Selsed, Co. Westmorland, and two messuages in the vill of Crosthwaite, and other property of the said William and his wife Thomasina. In 1548 he had granted to his mother Margaret, now wife of Robert Curwen, an annuity of £16.13.4. William's father Roland had granted a charter dated 11 Jan 1535 to William's brother Roland. William left as his son and next heir, a son Roland, aged 13 (D: 1:244).

Thomazine Thornborough d. 11 Aug 24 Eliz. (1582). Her inquisition post mortem was held at Kendall on 27 Sep 1583, She held two messuages in Longsledsale, five messuages in Selside, four messuages in Patton and 15 messuages in Whitewell. By a charter dated 20 July 1582 she had conveyed all the said messuages to her son Nicholas, still living. Her next heir was her son William, aged 35 and over (D: 1:244-245).

William and Thomasine had (D: 2:243-246; G; H): ROWLAND, b. c1541 (his inq.post mortem was taken 12 June 1557 and named as his heir his bro. William, aged 11); MARGARET, b. c1543; THOMASINE, b. c1545; CECILY, b. c1547; WILLIAM, b. c1547, of Hamsfield, Lancs.; DOROTHY, b. c1549; and NICHOLAS, b. c1550, at Kendall, Westmoreland.

15. NICHOLAS THORNBOROUGH, possibly son of Nicholas (13), or William (14), may have been b. c1550 at Kendal, d. 1598, having m. Janet Brockbank. She m. 2nd, in 1599, James Patton.

Nicholas and Janet had several children, including: THOMAS, b. 1596 at Hamsfield Hall, Cartmel.

16. WILLIAM THORNBOROUGH, son of William (14) and Thomasine, was b. 7 April 1547, and m. by 4 April 1574 his cousin, Ethelred, dau. of Sir Thomas Carus (E; G). On the latter date William and his wife, her mother Dame Katherine, and her brother, were arrested at the latter's house in Limehouse while preparing to hear Mass (G: cites *Catholic Record Society* 6:251-252).

On 20 Sep 1562 Elizabeth Bradley died and left her kinsman William Thornburgh the Broughton estates. Ethelred (Carus) Thornburgh died 3 March 1596 and was buried at Cartmel Priory. Her Inq. post mortem was dated 16 Sep 1609.

William and Ethelred were the parents of (G): THOMASINE, bapt. 2 Dec 1581 at Kendal; JOHN, b. and d. 1580; ROLAND, b. 1582, bapt. at Cartmel 14 April 1582/3; and ANN, bapt. 16 Jan 1584 at Cartmel.

17. THOMAS THORNBOROUGH, son of Nicholas (15) and Janet, was b. c1596, and emigrated to VA c1616. Delmar Leon Thornbury felt he might be the father of Roland of Baltimore County, but research by Snider and Fahy seem to have rejected this theory. He m. Alice Layne, b. c1594, in London (H).

Thomas Thornborough leased land from John Gundry in Kiquotan in 1626. He owned land in Elizabeth City Co., VA, in 1634 and 1638. In 1651 he was granted 700 a. in Northumberland Co., VA, for transporting 14 persons (Nell Marion Nugent, *Cavaliers and Pioneers*, pp. 20, 71, 89, 118, 212).

Thomas and Alice were in VA, and were the parents of (H): RICHARD, b. 1624; [-?-], b. 1626; SAMUEL, b. 1628/1630; [-?-], b. 1630; [-?-], b. 1632; (poss.) ROWLAND, b. 1634; m. Ann [-?-].

18. ROLAND THORNBOROUGH, son of William (16) and Ethelred, was bapt. 14 April 1582/3 at Cartmel, and d. 1612. By a marriage settlement dated 22 June 1598, when he was only 16, he m. Jane Dalton, dau. of Thomas Dalton and Anne, dau. of Sir Richard Molyneux of Sefton. Roland Thornborough died leaving a will dated 23 Aug 1611 (it has not survived), and his Inq. post mortem was held at Kendal on 14 Jan 1612 (G).

Roland and Jane had issue (G; H): WILLIAM, b. 20 June 1599; ROWLAND, b. 1600, bur. 12 July 1605 at Cartmel; JOHN, b. by 1609 (he had two illegitimate children, named Edward and Mary); FRANCIS, b. c1609 at Kirkham or Cartmel, Lancs., living in 1654; ROWLAND, b. c1612 at Cartmel, Lancs.; ETHELRED, b. c1614, m. John Gregson of Moore Hall; JANE, b. c1616, m. John Knipe of Rampside; ANN, m. at Cartmel on 6 May 1629, Henry Bigland of the Grange; and THOMAZINE, m. soon after 5 Dec 1635 Nicholas Withers of Longparish, Co. Southampton.

19. SAMUEL THORNBOROUGH, son of Thomas (17) and Alice (Layne), was b. 1628/1630, and settled in AA Co. by 1667, when he claimed land for service (Skordas cites MPL 11:167). He m. Sarah Birkhead, b. c1634. She m. 2nd, Richard Bedworth of AA Co.

On 6 Dec 1667 he and Richard Bedworth surveyed 100 a. called Hamm in AA Co. By 1707 this land had passed to Thomas Tench (*MRR*:126).

Bedworth died leaving a will dated 26 Feb 1683, proved 3 July 1683, naming his wife Sarah as extx., and sons-in-law Abraham to have his land after the death of Sarah, and then to pass in turn to his other sons-in-law, John and Richard Thornberry (MWB 4:17).

Sarah Birkhead may have m. 3rd, Matthew Axon of AA Co., who died leaving a will dated 23 Sep 1684, proved 27 April 1685, leaving his deceased's wife's thirds of Richard Bedworth's estate to son-in-law Abraham Thornberry, and sons-in-law Richard and John (MWB 4:89).

Samuel and Sarah were the parents of (H): ABRAHAM, b. 1660 or earlier;
JOHN, b. c1656/66; m. Elizabeth [-?-] b. c1656. 25; and RICHARD, b. c1658/62, m.
Elizabeth [-?-], b. c1662/6.

20. WILLIAM THORNBOROUGH, son of Rowland (18) and Jane (Dalton), was b. 20
June 1599 at Kirkham, Lancashire, England. He m. Catherine Langtree, b. c1620, dau. of
Edward Langtree.
    William and Jane were the parents of (H): ROWLAND, b. c1642; RICHARD,
b. c1642; RICHARD, b. c1643; CHARLES, b. c1645, at Methop, Eng., m. Elizabeth
Leyburn; ELIZABETH, b. c1649; CATHERINE, b. c1651; ROWLAND, b. c1651/3 at
Methop.

21. JOHN THORNBOROUGH, son of Roland (18) and Jane (Dalton), was b. c1600,
and no later than 1609; in August 1611 his father left him an annuity of £20 for life. He is
almost certainly the Mr. "John Thornburrow of Skelsmergh" buried at Kendal on 17
March 1673 (G).

22. ROWLAND THORNBOROUGH, son of Roland (18) and Jane (Dalton), was born
between 1606 and Aug. 1611. He m. Catherine Skelton, dau. of Thomas Skelton,
sometime Sheriff of Dublin.
    Rowland and Catherine were the parents of (G): THOMAS; and (poss.)
ROLAND who settled in Baltimore County.

23. ABRAHAM "THORNBURY,"son of Samuel (19) and Sarah, prob, d. by 1707. He
may have m. Katherine [-?-].
    On 12 Jan 1686 he served with Richard Thornbury as joint administrators of
the estates of Mathew Axon and Richard Bedworth of AA Co. (INAC 9:246).
    On 15 Jan 1701 Abraham Thornbury conv. to Thomas Tench land which
Richard Bedworth of AA Co., by his will, dated 26 Feb 1682/3, willed to his son-in-law
Abraham Thornbury (AALR WT#1:226).
    Abraham probably died by 1707 perhaps without issue as Bedworth's Addition
had passed to his brother John. However, it is possible (although firm proof is lacking
that he m. Katherine. who was the mother of: SABRAH [SARAH?], b. Aug 1703 in St.
Margaret's Parish, AA Co. (AACR:109). Sarah Thornbury, orphan, in 1706 was staying
with John Thornbury (AAJU, 1706, p. 353). She is almost certainly the Sarah who m.
William (not Benjamin) Anderson in April 1727 in All Hallows Parish (AACR:41).

24. JOHN "THORNBURY," son and heir of Samuel (19), d. by 1719. He m. Ann [-?-].
    He is not listed in Skordas or Gibb, but he was in AA Co. by 25 Jan 1676 when
he was listed as a debtor in the estate of John Benson of CV Co. (INAC 4:19). On 25 Aug
1684 he was listed as a debtor of the estate of Francis Holland (INAC 9:57).
    On 20 Jan 1686 he conv. 100 a. Hamm to Thomas Tench of AA Co. and his
"now wife" Margaret. The tract had formerly been occupied by Richard "Bosworth"
[Bedworth] and Samuel Thornbury, dec. (AALR IH#2:63, WT#1:56).
    On 21 May 1700 he was listed as a debtor of the estate of George Parker [of
AA Co.?] (INAC 20:67). As John Thorneborough he was a debtor in the undated
inventory of Elenor Wells of BA Co. (INAC 20:158).
    In 1707 he was listed in the Rent Rolls as owning 94 a. part of 100 a. Bersheba,
surveyed in 1663 for John Wilson (*MRR*:125). In 1707 he also owned 52 acres
Bedworth's Addition, surveyed in 1671 for Richard Bedworth (*MRR*:129). Bedworth had
left this to Abraham and if Abraham died without heirs it was to pass to his brothers John
and Richard.

John evidently d. by 1719, but no record of any will, inventory, or administration account has been found.

The estate of Anne Thornberry was inventoried on 8 Dec 1719 by Philip Dowell and Abell Hill. William Wooten and William Lock approved the inventory. No next of kin or administrator was mentioned (MINV 3:235).

Ann's estate was administered on 16 Aug 1720. Two inventories totaled £9.12.0 and £16.10.8. Payments were made to William Wootten, Stephen Warman, Thomas Reynolds and John Beall. The estate was admin. by John Powell (MDAD 3:196).

John Thornberry m. Ann [-?-]. They were the parents of: JOHN, b. 4 Feb 1703, bapt. 12 June 1706 in St. James Parish (AACR:155); and (prob.) SARAH, m. 1st, Richard Simmons in Oct 1713 in St. James Parish, AA Co. (AACR:162). She m. 2nd, by 16 Aug 1720, William Nichol. On that date the estate of Richard Symons of AA Co. was administered by Sarah Nichols wife of William Nichols. The account mentioned two inventories totalling £9.12.0 and £21.14.10 (MDAD 3:194).

25. RICHARD "THORNBURY," son of Samuel (19) and Sarah, was in AA Co. by 1677 when Francis Holland wife Margaret conveyed to him a certificate of sale for 200 a. of land, part of 900 a. patented to the said Francis Holland on 20 Aug 1670 (AALR IH#2:209).

On 25 Aug 1684 Richard was listed as a debtor of the estate of Francis Holland (INAC 9:57). On 12 Jan 1686 he and Abraham Thornbury served as joint admins. Of the estates of Matthew Axon and Richard Bedworth of AA Co. (INAC 9:246).

On 11 July 1691 Richard Thornborough sold 150 a. of 200 a. Broughton Ashley to John Cappell, merchant (AALR PK:22). However, in 1707 Richard was still listed in the Anne Arundel Rent Rolls as owning 50 a. part Broughton Ashley (MRR:122).

On 18 April 1694 he was listed as a debtor of Faith Gongo (INAC 13A:139).

He was involved in a dispute over land with Robert Gover, Sr., and agreed to abide by the decision of an arbitration panel (AALR WT#1:195)

On 7 Sep 1702 he was listed as a debtor of the estate of Abell Brown, Gent. (INAC 23:157).

By 26 Feb 1705 he and his wife Elizabeth were in Westmoreland Co., VA, when they appointed Richard Dallam their attorney to convey 50 a. of Broughton Ashley to Ephraim Gover of AA Co. (AALR WT#2:305-306).

26. CHARLES "THORNBURGH," son of William (20) and Catherine, was b. c1645 Methop, Lancs?, Eng. He m. Elizabeth Leyburne, b. 1645 Cunswick, Eng.

Charles and Elizabeth were the parents of (H): ROBERT, b. c1666 in Lancashire.

27. ROLAND THORNBOROUGH, son of Roland (22) and Catherine (Skelton), is placed by Fahy as the Roland who settled in Balto. Co. He m. Anne [-?-] who m. 2nd, John Royston.

Thornborough patented two tracts of land in BA Co.: 41 a. called Goose Harbour on 11 June 1688 (MPL 25:442, 31:201), and 900 a. Selsed, on 10 July 1695 (MPL 40:518).

Roland Thornborough d. leaving a will dated 25 July 1695, proved 23 June 1696. His three sons, John (the eldest), Roland, and Francis were to share in 900 a. Selsed. If they died without issue, the land was to pass to his next of kin the Thornboroughs of Hampsfield in Lancashire, and then the Thornboroughs at Selsad in Kendal, Westmoreland. His wife, Anne, extx., was to have two tracts of land, both called Goose Harbour, for life. His eldest dau. Catherine was to have the land at the death of his wife. Daus. Ann and Jane were to have personalty. Jno. Oldton, Geo. Chauncy, Edward

Stevenson, and Thomas Smallwood witnessed the will. By a codicil dated 25 Dec 1695, dau. Jane was to have 100 a. out of son Roland's tract, and dau. Ann was to have the use of 100 a. on Gunpowder River out of son Francis' tract (MWB 7:200).

Joseph Strawbridge and William Wilkeson appraised the personal estate of Rowland "Thornbury" on 24 June 1696, and valued it at £81.8.0 (INAC 14:30). Roland's widow Anne, now wife of John Royston, admin. the estate on 10 March 1697. The distribution was to the widow and five children (INAC 16:94).

Roland and Ann were the parents of (MWB 7:200): JOHN; ROLAND; FRANCIS; CATHERINE (eld dau.); JANE; and ANN.

Generation 16

28. ROBERT "THORNBURG," son of Charles (23) and Elizabeth, was b. c1666 Lancashire, Eng. He m. Sarah Jackson, b. c1666. They moved to Ireland and were the parents of (H): EDWARD, b. c1687, of Lurgan MM, Co. Armagh, Ireland; WALTER, b. c1688; JUDITH, b. c1689, Co. Cavan, Ireland, m. Alexander Miller, b. c1694; and THOMAS, b. c1690, Co. Cavan, Ireland.

Unplaced:

THORNBURY, ANNE, m. Ishmael Giles on 25 Dec 1711 in All Hallows Parish AA Co. (*AACR*:25).

THORNBOROUGH, FRANCIS, was in BA Co. by 13 Aug 1714 when he signed the inventory of Mathias Gray as a creditor (INAC 36A:92). On 10 Sep 1714 he received a payment from Gray's estate (INAC 36A:95).

THORNBERRY, JANE, of the Clifts, CV Co., d. leaving a will dated 16 Oct 1702 and proved 16 Nov 1702. She left personalty to Abraham Skippers, and named her sister Dorothy in England as her residuary legatee. Jno. Binyon, Cudbed Chilton, and Thomas Manning witnessed the will (MWB 11:246).

THORNBURY, JOHN, d. by 8 May 1744 when his dau. Elizabeth received a payment from the estate of Luke Stansbury of BA Co. (MDAD 20:156).

THORNBURY, THOMAS (or **JAMES**), d. in CV Co. d. by 20 Dec 1702, when his estate was appraised by Isaac Baker and James Robert, and valued at £21.6.6. (INAC 22:91)

THORNBURY, THOMAS, bookkeeper of the Widow Smith, d. 18 July 1723 in St. Anne's Parish, AA Co. (*AACR*:91). He witnessed the will of Edward Smith of Annapolis, innholder, on 27 April 1723 (MWB 18:149).

THE THROCKMORTON FAMILY

Refs.: A. Brice McAdoo Clagett, "The Ancestry of Capt. James Neale," *MGSB* 31 (2) 137-153. B: *PASC.* C: *MCS4.* D: *WAR7.* E: *RD500.* F: "Evidences of Throckmorton Family," *EONE1* 3:46-52. G: G. Andrews Moriarty. "The Ancestry of John Throckmorton of Providence." *EONE2* 3:478-483. H: -------. "Evidences on Throckmorton Family." *EONE2* 3:484-498. I: "Throckmorton of Ellington." *The Visitation of the County of Huntington 1684, Made by Sir Henry St. George, Knight, Clarenceux King of Arms. HSPV* new ser. 13:88.

ARMS: Gules, on a chevron Argent, three bars gemel Sable (B:213). Throckmorton of Ellington added a crescent surmounted by another for difference, and bore the following CREST: A falcon Argent, jessed and belled Or, differenced as in the arms (I).

Generations 1-5

1. **THOMAS THROCKMORTON** of Fladbury, Co. Warwick, was b. c1355, and d. c1412. He m. c1380 Agnes de Besford, living 1428, dau. of Alexander and Beatrice de Besford. Thomas and Agnes were the parents of (D:Line 29A; H:488): JOHN.

2. **JOHN THROCKMORTON**, son of Thomas (1) and Agnes, of Throckmorton in Fladbury, and *jure uxoris* (in right of his wife) of Coughton in Spernore, Warwickshire, was b. c1380, and d. 13 April 1445. He m. 1409, Eleanor Spinney, dau. of Sir Guy Spinney. John Throckmorton was an M. P., and Under Treasurer of England (A:143D:Line 29A).

   John and Eleanor were the parents of (D:Line 29A; H:488): Sir THOMAS; ELIZABETH, m. Robert Russell; AGNES, m. Thomas Wynslow of Burton Co. Oxford. (They were ancestors of **Alice Freeman who m. John Thompson and settled at New London, CT**); MARGARET, m. John Rous; MARY, m. Robert Gifford; MAUD, m. Thomas Green; ELEANOR, m. Richard Knigthly; and JOHN, d. by 1473 when his Inq. P. M. was held.

3. **Sir THOMAS THROCKMORTON**, of Coughton, Warwick, son of John (2) and Eleanor, was b. 1415, and d. 1472. His Inq. P. M. was held in 1473. He m. Margaret Olney, fl.1446-72, heiress of Weston Olney.

   He held Throckmorton in Fladbury, and Black Nauton in Warwickshire, and *jure uxoris* Weston Olney, Bucks., Roxton, Bedfordshire, and Bruggeton, Warwickshire (A:142). In 1443 he received a pardon for assaults made by him in the Palace of Westminster. Among the offices he held was Sheriff of Warwick and Leicester; Attorney General to Edward, Prince of Wales; and Steward of the lands and castles of the Bishop of Worcester (A:142). He was a J. P. 1458-1472, and an M. P. 1445/6-1449 (G:488).

   Sir Thomas and Margaret were the parents of (A; G:488): Sir ROBERT; MARY, m. John Middlemore; MARGARET, m. William Tracy; JUDITH, m. Edw. Peyton; JOHN, m. Jane Baynard; ELIZABETH, Abbess of Denny, d. 1547; Dr. WILLIAM of Shotesbrook College, d. 1547; and RICHARD.

4. **Sir ROBERT THROCKMORTON, K.B.**, son of Sir Thomas (3) and Margaret, was b. c1451, and d. 1518/9 beyond the seas, while on a pilgrimage to the Holy Land (A:141). He m. 2nd, Katherine Marrow (Marowe), dau. of William Marrow, Lord Mayor of London, and his wife Katherine Rich, fl. 1466.

   He held various manors in Warwickshire, Worcestershire, Hunts., Beds., and Bucks.

   Sir Robert and Katherine were the parents of (A; B:40; G:481); RICHARD; Sir GEORGE; MICHAEL, was granted Haseley, Co. Warwick, by Mary I, and d. in Mantua, Italy.

5. **JOHN THROCKMORTON**, son of Sir Thomas (3) and Margaret, was b. c1460, and d. testate c1507. His Inq. P. M. was not held until 1510. He m. Jane Baynard who d. testate c1539. She was a dau. of Henry Baynard.

   His descendants bore for arms: Gules, on a chevron Argent, two bars gemel sable (B:267).

John and Jane were the parents of (G:488): FRANCIS, b. c1490, m. and had issue; SIMON; ELIZABETH, m. William Claxton; MARGARET, m. Thos. Shardlow; ELEANOR; MARGERY, m. John? Fiske.

6. RICHARD THROCKMORTON, of Higham Ferrers, Northants., son of Sir Robert (4), d. 1547. He m. Jane Beaufou, dau. of Humphrey Beaufou (b. c1454, d. 1485), and his wife Joan Hugford/Higford/Higgeford (who d. by 1485).

Richard Throckmorton was brother of Michael Throckmorton, of Mantua, Italy, Secretary of Reginald, Cardinal Pole. He was uncle of Sir Nicholas Throckmorton, Ambassador to France and Scotland, and great-uncle of Francis Throckmorton who was executed for conspiring for a Catholic restoration in 1584 (A:140).

Richard and Jane were the parents of (A:140; C:Line 8B): GODITHA, m. Thomas Neale (ancestors of **Capt. James Neale of MD**), MARY, m. George Boteler of Tofte, Shambrook, Beds. (ancestors of **Capt. John, Thomas, and Elizabeth Boteler who m. William Claiborne of MD and VA:** C: Line 61).

7. Sir GEORGE THROCKMORTON, son of Sir Robert (4) and Katherine, d. testate 6 Aug 1552. He m. Katherine Vaux, dau. of Nicholas and Elizabeth (Fitzhugh) Vaux. Her Royal Descent from Edward III is given in B:40, and E:125.

Sir George was High Sheriff of Warwickshire (B::40).

Sir George and Katherine were the parents of (A; B:40; G:481): Sir ROBERT of Coughton; CLEMENT; Sir NICHOLAS, Ambassador of Queen Elizabeth, d. 12 Feb 1570; six other sons, and ten daus.

8. SIMON THROCKMORTON, of Barsham, Suffolk, son of John (5) and Jane (Baynard), m. Anne, dau. of Edmund Louthe of Sawtry, Hunts. They were the parents of (B:267): LIONEL.

Generation 6

9. GODITHA THROCKMORTON, dau. of Richard (6) and Jane, was living in 1544. She m. Thomas Neale, d. 1544, of Yielden, Bedfordshire of Newton Bromshold, Northants. (A). They were the ancestors of James Neale of MD.

10. GABRIEL THROCKMORTON, son of Richard (6) and Jane, d. 1552. He m. Emma, dau. of John Lawrence of Ramsay. They were the parents of (C:Line 8B): ROBERT.

11. CLEMENT THROCKMORTON, of Haseley, Co. Warwick, 3rd son of Sir George (7) and Katherine, M. P. for Warwickshire, d. 14 Dec 1573, and was buried at St. Mary's Haseley. He m. Katherine Neville, dau. of Sir Edward and Eleanor (Windsor) Neville, granddau. of George Neville, Lord Bergavenny, and a descendant of Edward III (B:213; G:481).

Clement Throckmorton received the Manor of Haseley from his uncle Michael in 1554 (G:481).

Clement and Katherine were the parents of (B:213; E:125, 126; G:481): JOHN of Haseley, "the Puritan (b. 1545, d. 1599/1600); MARY, m. Giles Foster of Bois, Glos.; CLEMENT (d. 1612, m. and had issue); URSULA, m. Theodore Bigges of Lenwick, Worcs.; KATHERINE, m. Thomas Harby; MARTHA, m. George Lynne; FRANCES, m. Henry Medley of Tetley, Isle of Wight; EDWARD; HENRY; AMPHILLIS; KENELM, settled Jamestown, VA; JOSIAS; and SUSANNA.

12. LIONEL THROCKMORTON, son of Simon (8), was b. 1525 and d. 24 Nov 1599. He m. 1st, Elizabeth Kemp (by whom he had no issue), and 2nd, Elizabeth Blennerhasset, a descendant of the Cornwallis Family (See *British Roots*, Vol. 1), and a descendant of Edward I. She d. leaving a will dated 30 June and proved 7 Nov 1608 (B:266).

Lionel founded Bungay Grammar School (B:267; C:Line 117).

Lionel and Elizabeth Blennerhasset were the parents of three sons and two daus., including (B:213; E:236; G:488): JOHN; ELIZABETH, m. Richard Vineor; KATHERINE; BASSINGBORNE; and ROBERT, m. and had issue.

Generation 7

13. ROBERT THROCKMORTON, of Ellington, Hunts., son of Gabriel (10) and Emma (Lawrence), was bapt. 1 Oct 1551, and d. 12 Jan 1631. He m. Elizabeth Pickering, dau. of John and Lucy (Kaye) Pickering, and a descendant of William I, the Lion of Scotland. Robert and Elizabeth were the parents of (C:Line 8B; E:340): GABRIEL.

14. KATHERINE THROCKMORTON, dau. of Clement (11) and Katherine (Neville), m. Thomas Harby of Adston, Northants., d. 1572, son of William and Emma (Wilmore) Harby of Ashby. Katherine m. 2nd, George Dryden, bro. of Sir Erasmus Dryden, Bart., and 3rd, John Wilmer of Shrowley (B:213).

Thomas and Katherine were the parents of (B:214; C:Line 94, 94A; E:125, 126): KATHERINE, m. Daniel Oxenbridge, and was in turn the mother of **Rev. John Oxenbridge, 1608/9-1674, of MA**; and EMMA, m. Robert Charlton and was the great-grandmother of **John Coke of VA**.

15. MARTHA THROCKMORTON, dau. of Clement (11) and Katherine (Neville), m. George Lynne (From them descend (E:125, 126): **Harman Blennerhasset, 1765-1831 of VA**, and **Thomas Addis Emmet, 1764-1827 of NY**).

16. BASSINGBORNE THROCKMORTON, Grocer, Citizen, and Alderman of Norwich, son of Lionel (12) and Elizabeth, was b. 1564, and d. on 21 Sep 1638. He m. 1st, Mary Hill, d. 1615, dau. of William and Joan (Annabel), Lionel m. 2nd, Hester Pye, but there were no children by this marriage (B:267).

Basssingborne and Mary (Hill) Throckmorton were the parents of (B:267; C:Line 117; E:236): LIONEL; THOMAS; **JOHN THROCKMORTON, who settled in RI**; MILES; ROBERT; GEORGE; SIMON; MARY, m. William Rawley; and ELIZABETH, m. John Layer.

Generation 8

17. GABRIEL THROCKMORTON of Ellington, son of Robert (13) and Elizabeth, was b. c1586, aged 27 in 1613. He m. Alice Bedell, dau. and heir of William Bedell of Beds. They were the parents of (E:341; I): ROBERT THROCKMORTON, of VA.

Generation 9

18. ROBERT THROCKMORTON, of Ellington, son of Gabriel (17), d. 1652. He m. [-?-], dau. of [-?-] Chare. They were the parents of (I): ALBION, of Stow, d. 1680 unm.; ROBERT of Stow, d. unm. 1681, unm.; and JOHN.

Generation 10

19. JOHN THROCKMORTON, of Ellington, son of Robert (18), d. 1678, age 45. He m. Mary [-?-], widow of Richard Powell and Henry Keene (I).

John and Mary were the parents of (I): ROBERT, age 22 in 1684, unm.; **GABRIEL, age 19 in 1684, living in VA**; ALBION, age 12 in 1684; and ANNE, age 9 in 1684.

Unplaced:

THROCKMORTON, Sir THOMAS, m. Elizabeth Berkeley, dau. of Sir Richard and Elizabeth (Reade) Berkeley. They were the parents of (E:205): **Elizabeth Throckmorton of VA**, m. **Sir Thomas Dale, d. 1619, Gov. of VA**.

THE TOLSON FAMILY EXPANDED

Refs.: A: "Tolson of Bridekirk," *Burke's Commoners*, 2:133-136. B: Register of St. John's Piscataway Parish, PG Co., MD. C: *The Records of Bridekirk Parish, Cumberland, 1584-1812*. Transcribed by J. F. Haswell. Pub. No. 14 of the Cumberland and Westmorland Parish register Society. Penrith: The Society, 1926. D: Tolson entries in IGI, 1988 ed.

ARMS: Vert, on a chief Azure, three martlets Or, all within a bordure of the third pellety (Sometimes the bordure is omitted or is Argent). **CREST**: Out of a ducal coronet Or, a lion's gamb Ermine holding two ostrich feathers Vert and Azure. MOTTO: Ferro comite (*CFAH*).

NB: Many of the baptisms contain the phrase *cujus susceptores fuere* followed by several names. These may have been godparents and are indicated here by an asterisk.

1. HENRY TOLSON was granted the Manor of Bridekirk, which had formerly belonged to Gisburn Priory. He was the father of (A; *CFAH*): HENRY.

2. HENRY TOLSON, son of Henry (1), was buried 12 June 1585 (C). He was High Sheriff of Cumberland, and was the father of (A; *CFAH*): RICHARD, and JOHN, d. 1644, Provost of Oriel College.

3. RICHARD TOLSON, son of Henry, was buried 26 May 1650 at Bridekirk (C). He m. Eleanor, daughter and eventual heiress of Francis Lamplugh of Dovenby.

Richard and Eleanor were the parents of (A; C): HENRY; MARIA, m. William Osmotherly on 24 April 1609; FRANCES, bur. 26 Nov 1597; JANETTA, bapt. 12 Feb 1593 (godparents were Johes Lamplugh, Janetta Lamplugh, and Joesen Tolson), bur. 16 Feb 1593; MARIE, bapt. 15 Jan 1595/6; KATHERINE, bapt. 7 Aug 1597, m. Richard Egglesfield on 6 April 1613; JANETA, bapt. 25 Aug 1598; FRANCIS, bur. 30 June 1600; LUCIA, bapt. 6 June 1603, m. Thomas Lamplugh on 26 Nov 1622; FRANCES, bapt. 18 Aug 1604; LANCELOT, bapt. 8 Sep 1607; JOHES [JOHN?], bapt. 6 Nov 1608; JOSEPH, bapt. 15 June 1610, bur. 9 June 1612; HELENA of Richard, bur. 14 Sep 1612; GEORGE of Richard, bur. 19 Feb 1612.

4. HENRY TOLSON, son of Richard (3) and Eleanor, Sheriff of Cumberland, was b. c1593 and was buried 30 Oct 1663 at Bridekirk. His wife was Margaret, dau. and heir of Henry Savile of Wath upon Dearne, whose will was proved Sep 1641 at York (A). Margaret was bur. 24 Jan 1631/2 (C).

Henry Tolson of Cumberland, Gent., matriculated at Oriel College, Oxford, on 2 Dec 1608 at age 15. He was a student at Gray's Inn in 1611 as Henry, son and heir of Richard of Bridekirk (*ALOX*).

Henry was the father of (A; C; D): (poss.) AGNETA, bapt. 26 March 1607 [but Henry was still at Oxford]; SIMON, bapt. 7 April, bur. 9 April 1609; WILLIAM, bapt. 28 March 1610; THOMAS, bapt. 25 July 1614; HELENA, bapt. 14 March 1621; RICHARD, bapt. 6 June 1622 (godparents were Thomas Lamplugh, Kt., Richard Tolson, armiger, and Maria Osmotherly); HENRY, bapt. 28 June 1626 (godparents were Henry Blancon, Kt., George Lamplugh, "clus?," and Doia [Lady?] Fletcher de Moresby); and MARGARETTA, bapt. 26 Jan 1631/2.

5. JOHN TOLSON, son of Richard (3) and Eleanor, was bapt. 6 Nov 1608. He may be the John who had an illegitimate child by Elena Thompson (C): GULIELMUS, bapt. 7 June 1646.

John may be the John who m. Mabel Lowes on 23 May 1646 (she was bur. 16 May 1648), and then Helena Longthaite on 13 Dec 1656. He was the father of (C): LANCELOT, bapt. 17 Nov 1646; JOHN, bur.7 May 1656; and HENRY, bur. 21 June 1656.

6. THOMAS TOLSON, son of Henry (4) and Margaret, was bapt. 25 July 1614. He may be the Thomas Tolson of Cockermouth who was "defuncti" in June 1669. Thomas of Cockermouth, m. Grace Benson of Dovenby 9 April 1665.

John was the father of (C): MARIA, bapt. 15 June 1669.

7. RICHARD TOLSON, son of Henry (4) and Margaret, was bapt. 6 June 1622 and was buried 2 July 1690 at Wath upon Dearne, Yorkshire. He m. Anne Gregory, dau. of Gilbert Gregory of Barnaby upon Dun, Yorkshire. Anne was 42 in 1665, and d. March 1714 (A).

Richard Tolson, son of Henry Tolson, of Bridekirk, Cumberland, matriculated at Oriel College, Oxford, on 11 Oct 1639 at age 17. He was of Lincoln's Inn in 1656 and Sheriff of Cumberland in 1647, and M.P. from March 1646 until he was secluded in Dec 1648. He was M.P. again in 1660, from Cockermouth (*ALOX*).

Richard and Anne were the parents of (A; C): HENRY, bapt. 15 April 1651; WILFRID, bapt. 19 Sep 1664; EDWARD, bapt. 16 Dec 1666 (Edward Musgrave, Bart., Christopher Musgrave, armiger, and Frances Tolson, "generosa"); ANNA, bapt. 31 July 1668 (Thomas Curwen, armiger, Mr. Senhouse, and Mr. Wmson [Williamson?]).

8. HENRY TOLSON of Wood Hall, Bright Church Parish, Cumberland, son of Richard (7) and Anne, was bapt. 15 April 1651. He was buried at Bridekirk on 17 Sep 1724 (*ALOX*).

. On 19 April 1666 he married on 16 April 1666, at Bridekirk, Frances Lawson, buried 19 June 1695, daughter of Sir Wilfride Lawson, Bart., by his wife Jane Musgrave (C; D).

Henry Tolson, son of Richard of Bridekirk, Cumberland, armiger, matriculated at St. Alban Hall, Oxford, on 19 Oct 1666 at age 15 (*ALOX*).

Henry and Frances were the parents of (A; D): RICHARD, bapt. 23 Sep 1668 (Guilielmus Lawson, Richard Tolson, Armiger, and [Lady?] Barwise; WILFRID, bapt. 29 Sep 1669 (Sir Wilfrid Lawson, Kt., Miles Pennington, armiger, and [Lady?] Tolson); JANA, bapt. 24 May 1671 (godparents were Thomas Curwen of Workington, armiger, [Lady] Musgrave of Hayton, and [Lady?] Lawson of Isell); ANNA, bapt. 30 Oct 1672 (Wilfrid Lawson, armiger, [Lady] Huddleston, and [Lady] Senhouse of Haimeshall); HENRY, bapt. 31 Dec 1673 (godparents were Sir John Lamplugh of Lamplugh, Kt., Leo: Dykes of Worth-Hall, and [Lady] Wyburgh of Cockermouth); WILLIAM, bapt. 23 May 1677 (godparents were Edward Lawson, Gent., Edw. Musgrave, Gent., and [Lady]

Lawson of Useworth); (poss.) MARIA, bapt. 3 July 1677; MILCAH, bapt. 12 Feb 1678/9; HEN[RI]CUS, bapt. 13 Apr 1680; FRANCES (twin), bapt. 2 Feb 1681; SARAH (twin), bapt. 2 Feb 1681; CATHARINE, bapt. 18 Oct 1682; FRANCIS, bapt. 22 April 1686; and LUCY, bapt. 16 June 1688.

9. FRANCIS TOLSON, son of Henry (8) and Frances, was bapt. 22 April 1686 at Woodhall, Bridekirk Parish, came to MD, where he m. Mary Clark, dau. of Robert Clark, on 22 Sep 1707 in St. John's Piscataway Parish, PG Co. (B).

Additional Records from Bridekirk Parish Register (C):

Baptisms (to 1695)

Henry, son of Guil[ielmi, b. 27 Aug, bapt. 30 Aug 1646.
Maria, dau. of Guilielmi, 6 May 1649.
Johes, son of William of Popescastle, 23 Feb 1654.
Symon, son of William of Popescastle, 23 Feb 1657.
George, son of William of Popescastle, 5 May 1661.
Martha, dau. of Henry of Popescastle, 3 Nov 1674.
Maria, dau. of Henry of Popescastle, 3 July 1677.
Henry, son of Simon of Popescastle, 8 Aug 1679.
Catherine, dau. of Henry of Popescastle, 18 Oct 1682.
William, son of Symon, 26 July 1683.

Marriages (to 1696)

Frances, to Edward Briscoe, 12 Oct 1641.
Gulielmus, to Katherine Parker, 7 June 1642.
Anne, to Richard Brumfield, 21 Jan 1644.
Jane, of Popescastle, m. William Bragg of the same, on 18 June 1674.

Burials (to 1668)

Jane, wife of William, 13 Aug 1587.
Agnes, wife of William, 30 Oct 1602.
Agnes, wife of Simon, 25 Dec 1616.
Janeta, wife of Simon, 24 Nov 1620.
Henry, 23 April 1623.
Dorothea, 6 July 1623.
Johis, son of Richard, armiger, 16 July 1628.
William, aged, of Popescastle, 20 Jan 1628/9.
Agnes, relict of Simon, 9 Sep 1640.
Anne, wife of Henry, armiger, 29 April 1654.
Johanes, son of William of Popescastle, 12 Aug 1656,
Catherine, wife of William of Popescastle, 23 Oct 1665.

THE TOMLINS FAMILY

Refs.: A: *Parish Registers of St. Chad, Shrewsbury, Shropshire* (Shropshire Parish Register Society; vols. 15, 16, and 17).

1. RICHARD TOMLINS of St. Chad m. Eleanor Lawrence on 24 July 1774 (B:1801). She was buried on 11 Feb 1782 (A:1801). (Richard may have m. 2nd, Ann Williams, on 6 Aug 1798 (A:1859).

Richard and Eleanor were the parents of (A:1342, 1358, 1371, 1375, 1382, 1403): WILLIAM, b. 8 March, bapt. 12 March 1775, buried 5 Sep 1776; RICHARD, b. 23 Oct, bapt. 30 Oct 1777, bur. 23 Feb 1778; THOMAS, b. 20 Dec, bapt. 26 Dec 1778; and JAMES, b. 5 Oct, bapt. 11 Oct 1780.

2. JAMES TOMLINS, son of Richard and Eleanor, was b. 5 Oct 1778 (A:1403). Formerly of Shrewsbury, Shropshire, later of Bath, Somerset, but most recently of Baltimore, MD, he died by June 1827 when admin. was granted to William Tomlins, atty. for the relict, Ann Tomlins in Balto. (*AWAP*:315).

THE TUBMAN FAMILY

Refs.: A: *The Records of Bridekirk Parish, Cumberland, 1584-1812*. Transcribed by J. F. Haswell. Pub. No. 14 of the Cumberland and Westmorland Parish Register Society. Penrith: The Society, 1926. B: *CFAH*: C. Roy Hudleston and R. S. Boumphrey. *Cumberland Families and Heraldry, With a Supplement to An Armorial for Westmorland and Lonsdale*. The Cumberland and Westmorland Antiquarian and Archaeological Society, 1978).

ARMS: Azure, on a bend between six lozenges Or, five escallops Sable (Shield on an altar frontal, dated 1768 (B).

1. NICHOLAS TUBMAN d. 8 July 1623 (A).

Nicholas was the father of (A): ANTHONY, bapt. 1 Oct 1596, bur. 1 Jan 1611/2; JOHN, bapt. 1 Nov 1600; CHRISTOPHER, bapt. 11 Aug 1603; MARIE, bapt. 12 Aug 1604, bur. --- 1611/2; JANETA, bapt. 21 June 1607

2. RICHARD TUBMAN of Tallentyre, relationship to Nicholas (1) not established. He married Elizabeth Dickerson on 6 Oct 1656 (A:197). Mr. Richard Tubman of Tallantyre was buried 23 July 1706 (A:307).

Richard was the father of (A: 51, 52, 54, 566, 58, 61, 65, 67, 294, 299): JANETA (twin), bapt. 24 Jan 1659/60; ELIZABETH (twin), bapt. 24 Jan 1659/60; WILLIAM, bapt. --- 1661; ROBERT [not Richard], bapt. 19/26 May 1663; ISABELLA, bapt. 18 Oct 1665; GEORGE, bapt. 4 June 1668; EDWARD, bapt. 27 Jan 1670/1, bur. 9 June 1683; DANIEL, bapt. 25 Nov 1673 (sponsors?: Thomas Belman, cler., Antony Wilkes, Gent., and Mrs. Dickinson of Lamplugh), bur. 22 Oct 1675; HENRY, bapt. 13 April 1676.

3. GEORGE TUBMAN, son of Richard (2), was bapt. 4 June 1668 (A). He settled in CH Co., MD, and m. Elinor, dau. of Henry Hawkins. Elinor m. 2nd, Edward Philpot.

George Tubman, son of Richard of Tallantyre, Cumberland, pleb., matriculated at Queen's College, Oxford, on 16 March 1696/7, age 18. He took his B.A. in 1690 and his M.A. in 1693 (*ALOX*).

Rev. George Tubman was in CH Co. by 17 July 1694 when he witnessed a deed (CHLR S:423).

On 11 March 1697 he was left personalty in the will of Eliza Smith (MWB 6:84). On 7 May 1698 he was left personalty in the will of Richard Hibart of CH Co. (MWB 6:181).

Henry Hawkins of CH Co. made his will on 18 Oct 1698. He named several children including a dau. Elinor Hawkins alias Tubman, to whom he left 238 a. Hawkins Addition, 100 a. Come By Chance, and 50 a. part of Moore's Branch (MWB 6:310). When Eliza Hawkins, widow [of Henry] made her will on 12 June 1716 she left personalty to Richard Tubman, son of Rev. George Tubman (MWB 14:510).

On 4 June 1705 Elinor Tubman, widow, made a deed of gift to her son Richard at age 18, and dau. Elizabeth at age 16 or marriage, of household goods, etc. Her son was to be taught to read, write, and count "to the rule of three." The deed was recorded at the request of Mrs. Elinor Philpot, wife of Edward Philpot (CHLR C#2:129).

George and Elinor had two children: RICHARD; and ELIZABETH.

Unplaced:

TUBMAN, RICHARD, was in CV Co. by 9 Dec 1669 when he witnessed the will of William Chapline (MWB 1:263).

TUBMAN, ROBERT, mercer, and a member of a leading Cockermouth family, d. 1727. He m. Frances, dau. and coheir of the Rev. George Lamplugh. Robert and Frances were the parents of (*CFAH*:145): ROBERT.

TUBMAN, ROBERT, of Cockermouth Castle, son of Robert and Frances, d. 1745. Robert was a merchant with an interest in the Virginia trade. He m. Martha Christian. Their two sons d.s.p., but they had a surviving daughter (*CFAH*:145).

Unplaced:

TUBMAN, WILLIAM, was in DO Co. by 25 Oct 1698 when he witnessed the will of William Deane of Cox Creek, near Hungar River, DO Co. (MWB 6:304).

THE VENABLES FAMILY

Refs.: A: Henrietta Brady Brown. *Some Venables of England and America and Brief Accounts of Families into which Captain Venables Married.* Cincinnati: Kinderton Press, 1961. MHS. B: *WAR7.* C: *MCS5.*

Generations 1-5

1. GILBERT de VENABLES, alias "Venator," living 1086, may have been a son of Eudo, Earl of Blois and a younger brother of Stephen, Earl of Blois. He was the father of (A:9): [-?-] de Venables.

2. [-?-] de VENABLES, son of Gilbert (1), was the father of (A:9): GILBERT.

3. GILBERT de VENABLES, son of [-?-] (2), was Baron of Kinderton and died temp. Henry II (c1154-1189). He m. Margery, dau. of Waltheof or Walthew, son of Wolfric, Lord of Hatton.

Gilbert and Margery were the parents of (A:9): Sir WILLIAM; HAMON (grantee of lands in Wicham, and of his brother Michael's lands in Marston; may be the Hamon who was ancestor of Leigh of West Hall); GILBERT; MICHAEL (a witness to deeds in 1156 and 1188); R.(?); HUGH, parson of Eccleston, Astbury and Rosthorne; MAUD, m. 1st Ralph son of Roger, and 2nd, Hugh de Brixis; and AMABIL, m. Richard of Davenport.

4. Sir WILLIAM de VENABLES, son of Gilbert (3) and Margery, Baron of Kinderton in 1188. He was living 12 Henry III (1228). He was the father of (A): HUGH; ROBERT, parson of Rosthorne, d. 1260; [-?-], parent of William de la Mere; WILLIAM, married and had two daughters (a. Lettice, m. 1st, Philip de Bemvyle, 2nd, Richard de Wilburham, and 3rd, Robert de Crosslegh; and b. Beatrix, m. Ralph Wasteneys of Tyxale); and HAMON.

5. HUGH de VENABLES, Baron of Kinderton, son of Sir William (4), m. 1st, Wentiland [-?-], whom he divorced. and 2nd, Agnes, dau. of Ranulph de Oxton. By his 2nd wife Hugh was the father of the following (A:9): Sir ROGER; ELIZABETH (was living in 1258, and was an aunt of Sir William, in 1267); and BEATRIX, m. Roger de Toft, Lord of Toft.

Generations 6-9

6. Sir ROGER de VENABLES, son of Hugh (5), d. c1261, and was Baron of Kinderton in the County Palatine of Chester. His arms: Azure, two bars argent, are displayed in Westminster Abbey, on the south side of the Nave (C. W. Scott-Giles, "Heraldry in Westminster Abbey," *Coat of Arms*, 7 (52) 159).

Sir Roger married Alice, daughter of Alan de Peninton of Peninton Hall, Lancs. Sir Roger and Alice were the parents of (A:9-10): Sir WILLIAM; ROSE, m. Alexander de Bamvyle; (prob.) ROGER, parson of Rosthorne, temp Edward I; and (prob.) AMY, m. Hugh de Hatton.

7. Sir WILLIAM de VENABLES, Knight, Baron of Kinderton, son of Sir Roger (6), died 20 Edward I (1291). He m. 1st, [-?-], and 2nd, Margaret, daughter of Sir Thomas de Dutton. Margaret was living in 1293. Sir William's 1st daughter may have been by his 1st wife, but the rest of his children were by his 2nd wife (A:10):

Sir William was the father of: CECILY (poss. by 1st wife), m. Adam, clerk of Allehulme; Sir HUGH; Sir WILLIAM (was given lands in Bradwall by his father. He m. 1st, Agnes, widow of Richard de Lymme, dau. and heiress of Richard de Legh of West Hall. Sir William m. 2nd, Katherine, widow of Sir Randle de Thornton, and dau. of Urian de St. Pierre. He had issue by both wives).

8. Sir HUGH de VENABLES, Baron of Kinderton, son of Sir William (7) and Margaret, died 4 Edward II (1311). He m. Agatha, dau. of Sir Ralph de Vernon, Baron of Shipbrooke, c1295. Agatha m. 2nd David de Hulgraves by 1313.

Sir Hugh and Agatha were the parents of (A:10): Sir HUGH; REGINALD (given one-fourth of the lands in Hope. He m. and had issue); ROGER, living 1336; JOHN, living 1336; WILLIAM; ALICE, m. John Arderne, son of Sir John (B:Line 230); ISABEL, m. David de Egerton; ANILLA, m. Sir William Brereton of Brereton; and ELIZABETH, m. Richard Done of Utkinton.

9. Sir HUGH de VENABLES, son of Sir Hugh (8) and Agatha, was a minor in 1311, and died 41 Edw. III (1368). He m. 1st, Elizabeth, daughter and coheiress of Ralph, Lord of Mobberlagh, and 2nd, Katherine, dau. of Richard de Houghton, Lord of Houghton.

Sir Hugh had two children by his first wife and five children by his 2nd wife (A:10-11; C:Line 103): (by Elizabeth): WILLIAM, d. before his father in 1350; JOHN, m. Isabel, dau. of Philip de Egerton (by Katherine): HUGH; ROGER, m. Elizabeth, married and had issue; THOMAS, living 1368; RICHARD, m. and had issue; and JOANE, m. Sir Thomas de Lathom, Lord of Lathom (Ancestors of **Rowland Cotymore of the Virginia Company**; Her parentage is confirmed in B:Line 57, which cites the *NCP* IV, 205; see The Lathom Family elsewhere in this work).

THE WALDEGRAVE FAMILY

Refs.: A: *HSPV 13*:119, 307. B: *PECD* 2:308. C: "Waldegrave." *Burke's Peerage and Baronetage*, 1956 ed. D: "Waldegrave." *HSPV 32*:295-300. E: *WAR7*:Line 200. F: *MCS5*:Line 75A. X: Undocumented Waldegrave data in the LDS Ancestral File.

ARMS: Per pale Argent and Gules (plus 11 other quarterings) (D:295).

Generations 1-5

1. WARREN WALDEGRAVE, Esq., m. [-?-] Ryston. They were the parents of (D:296): JOHN.

2. JOHN WALDEGRAVE, Esq., son of Warren (1), m. [-?-] Hastings. They were the parents of (D:296): WALTER.

3. WALTER WALDEGRAVE, son of John (2), m. [-?-], dau. of Sir James Neville of Co. Nottingham. They were the parents of (D:296): Sir RICHARD.

4. Sir RICHARD WALDEGRAVE, Kt., son of Walter (3), m. Agnes, dau. of [-?-] Dawbeny. They were the parents of (D:296): Sir RICHARD.

5. Sir RICHARD WALDEGRAVE, of Smallbridge, Suffolk, son of Sir Richard (4) and Agnes, d. c1400. He represented Suffolk in the reigns of Edward III and Richard II, and was Speaker of the House of Commons. He m. Joan, dau. and heiress of Silvester and Bures, Suffolk. She d. 1406.

Sir Richard Waldegrave, Kt., d. 1400; his wife Johann d. 10 June 1406. Both are buried in Bures Church (D:296).

Sir Richard and Joan were the parents of (C; D:296): Sir RICHARD.

Generation 6

6. Sir RICHARD WALDEGRAVE, son of Sir Richard (5) and Joan, d. 1436. He succeeded his mother in her estates, and was styled Lord of Bures or Buers and Silvesters. With Lords Clinton and Falconbridge, and Sir John Howard, he was appointed to keep the seas. He landed 10,000 men in Brittany and captured the Town of

Conquet and the Isle of Rhe (C). He was Vice Admiral of England in the reign of Edward IV (D:296).

By his wife Jane, dau. and heiress of Thomas Montechensey, Suffolk, he was the father of (C): Sir WILLIAM.

Generation 7

7. Sir WILLIAM WALDEGRAVE, Kt., son of Sir Richard (6) and Jane, d. 1461. He m. Joane Dureward, by whom he had a son (C; D:296): Sir THOMAS.

Generation 8

8. Sir THOMAS WALDEGRAVE, son of Sir William (7), d. 1500. He was knighted for bravery at the Battle of Towton Field, 20 March 1461. He m. Elizabeth, eldest dau., and coheiress of her father, Sir John Fray, Kt., Lord-Chief-Baron of the Exchequer.

Sir Thomas Waldegrave, Kt., d. 28 ... 1500. He and his wife, Elizabeth are buried in Bures Church (D:295).

Sir Thomas and Elizabeth were the parents of three sons and three daus., including (C): WILLIAM; EDWARD; and RICHARD.

Generation 9

9. Sir WILLIAM WALDEGRAVE, son of Sir Thomas (8), K.B., was buried at Bures, Suffolk, on 30 Jan 1527/8. He m. Margery Wentworth, dau. of Henry and Elizabeth (Howard) Wentworth. She was buried at Bures on 7 May 1540.

Sir William and Margery were the parents of (E: F): GEORGE; and ANTHONY.

10. EDWARD WALDEGRAVE, second son of Sir Thomas (8) and Elizabeth, settled at Boreley, Essex. He m. Mabel, dau. and heir of John Cheyney of Pynhoo, Co. Devon. Edward d. 1506 and Mabel d. 7 June 1505. Both are buried in Bures Church (D:295).

Edward and Mabel were the parents of (A; B; C; D:297): JOHN; THOMAS, d. s.p.; MARGERY, m. Robert Ryce of Preston, Suffolk; and GRACE, m. Thomas Edon of Sudbury, Co. Suffolk, Clerk of the Star Chamber.

Generation 10

11. GEORGE WALDEGRAVE, son of Sir William (9) and Margery, m. Anne, dau. of Sir Robert Drury of Hawstead, Suffolk. She d. 1572 having m. 2nd, Sir Thomas Jermyn of Rushbrook (For her ancestry see E:Line 257). George d. 8 July 1528 and is buried in All Hallows Church, Sudbury (D:296).

George and Anne were the parents of (E; *PASC*:273; *RD500*:317): Sir WILLIAM; EDWARD; PHILLIS, m. Thomas Higham of Higham, Suffolk (They were the ancestors of **Nathaniel Burroughs** of MA and MD); ANNE, m. 1st, Henry Buers of Acton, and 2nd, Sir Clement Higham; and MARGARET, m. Sir John St. John (Their great-granddau. Alice Apsley, m. 1st, **Sir John Boteler**; and 2nd, **George Fenwick of Saybrook, CT**).

12. ANTHONY WALDEGRAVE, of the Friers in Bures, 2nd son of Sir William (9) and Margery, m. Elizabeth, daughter and coheiress of Ralph Gray of Burnt Pelham, Co. Hertford, a Baron of the Exchequer.

Anthony and Elizabeth were the parents of (D:298; F): WILLIAM; THOMAS; BARNABY; and JULYAN.

13. JOHN WALDEGRAVE, son of Edward (10) and Mabel, of Borley, Essex, d. 6 Oct 1543 (B), of 1514 (A:119, Visit. of Essex, 1558). He m. Lora Rochester, sister of Sir Robert Rochester, Chancellor of the Duchy of Lancaster, and dau. of Sir John.

John and Lora were the parents of (B; D:297): Sir EDWARD; ROBERT, m. [-?-], dau. and coheir of [-?-] Forster; JOHN; ANNE; and MARY, m. [-?-] Abell of Coghall in Fordham, Essex.

Generation 11

14. Sir WILLIAM WALDEGRAVE, son of George (11) and Anne, d. at Calais, France, on 2 May 1554. He m. Julian Rainesford, dau. and heiress of Sir John Rainesford, Kt. A monument in All Hallows Church, Sudbury, states that Sir William Waldegrave of Bures died in Calais, France, on 12 May 1554 (D:296).

Sir William and Julian had one son and four daus., including (d:298; *PASC*:273): Sir WILLIAM; DOROTHY, m. Arthur Harris (from whom descend **The Kempe Family of VA**); MARGERY, m. John Wiseman of Canfield, Co. Essex (Ancestors of **Robert Wiseman, Passenger on the Ark and Dove to MD in 1634**); and MARY, m. 1st, Edward Wyatt, and 2nd, Walter Mildmay of Essex.

15. EDWARD WALDEGRAVE of Rivers Hall, Boxted, and later of Lawford Hall, Essex, son of George (11) and Anne, was b. 1514, and d. leaving a will dated 12 Aug 1584 and proved 5 Dec 1584. He m. by June 1556 Joan Ackworth, widow of William Bulmer, and dau. of George Ackworth. She was buried on 10 Dec 1590 (*PASC*:68-69).

He was imprisoned in the Tower of London because he was accused of withholding information from Henry VIII relative to the trial of Queen Katherine Howard for adultery (*PASC*:68).

Edward and Joan were the parents of (*PASC*:69; *RD500*:222): MARGARET, m. William Clopton (They were the parents of Thomasine Clopton who m. **John Winthrop, Governor of Massachusetts Bay Colony**; they were also ancestors of **William Clopton of VA**).

16. THOMAS WALDEGRAVE of the Friers in Bures, Suffolk, fourth son of Anthony (12) and Elizabeth, d. leaving a will dated 1 June 1611. He m. 1st, Elizabeth, dau. of Robert Gurdon of Waldingfield, and 2nd, Mary Badby (F).

Thomas and Elizabeth were the parents of (D:298; F): THOMAS; JOHN; WILLIAM; and ELIZABETH, m. John Wincole.

17. Sir EDWARD WALDEGRAVE, son of John (13) and Lora, was b. 1517 at Borley, and d. 1 Sep 1561 in the Tower of London. He m. Frances Neville, dau. of Sir Edward and Eleanor (Windsor) Neville of Adlington. She m. 2nd, Chideok Paulet (D:297).

Sir Edward was Chancellor of the Duchy of Lancaster and Privy Counselor to Queen Mary. He was Principal Officer in the Household of Lady Mary (later Queen

Mary I). He incurred the displeasure of Henry VIII when he refused to permit the celebration of mass in Mary's house. He was sent to the Tower of London but later released. During the reign of Elizabeth he was sent back to the Tower where he died (C).

Sir Edward and Frances were the parents of (B; C; D:197): MAGDALEN, b. c1543 [or c1557] at Borley, Essex, d. 8 Sep 1598, m. c1572, Sir John Southcote; CATHERINE, b. c1547 [or c1559] at Borley, Essex, m. Thomas Gowan or Gawen; MARY, b. c1549 [or c1555] at Borley, d. 29 Aug 1604 at Ingatestone, Essex, where she m. 17 April 1570, John Petre (See **The Petre Family, ancestors of George Atwood of MD**, both of which families are discussed elsewhere in this work); CHARLES, b. 5 April 1551 at Stanninghill, Norfolk, d. 10 Jan 1632 at Cotessey, Norfolk, m. Jeronimia Jerningham (ancestor of the Earls Waldegrave); FRANCES, b. c1553/7 at Borley, m. John Peter; NICHOLAS, b. c1554; and CHRISTOPHER, b. c1553, m. [-?-] Jerningham.

Generation 12

18. THOMAS WALDEGRAVE, of Mount Bures, Essex, eldest son of Thomas (16) and Elizabeth, d. leaving a will dated 4 Sep 1640. He m. Margaret, d. c1637, dau. and coheir of John Holmstead [or Hollinshed of Hawsted, Essex], of Halstead, Essex (D:298).

Thomas and Margaret were the parents of (F): JEMIMA, b. c1606, m. **Herbert Pelham, III**, who settled in New England.

19. NICHOLAS WALDEGRAVE, son of Sir Edward (17) and Frances (Neville), of Borley, Essex, was b. c1554 and d. 19 June 1621, having m. Catherine, dau. and coheir of Sir Weston Browne, d. 1580 of Roding Abesell, Sussex.

Nicholas and Catherine were the parents of (B; D:297): FRANCES, d. by 5 April 1641, m. by 1605, Sir Richard Weston (q.v.), Earl of Portland (from whom descend **Jerome and Frances White** of MD).

THE WESTON FAMILY

Refs.: A: Alfred Rudulph Justice, "Addendum: The Weston Family," Repr. in *Eng. Origins of New England Families*, 1st ser., I:582-588. B: "Weston," *HSPV* 13:318-319.

ARMS: Ermine on a chief Azure, five bezants, a martlet for difference. These arms were found on the tomb of Richard Weston's daughter, Lady Tichborne, and were allowed to his grandson, Sir Richard Weston, later Earl of Portland in the Visitation of Essex, 1612 (A:584).

1. WILLIAM WESTON of Prested Hall, Feering, Co. Essex, was prob. a descendant of Michael de Weston who settled in Essex c1286, and whose son Humfrey de Weston was living at Prested Hall by 1360. William d. leaving a will dated 20 June 1514, proved 6 Feb 1514/5. At the time he made his will he was married to Margaret [-?-], but she was not his first wife.

William was the father of (A:583): (by first wife): RICHARD, d. 1541 (by 2nd wife): WILLIAM; THOMAS; JOHN; and MARY, unm. on 20 June 1514.

2. JOHN WESTON, fourth son of William (1), was probably the father of (A:584): RICHARD, b. 1510; [-?-] (dau.), m. John Slade of Coventry, Co. Warwick.

3. RICHARD WESTON, Justice of the Peace and Common Pleas, probably son of John (2), was b. 1510, and d. 6 July 1572. He m. 1st, c1549, Wiburga (or Wyborow) Catesby Jenour, d. 1553, widow of Richard Jenour of Great Dunmow, Co. Essex, and dau. of Anthony Catesby of Whiston, Northants. She d. 1553 (B).

Richard m. 2nd, by 1558, Margaret Burnaby, bur 10 April 1565; m. 3rd, at Chicheley, Bucks, 7 July 1566, Elizabeth Lovett Cave Newdigate, widow of Anthony Cave and of John Newdigate of Harefield, Mddx., and dau. of Thomas Lovett [or Lovell] of Astwell, Northants. Weston was a Member of Parliament, and Justice of the Court of Common Pleas. He was granted two manors, Garnett and Marks, and Long Barnes, by Queen Mary.

Richard was the father (A:584-585; B) (by first wife): Sir JEROME, b. c1550; AMPHILIS, m. Sir Benjamin Tichborne of Tichborne, Hants., Bart. (by 2nd wife): NICHOLAS, minor on 4 July 1572; WINIFRED, bur. at Roxwell, 3 March 1590/1; MARGARET, bapt. 3 May 1564, m. 1st, John Loveday, and 2nd, Andrew Glascock.

4. Sir JEROME WESTON, son of Richard (3), was b. c1550 (he was age 22 at his father's death). He d. 31 Dec 1603, and was bur. at Roxwell on 17 Jan 1603/4. He m. 1st, at Chicheley, Bucks, Mary Cave, b. 1 Nov 1556, bur. at Roxwell 6 Oct 1593, dau. of Anthony Cave and Elizabeth Lovett (who m. as his 3rd wife, Jerome's father, Richard Weston). By this marriage the Cave **Arms**: Azure, fretty Argent, were brought into the Weston arms (B).

Sir Jerome m. 2nd, Margery Pert Thwaites, widow of William Thwaites, Alderman of London, and dau. of George and Alice Pert of Mountnessing, Essex. She m. 3rd, Sir John Savell [Savile?], Baron of the Exchequer (B).

Jerome Weston was High Sheriff of Essex in 1599, and was knighted by James I at the Charterhouse on 11 May 1603.

By his first wife Sir Jerome was the father of (A:586-588; *MCS* 5th ed., Line 100): ANNE, b. c1574, m. 6 Dec 1590, John Williams of Brentwood, Essex; Sir RICHARD; WILLIAM; MARY, bapt. 26 April 1579, m. William Clerke of St. Botolph Aldgate (They were parents of **Jeremy Clarke of RI**); JOHN, d. in inf.; ELIZABETH, b. c.1582, m. Nicholas Cotton; DOROTHY, b. c1584, m. Sir Edward Pinchon; JEROME, d. in inf.; WINIFRED, bapt. 3 March 1589/90, m. at Roxwell, Richard Gardiner; MARGARET, bapt. 5 Aug 1593, m. Edward Leventhorpe.

5. Sir RICHARD WESTON, K.G., Earl of Portland, son of Sir Jerome (4) and Mary (Cave) Weston, was bapt. at Chicheley, Bucks, 1 March 1576/7, d. 13 March 1634/5 at Wallingford House, Westminster. He m. 1st, Elizabeth Pinchon; and 2nd, Frances Waldegrave, d. 1615, dau. of Nicholas and Catherine (Browne) Waldegrave. The latter marriage brought the Waldegrave **Arms** (Per pale Argent and Gules, a crescent for difference), into the Weston Family (B).

Sir Richard was made Knight of the Garter on 9 April 1630, and Earl of Portland on 17 Feb 1632/3. He was a Member of Parliament and a Member of the Privy Council, and was a great favorite of King Charles I. He was Chancellor of the Exchequer in 1622, and Ambassador to the States of Germany 7 July 1629 (A; B).

Sir Richard had three children by his first wife and eight by his second.

By his first wife Sir Richard was the father of (B): RICHARD; ELIZABETH; and MARY

Among his children by Frances Waldegrave were (A:587; B): JEROME; THOMAS; and CATHERINE, bapt. 8 June 1607 at Roxwell, d. 22 Oct 1645 in Rome, m. as his 2nd wife, Richard White of Hutton, Essex (Their children **Frances and Jerome White** settled in MD).

THE WHICHCOTE FAMILY

Refs.: A: "Whichcote" *HSPV* 17:344; B: Data generously provided by Robert Hall, 3903 Conifer Lane, Bowie, MD, 20715 (301)-262-8749. C: "The Whichcote Family of Stoke, Shropshire," compiled by Burke's Peerage, Ltd.

ARMS: Ermine, two boars statant Gules, a crescent for difference. **CREST**: On a wreath of the colors, a boar's head erect Gules, armed and langued [Azure?], a crescent for difference (A).

Generations 1-5

1. JOHN WHICHCOAT was b. 1399 in Lancs., and d. 1441. He m. Elizabeth Tyrwhitt, b. 1399, d. 1444. They were the parents of (B): JOHN.

2. JOHN WHICHCOAT, son of John (1) and Elizabeth, was b. 1433 in Harpswell, Lincs., and d. 1470. He m. Catherine Bussey, b. 1443 in Hougham, Lincs., d. 1472. They were the parents of (B): THOMAS.

3. THOMAS WHICHCOAT, son of John (2) and Catherine, was b. 1465 at Harpswell, Lincs., and d. 1504. He m. Catherine Norton, b. 1465 in Kent, Eng., and d. 1510. Thomas and Catherine were the parents of two children, including (B): CHRISTOPHER, b. 31 July 1571/2 in Stoke, Salop.

4. CHRISTOPHER WHICHCOTE, son of Thomas (3) and Catherine, was b. 31 July 1571 in Stoke, Shropshire, Eng., and d. 5 March 1607. He m. c1597 Elizabeth Fox, dau. and sole heir of Edw. Fox, Esq. She was b. at Grete, Shropshire.

Christopher and Elizabeth had 12 children, including (A; B): Col. CHRISTOPHER, b. 20 March 1601/2; EDWARD; CHARLES; THOMAS; BENJAMIN, b. 1609; SAMUEL; JEREMY, b. 1614, of the Inner Temple, and Deputy Lieutenant of Middlesex; LUCY; ELIZABETH; SARAH; KATHERINE, and ANNE, m. Thomas Hayes.

5. Col. CHRISTOPHER WHICHCOTE, son of Christopher (4) and Elizabeth, was born 20 March 1601/2 in Burford, Shropshire. About 1635 he m. Lucy Bosville, b. New Hall, Yorks. (A; B).

He was a Col. in the Army and Governor of Windsor Castle from 1650 at least until 1659 (B: cites the *Calendar of State Papers Domestic for Charles I*).

In Feb 1637 Christopher Whichcote, son of Christopher Whichcote of Stoke Salop, was granted the Freedom of the Merchant Taylor's Company, having been apprenticed in 1618 (B: cites the Freedom and Apprenticeship Registers of the Livery Company of Merchant Taylors).

Christopher and Lucy were the parents of the following children [who some undocumented sources state were born at Stoke Lacy, Salop] (A; B: BENJAMIN; ELIZABETH, m. Matthias Crabbe in 1662; and MARY, m. Dr. John Worthington

6. BENJAMIN WHICHCOTE, son of Christopher (4) and Elizabeth, was b. 4 May 1609 at Stoke, Shropshire, and d. 1683. He was Provost of King's College, Cambridge. He m. Rebecca, widow of Matthew Craddock, Governor of MA (*DNB* 15:1196-1198).

Generation 6

7. BENJAMIN WHICHCOTE, son of Col. Christopher (5) and Lucy, was born 1640 in St. John Zachary, London, and died 1707 at Wood St., London.

Benjamin Whichcote, son of Christopher, was apprenticed in Feb 1662 to William Barret of the Merchant Taylor's Company. He was given the Freedom of the Company in 1670 (D: cites the Freedom and Apprenticeship Registers of the Livery Company of Merchant Taylors).

Benjamin Whichcote of St. Alban, Wood St., London, citizen and merchant taylor, age 28, and Mrs. Ann Archer of Islington, Mddx., spinster, age 18, on 14 Sep 1674, with the consent of her mother, Mrs. Archer, widow, were granted a license to marry either at the parish church or the chapel of the Guildhall, London (*HSPV* 23:231). Some four years later, on 27 Feb 1678/9, Benjamin Whichcote, of Love Lane, London, merchant taylor, widower, age c31, and Mrs. Ann Enos of the same Parish, spinster, age 16, with the consent of her mother, Mrs. Susanna Enos, widow of St. Lawrence, London, were granted a license to marry (*HSPV* 23:294). Anne Enos was b. 7 July 1663.

Benjamin Whichcote of St. John Zachary, London, d. leaving a will dated 14 April 1707 and proved 2 Oct 1707. He named his sons Christopher, Enos, Paul, Benjamin, Samuel, and Anne. He mentioned his trading activities with Africa and Nevis in America. He also mentioned his aunt Elizabeth Hundson, kinswoman Elizabeth Crabb, cousin Mr. Christopher Whichcote of London, and nephew Mr. John Worthington (B: cites a PCC Will).

Benjamin and Anne were the parents of nine children including (B; D: cites baptisms at St. Alban's, Wood St., found in the IGI): ANNE, bapt. 5 Nov 1676; BENJAMIN, bapt. 5 Dec 1677 [but almost certainly d. young]; CHRISTOPHER, bapt. 22 July 1686; ENOS; PAUL, b. 1685, bapt. 18 Aug 1689; BENJAMIN of St. Maryebone [Mary le Bon], Mddx. [under 21 in 1707]; SAMUEL; and ANNE.

Generation 7

8. PAUL WHICHCOTE, son of Benjamin (7) and Anne, was born 1685, baptized 18 Aug 1689 at St. Alban, Wood St., London, and died in MD 1752/7. He married c1715, prob. in England, Mary [-?-], who d. 1762 (B).

He attended Merchant Taylor's School from 1699 to 1701 and Cambridge in 1706/7. There was another Paul Whichcote, son of Henry of Finchley, who was also a Fellow Commoner at Cambridge, and it is possible that some of the records may have gotten mingled (B).

Paul Whichcote, commander of the Brig *Baltimore*, bound for Dublin, arrived in Annapolis on 17 Sep 1734 (*AMG* 27 Sep 1734).

In 1737 he and his son Paul, Jr., were living in Lower Back River Hundred in BA Co. Whichcote had moved to KE Co., MD, by 1739. On 29 Aug 1739 William Woodland and his wife Mary of KE Co., conv. to Paul Whichcote of the sd. county, mariner, part of two tracts, Perch Meadows bought by said Woodland from Doctor Richard Hill, and Woodlands Intention surveyed for the said Woodland, 100 a. (KELR JS#22:449; for other land transactions, see KELR JS#25:247, 248).

From 1747 to 1751 Whichcote was a Justice of the KE Co. Court. His home, built in 1751 in the Fairleigh Section of Chestertown, MD, is still occupied,

Whichcote, describing himself as a mariner, in the 67th year of his age, died leaving a will dated 1752 and proved on 11 April 1757. He mentioned a wife and named his children Paul and Sarah, and a grandson Benjamin Wright, who was to have land next to John Read. His wife and son Paul were named execs. William and John Browning witnessed the will (MWB 30:311).

John Carville and Joseph Wicks appraised the personal estate of Paul Whitchcoat at £48.8.6. Mary and Paul Witchcoat, execs., filed the inventory on 27 May 1758 (MINV 64:320).

Mary and Paul Whichcote administered the estate of Paul Whichcote on 2 Dec 1761. They cited three inventories, totaling £436.1.0, £40.8.6, and £0.15.0, and payments coming to £29.17.8, including one to David Griffith (MDAD 47:278).

Paul Whichcote was the father of (B): SARAH, b. c1715, d. c1780, m. 1st, in 1736, Samuel White d. 1750/1; 2nd, c1755, David Griffith, d. by 1764, and 3rd, after 1765, Jonathan Allawn who d. 1787; and PAUL, b. 1717, d. 1771.

9. **BENJAMIN WHICHCOTE** of St. Marylebone, Mddx., son of Benjamin (7), died leaving a will proved in the PCC in 1782. He mentioned his bro. Paul Whichcote of MD, and left £4000 to Paul's children Paul and Sarah, and to Martha, widow of Paul, Jr. Benjamin gave his executors three years to find the American heirs.

THE ROBERT WHITE FAMILY
A line in question

Refs.: A: *Pedigrees of Some of the Descendants of the Emperor Charlemagne*, 2:308-309. B: *ESBE*:144 (cites the 1634 Visitation of Essex). C: *HSPV 13*. D: James Duvall Trabue, "A Reconsideration of the Wells-White Marriage," *MGSB* 40 (1) 3-25.

This line was formerly questioned by Brice M. Clagett and John D. Baldwin, III, in Letters to the Editor of the *MGSB*, 35 (3) 468-469. He stated that no documentary proof of the marriage of Richard Wells to Frances White has been found and that the line was not recognized by either Harry Wright Newman or Gary Boyd Roberts. However the line was included in Volume 2 of *Pedigrees of Some of the Descendants of the Emperor Charlemagne*, edited by Aileen Lewers Langston and J. Orton Buck, Jr., with a Foreword by Timothy Field Beard, Genealogist General of the Crown of Charlemagne in the United States of Americas Repr.: Baltimore: GPC, 1986).

ARMS: Argent, a chevron Gules, between three popinjays Vert, beaked, legged and collared of the 2nd, within a bordure charged with eight bezants. CREST: Between two wings Argent, a popinjay's head Vert, collared Gules, holding in the beak a rose Gules, slipped and leaved of the 2nd (B).

Generations 1-5

1. ROBERT WHITE of Yeatley and Farnham m. Alice [-?-]. They were the parents of (B): ROBERT of Swanbourne (His descendants are traced *in Berry's Hampshire Families*; and a descendant Frances m. Thomas Yate of Berkshire, and was the ancestor of **George Yate of MD**; D:10); and JOHN.

2. JOHN WHITE, 2nd son of Robert (1) and Alice, m. Eleanor, daughter of Robert, Lord Hungerford. They were the parents of (A): RICHARD of Hutton.

3. RICHARD WHITE of Hutton, Essex, son of John and (2) Eleanor, m. Maud, sister of Sir William Tyrrell of Heron [**The Gorsuch Family of MD** also descends from the Tyrrells]. Richard and Maud were the parents of (B): RICHARD of Hutton; SUSAN, m. Thomas Tong, Clarenceux King of Arms; MARY, m. 1st [-?-] Whitehed, and 2nd, [-?-] Spencer; JOAN, m. [-?-] Wilcock.

4. RICHARD WHITE of Hutton, son of Richard (3) and Maud, m. Margaret, dau. of [-?-] Strelley of Notts. They were the parents of (B): GEORGE of Hutton; HUMPHREY; JOHN; DOROTHY, m. [-?-] Staunton; ANNE, m. [-?-] Setyll; ELIZABETH, m. [-?-] Sheppard; MARY; THOMAZINE; and CATHERINE.

5. GEORGE WHITE of Hutton, son of Richard (4) and Margaret, m. Katharine, dau. of William Stroud of Ployden, Salop. They were the parents of (B): RICHARD of Hutton; EDWARD of Notley Hall, Essex, m. Anne Wright; SUSAN, d. in inf.; GEORGE, d. unm. 1609; RICHARD; SUSAN, m. Sir George Kingston.

Generation 6

6. RICHARD WHITE of Hutton, Essex, son of George (5) and Katharine, d. 19 Aug. 1614; m. Mary, dau. of Edward Plowden of Plowden, Salop. They had at least two children (A: B; C: 314): RICHARD; MARY, m. Philip Waldegrave of Borley, Essex, and d. 3 or 4 years after her marriage.

Generation 7

7. RICHARD WHITE, son of Richard (6) and Mary, was buried in the Church of Sta. Maria Maggiore, Rome. He m. 1st, Anne, dau. and heir of Andrew Grey of the Inner Temple. He m. 2nd, Lady Katherine Weston, b. 1607, d. 31 Oct 1645 in Rome, buried in the Church of Sta. Maria Maggiore. She was a daughter of Richard Weston, Earl of Portland, K.G., and her epitaph states that she was the mother of eight children (D:8).

By his first wife Richard White was the father of (B; D:8): MARY, heir to her mother, m. Robert Brett of Whitstanton; (by his 2nd wife; the first four are named in the 1634 Visitation of Essex): FRANCES; GEORGE, age 6 in 1634; ELIZABETH; CATHERINE; and JEROME, evidently born after 1634; ANN (named in the will of Jerome White); and EDWARD, appointed by John Petre as overseer of his will.

Generation 8

8. FRANCES WHITE, dau. of Richard (7) and Katherine, was named in the 1634 Visitation of Essex, and is believed to have come to VA in 1637. She m. 1st, Capt.

Richard Wells (who settled in VA prior to Sep 1637 when he was granted 50 a.). She m. 2nd, c1681, John Petre (D:14).

At the time of Richard Wells' arrival in VA, he appearsto have been single (D:5-6). Frances White was brought to VA by Aug 1637 when John Graves claimed land for her transportation (D:7).

Richard and Frances both settled in AA Co., MD by c1658, with their 11 children (A; Skordas cites MPL ABH:347; D:6). Richard Wells was a Justice of the Peace in AA Co. from 1657 to 1661. He d. leaving a will dated 22 June 1667 and proved in AA Co. on 21 Aug 1667, but was proved in the PCC in 1668 (D:6).

Richard and Frances were the parents of: ANN; BENJAMIN; ELIZABETH; FRANCES; GEORGE; JOHN; MARY; RICHARD, and ROBERT.

9. JEROME WHITE, son of Richard (7) and Katherine, with his sister FRANCES, came to MD where he was Surveyor General, Councilor, and Justice of the Provincial Court until he returned to England in 1670 (MPL 5:421, 428-429; 12:558; D:9).

White died prior to 9 Nov 1678 leaving as bro. and heir George White of Runwell, Co. Essex, who prior to that date conveyed (through Thomas Taylor of the Ridge, AA Co., atty. for said George White) to Ann Coppen of DO Co., 1000 a. Weston, on the Nanticoke River (DOLR 3 Old: 144).

THE WILSFORD FAMILY

Refs.: "Wilsford," *HSPV* 42:53, 104. B: William Bailey Willford. *Williford and Allied Families*. Atlanta: Privately printed, 1961. C: "Wilford," *Visitations of Kent, 1574, 1592*.

ARMS: Gules, a chevron engrailed between three leopards' faces Or. **CREST**: Out of a crest coronet per pale Gules and Or, a leopard's face per pale Or and Gules (C:46, 116).

Generations 1-5

1. WILLIAM WILSFORD of Hartridge, Parish of Cranbrook, Co. Kent, m. Margaret, dau. and coheir of Walter Corneus, son and heir of Sir Walter Corneus, Kt. William and Margaret were the parents of (B:1); ROBERT.

2. ROBERT WILSFORD, son of William (1) and Margaret, m. and was the father of (B:1): JAMES; and EDMUND, Provost of Oriel College, Oxford, 1507-1516.

3. JAMES (or JACOBUS) WILSFORD, son of Robert (2), m. Elizabeth, dau. of John Betenham of Buckley.

James served as Alderman and Sheriff of London in 1499 (B:1).

James and Elizabeth were the parents of (A): THOMAS; JOHN; WILLIAM; ROBERT; and NICHOLAS.

4. THOMAS WILSFORD, of Hartridge, Cranbrook, Co. Kent, son of James (3), m. 1st, Elizabeth, dau. of Walter Colepepper of Bedgebury, and 2nd, Rose, dau. of William Whetenhall of Peckham, Kent.

William Cecil, Lord Burleigh, alienated to him the Manor of Lenham, Kent (B:1).

By his first wife Thomas was the father of: Sir JAMES of Cranbrooke; ELIZA, m. George Clerke of Wrotham (They were the great-grandparents of Jeremiah Clarke of RI: *RD500*:248); ANNA, m. Richard Tuck or Tooke; FRANCIS (m. and had issue: C:47); WINIFRED, m. Nicholas Snyth; JOANNA; CATHERINE, m. Hen: Hadd; CONSTANTIA, m. John Dingley; BRIDGETT, m. Leonard Digges (They were the ancestors of **Dudley Digges** of VA); and MARIA, m. George Covert of Slaugham in Sussex. By Rose, Thomas was the father of Sir THOMAS; and CECILIA, m. Edwin Sandys, Archbishop of York (They were the ancestors of **The Gorsuch Family** of Maryland: see *British Roots*, vol. 1; they were also the parents of **George Sandys**, Treasurer of VA, and the grandparents of **Margaret Sandys** who m. Sir Francis Wyatt, Gov. of VA: *RD500*:430).

5. Sir JAMES WILSFORD, son of Thomas (4) and Elizabeth (Colepeper), was b. c1516, and d. 1550. He fought in the French War of 1544-1545. He was Governor of Haddington. He was described by one writer as "such a one as was able to make of a cowardly beaste a courageous man." He d. Nov 1550, and was buried in Little St. Bartholomew beside St. Anthony's (B:2-3).

James m. Joyce, dau. of John Barrett. She was buried beside him on 15 Sep 1580 (B:3). They were the parents of (C:47): THOMAS; and ELIZABETH.

6. Sir THOMAS WILSFORD, son of Thomas (4) and Rose (Whetenhall), was b. c1530, and d. c1604. He went into exile because he could not accept the Roman Catholic faith which Mary Tudor had reestablished in England. He was also brought up as a soldier, and in 1585 commanded a company at Ostend. In 1593 he was made Governor of Camber Castle (B:3).

He m. Mary, only dau. of Edward Poynings. They were the parents of (B:3, 12): Sir THOMAS.

Generation 6

7. Sir THOMAS WILSFORD, son of Sir Thomas (6) and Mary (Poynings), married Margaret Sandys, child of Sir Edwin and Lady Margaret (Eveleigh) Sandys, and granddau. of Archbishop Edwin and Cecily (Wilsford) Sandys.

The younger Sir Thomas was a stockholder in the Virginia and Bermuda Companies, and a member of the first Parliament of the reign of Charles I. Sir Thomas died while supporting King Charles against Parliament (B:12-13).

Sir Thomas Wilsford and Margaret (Sandys) were the parents of at least two sons, the second of whom was (B:13): Capt. THOMAS.

Generation 7

8. Capt. THOMAS WILSFORD, second son of Sir Thomas (7) and Margaret (Sandys), settled in the Northern Neck of VA. He d. by 11 Sep 1667, leaving three sons (B:13-16): ANDREW; JAMES; and THOMAS, d. s.p., 1703.

THE WINTOUR FAMILY

Refs.: A: "Sir William Winter or Wynter." *DNB* 21:691-693. B: "Sir John Winter." *DNB*

21:684-686. C: "Wynter." *Visitation of Gloucestershire, 1623. HSPV* 21:274-279. D: "Winter." *Visitation of Worcestershire, 1569. HSPV* 27:147-149.

ARMS: Sable, a fess Ermine, in chief a crescent ... [plus 14 other quarterings]. **CREST**: Out of a ducal coronet Or, a cubit arm in armour Argent, garnished gold [*sic*], in the gauntlet a plume of ostrich feathers ... [plus two other crests] (D).

Although Frederick, Edward, and Robert Wintour came to Maryland with the *Ark* and *Dove* Expedition in 1634 they are not known to have left descendants. Their lineage is included here as a matter of historical, rather than genealogical, interest.

Generations 1-5

1. Sir ROGER WINTER, Kt., m. Margaret, widow of John, Lord Mohun of Dunster. Sir Roger and Margaret were the parents of (D): Sir ROBERT.

2. ROBERT WINTER, Esq., son of Sir Roger (1) and Margaret, m. Elizabeth, dau. of William Hotot of Co. Glos. Robert and Elizabeth were the parents of (D): RICHARD.

3. RICHARD WINTER, Esq., son of Robert (2) and Elizabeth, m. Margaret, dau. of Walter Burghill of Co. Warwick. Richard and Margaret were the parents of (D): WILLIAM.

4. WILLIAM WINTER, Esq., son of Richard (3) and Margaret, m. Elizabeth, dau. of Sir Henry Appleby, by whom he was the father of (D): Capt. JOHN.

5. Capt. JOHN WINTER, son of William (4) and Elizabeth, was Captain of the Castle of Mayett in France, under John Duke of Bedford. He was the father of (D): ROGER.

Generations 6-10

6. ROGER WINTER of Wych in Co. Worcester, son of Capt. John (5), m. Joane, dau. and coheir of Thomas Hodington. As an heraldic heiress she brought the Hodington arms (Argent, a saltire Gules, within a bordure Sable charged with ten mullets Or) to be quartered by her descendants.
Roger and Joan were the parents of (D): ROGER.

7. ROGER WINTER, Esq., son of Roger (6) and Joan, m. Anne, dau. of Richard Washborne, by whom he was the father of (D): ROGER.

8. ROGER WINTER, son of Roger (7), m. Joan, dau. of Sir John Hungerford od Cawton in Co. Warwick. Roger and Joan were the parents of (D): GILBERT; and ROBERT.

9. ROBERT WINTER, of Cawdwell, Co. Glos., son of Roger (8) and Joan, m. [1st?] Catherine, widow of Thomas Smyth of Campden, Glos., and dau. of Sir George Throckmorton of Cawton, Warwick. Robert Winter m. 2nd, Elizabeth, dau. of William Wirrall (D).

Robert and Catherine were the parents of (D): GEORGE, m. Jane, dau. of William Ingleby of Ripley, Co. York (Their son Thomas was son and heir in 1584); and ELIZABETH, m. Thomas Bushell of Brodmerston in Co. Glos.
Robert and Elizabeth were the parents of (D): JOHN.

10. JOHN WYNTER, Merchant and sea captain of Bristol, son of Robert (9) and Elizabeth, d 1546. He m. Alice, dau. and heiress of William Tirrey of Cork (A: D). The Tirrey Arms were: Or, two bars lozengy Gules (D).
John and Alice were the parents of (A): ARTHUR, d. s.p.; MARIA, d. s.p.; Sir WILLIAM; GEORGE; RANDOLPH; WILLIAM; and AGNES, m. 1st, William Brooke (See 1623 Vis. of Gloucestershire, p. 274), and 2nd, as his 2nd wife Dr. Thomas Wilson (c1525-1581), Secretary of State and scholar (See "Thomas Wilson." *DNB* 21:603-606).

Generation 11

11. Sir WILLIAM WINTER, Kt, Admiral, son of John (10) and Alice, d. 1589. He m. Mary, dau. and heiress of Thomas Langton. (The Langton arms were: Gules, a chevron Ermine between three lions rampant Argent (D).
William Winter entered the service of the Crown at an early age, was on an expedition in 1544, and in Nov 1557 was appointed Master of the ordnance of the navy, and was also surveyor of the navy. He was knighted on 12 Aug 1573 (A). In Nov 1561 he bought the manor of Lydney in Gloucestershire (A).
Sir William and Mary were the parents of four sons and four daus., including (A; D): Sir EDWARD; NICHOLAS, d. s.p. JAMES, d. s.p.; WILLIAM, saw action with Drake; MARIA, m. Thomas Baynham [or Braynham]; ELIZABETH, m. Thomas Morgan, son and heir of Thomas Morgan of Machen in Co. Monmouth; JANE; and ELEANOR, m. George Huntley.

12. GEORGE WINTER, son of John (10) and Alice, m. [-?-], dau. of [-?-] Brayne of Co. Glos. (C:274).
In 1571 he bought the manor of Dyrham in Gloucestershire.
George Winter was the father of (A; C:274; d): JOHN; WILLIAM; BENEDICT, slain at sea in the fight made against the Spaniards in 1588; ELIZABETH, m. Ferdinand Inge [or Ivy] of Wilts.; THOMAZINE, d. s.p; BRIDGET, m. George Wyrral; MARGARET, m. Thomas Weekes; ANNA, m. George Price; and MARIA, m. Anselm Huntley.

Generation 12

13. Sir EDWARD WINTER, of Lydney, Gloucestershire, son of Sir William (11) and Mary, m. on 11 Aug 1595 Anne, dau. of Sir Edward Somerset, K.G., 4th Earl of Worcester (B; D).
Edward commanded the *Aid* with Drake in 1585/6, fought against the Armada in 1588, and represented Gloucestershire in the Parliaments of 1589 and 1601, and was knighted in 1595. He was Sheriff in 1598/9 (A).
Sir Edward and Anne were the parents of (B): Sir JOHN, b. c1600, d. 1673; and prob. EDWARD; FREDERICK; and Capt. ROBERT.

14. JOHN WINTER, son of George (12), commanded the *Elizabeth* in 1578, and was lieutenant of the Vanguard in 1588, in the battle against the Spanish Armada (A).

Generation 13

15. Sir JOHN WINTER, son of Sir Edward (13) and Anne, was b. c1600 and d. c1673. He m. Mary [-?-] (B).

He was knighted on 7 Aug 1624. Like his father, he leased the ironworks and forests in the Forest of Dean from the King. He was a devout Catholic, a loyal follower of the King, an opponent of the Parliamentarians (B).

Sir John Winter was the author of "A True Narrative concerning the Woods and Ironworks of the Forest of Dean," and of "Observations on the Oath of Supremacy (B).

Sir John and Mary were the parents of several children including (B): Sir CHARLES, d. 1698.

16. FREDERICK AND 17. EDWARD WINTOUR, possibly sons of Sir Edward (13) and Lady Anne (Somerset) Winter, and were described by Lord Baltimore as brothers, sons of Sir John [more likely Edward] and Lady Anne Wintour. They may have been a brother of Robert Wintour (noticed separately), and they may have been sons of Sir Edward and Anne (Somerset) Wintour ("Robert Wintour." *BDML* 2:905).

They brought seven Adventurers to Maryland. Both probably died in Maryland without issue, or returned to England (*NFMP*:271).

18. Capt. ROBERT WINTOUR, son of Sir Edward (13) and Lady Anne (Somerset) Winter, was Commander of the Ark. Newman did not connect him with Frederick and Edward Wintour (*NFMP*:271). Papenfuse *et al* state that he was probably the son of Sir Edward Wintour of Sydney, Gloucs., and of the Lady Anne Somerset. He may have been a brother of Frederick and Edward Wintour, noticed above, and a brother of Sir John Winter [*sic*], Secretary of Queen Henrietta Maria ("Robert Wintour." *BDML* 2:905).

On 8 April 1638 he agreed to lease to George Evelin five of his servants (ARMD 4:27).

He d. by 4 Sep 1638 when James Baldridge and Thomas Hebden appraised his property at 9092 lbs tob. plus 3047 lbs tob. in debts and 338 lbs. tob. in desperate debts (*ARMD* 4:88-89). The account of his estate was filed 4 Sep 1639 (*ARMD* 4:106).

THE WORKMAN FAMILY

Generation 1

1. WILLIAM WORKMAN of Colford, dec., was the father of several children, whose births are registered in the Parish of Newland, Gloucestershire (QALR RTA:68 cites a certificate from the Churchwardens and Overseers of the Poor of Newland; MDTP 22:347-348): ANTHONY; WILLIAM; MARTIN; MATTHEW; and perhaps several other sons who died s.p.

Generation 2

2. ANTHONY WORKMAN, eldest son of William (1), died by Oct 1708. He married 1st, Elizabeth [-?-], and 2nd, Susannah [-?-].

He may be the Anthony Workman who, on 21 Nov 1668, was apprenticed to George Marks for 4 years in VA (*CBE2*:139). Anthony Workman of SM Co. claimed land for his service in 1673. His wife Elizabeth claimed land for her service in 1680 (MPL CB#2:128, 433, 17:548-9).

By Aug 1688 Anthony was living on Kent Island, when he was mentioned in the will, made 26 Aug, of Charles Stuart (MWB 6:12).

On 29 Oct 1707 Anthony Workman and wife Susannah conv. land to Isaac Harris, planter (QALR RTA:13).

Workman died leaving a will dated 6 Sep 1708 and proved 14 Oct 1708. He left £50.0.0 to Christ Church Parish for erecting a church. He named Hannah Distan, William Rakes, Edward Brown, Benjamin Wickes, and Francis Barnes, who were to have personalty. The rest of his estate was left to his wife Susannah. William Rakes, Hannah Distan, and Mary Wellshand witnessed the will (MWB 12:305).

Susannah Workman was living on Kent Island on 26 May 1710 when she conveyed property to her granddaughter Susanna Harris, dau. of Isaac Harris, granddaughter Rhoda Harris, and grandson Workman Harris (A:62). On or about Jan. 1710 John Ravenhill and wife Sarah, Alice Prees, John Long, Barnaby Vaughn and wife Eleanor, Richard Ambrow and wife Hannah, and Elizabeth Hill, all of Great Britain, assigned their discretionary shares in Anthony *als*. William Workman's personal estate to Richard Frensham and Thomas McNamara of QA Co. (QALR RTA:104).

Anthony left at least one son (QALR RTA:63-68): ANTHONY.

3. WILLIAM WORKMAN, son of William (1), was bapt. 20 May 1646 at Colford, Parish of Newland, Glos., and died by 1722 (MDTP 22:347-348)

He was brought up as a butcher at Colford, and went away beyond the seas c1669, and was living in MD.

4. MARTIN WORKMAN, son of William (1), was bapt. at Colford, Parish of Newland, Glos. on 13 Nov 1659 (MDTP 22:347-348). In 1709 he was living at Colford (QALR RTA:63-68).

5. MATTHEW WORKMAN, son of William (1), died by 1711 (MDTP 22:347-348).

Generation 3

6. ANTHONY WORKMAN, son of Anthony (2), in 1709 was a butcher living in the City of Gloucester. As heir of his uncle William (3) of MD, he and his wife Anne, and son James, sold land in MD to Humphrey Pellew of Flushing, Parish of Mylor, Cornwall (QALR RTA:63-68).

By his wife Anne, Anthony was the father of: JAMES,

THE WORTHINGTON FAMILY
An Revised Line of Descent

The compiler is indebted to the late Bryden Bordley Hyde for bringing this material to his attention. It should be noted that references B, C, D, and E are at the George Peabody Division (formerly The Peabody Library) of the Milton Eisenhower Library of The Johns Hopkins University.

Refs.: A: "Chart of the Worthington Family," by Bryden Bordley Hyde, Filing Case A, MHS. B: *LPRS 31: The Registers of the Cathedral Church of Manchester, Christenings, Burials, and Weddings, 1573-1616*. Cambridge: The Society, 1908. C: *Register of Prestwick, Manchester*. LPRS. Vol. 34. D: *The Great Historical, Geographical Genealogical and Poetical Dictionary*. Vol. 2. By Jeremy Collier. London, 1701. E: *Diary and Correspondence of Dr. John Worthington* (942.72 C526). F: *Anne Arundel Gentry*. By Harry Wright Newman. 1933, pp. 343-344. G: "The Presumed Ancestors of Capt. John Worthington ... <Mdgenweb>. H: CS 88:342: "Worthington of Crawshaw," *Visitation of Lancashire, 1664/5, taken by Sir William Dugdale*. Chetham Society, 88:342). I: LPRS 46: *Register of the Parish Church of Standish in the County of Lancaster, 1560-1653*. Cambridge: The Society, 1912. J: *LPRS 55: The Registers of the Cathedral Church of Manchester, Baptisms and Marriages, 1616 to 1653*. Trans. by Henry Brierly. Wigan: The Society, 1918. K: LPRS 56: *The Registers of the Cathedral Church of Manchester, Burials, 1616 to 1653*. Trans. by Henry Brierly. Wigan: The Society, 1919. L: LPRS 89: *The Registers of the Cathedral Church of Manchester, 1653 to 1665/6*. Preston: The Society, 1949. M: *The Worthington Families of Medieval England*. By Philip Michael Worthington. Phillimore, n.d.

Standish Parish includes the townships of Standish-with-Langtree, Shevington, Welsh-Whittel, Charnock Richard, Duxbury, Adlington, Heath Charnock, Anderton, Worthington, and Coppull (I).

ARMS: Argent, three dungforks [pitchforks] Sable.

1. CHRISTOPHER WORTHINGTON of Crawshaw, Lancs., the first definitely proven ancestor of the family, was living in 1433 and d. between 1486 and 1501. He m. Joan, dau. and heiress of William de Thornton of Thornton, Lancs., when she was only 5! She d. 1501 (M:206, 209).

   Christopher and Joan were the parents of (M:211): LAWRENCE, b. c1471.

2. LAWRENCE WORTHINGTON, son of Christopher (1) and Joan, was b. c1471 and d. 1563 at the age of 92. He was buried at Standish Church on 24 Sep 1563 (M:212). He m. Margaret Carleton of Carleton, Lancs., who d. c1536. Lawrence and Margaret were the parents of (M:206): CHRISTOPHER.

3. CHRISTOPHER WORTHINGTON of Crawshaw, son of Lawrence (2) and Margaret, d. in 1558, having predeceased his father (M:213). He m. Alice, dau. of John Holcroft of Holcroft, Lancs. She d. 1578 (M:206).

   Christopher and Alice were the parents of (M:206): LAWRENCE, d. 1606; and GILBERT of Adlington, d. 1572.

4. LAWRENCE WORTHINGTON of Crawshaw, son of Christopher (3) and Alice, d. in April 1607, and was buried at Standish Church on 28 April 1607. He m. Jane Lever of Little Lever. She was buried 11 May 1607 (M:215).

   Lawrence and Joan or Jane were the parents of (H; M:206): THOMAS, d. Dec 1626; JAMES of Snidale (or Sneithell), b. 1591, d. 1650; ROGER of Rufford, b. 1583; WILLIAM of Adlington, b. 1595, d. 1650; ELIZABETH, m. Henry Johnson of Appleton; HELEN, m. George Holcroft of Hurst; and JANE, m. [-?-] Holland.

5. THOMAS WORTHINGTON, son of Lawrence (4) and Jane, d. Dec 1626. He m. Agnes, dau. of John Gillibrand of Chorley. Thomas and Agnes Worthington of Adlington were the parents of (H; I:43, 47, 52, 58): (prob.) ROGER, b. c1593; LAWRENCE, b. c1598 [he was 67 in April 1665 when he signed the Visitation; he m. twice and had issue]; WILLIAM; JANE; ELIZA; MARGARET, bapt. at Standish Church 1 April 1602; ANNE, bapt. at Standish on 23 April 1604; DOROTHY; ALICE, bapt. at Standish on 22 March 1607; ELLEN; and MARY, bapt. 8 July 1611.

6. ROGER WORTHINGTON of Rufford, son of Lawrence (4) and Jane, was listed in the 1664/5 Visitation of Lancashire (H). As the third son, it is entirely possible that he was the Roger Worthington who was b. c1544 in Standish, Lancs., Eng., and d. in 1604. On 17 May 1568, in Standish, he m. Margaret Brownlowe (I:112). She was b. 1547, d. 25 Feb 1640 (G). Either she or another Margaret, wife of Roger Worthington of Manchester, was buried in the Cathedral on 2 April 1611 (B:393).

Roger and Margaret were the parents of (I:11, 14, 14, 16, 18, 20, 24, 27, 29): ANNA, bapt. 27 Aug 1558; THOMAS, bapt. 24 Sep 1570; AGNES, bapt. 18 May 1573; GILBERT, bapt. 27 March 1575; JANE, bapt. 4 Feb 1576/7; MARGARET, bapt. 7 Oct 1581; ELIZABETH, bapt. 13 Jan 1583/4; and NICHOLAS, bapt. 4 Sep 1585.

7. ROGER WORTHINGTON, of Worthington (or Rufford: G), in the Parish of Standish, Lancs., prob. son of Thomas (5) and Agnes, was b. 1593 in Manchester, Eng. However no baptismal record could be found for him there or in Standish.

A Roger Worthington of Thomas and Jane, was bapt. 3 Jan 1596/7 at Standish (I:38), but he was prob. too young to have been the Roger who m. Katherine Heywood of Heywood, Lancs., on 25 Feb 1611/2. Roger Worthington, woollen draper, of Manchester, was buried 23 Aug 1649 (K:597).

On 25 Feb 1611/2 he m. at Manchester Cathedral Katherine Heywood (B:471). Katherine Heywood of Heywood, Lancs., bapt. 25 Oct 1587, and as widow of Roger Worthington, was buried on 19 Feb 1652 (K:609).

Roger and Katherine were living in Manchester, where he is referred to as a linen draper.

Roger and Katherine were the parents of (A; G; J:18, 39, 53, 70, 93, 104; K:345, 359, 417, 451, 492, 501, 584): JOHN, bur. 4 Aug 1616; JOHN, D.D., bapt 8 Feb 1617/8 in Manchester (He was Master of Jesus College, Cambridge, and Vice Chancellor of the University, and d. 26 Nov 1671); ANN, bur. 30 Jan 1618; EDMUND, bapt. 27 Aug 1620, bur. 16 Nov 1625; WILLIAM, b. 24 March 1621/2, d. 26 Feb 1636; FRANCIS, bapt. 15 Oct 1624 at Manchester; KATHERINE, bapt. 16 Dec 1627, bur. 17 May 1647 at Roger Worthington's, m. 31 Aug 1646 James Peak of Warington; SAMUEL, bapt. 16 Jan 1627/8, d. 12 March 1645/6, Student at Cambridge; and ROBERT, bapt. 17 April 1629, bur. 22 April 1638.

8. FRANCIS WORTHINGTON, son of Roger (7) and Katherine, was b. 10 Sep 1624 in Manchester, Eng., and bapt. 15 Oct 1624 (B). He was a draper or tailor at Manchester. On 15 Sep 1646 at Prestwick, Manchester, he m. Mrs. Sarah Byram, Spinster, dau. of Ed. Byram of Manchester. She was bapt. 20 March 1625 at Manchester, and buried 30 Oct 1664 (G). The records of Manchester Cathedral show that Francis Worthington married Sarah Browne [*sic*] on 15 Sep 1646 (J:333). Sarah, wife of Francis Worthington of Manchester, woollen draper, was bur. 3 Oct 1664 (K:145).

Francis was too young to have been the Francis, father of the Thomas who was bapt. 21 April 1636 (J:161)

Francis and Sarah were the parents of (A: cites C: Register of Prestwick, but see J:246, 255, 262; K:582; L:10, 15, 149): [-?-], bur. 17 Feb 1646/7; KATHERINE, bapt. 30 Jan 1647/8 at Manchester; SARAH, bapt. 14 Oct 1649 at Manchester; Capt. JOHN, b. 1650 at Sharston Hall, Manchester, bapt. 5 Oct 1651 at Manchester; FRANCIS, b. 2 April 1657; FRANCES, d. 23 Sep 1678 at Manchester; MARY, b. 20 Oct 1658 in Manchester, and was bur. 7 July 1665.

9. Capt. JOHN WORTHINGTON, son of Francis (8) and Sarah (Byram), was b. 1650 at Sharston Hall, Manchester, and bapt. 2 Oct 1651 at the Cathedral in Manchester (G). He d. 6 April 1701 in MD. He m. Sarah Howard, d. 21 Dec 1726. She was a daughter of Matthew Howard, Jr., by his wife Sarah Dorsey. Sarah Howard Worthington m. 2nd on 16 Dec 1701, John Brice.

John Worthington and his wife Sarah were the par. of (A): JOHN, Jr., b. 12 Jan 1689; THOMAS, b. 8 Jan 1692; WILLIAM, b. 16 April 1694; SARAH, b. 10 Jan 1697, m. Nicholas Ridgely; CHARLES, b. 1699, d. in infancy; CHARLES, b. 20 Oct 1701, d. BA Co., 1774; m. 1st, Hammutal Hammond; and 2nd, Sarah Chew.

THE WIAT/WYATT FAMILY

Refs.: A: J. Cave-Brown. *The History of Boxley Parish: The Abbey, Rood of Grace, and Abbots; The Clergy; The Church, Monuments and Registers; Including an Account of the Wiat Family, and of the trial on Peneden Heath in 1076*. Maidstone: Printed for the Author by E. J. Dickinson, 1892. B: William Colwell Bibb. Six Wyatts of Kent. Anniston [AL]: Higginbothom, Inc., c1982.

Baptisms from the Registers of Boxley (A).
Hawte, Frances, dau. of Timothy, 14 Sep 1595.
Wyatt, Thomas, son of George, armiger, 4 March 1603.
Wyatt, Henry, son of Francis, Kt., 4 April 1619.
Wyatt, George, son of Sir Francis, 8 Sep 1620.
Wyatt, Robert, son of William, 22 July 1621.
Wyatt, Eleanor, dau. of Henry, gent., 1 Sep 1624.
Wyatt, Thomas, son of Hawte, 15 Oct 1626.
Wyatt, Anna, dau. of Hawte, 19 Feb 1631.

Marriages from the Registers of Boxley (A).
Wyat, Mariannam, and William Bened, 20 Jan 1560.

Burials from the Registers of Boxley (A).
Wyatt, Edward, "generosus," buried 26 Nov 1590.
Wyatt, Katherine, "virgo," 10 May 1608.
Wyatt, Anna, dau. of George, "generosus," 7 Sep 1611.
Wyatt, Cecila, "virgo," 20 July 1614.
Wyatt, Helen, wife of John Finch, 7 Dec 1623.
Wyatt, George, Armiger, 1 Sep 1624 (son of Sir Thomas Wyatt who had been beheaded by Queen Mary in 1554).
Wyatt, Henry, M.A., and minister, 10 day of new year/1 Jan 1624.

Wyatt, Elizabeth, wife of Hawte, 31 Oct 1626.
Wyatt, Anne. "ejusdem uxor" of Hawte, ult. Feb 1631.
Wyatt, William, son of Sir Francis and Lady Margaret, 24 March 1636.
Wyatt, George, son of Sir Francis and Lady Margaret, 12 Oct 1637.
Wyatt, Mr. Hawte, Vicar of this Parish, and son of George Wyatt, 1 Aug 1638.
Wyatt, Domina (Jane, widow of George), 1 March 1644.
Wyatt, Sir Francis, Kt., 24 Jan 1644.

1. ADAM WIAT of Southange, m. [-?-], dau. of Wigton. They were the parents of (A: chart opp. 133): WILLIAM.

2. WILLIAM WIAT of Southange, son of Adam (1), m. Jane, dau. of Roger Bailiffe of Barnsley. They were the parents of (A: chart opp. 133): ROBERT.

3. ROBERT WIAT, of Southange, son of William (2), m. Jane, dau. of Richard Skipwith of Southange. They were the parents of (A: chart opp. 133): ANNA.

4. ANNA WIAT, dau. of Robert (3), m. Galfridus (Geoffrey) Wiat. They were the parents of (A: chart opp. 133): RICHARD.

5. RICHARD WIAT of Southange, son of Galfridus and Anne (4) (Wiat) Wiat, m. Margaret, dau. of William Bailiffe *als.* Clarke of Southange. They were the parents of (A: chart opp. 133): Sir HENRY.

6. Sir HENRY WIAT of Allington Castle, son of Richard (5) and Margaret, d. 1537, having been imprisoned at one time by Richard III. He is buried at Milton, near Gravesend. He m. Anna, dau. of John Skinner, Co. Surrey.
      Sir Henry and Anna were the parents of (A: chart opp. 133): Sir THOMAS, The Elder.

7. Sir THOMAS WIAT, The Elder, of Allington Castle and Boxley, son of Sir Henry (6) and Anna, was b. in 1503 and d. on 10 Oct 1542; he was buried at Sherborne. He m. Elizabeth, dau. of Thomas Brooke, Lord Cobham (who had been beheaded in 1537). Elizabeth was a descendant of King Edward I. She m. as her 2nd husband, Sir Edward Warner, Kt. (*PASC*:288).
      Sir Thomas and Elizabeth were the parents of (A: chart opp. 133): Sir THOMAS, The Younger.

8. Sir THOMAS WIAT, The Younger, son of Sir Thomas (7) and Elizabeth, was b. c1522, and m. in 1537 Jane, dau. of Sir William Hawte of Bourne and Wavering by Mary, dau. of Sir Richard Guildford, Kt. (*PASC*:288).
      Sir Thomas led an armed conspiracy against Queen Mary when she m. Philip II of Spain, but the plot failed, and Wiat was beheaded in the Tower of London on 11 April 1554 (*PASC*:288).
      Sir Thomas and Jane were the parents of ten children, only three of whom left issue (A: chart opp. 133; *PASC*:288): GEORGE, d. 1644; ANNA, m. Sir Roger Twisden (They were ancestors of **Sir Henry Vane**, Governor of Massachusetts Bay, 1636-1637, and of Philadelphia Pelham who m. Francis Howard, 5th Baron Howard of Effinbgham,

Gov. of VA: see *MCS5*: Line 72, and *RD500*:123); and JANE, m. Sir Charles Scott of Egerton.

9. GEORGE WIAT, son of Sir Thomas (8) and Jane, was b. 1550 and d. 1644. He m. on 8 Oct 1582 Jane, dau. of Thomas Finch of Wastwell by his wife Katherine. Jane also d. 1644 (PASC:288).

George Wiat had Boxley Manor restored to him in 13 Elizabeth.

George and Jane were the parents of (A: chart opp. 133): Sir FRANCIS; Rev. HAWTE; and ELEANOR, d. 1623, m. in 1612, Sir John Finch, Lord Finch of Fordwick, who d. 1660.

10. JANE WIAT, dau. of Sir Thomas Wiat the Younger (8), m. in 1537 Sir Charles Scott of Egerton who d. 1617. A younger son of Sir Reynold and Mary (Tuke) Scott, he purchased the Manor of Egerton in Godmersham (*PASC*:112).

Charles and Jane had two sons and two daus. including (*PASC*:112): DEBORAH, m. William Fleete of Chatham, Kent; their son **Capt. Henry Fleete** was one of the Adventurers who came to MD with the Ark and the Dove expedition.

11. Sir FRANCIS WIAT, Kt., of Boxley Abbey, and Governor of VA, son of George (9) and Jane, d. 1644. He m. Margaret, dau. of Sir Samuel Sandys, Kt. She d. 1687.

Sir Francis and Margaret were the parents of (A: chart opp. 133): HENRY, b. 1618; EDWIN, b. 1629, m. and had two children, both of whom d. s.p.; and ELIZABETH, b. 1630, d. 1711, m. Thomas Bosville Of Little Mote, Eynsford.

12. Rev. HAWTE WYATT, son of George (9) and Jane, was b. 1596 and was bur. at Boxley at 1 Aug 1638. He m. 1st, on 6 Feb 1618/9, Barbara Mitford; and 2nd, Elizabeth [-?-] who d. 1626; and 3rd, Anne Lee, who d. 1632. He was Vicar of Boxley (*PASC*:289).

Hawte Wyatt matriculated at Queen's College, Oxford, on 25 Oct 1611, when he was age 17. He went to VA with his bro. in 1621, and was minister at Jamestown from 1621 to 1625. He returned to Eng., and was Vicar of Boxley until his death (*PASC*:289).

Rev. Hawte Wyatt had two sons by his first marriage, one by his second marriage, and two children by his third marriage. He was the father of (*PASC*:289; B) (by Barbara Mitford): **GEORGE, bapt. 12 Dec 1619, and settled in York Co., VA**; **EDWARD, b. c1621, settled at Boxley, Gloucester Co., VA**; THOMAS, bapt. at Boxley 15 Oct 1626, and buried there on 10 April 1627; (by Anne): JOHN, b. 1630, living in 1648/9; and ANNE, bapt. at Boxley on 14 Feb 1631/2, living 1648/9.

Unplaced:

WYATT, Sir DUDLEY, came to VA (*MCS5*; Line 47).

WYATT, NICHOLAS, who m. Damaris [-?-], and settled in MD. Many researchers have tried to place Nicholas in this Wiat Family of Boxley, but no documentation has been found to establish the claim.

Some writers have suggested he was a son of Anthony of Charles City Co., but that Nicholas was living long after Nicholas of MD died.

Nicholas and Damaris were the parents of: SARAH, m. Edward Dorsey, Jr.

Heraldic Glossary

The following definitions of heraldic terms are included to assist the reader in determining exactly what the coat of arms may have looked like. Definitions could not be found for two of the terms used in the blazons: *Excausion* and *Flint-stone*. Every effort was made to compile definitions that could be understood by anyone who does not have a knowledge of heraldry.

Sources used for definitions:

Friar, Stephen, ed. *A Dictionary of Heraldry*. New York: Harmony Books, 1987.

Parker, James A. *A Glossary of Terms Used in Heraldry*. Repr.: Rutland, VT: Tuttle, 1970.

Rothery, Guy Cadogan. *Concise Encyclopedia of Heraldry*. Originally published in 1915 by Stanley Paul & Co. as *An ABC of Heraldry*. Repr. Studio Editions Ltd.: London, 1994.

Zieber, Eugene. *Heraldry in America*. (1908). Repr.: Baltimore: Genealogical Publishing Co., 1977.

Addorsed: Said of two animals, or objects such as axes or keys, placed back to back.

Affrontee: Said of animate creatures when placed full face.

Annulet: A ring; as a mark of cadency it represents the fifth son.

Antelope: An animal that has the head of an heraldic tiger, tusks, serrated horns, the body of an antelope, a lion's tail, and tufts down its spine. It is usually described as an heraldic antelope, to distinguish it from the natural animal, which may also be used in heraldry.

Argent: The color silver; often depicted as white.

Armed: Used to describe the teeth, tusks, horns, claws, and talons of birds or beasts when they are of a different color from that of the body.

Azure: The color blue.

Badge: A device not worn on the helm, or as a crest, but intended to be worn on clothing or placed on property.

Banded: When a sheaf of wheat or other object(s) are tied together by a band of a different color, they are said to be banded of that color.

Bar: A horizontal stripe across the shield that occupies one-fifth of the field.

Barnacles: Instruments used to curb horses.

Barrulets: A diminutive of the bar.

Barry: A field that is horizontally divided into an even number of strips.

Bars gemmel: A pair of barrulets.

Base: The lower portion of the shield.

Beaked: Used when the beak of a bird is of a different color than the rest of the bird.

Bend: A broad band, one-third the width of the shield, stretching from dexter chief to sinister base.

Bend sinister: A bend stretching from dexter base to sinister chief.

Bezant: A roundel Or, representing a coin of Byzantium.

Bezantee: Used to describe a shield that is covered with bezants.

Billets: Small oblong figures.

Boar: the wild boar.

Bordure: A border that occupies one-fifth of the shield.

Bouget (or **Water Bouget**): A yoke with two large skins attached, used for carrying water to an army.

Bridled: Having a bridle.

Buckle: A belt buckle, circular or lozenge in shape.

Caboshed: An animal's head shown affrontee and cut off with no part of the neck showing. When the animal is a lion or a leopard, the term "face" is used.

Cadency: A system of varying the original arms of the family so that junior branches have slightly different arms than the senior branch.

Caltrap: A device intended to maim horses, so constructed that when thrown on the ground, one of its four points would always remain upright.

Canton: A device smaller than a quarter; it may itself be charged.

Charge: Any device placed on a shield.

Chaplet: A wreath of flowers.

Chequy: Divided into two or more rows of squares of alternating colors.

Chevron: A charge resembling an inverted letter V (or the rafters of a house), that occupies one-fifth of the shield.

Chevronel: A diminutive of the chevron.

Chief: A horizontal band covering approximately the top one-third of the shield.

Cinquefoil: A charge consisting of five leaves (compared with the three leaves of a shamrock or trefoil). The center is often pierced.

Collared: Having a plain collar.

Color: Argent, Azure, Gules, Purpure, Sable, and Vert. See also Metal and Fur.

Combatant: Two rampant beasts shown facing each other, as if they are ready to do combat.

Cornish chough: A member of the crow family; a bird Sable, with legs Gules.

Cotise (or Cottise): A narrow strip, usually borne in pairs on either side of a bend.

Couchant: An animal lying on all four paws, but with head erect.

Counterchanged: Used when a shield is divided by any of the lines of partition and the metals and colors of the shield and any charges are reversed on either side of the line.

Counterembattled: Embattled on both sides.

Couped: Cut off by a straight line.

Courant: An animal that is running at speed.

Crescent: A half-moon with the horns pointing upwards.

Crest: A three-dimensional device mounted on a helmet and so depicted on the coat of arms. At one time not all crests were three dimensional.

Crined: Used to describe the hair on a man's head or the mane of an animal when it is a different color than the rest of the charge.

Cross: A charge that occupies one-fifth of the shield unless it is charged, when it occupies one-third of the shield. There are many varieties, derived from variations in how the arms of the cross terminate.

Cross bottony: A cross whose arms end in three buttons or trefoils.

Cross crosslet: A plain cross in which each of the four arms ends in another cross.

Cross flory: A cross whose arms end in fleurs-de-lis.

Cross moline: A cross whose ends are bifurcated, and turned down like the two side lobes of a fleur-de-lis.

Cross patonce: A cross whose arms expanded, but whose arms end somewhat like a cross flory.

Cross pattee: A cross whose arms are expanded, ending in a straight line before reaching the edge of the shield.

Crowned: Having a crown.

Cuffed: Having cuffs that are of a different color than the sleeve.

Dancetty: A zig-zag line of partition; there are fewer indentations than if the line is described as indented.

Demi-: Half of anything; when applied to an animal, as a demi-lion, the upper fore half is intended; when describing an inanimate object, the dexter half per pale is meant.

Dexter: The right side of the shield as carried by the knight in front of him, but on the spectator's left.

Difference: Any change or addition to a coat of arms used to indicate cadency.

Displayed: Said of an eagle shown with its wings expanded.

Divided: Said of a shield or charge made up of two or more colors.

Doubled: The lining of a mantling.

Ducal coronet: (also crest coronet): This is not the coronet of a duke, but a coronet made up of four strawberry leaves or fleurs-de-lis, with three visible.

Ducally crowned: Wearing a ducal coronet.

Eagle: A bird noted for its sharp beak, outstretched wings, and long sharp talons or claws.

Elevated: Pointing upwards.

Embattled: (or crenelated): Decorated with an outline of alternate depressions and square projections as a fortified wall.

Embowed: Bent. When applied to arms or legs, the elbow or knee is to the dexter.

En arriere: With back to the spectator.

En crey: Possibly en croix, or in cross; placed in the form of a cross.

Engrailed: A partition line formed by a row of small concave indentations, the points turned outward.

Environed: Encircled by.

Eradicated: Said of a tree torn out by its roots.

Erased: Torn off with a jagged edge.

Erect: Upright; used only for charges that are not normally so.

Ermine: One of the furs, Argent with sable spots.

Escallop: A scallop shell usually depicted with the point upwards.

Escutcheon: A shield.
Escutcheon of pretense: A small shield borne in the center of a larger one.
Estoile: A star with wavy points, or with alternate wavy points. There are usually six points unless another number is specified.

Falchion: A sword with a broad blade and a curved front edge.
Fess: A broad horizontal band across the middle of the shield.
Fetterlock: A shackle for a horse.
Fired: Ignited.
Fitchee: Having the foot end in a point; usually used to describe a cross.
Flank: A side, as a side of the escutcheon.
Flaunches: a charge consisting of a pair of concave indentations, one on each side of the shield.
Fleurs-de-lis: A stylized lily having three lobes.
Floretty: A field strewn with tiny fleurs-de-lis.
Flory: Said of charges terminating in, or decorated with, fleurs-de-lis.
Flory counter-flory: Charges decorated with fleurs-de-lis alternately on either side.
Fretty: A field made up of interlaced bendlets and bendlets sinister.
Fur: One type of tincture. The two most common furs in heraldry are Ermine and Vair (q.v.).

Gamb: The leg of an animal.
Garb: A sheaf of wheat unless another type of grain is stated.
Garnished: Ornamented with a color other than the main part of the object.
Gauntlet: A glove of mail (armor).
Gauntleted: Said of hand wearing a glove.
Gorged: Encircled about the throat with a collar or a crown, etc.
Goutee: Strewn with drops of liquid. The tinctures may vary.
Grenade: A spherical ball with flames coming out of the top, a bomb; sometimes used to mean a pomegranate.
Guardant: An animal that has its head turned to face the observer.
Gules: The color red.
Guttee: See Goutee, above.
Gyronny: Used when the field is divided into triangular pieces radiating from the center; a shield divided per cross and per saltire, creating eight triangular sections. (The usual number of sections is eight, but there may be eight, ten, or twelve.)

Hand: The palm, thumb and fingers cut off at the wrist.
Haurient: Said of a fish depicted with its head upwards.
Hind: A female deer.
Humettee: See couped.
Hurt: A roundel or disc Azure.

Indented: A line of partition like dancetty, but with more teeth.

Interlaced: Interwoven; sometime called Braced.

Invected: A line of partition, the reverse of engrailed because the points go into the charge.

Issuant: Emerging from behind, or proceeding from.

Keys: The emblem of St. Peter; may be borne singly or in pairs.

Langued: Describing the tongue of a creature.

Leopard: Originally, any lion that was not rampant; more recently, the zoological animal.

Lined: Having an inside lining of a different color than the outside; having chains or cords attached.

Lodged: Used of a stag that is couchant.

Lozenge: A four cornered diamond shape figure, resembling the diamond in modern playing cards.

Lozengy: A field or charge composed of lozenges.

Lure: Two wings with their tips downward, joined by a line and a wing, originally used by falconers who tossed it into the air to decoy hawks

Mail: Armor.

Mantling: A piece of cloth hanging down the back of the helmet, originally designed to protect the back of the knight's head from sun or sword stroke. It is often depicted as being cut and twisted so that it hangs down both sides of the shield.

Martlet: A swallow or martin depicted with a short beak, long wings and thighs, but no legs or claws. As a mark of cadency it is used to denote the fourth son.

Metal: The heraldic tinctures Or (gold, or yellow) and Argent (silver, or white).

Millrind: Sometimes called a fer-de-moline. The piece of iron that upholds the moving millstone. It may be depicted in a variety of ways.

Mitre, Miter: A headdress denoting the rank of bishops, abbots, and priors.

Motto: A word, phrase, or sentence placed on a scroll. The scroll is usually below the shield, but sometimes it is found above the crest.

Mound: (Also Mount): A section at the bottom of the shield with curved sides, colored Vert, representing a hill or mountain of grass. Sometimes the hill is divided into three lobes.

Mullet: A star of five points unless another number is specified; if pierced it represents the rowel of a spur. See also Estoile.

Mural coronet: A coronet formed of battlements masoned (the mortar is a different color than the coronet).

Muzzled: Said of bears or other animals whose mouths are strapped shut with strips of leather or metal.

Nebulee: A line of partition representing clouds.

Ogress: A roundel Sable.

Or: The color gold, often depicted as yellow.

Pale: A horizontal stripe occupying one-third of the shield.

Pallet: One-half of a pale, and usually borne in pairs.

Paly: Used when the shield is divided into an even number of horizontal stripes, the first of which is usually a metal and the second a color.

Party: Used when the shield is divided or parted.

Passant: Used when an animal, usually a lion, is walking past, with his head straight before him (unless the term guardant is used).

Pellet: A roundel Sable.

Pellety: Strewn with pellets.

Pendant: Hanging from, or an object that hangs from another.

Pennon: A flag that ends in a point; it should not be charged with any arms, but may bear a crest, a badge, or motto.

Per chevron: A shield divided in the shape of a chevron (an inverted letter "V").

Per fess: A shield divided by a horizontal line across the middle.

Per pale: A shield divided by a vertical line down the middle.

Pheon: The head of a dart, barbed, point downward (unless otherwise specified), and engrailed on the inner side.

Pheoned: Used to describe arrows when the heads are of a different color than the shaft.

Pierced: Said of any charge that is perforated so that the field shows through.

Plate: A roundel Argent.

Plummet: A metal weight attached to a cord, used by mariners to test the depth of the water and by builders to make sure that a wall is perpendicular.

Powdered: The same as semee (q.v.).

Powit: A tadpole.

Proper: Said of a charge that is shown in its natural color.

Purpure: the color purple.

Quarterly: Said of a shield divided into (usually) four sections.

Queue-fourchee: An animal's tail that is forked, or doubled.

Raguly: An ordinary or the limb of a tree having projecting pieces alternating on each side, and couped.

Rampant: An animal rearing on its hind legs.

Reflecting: Bent back; applied to a cord or chain attached to the collar of an animal and curved over its back.

Reguardant: Said of an animal that is looking over its shoulder.

Respecting: Said of two beasts that are facing each other.

Rising: Said of a bird about to take flight.

Roundel: A flat colored disc.

Sable: The color black.

Saltire: A cross whose arms are diagonal; a cross of St. Andrew.

Saltirewise: Said of charges placed in the form of a saltire.

Saracen's head: The head of a man Sable, with a wreath of twisted linen across his forehead.

Segreant: Said of a griffin that is rampant.

Sejant: The color black.

Semee: Sprinkled with small charges.

Sinister: The left hand side of a shield as carried by a knight, but it is to the observer's right.

Slipped: Used to describe the stalk and leaves of trefoils, flowers, and other plants.

Sphere: A ball, globe, or a representation of a model of the Earth.

Statant: Said of an animal that is standing still with all four paws or feet on the ground.

Stringed: Applied to musical instruments or weapons when the strings are of a different color.

Supporters: Figures placed on either side of a shield appearing to hold it up.

Surmounted: Said of a bearing that is placed over another one of a different color.

Sustaining: Or Sustained, said of a charge supported by another.

Talbot: A dog having the body of a mastiff, long ears of a bloodhound, and the head of a hound.

Tincture: A metal, color, or fur used in heraldry.

Torse: French term for a crest wreath.

Tower: A structure of several stories having but one door.

Trefoil: A leaf with three lobes.

Trippant: Used to describe a stag or hind that is walking.

Truncheon: Short staff, a baton.

Turned Up: Having the edge folded outward so that the tincture is shown.

Unicorn: An animal with the body of a horse, but with cloven feet, a lion's tail, the beard of a goat, and a long spiraling horn on its forehead.

Vair: A fur made up of pieces of alternating colors, usually Argent and Azure.

Vert: The color green.

Vested: Clothed or habited.

Volant: Flying horizontally.

Wavy: A line of partition like waves, undulating; it always has three risings.

Wreathed: Decorated with a wreath, garland, or chaplet; as a figure wreathed about the loins and temples.

Bibliography

SOURCES AND ABBREVIATIONS

AA Co.: Anne Arundel Co., MD.

AACR: F. Edward Wright. *Anne Arundel Co. Church Records of the 17th and 18th Centuries.* FLP, no d.

AAJU: ANNE ARUNDEL CO. COURT Judgment Record (MSA C 91).

AALR: ANNE ARUNDEL CO. COURT Land Records (MSA C 97). See also *Abstracts of Land Records of Anne Arundel County, Maryland. 1662-1719.* 3 vols. Abstracted by Rosemary B. Dodd and Patricia Bausell. 1662-1719. Pasadena: The Anne Arundel Co. Genealogical Society.

AAWB: ANNE ARUNDEL CO. REGISTER OF WILLS Will Book (MSA CM 122).

ALCA: Alumni Cantabrigensis. Comp. by J. A. Venn. Cambridge University Press, 1927.

ALOX: Alumni Oxoniensis, 1500-1714. Comp. by Joseph Foster. Oxford: Parker and Co., 1891.

Ancestors of American Presidents. By Gary Boyd Roberts. Santa Clarita: Carl Boyer, 3rd, 1995.

AMG: The [Annapolis] *Maryland Gazette* [newspaper]. See also Karen Green. *The Maryland Gazette, 1727-1761.* Galveston: Frontier Press, 1989.

Annapolis Maryland Families. By Robert McIntire. 2 vols. Baltimore: Gateway Press, Inc.

APPD: J. Fred Dorman. *Adventurers of Purse and Person, 1607-1625.* 3rd Ed.

APPJ: Annie Lash Jester. *Adventurers of Purse and Person, 1607-1625.* Sponsored by the Order of First Families of Virginia, 1956.

ARCA: Archaelogia Cantiana: Being Transactions of the Kent Archaeological Society. London. [periodical].

ARMD: The Archives of Maryland. Vol. 1 - . Baltimore: The Maryland Historical Society, 1883 - .

AWAP: Peter Wilson Coldham. *American Wills and Administrations in the Prerogative Court of Canterbury, 1610-1857.* GPC, 1989.

AWLH: R. S. Boumphrey, C. Roy Hudleston, and J. Hughhes. *An Armorial for Westmorland and Lonsdale.* Printed for Lake District Museum Trust and Cumberland and Westnorland Antiquarian and Archaeological Society, 1975.

AWPL: Peter Wilson Coldham. *American Wills Proved in London, 1611-1775.* GPC, 1992.

B.A.: Bachelor of Arts.

BA: The Baltimore American [newspaper].

BA Co.: Baltimore Co., MD.

BAAB: BALTIMORE CO. REGISTER OF WILLS Administration Bonds (MSA C 264).

BAAD: BALTIMORE CO. REGISTER OF WILLS Administration Accounts (MSA CM 127).

BACP: BALTIMORE CO. COURT Proceedings (MSA C 400).

BACT: BALTIMORE CO. COURT Chattel Records (MSA C 298); also at MHS.

BADB: LAND OFFICE: Baltimore Co. Debt Book (MSA. S 12).

BAF: Burke's American Families with British Ancestry (1939). Repr. GPC, 1977.

BALR: BALTIMORE CO. COURT Land Records (MSA C 352). See also: *BALRb: Baltimore County, Maryland, Deed Abstracts, 1659-1750*. By Robert Barnes. FLP. *BALRs: Baltimore County Land Records, 1665-1687*. By Louis Dow Scisco. GPC.

BAML: BALTIMORE CO. COURT Marriage Licenses (MSA CM 174).

BAPA: Records of St. Paul's Parish. 2 Vols. By Bill and Martha Reamy. FLP, 1988.

Barbados Records: Baptisms, 1637-1800. By Joanne McRee Sanders. GPC, 1984.

Barbados Records: Wills and Administrations. Comp. and Ed. by Joanne McRee Sanders. 3 vols. Houston: Sanders Historical Publications, 1979-1981.

BARD7: Charles H. Browning. *Americans of Royal Descent*. 7th ed. (1911). Repr.: GPC, 1986.

Barnes, Robert. *British Roots of Maryland Families*. GPC, 1999.

BARP: Henry C. Peden, Jr. *Revolutionary Patriots of Baltimore Town and Baltimore County, Maryland, 1775-1783*. FLP, 1988.

BATH 1: St. Thomas' Parish Registers, 1732-1850. By Bill Reamy and Martha Reamy. FLP, 1987.

BAWB: BALTIMORE CO. REGISTER OF WILLS Will Book (MSA C 435).

BCF: Robert W. Barnes. *Baltimore County Families, 1659-1759*. GPC, 1989.

BCMR: Henry C. Peden. *Methodist Records of Baltimore City, 1799-1839*. 2 vols. FLP, 1994.

BCPR: Presbyterian Records of Baltimore City, Maryland, 1765-1840. By Henry C. Peden, Jr. FLP, 1995.

B.D.: Bachelor of Divinity.

BDEP: Sir Bernard Burke. *A Genealogical History of the Dormant, Abeyant, Forfeited and Extinct Peerages of the British Empire* (1883). Rewrinted Baltimore: Genealogical Publishing Co., Inc., 1985.

BDI: Baltimore Daily Intelligencer [newspaper].

BDML: Edward C. Papenfuse et al. *Biographical Dictionary of the Maryland Legislature, 1635-1789*. 2 vols. New York: The Johns Hopkins University Press.

BDR: Baltimore Daily Repository [newspaper].

BEDB: John Burke and John Bernard Burle. *A Genealogical and Heraldic History of the Extinct and Dormant Baronetcies of England, Scotland, and Ireland*. 1841. Repr.: London and Baltimore: Burke's Peerage/Genealogical Publishing Co., 1985.

Berry, *Essex*. See *ESBE*.

Berry, *Hants*. See *HABE*.

Berry, *Kent*. See *KEBE*.

Berry, *Sussex*. See *SUBE*.

Betham's Baronetage: The Baronetage of England. By William Betham. 5 vols. Ipswich: 1801-1805.

Betham's Genealogical Table: Genealogical Table of the Sovereigns of the World ... . By William Betham. London: W. Bennett, 1795.

BFD: Maryland Prerogative Court Balance Books (of Final Distributions). (MSA S 533).

BFG: The [Baltimore] *Federal Gazette*. [newspaper].

BFI: The [Baltimore] *Federal Intelligencer and Baltimore Daily Gazette* [newspaper].

BGAS: Bristol and Gloucestershire Archaeological Society: Records Section.

------- 1: *Marriage Bonds for the Diocese of Bristol, Excluding the Diocese of Dorset, Volume I, 1637-1700*. Trans. by Denzil Hollis, ed. by Elizabeth Ralph. The Society, 1952.

------ 3: *Registers of the Church of St. Augustine the Less, Bristol, 1577-1700.* Trans. and ed. by Arthur Sabin. The Society, 1956.

Blaydes. See *Genealogica* ... .

BLG: *Burke's Landed Gentry* (followed by the year of the edition).

BMG:[Baltimore] *Maryland Gazette or Baltimore Advertiser* [newspaper.]

BMGS: See *MGSB*.

BMJ: See *MJBA*.

BPR: *Bedfordshire Parish Registers*. Ed. by F. W. Emmison. Bedford: County Record Office, 1933-.

------ 7: "Knotting, 1592-1812," "Yelden, 1602-1812," et al.

------ 24: "Sharnbrook, 1596-1812." et al. 1941.

BRCO: Peter Wilson Coldham. *The Bristol Registers of Servants Sent to Foreign Plantations, 1654-1686*. GPC, 1988.

Browning: Charles H. Browning. *Some Colonial Dames of Royal Descent* (1900). Repr: GPC, 1969.

BRS: British Record Society. See *IL (Index Library)*.

Bruce: *Calendar of State Papers, Domestic Series of the Reign of Charles I, 1637*. Ed. by John Bruce. London: Longmans, Green, Reader, and Dyer, 1868.

Buck: See *PECD*.

Buckler, Charles Alban: *Bucleriana: Notices of the Family of Buckler*. By Charles Alban Buckler. London: Mitchell and Hughes, 1886.

Buckler, William Harold, and Katherine Hollenbach Buckler: *Buckleriana: Notices of the Family of Buckler*. By William Harold Buckler and Katherine Hollenbach Buckler. Baltimore: Gateway Press, 1988.

BULI: *The History and Antiquities of the County of Buckingham*. By George Lipscomb. London: J. & W. Robins, 1847.

Burke, Arthur: *Memorials of St. Margaret's Church, Westminster: The Parish Registers, 1539-1600*. Ed. by Arthur Meredyth Burke. London: Eyre and Spottiswoode, 1915.

Burke's Commoners: *A Genealogical and Heraldic History of The Commoners of Great Britain and Ireland* ... . Ed. by John Burke. 4 vols. 1833-37. Repr. Baltimore: GPC, 1977.

Burke's Family Records. Ed. by Ashworth P. Burke. 1897. Repr: Baltimore: Clearfield Co., 1965.

Burke's Peerage, 1956 ed.

BUWB: Bucks Co., PA, Will Book.

Cal. Doc. Scot.: Joseph Bain, ed. *Calendar of Documents Relating to Scotland, Preserved in Her Majesty's Public Record Office*. 4 vols. Edinburgh: Generak Register House, 1881-1888.

Calendar of Charter Rolls, 1226-1516. HMSO.

Calendar of Close Rolls, 1318-1323. HMSO.

Calendar of Inquisitiones Post Mortem, 1216-1377. 14 vols. 1865-.

Calendar of the Fine Rolls Preserved in the Public Record Office from Edward I, 1272- . Vols. 1-19. London: 1911-.

Calendar of Patent Rolls Preserved in the Public Record Office from Henry III, 1216- . London: 1901-.

Cawood: Richard Lawrence Cawood. *Who is This Fellow Cawood: A History of the Cawood Family*. No pl.: no pub., 1962.

CBE1: Peter Wilson Coldham. *Complete Book of Emigrants, 1607-1660*. GPC, 1987.

CBE2: ------. *Complete Book of Emigrants, 1661-1699*. GPC, 1990.

CBE3: ------. *Complete Book of Emigrants, 1700-1750*. GPC, 1992.

CBE4: ------. *Complete Book of Emigrants, 1751-1776*. GPC, 1993.

CBEB: ------. *Complete Book of Emigrants in Bondage, 1607-1775*. GPC, 1988.

CE Co.: Cecil Co., MD.

CECH: Henry C. Peden, Jr. *Cecil County, Maryland, Church Records*. FLP, 1990.

CELR: CECIL CO. COURT Land Records (MSA C 626).

CFAH: C. Roy Hudleston and R. S. Boumphrey. *Cumberland Families and Heraldry, With a Supplement to An Armorial for Westmorland and Lonsdale*. The Cumberland and Westmorland Antiquarian and Archaeological Society, 1978).

Charles County Gentry. By Harry Wright Newman. Repr. Baltimore: Clearfield Co., 1997.

Chauncey. See *HECH*.

CHLR: CHARLES CO. COURT Land Records (MSA C 670).

CHOR: George Ormerod and Thomas Helmsby. *The History of the County Palatine and City of Cheshire*. 3 vols. London: G. Routledge and Sons, 1882.

CHWB: CHARLES CO. REGISTER OF WILLS Will Book (MSA CM 412).

CLAY, J. W. *Extinct and Dormant Peerages of the Northern Counties*. London: 1913.

Clutterbuck. See *HECL*.

CMCR: Henry C. Peden, Jr. *A Collection of Maryland Church Records*. FLP, 1997.

CMSP: *Calendar of Maryland State Papers*. Annapolis: The Maryland Hall of Records Commission, 1943-1958.

------ *No. 1: The Black Books.*

------ *No. 3: The Brown Books.*

------ *No. 5: Executive Miscellanea.*

CN76: Bettie S. Carothers. *1776 Census of Maryland*. Lutherville: Carothers, n.d.

CN90: *Heads of Families at the First Census of the United States Taken in the Year 1790: Maryland*. Repr. GPC, 1972.

Collectanea Topographica et Genealogica. Vols. 1-8. 1834-1843.

Crawfurd: Gibbs Payne Crawfurd, ed. *Registers of the Parish of St. Mary's, Reading, Berkshire, 1538-1812*. Reading: Bradley and Son, 1892.

CRSM: Elise Greenup Jourdan. *Colonial Records of Southern Maryland*. FLP, 1997.

CS: The Chetham Society.

------ 38, 39, 40, 43, 57, 64: William Farrer, ed. *The Cockersand Chartulary. The Chartulary of Cockersand Abbey ... .* 3 vols. in 7 (Vols. 38, 39, 40, 43, 56, 57, 64). [Manchester]: *The Chetham Society*, 1898-1909.

------ 84-88: *The Visitation of Lancashire, 1664/5, taken by Sir William Dugdale.*

------ 104: n.s. Col. W. W. Chippindall. *A History of the Parish of Tunstall*. 1940.

CSM: *Chronicles of St. Mary's* [periodical].

CSSC: Mary Louise Donnelly. *Colonial Settlers of St. Clement's Bay, 1634-1780*. Ennis [TX]: The Author, 1996.

CV Co.: Calvert Co., MD.

CWAA: *Transactions of the Cumberland and Westmorland Antiquarian and Archaeological Society* [periodical].

CWFO: Joseph Foster, ed. *Pedigrees Recorded at the Heralds' Visitations of the Counties of Cumberland and Westmorland, Made by Richard St. George, Norroy King of Arms in 1615, and William Dugdale, Norroy King of Arms in 1666*. Kendal: T. Wilson.

CWPRS: *Cumberland and Westmorland Parish Register Society*.

------ 7: Henry Brierly, trans. *The Registers of Kendal, Westmorland, 1558-1687*. Vol. 7. 1921.

------ 8: ------. *The Registers of Kendal, Westmorland, Marriages and Burials 1558-1587. Baptisms 1591-1595*. Vol. 8. 1922.

------ 36: R. N. Birley, trans. *The Registers of Kendal, Part III, Baptisms, 1596-9, 1603-31, Marriages and Burials, 1691-9*. Vol. 36. 1952.

d'Angerville: See *LDBR*.

DCNI: Frank J. Metcalf and George H. Martin. *Marriages and Deaths, 1800-1820, from the National Intelligencer: Washington, DC*. Washington: The National Genealogical Society, 1968. Marriages and Deaths, 1821- , were published in the *National Genealogical Society Quarterly*.

DEGL: Stephen Glover and Thomas Noble. *The History and Gazetteer of the County of Derby*. 2 vols. 1829-1833.

DCRS: *Devon and Cornwall Record Society*.

------ 14: *The Register of Baptisms, Marriages, & Burials of the Parish of Ottery St. Mary, Devon, 1601-1837 (Part I, pp. 1-592)*. Trans. and ed. by H. Tapley-Soper. Exeter: The Society, 1908-1929.

------ 15: ------. (Part II, pp. 593-1157). Exeter: The Society, 1908-1929.

------ 26: *Register of Baptisms, Marriages and Burials of the Parish of St. Andrew's, Plymouth, Co. Devon, A. D. 1581-1618, with Baptisms 1619-1633*. Ed. by M. C. S. Cruwys. Exeter: The Society, 1954.

D.D.: Doctor of Divinity.

DNB: *The Dictionary of National Biography*. 21 vols. 1885-1900. Plus 4 supplements. 1908-1912.

DO Co.: Dorchester Co., MD.

DOLR: DORCHESTER CO. COURT Land Records (MSA C 710).

DOPR: *Dorset Parish Registers*. Phillimore's Parish Register Series

------ 7: "Netherbury Marriages." Ed. by Thomas M. Blagg. London: Phillimore and Co., 1914.

DSAC: David Dobson. *Scottish American Court Records, 1733-1783*. GPC, 1991.

DSBA: David Dobson. *Directory of Scots Banished to the American Plantations, 1650-1775*. GPC, 1983.

DSEW: Donald Whyte. *A Dictionary of Scottish Emigrants to the U. S. A.* (1972) Repr.: Baltimore: Clearfield Co., Inc., 1992.

DSSA: David Dobson. *Directory of Scottish Settlers in North America, 1625-1825*. Volume I. GPC, 1984.

DSSB: ------. ------. Volume II. GPC, 1984.

DSSC: ------. ------. Volume III. GPC, 1984.

DSSD: ------. ------. Volume IV. GPC, 1985.

DSSE: ------. ------. Volume V. GPC, Inc., 1985.

DSSF: ------. ------. Volume VI. GPC, 1986.

DSSG: ------. ------. Volume VII. GPC, 1993.

EAQG: William Wade Hinshaw, ed. *Encyclopedia of American Quaker Genealogy*. 7 Vols. 1936-1972. Vols. 1-6 repr.: GPC, 1969-1973.

ECEA: John Parsons Earwaker. *East Cheshire: Past and Present: or a History of the Hundred of Macclesfield in the County Palatine of Chester*. 2 vols. No pl.: no pub., 1877-1880.

Emison: James Wade Emison. *1962 Supplement to the Emison Families Revised*.

England: C. Walter England. *Joseph England and His Descendants*. Boyce, VA: Carr Publishing Co., 1975.

EONE1: *English Origins of New England Families from the New England Historic Genealogical Register. 1st ser*. 3 vols. GPC. 1984.

EONE2: *English Origins of New England Families from the New England Historic Genealogical Register. 2nd ser*. 3 vols. GPC. 1985.

ES: Isenburg, Wilhelm Karl, Prinz von, Frank, Baron Freytag von Loringhoven, and Detlev Schwennicke. *Europaische Stammtaffeln* New series, vol. 1-15. 1978-1993.

ESBE: Berry, William. *County Genealogies: Pedigrees of the Families in the County of Essex*. London: Sherwood Gilbert and Piper.

ESVR: F. Edward Wright. *Eastern Shore Vital Records*. 5 vols. FLP.

EWS: *The* [Elizabeth-Town] *Washington Spy* [newspaper}.

Farrar, William. *Early Yorkshire Charters*. Edinburgh: Ballentyne, Hanson & Co., 1914-.

Farrer, William. *Honours and Knights Fees*. 3 vols. London, 1923-1924.

FCLR: Frederick Co. Land Records; MSA.

Feet of Fines for Lancashire, 1196-1558. Ed. by William Farrer. Lancashire and Cheshire Record Society. Vols. 16, 39, 46, 50.

FFAA1: Donna Valley Russell. *First Families of Anne Arundel County, Maryland, 1649-1658. Volume 1: the Landowners*. New Market: Catoctin Press, 1999.

Final Concords of The County of Lancaster. Trans. by William Farrer. Printed for The Record Society of Lancashire and Cheshire, 1899-1910, Vols. 39, 46, 50.

Flowering: *Flowering of the Maryland Palatinate*. By Harry Wright Newman. 1961. Repr.: GPC, 1984.

FLP: Westminster: Family Line Publications.

FOLO: Joseph Foster. *London Marriage Licenses, 1521-1869*. London: bernard Quarritch, 1889.

FR Co.: Frederick Co., MD.

FR1 or FR2: T. J. C. Williams and Folger McKinsey. *History of Frederick Co., Maryland, With a Biographical Record of Representative Families*. (1910). Repr. Baltimore: Regional Publishing Co., 1979, with added index by Jacob Mehrling Holdcraft.

FRLR: FREDERICK CO. COURT Land Records (MSA CM485).

FRML: FREDERICK CO. COURT Marriage Licenses (MSA C 825).

GAVN: Robert K. Headley, Jr., *Genealogical Abstracts from 18th Century Virginia Newspapers*. GPC, 1987.

The Gen.: *The Genealogist* (periodical)

Genealogica Bedfordiensis. By Frederick Augustus [Frederick Augustus Page-Turner] Blaydes. London: The Chiswick Press, 1890.

GGE: Henry F. Waters. *Genealogical Gleanings in England*. 2 vols. 1901. Repr. GPC, 1969.

Ghirelli. See *LEMG*.

Gleanings from Maryland Newspapers, 1727-1775. By Robert Barnes. Lutherville: Bettie S. Carothers, 1976.

Gleanings from Maryland Newspapers, 1776-1785. By Robert Barnes. Lutherville: Bettie S. Carothers, 1975.

Gleanings from Maryland Newspapers, 1786-1790. By Robert Barnes. Lutherville: Bettie S. Carothers, 1975.

Gleanings from Maryland Newspapers, 1791-1795. By Robert Barnes. Lutherville: Bettie S. Carothers, 1976.

GM: The Genealogists' Magazine. There are several series, including the Official Organ of the Society of Genealogists.

GME: Genealogical and Memorial Encyclopedia of the State of Maryland: A Record of the Achievements of Her People in the Making of a Commonwealth & the Founding of a Nation under Editorial Supervision of Richard Henry Spencer. New York: The American Historical Society, Inc., 1919.

GPC: Baltimore: Genealogical Publishing Co., Inc.

GPR: Gloucestershire Parish Registers: Marriages. Ed. by W. P. R. Phillimore.

------ 1: "Rendcomb Marriages" et al.

Green: Karen Mauer Green. *The Maryland Gazette, 1727-1761.* Galveston: The Frontier Press, 1990.

GSV: The Green Spring Valley: Vol. 1: Its History and Heritage By Dawn F. Thomas. *Vol. 2: Genealogies.* By Robert Barnes. MHS, 1978.

Groome: Harry Connelly Groome. *The Groome Family and Connections: A Pedigree with Biographical Sketches.* Philadelphia: J. B. Lippincott, 1907.

GVFT: Genealogies of Virginia Families from Tyler's Quarterly. 4 vols. GPC.

GVFV: Genealogies of Virginia Families from the Virginia Magazine of History and Biography. 5 vols. GPC, 1981.

GVFW: Genealogies of Virginia Families from the William and Mary College Quarterly. 5 vols. GPC, 1982.

HA Co.: Harford Co., MD.

HABE: William Berry. *County Genealogies: Pedigrees of the Families in the County of Hants.* London: Sherwood Gilbert and Piper, 1833.

Hall's Baltimore: Baltimore: Its History and People. Ed. by Clayton Coleman Hall. 3 Vols. New York: 1912.

Harper, Irma S. *Maryland Marriage Clues.* 3 vols. Pub. by the Compiler.

Hasted. See *KEHA.*

HAWB: HARFORD CO. REGISTER OF WILLS Will Book (MSA CM 634).

Haydn, Joseph. *The Book of Dignities.* (1894). Repr.: GPC, 1970.

HECH: The Historical Antiquities of Hertfordshire. By Sir Henry Chauncey. 2 vols. 1826. Repr.: Dorking: Kohler and Coombes, 1975.

HECL: Robert Clutterbuck. *History and Antiquities of the County of Hertford.* 3 Vols. 1815-1827.

HEMA: Harry Wright Newman. *Heraldic Marylandiana.* Washington, D.C.: The Author, 1968.

HIJA: Frances McDonnell. *Highland Jacobites, 1745.* Baltimore: Clearfield Co., Inc., 1999.

Hist. of Durham: The History and Antiquities of the County Palatine of Durham. By Robert Surtees. 4 Vols. 1816-1840.

HLPO: Donnell M. Owings. *His Lordship's Patronage*. Baltimore: MHS, 1950

HMSO: His [Her] Majesty's Stationer's Office.

HSPR: *Harleian Society Publications, Registers Series*.

------- 1: *Register of All the Christninges Burialles & Weddinges Within the Parish of Saint Peeter's upon Cornhill* .... Ed. by W. G. Leveson Gower. London: Harleian Society, 1877.

-------- 2: *The Register Booke of Christnings, Marriages, and Burials Within the Precinct of the Cathedral and Metropolitiocall Church of Christe of Canterburie*. Ed. by Robert Hovenden. London: The Society, 1878.

------- 3: *The Register Booke of Saynte De'nis Backchurch Parishe for Maryages, Christenynges, and Buryalles Begynnynge in the Yeare of O'r Lord God 1638*. Ed. by Joseph Lemuel Chester. London: The Society, 1878.

------- 4: *A Register ... Saint Peeters upon Cornhill ... Pt. II*. The Society, 1879.

------- 5.: *Register of St. Mary Aldemary, London, ... , 1558 to 1754*. Edited by Joseph Lemuel Chester. London: The Society, 1880.

------- 7: *The Parish Registers of St. Michael Cornhill, London, Containing the Marriages, Baptisms, and Burials from 1546 to 1754*. Partly Edited by Joseph Lemuel Chester. London: The Harleian Society, 1882.

------- 17: *A True Register ... St. James Clerkenwell ... Vol. IV, Burials, 1551 to 1665*. Ed. by Robert Hovenden. London: The Society, 1891.

------- 25: *Register of Baptisms, Marriages and Burials in the Parish of St. Martins in the Fields in the County of Middlesex from 1550 to 1619*. London: The Society, 1898.

------- 31: *The Registers of St. Helen's Bishopsgate, London*. Ed. by W. Bruce Bannerman. London: The Society, 1904.

------- 38: *The Registers of St. Bene't and St. Peter's, Paul's Wharf, London*. Ed. by Willoughby A. Littledale. Vol. I: Christenings, St. Bene't 1619-1837, St. Peter, 1607-1837, London: The Society, 1909.

------- 39: *The Registers of St. Bene't and St. Peter's, Paul's Wharf, London*. Ed. by Willoughby A. Littledale. Vol. II: Marriages, St. Bened't, 1619-1730. London: The Society, 1910.

------- 40: *The Registers of St. Bene't and St. Peter's, Paul's Wharf, London*. Ed. by Willoughby A. Littledale. Vol. III, Marriages, St. Bene't, 1731 to 1837; St. Peter, 1607 to 1834. London: The Society, 1911.

------- 43. *The Registers of All Hallows, Bread Street, and St. John the Evangelist, Friday St., London*. Ed. by W. Bruce Bannerman. London: The Society, 1913.

------- 49: *The Registers of St. Stephen's Walbrook and St. Benet Sherehog, London*. Part I. Ed. by Wm. Bruce Bannerman and W. Bruce Bannerman. London: The Society, 1919.

------- 50: -------. Part II. Ed. by Wm. Bruce Bannerman and W. Bruce Bannerman. London: The Society, 1920.

------- 64: *The Register of St. Margaret's Westminster London, 1660-1675*. Trans. by Herbert F. Westlake. Ed. by Lawrence E. Tanner. London: The Society, 1935.

------- 67: *The Register of St. Clement East Cheape and St. Martin Orgar*. Part I. Trans. by A. W. Hughes Clerke (London: The Society, 1931).

------- 68: -------, Part II. London: The Society, 1938.

------ 72. *The Registers of St. Mary Magdalen, Milk St., 1558-1666, and St. Michael Basishaw, 1538-1625.* Part I. Trans. and ed. by A. W. Hughes Clark. London: the Society, 1942.

------ 73. *The Registers of St. Michael Basishaw.*, Part II. Trans. and ed. by A. W. Hughes Clark. london: the Society, 1943.

------ 76. *The Registers of St. Katharine by the Tower, London.* Trans. And ed. by A. W. Hughes Clarke. Pt. ii, 1626-1665. London: The Society, 1946.

------ 80-81. *The Registers of St. Katherine by the Tower.* Pts. vi and vii: Baptisms, 1666-1695; Burials, 1666-1695. London: The Society, 1952.

------ 88: *The Register of St. Margaret's Westminster London*, Part II. Ed. by Winefride Ward. The Society, c.r. 1956.

------ 89: *The Register of St. Margaret's Westminster London.* Part III. Ed. by Winefride Ward. The Society, c.r. 1977.

HSPV: Harleian Society Publications, Visitation Series.

------ 1: *Visitation of London, 1568.* London: The Society.

------ 3: *Visitation of the County of Rutland In the Year 1618-19.* By William Camden. London: The Society, 1870.

------ 4: *Visitation of Nottingham in the Years 1569 and 1614.* Ed. by George William Marshall. The Society, 1871.

------7: *The Visitation of the County of Cumberland in the Year 1615, Taken by Richard St. George, Norroy King of Arms.* Ed. by John Fetherston. London: The Society, 1872.

------ 9: *The Visitation of the County of Cornwall in the Year 1620.* Ed. by J. Vivian and Henry H. Drake. The Society, 1874.

------ 10: *The Marriage, Baptismal and Burial Registers of the Collegiate Church or Abbey of St. Peter, Westminster.* Ed. and Annotated by Joseph Lemuel Chester. London: The Society, 1876.

------ 12: *The Visitation of the County of Warwick in the Year 1619.* Ed. by John Fetherston. The Society, 1877.

------ 13: *The Visitations of Essex by Hawley, 1552; Hervey, 1558; Cooke 1570; Raven, 1612; and Owen and Lilly, 1634, to Which Are Added Miscellaneous Essex Pedigrees from Various Harleian Manuscripts, And an Appendix Containing Berry's Essex Pedigrees.* Ed. and Indexed by Walter C. Metcalfe. London: The Society, 1878.

------ 14: *The Visitations of Essex.* Part II. London: the Society, 1879.

------ 15: *The Visitation of London ... 1633, 1634, 1635 ...* Ed. by Joseph Jackson Howard and Joseph Lemuel Chester. London: The Society, 1880.

------ 17: *The Visitation of London, ... 1633, 1634, 1635 ....* Ed. by Joseph Jackson Howard and Joseph Lemuel Chester. London: The Society, 1883.

------ 18: *The Visitation of Cheshire in the Year 1580, Made by Robert Glover, Somerset Herald, and William Flower, Norroy King of Arms, With Numerous Addditions and continuations, ... 1566, ... 1533, ... and ... 1591.* Ed. by John Paul Rylands. The Society, 1882.

------ 19: *The Visitation of Bedfordshire ... 1566, 1582, and 1634 ...* Ed. by Frederic Augustus Blades. The Society, 1884.

------ 20: *The Visitation of the County of Dorset Taken in the Year 1623 ...* Ed. by John Paul Rylands. The Society, 1885.

------ 21: *The Visitation of the County of Gloucester, Taken in the Year 1623, by Henry Chitty and John Phillipot, as Deputis to William Camden, Clarenceux, King of Arms, With Pedigrees from the Heralds' Visitations of 1569 and 1582/3, and Sundry Miscellaneous Pedigrees*. Ed. by Sir John Maclean and W. C. Heane. The Society, 1885. [This edition contains notes from Dowdeswell and Whittington Parish Registers as well as other sources.]

------ 22: *Visitation of Hertfordshire, Made by Robert Cooke, Esq., Clarenceux, in 1572, and Sir Richard St. George, Kt., Clarenceux, in 1634, With Hertfordshire Pedigrees from Harleian Mss. 6147 and 1546.* Ed. by Walter C. Metcalfe. The Society, 1886.

------ 23: *Allegations for Marriage Licenses Issued by the Dean and Chapter of Westminster, 1588-1699; also for Those Issued by the Vicar-General of the Archbishop of Canterbury, 1660 to 1679.* Extracted by Joseph Lemuel Chester. Ed. by Geo. J. Armytage. The Society, 1886

------ 24: *Allegations for Marriage Licenses Issued from the Faculty Office of the Archbishop of Canterbury in London, 1543-1869.* Extracted by Joseph Lemuel Chester and Geo. J. Armytage. The Society, 1886.

------ 25: *Allegations for Marriage Licenses Issued by the Bishop of London, 1520-1610.* Extracted by Joseph Lemuel Chester and ed. by Geo. J. Armytage. Vol. I. The Society, 1887.

------ 26: *Allegations for Marriage Licenses Issued by the Bishop of London, 1611-1828.* Vol. II. London: The Society, 1887.

------ 27: *The Visitation of the County of Worcester Made in the Year 1569 ... .* Ed. by W. P. W. 7Phillimore. London: The Society, 1888.

------ 28: *The Visitation of Shropshire, Taken in the Year 1623 by Robert Tresswell, Somerset Herald, and Augustine Vincent, Rouge Croix Pursuivant ...* Ed. by George Grazebrook and John Paul Rylands, Part I. The Society, 1889.

------ 29: *The Visitation of Shropshire, Taken in the Year 1623, by Robert Tresswell, Somerset Herald, and Augustine Vincent, Rouge Croix Pursuivant ...* Ed. by George Grazebrook and John Paul Rylands, Part II. The Society, 1889.

------ 32: *The Visitation of Norfolk, made and taken by William Harvey, Clarencieux King of Arms, Anno 1563, Enlarged with another Visitation made by Clarencieux Cooke ... ; as also the Visitation Made by John Raven, Richmond, Anno 1613.* Ed. by Walter Rye. London: The Society, 1891.

------ 33: *Marriage Licenses of the Vicar General of the Archbishop of Canterbury, 1660-1668.* Ed. by George J. Armytage. The Society, 1892.

------ 34: *Marriage Licenses of the Vicar General of the Archbishop of Canterbury, 1669-1679.* Ed. by George J. Armytage. The Society, 1892.

------ 35: *Allegations for Marriage Licenses in the Archdeaconry of the Bishop of Winchester, 1689-1837, Vol. I.* Extracted and ed. by William J. C. Moens. The Society, 1893.

------ 36: *Allegations for Marriage Licenses in the Archdeaconry of the Bishop of Winchester, 1689-1837.* Vol. II. Extracted and ed. by William J. C. Moens. The Society, 1893.

------ 37: *Familiae Minorum Gentium.* Ed. by John W. Clay. Vol. 1. The Society, 1894. [Pagination is continuous throughout the four vols., and the index is in Vol. 4.]

------ 38: ------: Ed. by John W. Clay. Vol. 2. The Society, 1895.

------ 39: ------: Ed. by John W. Clay. Vol. 3. The Society, 1895.

------ 40: ------: Ed. by John W. Clay. Vol. 4. The Society, 1896.

------ 42: *The Visitation of Kent ... 1619-1621.* Ed. by Robert Hovenden. The Society, 1898.

------ 44, 50, 51, 52: *Lincolnshire Pedigrees.* Ed. by A. R. Maddison. London: The Society, 1902-1906.

------ 49: *Obituary Prior to 1800 ...* Comp. by Sir William Musgrave, 6th Bart. Vol. VI. The Society, 1901.

------ 53: *The Visitation of the County of Sussex ... 1530.* Ed. by W. Bruce Bannerman. The Society, 1905.

------ 56: *The Four Visitations of Berkshire Made and Taken By Thomas Benolte, Clarenceux, 1532; William Harvey, Clarenceux, 1566; Henry Chtting, Chester Herald, John Phillipott, Rouge Dragon for William Camden, Clarenceux, 1623, and Elias Ashmole, Windsor Herald for Sir Edward Bysshe, Clarenceux, 1665/6.* Ed. by W. Harry Rylands, Vol. I. The Society, 1907.

------ 58: *The Visitation of the County of Buckingham made in 1634 ...* Ed. by W. Harry Rylands. London: The Society, 1909.

------ 59: *Pedigrees Made at the Visitation of Cheshire, 1613, Made by Richard St. George, Esq., Norroy King of Arms, and Henry Sr. George, Gent., Bluemantle Pursuivant of Arms ... .* Ed. by Sir George J. Armytage, Bart., and J. Paul Rylands. The Society, 1909

------ 62: *The Visitation of the County of Warwick ... 1682 ... 1683.* Ed. by W. Harry Rylands. The Society, 1911.

------ 63: *Staffordshire Pedigrees; Based on the Visitation ... Made by William Dugdale ... 1663-1664, Written by Gregory King ... 1680-1700.* Ed. by Sir George J. Armytage and W. Harry Rylands. The Society, 1912.

------ 64: *Pedigrees from the Visitation of Hampshire ... 1530 ... 1574 ... 1622, ... 1634.* The Society, 1913.

------ 65: *Middlesex Pedigrees.* Edited by Sir George John Armytage, Bart. London: The Society, 1914.

------ 73: *The Visitation of the County of Rutland Begun by Fran. Burghill, Somerset [Herald] and Gregory King, Rougedragon [Pursuivant] in Trinity Vacation, 1681 ... .* Ed. by W. Harry Rylands and W. Bruce Bannerman. London: The Society, 1922.

------ 75: *The Visitation of Kent.* Part II. Ed. by W. Bruce Bannerman. The Society, 1924.

------ 80: *Knights of Edward I.* Notices Collected by C. Moor. Vol. I. The Society, 1929.

------ 86. *The Visitation of Norfolk ... 1664, Made by Sir Edward Bysshe, Clarenceux King of Arms.* Ed. and annotated by A. W. Hughes Clarke and Arthur Campling. The Society, 1934.

------ 92: *London Visitation Pedigrees, 1664.* By J. B. Whitmore and A. W. Hughes Clark. The Society, 1940.

------ 93: *Cheshire Visitation Pedigrees 1663.* Ed. by Arthur Adams. London: The Society, 1941.

------ 113, 114: *Rolls of Arms, Henry III.* Ed. by Thomas Daniel Tremlett and Hugh Stanford London, Additions and corrections by Sir Anthony Wagner. No pl.: the OSciety, 1967.

------ 8 n.s.: *The Visitation of Derbyshire Begun in 1662 and Finished in 1664, Made by William Dugdale, Norroy King of Arms.* Ed. by G. D. Squibb, Norfolk Herald Extraordinary. The Society, 1989.

------- 13 n.s.: *Visitation of the County of Huntingdon, 1684.* Made by Sir Richard St. George, Knight. Trans. and Ed. by John Bedells. The Society, 1994.

Hedley: Hedley, W. P. *Northumberland Families.* 2 Vols. 1968-1970.

Humphery-Smith: *The Phillimore Atlas and Index of Parish Registers.* Ed. by Cecil Humphery-Smith. GPC, 1984.

Hutchins' Dorset: John Hutchins. *History and Antiquities of the County of Dorset.* 2nd ed., 4 vols. Westminster: J. B. Nichols and Sons, 1796-1815.

IBCP: Henry C. Peden, Jr. *Inhabitants of Baltimore County, 1763-1774.* FLP.

IBCW: F. Edward Wright. *Inhabitants of Baltimore County, 1691-1763.* FLP, 1987.

IGI: International Genealogical Index; microfiche at local LDS Family History Library Centers (1988 edition); CD-Rom availiable. It is available on line at www.familysearch.org.

IL: Index Library. Published by the British Record Society.

------- 26: *Inquisitiones Post Mortem, London, 1561-1577.*

------- 43: *Prerogative Court of Canterbury Wills, 1605-1619.*

------- 44: *Prerogative Court of Canterbury Wills, 1620-1629.*

------- 50: *Prerogative Court of Canterbury Wills, 1396-1558, 1640-1650.*

------- 54: *Prerogative Court of Canterbury Wills, 1653-1656.*

------- 61: *Prerogative Court of Canterbury Wills, 1657-1660.*

------- 62: *Calendar of the Marriage Allegations in the Registry of the Bishop of London, 1597-1700.* [Part 1], 1937.

------- 67: *Prerogative Court of Canterbury Wills, 1671-1675.*

------- 68: *Prerogative Court of Canterbury Wills, 1649-1654.*

------- 71: *Prerogative Court of Canterbury Wills, 1676-1685.*

------- 77: *Prerogative Court of Canterbury Wills, 1686-1693.*

------- 80: *Prerogative Court of Canterbury Wills, 1694-1700.*

INAC: Maryland Prerogative Court Inventories and Accounts (MSA S 536).

INCE: Henry C. Peden, Jr. *Inhabitants of Cecil County.* FLP.

INKE: Henry C. Peden, Jr. *Inhabitants of Kent County.* FLP.

JANE: Frances McDonnell. *Part 1: Jacobites of 1715: Northeast Scotland. Part 2: Jacobites of 1745: Northeast Scotland.* Baltimore: Clearfield Co., Inc., 1997.

JAPE: Frances McDonnell. *Jacobites of Perthshire, 1745.* Baltimore: Clearfield Co., Inc., 1999.

K.B.: Knight Bachelor; Knight of the Bath.

K.C.: King's Councillor.

KEBE: William Berry. *County Genealogies: Pedigrees of the Families in the County of Kent.* London: Sherwood Gilbert and Piper, 1830.

KE Co.: Kent Co., MD.

KEHA: Edward Hasted. *The History and Topographical Survey of the County of Kent.* Canterbury: Simmons and Kirby.

KELR: KENT CO. COURT Land Records (MSA C 1068).

K.G.: Knight of the Garter.

KI: Kent Island.

Kindred: Davis-Stansbury Lines. By Helen E. Davis. Philadelphia: Dorrance and Co., 1977.

KPMV: Peter Wilson Coldham. *The King's Passengers to Maryland and Virginia.* FLP, 1997.

LAFO. Pedigrees of the County Families of England, Lancashire. By Joseph Foster. 1873.

The Lancashire Pipe Rolls. Ed. by William Farrer. Liverpool: H. Young and Sons, 1902.

Langston: See *PECD*. Vol. II.

Lawson: Sir Henry Lawson. *Genealogical Collections Illustrating the History of Roman Catholic Families of England*. London; privately printed, 1887-1892 [located at The Library of Congress, Microfilm 27722CS].

LCRS: Record Society of Lancashire and Cheshire.

LDBR: *Living Descendants of the Blood Royal*. By the Count d'Angerville. Vols. 1- [These volumes must be used with care.]

LEMG: Michael Ghirelli. *List of Emigrants to America, 1682-1692*. (1968) Repr. GPC, 1989.

LEMK: Jack and Marion Kaminkow. *List of Emigrants to America, 1718-1759*. Repr. GPC, 1989.

Lipscomb. See *BULI*.

LMCD: Peter Wilson Coldham. *Lord Mayor's Court of London: Depositions Relating to Americans, 1641-1726*. Washington: The National Genealogical Society, Special Publication no. 44, 1980.

LPRS: *Lancashire Parish Register Society*.

------- 2: *Parish Registers of Burnley, 1562-1653*.

------- 3: *Registers of Parish of Whittington, Lancs*.

------- 4: *Wigan Parish Register*.

------- 28: *The Registers of the Parish Church of Cartmel, in the County of Lancaster ... 1559-1661*. Trans. by Henry Brierly. Rochdale: Printed for The Lancashire Parish Register Society, 1907.

------- 31: *The Registers of the Cathedral Church of Manchester, Christenings, Burials, and Weddings, 1573-1616*. Cambridge: The Society, 1908.

------- 40: *Tunstall Parish Register, 1626-1685*.

------- 46: *Register of the Parish Church of Standish in the County of Lancaster, 1560-1653*. Cambridge: The Society, 1912.

------- 47: *Registers of the Parish Church of Gorton, 1599-1741*. Transc. by Henry Brierly. Wigan: The Society, 1913.

------- 55: *The Registers of the Cathedral Church of Manchester, Baptisms and Marriages, 1616 to 1653*. Trans. by Henry Brierly. Wigan: The Society, 1918.

------- 56: *The Registers of the Cathedral Church of Manchester, Burials, 1616 to 1653*. Trans. by Henry Brierly. Wigan: The Society, 1919.

------- 80: *Register of Farnworth Chapel in Parish of Prescott, 1558-1612*. Trans. by F. A. Bailey. Preston: The Society, 1941.

------- 89: *The Registers of the Cathedral Church of Manchester, 1653 to 1665/6*. Preston: The Society, 1949.

------- 96: *Registers of the Parish Church of Cartmel, Part II, 1660-1723*. Trans. and ed. by Robert Dickinson. Macclesfield: The Society, 1957.

-------122: *Registers of Childwall, Lancs., 1681-1753*.

M.A.: Master of Arts.

The Manors of Suffolk. By Walter Copinger. Vol. 1- , 1905- .

"Maryland Gleanings in England," by Lothrop Withington, *MHM*, Vols. 1-5.

Maryland Marriages, 1801-1820. By Robert Barnes. GPC, 1993.

McAllister: *Land Records of Dorchester Co., MD*. By James A. McAllister. Books A-E Repr.: FLP.

MCHP: MARYLAND CHANCERY COURT Chancery Papers (MSA S 512).

MCHR: MARYLAND CHANCERY COURT Chancery Record (MSA S 517). See also Debbie Hooper. *Abstracts of Chancery Court Records of Maryland, 1669-1782*. FLP.

MCS4: Frederick Lewis Weis. *The Magna Charta Sureties, 1215*. 4th Edition. GPC, 1991

MCS5: --------. *The Magna Charta Sureties, 1215*. 5th Edition, With Additions and Corrections by Walter Lee Sheppard, Jr., with William R. Beall. GPC, 1991.

MCW: *The Maryland Calendar of Wills*. Comp. by Jane Baldwin Cotton. 8 vols. Baltimore: Kohn and Pollock, 1904). Vol.s 9-16 pub. By FLP.

MDAD: MARYLAND PREROGATIVE COURT Administration Accounts (MSA S 531).

MDC: *The Biographical Cyclopedia of Representative Men of Maryland and District of Columbia*. Baltimore: National Biographical Publishing Co., 1879.

Mddx: Middlesex, England.

MDG: Raymond B. Clark, Jr. *The Maryland and Delaware Genealogist*. [periodical].

MDP: Henry C. Peden, Jr. *Maryland Deponents, 1634-1799*. FLP.

MDTP: MARYLAND PREROGATIVE COURT Testamentary Proceedings (MSA S 541).

Medics: P. J. and R. V. Wallis. *Eighteenth Century Medics*. NewCastle Upon Tyne: Project for Historical Bibliography, 1988.

MEMO: *Memoirs: Memoirs of the Dead and the Tomb's Remembrancer (1806)*. Transcribed by Martha Reamy and Marlene Bates. Published by the transcribers and by FLP, 1989.

MG: *Maryland Genealogies*. 2 vols. GPC, 1980.

MGH: *Miscellanea Genealogica et Heraldica*. Several series.

MGSB: *Maryland Genealogical Society Bulletin*.

MHM: *Maryland Historical Magazine*.

MHS: Maryland Historical Society, Baltimore, MD.

M.I.: Monumental Inscription, usually erected in a church.

MINV: MARYLAND PREROGATIVE COURT Inventories (MSA S 534).

MJBA: (or *BMJ*): *The Maryland Journal and Baltimore Advertiser*. [newspaper].

MM1: Robert Barnes. *Maryland Marriages, 1634-1777*. GPC, 1978.

MMDP: Henry C. Peden. *More Maryland Deponents, 1716-1799*. FLP.

MNA: Robert Andrew Oszakiewski. *Maryland Naturalization Abstracts*. 2 vols. FLP.

MOPG: Prince George's Parish Register, MO Co.

MOWB: MONTGOMERY CO. REGISTER OF WILLS Will Book, MSA has various series..

M. P.: Member of Parliament.

MPL: MARYLAND LAND OFFICE Patent Liber (MSA S 11).

MRR: *Maryland Rent Rolls: Baltimore and Anne Arundel Counties*. GPC.

MSA: Maryland State Archives.

MWB: MARYLAND PREROGATIVE COURT Will Book (MSA SM 16).

Name Unknown is designated as [-?-].

NCP: *The New Complete Peerage*. 13 Vols. Ed. by Vicary Gibbs *et al*. 1910-1959.

NEHG Reg. *The New England Historical and Genealogical Register*.

NERA 1: "A Roll of Arms Registered by the Committee on Heraldry of the New England Historical and Genealogical Society." *NEHG Reg*. 82:146-168.

-------- 2: "A Second Roll of Arms" [Registered as above]. *NEHG Reg*., July 1932.

-------- 3: "Third Part of a Roll of Arms" [Registered as above]. *NEHG Reg*., July, Oct 1952.

------ 4: "Fourth Part of a Roll of Arms" [Registered as above]. c.r. 1940. *NEHG Reg.*, Jan 1953.

------ 5: "Fifth Part of a Roll of Arms" [Registered as above]. c.r. 1946. *NEHG Reg.*, April, July 1953.

------ 6: "Sixth Part of a Roll of Arms" [Registered as above]. c.r. 1954. *NEHG Reg.*, Oct 1953.

------ 7: "Seventh Part of a Roll of Arms" [Registered as above]. *NEHG Reg.*, July 1958.

------ 8: "A Roll of Arms Registered by the Committee on Heraldry ... Eighth Part" [Registered as above]. *NEHG Reg.*, Jan, April and July 1968, and Oct 1971.

------ 9: "A Roll of Arms Registered by the Committee on Heraldry Ninth Part." [Registered as above]. *NEHG Reg.*, 133:83 ff.

------ 10: "A Roll of Arms: Registered by the Committee on Heraldry Tenth Part," *NEHG Reg.*, 145:367 ff.

A [New] History of Northumberland. 15 Vols. Newcastle-upon-Tyne, 1893-1940.

NGSQ: National Genealogical Society Quarterly (periodical).

Nichols: *The History and Antiquities of Leicestershire.* London: John Nichols, 1791. Repr. No pl.: S. R. Publishers, Unlimited, 1971.

Nicholson. See *SEEA*.

Nicholson, J., and R. Burn. *The History and Antiquities of the Counties of Cumberland and Westmorland.* 1777.

NOFO. Pedigrees Recorded at the Heralds' Visitations of the County of Northumberland, Made by Sir Richard St. George, Norroy King of Arms in 1615, and William Dugdale, Norroy King of Arms in 1662. Ed. by Joseph Foster. Newcastle-upon-Tyne: Browne and Browne, n.d.

Northumberland, A History of, in Three Parts. By John Hodgson. Newcastle, 1832.

Northumberland Families. See Hedley, above.

NQBD: Alice L. Beard. *Births, Deaths and Marriages of the Nottingham Quakers, 1680-1899.* FLP, 1989.

Nugent, Nell M. *Cavaliers and Pioneers.* (1934). Repr. GPC, 1974.

OAAA: Order of Americans of Armorial Ancestry. Comp. by Arthur Louis Finnell. Baltimore: Clearfield Co., Inc., 1997.

OAJP: Sir James Balfour Paul. *An Ordinary of Arms.* (1893). Repr. Baltimore: Clearfield Co., 1991.

Ormerod. See *CHOR*.

Overman: Michael Overman. *A Gorsuch Pedigree.* No p.: no pub., 1982.

PAG: Franklin's Pennsylvania Gazette (newspaper).

Papenfuse et al. See *BDML*.

PASC: David Faris. *Plantagenet Ancestors of Seventeenth Century Colonists.* GPC, 1996.

PASC2: David Faris. *Plantagenet Ancestors of Seventeenth Century Colonists. English Ancestry Series, Volume 1.* 2nd ed. New England Historic Genealogical Society, 1999.

PCC: Prerogative Court of Canterbury.

PCLR: PROVINCIAL COURT Land Records (MSA S 552).

PECD: Pedigrees of Some of the Emperor Charlemagne's Descendants. 3 vols. Repr.: GPC, 1988

------ *Vol. II.* Ed. by Aileen Lewers Langston and J. Orton Buck, Jr. 1974. Repr.: GPC, 1986.

------- *Vol. III.* Comp. by J. Orton Buck and Timothy Field Beard (1987). Repr. GPC, 1988.

PG: Prince George's Co., MD.

PGEJ: PROVINCIAL COURT Prince George's Co. Ejectment Papers (MSA S 549).

PGGS: Prince George's Co. Gen. Soc. Bulletin [periodical].

PGKG: King George's Parish Register, PG Co., MSA.

PGLR: PRINCE GEORGE'S CO. COURT Land Records (MSA C 1237).

PGQA: Queen Anne's Parish Register, PG Co.; MSA.

PGWB: Prince George's Co., MD, Register of Wills Will Book (MSA C1326).

PHSL: Publications of the Huguenot Society of London. Vol. 1- , 1887-.

------- 5: *Registers of the Walloon or Strangers Church in Canterbury.* The Society, 1891.

------- 9: *Registers of French Church in Threadneedle St., London.* Part 1. The Society, 1896.

------- 13: *Registers of the French Church in Threadneedle St., London.* Part 2. The Society, 1899.

------- 15: *Registers of the French Church in Threadneedle St., London.* Part 3. The Society.

------- 18: *Letters of Denization and Acts of Naturalization for Aliens in England and Ireland, 1603-1700.* Ed. by William A. Shaw. Lymington: The Society. 1911.

------- 20: *Livre des Tesmoignages [Book of Certificates] of the French Church in Threadneedle St., London.* Trans. and ed. by William Minet and Susan Minet. London: The Society, 1905.

------- 21: *Registers of the French Church in Threadneedle St., London.* Part 4. Ed. by T. Colyer Ferguson. London: The Society, 1916.

------- 25: *Register of the Church of Le Carre and Berwick St., 1690-1788.* The Society, 1921.

------- 27: *Letters of Denization and Acts of Naturalization for Aliens in England and Ireland, 1701-1800.* Ed. by William A. Shaw. The Society, 1923.

------- 31: *Register of the Church of Hungerford Market, Later Castle St.* Ed. by William Minet and Susan Minet. The Society, 1928.

"Planche's Roll of Arms" [prob. compiled near the end of the reign of Henry III, d. 1272], *The Genealogist*, n.s., beginning 3:148).

The Plantagenet Ancestry of King Edward III and Queen Philippa. By George Andrews Moriarty. Salt Lake City: Mormon Pioneer Genealogy Society, 1985.

PMD: Maryland Deponents. By Henry C. Peden. FLP.

PRBRE: The Plantaganet Roll of the Blood Royal: Essex. By The Marquis of Ruvigny. Repr.: GPC, 1994.

PRHE: J. H. and R. V. Pinches. *The Royal Heraldry of England.* London: Heraldry Today, 1974.

PROE: Public Record Office of Exeter [Devonshire, England].

PRS: The Parish Register Society.

------- 6: *Registers of Stratford-on-Avon, Co. Warwick.* 1897.

------- 32: *The Registers of Bitton, Co. Gloucester, 1572-1674.* Trans. by P. W. P. Carylon-Britton. London: The Society, 1900.

------- 53: *The Register of Solihull, Co. Warwick, Volume I, 1538-1668.* No pl.: The Society, 1904.

------- 64: *The Register of St. Mary, Leicester, Co. Leicester. Volume I: Baptisms, Marriages and Burials, 1600-1738.* Transcribed by Henry Hartopp. London: The Society, 1909.

PTAT: *Passengers to America: A Consolidation of Ship Passenger Lists from the New England Historical and Geenalogical Register*. Ed. by Michael Tepper. GPC, 1988.

QA Co.: Queen Anne's Co., MD.

QALR: QA CO. COURT Land Records (MSA C 1426). See Published abstracts by R. Bernice Leonard.

QRNM: Henry C. Peden, Jr. *Quaker Records of Northern Maryland*. FLP, 1993.

QRSM: --------. *Quaker Records of Southern Maryland*. FLP, 1992.

Raine, Rev. James. *The History and Antiquities of North Durham*. 1852.

RBRB: Marquis of Ruvigny. *The Blood Royal of Britain (The Tudor Volume)*. GPC, 1994.

RD500: Gary Boyd Roberts. *Royal Descents of 500 Immigrants to the American Colonies or the United States*. GPC, 1993.

Reg. Pal. Dnrham. Registrum Palatinum Dunelmense. Register of Richard de Kellaw. Rolls Series, 4 vols., 1873-1878.

RMHF: Alice N. Parran. *Register of Maryland Heraldic Families*. 2 vols. 1935-1938. [These books must be used with extreme care!]

RUWR: James Wright. *History and Antiquities of the County of Rutland*. London: Bennet Griffin, 1684.

Sanders: Ivor J. Sanders. *English Baronies*. New York: Oxford University Press, 1960.

SCBC: Sallie Mallick. *Sketches of Citizens of Baltimore City and Baltimore County*. FLP.

Scott1: Kenneth Scott. *Abstracts of Franklin's Pennsylvania Gazette, 1728-1748*. GPC, 1977.

Scott2: Kenneth Scott & Janet r, Clarke. *Abstracts from the Pennsylvania Gazette, 1746-1755*. GPC, 1977.

SCWM 2: *Society of Colonial Wars in the State of Maryland: Genealogies of the Members and Services of Ancestors*. Ed. by Francis B. Culver. Baltimore: William & Wilkins Co., 1940.

SAEA: John Parsons Earwaker. *The History of the Ancient Parish of Sandbach, Co. Chester*. London and Redhill: The Hansard Publishing Union, 1890.

SEEA: Cregoe P. D. Nicholson. *Some Early Emigrants to America*. Repr. GPC, 1996.

SEEW: John Wareing. "Some Early Emuigrants to America, 1683-4: A Supplementary List." *The Genealogists' Magazine* 18:239-246.

The Shapley Connection. [newsletter].

SJSG: Henry C. Peden, Jr. *St. John's & St. George's Parish Regsters, 1696-1851*. FLP, 1987.

Skordas, Gust. *The Early Settlers of Maryland, 1633-1680*. GPC, 1979.

SM Co.: St. Mary's Co., MD.

Smith, Frank A. *A Genealogical Gazetteer of England*. GPC. 1982.

-------. *Immigrants to America Appearing in English Records*. No pl.: Everton Publishers, 1976.

SO Co.: Somerset Co., MD.

SOCD: David Dobson. *Scots on the Chesapeake, 1607-1830*. GPC, 1992.

SOLR: SOMERSET CO. COURT Land Records (MSA CM 963).

A Somerset Sampler. By Pauline Manning Batchelder. Lower Delmarva Genealogical Society, 1994.

SSLM: Alan F. Day. *A Social Study of Lawyers in Maryland, 1660-1775*. New York: Garland Publishing Co., Inc., 1989.

SMMD: Margaret K. Fresco. *Marriages and Deaths: St. Mary's County, Maryland, 1634-1900.* Ridge, MD: The Author, 1982.

Stanard: W. G. Stanard. *Some Emigrants to Virginia: Second Edition Enlarged.* (1915). Repr.: GPC, 1983.

STDU: Thomas Colyer Ferguson. *Marriage Registers of St. Dunstan's, Stepney, in the County of Middlesex.* 3 vols. Canterbury: Cross and Jackson, 1898-1901.

SUBE: William Berry. *County Genealogies: Pedigrees of the Families in the County of Sussex.* London: Sherwood Gilbert and Piper, 1830.

TA Co.: Talbot Co., MD.

Tabb: Jeanne Mitchell Jordan Tabb. *Ancestor Lineages of Members, Texas Society, National Society, Colonial Dames Seventeenth Century.* Balto.: Clearfield Co., 1991.

TAG: The American Genealogist (periodical).

TAJU: TALBOT CO. COURT Judgment Record (MSA C 1875).

TALR: TALBOT CO. COURT Land Records (MSA C 1880).

TATH: Third Haven Monthly Meeting; Records published in *ESVR* (q.v.).

TAPE: St. Peter's Parish, Talbot Co.; Records published in *ESVR* (q.v.).

TAWB: TALBOT CO. REGISTER OF WILLS Will Book (MSA C 1925).

Thomas Family of Talbot County, Maryland, and Allied Families. By Richard H. Spencer. Baltimore: 1914

TMFO: Harry Wright Newman. *To Maryland From Overseas.* (1982). Repr.: GPC, 1985.

The Topographer and Genealogist. 3 vols. 1846-1858.

Turton: Plantagenet Ancestry. By Lt. Col. W. H. Turton. 1928. Repr.: GPC. [Must be usd with care.]

VHC: Victoria Histories of the Counties of England.

-------- *Beds.: The Victoria History of the County of Bedfordshire.* Ed. by William Page. London: Constable and Co., 1969.

------- *Bucks.: The Victoria History of the County of Buckingham.* Ed. by William Page. London: A. Constable and Co., 1905-1927.

------- *Herts. The Victoria History of the County of Hertfordshire.* London: A. Constable and Co., Ltd.

------- *Hunts. The Victoria History of the County of Huntingdon.* Ed. by William Page et al. 3 vols. London: St. Catherine Press, 1926-1936.

------- *Lancs. The Victoria History of the County of Lancaster.* Ed. by William Farrer and J. Brownbill. 8 vols. London: A. Constable and Co., Ltd., 1906-1914.

------- *Rutland. The Victoria History of the County of Rutland.* Ed. by William Page. 2 vols. London: A. Constable and Co., Ltd., 1908-1935.

------- *Staffs. The Victoria History of the County of Stafford.* Ed. by William Page. London: A. Constable, 1908-.

------- *Wilts. The Victoria History of the County of Wiltshire.* Ed. by R. B. Pugh and Elizabeth Crittell. Pub. for the Institute of Historical Research by Oxford University Press, 1953-.

Venn. See *ALCA*.

VGEW: Lothrop Withington. *Virginia Gleanings in England.* GPC, 1980.

VMHB: The Virginia Magazine of History and Biography.

WALR: WASHINGTON CO. COURT Land Records (MSA CM 1130).

Warfield Records. By Evelyn Ballenger. Annapolis: Thomas Ord Warfield, 1970

Waters. See *GGE*.

WAR7: Frederick Lewis Weis. *Ancestral Roots of Certain American Colonists Who Came to America bewfore 1700*. 7th Edition, With Additions and Corrections by Walter Lee Sheppard, Jr. GPC, 1992.

Whalley Coucher. *The Coucher Book of Whalley Abbey*. 3 vols. The Chetham Society. Vols. 10, 11, 20.

Whellan. Whellan, W. *The History and Topography of the Counties of Cumberland and Westmorland*. 1860.

WILR: Ruth Dryden. *Wicomico Co. Land Records*. Repr. FLP, 1992.

WIPR: Wiltshire Parish Registers.

-------- 2: *Marriages of St. Peter's, Marlborough, Wilts.; Marriages of St. Mary's, Marlborough.*

WMC4: See *MCS4*.

WMG: Western Maryland Genealogy [periodical].

WMQ: William and Mary Quarterly. [periodical].

WOLR; Worcester Co. Land Records.

Wright: See *RUWR*.

Wyker: Clara B. Wyker. *Andrews Genealogy and Alliances*. Decatur, AL: 1917.

YASP: Yorkshire Archaeological Society, Parish Register Division.

------- 1: *Register of St. Michael Belfrey, York, Part I, 1565-1653.*

------- 3: *Parish Register of Atwick, 1538-1708.*

------- 33: *The Parish Registers of Otley, Co. York, Part I, 1562-1672*. Leeds: The Society, 1908.

------- 42: *Parish Registers of Thirsk, Yorkshire.*

------- 67 & 68: *Parish Register of Clapham, Yorkshire, Part 1: 1595-1683*. Trans. and ed. by John Charlesworth. The Society. 1921.

------- 70: *Parish Register of St. Crux, York, Part I, 1539-1716*. Trans. and ed. by R. B. Cook and Mrs. F. Harrison. 1922

------- 78: *Parish Registers of Heptonstall, Vol. I, 1593-1660*. Ed. and indexed by Edith Horsfall. No p., The Society, 1925.

------- 79: *Register of Ripon Cathedral.*

------- 100: *Parish Register of All Saints Church, Pavement, in the City of York. Vol. I, 1554-1690*. Trans. and ed. by T. M. Fisher. The Society, 1935 (The index is in Vol. 102).

------- 140: *Parish Register of Giggleswick, Vol. I, 1558-1669.*

YPRS: See *YASP*.

334   *Index*